W9-BWS-485

The Princeton Review

Cracking the GMAT®

2015 Edition

Geoff Martz and Adam Robinson

PrincetonReview.com

PENGUIN RANDOM HOUSE

The Princeton Review

The Princeton Review
24 Prime Parkway, Suite 201
Natick, MA 01760
E-mail: editorialsupport@review.com

Published in the United States by Random House LLC, New York, and simultaneously in Canada by Random House of Canada Limited, Toronto.

A Penguin Random House Company.

ISBN: 978-0-8041-2492-8
eBook ISBN: 978-0-8041-2493-5
ISSN: 1549-263X

Editor: Meave Shelton
Production Artist: Sandra Schmeil
Production Editor: Kathy Carter

Printed in the United States on partially recycled paper.

10 9 8 7 6 5 4 3 2 1

2015 Edition

Editorial
Rob Franek, Senior VP, Publisher
Casey Cornelius, VP Content Development
Mary Beth Garrick, Director of Production
Selena Coppock, Managing Editor
Calvin Cato, Editor
Meave Shelton, Editor
Alyssa Wolff, Editorial Assistant

Random House Publishing Team
Tom Russell, Publisher
Alison Stoltzfus, Publishing Manager
Dawn Ryan, Associate Managing Editor
Ellen Reed, Production Manager
Erika Pepe, Associate Production Manager
Kristin Lindner, Production Supervisor
Andrea Lau, Designer

Acknowledgments

Our GMAT course is much more than clever techniques and powerful computer score reports; the reason our results are great is that our teachers care so much about their students. Thanks to all the teachers who have made the GMAT course so successful, but in particular the core group of teachers and development people who helped get it off the ground: Alicia Ernst, Tom Meltzer, Paul Foglino, John Sheehan, Mark Sawula, Nell Goddin, Teresa Connelly, Phillip Yee, Kimberly Beth Hollingsworth, Bobby Hood, Chris Chimera, Chris Hinkle, Peter Hanink, and Cathy Evins.

Special thanks to John Fulmer and Geoff Martz for their revisions to the current edition.

Special thanks to Adam Robinson, who conceived of and perfected the Joe Bloggs approach to standardized tests and many of the other successful techniques used by The Princeton Review.

Contents

...So Much More Online!

Register your book now!

- Go to PrincetonReview.com
- You'll see a welcome page where you should register your book using the ISBN. Type in 9780804124928 and create a username and password so that next time you can log into PrincetonReview.com easily.
- Now you're good to go!

Once you've registered, you can...

- Take 2 full-length practice GMAT exams.
- Take one as a diagnostic test before you work through *Cracking the GMAT.*
- Work through the chapters and practice questions found in this book, focusing on the sections where you need specific review.
- Then take the second practice GMAT and see how much you improved.
- Review all of the content to sharpen your skills one last time.
- Then, prepare to tackle the GMAT with skill and ease!

Offline Resources

If you are looking for more review or business school advice, please feel free to pick up these books in stores right now!

- *Business School Essays That Made A Difference*
- *The Best Business Schools*
- *Verbal Workout for the New GMAT, 3rd Edition*
- *Math Workout for the New GMAT, 4th Edition*
- *1,037 Practice Questions for the New GMAT, 2nd Edition*

PrincetonReview.com

Look For These Icons Throughout The Book

Online Articles	Applied Strategies
Online Practice Tests	Study Break
Proven Techniques	More Great Books

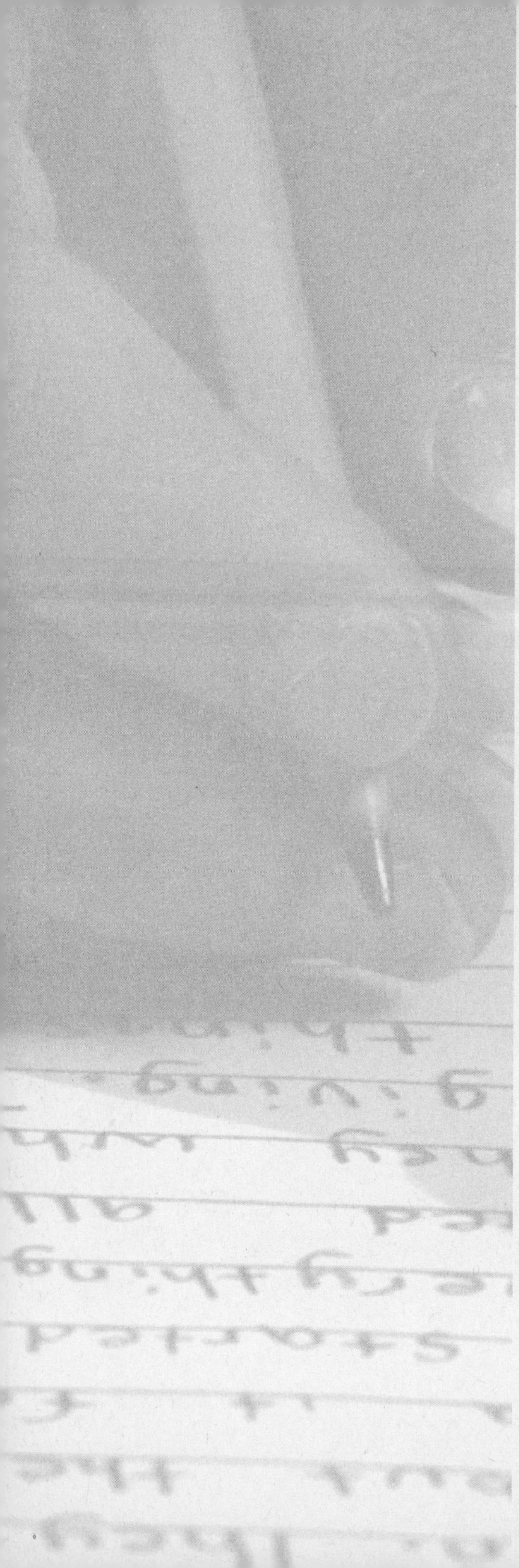

Part I
Orientation

Chapter 1
Introduction

Congratulations on your decision to attend business school! Preparing for the GMAT is an important part of the process, so let's get started. This chapter will provide you with a strategic plan for acing the GMAT, as well as an overview of the test itself, including question formats and information on how the test is scored.

HOW TO USE THIS BOOK: A STRATEGIC PLAN FOR ACING THE GMAT

1. Learn the Famed Princeton Review Test-Taking Strategies

In the next few chapters, you'll find the strategies that have given our GMAT students the edge for the past 20 years.

2. Learn the Specific Math and Verbal Skills You'll Need

Our courses include an extremely thorough review of the math and verbal skills our students need to ace the GMAT, and this book will give you that same review.

Important Phone Numbers:
To register for the GMAT: 800-717-GMAT

To reach GMAC Customer Service: 866-505-6559 or 703-668-9605

3. Practice Each Type of Question—at the Difficulty Level You Need to Master

Two of the GMAT's sections, the Quantitative and Verbal sections, are computer adaptive. These sections quickly hone in on your ability level and then mostly give you questions at or just above that level. It makes sense for you to practice on the level of problem you will actually see during the test. *Cracking the GMAT* is the only book out there with practice questions grouped by difficulty. Page after page of practice questions are arranged at the back of this book in difficulty "bins"—just like the questions on the real GMAT—so that you can concentrate on the question level you will have to answer on the actual test in order to get the score you need.

The recently added Integrated Reasoning section of the GMAT is not computer adaptive. We've provided two complete Integrated Reasoning sections at the back of this book to help you prepare for this section of the test.

4. Periodically Take Simulated GMATs to Measure Your Progress

As you work through the book, you'll want to take our online practice tests to see how you're doing. These tests closely mimic the GMAT so you can become familiar with the test's content and structure. Our tests include adaptive sections for the Quantitative and Verbal sections and a non-adaptive section for the Integrated Reasoning section. Our practice tests can be found at **PrincetonReview.com.** In addition, we actively encourage students to use *The Official Guide for GMAT Review,* which is published by the Graduate Management Admission Council (GMAC). It contains actual test questions from previous administrations of the GMAT. You should also take at least one of the real practice tests available through the GMAT website, **www.mba.com.**

5. Hone Your Skills

Using the detailed score reports from your practice exams, you'll be able to zero in on problem areas and quickly achieve mastery through additional practice. And as your score rises on the adaptive sections, this book is ready with more difficult question bins to keep you on track for the score you need. You can use the two practice Integrated Reasoning sections in this book to help you prepare for your practice tests and your real GMAT.

6. Keep Track of the Application Process

Throughout the book, you will find informative sidebars explaining how and when to register for the test, how and when to apply to business school, the advantages and disadvantages of applying early, and much more. Plus, at **PrincetonReview.com**, you'll be able to take advantage of our powerful web-based tools to match yourself with schools that meet your needs and preferences.

Important Websites
To register for the GMAT:
www.mba.com

WHAT IS THE GRADUATE MANAGEMENT ADMISSION TEST?

The Graduate Management Admission Test (GMAT) is a standardized test used by business schools as a tool to decide whom they are going to let into their M.B.A. programs.

More Great Books!
Check out our survey-driven guide, *The Best Business Schools*, for profiles of the nation's top b-schools.

Where Does the GMAT Come From?

The GMAT is published and administered by the Graduate Management Admission Council (GMAC). GMAC is a private company. We'll tell you more about them later on in this book.

What Does the Test Look Like?

The GMAT is offered only on computer. The 3.5 hour test is administered at a secure computer terminal at an approved testing center. You enter your multiple-choice answers on the screen with a mouse; you must compose your essay for the Writing Assessment section on the computer as well.

1. One 30 minute essay to be written on the computer using a generic word processing program.
2. One 30 minute, 12 question, multiple choice Integrated Reasoning section. Some Integrated Reasoning questions can have multiple parts.
(optional break)
3. A 75 minute, 37 question multiple choice Math section
(optional break)
4. A 75 minute, 41 question multiple choice Verbal section

On average, this would give you two minutes for each math question and a little less than two minutes for each verbal question—but you will find that our Princeton Review strategies will slightly revise these times. You must answer a question in order to get to the next question—which means that you can't skip a question and come back to it. And while you are not required to finish any of the sections, your score will be adjusted downward to reflect questions you did not complete.

On each of the Math and Verbal sections, approximately one quarter of the questions you encounter will be experimental and will not count toward your score. These questions, which will be mixed in among the regular questions, are there so the test company can try out new questions for future tests. We'll have much more to say about the experimental questions later.

What Information Is Tested on the GMAT?

You will find several different types of multiple-choice questions on the GMAT.

Math (37 questions total)

- Problem Solving—approximately 19 questions
- Data Sufficiency (a strange type of problem that exists on no other test in the world)—approximately 18 questions

Verbal (41 questions total)

- Reading Comprehension (tests your ability to answer questions about a passage)—approximately 13 questions
- Sentence Correction (a grammar-related question type)—approximately 17 questions
- Critical Reasoning (a logic-based question type recycled from the LSAT)—approximately 11 questions

Integrated Reasoning (12 questions total)

- Table Analysis—data is presented in a sortable table (like an Excel spreadsheet); each question usually has three parts.
- Graphics Interpretation—a chart or graph is used to display data; each question usually has two parts; answers are selected from drop-down boxes.
- Multi-Source Reasoning—information (a combination of charts, text, and tables) is presented on two or three tabs; each set of tabbed information is usually accompanied by three questions.
- Two-Part Analysis—each question usually has five or six options and you need to pick two.

How Is the GMAT Scored?

As soon as you've finished taking the GMAT, your computer will calculate and display your unofficial results, not including your Writing Assessment score. You can print out a copy of your unofficial results to take with you. Within 20 days, you will receive your score report online; a written report will be available only by request.

Most people think of the GMAT score as a single number, but in fact there are five separate numbers:

1. Math score (reported on a scale that runs from 0 to 60)
2. Verbal score (reported on a scale that runs from 0 to 60)
3. Total score (reported on a scale that runs from 200 to 800 and based only on the results of Math and Verbal sections)
4. Analytic Writing Assessment score (reported on a scale of 0 to 6, in half point increments; 6 is the highest score)
5. Integrated Reasoning score (reported on a scale from 1 to 8 in one point increments)

The report will look something like this:

Math	%	Verbal	%	Total	%	AWA	%	Integrated Reasoning	%
36	42	30	56	550	48	4.5	38	6	75

Many business schools tend to focus on the total score, which means that you may make up for weakness in one area by being strong in another. For example, if your quantitative skills are better than your verbal skills, they'll help pull up your total score—although some of the more selective schools say they prefer to see math and verbal sub-scores that are balanced. Total scores go up or down in ten-point increments. In other words, you might receive 490 or 500 on the GMAT, but never 494 or 495.

Since the Integrated Reasoning section is still relatively new, it's unclear how much importance schools will attach to your score on this section. Be sure to check with your schools to see how they plan to use the Integrated Reasoning score. Your schools should also be able to tell you what they consider a competitive score for this section. For more information on how schools weigh the Analytical Writing Score, refer to Chapter 21.

You will also see a percentile ranking next to each score. For example, if you see a percentile of 72 next to your Verbal score, it means that 72 percent of the people who took this test scored lower than you did on the Verbal section.

WHAT IS THE PRINCETON REVIEW?

The Princeton Review is a test-preparation company founded in New York City. It has branches in more than 50 cities across the country, as well as abroad. The Princeton Review's techniques are unique and powerful, and they were developed after a study of thousands of real GMAT questions. They work because they are based on the same principles that are used in writing the actual test. The Princeton

Review's techniques for beating the GMAT will help you improve your scores by teaching you to

- think like the test writers
- take full advantage of the computer-adaptive algorithms upon which the GMAT is based
- find the answers to questions you don't understand by using Process of Elimination
- avoid the traps that test writers have set for you (and use those traps to your advantage)

A Warning

Many of our techniques for beating the GMAT may be very different from the way that you would naturally approach problems. Some methods may even seem counterintuitive. Rest assured, however, that many test takers have used our methods to get great GMAT scores. To get the full benefit of our techniques, you must trust them. The only way to develop this trust is to practice the techniques and persuade yourself that they work.

Practice with Real Questions

One reason coaching books do not use real GMAT questions is that GMAC won't let them. So far, the council has refused to let anyone (including us) license actual questions from old tests. As we mentioned above, the council has its own review book called *The Official Guide for GMAT Review*, which we heartily recommend that you purchase. GMAC also puts out preparation software called *GMATPrep*, which can be downloaded for free from **www.mba.com**. This software includes two computer-adaptive tests plus additional practice sets, all of which feature real GMAT questions. By practicing our techniques on real GMAT items, you will be able to prove to yourself that the techniques work and increase your confidence when you actually take the test.

And, remember, by using The Princeton Review's practice questions grouped by level of difficulty at the back of this book, you'll be able to concentrate on types of questions you are actually likely to see.

There's More to This Book Than This Book

Don't forget to register your book at **PrincetonReview.com** to gain access to our computer-adaptive tests. Also check out **PrincetonReview.com/gmat**, where you'll find a ton of useful information on b-school programs, financial aid, and everything else related to b-school.

Summary

- By using a combination of The Princeton Review's Integrated Reasoning introduction, math and verbal reviews, the practice questions contained in this book, and periodic simulated tests, you will be able to improve your score on the GMAT.
- The test itself is taken on computer. It consists of the following:

Analytical Writing Assessment			
• Analysis of an Argument	1 essay on business or a topic of general interest.	30 minutes	Scoring: 0–6 in half point increments
Quantitative Section			
• Problem Solving • Data Sufficiency	37 questions total. Roughly 50% Problem Solving.	75 minutes	Scoring: 0–60

Verbal Section			
• Sentence Correction • Critical Reasoning • Reading Compre-hension	41 questions total. Roughly 40% Sentence Correc-tion and 30% each for Read-ing and Critical Reasoning.	75 minutes	Scoring: 0–60
Overall score: 200–800 (based only on the Quantita-tive and Verbal sections)			
Integrated Reasoning Section			
• Table Analysis • Graphics Interpreta-tion • Multi-Source Reasoning • Two-Part Analysis	12 questions total. But most questions require multiple responses.	30 minutes	Scored on a scale from 1 to 8 in one point increments.

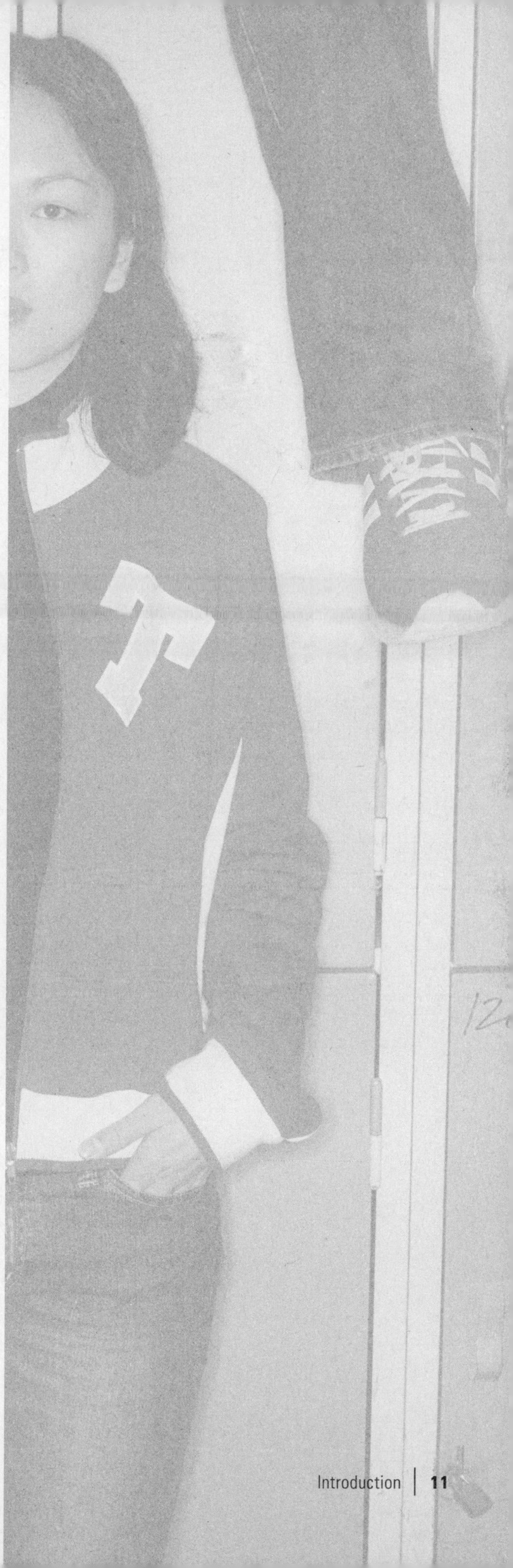

Chapter 2
How to Think About the GMAT

If you think the GMAT tests your business knowledge or shows how smart you are, you're in for a surprise. This chapter will give you a new way to look at the GMAT to guide your studies in the right direction.

Are You a Genius Or an Idiot?

If you're like most people, you think standardized tests measure how smart you are. If you score 800 on the GMAT, you may think of yourself as a genius (and the future manager of a corporate empire). If you score 200, you may think of yourself as an idiot (and the future manager of… well… nothing). You may think that the GMAT measures your verbal and math abilities. At the very least, you probably believe the GMAT is an accurate predictor of how you'll do in business school.

What Does the GMAT Measure?

The GMAT is not a test of how smart you are. Nor is it a test of your business acumen or even a predictor of your grades in business school. It's simply a test of how good you are at taking the GMAT. In fact, you will learn that by studying the very specific knowledge outlined in this book, you can substantially improve your score.

The GMAT as a Job Interview

The first axiom of any how-to book on job interviewing is that you must always tell your interviewer what he or she wants to hear. No matter whether this is good job-hunting advice, it happens to be a very useful strategy on the GMAT. The test writers think in predictable ways. You can improve your score by learning to think the way they do and anticipating the kinds of answers that they think are correct.

How Closely Does The Princeton Review Monitor the GMAT?

Very closely. Each year, we publish a new edition of this book to reflect the subtle shifts that happen over time, or, in the case of the introduction of the new Integrated Reasoning section last year, the major changes to the GMAT. For the latest information on the GMAT, please visit our website at **PrincetonReview.com**.

Is This Book Just Like The Princeton Review Course?

No. You won't have the benefit of taking ten computer-adaptive GMATs that are scored and analyzed by our computers. You won't get to sit in small classes with only three other highly motivated students who will spur you on. You won't get to work with our expert instructors who can assess your strengths and pinpoint your weaknesses. There is no way to put these things in a book.

What you *will* find in this book are some of the techniques and methods that have enabled our students to crack the system—plus a review of the essentials that you cannot afford not to know.

If at all possible, you should take our course. If that is not possible, then there is this book.

How to Crack the System

In the following chapters we're going to teach you our method for cracking the GMAT. Read each chapter carefully. Some of our ideas may seem strange at first. For example, when we tell you that it is sometimes easier to answer GMAT questions without actually working out the entire problem, you may think, "This isn't the way I conduct business."

But the GMAT Isn't About Business

We're not going to teach you business skills. We're not going to teach you math and English. We're going to teach you the GMAT.

Chapter 3 Cracking the Adaptive Sections: Basic Principles

This chapter will show you how the computer-adaptive sections of the GMAT really work. You will learn to pace yourself and to take advantage of the test's limitations.

HOW THE COMPUTER-ADAPTIVE GMAT SECTIONS WORK

To check out which b-schools are the "Toughest to Get Into," take a look at the Business School Ranking lists at PrincetonReview.com.

To understand how to beat the computer-adaptive sections (Math and Verbal) of the GMAT, you have to understand how they work.

Unlike paper-and-pencil standardized tests that begin with an easy question and then get progressively tougher, the computer-adaptive sections always begin by giving you a medium question. If you get it right, the computer gives you a slightly harder question. If you get it wrong, the computer gives you a slightly easier question, and so on. The idea is that the computer will zero in on your exact level of ability very quickly, which allows you to answer fewer questions overall and allows the computer to make a more finely honed assessment of your abilities.

What You Will See on Your Screen

During the test itself, your screen will display the question you're currently working on, with little circles next to the five answer choices. To answer the question, you use your mouse to click on the circle next to the answer choice you think is correct. Then you press a button at the bottom of the screen to verify that this is the answer you want to pick.

What You Will Never See on Your Screen

What you will *never* see is the process by which the computer keeps track of your progress. When you start each adaptive section, the computer assumes that your score is average. So, your starting score for each section is around a 30. As you go through the test, the computer will keep revising its assessment of your score based on your responses.

Let's watch the process in action. In the left-hand column on the next page, you'll see what a hypothetical test taker—let's call her Jane—sees on her screen as she takes the test. In the right-hand column, we'll show you how GMAC keeps track of how she's doing. (We've simplified this example a bit in the interest of clarity.)

WHAT JANE SEES:

To regard the overwhelming beauty of the Mojave Desert is <u>understanding the great forces of</u> nature that shape our planet.

◯ understanding the great forces of
◯ to understand the great forces to
◯ to understand the great forces of
◯ understanding the greatest forces in
◯ understanding the greater forces on

WHAT JANE *DOESN'T* SEE:

When you start each adaptive section, the computer assumes that your score is average. So, your starting score for each section is around a 30. Jane gets the first question right (the third answer down), so her score goes up to a 35, and the computer selects a harder problem for her second question.

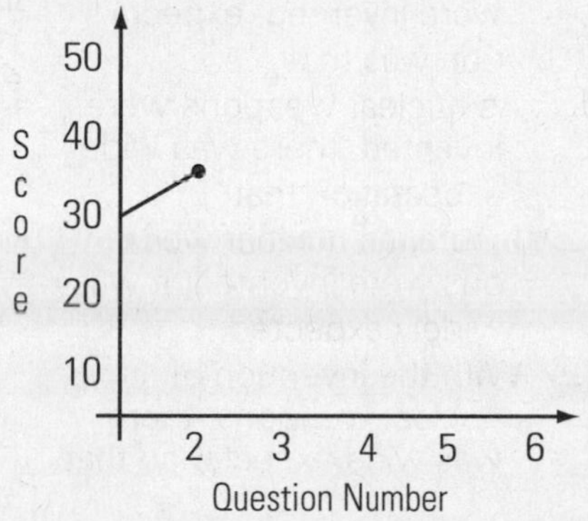

WHAT JANE SEES:

Hawks in a certain region depend heavily for their diet on a particular variety of field mouse. The killing of field mice by farmers will seriously endanger the survival of hawks in this region.

Which of the following, if true, casts the most doubt on the conclusion drawn above?

◯ The number of mice killed by farmers has increased in recent years.
◯ Farmers kill many other types of pests besides field mice without any adverse effect on hawks.
◯ Hawks have been found in other areas besides this region.
◯ Killing field mice leaves more food for the remaining mice, who have larger broods the following season.
◯ Hawks are also endangered because of pollution and deforestation.

WHAT JANE *DOESN'T* SEE:

The computer happens to select a Critical Reasoning problem.

Oops. Jane gets the second question wrong (the correct answer is the fourth answer down), so her score goes down to a 32, and the computer gives her a slightly easier problem.

current score: 32

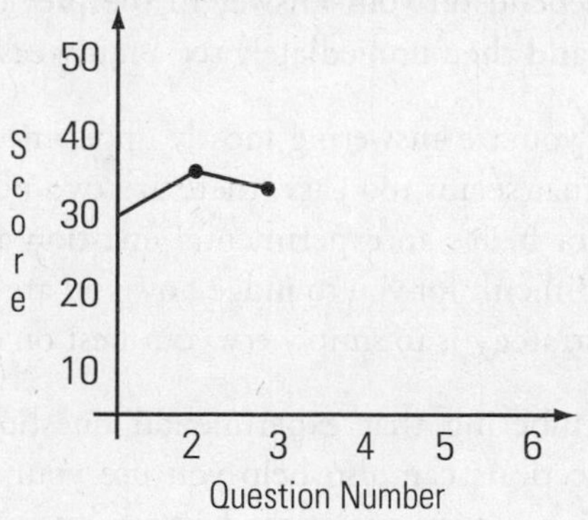

WHAT JANE SEES:

Nuclear weapons being invented, there was wide expectation in the scientific community that all war would end.

- Nuclear weapons being invented, there was wide expectation in the scientific community that
- When nuclear weapons were invented, expectation was that
- As nuclear weapons were invented, there was wide expectation that
- Insofar as nuclear weapons were invented, it was widely expected
- With the invention of nuclear weapons, there was wide expectation that

WHAT JANE *DOESN'T* SEE:

Jane has no idea what the correct answer is on this third question, but she guesses choice E and gets it correct. Her score goes up to a 33.

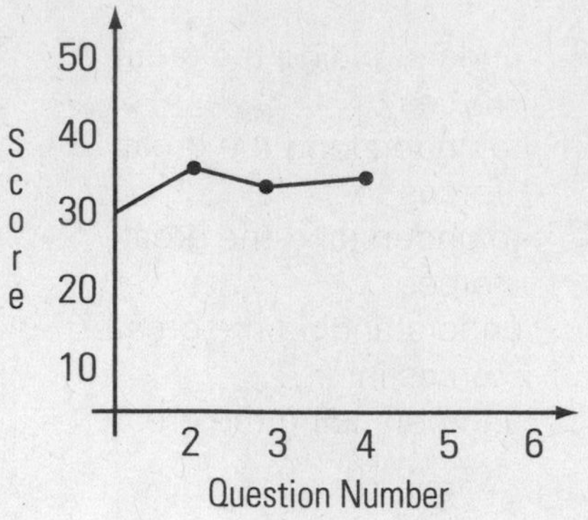

You get the idea. At the very beginning of the section, your score moves up or down in larger increments than it does at the end, when GMAC believes it is merely refining whether you deserve, say, a 42 or a 43. The questions you will see on your test come from a huge pool of questions held in the computer in what the test writers call "difficulty bins"—each bin with a different level of difficulty.

The Experimental Questions

Unfortunately, approximately one-fourth of the questions in each adaptive section (Math and Verbal) won't actually count toward your score; they are experimental questions being tested out on you. The difficulty of an experimental question does not depend on your answer to the previous question. You could get a question right and then immediately see a fairly easy experimental question.

So, if you are answering mostly upper-medium questions and suddenly see a question that seems too easy, there are two possibilities: a) you are about to fall for a trap, or b) it's an experimental question and really is easy. That means it can be very difficult for you to judge how you are doing on the section. So, don't try! Your best strategy is to simply try your best on every question.

Remembering that experimental questions are included throughout the adaptive sections can also help you use your time wisely. When you get stuck on a question—even one of the first ten questions—remember that it might be experimental. Spending an inordinate amount of time on one question could cause you to rush and make silly mistakes later. Would you really want to do that if the question turned out to be experimental?

Eliminate what you can, guess, and move on in those situations.

What the Computer-Adaptive GMAT Uses to Calculate Your Score

The GMAT keeps a running tally of your score as it goes, based on the number of questions you get correct and their levels of difficulty—but there are two other important factors that can affect your score:

- Early questions count more than later questions.
- Questions you leave unanswered will lower your score.

How much can leaving questions at the end unanswered damage your score? GMAC says that somebody who was on track to score in the 91st percentile will drop to the 77th percentile by leaving just five questions unanswered.
Answer every question!

Why Early Questions Count More Than Later Questions

At the beginning of the test, your score moves up or down in larger increments as the computer hones in on what will turn out to be your ultimate score. If you make a mistake early on, the computer will choose a much easier question, and it will take you a while to work back to where you started from. Similarly, if you get an early problem correct, the computer will then give you a much harder question.

However, later in the test, a mistake is less costly—because the computer has decided your general place in the scoring ranks and is merely refining your exact score.

While it is not impossible to come back from behind, you can see that it is particularly important that you do well at the beginning of the test. Answering just a few questions correctly at the beginning will propel your interim score quite high.

Pace Yourself

Make sure that you get these early questions correct by starting slowly, checking your work on early problems, and then gradually picking up the pace so that you finish all the problems in the section.

Still, if you are running out of time at the end, it makes sense to spend a few moments to guess intelligently on the remaining questions using Process of Elimination (POE) rather than random guesses or (let's hope it never comes to this) not answering at all. You will be pleased to know that it is possible to guess on several questions at the end and still end up with a 700.

On the next page, you'll find our pacing advice for math and verbal. The charts will tell you how much time you should spend for each block of ten questions based on a practice test score.

MATH				
	Question numbers			
Score	1–10	11–20	21–30	31–37
Under 35	30 min.	25 min.	15 min.	5 min.
35–42	30 min.	20 min.	15 min.	10 min.
Above 42	25 min.	20 min.	20 min.	10 min.

VERBAL				
	Question numbers			
Score	1–10	11–20	21–30	31–41
Under 28	30 min.	25 min.	10 min.	10 min.
28–34	27 min.	20 min.	18 min.	10 min.
Above 34	25 min.	20 min.	15 min.	15 min.

The Princeton Review Approach to the GMAT

To help you ace the computer-adaptive sections of the GMAT, this book is going to provide you with

- Test-taking techniques that have made The Princeton Review famous and that will enable you to turn the inherent weaknesses of the computer-adaptive sections of the GMAT to your advantage
- A thorough review of all the major topics covered on the GMAT
- A short practice test to help you predict your current scoring level
- Practice questions to help you raise your scoring level

Know Your Bin

According to classic theory, the average test taker spends most of his or her time answering questions at his level of competency (which he gets right) and questions that are just above his level of competency (which he gets wrong). In other words, most test takers will see questions from only a few difficulty "bins."

This means that to raise your score, you must learn to answer questions from the bins immediately *above* your current scoring level. At the back of this book, you will find a short diagnostic test to determine your current scoring level and then bins filled with questions at various scoring levels. When combined with a thorough review of the topics covered on the GMAT, this should put you well on your way to the score you're looking for.

But first, let's learn with some test-taking strategies.

Summary

- The computer-adaptive sections of the GMAT always start you off with a medium question. If you get it right, you get a harder question; if you get it wrong, you get an easier question. The test assigns you a score after each answer and quickly (in theory) hones in on your level of ability.
- Mixed in with the questions that count toward your score will be experimental questions that do not count toward your score. The testing company is using you as an unpaid guinea pig to try out new questions. Approximately one-fourth of the questions in each of the adaptive sections are experimental.
- Because the test is taken on a computer, you must answer each question to get to the next question—you can't skip a question or come back to it later.
- Because of the scoring algorithms, early questions count more than later questions—so check your work carefully at the beginning of the test.
- The GMAT computer-adaptive sections select questions for you from "bins" of questions at different levels of ability. The Princeton Review method consists of finding your current bin level through diagnostic tests and then practicing questions from that bin, gradually moving to higher bins as you become more proficient.

Chapter 4
Cracking the Adaptive Sections: Intermediate Principles

This chapter provides an introduction to one of the key Princeton Review techniques: Process of Elimination.

Imagine for a moment that you are a contestant on the latest reboot of *Deal or No Deal*. You're down to the final two briefcases. The host asks you, "Do you want briefcase number two, or briefcase number three?"

As you carefully weigh your options, the members of the audience are shouting out *their* suggestions. But you can bet that there is *one* thing no one in the audience is going to shout at you: "Skip the question!"

B-School Lingo
If you want to be an MBA student, you'll have to learn to talk like one.

air hogs: students who monopolize classroom discussion and love to hear themselves speak.

B2B: "Business-to-Business": a company that sells not to retail consumers, but to other enterprises.

B2C: Business-to-Consumer: a company that sells primarily to individual retail consumers.

Source: *The Best Business Schools*

It's just not an option. You have to make a choice—and you have to make it *now*. In one briefcase there is a million dollars with which you could buy a yacht; in the other, $50 which won't even pay for the gas you used to drive to the studio. One of these choices is much better than the others, but on *Deal or No Deal*, you have no idea which is which.

Let's Make a GMAT

Normally when you don't know the correct answer on a test, you skip the question and come back to it later. But on the computer-adaptive sections of the GMAT, as in *Deal or No Deal*, you can never skip the question.

To Get to the Next Question, You Have to Answer This One

Because of the way the computer-adaptive sections of the GMAT's scoring algorithm works, the question you see on your computer screen at any particular moment depends on your response to the previous question. This creates an odd situation for the test designers: If they allowed you to skip a question, they wouldn't know which question to give you next.

It's clear from articles that GMAT test designers have published that they know test takers are at a real disadvantage when they can't skip a problem and come back to it later. Still, the idea of using a computer to administer tests was too tempting to give up. In the end, GMAC decided that you should generously be willing to make the sacrifice in the name of progress.

So whether you know the answer to a problem or not, you have to answer it in order to move on.

This means that, like it or not, you may have to do some guessing on the GMAT. Ah, but there's guessing, and then there's *guessing*.

If You Don't Know the Right Answer, Don't You Dare Just Pick an Answer at Random

This may sound a little loony, but it turns out that you don't always have to know the correct answer to get a question right.

Try answering the following question:

> What is the unit of currency in Sweden?

What? You don't know?

Unless you work for an international bank or have traveled in Scandinavia, there is no reason why you should know what the unit of currency in Sweden is. (By the way, the GMAT doesn't ask such factual questions. We're using this one to make a point.) As it stands now, because you don't know the answer, you would have to answer this question at random, right?

Not necessarily. GMAT questions are written in multiple-choice format. One of the five choices has to be the answer. You just have to find it.

Inappropriate Use of GMAT Scores

The following is a list of what GMAC considers "inappropriate uses" of GMAT scores:

1. As a requisite for awarding a degree
2. As a requirement for employment, for licensing or certification to perform a job, or for job-related rewards (raises, promotions, etc.)
3. As an achievement test

Source: *Graduate Management Admission Council*

Look for Wrong Answers Instead of Right Ones

Let's put this question into multiple-choice format—the only format you'll find on the GMAT—and see if you still want to answer at random.

> What is the unit of currency in Sweden?
>
> ○ the dollar
> ○ the franc
> ○ the pound sterling
> ○ the yen
> ○ the krona

PROCESS OF ELIMINATION

Suddenly this question isn't difficult anymore. You may not have known the right answer, but you certainly knew enough to eliminate the wrong answers. Wrong answers are often easier to spot than right answers. Sometimes they just sound weird. Other times they're logically impossible. While it is rare to be able to eliminate all four of the incorrect answer choices on the GMAT, you will almost always be able to eliminate at least one of them—and frequently two or more—by using Process of Elimination. Process of Elimination (POE for short) will enable you to answer questions that you don't have the time to figure out exactly. We will refer to POE in every single chapter of this book. It is one of the most important and fundamental tools you will use to increase your score.

Try another example:

> Which of the following countries uses the peso as its unit of currency?
>
> ◯ Russia
> ◯ Canada
> ◯ Venezuela
> ◯ England
> ◯ Chile

This time you can probably get rid of only three of the five answer choices using POE. The answer is clearly *not* Russia, Canada, or England, but most people probably don't know for sure whether the answer is Venezuela or Chile.

You've got the question down to two possibilities. What should you do?

Heads or Tails

A Chilean might flip a peso. You have a fifty-fifty chance of getting this question right, which is much better than if you had guessed at random. And because the GMAT forces you to guess anyway, it makes sense to guess intelligently.

In the chapters that follow, we'll show you specific ways to make use of POE to increase your score. You may feel uncomfortable about using these techniques at first, but the sooner you make them your own, the sooner you'll start to improve your score.

Is It Fair to Get a Question Right When You Don't Know the Answer?

If you took any math courses in college, you probably remember that the correct answer to a problem, while important, wasn't the only thing you were graded on. Your professor was probably more interested in *how* you got the answer, whether you wrote an elegant equation, or if you used the right formula.

If your equation was correct but you messed up your addition at the end, did you get the entire question wrong? Most college professors give partial credit for an answer like that. After all, what's most important is the mental process that goes into getting the answer, not the answer alone.

On the GMAT, if you don't click the correct circle with your mouse, you're wrong. It doesn't matter that you knew how to do the problem, or that you clicked the wrong answer by mistake. GMAC doesn't care: You're just wrong. And a wrong answer means that the running score GMAC is keeping on you will go down by 10 or 20 points and you'll be forced to answer several easier questions correctly before you get back to the level at which you were.

This really isn't fair. It seems only fitting that you should also be able to benefit from the flip side of this situation: If you click on the correct circle, GMAC doesn't care how you got that answer either.

So, What Are the Appropriate Uses?

1. Selection of applicants for graduate study in management
2. Selection of applicants for financial aid on the basis of academic potential
3. Counseling and guidance

Source: *Graduate Management Admission Council*

Scratch Work

Process of Elimination is a powerful tool, but it's powerful only if you keep track of the answer choices you've eliminated. On a computer-adaptive test, you obviously can't cross off choices on the screen—but you can cross them off on your scratch paper.

The testing center provides each tester with a blank ten-page booklet and a fine-tipped black marker for scratch work. The pages are laminated and printed with a faint grid pattern useful for drawing math diagrams. In our course, we encourage our students to divide up each page into boxes and label each box with five answer choices as shown on the next page.

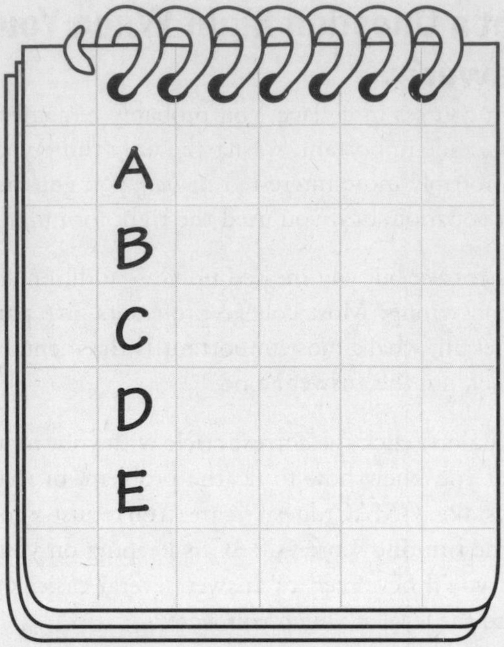

Each letter corresponds to an answer. Of course, the answers on the computer-adaptive sections of the GMAT are no longer labeled with letters, but to be able to track the answers you've crossed off, it helps to think of them as if they are. The first answer choice is equivalent to A, the second to B, and so on.

Throughout this book, you will see us using the scratch booklet to keep track of the answer choices that have already been eliminated. By making this part of the ritual of how you take the GMAT, you will be able to prevent careless errors and make your guesses count.

Summary

- Because of the way the GMAT is designed, you will be forced to answer questions whether or not you know the correct answer.
- However, not knowing the exact answer to a question does not mean that you have to get it wrong.
- When you don't know the right answer to a question, look for wrong answers instead. This is called POE, or Process of Elimination.
- The best way to keep track of the answer choices that you've eliminated is to use your scratch work to cross them off as you go.

Chapter 5
Cracking the Adaptive Sections: Advanced Principles

In this chapter, you will make a new friend named Joe Bloggs. You will also learn how to use the way the GMAT is constructed to radically increase your score.

The people who write the computer-adaptive section of the GMAT think that this part of the test is wonderful—and not just because they wrote it, or because it makes them a lot of money. They like it because it ensures that the only problems a test taker gets to see are problems at, and slightly above and below, her level of ability. One of the things they always hated about the paper-and-pencil test was that a student scoring 300 could guess the correct answer to a 700-level question.

But They Have This Little Problem

The questions on the GMAT are still multiple-choice.

That may not seem like a problem to you, but consider the following situation. Suppose an average student takes the GMAT. He's answered 36 of the 37 problems on the Math section. There's one left, and as he looks at this last question, he realizes he has absolutely no idea how to answer it. However, one of the answer choices just "seems" right. So he picks it.

And he gets it right.

The test writers get nightmares just thinking about this situation. That average student was supposed to get 500. He "deserved" 500. But by guessing the correct answer to one last problem, he may have gotten 510.

Ten points more than he "deserved."

GMAC's Solution

GMAC's tests wouldn't be worth much if students could routinely guess the correct answer to difficult questions by picking answers that seemed right.

So the test writers came up with a wonderful solution:

On some difficult questions, answer choices that seem right to the average student are wrong.

Choosing Answers That Seem Right

Almost everybody gets stuck on at least a few questions when they take the computer-adaptive sections of the GMAT. After all, the questions keep getting harder as you get questions right. Sooner or later, you may run into a question that you just don't know how to do. If you're like most people, you'll get as far as you can, and then choose the answer that seems correct. In other words, you play a hunch. For some questions, you may pick an answer because it "just looks right" or something about it seems to go naturally with the question.

What Happens When the Average Person Takes the GMAT?

The average person picks the answer that seems right on every problem. Sometimes these hunches are correct; sometimes they are not.

- On easy questions, the average person tends to pick the correct answer. The answers that seem right to the average person actually are right on the easy questions.
- On medium questions, the average person's hunches are right only some of the time. Sometimes the answers that seem right to the average person really are right and sometimes they're wrong.
- Finally, on difficult problems, the average person's hunches are almost always wrong. The answers that seem right to the average person on these questions are invariably wrong.

Question Difficulty

GMAT questions are rated based on how many people get them wrong not the question content.

Hard = 70 percent or more of people get it wrong

Medium = about half of people get it wrong

Easy = fewer than 30 percent of people get it wrong

MEET JOE BLOGGS

We're going to talk a lot about "the average test taker" from now on. For the sake of convenience, let's call him Joe Bloggs. Joe Bloggs is just the average prospective business school student. Joe gets an average score—around 500—when he takes the GMAT because Joe always does what the test writers expect. Joe tends to answer questions quickly because he just picks answers that seem right.

There's a little bit of Joe in everybody. If you've ever wanted to pick an answer immediately after reading a question, you're in touch with your inner Joe. The problem only emerges later when you reread some of these questions and realize you missed something. The quick, obvious answer was wrong!

No matter what your score, Joe can help you do better on the GMAT. Any time you have the impulse to pick an answer within a few seconds of reading the question, you may be about to pick a "Joe Bloggs answer." Ask yourself, "Are they really going to let me go to a good business school for doing something that easy?" Probably not. Go reread the question!

How Does Joe Bloggs Approach the GMAT?

Joe Bloggs, the average test taker, spends most of his time answering questions of medium difficulty. But whenever he gets several questions correct in a row, the computer gives him a more difficult question.

Joe approaches the GMAT just as the test writers expect. Whether the question is hard or easy, he always chooses the answer that *seems* to be correct.

Here's an example of what a more difficult problem might look like on a GMAT Problem Solving section:

> The output of a factory is increased by 10% to keep up with rising demand. To handle the holiday rush, this new output is increased by 20%. By approximately what percent would the output of the factory now have to be decreased in order to restore the original output?
>
> ○ 20%
> ○ 24%
> ○ 30%
> ○ 32%
> ○ 79%

This question is from an upper medium difficulty bin. Don't bother trying to work the problem out now. You will learn how to do this type of problem (percentage decrease) in the first math chapter.

How Did Joe Bloggs Do on This Question?

He got it wrong. Why? Because GMAC set a trap for him. In fact, this question was rated upper medium *because* the trap answer made it so easy to get the question wrong!

Which Answer Did Joe Bloggs Pick on This Question?

Joe didn't think this was a hard problem. The answer seemed perfectly obvious. Joe Bloggs picked the middle choice—what we call C. (Please note that the first answer choice is called A, the second B, etc.) Joe assumed that if you increase production first by 10% and then by 20%, you have to take away 30% to get back to where you started.

The test writers led Joe away from the correct answer by giving him an answer that seemed right. In fact, the correct answer is B. Here's the same problem with slightly different answer choices. We've changed the choices to make a point:

> The output of a factory is increased by 10% to keep up with rising demand. To handle the holiday rush, this new output is increased by 20%. By approximately what percent would the output of the factory now have to be decreased in order to restore the original output?
>
> ◯ 21%
> ◯ 24%
> ◯ 34.2%
> ◯ 37%
> ◯ 71.5%

If Joe had seen this version, he actually would have been more likely to get the question right. He still would have thought, "That's easy—30 percent" two seconds after reading the question. However, when he looked at the answers and 30% wasn't there, he would have been forced to go back and think about how he should really solve the question. But the test writers wanted him to get it wrong, so they supplied the trap answer.

B-School Lingo

back of the envelope: a quick analysis of numbers, as if scribbled on the back of an envelope

benchmarking: comparing a company to others in the industry

burn rate: the amount of cash a money-losing company consumes during a period of time

Source: *The Best Business Schools*

Could GMAC Have Made This an Easy Question Instead?

Sure, by writing different answer choices.

Here's the same question with choices we've substituted to make the correct answer choice obvious:

> The output of a factory is increased by 10% to keep up with rising demand. To handle the holiday rush, this new output is increased by 20%. By approximately what percent would the output of the factory now have to be decreased in order to restore the original output?
>
> ◯ a million %
> ◯ 24%
> ◯ a billion %
> ◯ a trillion %
> ◯ a zillion %

When the problem is written this way, Joe Bloggs can see that the answer has to be choice B. It seems right to Joe because all the other answers seem obviously wrong.

Profiting from Other People's Bankruptcy

Let's look at a textbook example of how *not* to run a company.

Suppose you started your own company, with three partners: Kenneth Lay (formerly of Enron), Bernie Madoff (former head of Madoff Investment Securities), and Martha Stewart (now back with Martha Stewart Omnimedia). You have an important business decision to make, and each of your partners gives you his or her advice. Lay says, "Take an established company with actual assets and turn it into an Internet company without assets. It always worked for me." Madoff says, "Just pretend you're actually making money—the investors will never know the difference." Stewart says, "What you need is inside information."

Are you going to make use of the advice of these people? Of course not! Now you know three things you're *not* going to do.

Joe Bloggs is our textbook example of how *not* to take a test.

YOUR PARTNER ON THE TEST: JOE BLOGGS

When you take the GMAT a few weeks or months from now, you'll have to take it on your own, of course. But suppose for a moment that GMAC allowed you to take it with Joe Bloggs as your partner. Would Joe be any help to you on the GMAT?

You Probably Don't Think So

After all, Joe is wrong as often as he's right. He knows the answers to the easy questions, but so do you. You'd like to do better than average on the GMAT, and Joe earns only an average score (he's the average test taker, remember). All things considered, you'd probably prefer to have someone else for your partner.

But Joe might turn out to be a pretty helpful partner, after all. Because his hunches on difficult questions are always wrong, couldn't you improve your chances on those questions simply by finding out what Joe wanted to pick and then picking something else?

If you could use what you know about Joe Bloggs to eliminate one, two, or even three obviously incorrect choices on a hard problem, wouldn't you improve your score by guessing among the remaining choices?

Whatever Your Current Scoring Level, the Joe Bloggs Principle Can Help You

We're going to teach you how to use Joe Bloggs while taking the GMAT.

After you've taken the practice test at the back of this book, the free tests on our website, or the practice tests available in *GMATPrep*, you will have some idea of how you are scoring at any given moment on the GMAT. This means that you'll know approximately the level of difficulty of most of the problems you'll face.

However, it's not a good idea to worry about the difficulty levels of questions as you are taking the test. You really don't have time for that! Instead, anytime that you get an answer with very little work, consider that you might be about to pick a Joe Bloggs answer. At the very least, reread the question stem before selecting your answer. If you know from your practice tests that you generally do well on the section, you probably want to eliminate that easy answer.

Harvard and the GMAT

For 12 years, Harvard University's Business School would not even look at the GMAT scores of its applicants. The class of 1997 was the first in more than a decade that was required to submit GMAT scores.

Should You Always Just Eliminate Any Answer That Seems to Be Correct?

No! Remember what we said about Joe Bloggs:

1. His hunches are often correct on easy questions.
2. His hunches are sometimes correct and sometimes incorrect on medium questions.
3. His hunches are always wrong on difficult questions.

Putting Joe Bloggs to Work for You

In the following chapters, we'll teach you many specific problem-solving techniques based on the Joe Bloggs principle. The Joe Bloggs principle will help you:

1. Use POE to eliminate incorrect answer choices.
2. Avoid careless mistakes.

Bloggs and Your Bin

Knowing your bin is key to knowing how to use Joe Bloggs. Based on your scores on practice tests, you will have a good sense of what bins the test writers will be drawing from during the real test. If those bins are from the upper medium or difficult problems, then you can expect to see Joe Bloggs answers in some of these questions—and you will know that they are almost certainly wrong. On the other hand, if you know that you are drawing questions from the easy and early medium questions, then you will also know that the Joe Bloggs answer you spot could well be correct.

Summary

- Almost everyone approaches the GMAT by choosing the answer that seems correct, all things considered.
- Joe Bloggs is the average GMAT test taker. He earns an average score on the GMAT. On easy GMAT questions, the answers that seem correct to him are usually correct. On medium questions, his answers are sometimes correct and sometimes not. On hard questions, the answers that seem correct to him are always wrong.
- By taking a practice test from time to time, you can predict your current scoring level—which, in turn, will tell you what type of questions you will generally be answering: easy, medium, or difficult.
- Whatever your current scoring level, the Joe Bloggs principle can help you to eliminate answer choices when you don't know the correct answer.

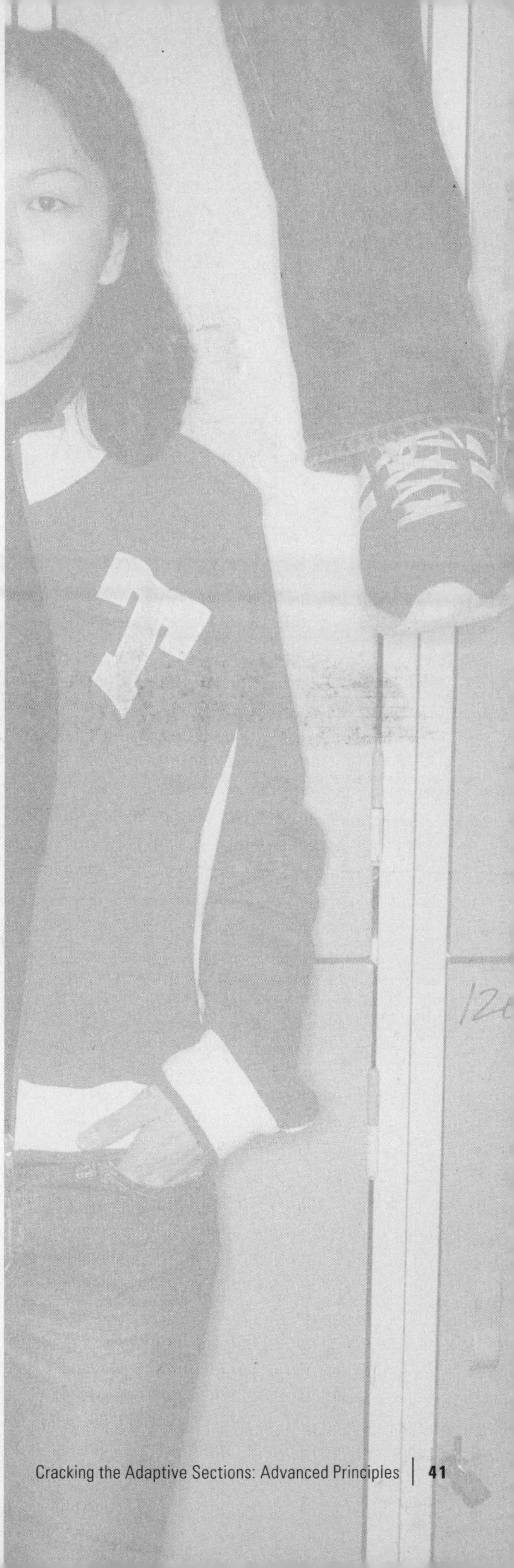

Chapter 6
Taking the GMAT

How do you register and practice for the GMAT? What is taking the actual test really like? What do you do if something goes wrong? This chapter will answer these and other practical questions.

REGISTERING TO TAKE THE GMAT

To register for the GMAT, call 1-800-717-GMAT or visit the website at **www.mba.com.**

The easiest way to register for the exam is by telephone or online. You will be given a list of dates, times, and testing centers that are located near you. One of the actual advantages of the GMAT is that you get to schedule the time of the exam. If you are not a morning person, ask for an afternoon time slot. If you can't think after midday, ask for a morning time slot.

Keep in mind that certain slots get filled quickly, so be sure to call ahead of time. The registration fee is $250 (worldwide). Those who schedule an exam in certain countries will incur taxes. Tax rate information is available at **www.mba.com** in the GMAT registration section. Note that checks or money orders payable in U.S. dollars must be drawn from banks located in the United States or Canada.

PRACTICING TO TAKE THE GMAT

As you prepare for the GMAT, it's important to know—in advance—what the experience of taking the test is like, so that you can mimic those conditions during practice tests. When you are taking a practice test, turn off your telephone, and try to strictly observe the time limits of the test sections, and even the time limits of the breaks in between sections. To mimic the experience of working with a scratch booklet, buy a spiral notebook filled with grid paper. If you know when you will be taking the real GMAT, try to schedule your practice tests around the same time of day.

If you are the sort of person who likes to have a mental picture of what a new experience will be like, you might even consider visiting the test center ahead of time. This serves two purposes: first, you'll know how to get there on the day of the test, and second, you'll be familiar with the ambiance in advance.

The Days Before the Test

Try to keep to your regular routine. Staying up late to study the last few nights before the test is counterproductive. It's important to get regular amounts of exercise and sleep. Continue the study plan you've been on from the beginning, but taper off toward the end. You'll want to take your last practice exam no later than several days before the real test, so you'll have time to go over the results carefully. The last day or so should be devoted to any topics that still give you trouble.

The Night Before the Test

Get together the things you will need to take with you for the test: directions to the test center (if you haven't already been there); a mental list of the schools you wish to receive your test scores (if you can't identify these when you take the test, you will have to pay $28 extra per school to get scores sent out later); a snack, and some water. Snacks and water are not allowed in the testing room, but they can be placed in your locker and consumed during a break. Don't bother to take a calculator—no calculators are permitted for the adaptive sections (Quantitative and Verbal) of the GMAT. An onscreen calculator is provided for the Integrated Reasoning section.

> What to Take to the Test Center
> 1. A government-issued ID
> 2. A snack
> 3. A bottle of water

Once you have gathered everything you need, take the night off. Go to a movie. Relax. There is no point in last-minute cramming. You are as ready as you are going to be.

The Day of the Test

If you are taking the test in the morning, get up early enough that you have time to eat breakfast, if that is your usual routine, and do a couple of GMAT questions you've already seen in order to get your mind working. If you are taking the test in the afternoon, make sure you get some lunch, and, again, do a few GMAT problems. You don't want to have to warm up on the test itself.

Take a snack to the test center. Use your breaks to eat the food you've brought, or to run to the bathroom.

At the Testing Center

Unlike testing sessions you may have attended in the past, where hundreds of people were lined up to take the same test, you may well be the only person at your testing center taking the GMAT. You'll be asked to present your government-issued ID, and an employee will take your photograph and scan your palm using a palm vein scanner. Finally, you'll be led to the computer station where you will take the test. The station consists of a desk with a computer monitor, a keyboard, a mouse, a scratch booklet, and a black, fine-tipped marker. The marker they will give you to write in your scratch booklet has tendency to dry up when left uncapped—so during breaks, remember to cap it. If you need another marker or another scratch booklet during the test, simply raise your hand, and a proctor will bring it. However, the timer won't stop while the proctor brings you another scratch booklet or marker. Use your practice tests to learn to fit your scratch work into one scratch booklet. Before the test starts, make sure you're comfortable. Is there enough light? Is your desk sturdy? Don't be afraid to speak up; you're going to be spending four hours at that desk.

There will almost certainly be other people in the same room at other computer stations taking other computer-adaptive tests. You might be seated next to someone taking the licensing exam for architects or a test for school nurses, or even a test for golf pros.

None of the people in the room will have necessarily started at the same time. The testing center employee will show you how to begin the test, but the computer itself will be your proctor from then on. It will tell you how much time you have left in a section, when your time is up, and when to go on to the next section.

The test center employees will be available if you have a question. They will also monitor the room for security purposes. Just in case their eagle eyes aren't enough, video and audio systems will record everything that happens in the room.

The process sounds less human than it really is. Our students have generally found the test center employees to be quite nice.

What Your Screen Will Look Like

During most of the test, your screen will look a lot like this:

Admissions Insight No. 1: Timeline
January–May: Research schools; study for the GMAT
June–July: Take the GMAT; request official undergraduate transcripts; ask mentors for recommendations
July–August: Start essays; follow up with recommenders; update resume
September: Fine-tune essay; make sure recommenders meet deadlines
October: Begin to submit applications; send thank-you notes to recommenders

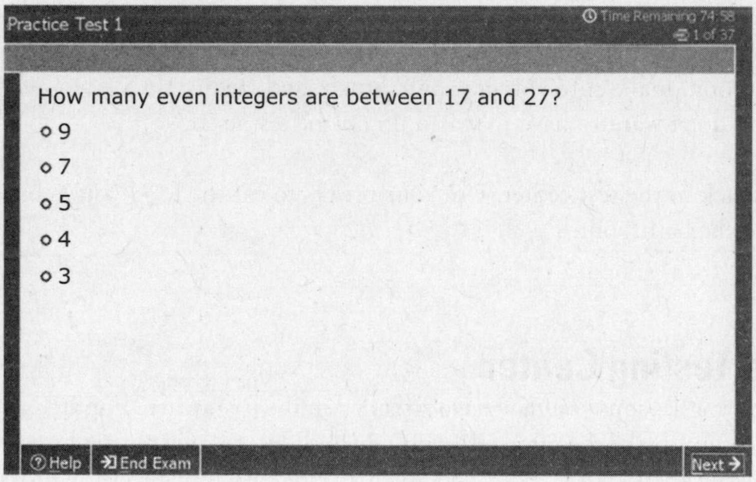

The problem you're working on at any particular moment will be near the top of the screen (by the way, the answer to this one is the third choice). At the top right will be a readout of the time remaining in the section, the number of the question you're working on, and how many total questions there are in the section. Here are the main interface items you will see on the screen:

End Exam—By clicking on this button, you can end the test at any moment. We don't recommend that you do this unless you actually become ill. Even if you decide not to have your test scored (an option they will give you at the end of the exam), you might as well finish—it's great practice, and besides, GMAC has no intention of giving you a refund.

Time—The time you have left to complete the section is displayed in the upper right of the screen. You can hide the time by clicking on it, and you can make it reappear by clicking on the icon in its place. During the last few minutes of the test, the time is automatically displayed and you cannot hide it.

Question Number—The question number that you are on is also displayed in the upper right, and it works just like the time display: You can hide it by clicking on it or make it reappear by clicking on the icon. During the last few minutes of the test, the question number is automatically displayed and cannot be hidden.

Help—During the test this button provides test and section directions and information about using the software.

Next—When you've answered a question by clicking on the small bubble in front of the answer you think is correct, you press this button.

Confirm—After you press "Next," a pop-up window will open and ask you to confirm your answer. Select "yes" to continue to the next question.

What Happens If You Get Stuck on a Question?

Everyone knows that sinking feeling of not knowing how to do a test problem, but before you start panicking, there are a few things to bear in mind about the GMAT.

First of all, as any Princeton Review graduate will tell you, seeing hard questions on the adaptive (Math and Verbal) sections of the GMAT is a good sign. Because these sections are adaptive, you don't get a hard question until you've answered a bunch of increasingly difficult medium questions correctly—which means you are probably already on track for a good score.

Second, if you have gone through this book and taken the practice tests, then chances are good that if you reread the question and think about it for a few seconds, you may get an idea of how to start it (and starting is half the battle).

Third, you should remember that approximately one-fourth of the questions on the adaptive sections of this test don't even count. They are "experimental questions" being tried out for future versions of the GMAT, so there's no point in getting too upset over a question that might not even get scored.

And fourth, if you are really stuck, then you can pull out The Princeton Review's arsenal of POE (Process of Elimination) techniques to do some very shrewd guessing.

Admissions Insight No. 2: Research
All business schools are NOT alike. To begin your admissions research, go to **PrincetonReview.com**, and take advantage of our Advanced Business School Search tool. Our school profiles present detailed facts and figures on admissions, academics, student body, and career outlook.

What Happens If You Don't Get to Every Question in a Section?

If you run out of time without having answered all the questions in one of the adaptive sections, the computer just moves you on to the next section. As we said earlier, for adaptive sections, the computer keeps an updated estimate of your score as you move through the section. If you don't get to answer some questions, the computer deducts points (based on an algorithm) and gives you a score based on the questions you *have* answered. So, you could get a score on the adaptive sections by answering only one math and one verbal question. Of course, that score would be pretty low!

For the Integrated Reasoning section, you also cannot skip a question and move on to the next question. For questions that have multiple parts, you also need to answer every part of the question before you move onto the next question. Like the adaptive sections, you can run out of time, however, and leave questions unanswered. Doing so, however, can have a drastic impact on your Integrated Reasoning score. With scores that range from only 1 to 8, and only 12 questions that are scored all or nothing, answering every question is important on this section.

It Is Actually in Your Interest to Answer *All* the Questions—Even If You Have to Guess

You might think it would be better to skip any questions you don't have time to answer at the end of an adaptive section—but in fact, the reverse is true: If time is running out, you will almost certainly get a higher score by clicking through and answering any remaining questions at random. This is because the penalty for getting a question wrong diminishes sharply toward the end of each adaptive section (when the computer has already largely decided your score). The penalty for each question skipped at the end of an adaptive section is actually greater than the penalty for getting one of those last questions wrong.

But You Can Do Much Better Than Guessing at Random

In the following chapters, we will give you all the specific math and verbal skills you need to ace the Math, Verbal, and Integrated Reasoning sections. We will also raise the Process of Elimination to a fine art—in case you have to guess.

Zen and the Art of Test Taking

As you begin each new question, put the previous question behind you. Don't get rattled if you think you got the previous question wrong. Even if your current question seems easier, it could be experimental. Just do your best to answer the current question correctly.

At the End of the Test

When you finish, the computer will ask you if you want the test to count. If you say no, or you just walk away, the computer will not record your score, and no schools will ever see it. Of course, neither will you. GMAC will not let you look at your score and then decide whether you want to keep it. You should also know that if you do cancel your scores, your future score reports will show this.

If you tell the computer that you want the test to count, then it will give you your unofficial score right then and there on the screen. This will include your Integrated Reasoning score but not your essay score. (Test center employees can print out the unofficial score report for you.) Within 20 days, you'll receive your official results online. If you choose to cancel at the test site, you will not be able to change your mind later. By the same token, once you've chosen to see your score, you can't cancel it.

If Something Weird Happens at the Test Center...

We have found that almost nothing ever goes wrong at the test centers. They are professionally run. But in the unlikely event that there is a technical glitch with your assigned computer, or if you want to complain about test center conditions or some other anomaly, it is best to start the process before you leave the test center by filing a complaint immediately after the test is over. If possible, get the test center staff to corroborate your complaint. Then, as soon as possible after the test is over, contact either Pearson VUE or GMAT Customer Service by one of the following methods:

E-mail: pvtestsecurity@pearson.com
Web: www.pearsonvue.com/contact/gmat/security
Phone: 800-717-GMAT or 952-681-3680

Admissions Insight No. 3: When to Apply
Although many schools have a filing range that stretches from six to eight months, early applications often have a better chance. This is because there are more spots available in the beginning of the process.

One Final Thought Before You Begin

No matter how high or low you score on the test and no matter how much you improve your performance with this book, you should *never* accept the score GMAC assigns you as an accurate assessment of your abilities. The temptation to see a high score as evidence that you're a genius, or a low score as evidence that you're an idiot, can be very powerful.

When you've read this book and practiced our techniques on real GMAT questions, you'll be able to judge for yourself whether the GMAT actually measures much besides how well you do on the GMAT.

Think of this as a kind of game—a game you can win.

Summary

- Register for the GMAT either online or by telephone. Schedule the test for a time that is convenient for you, but that meets your schools' deadlines.
- In the days leading up to the test, follow the study plan you set up in the beginning. Be sure to get plenty of rest, particularly the night before the test.
- Get together all the things you'll need on the day of the test: directions to the test center, a list of schools to which you want to submit scores, a snack, water, and photo-ID.
- At the testing center, make sure you are comfortable at the computer they assign to you. Tune out everyone else. Start working through the test. It should look exactly like the practice tests you have taken online. If you get stuck on a question, use POE and Joe Bloggs to make an educated guess and move on. Remember, some of the questions are experimental and may not even have an answer.
- Because there is a penalty for unanswered questions at the end of the test, it makes sense to use POE to guess on any remaining questions rather than to leave them blank.

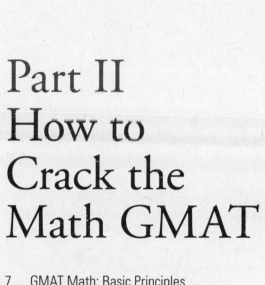

Part II How to Crack the Math GMAT

Chapter 7 GMAT Math: Basic Principles

If *absolute value* sounds familiar, but you can't quite remember it, this chapter can help. It provides a comprehensive review of the math terms and rules you haven't had to think about since high school.

Math and the Integrated Reasoning Section

Before we get started talking about the Quantitative section of the GMAT, let's take a moment to talk about the Integrated Reasoning section. The Integrated Reasoning section tests a blend of math and critical reasoning (verbal) skills. However, some questions test math skills. The good news is that those math skills are the same math skills that the GMAT has been testing for years. So, while we'll be mostly discussing the Quantitative section in this and the following chapters, you'll want to remember that you'll also use the math reviewed in these chapters to answer some of the Integrated Reasoning questions.

What's Covered in the Math Section

B-School Lingo

cold call: an unexpected, often dreaded request by the professor to open a case discussion

cycle time: how fast you can turn something around

Source: *The Best 296 Business Schools*

The 37 math questions on the GMAT come in two different formats. About half of the questions are regular Problem Solving questions of the type you're familiar with from countless other standardized tests, such as the SAT. The other half of the questions, mixed in among the regular Problem Solving questions, are of a type unique to the GMAT: They're called Data Sufficiency questions, and they ask you to determine whether you can answer a math question based on two pieces of information. We've devoted two entire chapters to Data Sufficiency.

But whether the question falls into the category of Problem Solving or Data Sufficiency, GMAT questions test your general knowledge of three subjects:

1. Arithmetic
2. Basic algebra
3. Basic geometry

What Isn't Covered in the Math Section

The good news is that you won't need to know calculus, trigonometry, or any complicated geometry. The bad news is that the specialized, business-type math you're probably good at isn't tested, either. There will be no questions on computing the profit on three ticks of a particular bond sale, no questions about amortizing a loan, no need to calculate the bottom line of a small business.

Ancient History

For the most part, what you'll find on the GMAT is a kind of math that you haven't had to think about in years: junior high school and high school math. Because most people who apply to business school have been out of college for several years, high school math may seem a bit like ancient history. In the next few chapters, we'll give you a fast review of the important concepts, and we'll show you some powerful techniques for cracking the system.

Order of Difficulty

The first problem on the computer-adaptive Math test is of medium difficulty. Based on your response to that first question, you will next be presented with an easier or a more difficult problem.

The Princeton Review Approach

Because it's probably been a long time since you've needed to reduce fractions or remember how many degrees there are in a quadrilateral, the first thing to do is review the information tested on the GMAT by going through our math review. Along the way, you'll learn some valuable test-taking skills that will allow you to take advantage of some of the inherent weaknesses of standardized testing.

When you've finished the math review, you should read our chapter on Data Sufficiency and then take our diagnostic math test. Based on your approximate score on our diagnostic, you can then practice working through problems at, or just above, your scoring range. By becoming familiar with the general level of difficulty of these problems and the number of steps required to solve them, you can increase your score on the real GMAT.

Stay focused!
Always keep in mind that if your purpose is to raise your GMAT score, it's a waste of time to learn math that won't be tested. Don't get us wrong, we think the derivation of ϖ is fascinating, but...

Extra Help

Although we can show you which mathematical principles are most important for the GMAT, this book cannot take the place of a basic foundation in math. We find that most people, even if they don't remember much of high school math, pick it up again quickly. Our drills and examples will refresh your memory if you've gotten rusty, but if you have serious difficulties with the following chapters, you should consider a more thorough review, like *Math Workout for the New GMAT*, from The Princeton Review. This book will enable you to see where you need the most work. Always keep in mind, though, that if your purpose is to raise your GMAT score, it's a waste of time to learn math that won't be tested.

No Calculators on Quant!
One form of extra help you won't be allowed during the Quantitative section of the GMAT is a calculator. (For the Integrated Reasoning section, there's an onscreen calculator.) All calculations for the Quant section must be done the old fashioned way—by hand. To get used to this, you should retire your calculator (especially during practice tests) until after you have finished with your real GMAT.

BASIC INFORMATION

Try the following problem:

How many even integers are between 17 and 27?

- 9
- 7
- 5
- 4
- 3

This is an easy GMAT question. Even so, if you don't know what an integer is, the question is impossible to answer. Before moving on to arithmetic, you should make sure you're familiar with some basic terms and concepts. This material isn't difficult, but you must know it cold. (The answer, by the way, is C.)

Integers

Integers are the numbers we think of when we think of numbers. Integers are sometimes called whole or natural numbers. They can be negative or positive. They do not include fractions. The positive integers are:

1, 2, 3, 4, 5, etc.

The negative integers are:

–1, –2, –3, –4, –5, etc.

Zero (0) is also an integer. It is the only number that is neither positive nor negative.

Ancient History 101
The GMAT will test your (probably rusty) knowledge of high school math.

Positive integers get bigger as they move away from 0; negative integers get smaller. Look at this number line:

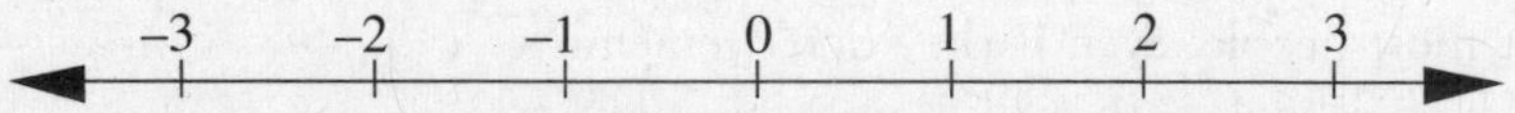

2 is greater than 1, but –2 is less than –1.

Positive and Negative

Positive numbers lie to the right of zero on the number line. Negative numbers lie to the left of zero on the number line.

There are three rules regarding the multiplication of positive and negative numbers:

> positive × positive = positive
>
> positive × negative = negative
>
> negative × negative = positive

If you add a positive number and a negative number, subtract the number with the negative sign in front of it from the positive number.

$$4 + (-3) = 1$$

If you add two negative numbers, you add them as if they were positive, then put a negative sign in front of the sum.

$$-3 + -5 = -8$$

Having Trouble Memorizing?

If you're having trouble memorizing GMAT math terminology, consider making flashcards to help you review.

Digits

There are ten digits:

0, 1, 2, 3, 4, 5, 6, 7, 8, 9

All integers are made up of digits. In the integer 246, there are three digits: 2, 4, and 6. Each of the digits has a different name:

6 is called the units (or ones) digit.
4 is called the tens digit.
2 is called the hundreds digit.

A number with decimal places is also composed of digits, although it is not an integer. In the decimal 27.63 there are four digits:

2 is the tens digit.
7 is the units digit.
6 is the tenths digit.
3 is the hundredths digit.

Remainders

If an integer cannot be divided evenly by another integer, the integer that is left over at the end of division is called the **remainder**. Thus, remainders *must* be integers.

$$\begin{array}{r} 3 \\ 2\overline{)\,7} \\ \underline{-6} \\ 1 \end{array} \leftarrow \text{remainder}$$

Odd or Even

Q: 20,179.01792
In the number above, which of the following two digits are identical?
(A) the tens digit and the hundredths digit
(B) the ones digit and the thousandths digit
(C) the hundreds digit and the tenths digit
(D) the thousands digit and the tenths digit
(E) the thousands digit and the hundredths digit
Turn the page for the answer.

Even numbers are integers that can be divided evenly by 2, leaving no remainder. Here are some examples:

–6, –4, –2, 0, 2, 4, 6, etc.

Any integer, no matter how large, is even if its last digit is divisible by 2. Thus 777,772 is even.

Odd numbers are integers that cannot be divided evenly by 2. Put another way, odd integers have a remainder of 1 when they are divided by 2. Here are some examples:

–5, –3, –1, 1, 3, 5, etc.

Any integer, no matter how large, is odd if its last digit is not divisible by 2. Thus 222,227 is odd.

There are several rules that always hold true for even and odd numbers:

even × even = even

odd × odd = odd

even × odd = even

even + even = even

odd + odd = even

even + odd = odd

It isn't necessary to memorize these, but you must know that the relationships always hold true. The individual rules can be derived in a second. If you need to know *even* × *even*, just try 2 × 2. The answer in this case is even, as *even* × *even* always will be.

Consecutive Integers

Consecutive integers are integers listed in order of increasing value without any integers missing in between. For example, –3, –2, –1, 0, 1, 2, 3 are consecutive integers. Only integers can be consecutive.

Some consecutive even integers: –2, 0, 2, 4, 6, 8, etc.

Some consecutive odd integers: –3, –1, 1, 3, 5, etc.

Distinct Numbers

If two numbers are **distinct**, they cannot be equal. For example, if x and y are distinct, then they must have different values.

Prime Numbers

A **prime number** is a positive integer that is divisible only by two numbers: itself and 1. Thus 2, 3, 5, 7, 11, 13 are all prime numbers. The number 2 is both the smallest and the only even prime number. Neither 0 nor 1 is a prime number. All prime numbers are positive.

Divisibility Rules

If there is no remainder when integer x is divided by integer y, then x is said to be **divisible** by y. Put another way, divisible means you can evenly divide the greater number by the smaller number. For example, 10 is divisible by 5.

Some Useful Divisibility Shortcuts:

- An integer is divisible by 2 if its units digit is divisible by 2. Thus 772 is divisible by 2.
- An integer is divisible by 3 if the sum of its digits is divisible by 3. We can instantly tell that 216 is divisible by 3, because the sum of the digits (2 + 1 + 6) is divisible by 3.
- An integer is divisible by 4 if the number formed by its last two digits is divisible by 4. 3,028 is divisible by 4, because 28 is divisible by 4.
- An integer is divisible by 5 if its final digit is either 0 or 5. Thus, 60, 85, and 15 are all divisible by 5.
- An integer is divisible by 6 if it is divisible by both 2 and 3, the factors of 6. Thus 318 is divisible by 6 because it is even, and the sum of 3 + 1 + 8 is divisible by 3.
- Division by zero is undefined. The test writers won't ever put a zero in the denominator. If you're working out a problem and you find yourself with a zero in the denominator of a fraction, you've done something wrong. By the way, a 0 in the numerator is fine. Any fraction with a 0 on the top is 0.

$$\frac{0}{1} = 0$$

$$\frac{0}{4} = 0$$

$$\frac{4}{0} = \text{undefined}$$

Factors and Multiples

An integer, *x*, is a factor of another integer, *y*, if *y* is divisible by *x*. So, in other words, $y = nx$, where *y*, *n* and *x* are all integers. For example, 3 is a factor of 15 because 15 = (3)(5). All the factors of 15 are 1, 3, 5, and 15.

A: D. Both the thousands digit and tenths digit are 0.

The **multiples** of an integer, *y*, are all numbers 0, ±1*y*, ±2*y*, ±3*y*..., etc. For example, 15 is a multiple of 3 (3 × 5); 12 is also a multiple of 3 (3 × 4). When you think about it, most numbers have only a few factors, but an infinite number of multiples. The memory device you may have learned in school is "factors are few; multiples are many."

Every integer greater than 1 is both its own greatest factor and least positive multiple.

Q: Which of the following numbers is prime?
0, 1, 15, 23, 33
Turn the page for the answer.

Least Common Multiples

If an integer, *x*, is divisible by two integers *n* and *m*, then *x* is a common multiple of *n* and *m*. For example, 30 is a common multiple of 5 and 6. The smallest common multiple of two integers is called the **least common multiple**. For our example, 30 is also the least common multiple of 5 and 6.

The most straightforward way to find a least common multiple is to simply start listing the positive multiples of both integers. When you find a number that is on both lists, that number is the least common multiple.

For example, here's how you find the least common multiple of 4 and 6.

Multiples of 4: 4, 8, 12, 16, 20,...

Multiples of 6: 6, 12,...

Since 12 is on both lists, 12 is the least common multiple of 4 and 6.

Greatest Common Factor

If two integers, *n* and *m*, are both divisible by an integer, *x*, then *x* is a common factor of *n* and *m*. For example, 6 is a common factor of both 12 and 18. The largest factor that two numbers have in common is referred to as the **greatest common factor**. For our example, 6 is also the greatest common factor of 12 and 18.

The most straightforward way to find a greatest common factor is to simply list the factors of both numbers. Then you just need to find the greatest number that is on both lists.

For example, here's how you find the greatest common factor of 12 and 18.

Factors of 12: 1, 2, 3, 4, 6, 12

Factors of 18: 1, 2, 3, 6, 9, 18

Since 6 is the greatest number on both lists, 6 is the greatest common factor of 12 and 18.

Prime Factors

If an integer, x, that is a factor of an integer, y, is also prime, then x is called a **prime factor** of y. For example, 3 and 5 are prime factors of 15.

To find the prime factors of an integer, use a factor tree:

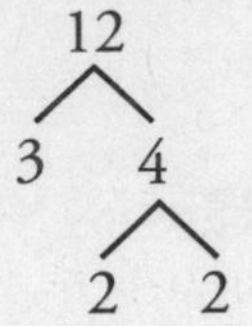

All positive integers greater than 1 have unique prime factorizations, a fact that the GMAT frequently tests. So, it doesn't matter which pair of factors you start with when you use the factor tree.

Here are some symbols you should know for the GMAT:

Symbol	Meaning
=	is equal to
≠	is not equal to
<	is less than
>	is greater than
≤	is less than or equal to
≥	is greater than or equal to

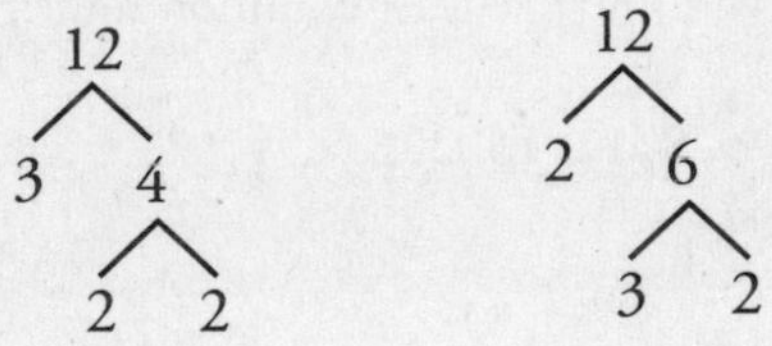

The prime factorization of 12 is $2 \times 2 \times 3$.

Absolute Value

The **absolute value** of a number is the distance between that number and 0 on the number line. The absolute value of 6 is expressed as $|6|$.

$$|6| = 6$$

$$|-5| = 5$$

NOW LET'S LOOK AT THE INSTRUCTIONS

During the test, you'll be able to see test instructions by clicking on the "Help" button at the bottom of the screen. However, to avoid wasting time reading these during the test, read our version of the instructions for Problem Solving questions now:

> Problem Solving Directions: Solve each problem and choose the best of the answer choices provided.
>
> Numbers: This test uses only real numbers; no imaginary numbers are used or implied.
>
> Diagrams: All problem solving diagrams are drawn as accurately as possible UNLESS it is specifically noted that a diagram is "not drawn to scale." All diagrams are in a plane unless stated otherwise.

A: 23. Remember, neither 0 nor 1 is prime.

Summary

- Without a review of the basic terms and rules of math tested on the GMAT, you won't be able to begin to do the problems.
- Study the vocabulary and rules in the preceding chapter to get this stuff back into your head. If you find that you need an even more comprehensive review, consider getting *Math Workout for the New GMAT* or *Math Smart*, both published by The Princeton Review.

Chapter 8
POE and GMAT Math

This chapter shows you how to use one of the most powerful Princeton Review techniques—Process of Elimination—and apply it to GMAT math, with startling results!

In Chapter 4, we introduced you to the Process of Elimination—a way to find correct answers by eliminating wrong answers. Now, we're going to show you how to turn POE into a science.

Here's an example of a typical medium-level problem—the sort of problem that the computer might give you for your very first math question:

> Twenty-two percent of the cars produced in the United States are manufactured in Michigan. If the United States produces a total of 40 million cars, how many cars are produced outside of Michigan?
>
> ◯
> ◯
> ◯ 31.2 million
> ◯
> ◯

Zen and the Art of Test Writing

Let's put ourselves in the place of the GMAC test writer who has just written this medium-level math problem. He's finished with his question, and he has his correct answer (31.2 million), but he isn't done yet. He still has four empty slots to fill in. He needs to come up with incorrect numbers for answer choices A, B, C, and D.

He *could* simply choose numbers at random, or numbers that are closely clustered around the correct answer. However, if he did that, test takers who didn't know how to do the problem wouldn't see an obvious answer and might therefore guess at random. The test writer does *not* want test takers to guess at random. If they did, they might actually pick the right answer.

By the same token, if the test writer chooses numbers at random for his empty slots, test takers who actually understood the problem but made a careless error, wouldn't see their result among the answer choices—and would know to go back and fix their mistake. The test writer doesn't want that either.

So our test writer comes up with incorrect answer choices that whisper seductively, "Pick *me.*" He tries to figure out all the mistakes a careless test taker might make; then he includes those answers among the choices. Here's that same question, now that the test writer has finished it:

> Twenty-two percent of the cars produced in the United States are manufactured in Michigan. If the United States produces a total of 40 million cars, how many cars are produced outside of Michigan?
>
> ◯ 8.8 million
> ◯ 18 million
> ◯ 31.2 million
> ◯ 48.8 million
> ◯ 62 million

Partial Answers

People often go wrong on GMAT math problems by thinking that they are finished before they really are. The first step in this problem is to find out how many actual cars are produced in Michigan; in other words, we need to know what 22 percent of 40 million equals. If you aren't sure how to do this, don't worry; we'll show you how to do percent problems in the arithmetic chapter. For the moment, take our word for it that 22 percent of 40 million equals 8.8 million.

If you were feeling smug about having figured this out, you might just look at the answer choices, notice that the first answer choice is 8.8 million and figure that you're done. Unfortunately, the problem didn't ask how many cars were produced in Michigan; it asked how many cars were *not* produced in Michigan.

GMAC provided answer choice A just in case you got halfway through the problem and decided you'd done enough work. It was a *partial* answer. To find the correct answer, you have to subtract 8.8 from 40 million. The correct answer is choice C, 31.2 million.

How Do You Avoid Picking Partial Answers?

You can avoid this mistake by doing three things:

- When you finish a problem, always take two seconds to reread the problem to make sure you've actually answered the question.
- Remember the practice problems that you have done and the practice tests that you have taken. For the most part, only fairly easy questions can be solved after only one or two steps. You no doubt remember some practice questions that you got wrong by essentially doing too little work. So, when you get an answer after doing very little work, stop and ask yourself "Is that really all they expected me to do?" You don't want to psyche yourself out but you do want to be careful.
- Train yourself to look for complementary answers while you practice. A great number of questions that have partial answers are questions like the one we've been looking at. If the test writers are asking about the cars produced *outside* of Michigan, you just know they are going to include the number of cars produced *inside* Michigan as a partial answer. When you work practice questions, see if you can find complementary answers. As you do, you'll be training yourself to avoid a potential trap.

Crazy Answers

The GMAT test writers also know that people taking tests do crazy things under pressure. Thus, even though there is no good reason why a person would want to do this, some percentage of the test takers who see this question are going to correctly find 22 percent of 40, or 8.8, but then *add* it to the original 40. Thus, the test writer will want to include 48.8 among the answer choices. If it weren't there, test takers who'd gotten this answer might realize they had made a mistake and figure out the correct answer, but the test writer would prefer that they just get it wrong.

How else could a test taker go wrong on this problem?

Joe Bloggs and GMAT Math

In Chapter 5 we introduced you to Joe Bloggs—the average test taker. Joe just does the first thing that comes into his head. On easy problems, this often gets him the right answer. On difficult questions, his first response is *always* wrong. On medium problems Joe Bloggs's first response is wrong about half the time. On this particular medium problem, what might Joe want to do?

What about just adding the two numbers in the problem together? 22 + 40 equals 62. Or subtracting 22 from 40, which gives you 18. If there's a chance that Joe might pick it, GMAC wants it to be there. So the test writers will probably include 62 and 40 among the answer choices. Again, there's no good mathematical reason why a test taker would want to do these things, but GMAC knows that you don't always need a good reason to go wrong.

It might strike you that this is pretty unfair. If GMAC just picked answers at random, Joe would be much less likely to fall into their traps. However, there is one positive side to GMAC's obsession with trap answers…

Common Sense: The Antidote to Trap Answers

GMAC is so caught up in trying to provide answer choices that anticipate all the mistakes a test taker might make on a problem that it often forgets to make certain that all of these answer choices make sense. Let's just think about that problem again.

> Twenty-two percent of the cars produced in the United States are manufactured in Michigan. If the United States produces a total of 40 million cars, how many cars are produced outside of Michigan?
>
> ◯ 8.8 million
> ◯ 18 million
> ◯ 31.2 million
> ◯ 48.8 million
> ◯ 62 million

We want the number of cars produced in places other than Michigan. Forget about math for a moment. Let's just look at the answer choices in the cold light of day. Even if you're rusty on percentages, is there any way that the number of cars produced in the other states could be greater than the total number of cars produced altogether? No way. The answer has to be less than 40 million. Thus, in their zeal to anticipate your potential wrong answers, the test writers have given you two answer choices (48.8 and 62) that are just plain crazy.

Scratch Work

If these two answers are crazy, then cross them off in your scratch booklet. It's psychologically very uplifting to see your possible answers narrowed down to only three. Here's what your scratch work should look like for this question:

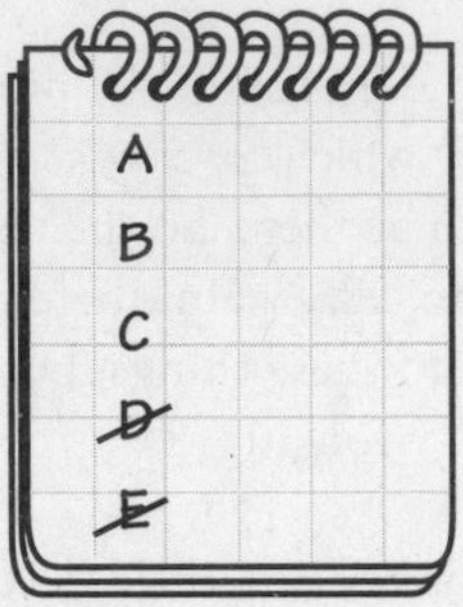

Admissions Insight No. 4: How Criteria Are Weighted

Although requirements vary from school to school, most rely on some combination of the following criteria (although not necessarily in this order):

1) GMAT score
2) Undergraduate GPA
3) Work experience
4) Essays
5) Letters of recommendation
6) Interviews
7) Extracurricular activities

The advantage of this system is that it allows applicants to compensate for weaknesses in some areas with strengths in other areas. And the single easiest thing to change in your admissions "package" is your GMAT score.

How Do You Prevent Yourself from Picking Crazy Answers?

You can prevent yourself from selecting crazy answers by doing these simple things:

- Before you even start doing any serious math, take a second to use common sense on the problem: Are there any answers that simply don't make sense? If so, cross them off in your scratch work. This will prevent you from picking them later through carelessness or desperation.
- If, based on your scores on practice tests, you expect to be seeing mainly medium and difficult problems on the Math section, take a second to see if there are any Joe Bloggs answers to cross off.
- Always be suspicious of answers that you get too easily. Five second answers or answers that can be found by doing things like simply adding the numbers in the problem are not usually correct on the GMAT.

Psst! Hey, Joe...

To come up with answers that will appeal to Joe Bloggs, the GMAT test writer has to know how Joe thinks. Fortunately for the test writer, she can draw on more than 30 years of statistical information GMAC has compiled. From this, she knows that:

1. On difficult math problems, Joe Bloggs is always attracted to easy solutions that he can find in one step.

For example, Joe might just add together the numbers mentioned in the problem.

2. On difficult math problems, Joe Bloggs is attracted to numbers that he has already seen in the problem.

It's pretty silly, but frequently Joe picks a number simply because he remembers it from the problem itself.

Now, let's look at the upper-medium problem we showed you in Chapter 5, complete with answer choices:

The output of a factory is increased by 10% to keep up with rising demand. To handle the holiday rush, this new output is increased by 20%. By approximately what percent would the output of the factory now have to be decreased in order to restore the original output?

- 20%
- 24%
- 30%
- 32%
- 70%

Here's How to Crack It

If the test writer has done her job properly, Joe Bloggs will never even consider the correct answer (24%). He's too smitten by the other answer choices. As we said in Chapter 5, Joe's favorite answer to this question is undoubtedly 30 percent (what we call choice C). Joe notices that the output seems to have increased by 30 percent and figures that to get rid of that increase, you would have to decrease it by 30 percent. Joe just added together the two numbers he saw in the problem.

> On medium and difficult math problems, Joe Bloggs is attracted to easy solutions that he can find in one step.

Another answer Joe might be attracted to is choice A. Twenty (20%) is simply one of the numbers from the problem. There is no logical reason to think this is the correct answer, but Joe isn't always logical.

> On medium and difficult math problems, Joe Bloggs is attracted to answer choices that simply repeat numbers from the problem.

Putting Everything Together

Here's one last example of an upper-medium problem to show how you can use both common sense and the Joe Bloggs principle to help eliminate answers:

A student took 6 courses last year and received an average (arithmetic mean) grade of 100 points. The year before, the student took 5 courses and received an average grade of 90 points. To the nearest tenth of a point, what was the student's average grade for the entire two-year period?

- ◯ 79
- ◯ 89
- ◯ 95
- ◯ 95.5
- ◯ 97.2

Here's How to Crack It

Don't worry if you aren't sure how to solve this problem right now; we'll cover average problems in the next chapter. Let's assume for a moment that you've done our math review and will be facing mostly medium questions on the Math portion of the GMAT.

Always be suspicious of answers that you get too easily. Five second answers or answers that can be found by doing things like simply adding the numbers in the problem are not usually correct on the GMAT. Let's begin by thinking about what Joe Bloggs would like to pick on this question. Joe likes answer choice C a lot. He figures that to find the average of the entire two-year period, all he has to do is find that the average of 90 and 100 is 95. If this were an easy problem, he might be right, but we're assuming for the moment that you will be seeing mainly medium problems—so cross off choice C in your scratch booklet.

There are no other obvious Joe Bloggs answers, but it *is* possible to eliminate a couple of other choices by using common sense. The student's average for the first year was 90. The student's average for the second year was 100. Obviously the student's second-year grades are going to bring his average *up*. We may not be sure by exactly how much, but the average for the entire two-year period has to be higher than it was for the first year. Both choices A and B are less than the first year's average. We can therefore eliminate both of them.

We've eliminated three answer choices. If you know how to solve the problem, go to it. If not, you have a fifty-fifty shot at getting it right anyway. The correct answer is choice D, 95.5.

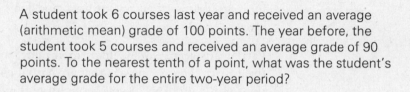

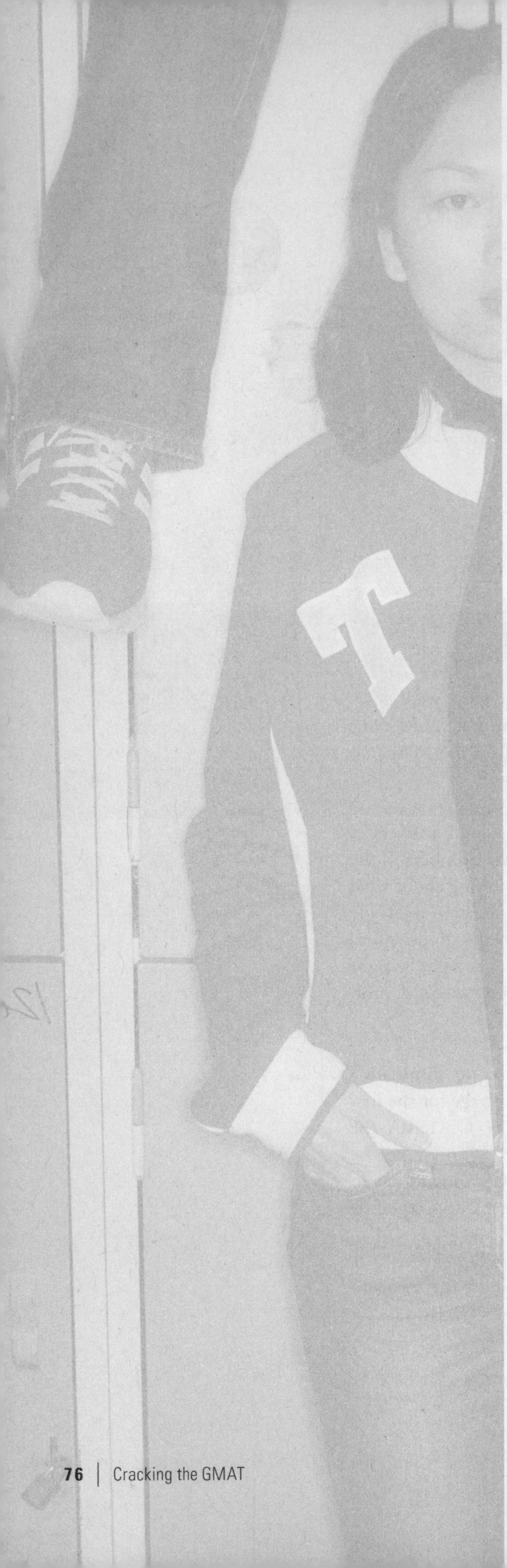

Summary

- The Process of Elimination allows you to eliminate answer choices even when you don't know how to do a problem. There are three types of answers to look for: partial answers, crazy answers, and Joe Bloggs answers.
- **Partial answers:** GMAC likes to include, among the answer choices, answers that are partial completions of the problem. If you get halfway through a problem and decide that you're done, the number you have arrived at will likely be there, waiting to trip you up. The way to avoid partial answers is to reread the problem before you pick an answer to make sure you're answering the question it has asked.
- **Crazy answers:** The test writers also like to include, among the answer choices, numbers that a test taker may arrive at—even though they don't make much sense. Crazy answer choices can be spotted by taking a step back and looking at the problem and its answers in the cold light of day.
- **Joe Bloggs answers:** GMAC also likes to plant, among the answer choices, numbers that would appeal to Joe Bloggs, the average test taker. Joe is attracted to easy solutions that he can arrive at in one step and answers that repeat numbers from the problem.

Chapter 9
Data Sufficiency: Basic Principles

Data Sufficiency is a question type you've never seen before. This chapter will show you how to use basic POE techniques to make this format your new favorite kind of math.

Almost half of the thirty-seven math questions on the GMAT will be Data Sufficiency questions. We're about to show you how to use POE to make this strange question type easy.

WHAT IS DATA SUFFICIENCY?

If you've never heard of Data Sufficiency, that's because this question type is unique to the GMAT and these questions definitely require some getting used to. If you have already taken a GMAT practice exam, or the actual GMAT, you may have spent several minutes just trying to understand the directions for Data Sufficiency questions.

However, Data Sufficiency questions really just test the same math concepts as Problem Solving questions, but with a twist—a strange question format.

Here's what a Data Sufficiency question looks like on the GMAT:

What is the value of y ?

(1) y is an even integer such that $-1.5 < y < 1.5$

(2) Integer y is not prime.

- ○ Statement (1) ALONE is sufficient, but statement (2) alone is not sufficient.
- ○ Statement (2) ALONE is sufficient, but statement (1) alone is not sufficient.
- ○ BOTH statements TOGETHER are sufficient, but NEITHER statement ALONE is sufficient.
- ○ EACH statement ALONE is sufficient.
- ○ Statements (1) and (2) TOGETHER are not sufficient.

Every Data Sufficiency question consists of a question followed by two statements. There are also five possible answer choices, as shown. The answers are the same for every Data Sufficiency question, so once you learn what each means, you won't need to spend time rereading them. You'll just be able to think about them as answers A, B, C, D, and E, which is how we'll refer to them.

Notice that there are two words that the answer choices keep repeating—alone and sufficient. So, it looks like we're supposed to evaluate the statements on their own—at least at first. Moreover, our task is evidently to determine whether we have sufficient information to answer the question.

That's how Data Sufficiency differs from Problem Solving. In Problem Solving questions you are asked to give a numerical answer to the question. In fact, the inclusion of five numerical answer choices tells you that you can assume that the question can be solved. For Data Sufficiency questions, however, you're not being asked to solve the question but to decide WHETHER the question can be solved. It may, in fact, turn out that the statements do not provide sufficient information to answer the question.

Here's How to Crack It

The first answer choice—answer A—indicates that we should first look at Statement (1) by itself to see if it is sufficient to answer the question.

In fact, the best way to work Data Sufficiency problems is to look at *one statement at a time.* So, ignore Statement (2). Here, we've replaced Statement (2) with question marks to indicate that we are looking only at the first statement—almost as though we had covered up the second statement.

What is the value of y ?

(1) y is an even integer such that $-1.5 < y < 1.5$

(2) ????

Now, we're ready to evaluate Statement (1) alone. There are three integers between -1.5 and 1.5: -1, 0, and 1. Of those, as you may recall from Chapter 7, only 0 is even. So, Statement (1) does provide sufficient information to answer the question.

We're not ready to choose the first answer—answer A—yet, however, because the second part of the answer choice states that Statement (2) alone is not sufficient. Now, forget that you have ever seen Statement (1).

What is the value of y ?

(1) ????

(2) Integer y is not prime.

The second statement only tells us that y is not prime. So, possible values for y include 1, 4, 6, 8, etc. Do we know the value of y? No way. So, Statement (2) is not sufficient. Because (1) is sufficient and (2) is not, the answer to this question is

◯ Statement (1) ALONE is sufficient, but statement (2) alone is not sufficient.

Or, in other words, the correct answer is A.

DATA SUFFICIENCY: GETTING STARTED

Now that you've seen and worked a Data Sufficiency question, it's time learn how to make this weird question type your own. The first step is to understand what each of the answer choices means.

By making small changes to the example you've just seen, we can provide examples of each of the answer choices. Next to each example, you'll find a graphic that provides a quick, down and dirty way to understand and remember each answer choice. Here's the example for choice A again:

○ Statement (1) ALONE is sufficient, but statement (2) alone is not sufficient.

What is the value of y ?

(1) y is an even integer such that $-1.5 < y < 1.5$

(A) ① ~~2~~

(2) Integer y is not prime.

Now, let's make some changes to the statements, to get an example of answer B.

○ Statement (2) ALONE is sufficient, but statement (1) alone is not sufficient.

What is the value of y ?

(1) Integer y is not prime.

(B) * ②

(2) y is an even integer such that $-1.5 < y < 1.5$

As you can see from this example, choice B is pretty much the flip side of choice A. In this case, the first statement provides no help in determining the value of y, but the second statement tells us that $y = 0$.

A few more changes produce an example of answer C.

○ BOTH statements TOGETHER are sufficient, but NEITHER statement ALONE is sufficient.

What is the value of y ?

(1) y is an even integer.

(C) (* ~~2~~)

(2) $-1.5 < y < 1.5$

The first statement tells us that y is even, but there are a lot of even integers. The second statement gives us a range of values for y, but, by itself, we don't even know that y is an integer from the second statement. So, neither statement is sufficient on its own. But, when we put them together, we know that $y = 0$.

Now, let's get an example of answer D.

◯ EACH statement ALONE is sufficient.

What is the value of y ?

(1) y is an even integer such that
$-1.5 < y < 1.5$

(D)①②

(2) For any integer $a \neq 0$, $ay = 0$

As pointed out in previous examples, the information in Statement (1) allows us to conclude that $y = 0$. The information in the second statement also tells us that y is 0 because the only way for the product of ay to equal 0 is if either a or y is 0. Since a can't be 0, y must be 0. Note how the statements independently allow us to arrive at the conclusion that $y = 0$ for answer choice D.

Finally, let's look at an example of choice E.

◯ Statements (1) and (2) TOGETHER are not sufficient.

What is the value of y ?

(1) y is an even integer.

(E) ~~1~~ ~~2~~

(2) Integer y is not prime.

For this example, there's no way to determine the value of y. The first statement doesn't work because y could be any even integer. The second statement also doesn't help because y can be any integer that isn't prime. Even when we combine the statements, we don't know the value of y because any even integer except 2 fits the conditions. So, E is the no way, no how answer.

Below, you'll find the full graphic for all of the answers. You may find it helpful to keep the graphic handy until you are completely comfortable with what each answer choice means.

(A) ① ~~2~~
(B) ~~1~~ ②
(C) (~~1~~ ~~2~~)
(D) ①②
(E) ~~1~~ ~~2~~

DATA SUFFICIENCY: BASIC POE STRATEGY

One of the reasons the test writers decided to include Data Sufficiency questions on the GMAT is that when this format was first dreamed up they thought these questions would be immune to Process of Elimination (POE). Were they ever wrong! If anything, it's even easier to apply POE to Data Sufficiency questions. Let's see why.

First, however, let's restate one of the most important strategies for working any Data Sufficiency question: *Evaluate the statements one at a time before you think about combining them.* Many people mistakenly pick C—you need both statements together—when it would have been possible to answer the question with only the information in the first statement or the second statement. Generally, people make this mistake when they read both statements right after reading the question stem. In fact, this mistake is the most common mistake that test takers make when working Data Sufficiency questions.

To avoid this common mistake, *read the question stem and only the first statement.* Ignore the second statement. Pretend it isn't there. You may even go as far as covering Statement (2) with your finger if you find the temptation to read both statements too overpowering. Once you have evaluated Statement (1), forget it. Ignore it. It doesn't exist anymore. Cover it up if you need to and read and evaluate Statement (2).

What happens when you evaluate the statements one at a time? Something magical, that's what! POE comes roaring back. Consider the following partial example:

What is the value of x ?

(1) $x + 7 = 12$

We don't even have Statement (2), but we can still do a lot with this partial question. (Don't worry. There won't be any partial questions on the real test!) First, you want to see if the statement is sufficient to answer the question. In this case, you could subtract 7 from both sides of the equation to discover that $x = 5$. We'll take this as an opportunity to remind you, however, that you don't really need to solve the equation—you just need to know that you *can* solve the equation. After all, to pick an answer to the problem, you just need to know if you have sufficient information.

Since Statement (1) is sufficient in this case, which answer choices can be eliminated? From the chart, you can see that there are only two answer choices—A and D—that have Statement (1) circled to indicate that, for that answer choice, Statement (1) is sufficient. So, you no longer need to worry about B, C, or E. They've been eliminated! If the first statement is sufficient, the answer to the problem must be A or D! You're down to fifty-fifty just based on looking at the first statement!

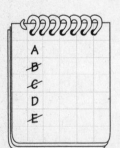

Now, check out this example:

What is the value of x ?

(1) x is an integer.

Now, what are the possible answers? If you said B, C, or E, you are well on your way to getting this Data Sufficiency stuff under control. If you said something else, take a look at the steps back on page 79. In this case, the first statement is insufficient to determine the value of x. So, you want the answer choices that have 1 crossed off, and that is B, C, or E.

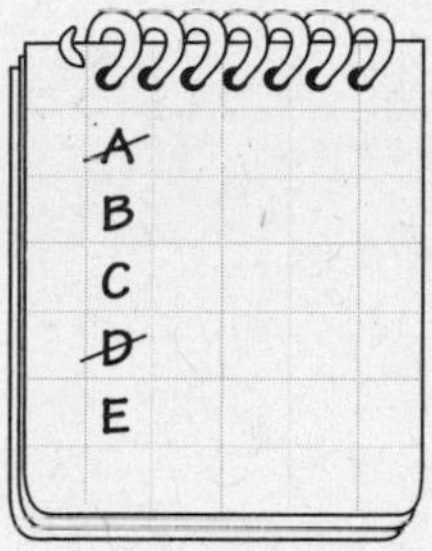

DRILL 1: (AD/BCE)

In the following drill, each question is followed by only one statement. Based on the first statement, decide if you are down to AD or BCE. The answers can be found in Part VI.

1. What is the value of x?

   (1) $y = 4$

   (2) ????

2. Is y an integer?

   (1) $2y$ is an integer.

   (2) ????

3. A certain room contains 12 children. How many more boys than girls are there?

   (1) There are three girls in the room.

   (2) ????

4. What number is x percent of 20?

   (1) 10 percent of x is 5.

   (2) ????

From AD or BCE to the Answer

Every time you start a Data Sufficiency question, you should read the question and only the first statement. If the first statement is sufficient, your possible answers are A or D. If the first statement is insufficient, your possible answers are B, C, or E. So, you can always get rid of either two or three answer choices just by evaluating the first statement. The AD/BCE split is so important that you'll want to write down AD or BCE on your noteboard as you work every Data Sufficiency question.

But what happens next? How do you get to the answer? Let's take a look.

If $x + y = 3$, what is the value of xy?

(1) x and y are integers

(2) x and y are positive

- Statement (1) ALONE is sufficient, but statement (2) alone is not sufficient.
- Statement (2) ALONE is sufficient, but statement (1) alone is not sufficient.
- BOTH statements TOGETHER are sufficient, but NEITHER statement ALONE is sufficient.
- EACH statement ALONE is sufficient.
- Statements (1) and (2) TOGETHER are not sufficient.

Here's How to Crack It

As always, ignore Statement (2) and look only at Statement (1). If x and y are integers and $x + y = 3$, do we know what they are? Not really—x could be 1 and y could be 2 (in which case, xy would be 2). But x could also be 0 (yes, 0 is an integer) and y could be 3 (in which case, xy would be 0). Because Statement (1) alone does not answer the question definitively, we are down to BCE, a one in three shot. Write it down in your scratch booklet.

Now, ignore Statement (1) and look at Statement (2). By itself, this statement doesn't begin to give us values for x and y—x could be 1 and y could be 2, but x could just as easily be 1.4 and y could be 1.6. Because there is still more than one possible value for xy, cross off answer choice B.

We're down to C or E. Now it's finally time to look at both statements at the same time. See how late in the process we combine the statements? Get into the habit of physically crossing off B before you think about combining the statements. That's how you can avoid making the most common GMAT Data Sufficiency mistake of putting the statements together too early.

Because we know from the first statement that x and y are integers, and from the second statement that they must be positive, do we now know specific values for x and y?

Well, we do know that there are only two positive integers that add up to 3: 2 and 1. (Remember, zero is an integer but it is neither positive nor negative.)

Do we know if $x = 1$ and $y = 2$, or vice versa? Not really, but frankly, it doesn't matter in this case. The question is asking us the value of xy.

Because neither statement by itself is sufficient, but both statements together are sufficient, the answer is choice C.

Here's a handy flowchart that shows you what to do for any Data Sufficiency problem. You should keep the flowchart next to you and consult it as you first start practicing Data Sufficiency questions. After you have done ten or twenty questions, you'll probably find that you have learned the basic POE process well enough that you don't need the chart anymore. However, if you ever find yourself having trouble with Data Sufficiency, pull out the chart again and do some more problems using it as a guide.

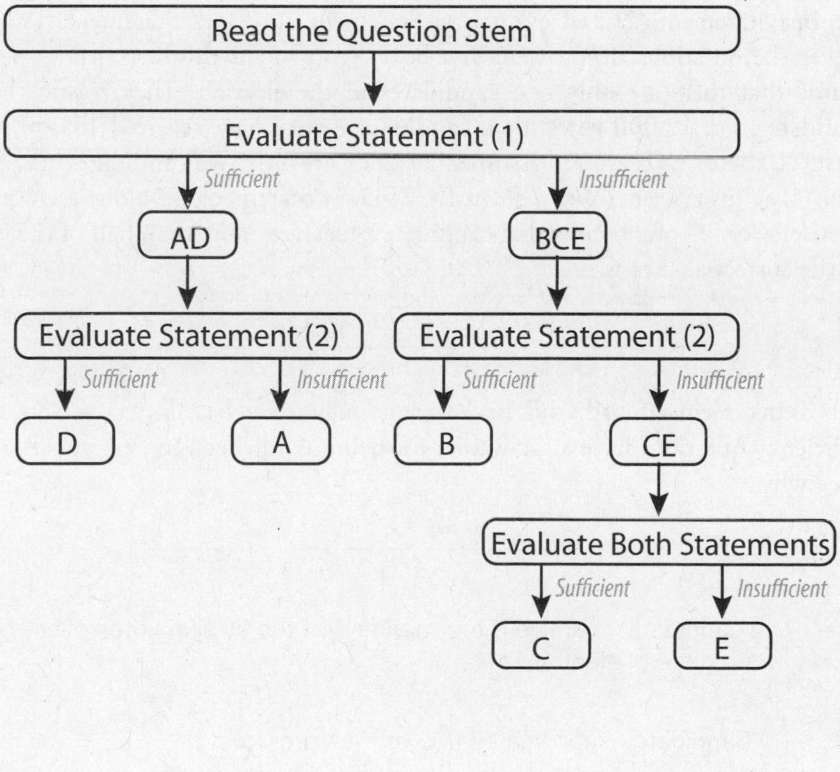

Combining the Statements

Notice how late in the process you combine the statements. Remember that one of the most common mistakes on Data Sufficiency is combining the statements before you have properly evaluated each statement on its own.

YES/NO DATA SUFFICIENCY: THE BASICS

If you were going to provide the answer to most Data Sufficiency questions, your response would be a number. However, as many as half of all the Data Sufficiency questions that you will see on your test will ask a yes-or-no question instead.

Leave it to GMAC to come up with a way to give you five different answer choices on a yes-or-no question. Let's look at an example.

Did candidate x receive more than half of the 30,000 votes cast in the general election?

(1) Candidate y received 12,000 of the votes cast.

(2) Candidate x received 18,000 of the votes cast.

Here's How to Crack It

When all is said and done, the answer to this question is either yes or no. Start by ignoring Statement (2) and evaluating Statement (1). Does Statement (1) alone answer the question? If you were in a hurry, you might think so. Many people assume that there are only two candidates in the election. They reason that if candidate y got 12,000 votes, then candidate x must have received 18,000 votes. However, there's no reason to assume that there are only two candidates. So, Statement (1) is insufficient. Write down BCE. Does Statement (2) alone answer the question? Yes, it's pretty clear that candidate x received more than half of the votes. So, the correct answer is B.

That didn't seem so bad, did it? Yet, you may have heard that yes/no Data Sufficiency questions have a reputation for being hard. Let's change our example to see why.

Did candidate x receive more than half of the 30,000 votes cast in the general election?

(1) Candidate y received 12,000 of the votes cast.

(2) Candidate x received 13,000 of the votes cast.

Here's How to Crack It

As always, start by ignoring Statement (2) so that you can properly evaluate Statement (1) alone. As in our previous example, Statement (1) is insufficient, so be sure to write down BCE. Statement (2) seems pretty straightforward. Candidate x received fewer than half of the votes cast. At this point many people say, "Since the guy clearly got fewer than half the votes, this statement doesn't answer the question, either." But those people are wrong!

Just Say No

Broken down to its basics, the question we were asked was, "Did he get more than half of the vote—yes or no?"

Statement (2) *does* answer the question. The answer is, "No, he didn't." So, the answer is the same as that of the first example. The answer is B.

On a yes/no Data Sufficiency problem, if the statement answers the question in either the affirmative or the negative, it is sufficient.

Yes/No/Maybe

Yes/no questions really should be called yes/no/maybe questions. Even if that's not their "official" name, it's still worthwhile to think about them in that fashion.

Let's look at one last example to see why.

Did candidate x receive more than half of the 30,000 votes cast in the general election?

(1) Candidate y received 12,000 of the votes cast.

(2) Candidate x received at least 13,000 of the votes cast.

Here's How to Crack It

Since the first statement of this question is the same as that of the previous two examples, we know that it is insufficient. So, write down BCE. Now, let's tackle Statement (2). Based on Statement (2), candidate x could have received exactly 13,000 votes, which would make the answer to the question "No, he did not receive more than half the votes cast." However, he could have also received 16,000 votes, and that would make the answer to the question, "Yes, he did receive more than half the votes cast." So, based on Statement (2), the best we can really say is that candidate x may have received more than half the votes. "Maybe" isn't good enough—we need a definitive yes or no answer. So, Statement (2) is insufficient. Cross off B. What if we combine the statements? We still have the same problem. We've accounted for at least 25,000 of the votes between the two candidates, but we don't know about the other 5,000. All of those votes could have gone to candidate x, making the answer to the question "yes." However, there could have been a third candidate who received those 5,000 votes. In that case, x would have received only 13,000 votes and the answer to the question is "no." Combining the statements didn't get us to a definitive answer. If the answer is sometimes "yes" and sometimes "no," the statement is not sufficient. Cross off C. The correct answer is E.

MORE ON DATA SUFFICIENCY

Although Data Sufficiency problems test the same material covered by regular Problem Solving questions, some readers find it distracting to learn the more complicated subtleties of this new question type at the same time that they are learning (or relearning) math concepts. That's why we've put our main chapter on Data Sufficiency at the end of our math review.

However, you will find Data Sufficiency problems sprinkled throughout the math drills—and you should feel free at any time to dip into Chapter 14, where you'll find everything in one place, including more advanced strategy, several more drills, and some great techniques to handle the most complicated yes/no questions.

Summary

- "Data Sufficiency" means just that, sufficiency. These questions are asking you if the data presented is enough to solve the problem.
- Every Data Sufficiency problem consists of a question followed by two statements. You must decide whether the question can be answered based on the information in the two statements.
- The best strategy for Data Sufficiency problems is to look at one statement at a time. Cover up the other statement with your hand, so that you can completely focus on one statement at a time.
- AD or BCE: These are always your options when you first start eliminating. Memorize them.

Chapter 10
Arithmetic

Do you remember all the rules for exponents? This chapter will review rules for those and other important mathematical concepts and teach you how to solve problems involving fractions, proportions, decimals, ratios, percentages, averages, medians, modes, standard deviation, exponents, and radicals.

Although arithmetic is only one of the three types of math tested on the GMAT, arithmetic problems comprise about half of the total number of math questions.

Here are the specific arithmetic topics tested on the GMAT:

1. Axioms and Fundamentals (properties of integers, positive and negative numbers, even and odd). These were covered in Chapter 7.
2. Arithmetic Operations
3. Fractions
4. Decimals
5. Ratios
6. Percentages
7. Averages
8. Exponents and Radicals

In this chapter, we will first discuss the fundamentals of each topic and then show how the test writers construct questions based on that topic.

ARITHMETIC OPERATIONS

There are six arithmetic operations you will need for the GMAT:

1.	**Addition** (2 + 2)	The result of addition is a sum or total.
2.	**Subtraction** (6 – 2)	The result of subtraction is a difference.
3.	**Multiplication** (2 × 2)	The result of multiplication is a product.
4.	**Division** (8 ÷ 2)	The result of division is a quotient.
5.	**Raising to a power** (x^2)	In the expression x^2 the little 2 is called an exponent.
6.	**Finding a square root** $\left(\sqrt{4}\right)$	$\sqrt{4} = \sqrt{2 \times 2} = 2$

Which One Do I Do First?

In a problem that involves several different operations, the operations must be performed in a particular order, and occasionally GMAC likes to see whether you know what that order is. Here's an easy way to remember the order of operations:

> Please Excuse My Dear Aunt Sally
> or
> PEMDAS

The first letters stand for Parentheses, Exponents, Multiplication, Division, Addition, and Subtraction. Do operations that are enclosed in parentheses first; then take care of exponents; then multiply and divide; then add and subtract, going from left to right.

DRILL 2

Just to get you started, solve each of the following problems by performing the indicated operations in the proper order. The answers can be found in Part VI.

1. $74 + (27 - 24) =$

2. $(8 \times 9) + 7 =$

3. $2[9 - (8 \div 2)] =$

4. $2(7 - 3) + (-4)(5 - 7) =$

Here's an easy question that shows how GMAC might test PEMDAS.

5. $4[-3(3 - 5) + 10 - 17] =$

- ○ –27
- ○ –4
- ○ –1
- ○ 32
- ○ 84

The Drill on Drills

- You can't use a calculator on the math section of the GMAT, so please don't use one as you work through the math drills in this book.
- To mimic the actual conditions of the test, get used to using scratch paper rather than writing in the book directly.

It is not uncommon to see a Data Sufficiency problem like this on the GMAT:

6. What is the value of x?

(1) $x^3 = 8$

(2) $x^2 = 4$

There are two operations that can be done in any order, provided they are the only operations involved: *When you are adding or multiplying a series of numbers, you can group or regroup the numbers any way you like.*

$2 + 3 + 4$ is the same as $4 + 2 + 3$
and
$4 \times 5 \times 6$ is the same as $6 \times 5 \times 4$

This is called the **associative law,** but the name will not be tested on the GMAT.

Another law that GMAC likes to test states that

$a(b + c) = ab + ac$ and $a(b - c) = ab - ac$.

This is called the **distributive law** but, again, you don't need to know that for the test. Sometimes the distributive law can provide you with a shortcut to the solution of a problem. If a problem gives you information in "factored form"—$a(b + c)$—you should distribute it immediately. If the information is given in distributed form—$ab + ac$—you should factor it.

DRILL 3

If the following problems are in distributed form, factor them; if they are in factored form, distribute them. Then do the indicated operations. Answers are in Part VI.

1. $8(10 + 5)$

2. $(55 \times 12) + (55 \times 88)$

3. $a(b + c - d)$

4. $abc + xyc$

A GMAT problem might look like this:

5. If $x = 6$ what is the value of $\frac{2xy - xy}{y}$?

- ⬭ –30
- ⬭ 6
- ⬭ 8
- ⬭ 30
- ⬭ It cannot be determined from the information given.

It is not uncommon to see a Data Sufficiency problem like this on the GMAT:

6. If $ax + ay + az = 15$, what is $x + y + z$?

   (1) $x = 2$

   (2) $a = 5$

FRACTIONS

Fractions can be thought of in two ways:

- A **fraction** is just another way of expressing division. The expression $\frac{1}{2}$ is exactly the same thing as 1 divided by 2. $\frac{x}{y}$ is nothing more than x divided by y. In the fraction $\frac{x}{y}$, x is known as the **numerator** and y is known as the **denominator**.

- The other important way to think of a fraction is as $\frac{\text{part}}{\text{whole}}$. The fraction $\frac{7}{10}$ can be thought of as 7 parts out of a total of 10 parts.

Adding and Subtracting Fractions with the Same Denominator

To add two or more fractions that have the same denominator, simply add up the numerators and put the sum over the common denominator. For example:

$$\frac{1}{7}+\frac{5}{7}=\frac{(1+5)}{7}=\frac{6}{7}$$

Subtraction works exactly the same way:

$$\frac{6}{7}-\frac{2}{7}=\frac{6-2}{7}=\frac{4}{7}$$

Adding and Subtracting Fractions with Different Denominators

Before you can add or subtract two or more fractions with different denominators, you must give all of them the same denominator. To do this, multiply the numerator and denominator of each fraction by a number that will give it a denominator in common with the others. If you multiplied each fraction by any old number, the fractions wouldn't have their original values, so the number you multiply by has to be equal to 1. For example, if you wanted to change $\frac{1}{2}$ into sixths, you could do the following:

$$\frac{1}{2}\times\frac{3}{3}=\frac{3}{6}$$

We haven't actually changed the value of the fraction, because $\frac{3}{3}$ equals 1.

If we wanted to add:

$$\frac{1}{2}+\frac{2}{3}$$

$$\frac{1}{2}\times\frac{3}{3}+\frac{2}{3}\times\frac{2}{2}$$

$$\frac{3}{6}+\frac{4}{6}=\frac{7}{6}$$

The Bowtie

The Bowtie method has been a staple of The Princeton Review's materials since the company began in a living room in New York City in 1981. It's been around so long because it works so simply.

To add $\frac{3}{5}$ and $\frac{4}{7}$, for example, follow these three steps:

Step One: Multiply the denominators together to form the new denominator.

$$\frac{3}{5}+\frac{4}{7}=\frac{\quad}{5\times 7}=\frac{\quad}{35}$$

Step Two: Multiply the first denominator by the second numerator ($5 \times 4 = 20$) and the second denominator by the first numerator ($7 \times 3 = 21$) and place these numbers above the fractions, as shown below.

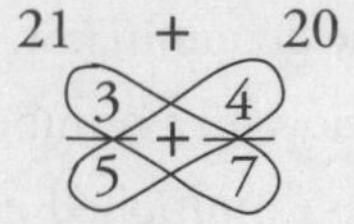

See? A bowtie!

Step Three: Add the products to form the new numerator.

$$\frac{3}{5}+\frac{4}{7}=\frac{21+20}{5\times 7}=\frac{41}{35}$$

Subtraction works the same way.

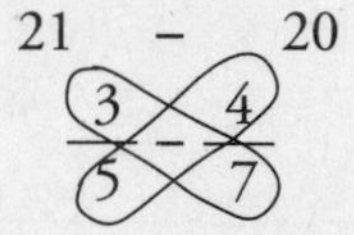

Note that with subtraction, the order of the numerators is important. The new numerator is 21 – 20, or 1. If you somehow get your numbers reversed and use 20 – 21, your answer will be $-\frac{1}{35}$, which is incorrect. One way to keep your subtraction straight is to always multiply **up** from denominator to numerator when you use the Bowtie.

Multiplying Fractions

To multiply fractions, just multiply the numerators and put the product over the product of the denominators. For example:

$$\frac{2}{3}\times\frac{6}{5}=\frac{12}{15}$$

Reducing Fractions

When you add or multiply fractions, you often end up with a big fraction that is hard to work with. You can usually reduce such a fraction. To reduce a fraction, find a factor of the numerator that is also a factor of the denominator. It saves time to find the biggest factor they have in common, but this isn't critical. You may just have to repeat the process a few times. When you find a common factor, cancel it. For example, let's take the product we just found when we multiplied the fractions above:

$$\frac{12}{15} = \frac{4 \times \cancel{3}}{5 \times \cancel{3}} = \frac{4}{5}$$

Get used to reducing all fractions (if they can be reduced) *before* you do any work with them. It saves a lot of time and prevents errors in computation.

For example, in that last problem, we had to multiply two fractions together:

$$\frac{2}{3} \times \frac{6}{5}$$

Before you multiplied 2×6 and 3×5, you could have reduced $\frac{6}{3}$ to $\frac{2}{1}$ and gotten the same answer even faster.

Dividing Fractions

To divide one fraction by another, just invert the second fraction and multiply:

$$\frac{2}{3} \div \frac{3}{4}$$

which is the same thing as...

$$\frac{2}{3} \times \frac{4}{3} = \frac{8}{9}$$

You may see this same operation written like this:

$$\frac{\frac{2}{3}}{\frac{3}{4}}$$

Again, just invert and multiply. This next example is handled the same way:

$$\frac{6}{\frac{2}{3}} = \frac{6}{1} \times \frac{3}{2} = \frac{18}{2} = 9$$

When you invert a fraction, the new fraction is called a **reciprocal.** $\frac{2}{3}$ is the reciprocal of $\frac{3}{2}$. The product of two reciprocals is always 1.

Converting to Fractions

An integer can be expressed as a fraction by making the integer the numerator and 1 the denominator: $16 = \frac{16}{1}$.

The GMAT sometimes gives you numbers that are mixtures of integers and fractions, for example, $3\frac{1}{2}$. It's easier to work with these numbers if you convert them into fractions. Simply multiply the denominator by the integer, then add the numerator, and place the resulting number over the original denominator. Because the fractional part of this number was expressed in halves, let's convert the integer part of the number into halves as well:

$$3 = \frac{6}{2}$$

Now just add $\frac{1}{2} + \frac{6}{2}$.

So, $3\frac{1}{2} = \frac{7}{2}$.

Comparing Fractions

In the course of a problem, you may have to compare two or more fractions and determine which is larger. This is easy to do as long as you remember that you can compare fractions directly only if they have the same denominator. Suppose you had to decide which of these three fractions is largest:

$$\frac{1}{2}, \frac{5}{9}, \text{ or } \frac{7}{15}$$

To compare these fractions directly you need a common denominator, but finding a common denominator that works for all three fractions would be complicated and time consuming. It makes more sense to compare these fractions two at a time. We showed you the classical way to find common denominators when we talked about adding fractions earlier.

Let's start with $\frac{1}{2}$ and $\frac{5}{9}$. An easy common denominator for these two fractions is 18 (9 × 2).

$$\frac{1}{2} \qquad \frac{5}{9}$$

$$\frac{1}{2}\times\frac{9}{9} \qquad \frac{5}{9}\times\frac{2}{2}$$

$$=\frac{9}{18} \qquad =\frac{10}{18}$$

Because $\frac{5}{9}$ is bigger, let's compare it with $\frac{7}{15}$. Here the easiest common denominator is 45. But before we do that...

Two Shortcuts

Comparing fractions is another situation where we can use the Bowtie. The idea is that if all you need to know is which fraction is bigger, you just have to compare the new numerators. Again, simply multiply the denominator of the first fraction by the numerator of the second and the denominator of the second by the numerator of the first, as shown below.

$$9 \times 1 = 9 \quad \frac{1}{2} \times \frac{5}{9} \quad 2 \times 5 = 10$$

$$10 > 9\text{, therefore } \frac{5}{9} > \frac{1}{2}$$

You could also have saved yourself some time on the last problem by a little fast estimation. Again, which is larger? $\frac{1}{2}$, $\frac{5}{9}$, or $\frac{7}{15}$?

Let's think about $\frac{5}{9}$ in terms of $\frac{1}{2}$. How many ninths equal a half? To put it another way, what is half of 9? 4.5. So $\frac{4.5}{9} = \frac{1}{2}$. That means $\frac{5}{9}$ is *bigger* than $\frac{1}{2}$.

Now let's think about $\frac{7}{15}$. Half of 15 is 7.5. $\frac{7.5}{15} = \frac{1}{2}$, which means that $\frac{7}{15}$ is less than $\frac{1}{2}$.

PROPORTIONS

A fraction can be expressed in many ways. $\frac{1}{2}$ also equals $\frac{2}{4}$ or $\frac{4}{8}$, etc. A **proportion** is just a different way of expressing a fraction. Here's an example:

If 2 boxes hold a total of 14 shirts, how many shirts are contained in 3 boxes?

Here's How to Crack It

The number of shirts per box can be expressed as a fraction. What you're asked to do is express the fraction $\frac{2}{14}$ in a different way.

$$\frac{2\text{ (boxes)}}{14\text{ (shirts)}} = \frac{3\text{ (boxes)}}{x\text{ (shirts)}}$$

To find the answer, all you need to do is find a value for x such that $\frac{2}{14} = \frac{3}{x}$. The easiest way to do this is to cross-multiply.

$2x = 42$, which means that $x = 21$. There are 21 shirts in 3 boxes.

DRILL 4

The answers to these questions can be found in Part VI.

1. $5\frac{2}{3} + \frac{3}{8} =$

2. Reduce $\frac{12}{60}$

3. Convert $9\frac{2}{3}$ to a fraction

4. $\frac{9}{2} = \frac{x}{4}$

A relatively easy GMAT fraction problem might look like this:

5. $$\frac{\left(\frac{\frac{4}{5}}{\frac{3}{5}}\right)\left(\frac{\frac{1}{8}}{\frac{2}{3}}\right)}{\frac{3}{4}} =$$

- ○ $\frac{3}{100}$
- ○ $\frac{3}{16}$
- ○ $\frac{1}{3}$
- ○ 1
- ○ $\frac{7}{16}$

Proportions and Ratios
Proportions are really ratios. Where a proportion question asks about the number of shirts *per* box, a ratio question might ask about the number of red shirts to blue shirts in a box.

Q: There are only roses, tulips, and peonies in a certain garden. There are three roses to every four tulips and every five peonies in the garden. Expressed as a fraction, what part of the flowers in the garden are tulips?

Turn the page for the answer.

Fractions: Advanced Principles

Now that you've been reacquainted with the basics of fractions, let's go a little further. More complicated fraction problems usually involve all of the rules we've just mentioned, with the addition of two concepts: $\dfrac{\text{part}}{\text{whole}}$, and the rest. Here's a typical medium fraction problem:

A cement mixture is composed of 3 elements. By weight, $\dfrac{1}{3}$ of the mixture is sand, $\dfrac{3}{5}$ of the mixture is water, and the remaining 12 pounds of the mixture is gravel. What is the weight of the entire mixture in pounds?

- ○ 4
- ○ 8
- ○ 36
- ○ 60
- ○ 180

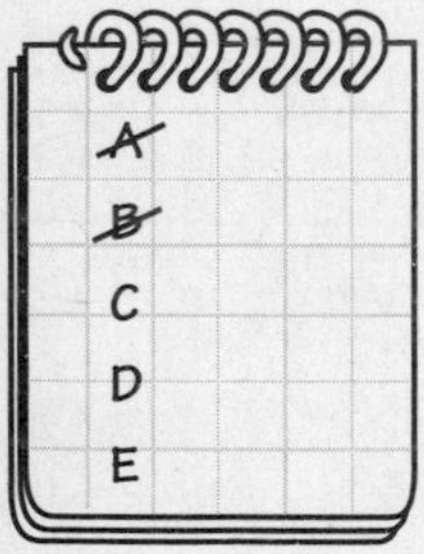

Easy Eliminations

Before we even start doing serious math, let's use some common sense. The weight of the gravel alone is 12 pounds. Because we know that sand and water make up the bulk of the mixture—sand $\dfrac{1}{3}$, water $\dfrac{3}{5}$ (which is a bit more than half)—the entire mixture must weigh a great deal more than 12 pounds. Answer choices A and B are out of the question. Eliminate them.

Here's How to Crack It

The difficulty in solving this problem is that sand and water are expressed as fractions, while gravel is expressed in pounds. At first there seems to be no way of knowing what fractional part of the mixture the 12 pounds of gravel represent; nor do we know how many pounds of sand and water there are.

The first step is to add up the fractional parts that we do have:

$$\frac{1}{3}+\frac{3}{5}=\frac{1}{3}\left(\frac{5}{5}\right)+\frac{3}{5}\left(\frac{3}{3}\right)=\frac{14}{15}$$

Sand and water make up 14 parts out of the whole of 15. This means that gravel makes up what is left over—the rest: 1 part out of the whole of 15. Now the problem is simple. Set up a proportion between parts and weights.

$$\frac{1}{15}=\frac{12}{x}\quad \begin{array}{l}\text{pounds (of gravel)}\\ \text{pounds (total pounds)}\end{array}$$

Cross-multiply: $x = 180$. The answer is choice E.

DECIMALS ARE REALLY FRACTIONS

A decimal can be expressed as a fraction, and a fraction can be expressed as a decimal.

$$0.6=\frac{6}{10}\text{, which can be reduced to }\frac{3}{5}$$

$$\frac{3}{5}\text{ is the same thing as }3 \div 5$$

Which would you rather figure out—the square of $\frac{1}{4}$ or the square of 0.25? There may be a few of you out there who've had so much practice with decimals in your work that you prefer decimals to fractions, but for the rest of us, fractions are infinitely easier to deal with.

A: The relationship between roses, tulips, and peonies was expressed as a ratio. To find the fractional part, first find the *whole*. We know the parts are 3 roses, 4 tulips, and 5 peonies. 3 + 4 + 5 = 12 = the whole. What fractional part of the flowers are tulips? 4 out of a total of 12, otherwise known as $\frac{4}{12}$ or $\frac{1}{3}$.

Occasionally, you will have to work with decimals. Whenever possible, however, convert decimals to fractions. It will save time and eliminate careless mistakes. In fact, it makes sense to memorize the fractional equivalent of some commonly used decimals:

$$0.2 = \frac{1}{5} \qquad 0.6 = \frac{3}{5}$$

$$0.25 = \frac{1}{4} \qquad 0.\overline{66} = \frac{2}{3}$$

$$0.\overline{33} = \frac{1}{3} \qquad 0.75 = \frac{3}{4}$$

$$0.4 = \frac{2}{5} \qquad 0.8 = \frac{4}{5}$$

$$0.5 = \frac{1}{2}$$

Adding and Subtracting Decimals

To add or subtract decimals, just line up the decimal points and proceed as usual. Adding 6, 2.5, and 0.3 looks like this:

$$\begin{array}{r} 6.0 \\ 2.5 \\ +\,0.3 \\ \hline 8.8 \end{array}$$

Multiplying Decimals

To multiply decimals, simply ignore the decimal points and multiply the two numbers. When you've finished, count all the digits that were to the right of the decimal points in the original numbers you multiplied. Now place the decimal point in your answer so that there are the same number of digits to the right of it. Here are two examples:

$0.3 \times 0.7 = 0.21$

There were a total of two digits to the right of the decimal point in the original numbers, so we place the decimal so that there are two digits to the right in the answer.

$14.3 \times 0.232 = 3.3176$

There were a total of four digits to the right of the decimal point in the original numbers, so we place the decimal such that there are four digits to the right in the answer.

Dividing Decimals

The best way to divide one decimal by another is to convert the number you are dividing by (in mathematical terminology, the **divisor**) into a whole number. You do this simply by moving the decimal point as many places as necessary. This works as long as you remember to move the decimal point in the number that you are *dividing* (in mathematical terminology, the **dividend**) the same number of spaces.

For example, to divide 12 by 0.6, set it up the way you would an ordinary division problem: $0.6\overline{)12.}$

To make 0.6 (the divisor) a whole number, you simply move the decimal point over one place to the right. You must also move the decimal one place to the right in the dividend. Now the operation looks like this:

$$0.6\overline{)12.}$$

$$6\overline{)120}$$

$$\begin{array}{r} 20 \\ 6\overline{)120} \end{array}$$

Rounding Decimals

9.4 rounded to the nearest whole number is 9.
9.5 rounded to the nearest whole number is 10.

When GMAC asks you to give an approximate answer on an easy question, it is safe to round numbers. But you should be leery about rounding numbers on a difficult question. If you're scoring in a high percentile, rounding off numbers will be useful to eliminate answer choices that are out of the ballpark, but not to decide between two close answer choices.

To round a decimal, look at the digit to the right of the digits place you are rounding to. If that number is 0–4, there is no change. If that number is 5–9, round up.

DRILL 5

Decimals or Fractions
Whether you prefer decimals or fractions, you must be able to work with both. The ability to work comfortably and confidently with decimals and fractions is vital to GMAT success.

The answers to these questions can be found in Part VI.

1. $\begin{array}{r} 34.26 \\ -\ 0.96 \\ \hline \end{array}$

2. $\begin{array}{r} 27.3 \\ \times 9.75 \\ \hline \end{array}$

3. $\frac{19.6}{3.22}$ (rounded to the nearest hundredth) =

4. $\dfrac{\frac{4}{0.25}}{\frac{1}{50}} =$

On the GMAT, there might be questions that mix decimals and fractions:

5. $\dfrac{\frac{3}{10} \times 4 \times 0.8}{0.32}$

- 0.96
- 0.333
- 3.0
- 30.0
- 96.0

6. If x and y are reciprocals, what is the value of $x + y$ rounded to the nearest hundredth?

(1) $x = 0.2$

(2) $y = 5$

RATIOS

Ratios are close relatives of fractions. A ratio can be expressed as a fraction and vice versa. The ratio 3 to 4 can be written as $\frac{3}{4}$ as well as in standard ratio format: 3 : 4.

There Is Only One Difference Between a Ratio and a Fraction

A fraction compares a part to whole relationship. A ratio compares a part to part relationship. It's that simple. Check out the box below for a handy visual representation.

Fraction:	Ratio:	
part: 3 women / whole: 7 people	part: 3 women / part: 4 men	(The whole is 7.)

First Things First

On *all* questions, before you do any serious calculations, take a moment to see whether the answer choices make sense. Eliminate crazy answer choices.

Do this first because those "crazy" choices usually reflect the result of a common (but incorrect) approach to the problem. Eliminate first and you won't think (falsely), "Aha, I've got it." Instead, you'll know you took a misstep somewhere.

Aside from That, All the Rules of Fractions Apply to Ratios

A ratio can be converted to a percentage or a decimal. It can be cross-multiplied, reduced, or expanded—just like a fraction. The ratio of 1 to 3 can be expressed as:

$$\frac{1}{3}$$

$$1 : 3$$

$$\frac{2}{6}$$

$$\frac{3}{9}$$

An Easy Ratio Problem

The ratio of men to women in a room is 3 to 4. If there are 20 women, what is the number of men in the room?

Here's How to Crack It

No matter how many people are actually in the room, the ratio of men to women will always stay the same: 3 to 4. What you're asked to do is find the numerator of a fraction whose denominator is 20, and which can be reduced to $\frac{3}{4}$. Just set one fraction equal to another and cross-multiply:

$$\frac{3}{4} = \frac{x}{20} \qquad 60 = 4x \qquad x = 15$$

The answer to the question is 15 men. Note that $\frac{15}{20}$ reduces to $\frac{3}{4}$.

A More Difficult Ratio Problem

> The ratio of women to men in a room is 3 to 4. If there are a total of 28 people in the room, how many are women?

This problem is more difficult because, while we are given the ratio of women to men, we are not given a specific value for either the women or the men. If we tried to set up this problem as we did the previous one, it would look like this:

$$\frac{3}{4} = \frac{x}{y}$$

Of course, you can't solve an equation that has two variables.

Here's How to Crack It

You need a way to see how the total number of people in the room, which you know is 28, can be broken down into groups of 3 women and 4 men.

A good way to solve the problem is to use a ratio box. Here's what that looks like for the information provided by the problem:

	Women	Men	Total
Ratio	3	4	
Multiplier			
Actual Number			28

To use a ratio box, you need a ratio and an actual number. Now, remember that ratios compare parts to parts. So, if you add up the parts, you get a group (or total) of 7 people.

Next, the key idea of a ratio is the multiplier, which allows you to make the group bigger or smaller while keeping everything in the same ratio. For this problem, you don't want a group of 7 people. You want a group of 28. So, you multiply $7 \times 4 = 28$.

To keep everything in the same ratio, you just need to remember that whatever you do to one part, you need to do to every part. So, multiply the ratio numbers for both the women and men by 4.

Here's what the box looks like when it is completed:

	Women	Men	Total
Ratio	3	4	7
Multiplier	4	4	4
Actual Number	12 = (3 × 4)	16 = (4 × 4)	28 = (7 × 4)

There are 12 women in the room.

PERCENTAGES

A **percentage** is just a fraction in which the denominator is always equal to 100. Fifty percent means 50 parts out of a whole of 100. Like any fraction, a percentage can be reduced, expanded, cross-multiplied, converted to a decimal, or converted to another fraction. $50\% = \frac{1}{2} = 0.5$

An Easy Percent Problem

Q: What is $\frac{1}{4}$% of 40?

Turn the page for the answer.

5 is what percent of 20?

Here's How to Crack It

Whenever you see a percent problem, you should be thinking $\frac{\text{part}}{\text{whole}}$. In this case, the question asks you to expand $\frac{5}{20}$ into another fraction in which the denominator is 100.

$$\frac{\text{part}}{\text{whole}} = \frac{5}{20} = \frac{x}{100}$$

$$500 = 20x$$

$$x = 25$$

$$\frac{x}{100} = 25\%$$

Percent Shortcuts

In the last problem, reducing $\frac{5}{20}$ to $\frac{1}{4}$ would have saved you time if you knew that $\frac{1}{4} = 25\%$. Here are some fractions and decimals whose percent equivalents you should know:

$$\frac{1}{4} = 0.25 = 25\%$$

$$\frac{1}{2} = 0.50 = 50\%$$

$$\frac{1}{3} = 0.333\ldots \text{ (a repeating decimal)} = 33\frac{1}{3}\%$$

$$\frac{1}{5} = 0.20 = 20\%$$

Some percentages simply involve moving a decimal point: To get 10 percent of any number, you simply move the decimal point of that number over one place to the left:

10% of 6 = 0.6
10% of 60 = 6
10% of 600 = 60

- To get 1 percent of any number, you just move the decimal point of that number over two places to the left:
  1% of 600 = 6
  1% of 60 = 0.6
  1% of 6 = 0.06

- To find a more complicated percentage, it's easy to break the percentage down into easy-to-find chunks:

20% of 60:	10% of 60 = 6; 20% of 60 is double 10%, so the answer is 2 × 6, or 12.
30% of 60:	10% of 60 = 6; 30% of 60 is three times 10%, so the answer is 3 × 6, or 18.
3% of 200:	1% of 200 = 2; 3% of 200 is just three times 1%, so the answer is 3 × 2, or 6.
23% of 400:	10% of 400 = 40. Therefore 20% equals 2 × 40, or 80. 1% of 400 = 4. Therefore 3% equals 3 × 4, or 12. Putting it all together, 23% of 400 equals 80 + 12, or 92.

A: There are a number of ways to calculate the answer, but the simplest is to first calculate 1% of 40 by moving the decimal point two places. This gives 0.4 as a result. Dividing this result by 4 gives us 0.1—the answer.

A Medium Percent Problem

Like medium and difficult fraction problems, medium and difficult percent problems often involve remembering the principles of $\frac{\text{part}}{\text{whole}}$ and the rest.

A motor pool has 300 vehicles of which 30 percent are trucks. 20 percent of all the vehicles in the motor pool are diesel, including 15 trucks. What percent of the motor pool is composed of vehicles that are neither trucks nor diesel?

- 165%
- 90%
- 65%
- 55%
- 10%

Here's How to Crack It

Do this problem one sentence at a time.

1. A motor pool has 300 vehicles, of which 30% are trucks. Thirty percent of 300 = 90 trucks, which means that 210 (the rest) are *not* trucks.
2. Twenty percent of all the vehicles are diesel, including 15 trucks. Twenty percent of 300 = 60 diesel vehicles, 15 of which are trucks, which means there are 45 diesel vehicles that are *not* trucks.
3. What percent of the motor pool is composed of vehicles that are neither truck nor diesel? We know from sentence number 1 that there are 210 nontrucks. We know from sentence number 2 that of these 210 nontrucks, 45 are diesel. Therefore 210 – 45, or 165, are neither diesel nor truck.

There's a handy formula for calculating mixed groups. It isn't a priority for you to memorize (you just saw the problem calculated without it), but the formula can be helpful on some questions. Here it is: Group 1 + Group 2 – both + neither = total. Here's what that looks like using the numbers from the vehicle problem. 90 trucks + 60 diesel – 15 diesel trucks + x = 300. 135 + x = 300. x = 165, or 55% of 300.

The question asks what percent of the entire motor pool these 165 nondiesel nontrucks are.

$$\frac{165}{300} = \frac{x}{100} \qquad 300x = 16{,}500$$

$x = 55$ and the answer is choice D.

Easy Eliminations

1. Because the problem asks us to find a portion of the entire motor pool, it's impossible for that portion to be larger than the motor pool itself. Therefore answer choice A, 165%, is crazy.
2. If the problem simply asked what percent of the motor pool was not made up of trucks, the answer would be 70%. But because there is a further condition (the vehicles must be both nontruck and nondiesel), the answer must be even less than 70%. This makes answer choice B impossible, too.
3. Answer choice C is probably a Joe Bloggs answer. You can get it simply by adding 30 + 20 + 15.

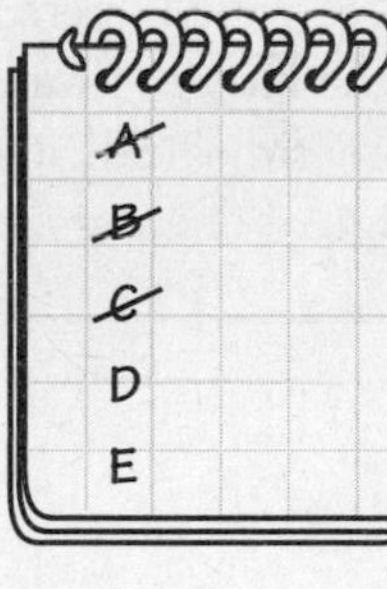

Percent Increase or Decrease

Another type of percent problem you may see on the GMAT has to do with *percent increase* or *percent decrease*. In these problems the trick is always to put the increase or decrease in terms of the *original* amount. See the following example:

The cost of a one-family home was $120,000 in 1980. In 1988, the price had increased to $180,000. What was the percent increase in the cost of the home?

- 60%
- 50%
- 55%
- 40%
- 33.3%

Here's How to Crack It

The actual increase was $60,000. To find the percent increase, set up the following equation:

$$\frac{\text{amount of increase}}{\text{original amount}} = \frac{x}{100}$$

In this case, $\frac{\$60,000}{\$120,000} = \frac{x}{100}$. So, $x = 50$ and the answer is choice B.

To solve a percent *decrease* problem, simply put the amount of the decrease over the original amount.

What's the Original Amount?

GMAT test writers like to see if they can trick you into mistaking which number was the original amount. On percent decrease problems (sometimes called "percent less" problems), the original is the larger number; on percent increase problems (sometimes called "percent greater" problems), the original is the smaller number.

Compound Interest

Another type of percent problem involves **compound interest.** If you kept $1,000 in the bank for a year at 6% simple interest, you would get $60 in interest at the end of the year. Compound interest would pay you slightly more. Let's look at a compound-interest problem:

Ms. Lopez deposits $100 in an account that pays 20% interest, compounded semiannually. How much money will there be in the account at the end of one year?

- ◯ $118.00
- ◯ $120.00
- ◯ $121.00
- ◯ $122.00
- ◯ $140.00

Easy Eliminations

Joe Bloggs doesn't know how to find compound interest, so he finds simple interest instead. In a compound-interest problem, always calculate simple interest first. $100 at 20% simple interest for one year would turn into $120, which is answer choice B. Because compound interest is always a *little bit* more than simple interest, we can eliminate answer choices A and B. Answer choice E is a great deal more than simple interest, so we can eliminate it, too. Only answer choices C and D are a *little bit* more than simple interest. We're down to a fifty-fifty guess.

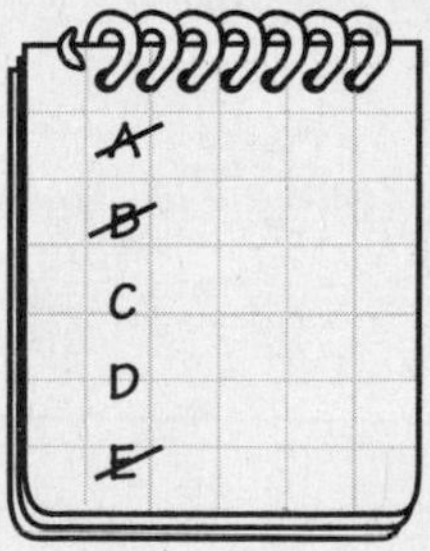

Here's How to Crack It

To find compound interest, divide the interest into as many parts as are being compounded. For example, if you're compounding interest semiannually, you divide the interest into two equal parts. If you're compounding quarterly, you divide the interest into four equal parts.

When Ms. Lopez deposited $100 into her account at a rate of 20% compounded semiannually, the bank divided the interest into two equal parts. Halfway through the year, the bank put the first half of the interest into her account. In this case, because the full rate was 20% compounded semiannually, the bank deposited 10% of $100 (10% of $100 = $10). Halfway through the year, Ms. Lopez had $110.

For the second half of the year, the bank paid 10% interest on the $110 (10% of $110 = $11). At the end of the year, Ms. Lopez had $121.00 in her account. She earned $1 more than she would have earned if the account had paid only simple interest. The answer is choice C.

AVERAGES

Reminder!
Averaging problems often have easy eliminations, so be sure to look for them—*before* you solve.

To find the **average** of a list of *n* numbers, you simply add the numbers and divide by *n*. For example:

$$\text{The average of 10, 3, and 5 is } \frac{10+3+5}{3} = 6$$

A good way to handle average problems is to set them up in the same way every time. Whenever you see the word *average*, you should think:

$$\frac{\text{total sum of the items}}{\text{total number of the items}} = \text{average}$$

A One-Step Average Problem

In a simple problem, GMAC will give you two parts of this equation, and it will be up to you to figure out the third. Let's warm up those old average skills.

What is the average (arithmetic mean) of the numbers 3, 4, 5, and 8?

Here's How to Crack It

In this case they've given us the actual numbers, which means we know the total sum (3 + 4 + 5 + 8 = 20) and the total number of items (there are four numbers). What we're missing is the average.

$$\frac{\text{total sum of the items}}{\text{total number of the items}} = \text{average} \qquad \frac{20}{4} = x \quad x = 5$$

Here's another one:

If the average (arithmetic mean) of 7 numbers is 5, what is the sum of the numbers?

Here's How to Crack It

In this case we know the total number of items and the average, but not the total sum of the numbers.

$$\frac{\text{total sum of the items}}{\text{total number of the items}} = \text{average} \qquad \frac{x}{7} = 5 \qquad x = 35$$

> **The Average Trap For Joe Bloggs**
>
> Joe thinks you can take the average of two averages.
>
> If Joe's average score on his first two tests was 70 and his average score on his next three tests was 80, what was his average score on all the tests?
>
> Joe wants to say 75 (the average of 70 and 80) because he forgot that his first average was based on two tests, while his second average was based on three tests. To find the real answer, you have to find the total number of points he got on all the tests (70 × 2 plus 80 × 3) and divide by the total number of tests (5). His real average: 76.

A Two-Step Average Problem

This is the same problem you just did, made a little more difficult:

The average (arithmetic mean) of 7 numbers is 5. If two of the numbers are 11 and 14, what is the average of the remaining numbers?

Here's How to Crack It

Always set up an average problem the way we showed you above. With more complicated average problems, take things one sentence at a time. The first sentence yields:

$$\frac{\text{total sum of the items}}{\text{total number of the items}} = \text{average} \qquad \frac{x}{7} = 5 \qquad x = 35$$

The sum of *all* the numbers is 35. If two of those numbers are 11 and 14, then the sum of the remaining numbers is 35 – (11 + 14), or 10. The question asks, "What is the average of the remaining numbers?" Again, let's set this up properly:

$$\frac{\text{total sum of the remaining numbers}}{\text{total number of the remaining numbers}} = \text{average} \qquad \frac{10}{5} = y \qquad y = 2$$

Why did we divide the total sum of the remaining numbers by 5? There were only 5 remaining numbers!

Medians and Modes

Calculating the average of a list of numbers is one way to find the "middle" of these numbers, but there are two other ways that yield slightly different results. To find the **median** of a list of *n* numbers, just reorder the numbers from least to greatest, and pick the middle number.

If *n* is odd, this is a piece of cake:

The median of 4, 7, 12, 14, 20 = 12.

If *n* is even, it's still easy—just add the two middle numbers together and divide by 2:

$$\text{The median of } 4, 12, 14, 20 = \frac{12+14}{2} = 13.$$

To find the **mode** of a list of *n* numbers, just pick the number that occurs most frequently...

The mode of 5, 6, 3, 9, 3, 28, 3, 5 = 3.

...but remember that a list of numbers *can* have more than one mode:

The modes of 3, 3, 3, 4, 5, 5, 5 = both 3 and 5.

Here's a relatively easy problem:

4, 6, 3, *y*

If the mode of the list of numbers above is 3, then what is the average (arithmetic mean) of the list?

- 7
- 3
- 4
- 9
- 12

Means

When a question refers to an average, the words "arithmetic mean" will often follow in parentheses. This is not just to make the problem sound scarier. **Arithmetic mean** is the precise term for the process of finding an average that we've illustrated in the problems above.

Here's How to Crack It

The mode of the list of numbers is 3, which means that y must also equal 3 (because the mode is the number that occurs most frequently in the list). So now all we have to do is find the average of 4, 6, 3, and 3. The correct answer is choice C.

RANGE AND STANDARD DEVIATION

To find the **range** of a list of n numbers, take the smallest number and subtract it from the largest number. This measures how widely the numbers are dispersed.

The range of 4, 3, 8, 12, 23, 37 = 37 – 3 = 34

Another way to measure the dispersion of a list of numbers is **standard deviation,** which measures the distance between the arithmetic mean and each of the numbers in that list. Even if you think you've never heard of this concept before, you've actually seen one example of standard deviation in the form of a graph that is near and dear to the test writers' hearts: the bell-shaped curve.

In the graph of approximate score frequencies below, you'll notice that many people's GMAT scores are clustered around the mean (500), with some people's scores below and other's above. The standard deviation is a number that expresses the degree to which the list of numbers vary from the mean, either above it or below it. The greater the standard deviation, the greater the degree of variation.

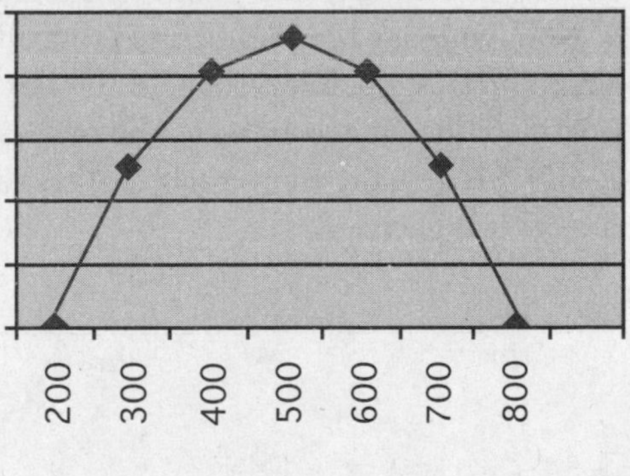

To calculate the standard deviation of a list of n numbers (not that the GMAT is likely to ask you to), first find the average (arithmetic mean) of the numbers. Then find the difference between that average and each number in the set and square each of the differences. And finally, find the average of the squared differences and take the square root of this average. The rather intimidating formula looks like this:

$$\sqrt{\frac{\sum\left(x-\bar{x}\right)^2}{n-1}}$$

Means, Medians, and Modes, Oh My!

Q: For the list of numbers {3, 2, 5, 8, 2, 16}, find the mean, the mode, the median, and the range.

Turn the page for the answer.

But you won't need it.

Standard deviation usually comes down to a single number such as 2.4 or 3.0. Most GMAT questions about standard deviation concern the difference between standard deviation and the mean. Here's a typical problem:

If the average (arithmetic mean) of a list of numbers is 12 and the standard deviation of that list of numbers is 1.3, then which of the following numbers is more than two standard deviations from the mean?

I. 14.7
II. 12.3
III. 9.3

- ◯ I only
- ◯ I and II only
- ◯ II only
- ◯ III only
- ◯ I and III only

Here's How to Crack It

One standard deviation above the mean of 12 is 13.3, and two standard deviations is 14.6. So 14.7 (Roman Numeral I) is definitely more than two standard deviations. Is the correct answer choice A? We don't know yet—but we can definitely cross off choices C and D because they don't include Roman Numeral I. Let's look at Roman Numeral II. 12.3 is definitely less than two standard deviations, so we can cross off choice B. Now, you may have wanted to cross off choice E as well, because 9.3 (Roman Numeral III) is much less than 14.6—but remember, standard deviation means a deviation either above *or below* the mean. Two standard deviations below 12 is 9.4, so 9.3 is actually more than two standard deviations from the mean. The correct answer is choice E.

EXPONENTS

An **exponent** is a short way of writing the value of a number multiplied several times by itself. $4 \times 4 \times 4 \times 4 \times 4$ can also be written as 4^5. This is expressed as "four to the fifth power." The large number (4) is called the base, and the little number (5) is called the exponent.

There are several rules to remember about exponents:

- **Multiplying numbers with the same base:** When you multiply numbers that have the same base, you simply add their exponents.

$$6^2 \times 6^3 = 6^{(2+3)} = 6^5 \qquad (y^4)(y^6) = y^{(4+6)} = y^{10}$$

- **Dividing numbers with the same base:** When you divide numbers that have the same base, you simply subtract the bottom exponents from the top exponents.

$$\frac{3^6}{3^2} = 3^{(6-2)} = 3^4 \qquad \frac{x^7}{x^4} = x^{(7-4)} = x^3$$

- **Raising a power to a power:** When you raise a number with an exponent to another power, you can simply multiply the exponents.

$$(4^3)^2 = 4^{(3\times 2)} = 4^6 \qquad (z^2)^4 = z^{(2\times 4)} = z^8$$

There are several operations that ***seem*** like they ought to work with exponents, but don't.

- Does $x^2 + x^3 = x^5$? NO!
- Does $x^6 - x^2 = x^4$? NO!
- Does $\dfrac{(x^2 + y^2 + z^2)}{(x^2 + y^2)} = z^2$? NO!

But note that in the first example, $x^2 + x^3$ can be written in another form, using the distributive property: $x^2 + x^3 = x^2(1 + x)$.

Means, Medians, and Modes, Oh My!

A: Always remember to reorder the numbers. In the list of numbers {2, 2, 3, 5, 8, 16}:
The mean is 6.
The mode is 2.
The median is 4.
The range is 14.

Strange Powers Revealed!
Why is any number to the 0 power equal to 1 when any other time we multiply by 0 the result is 0? The answer is that we aren't multiplying by 0 at all. Watch closely now: 3^0 should equal $3^{-1} \times 3^1$, because when you add the exponents you get 3^0. Now, $3^{-1} \times 3^1$ can be rewritten $\frac{1}{3} \times 3 = \frac{3}{3} = 1$.

The Strange Powers of Powers

If you raise a positive integer to a power, the result is *greater* than the original integer. For example, $6^2 = 36$. However, raising a number to a power can sometimes have unexpected results:

- If you raise a positive fraction that is less than 1 to a power, the result is *less* than the original fraction.

$$\left(\frac{1}{3}\right)^2 = \frac{1}{3} \times \frac{1}{3} = \frac{1}{9}$$

- If you raise a negative number to an odd power, the result is *less* than the original number.

$$(-3)^3 = (-3)(-3)(-3) = -27$$

  (Remember, –27 is smaller than –3.)
- If you raise a negative number to an even power, the result is positive.

$$(-3)^2 = (-3)(-3) = 9$$

  (Remember, negative times negative = positive.)
- Any number to the first power = itself.
- Any nonzero number raised to the 0 power = 1.

Even More Strange Powers
A radical can be rewritten as a fractional exponent, and vice versa. That is: $\sqrt[3]{5} = 5^{\frac{1}{3}}$.

RADICALS

The **square root** of a positive number x is the number that, when squared, equals x. By definition, you can take the square root of only a nonnegative number and the square root function returns only nonnegative values. The symbol for a square root is $\sqrt{\ }$. A number inside the $\sqrt{\ }$ is called a **radical**. Thus, in $\sqrt{4} = 2$, 4 is the radical and 2 is its square root.

The **cube root** of a positive number x is the number that, when cubed, equals x. For example, the cube root of 8 is 2, because $2 \times 2 \times 2 = 8$. The symbol for a cube root is $\sqrt[3]{\ }$. Thus, the cube root of 27 would be represented as $\sqrt[3]{27} = 3$, because $3 \times 3 \times 3 = 27$. The cube root of –27 would be represented as $\sqrt[3]{-27} = -3$ because $-3 \times -3 \times -3 = -27$.

There are several rules to remember about radicals:

1. $\sqrt{x}\sqrt{y} = \sqrt{xy}$. For example, $\sqrt{12}\sqrt{3} = \sqrt{36} = 6$.

2. $\sqrt{\frac{x}{y}} = \frac{\sqrt{x}}{\sqrt{y}}$. For example, $\sqrt{\frac{3}{16}} = \frac{\sqrt{3}}{\sqrt{16}} = \frac{\sqrt{3}}{4}$.

3. To simplify a radical, try factoring. For example, $\sqrt{32} = \sqrt{16}\sqrt{2} = 4\sqrt{2}$.

4. The square root of a positive fraction less than 1 is actually larger than the original fraction. For example, $\sqrt{\frac{1}{4}} = \frac{1}{2}$.

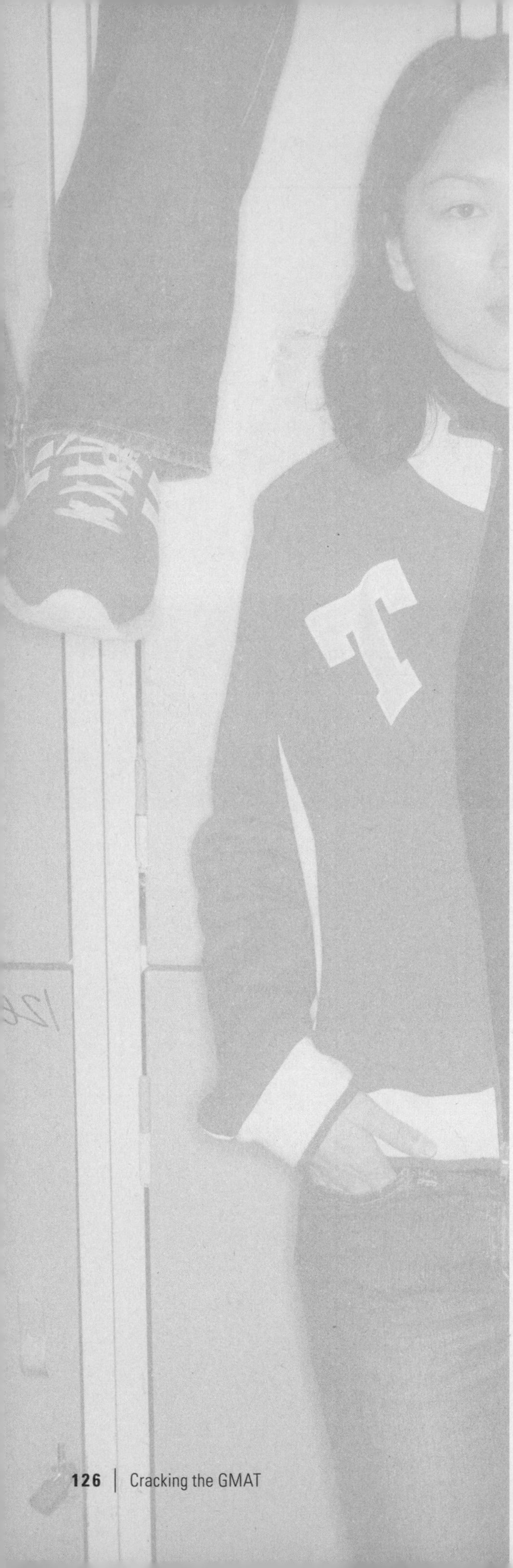

Summary

- The six arithmetic operations are addition, subtraction, multiplication, division, raising to a power, and finding a square root.
- These operations must be performed in the proper order (Please Excuse My Dear Aunt Sally).
- If you are adding or multiplying a group of numbers, you can regroup them in any order. This is called the **associative law.**
- If you are adding or subtracting numbers with common factors, you can regroup them in the following way:

  $$ab + ac = a(b + c)$$
  $$ab - ac = a(b - c)$$

  This is called the **distributive law.**
- A fraction can be thought of in two ways:
  - another way of expressing division
  - as a $\frac{\text{part}}{\text{whole}}$
- You must know how to add, subtract, multiply, and divide fractions. You must also know how to raise them to a power and find their roots.
- Always reduce fractions (when you can) before doing a complicated operation. This will reduce your chances of making a careless error.
- In tough fraction problems always think $\frac{\textit{part}}{\textit{whole}}$ and *the rest.*
- A decimal is just another way of expressing a fraction.
- You must know how to add, subtract, multiply, and divide decimals.
- In general it is easier to work with fractions than with decimals, so convert decimals to fractions.

- A ratio is a fraction in all ways but one:
    - A fraction is a $\frac{\text{part}}{\text{whole}}$.
    - A ratio is a $\frac{\text{part}}{\text{part}}$.
    - In a ratio, the whole is the sum of all its parts.
- A percentage is just a fraction whose denominator is always 100.
- You must know the percentage shortcuts outlined in this chapter.
- In tough percent problems, like tough fraction problems, think $\frac{\textit{part}}{\textit{whole}}$ and *the rest.*
- In a percentage increase or decrease problem, you must put the amount of the increase or decrease over the *original* amount.
- In compound interest problems, the answer will always be *a little bit more* than it would be in a similar simple interest problem.
- To find the average of several values, add the values and divide the total by the number of values.
- Always set up average problems in the same way:

$$\frac{\text{total sum of the items}}{\text{total number of the items}} = \text{average}$$

- To find the median of a list of n numbers, reorder the numbers from least to greatest, and pick the middle number if n is odd. Take the average of the two middle numbers if n is even.
- To find the mode of a list of n numbers, pick the number that occurs most frequently.
- To find the range of a list of n numbers, subtract the smallest number from the greatest number.

- Standard deviation measures the distance between a set of numbers and its arithmetic mean. Most GMAT problems about this concept hinge on the difference between the standard deviation and the arithmetic mean.
- An exponent is a shorter way of expressing the result of multiplying a number several times by itself.
- When you multiply numbers with the same base, you simply add the exponents.
- When you divide numbers with the same base, you simply subtract the exponents.
- When you raise a power to a power, you multiply the exponents.
- You *cannot* add or subtract numbers with the same or different bases by adding their exponents.
- The three radical rules you need to know:
  - $\sqrt{x}\sqrt{y} = \sqrt{xy}$
  - $\sqrt{\frac{x}{y}} = \frac{\sqrt{x}}{\sqrt{y}}$
  - $\sqrt{x^2 y} = x\sqrt{y}$
- There are some unusual features of exponents and radicals:
  - The square root of a positive fraction that's less than 1 is larger than the original fraction.
  - When you raise a positive fraction that's less than 1 to an exponent, the resulting fraction is smaller.
  - When you raise a negative number to an even exponent, the resulting number is positive.
  - When you raise a negative number to an odd exponent, the resulting number is still a negative number.

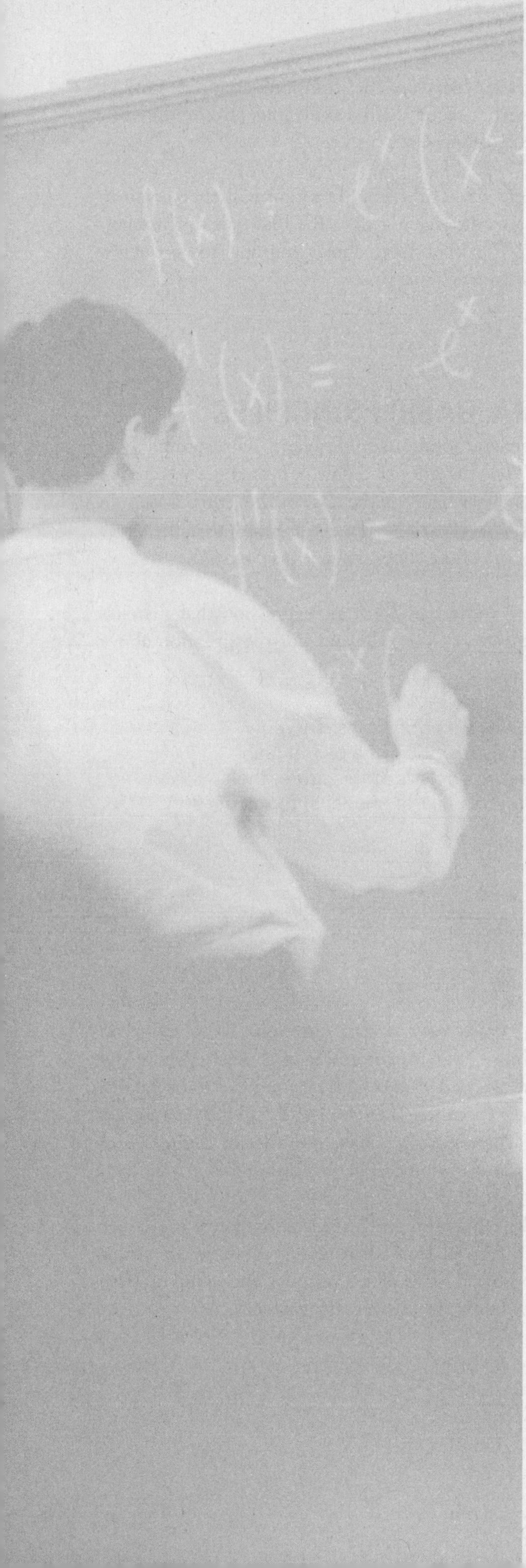

Chapter 11
Algebra

Algebra is usually all about writing equations. In this chapter, we'll show you a fool-proof way to write the equations you *need* to write, give you a review of the quadratic formula, and teach you how to do simultaneous equations. Plus, you'll learn two fantastic techniques that will allow you to avoid writing equations on most GMAT questions: *Plugging In* and *Plugging In the Answers* (PITA).

Approximately one-fourth of the problems on the computer-adaptive GMAT Math section involve traditional algebra. Your algebra skills may also be tested by some questions in the Integrated Reasoning section.

In this chapter, we'll show you some powerful techniques that will enable you to solve these problems without using traditional algebra. The first half of this chapter discusses these new techniques. The second half shows you how to do the few algebra problems that must be tackled algebraically.

NOT EXACTLY ALGEBRA: BASIC PRINCIPLES

Algebra is used to come up with general solutions to problems. For example, you might know (for whatever reason) that the price of a new pair of shoes in relation to the cost of a pair of jeans is $3j + 20$, where j is the cost of the jeans. Based on this formula, if you know that the jeans cost \$50, then you know that the shoes cost \$170. But, you also know the cost of the shoes if the jeans cost \$75.

In most algebra problems, you need to find an algebraic expression that matches the description of the relationship given in the problem. For the situation above, the problem might say

> At a certain store, the price of a pair of shoes is twenty dollars more than three times the price of a pair of jeans. If the price of a pair of jeans is j dollars at this store, then what is the price, in dollars, of a pair of shoes, in terms of j?
>
> ◯ $20 - 3j$
> ◯ $3j + 20$
> ◯ $3j - 20$
> ◯ $3j + 60$
> ◯ $20j + 3$

You might consider this question a fairly easy algebra question. To solve it, you might just start translating the phrase "the cost of a pair of shoes is twenty dollars more than three times the cost of a pair of jeans." But, you need to be careful while doing that. If you get confused about whether you should add 20 or subtract 20, you'll pick the wrong answer. The test writers have put a lot of thought into the ways that the key statement in the question can be misinterpreted.

So, if it's so easy to make a mistake while doing the algebra, is there a more foolproof way to do this question? Of course! Instead of trying to come up with a general solution—the algebraic approach—let's pick a number and come up with a specific solution. Then, we'll just choose the answer that matches.

We call this approach **Plugging In**. It is perhaps our most powerful math technique and will allow you to solve complicated problems more quickly than you might have ever thought possible. Plugging In is easy. There are three steps involved.

Plugging In

1. Pick numbers for the variables in the problem.
2. Using your numbers, find an answer to the problem. At The Princeton Review, we call this the target answer.
3. Plug your numbers into the answer choices to see which choice equals the answer you found in step 2.

Let's look at the same problem again:

At a certain store, the price of a pair of shoes is twenty dollars more than three times the price of a pair of jeans. If the price of a pair of jeans is j dollars at this store, then what is the price, in dollars, of a pair of shoes, in terms of j ?

- ◯ $20 - 3j$
- ◯ $3j + 20$
- ◯ $3j - 20$
- ◯ $3j + 60$
- ◯ $20j + 3$

Here's How to Crack It

Let's pick a number for j. Let's say that the jeans cost $10. (We don't need to worry about being realistic!) In your scratch booklet, write down "$j = 10$". We've now transformed the problem from an algebra problem into an arithmetic problem.

Here's what the problem now asks:

At a certain store, the price of a pair of shoes is twenty dollars more than three times the price of a pair of jeans. If the price of a pair of jeans is **10** dollars at this store, then what is the price, in dollars, of a pair of shoes, ~~in terms of j~~?

You'll notice that we've substituted 10 for the variable *j* in the original problem. You'll also notice that we've crossed out the phrase "in terms of *j*." Once we put a number into the problem, the phrase "in terms of" has no meaning so we can ignore it.

Using \$10 for the price of the jeans, the price of the pair of shoes is \$50. All we did was translate the phrase "the price of a pair of shoes is twenty dollars more than three times the price of a pair of jeans." Three times the price of the pair of jeans is 3 × \$10 = \$30. Twenty dollars more is just \$30 + \$20 = \$50. The numerical answer to our problem is \$50. Write that number down on your noteboard and circle it to indicate that it is your target answer.

Now, you just need to find the answer that matches \$50 when you substitute 10 for *j*. You should write down A, B, C, D, E on your noteboard and work out each answer choice. Here's what that looks like:

A) $20 - 3j = 20 - 3(10) = -10$
B) $3j + 20 = 3(10) + 20 = 50$
C) $3j - 20 = 3(10) - 20 = 10$
D) $3j + 60 = 3(10) + 60 = 90$
E) $20j + 3 = 20(10) + 3 = 203$

Answer B is the only answer that matches the target answer so it is the answer to this problem. You'll note that we checked all five answer choices. We did that to be sure we were picking the correct answer.

Scratch Work

The students in our GMAT course learn to automatically do scratch work. When plugging in, always write down the numbers you are plugging in for each variable. Be sure to clearly label the number for each variable by writing down something like $j = 10$. Next, do the work for each step in the problem. When you find the numerical answer to the problem, write that down and circle it. Then, try each of the answer choices, crossing them off as you eliminate them. Here's what your scratch work should have looked like for the last problem:

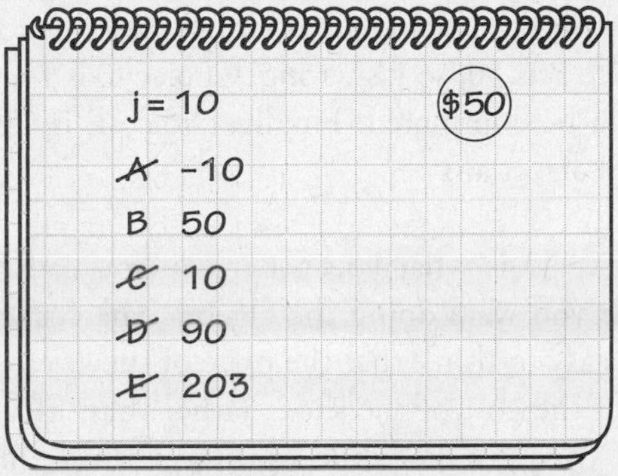

Why Plug In? Because It Makes Difficult Problems Easy!

You might be thinking, "Wait a minute! It was just as easy to solve this problem algebraically. Why should I plug in?" To see why, let's take a look at another version of the problem.

At a certain store, the price of a pair of shoes is twenty dollars more than three times the price of a pair of jeans and the price of a sweater is fifty percent more than the price of a pair of shoes. If the price of a pair of jeans is j dollars at this store, then what is the price, in dollars, of a pair of shoes, a sweater and a pair of jeans, in terms of j ?

- ◯ $1.5j + 10$
- ◯ $3j + 20$
- ◯ $4.5j + 30$
- ◯ $5.5j + 30$
- ◯ $8.5j + 50$

Another Reason to Plug In

Plugging numbers into a problem is a much more natural way to think for most folks than algebra. Has anyone ever asked a bartender, "Say, could I get $6x$ of whiskey, where $6x$ equals a standard shot?" The bartender might comply, but you can be sure he'd ask for your car keys first. Complicate the question with y, the ounces of alcohol in a standard shot, and z, the number of ice cubes in the glass, and you've got a real headache. Essentially, Plugging In is a matter of putting numbers back into a form that you are used to working with.

Here's How to Crack It

This version of the problem is wordier and that helps to make it more confusing. Let's try Plugging In. As before, we'll start by making $j = 10$. So, the jeans cost \$10. Next, we know the relationship between the price of the jeans and the cost of the shoes. The price of the shoes is "twenty dollars more than three times the price of the jeans." So, the price of the shoes is \$50. Finally, the sweater costs "fifty percent more than the price of the shoes." So, the sweater is \$50 + \$25, or \$75. So, the cost of all three items is \$10 + \$50 + \$75 = \$135. Be sure to circle \$135.

Now, it's time to find the answer that equals 135 when $j = 10$. Choice A is 25, so cross it off. Choice B is 50, so it's wrong. Choice C is 75, so it's also wrong. Choice D is 85, so it can be eliminated. Finally, choice E is 135. Choice E matches the target and is the correct answer.

By the way, choice D is what you get if you misread how to calculate the cost of the sweater. If you were doing the algebra, the cost of the shoes is $3j + 20$. It would be pretty easy to think that the price of the sweater is then $1.5j + 10$, which is fifty percent of the cost of the shoes rather than fifty percent *more.* Of course, you could make this mistake while working with the numbers, too. But, what's easier—to see that \$25 is not more than \$50 or to see that $1.5j + 10$ is not more than $3j + 20$?

To recap, there are two reasons why you'd want to plug in even if you are pretty good at algebra.

1. Plugging In can make even the hardest algebra problems much easier to solve.
2. The test writers have thought about all the possible ways you might mess up the algebra while working the problem. If you make one of those mistakes, your answer will be among the answer choices and you'll most likely wind up picking the wrong answer.

What Number Should I Plug In?

While you can plug in any number, you'll find that certain numbers work better than others. Ideally, you want a number that makes it easy to perform the calculations for the problem. For most problems, you can just use small, simple numbers such as 2, 5, or 10. However, you also want numbers that make sense within the context of the problem. For example, for a problem that uses percents, plugging in 100 would be a good idea. Different numbers work for different types of problems. As you practice, you'll get better at picking good numbers—especially if you keep asking yourself "What number will make this problem easy?" You also shouldn't be afraid to change your number if the calculations start to get messy.

What to Plug In

- Numbers that make the math easy!
- Try small simple numbers such as 2, 5, or 10
- Percents? Try 100
- Hours or Minutes? 30 or 120

What NOT to Plug In

- Avoid using 0 or 1
- Numbers in the problem or in the answer choices

Sometimes the best way to select a number is to use a little common sense. Here's an example:

If Jim drives k miles in 50 minutes, how many minutes will it take him to drive 10 miles, at the same rate?

- ○ $\frac{500}{k}$
- ○ $\frac{k}{500}$
- ○ $60k$
- ○ $10k$
- ○ $\frac{50}{k}$

Q: If 80% of a certain number x is 50% of y and y is 20% of z, then what is x in terms of z?

A. $5z$
B. $3z$
C. $z/4$
D. $z/5$
E. $z/8$

Turn the page for the answer.

Here's How to Crack It

GMAC would like you to use the formula *distance* = *rate* × *time*. There are variables in the answer choices, so we can plug in. Since it's a good bet that at least a few of the wrong answers are based on using the formula, let's plug in.

Any number you choose to plug in for k will eventually give you the answer to this problem, but there are some numbers that will make your task even easier.

We need to find a good number for k. Notice that we know that Jim is going to drive 10 miles. Suppose we just made k equal to half of 10? The question now reads as follows:

If Jim drives 5 miles in 50 minutes, how many minutes will it take him to drive 10 miles, at the same rate?

Now the problem is pretty easy. Since Jim is going to drive twice the distance, it's going to take him twice the time. So, the target is 100 minutes. Now, all we need to do is find the answer that matches the target when $k = 5$. Start with answer choice A. Divide 500 by 5 to get 100. Bingo! To double check, plug 5 into the other answer choices as well. None of them match the target.

A: The answer is E. If you plugged in 100 for *x*, then you found *y* must equal 160. The question tells us 160 (our *y*) equals 20% of *z*. That means *z* equals 800. Now it should be simple to see that *x* equals *z* divided by 8.

The answer to this question is choice A.

More Times to Plug In

So far, we've been looking at questions that have explicit variables in both the problem and the answer choices. When you see variables in the problem or answer choices, that's one of the signs to plug in.

However, sometimes GMAC expects you to use algebra to answer a question that doesn't have explicit variables. You can still plug in on these problems. In fact, *you should consider plugging in whenever you feel the urge to do algebra*. The urge to do algebra is the ultimate sign that the problem can be cracked using some form of Plugging In.

Let's take a look at some other ways to plug in.

Plugging In with Hidden Variables

Some problems have a hidden variable. For these problems, all the calculations are usually based off one item but you don't know the value of that item. There's a simple solution—just plug in a value for the item!

Let's look at an example:

A merchant reduces the original price of a coat by 20 percent for a spring sale. Finding that the coat did not sell, the merchant reduces the spring price by a further 15 percent at the start of the summer. The coat's summer price is what percent of its original price?

- ◯ 35%
- ◯ 64%
- ◯ 65%
- ◯ 68%
- ◯ 80%

Here's How to Crack It

You may have noticed that this problem never gave us the coat's original price. You may have felt the urge to do algebra starting to kick in as you read the problem. For example, you might have started to say to yourself "Well, if the price of the coat is x, then the spring price is..." That's your sign that you can do this problem as a Plug In! All you need to do is pick a price for the coat.

Let's make the original price of the coat $100. *When you are solving a percent problem, 100 is a great number to plug in.* The merchant discounts the price of the coat by 20% for the spring sale. Twenty percent of $100 is $20, so the spring price is $80. For the summer, the spring price of the coat is discounted by another 15%. Fifteen percent of $80 is $12, making the summer price $68.

The question asks for the summer price as a percent of the original price. In other words, $68 is what percent of $100? 68%. The answer is choice D.

Easy Eliminations

If you were running out of time, you'd need to make a guess. But, you could eliminate some obviously wrong answers first. When you read the problem fast, you might be tempted to think that the overall reduction is 20% + 15% = 35% but that's too easy. So, cross off choice A. Choice C is just 100 – 35 = 65. Also, too easy. Finally, choice E is what you get after the first reduction. The answer is probably B or D.

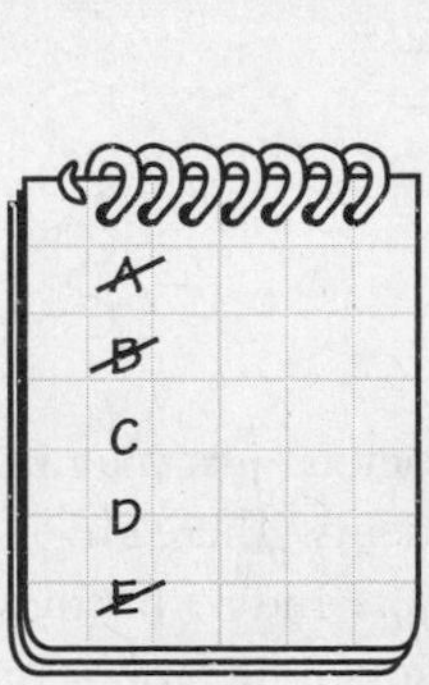

Another way to tell that you can probably solve a question as a hidden Plug In is to look at the answer choices. The answer choices for hidden Plug In questions are typically percents, fractions, or sometimes ratios. How can you tell that this problem is a hidden Plug In?

At College P, one–fourth of the students are seniors and one–fifth of the seniors major in business. If two–fifths of all students at the college major in business, the business majors who are not seniors are what fraction of all business majors?

- ◯ $\frac{1}{20}$
- ◯ $\frac{1}{8}$
- ◯ $\frac{7}{20}$
- ◯ $\frac{7}{15}$
- ◯ $\frac{7}{8}$

Here's How to Crack It

You may have noticed that while this problem provides lots of fractions to work with, it never reveals how many students attend College P. Of course, knowing the total enrollment at the college would make solving the problem fairly straightforward. So, before you start setting up equations based on *x* students at College P, let's plug in a number for the total students.

An easy way to come up with a good number when the problem has fractions is to simply multiply the denominators of the fractions together. In this case, that's $4 \times 5 \times 5 = 100$. Don't worry, by the way, that some of the denominators are not distinct. Multiplying by the extra 5 may help us to avoid getting a result that leads to some fractional part of a student!

It Works for Ratios, Too!

You can also plug in when the answer choices are expressed as ratios. Here's how the same question would be rewritten as a ratio problem.

...what is the ratio of the senior business majors to the business majors who are not seniors?

- ◯ 1:3
- ◯ 1:5
- ◯ 1:7
- ◯ 1:8
- ◯ 7:8

As before, just plug in 100 for the number of students. There are 5 seniors who are business majors and 35 business majors who are not seniors. The ratio is 5:35, which reduces to 1:7. The answer is C.

So, if there are 100 students at the college, there are 25 seniors and 75 students who are not seniors. Next, you know that one-fifth of the seniors major in business, so that's 5 seniors who are business majors. Since two-fifths of all students are business majors, the college has 40 business majors. Of those 40 business majors, 40 – 5 = 35 of the business majors are not seniors. So, the fraction of business majors who are not seniors is $\frac{35}{40} = \frac{7}{8}$. The correct answer is E.

Plugging In the Answers (PITA)

Some algebra questions ask for a numerical answer. GMAC expects you to write an equation, solve it and then pick the answer. However, the person who wrote the problem had to do all of that hard work. So, rather than duplicate all of the work the question writer did, why not just test out the answers to see which one works?

We call this method of solving the problem **Plugging In the Answers** (or PITA for short). You'll find that solving problems this way can save you a lot of time and help you to avoid common algebra mistakes. There are three steps involved when you Plug In the Answers.

Plugging In the Answers

1. Write down the answers, determine what they represent and label them.

2. Start with choice C and work the steps of the problem.

3. Look for some sort of condition that must be met to make the answer correct.

Let's take a look at an example.

At a certain restaurant, the price of a sandwich is $4.00 more than the price of a cup of coffee. If the price of a sandwich and a cup of coffee is $7.35, including a sales tax of 5%, what is the price of a cup of coffee, EXCLUDING the sales tax?

- $1.50
- $3.00
- $4.00
- $5.50
- $7.00

Here's How to Crack It

If there were no answer choices, you'd be forced to write an equation and solve it. However, because you know the answer must be one of the five provided choices, it will be easier and faster to simply try the answers.

Start by writing down the answers and labeling them as "coffee." Now, start with choice C. If the cup of coffee costs $4.00, what can you figure out? The problem states that the sandwich costs $4.00 more than the cup of coffee, so the sandwich is $8.00. Make a column for "sandwich" and write down $8.00 next to choice C. You now know that the cost for the sandwich and the cup of coffee is $12.00. Choice C is too big because the cost for the sandwich and the cup of coffee is supposed to be only $7.35 including the sales tax. Go ahead and cross off choice C.

Scratchwork

When you Plug In the Answers, make your scratch-work look like an Excel spreadsheet. Label your columns and put your results for each column next to the answer choice you are checking. Doing so will help you to cut down on mistakes and check subsequent answer choices more quickly.

So far, your work should look like this:

Coffee	Sandwich	Total
A) $1.50		
B) $3.00		
~~C) $4.00~~	$8.00	$12.00
D) $5.50		
E) $7.00		

Now, its time to decide if you need a bigger number or a smaller number. It's a pretty easy choice for this problem. Since $4.00 turned out to be too big, it makes sense to try a smaller number. Choices D and E are out of the question, so cross them off. There's no need to debate over choice A or B. One of them must be correct, so just try choice B. If it works, you're done. If it doesn't, choose choice A and you're still done.

If the cup of coffee costs $3.00 (choice B), then the sandwich is $7.00. That would make the total cost for both items $10.00. That's still too big! The answer must be A.

Here's what the work should look like at this point:

Coffee	Sandwich	Total
A) $1.50		
~~B) $3.00~~	$7.00	$10.00
~~C) $4.00~~	$8.00	$12.00
~~D) $5.50~~		
~~E) $7.00~~		

There's really no need to test choice A. However, if the coffee costs $1.50, then the sandwich costs $5.50. Together the two items cost $7.00. The tax on the two items is 5% of $7.00 or $0.35. So, the total with tax is $7.35, which meets the condition stated in the problem. The answer is choice A.

Plugging In the Answers: Advanced Principles

When you solve a problem using Plugging In the Answers (PITA), you'll usually know if you need a bigger or smaller number if choice C didn't work. However, there are times when you won't be sure. Rather than wasting time trying to decide if you need a bigger or smaller number, just pick an answer choice and try it. You'll actually waste less time testing an extra answer choice or two than you will trying to decide which type of number to try next.

Jim is now twice as old as Fred, who is two years older than Sam. Four years ago, Jim was four times as old as Sam. How old is Jim now?

- ◯ 8
- ◯ 12
- ◯ 16
- ◯ 20
- ◯ 24

Here's How to Crack It

This question has numbers in the answers and you probably started to think "Well, if Jim is *x* years old, then Fred is..." The urge to do algebra means that it's time to Plug In the Answers. Start with choice C.

The answers represent possible ages for Jim. If Jim is 16 years old, then Fred is 8 because Jim is twice as old as Fred. Next, you know that Fred is two years older than Sam, so Sam is 6. Now, you need to compare Jim's age and Sam's age four years ago. Four years ago, Jim was 12 and Sam was 2. Remember that there's always a condition in the problem that must be met by the correct answer.

> **When to Plug In the Answers**
> - There are numbers in the answer choices.
> - The question asks for a specific amount.
> - You have the urge to set up and solve an equation.

In this case, Jim's age four years ago must be four times that of Sam. Is 12 four times 2? No. So, choice C can be eliminated.

Here's what your work should look like up to this point.

	Now			4 years ago	
Jim	Fred	Sam		Jim	Sam
A)8					
B)12					
~~C)16~~	8	6		12	2
D)20					
E)24					

Now, it's time to choose a bigger or smaller number. But, it isn't really clear which direction to go, is it? So, rather than waste a lot of time trying to figure that out, just pick an answer and try it. If Jim is 20 years old now (choice D), then Fred is 10 and Sam is 8. Four years ago, Jim was 16 and Sam was 4.

Here's what your work should look like.

	Now			4 years ago	
Jim	Fred	Sam		Jim	Sam
A) 8					
B) 12					
~~C) 16~~	8	6		12	2
D) 20	10	8		16	4
E) 24					

Since $4 \times 4 = 16$, the condition in the problem is met. Choice D is the correct answer.

Most of the time, starting at C when doing PITA makes the most sense. By starting at C, you can usually cut down on the number of answer choices that you need to test. However, there can be times when it makes sense to start with a different answer choice.

If x is a positive integer such that $x^2 + 5x - 14 = 0$, what is the value of x ?

- ◯ –7
- ◯ –5
- ◯ 0
- ◯ 2
- ◯ 5

Here's How to Crack It

Notice that the question states that x is a positive integer. Don't waste time with choices A, B, or C—cross them off immediately. For this problem, it makes sense to start with choice D. Plug 2 into the equation for x to get $(2)^2 + 5(2) - 14 = 0$. Since the equation is true when $x = 2$, choice D is the correct answer.

Plugging In the Answers Advanced Tips

1. If you're not sure whether you need a bigger or smaller number, don't waste time. Just pick another answer choice and try it.
2. You may be able to eliminate some numbers that are too big or too small before you start plugging in. If you can, just start with the middle number that you have left.
3. If you have both easy to work with numbers and messy numbers in the answer choices, try the easy to work with numbers first.

Must Be

Some questions will use the words "must be." For example, the question may ask which of the expressions in the answers must be even or must be divisible by 3. These questions can be solved easily by plugging in. However, you'll probably need to plug in at least twice to find the answer.

Here's all you need to do.

Must Be Plugging In

1. Pick numbers for the variables in the problem. Be sure to satisfy any restrictions for the variables.
2. Eliminate any answer choices that don't match what you are looking for.
3. Plug in the most different kind of number you are allowed to try. For example, if you tried an even number, try an odd number.
4. Repeat until only one answer remains.

If n is a positive integer, which of the following must be even?

- ⬭ $(n - 1)(n + 1)$
- ⬭ $(n - 2)(n + 1)$
- ⬭ $(n - 2)(n + 4)$
- ⬭ $(n - 3)(n + 1)$
- ⬭ $(n - 3)(n + 5)$

Here's How to Crack It

Start by picking a value for n. How about $n = 2$? Now, evaluate each answer choice. For choice A, the expression equals 3, so cross it off. For choice B, the expression equals 0. Remember that 0 is an even number so keep this answer choice. But you aren't done yet. Just because you've found one case where this answer choice is even doesn't mean it will always be even. Keep checking the answers. Choice C is also equal to 0, so keep it as well. Choice D equals –3. Don't be fooled by the negative sign. Negative integers can also be even or odd. Since –3 is odd, cross this answer off. Choice E equals –7 and can also be eliminated.

Next, try a new number. Since this problem is about even and odd numbers, it makes sense to try an odd number next. How about $n = 3$? You need to check only the two answers that remain. Choice B equals 4, which is still even. However, choice C now equals 7, so can be eliminated. The correct answer is choice B.

When doing a must be question, it's very helpful to set up your scratchwork so that it looks like a chart. Write down A, B, C, D, E and the actual expressions. Make a new column for each number that you plug in. Be sure to cross off answers as you go.

Here's what your work should look like once you have worked through the entire problem.

	$n = 2$	$n = 3$
~~A) $(n - 1)(n + 1)$~~	3	
B) $(n - 2)(n + 1)$	0	4
~~C) $(n - 2)(n + 4)$~~	0	7
~~D) $(n - 3)(n + 1)$~~	–3	
~~E) $(n - 3)(n + 5)$~~	–7	

BASIC ALGEBRA

You can solve most GMAT algebra problems using some form of Plugging In. However, there are some questions that you may need to solve using some relatively basic algebra.

Two Simple Rules

Before we review some very specific types of algebra that GMAC likes to test, let's review the two basic rules that are true for any algebraic situation. These two rules are used pretty much any time that you solve a problem algebraically.

1. Collect like terms. Get all the *x*'s on one side of the equal sign and all the numbers on the other.
2. Whatever you do to one side of an equation, you need to do to the other side of the equation. Did you multiply one side by 5? Then, you need to multiply the other side of the equation by 5, as well.

Avoiding Common Errors

We'll add a third rule that you won't find written in any math book.

3. Equations cannot become expressions.

If you've ever started working with one side of an equation without writing down both sides of the equation, you've broken this rule. By always writing down both sides of the equation, you can avoid wasting time and making silly mistakes.

Solving Equalities

Even the simplest equalities can be solved by Plugging In the Answers, but it's probably easier to solve a simple equation algebraically. If there is one variable in an equation, isolate the variable on one side of the equation and solve it. Let's try an example of this type, although a question this easy wouldn't actually be seen on the GMAT. This one is just for practice.

If $x - 5 = 3x + 2$, then $x =$

- -8
- $-\frac{7}{2}$
- -7
- $\frac{10}{3}$
- $\frac{7}{5}$

Here's How to Crack It

Get all of the *x*'s on one side of the equation. If we subtract *x* from both sides we have:

$$\begin{aligned} x - 5 &= 3x + 2 \\ -x \quad &\quad -x \\ -5 &= 2x + 2 \end{aligned}$$

Now subtract 2 from both sides:

$$\begin{aligned} -5 &= 2x + 2 \\ -2 \quad &\quad -2 \\ -7 &= 2x \end{aligned}$$

Finally, divide both sides by 2:

$$\frac{-7}{2} = \frac{2x}{2}$$

$$x = -\frac{7}{2}$$

The answer is choice B.

Solving Inequalities

To solve inequalities, you must be able to recognize the following symbols:

>	is greater than
<	is less than
≥	is greater than or equal to
≤	is less than or equal to

As with an equation, you can add a number to or subtract a number from both sides of an inequality without changing it; you can collect similar terms and simplify them. In fact, an inequality behaves just like a regular equation except in one way:

> If you multiply or divide both sides of an inequality by a negative number, the direction of the inequality symbol changes.

For example,

$$-2x > 5$$

To solve for x, you would divide both sides by –2, just as you would in an equality. But when you do, the sign flips:

$$\frac{-2x}{-2} < \frac{5}{-2}$$

$$x < -\frac{5}{2}$$

Q: Are the following equations distinct?
(1) $3x + 21y = 12$
(2) $x + 7y = 4$
Answer in next page's margin.

Solving Simultaneous Equations

Simultaneous equations are almost always tested in Data Sufficiency format on the GMAT. It's impossible to solve one equation with two variables. But if there are two equations, both of which have the same two variables, then it is possible to solve for both variables. An easy problem might look like this:

If $3x + 2y = 6$ and $5x - 2y = 10$, then $x = ?$

To solve simultaneous equations, add or subtract the equations so that one of the variables disappears.

$$\begin{array}{rl} 3x + 2y &= 6 \\ \underline{+\ 5x - 2y} &\underline{= 10} \\ 8x \qquad &= 16 \end{array}$$

$$x = 2$$

Equation Tricks and Traps

$x + 3y - 7 = x^2(x^{-1}) + y$

This looks like two variables in one equation, which would mean we need at least one more equation to solve, but look again. Because $x^2(x^{-1}) = x^{(2-1)} = x$, each side of the equation has only one x. The x's can be subtracted, leaving you with just one variable, y. The equation can be solved.

In more difficult simultaneous equations, you'll find that neither of the variables will disappear when you try to add or subtract the two equations. In such cases you must multiply both sides of one of the equations by some number in order to get the coefficient in front of the variable that you want to disappear to be the same in both equations. This sounds more complicated than it is. A difficult problem might look like this:

If $3x + 2y = 6$ and $5x - y = 10$, then $x = ?$

Let's set it up the same way:

$$3x + 2y = 6$$

$$5x - y = 10$$

Unfortunately, in this example, neither adding nor subtracting the two equations gets rid of either variable. But look what happens when we multiply the bottom equation by 2:

$$\begin{array}{c} 3x + 2y = 6 \\ (2)5x - (2)y = (2)10 \end{array} \quad \text{or} \quad \begin{array}{rl} 3x + 2y &= 6 \\ \underline{+\ 10x - 2y} &\underline{= 20} \\ 13x \qquad &= 26 \end{array} \quad x = 2$$

Quadratic Equations

On the GMAT, quadratic equations always come in one of two forms: factored or expanded. Here's an example:

$$\underset{\textit{factored}}{(x + 2)(x + 5)} = \underset{\textit{expanded}}{x^2 + 7x + 10}$$

The first thing to do when solving a problem that involves a quadratic equation is to see which form the equation is in. If the quadratic equation is in an unfactored form, factor it immediately. If the quadratic equation is in a factored form, unfactor it. The test writers like to see whether you know how to do these things.

To unfactor a factored expression, just multiply it out using FOIL (First, Outer, Inner, Last):

$$(x + 2)(x + 5) = (x + 2)(x + 5)$$

$$= (x \text{ times } x) + (x \text{ times } 5) + (2 \text{ times } x) + (2 \text{ times } 5)$$

$$= x^2 + 5x + 2x + 10$$

$$= x^2 + 7x + 10$$

To factor an unfactored expression, put it into the following format and start by looking for the factors of the first and last terms.

$$x^2 + 2x - 15$$
$$= (\quad)(\quad)$$

For the first term of the unfactored expression to be x^2, the first term of each parentheses of the factored expression has to be x.

$$x^2 + 2x - 15$$
$$= (x \quad)(x \quad)$$

For the last term of the unfactored expression to be 15, the last term in each parentheses of the factored expression must be either 5 and 3 or 15 and 1. Since there is no way to get a middle term for the unfactored expression with a coefficient of 2 if the terms were 15 and 1, we are left with

$$x^2 + 2x - 15$$
$$= (x \quad 5)(x \quad 3)$$

To decide where to put the pluses and minuses in the factored expression, look to see how the inner and outer terms of the factored equation would combine to form the middle term. If we put a minus in front of the 5 and a plus in front of the 3, then the middle term would be $-2x$ (not what we wanted). Therefore, the final factored expression looks like this

$$x^2 + 2x - 15$$
$$= (x + 5)(x - 3)$$

A: No. Look at what equation #2 looks like multiplied by 3: $3(x + 7y) = 3(4)$ or $3x + 21y = 12$. Multiply both sides by 3 and equations #1 and #2 are identical. When one equation can be multiplied to produce the other, the equations are identical, not distinct.

Quadratic equations are usually set equal to 0. Here's an example:

What are all the values of x that satisfy the equation $x^2 + 4x + 3 = 0$?

- ○ –3
- ○ –1
- ○ –3 and –1
- ○ 3 and 4
- ○ 4

Here's How to Crack It

This problem contains an unfactored equation, so let's factor it.

$$x^2 + 4x + 3 = 0$$
$$(x \quad)(x \quad) = 0$$
$$(x \quad 3)(x \quad 1) = 0$$
$$(x + 3)(x + 1) = 0$$

In order for this equation to be correct, x must be either –3 or –1. The correct answer is choice C.

Note: This problem would also have been easy to solve by Plugging In the Answers. It asked a specific question, and there were five specific answer choices. One of them was correct. All you had to do was try the choices until you found the right one. Bear in mind, however, that in a quadratic equation there are usually two values that will make the equation work.

The Equation Rule
You must have as many equations as you have variables for the data to be sufficient. For example, $x = y + 1$ cannot be solved without another *distinct* equation.

Try the ZONEF Numbers
For some 'must be' questions, the different number you need is one of the ZONEF numbers. These are the numbers that most people forget to think about.

Zero
One
Negatives
Extremes (like 100)
Fractions

Favorites of GMAT Test Writers

There are three types of quadratic equations the GMAT test writers find endlessly fascinating. These equations appear on the GMAT with great regularity in both the Problem Solving format and the Data Sufficiency format:

$$(x + y)^2 = x^2 + 2xy + y^2$$

$$(x + y)(x - y) = x^2 - y^2$$

$$(x - y)^2 = x^2 - 2xy + y^2$$

Memorize all three of these. As with all quadratic equations, if you see the equation in factored form, you should immediately unfactor it; if it's unfactored, factor it immediately. Here's an example:

If $\frac{x^2 - 4}{x + 2} = 5$, then $x =$

- 3
- 5
- 6
- 7
- 9

Here's How to Crack It

It is unfactored, so let's factor it:

$$\frac{(x+2)(x-2)}{(x+2)} = 5$$

The $(x + 2)$s cancel out, leaving us with $(x - 2) = 5$. So $x = 7$, and the answer is choice D.

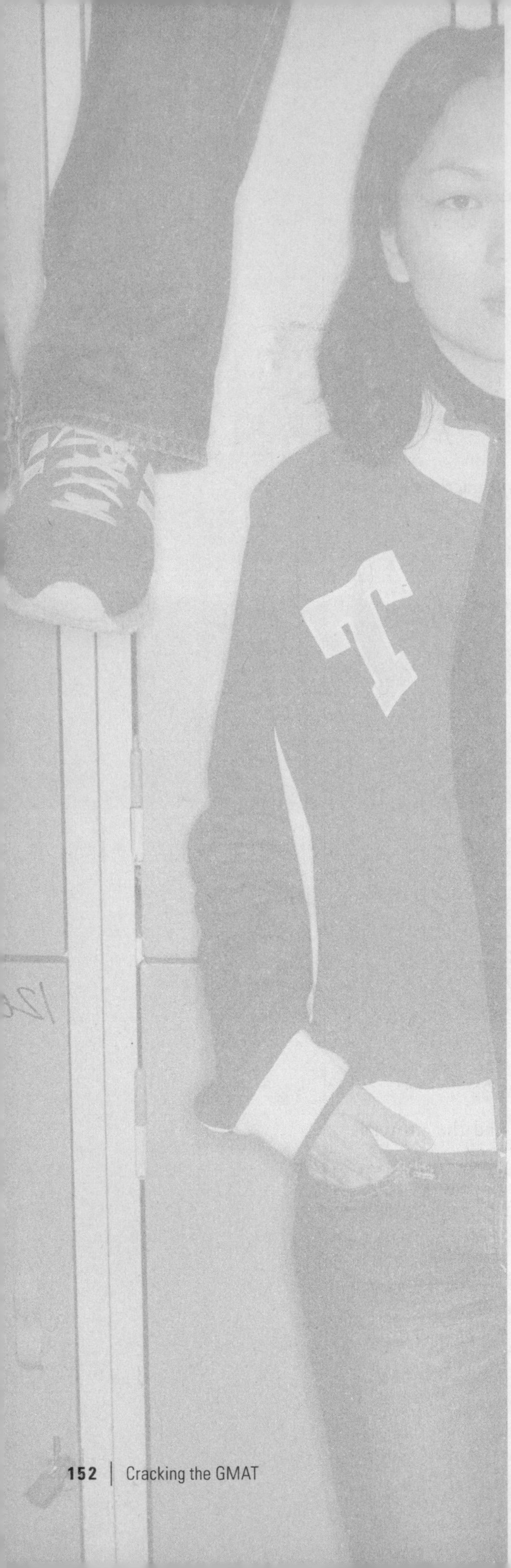

Summary

- Most of the algebra problems on the GMAT are simpler to solve *without* algebra, using two Princeton Review techniques: **Plugging In** and **Plugging In the Answers.**
- Plugging In is easy. There are three steps:
    - Pick numbers for the variables in the problem. (Write them down in your scratch booklet.)
    - Using your numbers, find an answer to the problem. (Write that answer down and circle it.)
    - Plug your numbers into the answer choices to see which choice equals the answer you found in the previous step.
- When you plug in, try to choose convenient numbers—those that are simple to work with and make the problem easier to manipulate.
- When you plug in, avoid choosing 0, 1, or a number that already appears in the problem or in the answer choices.
- On problems with variables in the answers that contain the words "must be" or "could be," you may have to plug in more than once to find the correct answer.
- Plugging In the Answers is easy. There are three steps:
    - Always start with answer choice C. Plug that number into the problem and see whether it makes the problem work.
    - If choice C is too small, try the next larger number.
    - If choice C is too big, try the next smaller number.
    - If you're not sure which way to go, don't sweat it. Just pick a direction and try it out!

- If you see a problem with a quadratic equation in factored form, the easiest way to get the answer is to expand the equation immediately. If the equation is expanded, factor it immediately.

- Memorize the factored and expanded forms of the two most common quadratic equations on the GMAT:

$$(x + y)^2 = x^2 + 2xy + y^2$$
$$(x + y)(x - y) = x^2 - y^2$$

- On problems containing inequalities, remember that when you multiply or divide both sides of an inequality by a negative number, the sign flips.

- In solving simultaneous equations, add or subtract one equation to or from another so that one of the two variables disappears.

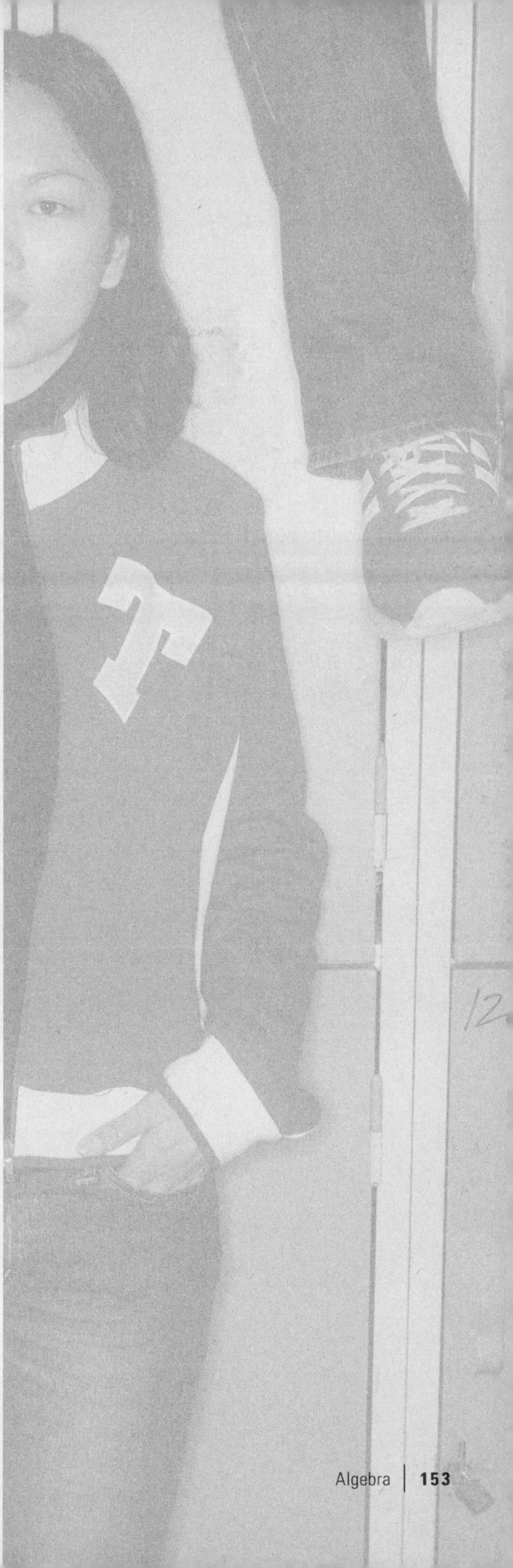

Chapter 12
Applied Arithmetic

Applied arithmetic involves knowing how to solve word problems involving rate and work, functions, probability, permutations, and combinations. In this chapter, we cover the important facets of each type of problem and show you how they appear on the GMAT.

It's time to look as some applied arithmetic subjects that the GMAT test writers love to use. In this chapter, we'll cover

1. Rate problems
2. Work problems
3. Function problems
4. Probability problems
5. Permutation and Combination problems

RATE PROBLEMS

Any problem that mentions planes, trains, cars, bicycles, distance, miles per hour, or any other travel-related terminology is asking you to solve a rate problem. You may remember that you can use the formula *distance* = *rate* × *time* to solve these types of problems.

We're going to use a **rate pie** to keep track of the information in a rate problem. Here's what it looks like:

Two Out of Three Ain't Bad
For Data Sufficiency problems, as soon as you have two of the pieces of the rate pie, you have sufficient information to find the other piece.

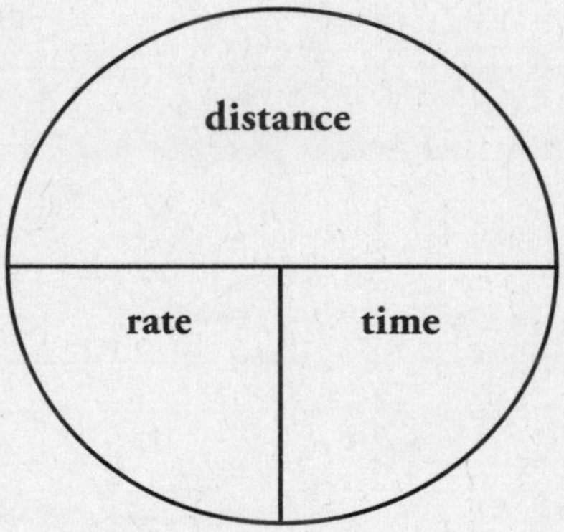

If a problem gives you the rate and time, the pieces on the bottom, you multiply to get the distance. If you have the distance, the piece on the top, and one of the pieces on the bottom, you divide to get the other bottom piece. As soon as you know that you are dealing with a rate problem, draw a rate pie and start filling in what you know.

The rate pie is really just a different way of writing the *distance* = *rate* × *time* formula. It works well for GMAT problems, however, because GMAT problems often involve multiple steps. So, the pie helps you to see what information you have and what you need to find.

Let's try a problem:

Pam and Sue drove in the same car to a business meeting that was 120 miles away. Pam drove to the meeting at 60 miles per hour and Sue drove back, along the same route, at 50 miles per hour. How many more minutes did it take Sue to drive the distance than it took Pam?

- ○ 4
- ○ 10
- ○ 20
- ○ 24
- ○ 30

Here's How to Crack It

Since the problem deals with rates, you need a rate pie. In fact, since there is rate information for both Pam and Sue, you need two rate pies—one for Pam and one for Sue.

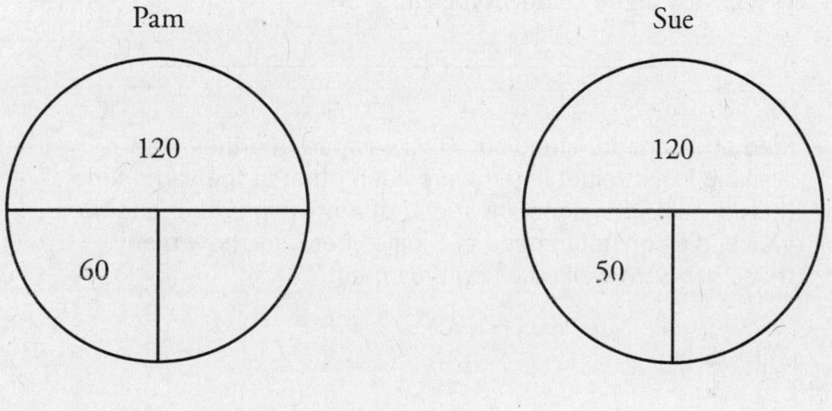

Once you draw the pies, you can transfer the information that you know to each pie. Since Pam and Sue drove along the same route, the distance is 120 miles for each pie. Pam's rate is 60 miles per hour and Sue's rate is 50 miles per hour. Transfer that information to the pies, too.

To use the pie, remember that if you have the piece at the top and one of the pieces on the bottom, you divide to find the other piece. So, Pam's time is $120 \div 60 = 2$ and Sue's time is $120 \div 50 = 2\frac{2}{5}$. The pies made it easy to see how to find the time for each driver.

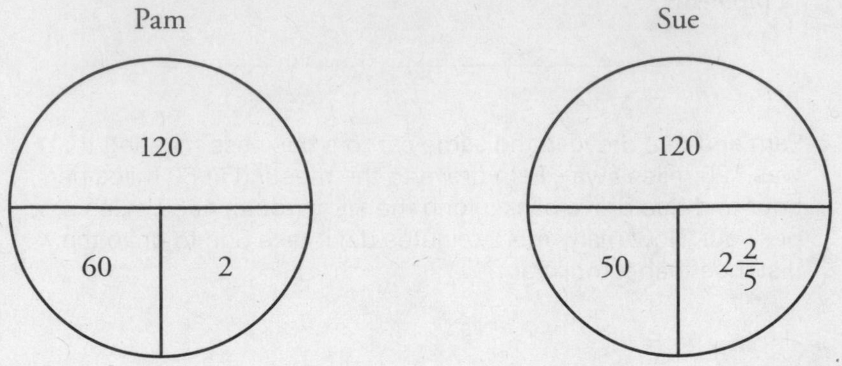

The problem asks how many more minutes it took Sue to drive the distance than it took Pam. Start by subtracting $2\frac{2}{5} - 2 = \frac{2}{5}$ to find that it took Sue $\frac{2}{5}$ of an hour longer. Now, just convert to minutes: $60 \times \frac{2}{5} = 24$. The answer is choice D.

Now, let's look at a slightly harder problem:

Easy Eliminations
Choices A and E are unlikely because they are numbers in the problem. Choice B is just 45 ÷ 5, which is Fred's time to walk the whole distance.

Fred and Sam are standing 45 miles apart and they start walking in a straight line toward each other at the same time. If Fred walks at a constant speed of 4 miles per hour and Sam walks at a constant speed of 5 miles per hour, how many miles has Sam walked when they meet?

- ◯ 5
- ◯ 9
- ◯ 25
- ◯ 30
- ◯ 45

Here's How to Crack It

Since the problem is about rates, draw a rate pie. In this case, you may be wondering if you need one pie or two. You actually need one. Here's why: When dealing with rates, it is often helpful to think about what happens in a certain amount of time like an hour. In one hour, Fred walks 4 miles and Sam walks 5 miles. Since they are walking toward each other in a straight line, they have covered 9 miles of the distance between them at the end of an hour. Wait! Nine miles in an hour? That means that their combined rate is 9 miles per hour. That's what goes on the pie for the rate.

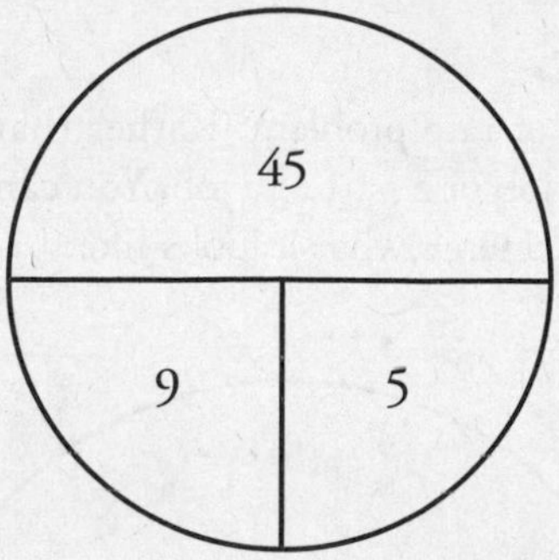

The other piece that you could fill in on the pie from the problem was the distance, 45 miles. Then, use the pie to find that Fred and Sam walk for 5 hours before they meet. (Remember that you divide the top piece of the pie by one of the pieces on the bottom to find the other bottom piece.)

The problem wants to know how many miles Sam had walked when he met Fred. So, set up one more pie. This time you know Sam's rate, 5 miles per hour, and you know that he walked for 5 hours.

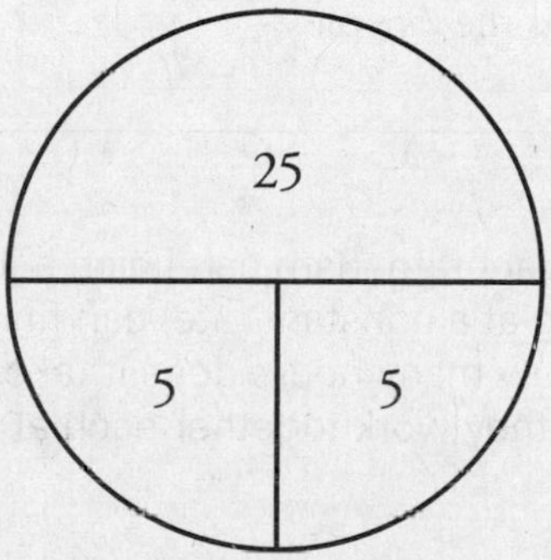

So, Sam walks 25 miles when he meets Fred. The answer is choice C.

Here's A Tip!
When two items travel in a straight line toward each other, you can add their rates.

WORK PROBLEMS

Work problems are a type of rate problem. Rather than asking about a distance, these problems ask about a job or a part of a job. You can use a variation of the rate pie to solve these problems. Here's what it looks like:

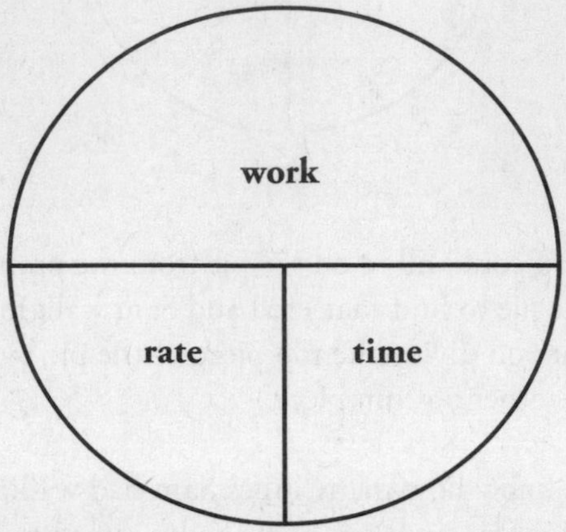

All that changes is that *work* replaces *distance* at the top of the pie. You use the **work pie** in the same way as the rate pie.

Working at a constant rate, Sam can finish a job in 3 hours. Mark, also working at a constant rate, can finish the same job in 12 hours. How many hours does it take Mark and Sam to finish the job if they work together each at his respective, constant rate?

- ◯ 1
- ◯ $2\frac{2}{5}$
- ◯ $2\frac{5}{8}$
- ◯ $3\frac{1}{4}$
- ◯ 4

Since the problem mentions a job being completed, you can use a work pie. You'll actually need two pies for the first step of the problem since you'll want to find each worker's individual rate. Once you draw your pies, you can put each worker's time on the pie. You can also put 1 for the work since they each complete 1 job.

Sam

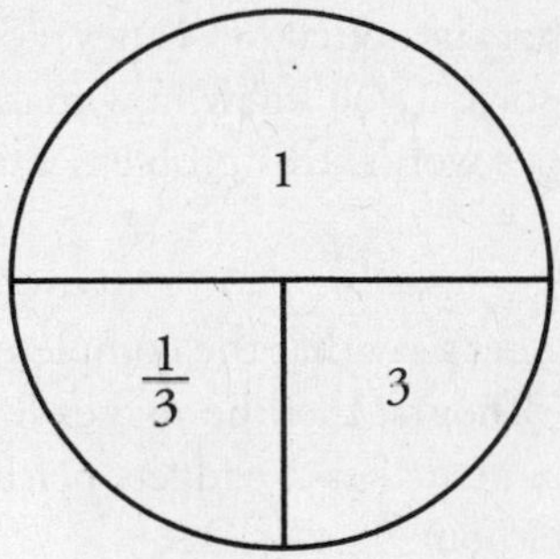

Mark

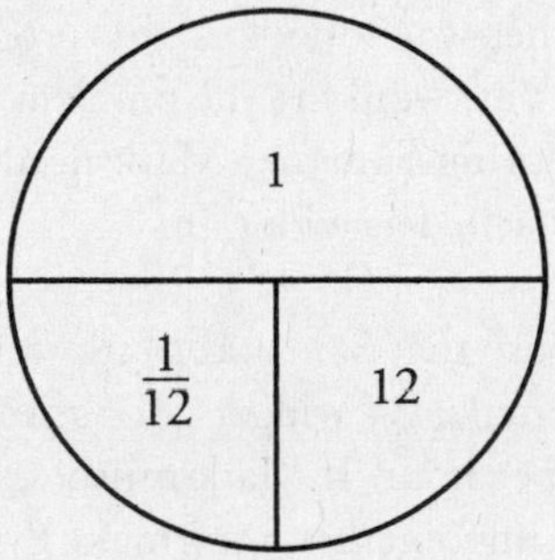

So, Sam's rate is $\frac{1}{3}$ and Mark's rate is $\frac{1}{12}$. What does that mean? Well, it means that Sam completes $\frac{1}{3}$ of the job every hour while Mark completes $\frac{1}{12}$ of the job every hour.

To finish the problem, note that Mark and Sam work together. Since they are working together, you can combine their rates to find that they complete $\frac{1}{3} + \frac{1}{12} = \frac{5}{12}$ of the job every hour. When people work together, you can combine their rates. Now, set up one more work pie. Use 1 for the amount of work and $\frac{5}{12}$ for the rate.

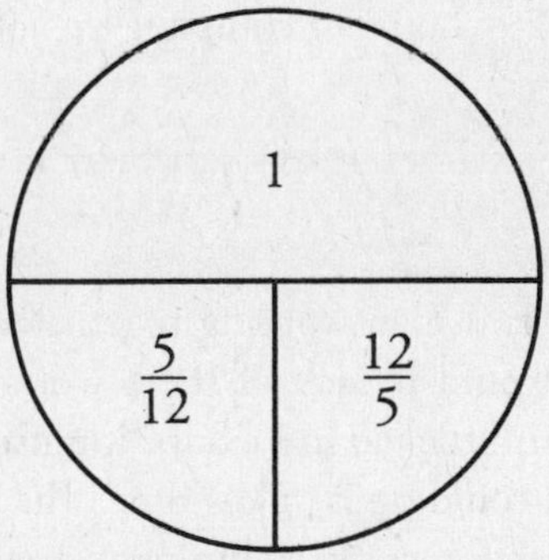

Divide the amount of work by the combined rate to find that the time to complete the job is $1 \div \frac{5}{12} = \frac{12}{5} = 2\frac{2}{5}$ hours. The correct answer is B.

Same Problem, Different Approach

Another way to look at this problem is to realize that the actual job is never specified. But, wouldn't the problem be much easier to solve if you knew how many of something Sam and Mark needed to make? In other words, this problem can be approached as a Plug In.

Suppose that Sam and Mark were making widgets. Let's say that the complete job is to make 24 widgets. If Sam finishes the job in 3 hours, then he makes 8 widgets per hour. If Mark finishes the job in 12 hours, he makes 2 widgets per hour. Working together, they make 8 + 2 = 10 widgets per hour.

Now, let's set the last step up using a work pie.

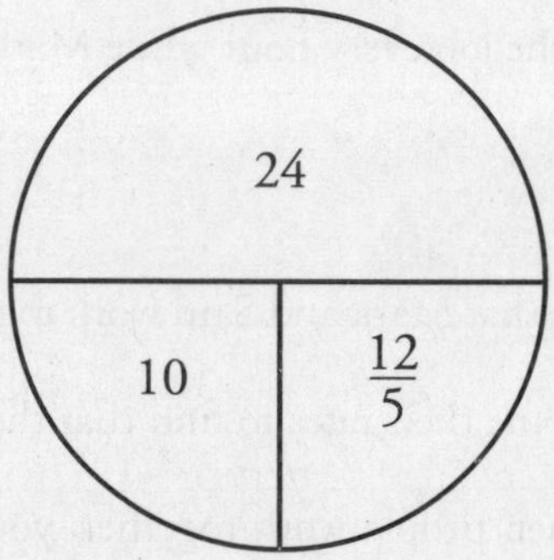

Again, it takes them $\frac{12}{5} = 2\frac{2}{5}$ hours to complete the job. The answer is choice B.

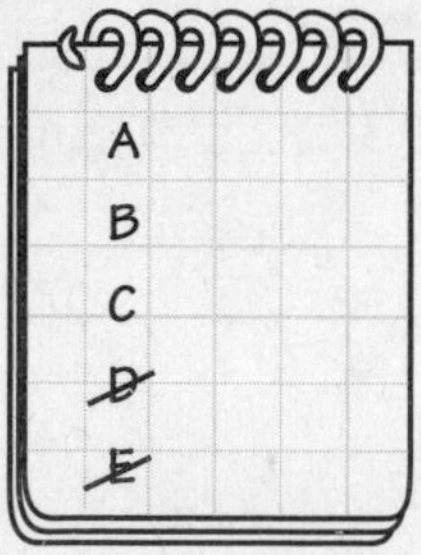

Easy Eliminations

It stands to reason that two men working together would take less time to finish a job than they would if each of them worked alone. Because Sam, working alone, could finish the job in 3 hours, it must be true that the two of them, working together, could do it in less time. The answer to this question has to be less than 3. Therefore we can eliminate answer choices D and E.

Here's a slightly harder version of the problem above:

Working at a constant rate, Sam can finish a job in 3 hours. Mark, also working at a constant rate, can finish the same job in 12 hours. If they work together for 2 hours, how many minutes will it take Sam to finish the job, working alone at his constant rate?

- ◯ 5
- ◯ 20
- ◯ 30
- ◯ 60
- ◯ 120

Here's How to Crack It

This problem starts in the same way so you can use the same work pies to find each worker's rate.

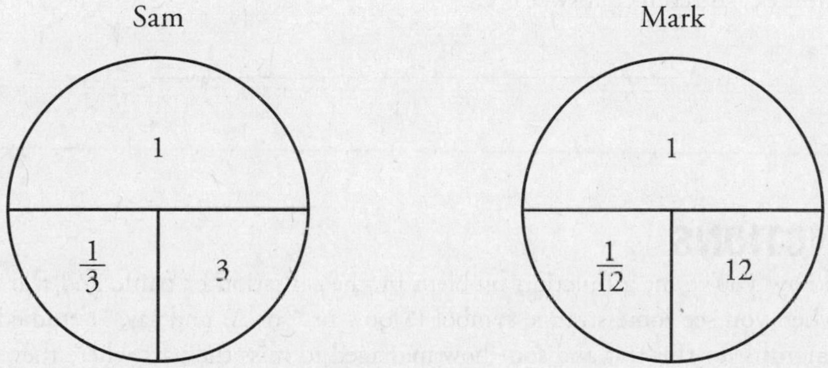

Now, you need a new pie. For this pie, you know the combined rate, $\frac{1}{3} + \frac{1}{12} = \frac{5}{12}$, and that they work together for two hours.

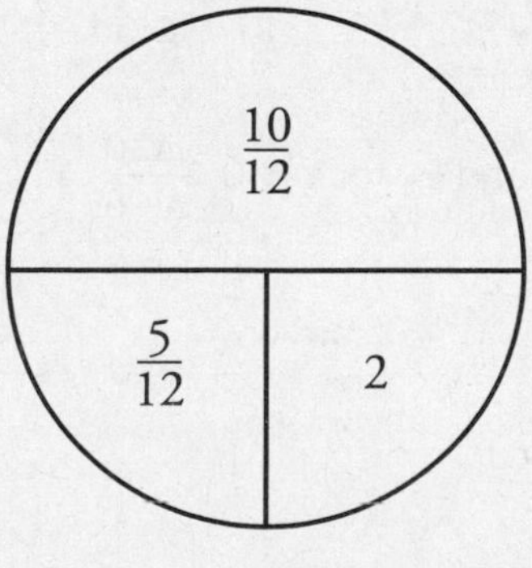

So, you now know that $\frac{5}{12} \times 2 = \frac{10}{12} = \frac{5}{6}$ of the job has been completed when Mark goes home. Sam must finish $\frac{1}{6}$ of the job on his own. Of course, you know Sam's rate, so just set up one last work pie.

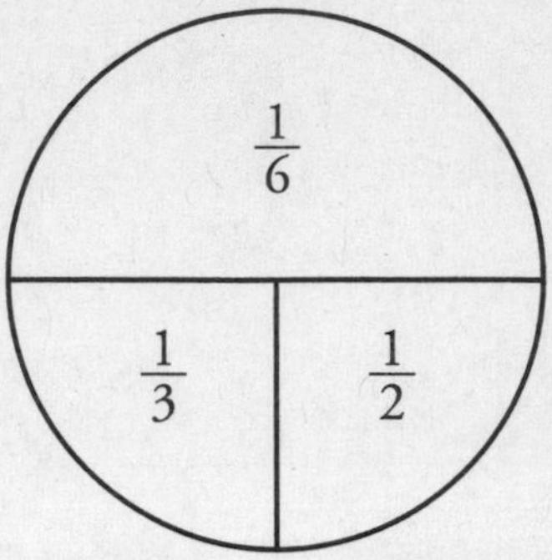

To find the time for Sam to finish the job, use the pie to find that $\frac{1}{6} \div \frac{1}{3} = \frac{1}{2}$ or 30 minutes. The correct answer is C.

FUNCTIONS

Functions? No Problem

If you can follow a recipe, you can do a GMAT function problem. Because function questions freak so many people out, they often show up in the medium to difficult area of a section. If you can become comfortable with function problems, you'll pick up a point on a question that you might otherwise feel tempted to guess on.

You know you've hit a function problem by the sensation of panic and fear you get when you see some strange symbol ($ or # or * or Δ) and say, "I studied for two months for this test and somehow managed to miss the part where they told me about # or * or Δ." Relax. Any strange-looking symbol on the GMAT is just a function, and on this test, functions are easy.

A function is basically a set of directions. Let's look at an example:

If $\Delta x = x$ for $x \geq 0$ and $2x$ for $x < 0$, $\frac{\Delta 30}{\Delta(-5)} =$

- ◯ –12
- ◯ –6
- ◯ –3
- ◯ 6
- ◯ 30

Here's How to Crack It

A function is basically a set of directions. In this case, the directions tell you what to do with the number that comes after the symbol Δ. If the number that follows the symbol is greater than or equal to 0, then the output of the function is just the number x. However, if the number that follows the symbol is negative, the output of the Δ function is $2x$. So, we can evaluate the given expression thus:

$$\frac{\Delta 30}{\Delta(-5)} = \frac{30}{2(-5)} = \frac{30}{-10} \text{ or } -3.$$ The answer is choice C.

Easy Eliminations

Joe has no idea what to do with Δ, so he just ignores it. Because $\frac{30}{-5} = -6$, Joe picks answer choice B. On the other hand, Joe might also think he can reduce functions. In other words, he might think he could do this:

$$\frac{\Delta 30}{\Delta(-5)} = \Delta(-6)$$

The function of –6 = –12, so Joe might also select answer choice A.

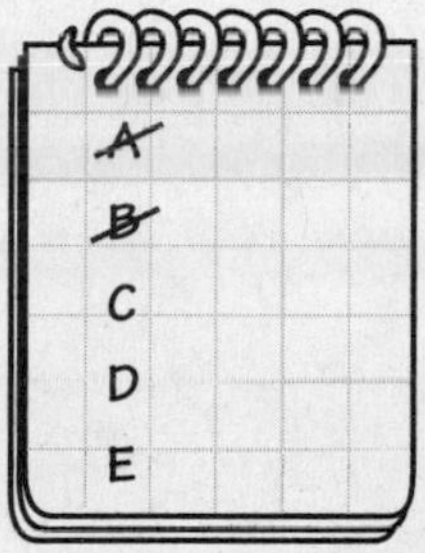

You may remember seeing a different notation for functions in school. The standard math notation for functions is $f(x)$—pronounced *f* of *x*—and the GMAT test writers will sometimes ask function questions using this notation, too.

Let's look at an example.

Working with $f(x)$

When you see $f(x)$, all you need to remember is that the number inside the parentheses gets plugged into the expression on the right of the equal sign. The output of a function is a *y*-value. So, $y = f(x)$ means that *x*-values go into the function and *y*-values come out.

For which of the following functions is $f(x) = f(-x)$ for all values of x?

- ◯ $f(x) = x^3 + 3$
- ◯ $f(x) = -x$
- ◯ $f(x) = 2x + 3$
- ◯ $f(x) = -x^2 + 2$
- ◯ $f(x) = 5x - 4$

Here's How to Crack It

Plug in a value for x and use that value to see if $f(x) = f(-x)$ for each of the functions in the answer choices. So, for example, look at answer A if $x = 2$. Does $(2)^3 + 3 = (-2)^3 + 3$? No, so eliminate answer A.

Only for answer D does $f(2) = f(-2)$. In this case, $f(2) = -(2)^2 + 2 = -2$ and $f(-2) = -(-2)^2 + 2 = -2$. So, D is the correct answer.

PROBABILITY

Probability, Part 1

Just the word is enough to cause math-phobes to run for the exits—but, at least as it appears on the GMAT, probability really isn't all that bad. Check out the easy example below:

> A six-sided die, with faces numbered one through six is rolled once. What is the probability that the face numbered 2 is facing upward?

Well, of course, there's only one possibility of this happening, and there are six possible outcomes, so there's a one-in-six chance. In essence, this is all that probability is about. On the GMAT, probability is usually expressed as a fraction: The total number of possibilities is always the denominator. The number of possibilities that match what you want is the numerator. In the example above, that translates to $\frac{1}{6}$.

$$\text{Basic probability formula} = \frac{\text{number of outcomes you want}}{\text{total number of possible outcomes}}$$

Let's make this example a little harder:

> A six-sided die with faces numbered one through six is rolled once. What is the probability that either the face numbered two or the face numbered three is facing up?

The total number of possible outcomes (the denominator) is still the same: 6. But the numerator is different now. There are two possibilities that would match what we want, so the numerator becomes 2. The probability is $\frac{2}{6}$, or $\frac{1}{3}$.

Let's make the example a little harder still.

> A six-sided die with faces numbered one through six is rolled twice. What is the probability that the face numbered 2 is facing up after both rolls?

Obviously, the odds of this happening are much smaller. How do you figure out the probability of something happening over a series of events? It's actually pretty easy. To find the probability of a series of events, you multiply the probabilities of each of the individual events. Let's start with the first roll of the die. We already figured out that the probability of the die landing with its "2" side facing up on a single toss is $\frac{1}{6}$. Now, let's think about the second toss. Well, actually, the probability of this happening on the second toss is exactly the same: $\frac{1}{6}$.

However, to figure out the probability of the "2" side facing upward on *both* tosses, you multiply the first probability by the second probability: $\frac{1}{6} \times \frac{1}{6} = \frac{1}{36}$.

The probability that A **and** B will both happen: A × B

Here's an example of a moderately difficult GMAT problem.

There are 8 job applicants sitting in a waiting room—4 women and 4 men. If 2 of the applicants are selected at random, what is the probability that both will be women?

- $\frac{1}{2}$
- $\frac{3}{7}$
- $\frac{1}{4}$
- $\frac{3}{14}$
- $\frac{1}{10}$

Here's How to Crack It

Admissions Insight No. 5: Letters of Recommendation, Part 1

Most MBA programs require two to three letters of recommendation. The best recommendations are from people who know you well in a professional capacity and can discuss the same points you have already made in your essays.

Unlike admissions committees for other graduate programs, MBA admissions committees generally prefer professional recommendations to academic ones.

Let's take the first event in the series. The total number of possibilities for the first selection is 8, because there are 8 applicants in the room. Of those 8 people, 4 are women, so the probability that the first person chosen will be a woman is $\frac{4}{8}$, or $\frac{1}{2}$. You might think that the probability would be exactly the same for the second choice (in which case you would multiply $\frac{1}{2} \times \frac{1}{2}$ and choose answer choice C), but in fact, that's not true. Let's consider: The first woman has just left the room, and they are about to choose another applicant at random. How many total people are now in the room? Aha! Only 7. And how many of those 7 are women? Only 3. So the probability that the second choice will be a woman is actually only $\frac{3}{7}$, which is choice B. But we aren't done yet. We have to figure out the probability that BOTH choices in this series of two choices will be women. The probability that the first will be a woman is $\frac{1}{2}$. The probability that the second will be a woman is $\frac{3}{7}$. The probability that they both will be women is $\frac{1}{2} \times \frac{3}{7}$, or $\frac{3}{14}$. The answer is choice D.

Easy Eliminations

The GMAT test writers like to see if they can trick you into picking partial answers—i.e., numbers that you get in the course of solving a problem that are not quite the final answer. The probability that the first choice will be a woman is $\frac{1}{2}$, choice A—but does it feel like you've done enough work to "deserve" to get this problem right yet? Nope—this is only an intermediate step. The probability that the second choice will be a woman is $\frac{3}{7}$, choice B. But again, this is just another intermediate step. Don't fall for these trick choices—cross off choices A and B.

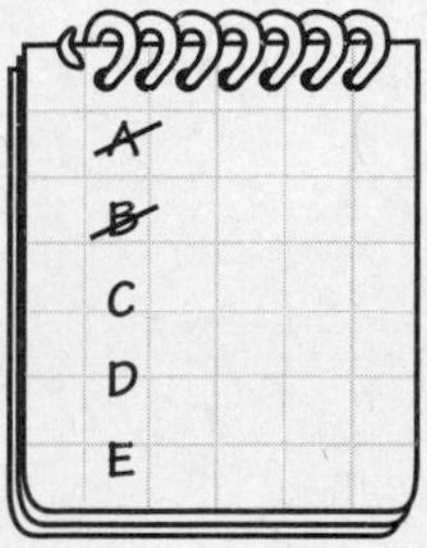

Probability, Part 2: One Thing or Another

So far, we've been dealing with the probability of one event happening and then another event happening (for example, in that last problem, the first event was choosing a female job applicant; the second event was choosing ANOTHER female job applicant). But what if you are asked to find the probability of either one thing OR another thing happening? To solve this type of problem, you simply add the probabilities. Note that pure versions of these 'or' problems are incredibly rare on the GMAT. Understanding the idea can be helpful on other problems, however.

The probability that A **or** B will happen: A + B

Here's an example:

Sally and Sam are watching a magician perform with 16 of their friends. If the magician chooses one audience member at random to assist with a trick, what is the probability that either Sally or Sam is chosen?

Here's How To Crack It

By this point, you should have no problem figuring out that the probability of Sally being chosen is $\frac{1}{18}$. And the probability of Sam being chosen? That's right: $\frac{1}{18}$. So what is the probability of Sally or Sam being chosen?

$$\frac{1}{18}+\frac{1}{18}=\frac{2}{18} \textit{ or } \frac{1}{9}$$

Probability, Part 3: The Odds That Something Doesn't Happen

But what if you are asked to find the probability that something will NOT happen? Well, think of it this way: If the probability of snow is 70% or $\frac{7}{10}$, what's the probability that it won't snow? That's right: 30% or $\frac{3}{10}$. To figure out the probability that something won't happen, simply figure out the probability that it WILL happen, and then subtract that fraction from 1.

WON'T = 1 – WILL

Here's an example:

Sally and Sam are watching a magician perform with 16 of their friends. If one audience member is chosen at random to assist with a trick, what is the probability that neither Sally nor Sam is chosen?

Here's How to Crack It

As we already know, the probability that Sally will be chosen is $\frac{1}{18}$. The probability that Sam will be chosen is also $\frac{1}{18}$. So what is the probability that neither Sally nor Sam will be chosen?

$$1-\frac{2}{18}=\frac{16}{18}=\frac{8}{9}$$

Probability, Part 4: The Odds That at Least One Thing Will Happen

What if the problem asks the probability of something happening at least once? To calculate the probability of at least one thing happening, just use this equation: The probability of what you WANT to happen plus the probability of what you DON'T want to happen equals one. Or, to put it another way:

WILL = 1 – WON'T

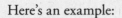

Here's an example:

Nine boys and nine girls are watching a magician perform. Four times during the performance a child is chosen at random to assist with a trick. If any of the children can be chosen to assist with each of the four tricks, what is the probability that at least one girl is chosen?

Here's How to Crack It

To find out the odds of at least one girl being chosen, let's begin by figuring out the odds that a girl isn't chosen. The magician will make a total of four choices. What are the odds that the magician will not pick a girl in the first round? If you said $\frac{9}{18}$ *or* $\frac{1}{2}$, you are doing just fine. And what are the odds that the magician will not pick a girl the second, third, and fourth round? Each time, the odds of not picking a girl stay the same, because the children are returned to the pool of possible candidates, so each time the odds will be $\frac{9}{18}$ *or* $\frac{1}{2}$. The probability of not picking a girl all four times is:

$$\frac{1}{2} \times \frac{1}{2} \times \frac{1}{2} \times \frac{1}{2} = \frac{1}{16}$$

But we aren't done. The probability of a girl being picked at least once is 1 minus the probability that she will not be picked. So the correct answer is:

$$1 - \frac{1}{16} = \frac{15}{16}$$

PERMUTATIONS AND COMBINATIONS

In general, permutation and combination problems tend to show up as medium-hard to hard problems on the GMAT.

Here's a very simple example of a combination problem:

At a restaurant, you must choose an appetizer, a main course, and a dessert. If there are 2 possible appetizers, 3 possible main courses, and 5 possible desserts, how many different meals could you order?

- ◯ 60
- ◯ 30
- ◯ 10
- ◯ 6
- ◯ 3

Here's How to Crack It

You could just carefully write down all the different combinations:

Shrimp cocktail with meatloaf with cherry pie
Shrimp cocktail with meatloaf with ice cream
Shrimp cocktail with meatloaf with…

You get the idea. But first of all, this is too time-consuming, and second of all, there's a much easier way.

For a problem that asks you to choose a number of items to fill specific spots, when each spot is filled from a different source, all you have to do is multiply the number of choices for each of the spots.

So, because there were 2 appetizers, 3 main courses, and 5 possible desserts, the total number of combinations of a full meal at this restaurant would be $2 \times 3 \times 5$, or 30. The answer is choice B.

Permutations: Single Source, Order Matters

The same principle applies when you're choosing from a group of similar items—with one slight wrinkle. Take a look at this easy permutation problem:

Three basketball teams play in a league against each other. At the end of the season, how many different ways could the 3 teams end up ranked against each other?

- 1
- 3
- 6
- 36
- 72

Admissions Insight No. 6: Letters of Recommendation, Part 2

What to give to your recommenders:

1) Background information about yourself, such as a resumé or statement of purpose, plus talking points (if appropriate) to get them started
2) A list of schools to which you're applying
3) Stamped envelopes already addressed to the schools
4) The recommendation deadlines for each of the schools
5) A thank-you note, mailed after the letters are submitted

In general, it is best to waive your right to see the recommendations, because this will give the schools more confidence in their veracity.

Here's How to Crack It

You could just carefully write down all the different combinations. If we call the three teams A, B, and C, then here are the different ways they could end up in the standings:

ABC ACB BAC BCA CAB CBA

But again, this approach is time-consuming (even more so for more difficult problems). As you probably suspected, there's a simpler and faster way to solve this problem.

> For a problem that asks you to choose from the same source to fill specific spots, all you have to do is multiply the number of choices for each of the spots—but the number of choices keeps getting smaller.

Let's think for a moment about how many teams could possibly end up in first place. If you said 3, you're doing just fine.

Now, let's think about how many teams could finish second. Are there still 3 possibilities? Not really, because one team has already finished first. There are, in fact, only 2 possible teams that could finish second.

And finally, let's think about how many teams could finish third. In fact, there is only 1 team that could finish third.

To find the number of different ways these teams could end up in the rankings, just multiply the number of choices for first place (in this case, 3) times the number of choices for second place (in this case, 2) times the number of choices for third place (in this case, 1).

$$3 \times 2 \times 1 = 6$$

The correct answer is choice C.

In general, no matter how many items there are to arrange, you can figure out the number of permutations of a group of n similar objects with the formula:

$$n(n - 1)(n - 2)\ldots \times 3 \times 2 \times 1, \text{ or } n!$$

So if there were 9 baseball teams, the total number of permutations of their standings would be $9 \times 8 \times 7 \times 6 \times 5 \times 4 \times 3 \times 2 \times 1$, also sometimes written as 9! If 4 sailboats sailed a race, the total number of permutations of the orders in which they could cross the finish line would be $4 \times 3 \times 2 \times 1$, also sometimes written as 4!

Single Source, Order Matters but Only for a Selection

The problems we've shown you so far were necessary to show you the concepts behind permutation problems—but were much too easy to be on the GMAT. Here's a problem that would be more likely to appear on the test:

Seven basketball teams play in a league against each other. At the end of the season, how many different arrangements are there for the top 3 teams in the rankings?

- ◯ 6
- ◯ 42
- ◯ 210
- ◯ 5,040
- ◯ 50,450

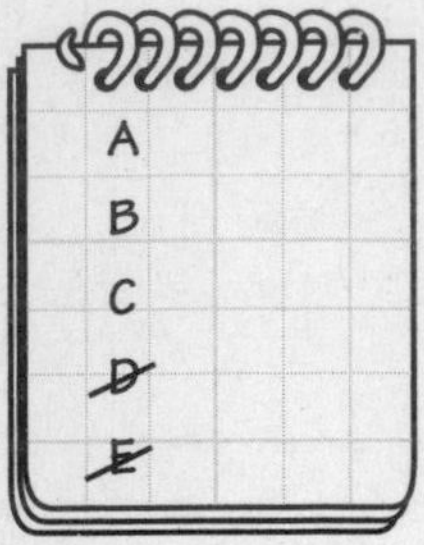

Easy Eliminations

If you were to see this problem on the computer-adaptive section of the actual GMAT, you should first stop and give yourself a pat on the back, because it means you're doing pretty well—permutation and combination problems usually show up only among the more difficult problems. But after you've congratulated yourself, stop and think for a moment. Could the answer to this difficult problem simply be a matter of finding $7 \times 6 \times 5 \times 4 \times 3 \times 2 \times 1$, choice D? Too easy. Because the question is asking for the permutations for only 3 of the 7 slots, the number must be less than that. So get rid of choices D and E.

Here's How to Crack It

To find all the possible permutations of the top 3 out of 7 baseball teams, simply multiply the number of combinations for each spot in the standings. How many teams are possibilities for the first place slot? If you said 7, you're right. How about for the second slot? Well, one team is already occupying the first place slot, so there are only 6 contenders left. And for the third place slot? That's right: 5.

So, the correct answer is $7 \times 6 \times 5 = 210$, or choice C.

In general, no matter how many items there are to arrange, you can figure out the number of permutations of r objects chosen from a set of n objects with the formula:

$$n(n-1)(n-2)\ldots \times (n-r+1)$$

So if there were 9 baseball teams (n), the total number of permutations of the top 4 teams (r) would be $9 \times 8 \times 7 \times 6$. If 4 sailboats sailed a race (n), the total number of permutations of the first 3 boats to cross the finish line (r) would be $4 \times 3 \times 2$. Here is another way to write this same formula:

$$\frac{n!}{(n-r)!}$$

(where n = total items and r = the number selected)

Because $9 \times 8 \times 7 \times 6$ is the same as $\frac{9\times8\times7\times6\times\cancel{5}!}{\cancel{5}!}$

Combinations: Single Source, Order Doesn't Matter

In the previous problems, the order in which the items are arranged actually matters to the problem. For example, if the order in which the three teams finish a season is Yankees, Red Sox, Orioles—that's entirely different than if the order were Red Sox, Yankees, Orioles, especially if you're from Boston.

But combination problems don't care about the order of the items.

> Not Sure If It's a Permutation or a Combination Problem?
>
> Here's a good clue:
> Permutation problems usually ask for "arrangements."
> Combination problems usually ask for "groups."

Six horses are running in a race. How many different groups of horses could make up the first 3 finishers?

- ◯ 6
- ◯ 18
- ◯ 20
- ◯ 120
- ◯ 720

Easy Eliminations

If we cared about the order in which the top 3 horses finished the race, then the answer would be the number of permutations: $6 \times 5 \times 4$, or 120. But in this case, we care only about the number of *unique* permutations, and that means the number will be smaller because we don't have to count the set of, for example, (Secretariat, Seattle Slew, and Affirmed) and the set of (Seattle Slew, Secretariat, and Affirmed) as two different permutations. If the correct answer must be smaller than 120, then we can eliminate choices D and E—they're too big.

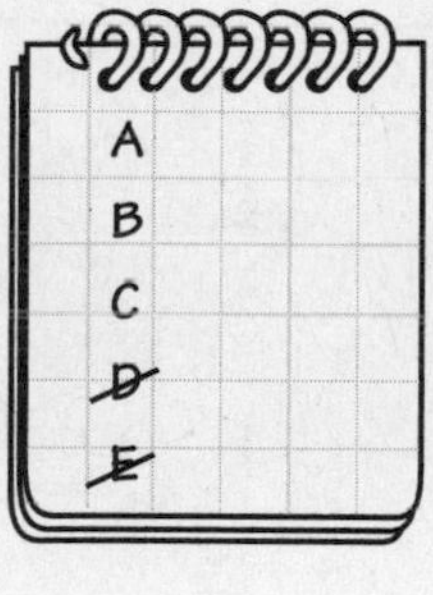

Here's How to Crack It

To find the number of combinations, first find the number of permutations. If 6 horses run in the race, and we are interested in the top 3 finishers, then the number of permutations would be 6 × 5 × 4, or 120. But if we don't care about the order in which they finished, then a bunch of these 120 permutations turn out to be duplicates.

How many? Let's think of one of those permutations. Let's say the first 3 finishers were Secretariat, Seattle Slew, and Affirmed. How many different ways could we arrange these 3 horses? If you said 6, you're thinking like a permutation master. There are 3!, or 3 × 2 × 1 permutations of any 3 objects. So, of those 120 permutations of the top 3 horses, each combination is being counted 3!, or 6 times. To find the number of combinations, we need to divide 120 by 6. The correct answer is choice C.

In general, no matter how many items there are to arrange, you can figure out the number of combinations of *r* objects chosen from a set of *n* objects with the formula:

$$\frac{n(n-1)(n-2)\ldots\times(n-r+1)}{r!}$$

So if there were 9 baseball teams, the total number of combinations of the top 4 teams would be:

$$\frac{9\times8\times7\times6}{4\times3\times2\times1}$$

Another way to write this same formula is:

$$\frac{n!}{r!(n-r)!}$$

because $\frac{9\times8\times7\times6}{4\times3\times2\times1}$ is the same as $\frac{9\times8\times7\times6\times\cancel{5}!}{(4\times3\times2\times1)\times\cancel{5}!}$

Summary

- Rate problems and work problems can be solved using your handy rate or work pies.
- The key to work problems is to think about how much of the job can be done in one hour. But remember, it is often easier to simply plug in.
- A function problem may have strange symbols like \$, Δ, or *, but it is really just a set of directions.
- Probability problems can be solved by putting the total number of possibilities in the denominator, and the number of possibilities that match what you are looking for in the numerator.
- Permutation and combination problems ask you to choose or arrange a group of objects.
    - To choose a number of items to fill specific spots, when each spot is filled from a different source, all you have to do is multiply the number of choices for each of the spots.
    - To choose from a set of n objects from the same source to fill specific spots, when order matters, all you have to do is multiply the number of choices for each of the spots—but the number of choices keeps getting smaller, according to the formula:

      $n(n-1)(n-2)\ldots \times 3 \times 2 \times 1$, or $n!$

    - To find the number of permutations of r objects chosen from a set of n objects, when order matters, use the formula: $n(n-1)(n-2)\ldots \times (n-r+1)$, also expressed as $\frac{n!}{(n-r)!}$
    - To find the number of combinations of r objects chosen from a set of n objects, use the formula: $\frac{n(n-1)(n-2)\ldots\times(n-r+1)}{r!}$

Chapter 13
Geometry

The geometry tested on the GMAT is but a small fraction of the geometry you probably studied during high school. In this chapter, we cover the geometry the test-makers actually test: angles, triangles, circles, quadrilaterals, volume, surface area, and coordinate geometry.

Fewer than one-quarter of the problems on the computer-adaptive math section of the GMAT will involve geometry. And while this tends to be the math subject most people remember least from high school, the good news is that the GMAT tests only a small portion of the geometry you used to know. It will be relatively easy to refresh your memory.

The bad news is that unlike some standardized tests, such as the SAT, the GMAT does not provide you with the formulas and terms you'll need to solve the problems. You'll have to memorize them.

The first half of this chapter will show you how to eliminate answer choices on certain geometry problems without using traditional geometry. The second half will review all the geometry you need to know in order to answer the problems that must be solved using more traditional methods.

CRAZY ANSWERS

Eliminating choices that don't make sense has already proven to be a valuable technique on arithmetic and algebra questions. On geometry questions you can develop this technique into an art form. The reason for this is that many geometry problems come complete with a diagram *drawn to scale.*

Most people get so caught up in solving a geometry problem geometrically that they forget to look at the diagram to see whether their answer is reasonable.

Crazy Answers on Easy Questions

How big is angle *x*?

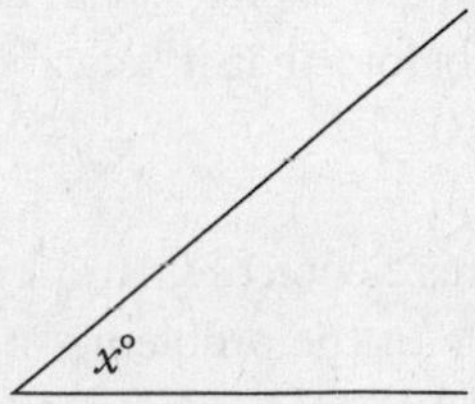

Obviously you don't know exactly how big this angle is, but it would be easy to compare it with an angle whose measure you *do* know exactly. Let's compare it with a 90-degree angle:

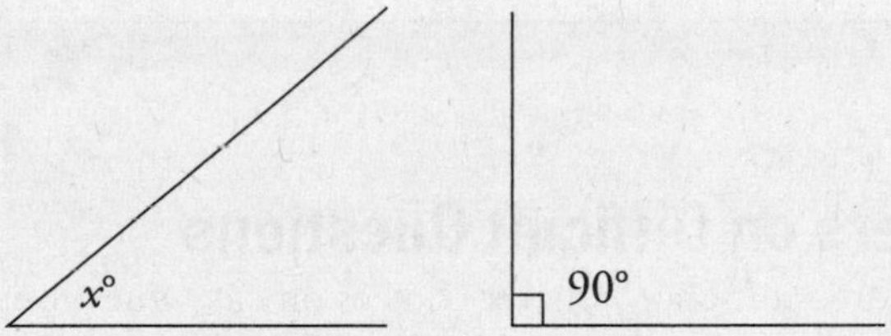

Angle *x* is less than 90 degrees. How much less? It looks as though it's about half of a 90-degree angle, or 45 degrees. Now look at the following problem that asks about the same angle, *x*.

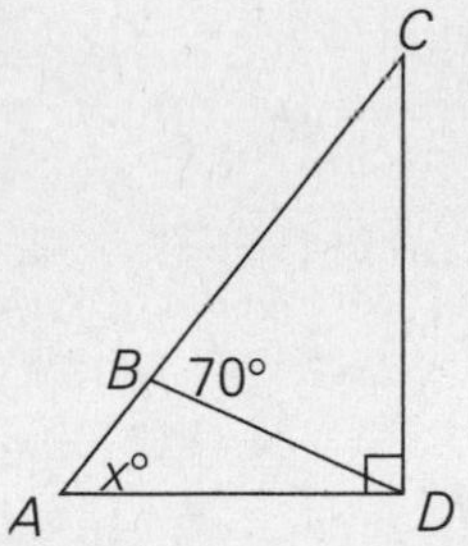

In the figure above, if $BC = CD$ and angle $ADC = 90$ degrees, then what is the value of x?

- 45
- 50
- 70
- 75
- 100

Easy Eliminations

We've already decided that angle x is less than 90 degrees, which means that the last answer choice (what we call choice E) can be eliminated. How much less is it? Well, we estimated before that it was about half, which rules out answer choices C and D as well.

There is another way to eliminate choices C and D. We can compare angle x with the other marked angle in the problem—angle *DBC*. If the answer to this problem is choice C, then angle x should look like angle *DBC*. Does it? No. Angle x looks a little bit smaller than angle *DBC*, which means that both choices C and D can be eliminated.

Eliminating crazy answers will prevent you from making careless mistakes on easy problems.

Crazy Answers on Difficult Questions

If it's important to cross off crazy answer choices on easy questions, it's even more important to eliminate crazy answer choices when you're tackling an average or difficult geometry problem. On these problems, you may not know how to find the answer geometrically, and even if you do, you could still fall victim to one of the traps the test writers have placed in your path. Take a look at the following difficult geometry problem:

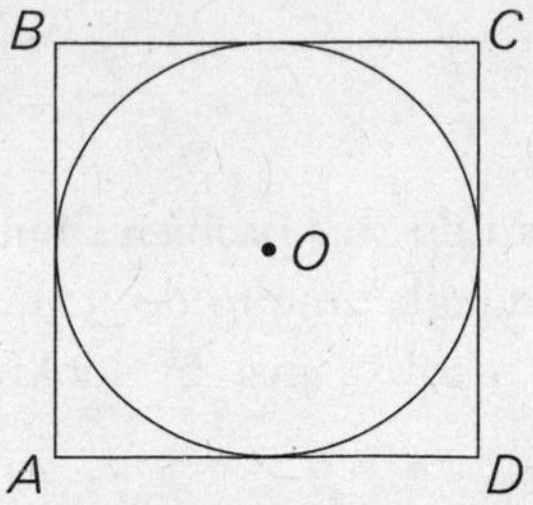

In the figure above, the circle with center O is inscribed inside square $ABCD$ as shown. What is the ratio of the area of circle O to the area of square $ABCD$?

- $\frac{\pi}{2}$
- $\frac{4}{\pi}$
- $\frac{\pi}{3}$
- $\frac{\pi}{4}$
- $\frac{\pi}{5}$

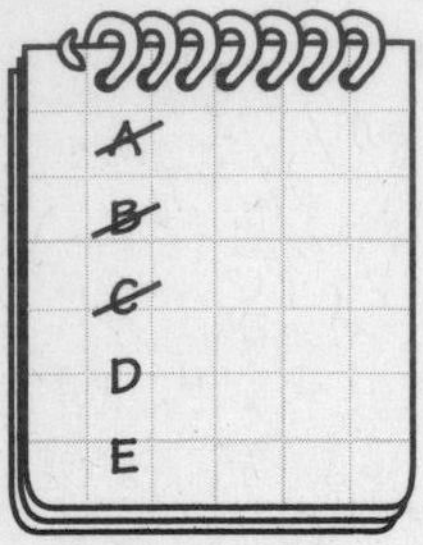

How to Drive Math Teachers Insane
Teachers will never know if you use our approximations. We promise. Use them. Many students freeze up when they see π: It's just a number. Think of it as 3 (and a little extra).

Easy Eliminations

Let's say that you knew how to do this problem, but it's near the end of the section and you don't have enough time to do it. Let's see whether you can eliminate any of the answer choices just by looking at the diagram and using some common sense.

The problem asks you for the ratio of the area of the circle to the area of the square. Just by looking at the diagram, you can tell that the circle is smaller than the square. The correct answer to this question has to be the ratio of a smaller number to a bigger number. Let's look at the answer choices.

In choice A, the ratio is π over 2. An approximate value of π is 3, so this really reads $\frac{3}{2}$.

Is this the ratio of a smaller number to a bigger number? Just the opposite. Therefore choice A is a crazy answer. Eliminate it.

In choice B, the ratio is 4 over π. This really reads $\frac{4}{3}$.

Is this the ratio of a smaller number to a bigger number? No. Choice B is a crazy answer. Eliminate it.

In choice C, the ratio is π over 3. This really reads $\frac{3}{3}$.

Is this the ratio of a smaller number to a bigger number? No. Choice C is a crazy answer. Eliminate it.

Answer choices D and E both contain ratios of smaller numbers to bigger numbers, so they're both still possibilities. However, we've eliminated three of the answer choices without doing any math. If you know how to solve the problem geometrically, then proceed. If not, guess and move on. (By the way, we will show you how to solve this problem using geometry later in the chapter.)

The Basic Tools

In eliminating crazy answers, it helps to have the following approximations memorized.

$$\pi \approx 3$$
$$\sqrt{1} = 1$$
$$\sqrt{2} \approx 1.4$$
$$\sqrt{3} \approx 1.7$$
$$\sqrt{4} = 2$$

It's also useful to have a feel for the way certain common angles look:

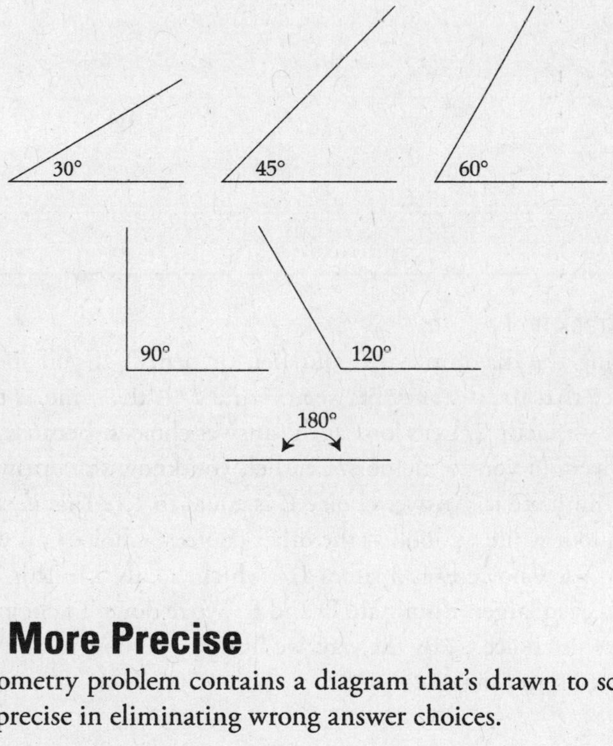

Getting More Precise

When a geometry problem contains a diagram that's drawn to scale, you can get even more precise in eliminating wrong answer choices.

How? By measuring the diagram.

Q: Is using your marker as a ruler considered cheating?
Turn the page for the answer.

Look at the problem below:

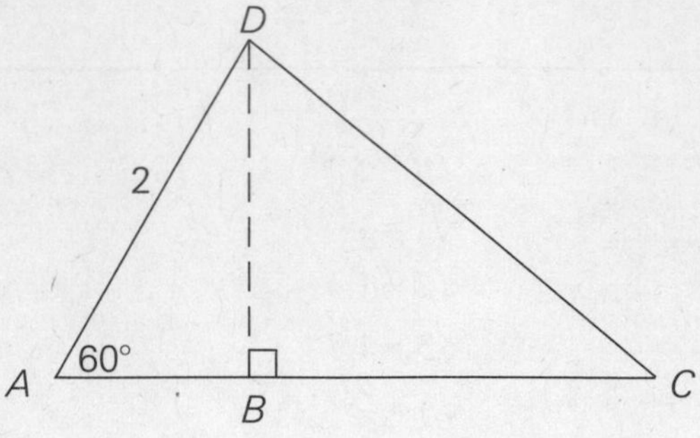

A: No.

In the figure above, if a line segment connecting points *B* and *D* is perpendicular to *AC* and the area of triangle *ADC* is $\frac{3\sqrt{3}}{2}$, then *BC* = ?

- ○ $\sqrt{2}$
- ○ $\sqrt{3}$
- ○ 2
- ○ $3\sqrt{3}$
- ○ 6

Here's How to Crack It

Practice measuring the diagram with your pen or pencil. If you measure carefully, you'll notice that the distance between *A* and *D* is the same as the distance between *B* and *C*—exactly 2. Let's look at the answer choices. Because you memorized the values we told you to memorize earlier, you know that answer choice A is equal to 1.4. Eliminate it. Answer choice B is equal to 1.7. This is close enough for us to hold on to it while we look at the other choices. Choice C is exactly what we're looking for—2. Choice D is 3 times 1.7, which equals 5.1. This is much too large. Choice E is even larger. Eliminate D and E. We're down to choices B and C. The correct answer is choice C. By the way, we'll show you how to do this problem geometrically later on the chapter.

Three Important Notes

1. Diagrams in questions using the Problem Solving format are drawn to scale (unless otherwise indicated).
2. Diagrams marked "not drawn to scale" cannot be measured. In fact, the drawings in these problems are often purposely misleading to the eye.
3. Data Sufficiency geometry diagrams have their own rules, which we will discuss in Chapter 14.

What Should I Do if There Is No Diagram?

Draw one. It's always difficult to imagine a geometry problem in your head. The first thing you should do with any geometry problem that doesn't have a diagram is sketch it out in your scratch booklet. And when you draw the diagram, try to draw it to scale. That way, you'll be in a position to estimate.

Geometry Hint
If there's no diagram, draw one yourself.

What Should I Do if the Diagram Is Not Drawn to Scale?

The same thing you would do if there were no diagram at all—draw it yourself. Draw it as accurately as possible so you'll be able to see what a realistic answer should be.

Basic Principles: Fundamentals of GMAT Geometry

The techniques outlined above will enable you to eliminate many incorrect choices on geometry problems. In some cases, you'll be able to eliminate every choice but one. However, there will be some geometry problems in which you will need geometry. Fortunately, GMAC chooses to test only a small number of concepts.

For the sake of simplicity, we've divided GMAT geometry into six basic topics:

1. degrees and angles
2. triangles
3. circles
4. rectangles, squares, and other four-sided objects
5. solids and volume
6. coordinate geometry

The 180° Rule, Part I

When you see a geometry problem that asks about angles, always look to see if two angles form a line, which tells you that the total of the two angles is 180 degrees. This is often the crucial starting point on the road to the solution. The test writers like to construct problems in such a way that it is very easy to miss this.

DEGREES AND ANGLES

There are 360 degrees in a circle. No matter how large or small a circle is, it still has precisely 360 degrees. If you drew a circle on the ground and then walked a quarter of the distance around it, you would have traveled 90 degrees of that circle. If you walked halfway around the circle, you would have traveled 180 degrees of it.

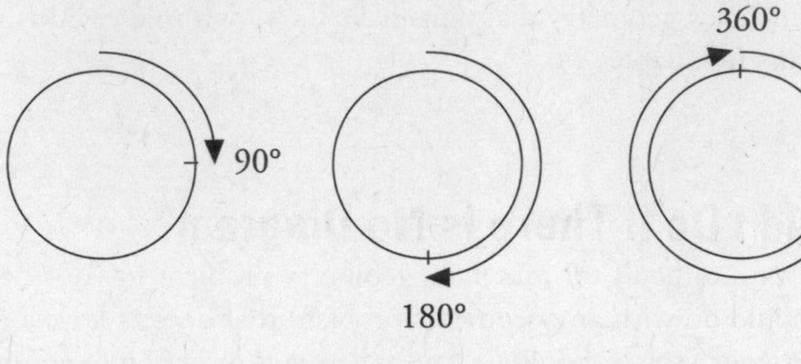

An angle is formed when two line segments extend from a common point. If you think of that point as the center of a circle, the measure of the angle is the number of degrees enclosed by the lines when they pass through the edge of the circle.

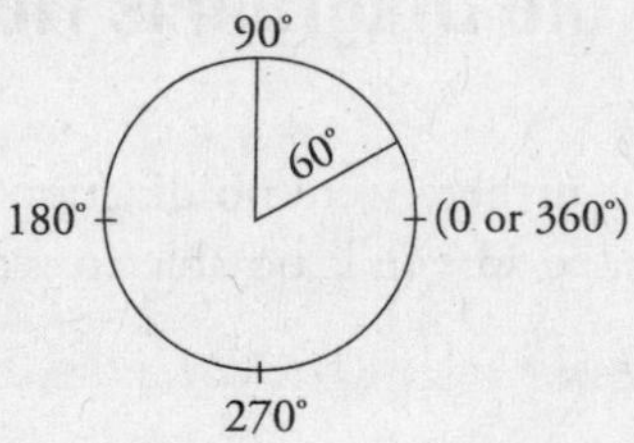

A line is just a 180-degree angle.

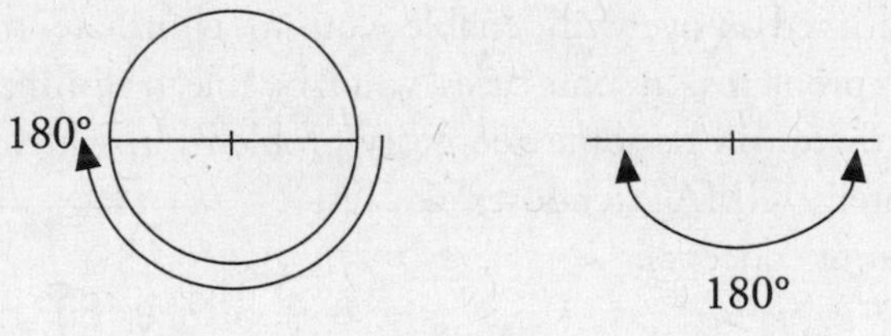

ℓ is the symbol for a line. A line can be referred to as ℓ or by naming two points on that line. For example, in the diagram below, both points *A* and *B* are on the line ℓ. This line could also be called line *AB*. Also, the part of the line that is between points *A* and *B* is called a line segment. *A* and *B* are the end points of the line segment.

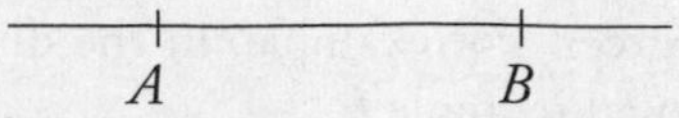

If a line is intersected by another line, as in the diagram below, angle x and angle y add up to one straight line, or 180 degrees. So, for example, if you know that angle x equals 120 degrees, you can find the measure of angle y by subtracting 120 degrees from 180 degrees. Thus angle y would equal 60 degrees.

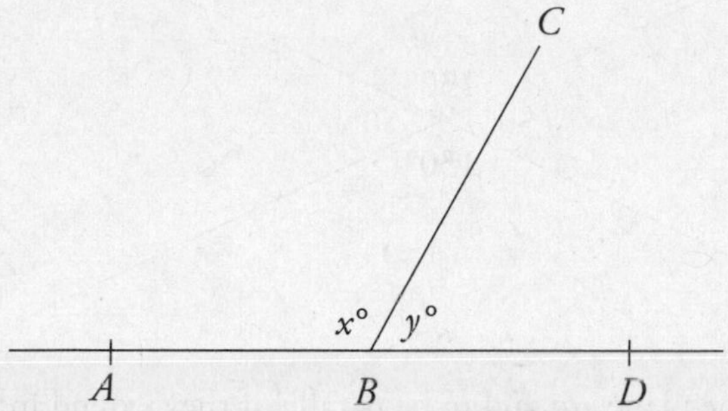

Note that in the diagram above, angle x could also be called angle ABC, with B being the point in the middle.

When two lines intersect—as in the diagram below—four angles are formed. The four angles are indicated by letters.

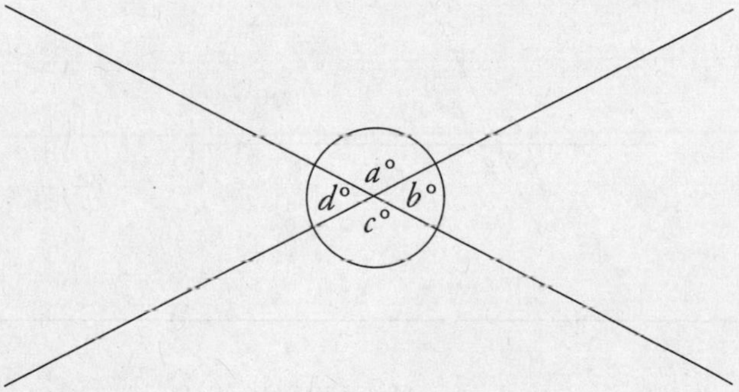

The four angles add up to 360 degrees (remember the circle).

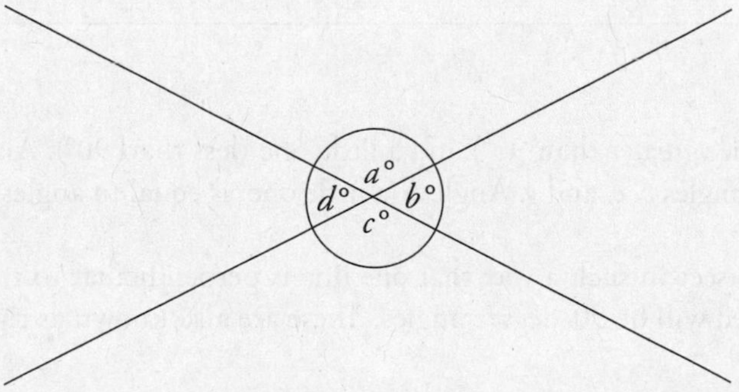

$a° + b° + c° + d° = 360$ degrees. Angle a + angle b, because they form a straight line, are equal to 180 degrees. Angle b + angle c also form a straight line, as do $c + d$ and $d + a$. Angles that are opposite each other are called *vertical angles* and have the same number of degrees. For example, in the diagram above, angle *a* is equal to angle *c*. Angle *d* is equal to angle *b*.

Therefore, when two lines intersect, there appear to be four different angles, but there are really only two:

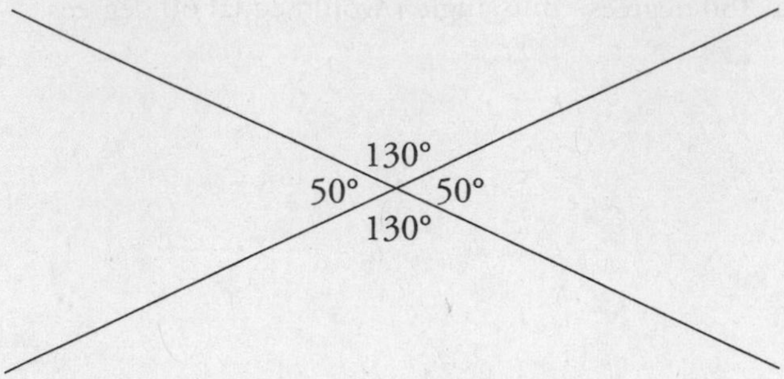

Two lines in the same plane are said to be parallel if they extend infinitely in both directions without intersecting. The symbol for parallel is ||.

Look at the diagram below:

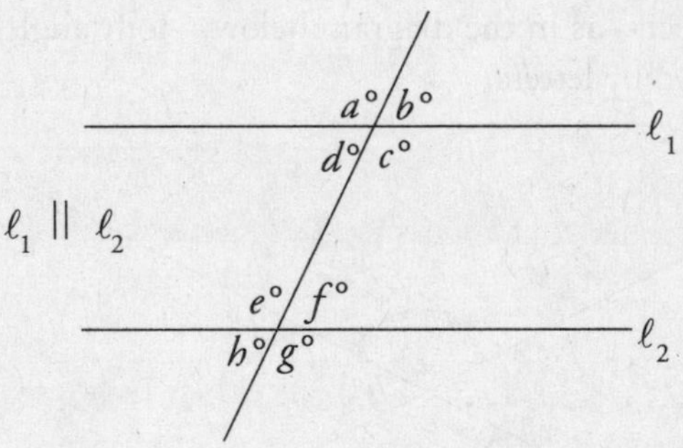

> When two parallel lines are intersected by a third line, there appear to be eight different angle measurements, but there are really only two.

There is a big one (greater than 90°) and a little one (less than 90°). Angle *a* (a big one) is equal to angles *c, e,* and *g.* Angle *b* (a little one) is equal to angles *d, f,* and *h.*

If two lines intersect in such a way that one line is perpendicular to the other, all the angles formed will be 90-degree angles. These are also known as right angles:

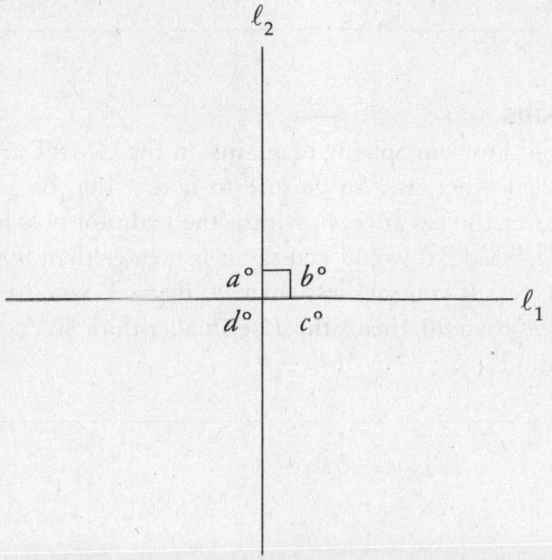

Angles *a, b, c,* and *d* each equal 90 degrees. The little box at the intersection of the two lines is the symbol for a right angle.

Let's practice on a problem:

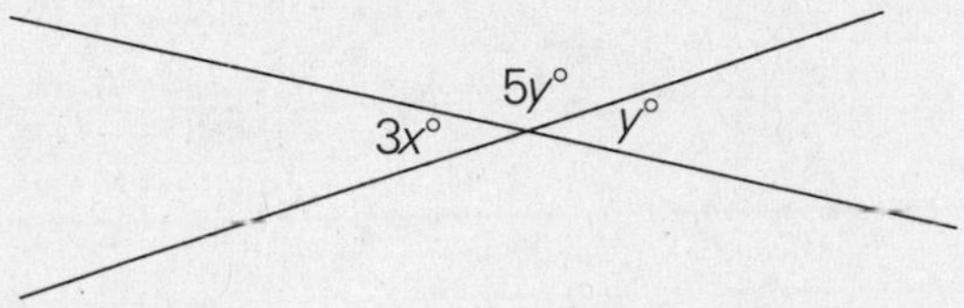

In the figure above, what is the value of *x*?

- ◯ 10
- ◯ 15
- ◯ 20
- ◯ 30
- ◯ 40

Here's How to Crack It

On a GMAT geometry problem, you may not know exactly how to solve at first glance, but there is almost always something you can do to get started. Did you notice that 5*y* and *y* together make up a straight line? In other words, $6y = 180$ degrees. Noticing this is the key to solving the problem. If $6y = 180$ degrees, then *y* equals 30 degrees. You might be tempted to pick choice D, but remember—we aren't looking for the value of *y*, we're looking for the value of *x*. Opposite angles formed by two straight lines are always equal—so *y* is equal to 3*x*. Therefore, 3*x* also equals 30 degrees, and the correct answer to this problem is choice A, 10 degrees.

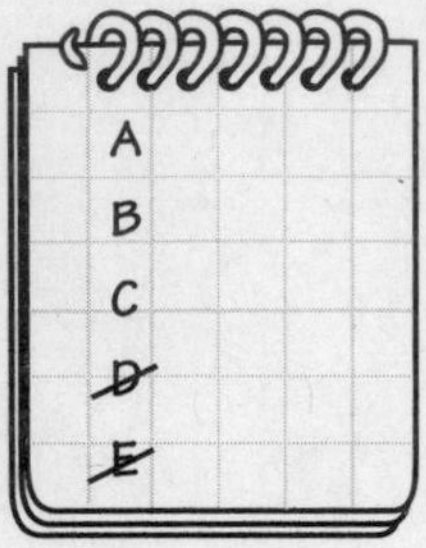

Easy Eliminations

Remember that all Problem Solving diagrams on the GMAT are drawn to scale unless labeled otherwise. So be sure to take a step back and think about which answer choices are even within the realm of possibility. Looking at the angle labeled $3x$, would you say it is greater than 90 degrees or less than 90 degrees? If you said less than 90 degrees, you are doing just fine. So if $3x$ is less than 90, then x must be smaller than 30 degrees. Eliminate choices D and E.

DRILL 6 (Angles and Lengths)

In the following figures, find numbers for all the variables. The answers to these problems can be found in Part VI.

1.

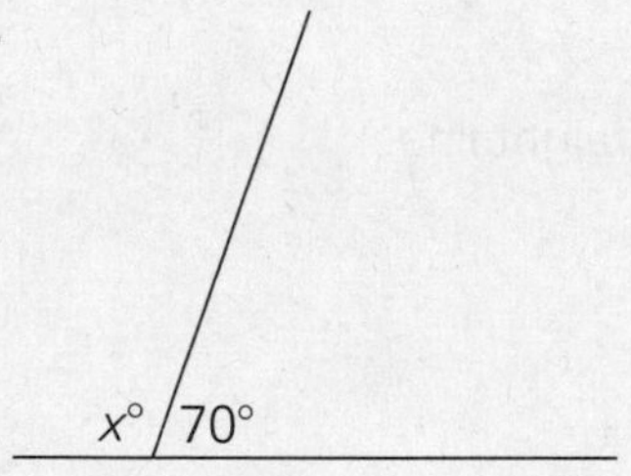

2.

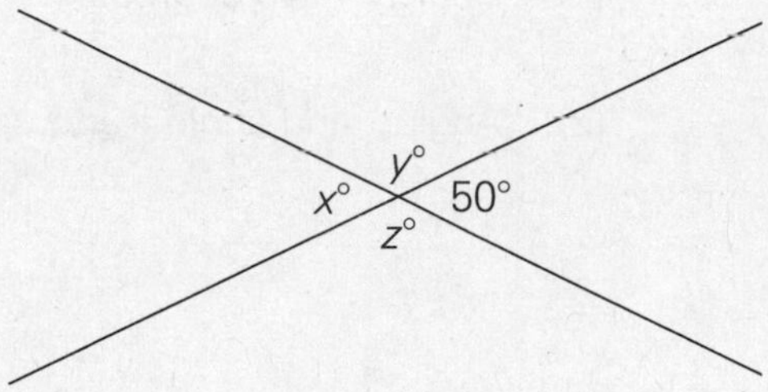

3.

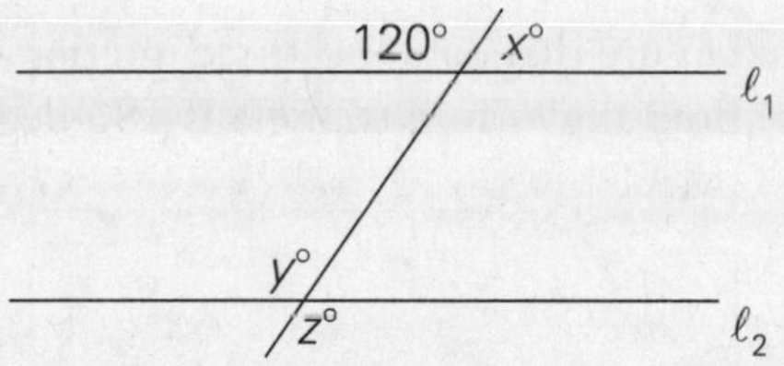

4. If a driver has traveled 270 degrees around a circular race track, what fractional part of the track has he driven?

Drawn to Scale?
In a Problem Solving question, if it doesn't say *not drawn to scale*, then it *is* drawn to scale. When they give you a scaled drawing, use it to eliminate answers that are out of proportion.

A real GMAT angle problem might look like this:

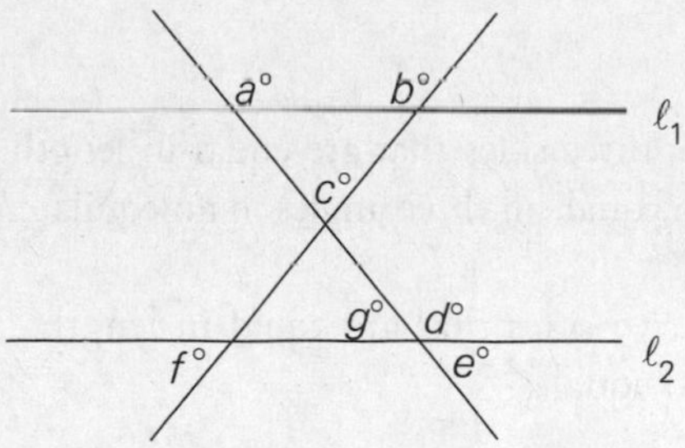

Note: Figure not drawn to scale.

5. In the figure above, if $\ell_1 \parallel \ell_2$, then which of the following angles must be equivalent?

- ○ *a* and *b*
- ○ *g* and *f*
- ○ *d* and *e*
- ○ *a* and *d*
- ○ *f* and *d*

You might see a very straightforward Data Sufficiency problem like this on the GMAT:

6. What is the degree measure of angle x?

   (1) Angle $y = 40$ degrees.

   (2) Angle x and angle y add up to a straight line.

TRIANGLES

A triangle is a three-sided figure that contains three interior angles. The sum of the degree measures of the three angles in a triangle is 180 degrees. Several kinds of triangles appear on the GMAT:

The 180° Rule, Part II

When a question involving angles has a triangle or several triangles in it, remember that the interior angles of a triangle add up to 180 degrees. Apply that rule in every possible way you can. It is one of the things that the GMAT writers love to test most.

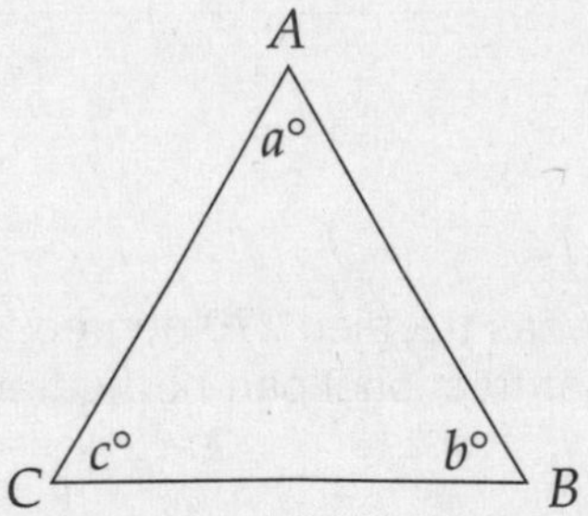

$AB = BC = CA$
$a = b = c = 60°$

An **equilateral triangle** has three sides that are equal in length. Because the angles opposite equal sides are also equal, all three angles in an equilateral triangle are equal.

Triangles

Triangles are by far the test writers' favorite geometric shape. If you get stuck on a geometry problem that doesn't have triangles in it, ask yourself: Can the figure in this problem be divided into triangles (especially right triangles) that I can work with? This will sometimes be the key to the solution.

An **isosceles triangle** has two sides that are equal in length. The angles opposite the two equal sides are also equal.

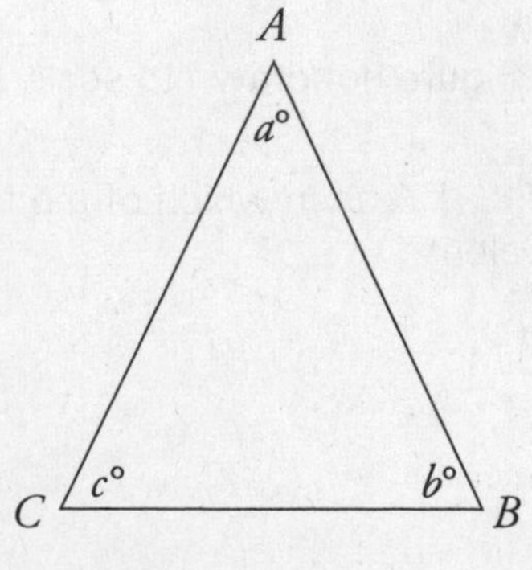

$AB = AC$
$b = c$

A **right triangle** has one interior angle that is equal to 90 degrees. The longest side of a right triangle (the one opposite the 90-degree angle) is called the *hypotenuse.*

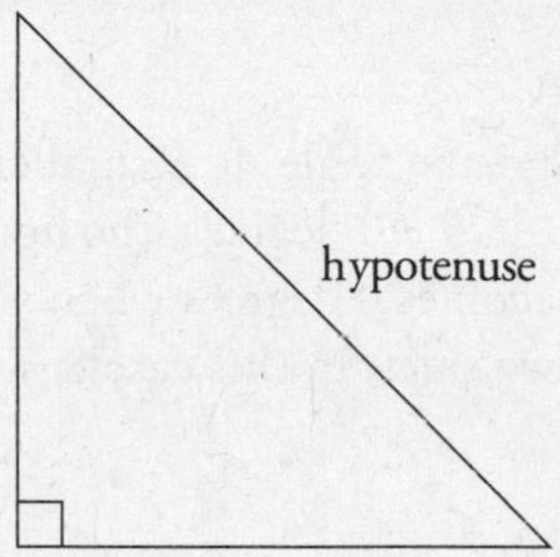

Everything Else You Need to Know About Triangles

1. The sides of a triangle are in the same proportion as its angles. For example, in the triangle below, which is the longest side?

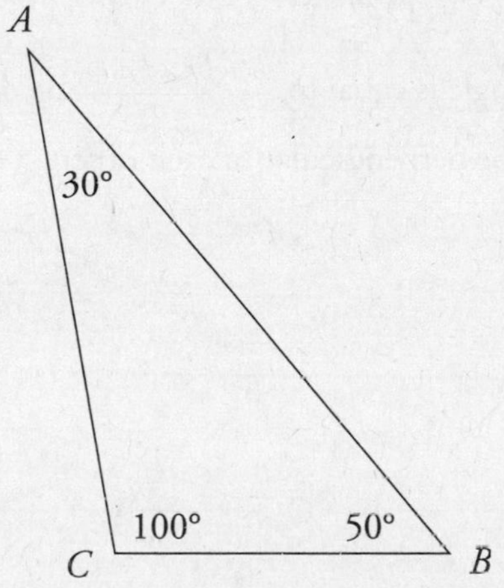

The longest side is opposite the largest angle. The longest side in the triangle above is *AB*. The next longest side would be *AC*.

2. One side of a triangle can never be longer than the sum of the lengths of the other two sides of the triangle, or less than their difference. Why? Look at the diagrams below:

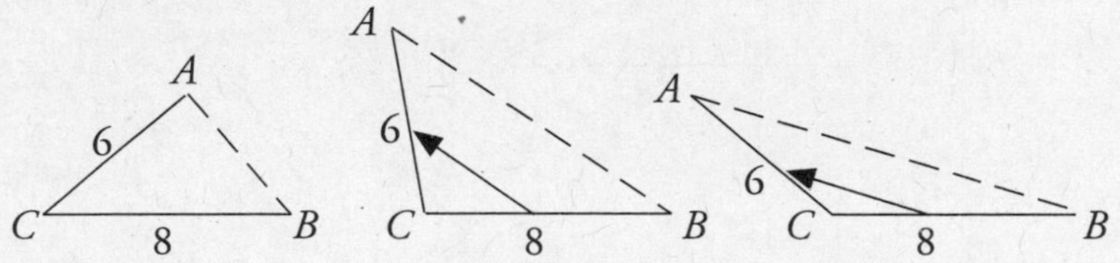

At the point where angle ACB = 180 degrees, this figure ceases to be a triangle. Angle ACB becomes 180 degrees when side AB equals the sum of the other two sides, in this case 6 + 8. Side AB can never quite reach 14.

By the same token, if we make angle ACB smaller and smaller, at some point, when angle ACB = 0 degrees, the figure also ceases to be a triangle. Angle ACB becomes 0 degrees when side AB equals the difference of the other two sides, in this case 8 – 6. So AB can never quite reach 2.

3. The *perimeter* of a triangle is the sum of the lengths of the three sides.

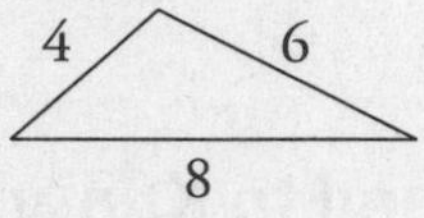

perimeter = 18

4. The *area* of a triangle is equal to $\frac{height \times base}{2}$. By definition, the base and height must be perpendicular to each other.

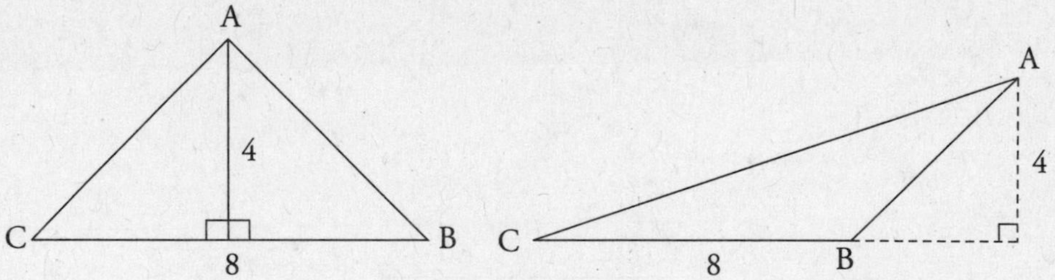

In both of the above triangles, the area = $\frac{4 \times 8}{2}$ = 16.

In a right triangle, the height also happens to be one of the sides of the triangle:

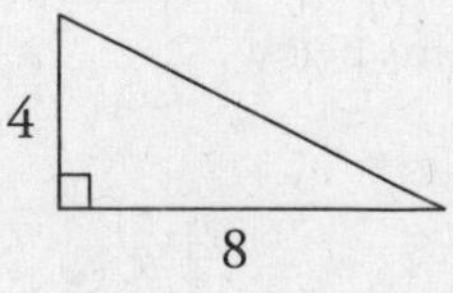

5. Don't expect triangles to be right side up:

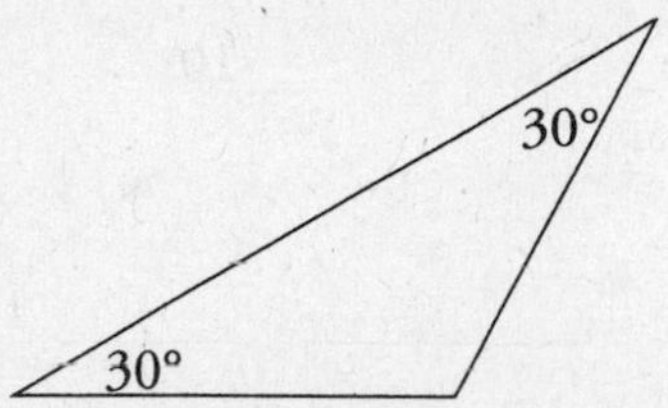

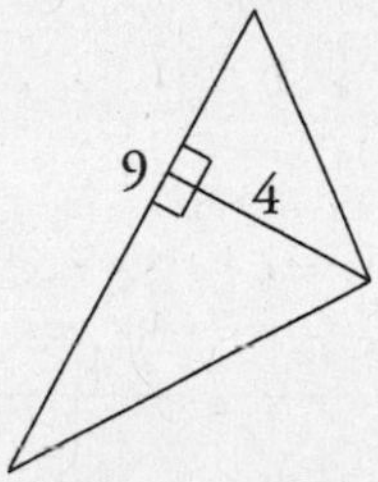

This is an isosceles triangle.

The area of this triangle is

$$A = \frac{9 \times 4}{2}, \text{ or } 18.$$

6. In a right triangle, the square of the hypotenuse equals the sum of the squares of the other two sides. In the triangle below:

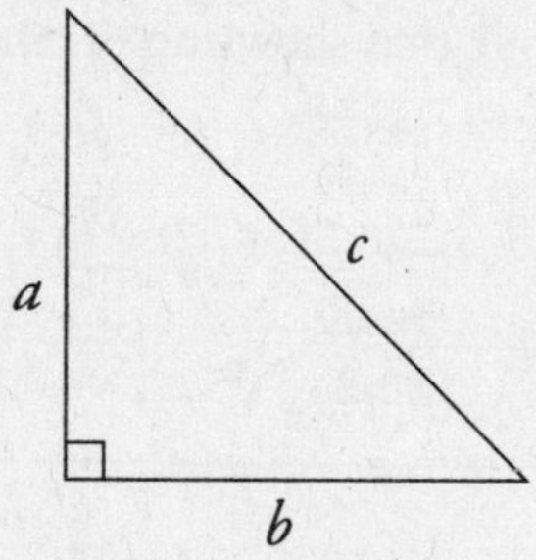

$$a^2 + b^2 = c^2$$

This is called the **Pythagorean theorem.** The test writers love to test this theorem, but usually you won't actually have to make use of it if you've memorized a few of the most common right-triangle proportions.

The Pythagorean triangle that comes up most frequently on the GMAT is one that has sides of lengths 3, 4, and 5, or multiples of those numbers. Look at the following examples:

Pythagoras's Other Theorem

Pythagoras also developed a theory about the transmigration of souls. So far, this theory has not been proven.

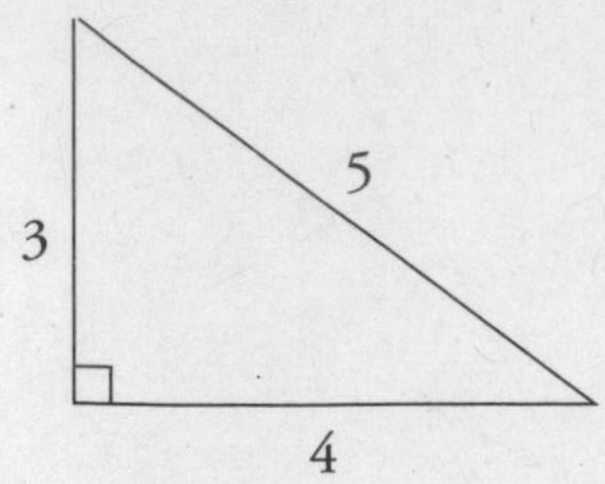

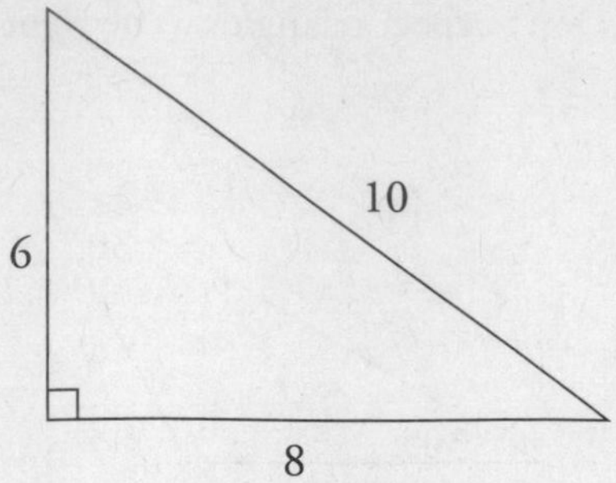

$3^2 + 4^2 = 5^2$ $\qquad$ $6^2 + 8^2 = 10^2$

$9 + 16 = 25$ $\qquad$ $36 + 64 = 100$

Pythagorean Triples

The right triangle in the ratio 3 : 4 : 5 is the most common Pythagorean triple, but it's not the only one that shows up on the GMAT. Here are the three triples you need to know:

3 : 4 : 5
5 : 12 : 13
7 : 24 : 25

There are two other kinds of right triangles that GMAC loves to test. These are a little complicated to remember, but they come up so often that they're worth memorizing.

7. A right isosceles triangle always has proportions in the ratio side: side: side $\sqrt{2}$.

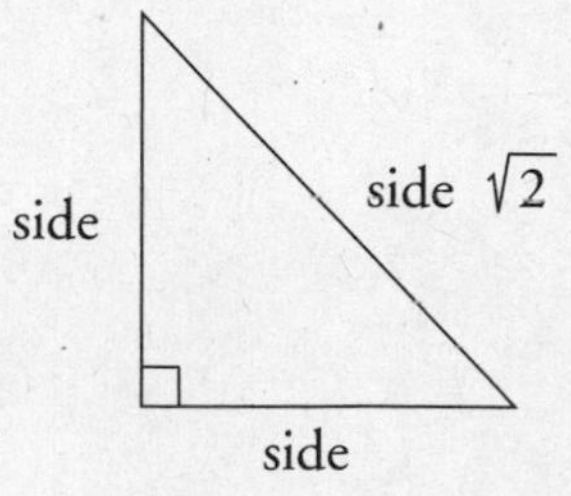

For example:

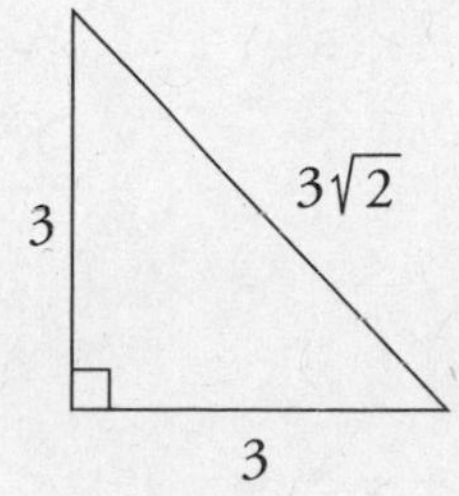

8. The second special right triangle is called the **30-60-90** right triangle. The ratio between the lengths of the sides in a 30-60-90 triangle is constant. If you know the length of any of the sides, you can find the lengths of the others. The ratio of the sides is always $x : x\sqrt{3} : 2x$.

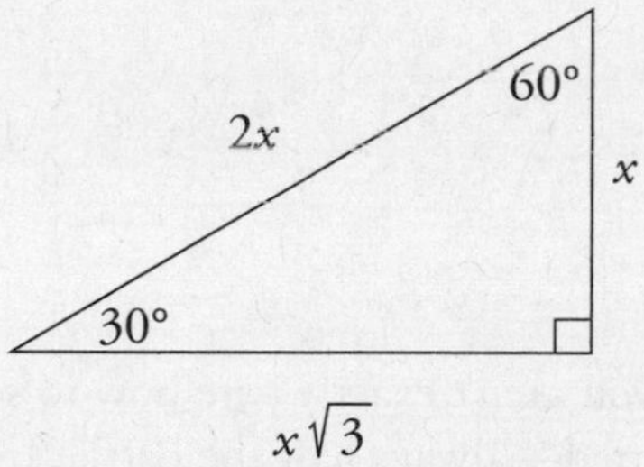

How to Label a 30-60-90 Triangle

Remembering how to label the 1, 2, $\sqrt{3}$ sides of a 30-60-90 triangle is easy if you remind yourself that the largest side goes opposite the largest angle and the smallest side opposite the smallest angle, *and* if you remind yourself that $\sqrt{3}$ is roughly 1.7, okay?

That is, if the shortest side is length x, then the hypotenuse is $2x$, and the remaining side is $x\sqrt{3}$.

Try this problem:

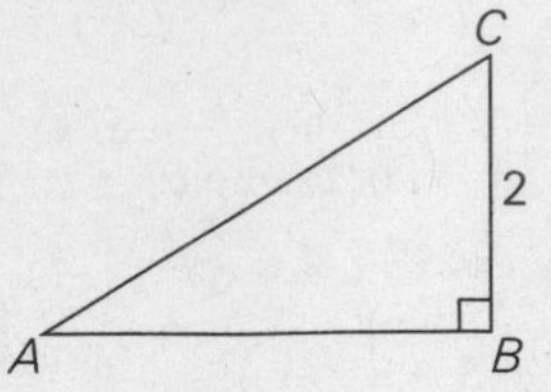

In ΔABC shown above, if $\angle CAB$ equals 30°, then what is the area of the triangle?

- 2
- $2\sqrt{2}$
- $2\sqrt{3}$
- $3\sqrt{2}$
- 4

Here's How to Crack It

As with all geometry problems, even if you aren't exactly sure how to solve, there may be something you can do to get started—always half the battle. In this case, since we know that ΔABC is a right triangle, and the problem tells you that $\angle CAB$ equals 30, do we know the value of $\angle ACB$? We do: it must be 60° (since there are a total of 180 degrees in a triangle). Because this is a 30-60-90 triangle (which always has sides in proportion of x, $2x$, and $x\sqrt{3}$), and the diagram gives us all the measurement of one of those sides, we actually know the measurement of all sides: $2, 2\sqrt{3}$, and 4. To find the area, we simply multiply the base times the height and divide by 2:

$A = \frac{2 \times 2\sqrt{3}}{2} = 2\sqrt{3}$, and the answer is choice C.

DRILL 7 (Triangles)

Find the value of the variables in the following problems. The answers can be found in Part VI.

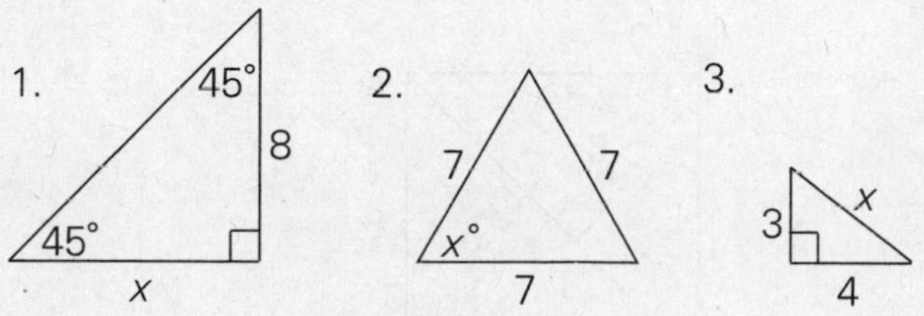

4. What value must x be less than in the triangle below? What value must x be greater than?

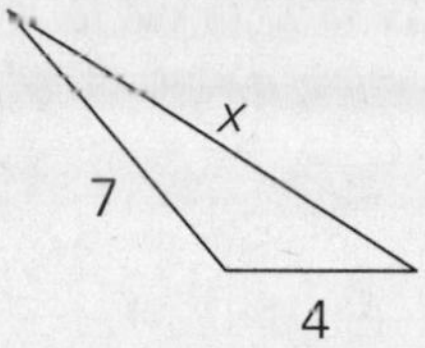

5. In the square $ABCD$ below, what is the length of line segment AC?

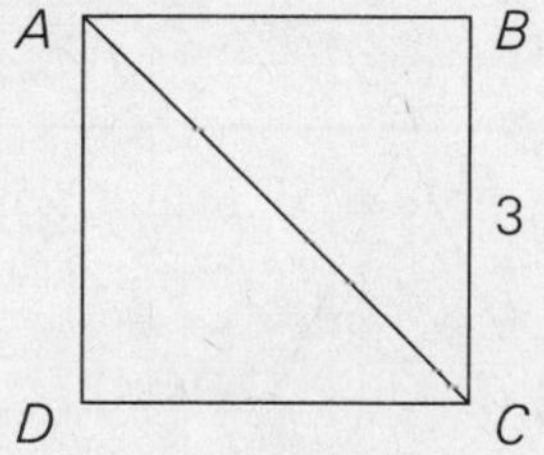

6. In the triangle below, what is the length of the line segment BC?

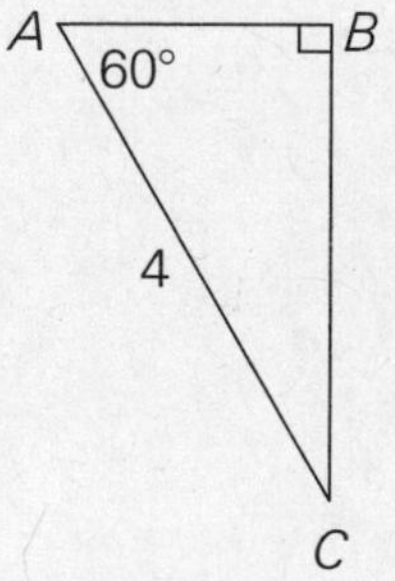

A real GMAT triangle problem might look like this:

7. In the diagram below, if the area of triangle *LNP* is 32, then what is the area of triangle *LMN*?

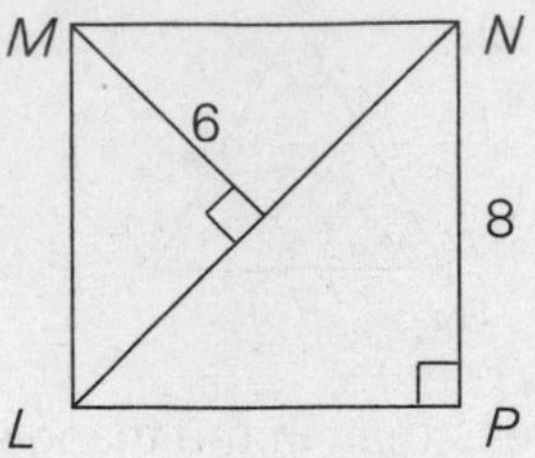

Note: Figure not drawn to scale.

- ◯ 24
- ◯ $24\sqrt{2}$
- ◯ $24\sqrt{3}$
- ◯ 32
- ◯ 48

You might see a Data Sufficiency problem like this on the GMAT:

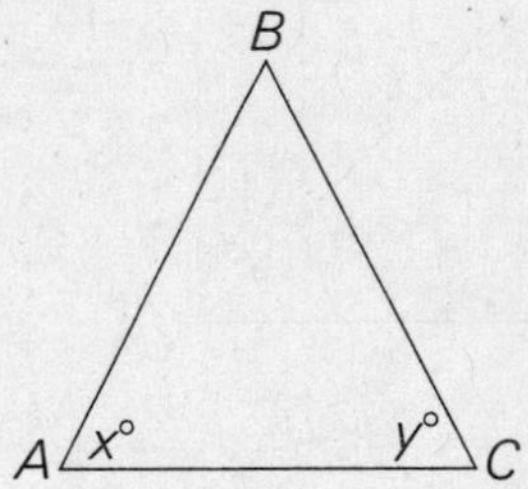

8. What is the value of x in triangle *ABC* shown above?

(1) Angle y = 80 degrees.

(2) $AB = BC$

CIRCLES

A line segment whose endpoints lie on a circle is called a **chord**. The distance from the center of the circle to any point on the circle is called the **radius.** The distance from one point on the circle through the center of the circle to another point on the circle is called the **diameter.** The diameter is equal to twice the radius.

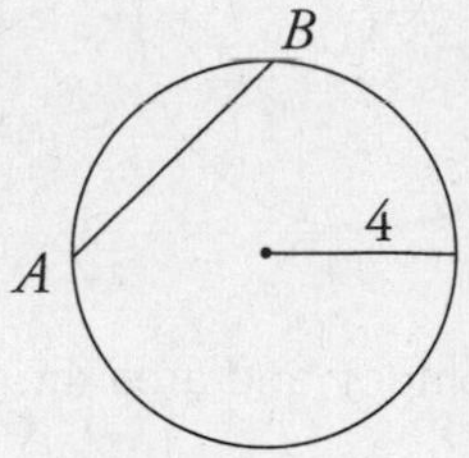

radius = 4

diameter = 8

AB is a chord.

The **circumference** (the length of the entire outer edge of the circle) = $2\pi r$ or πd.

The rounded portion of the circle between points *A* and *B* is called an **arc.**

The **area** of a circle = πr^2.

A circle cut in half by a diameter is called a **semicircle.**

A triangle is said to be **inscribed** inside a semicircle when one of its sides is the diameter of the circle itself, with the two other sides meeting at any point on the circle. A triangle inscribed inside a semicircle is always a **right triangle.**

A Perfect Circle

During the fourteenth century, Pope Boniface VIII commissioned artists to send samples of their work to demonstrate their abilities. One of the artists, Giotto, responded by dipping his paintbrush in red ink and in one continuous stroke created "a perfect circle." When the pope saw it, he instantly perceived that Giotto surpassed all other painters of his time.

Let's try a circle problem:

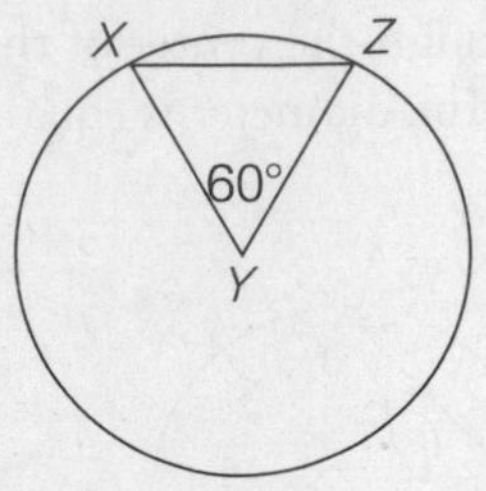

If the circle above has center y and area 4π, then what is the perimeter of triangle XYZ?

- 2
- 2π
- 4
- 6
- 6π

Here's How to Crack It

As always, the solution to this problem will probably only become apparent once you've started doing the problem. The only apparent information you've been given: the area of the circle, 4π. Since the formula for the area of a circle is πr^2, set that equal to 4π. Can you figure out what r equals? That's right, 2. And since both sides XY and YZ are radii of the circle, they must both equal 2. To find the perimeter of the triangle, the last thing we need to do is find the length of XZ. You might not think that you know what XZ equals, but the diagram tells us that angle XYZ equals 60 degrees. Since we know sides xy and yz are equal, that means that this triangle must be equilateral: all three sides have the same length, 2. Therefore, the perimeter of triangle XYZ is 6, and the answer is choice D.

DRILL 8 (Circles)

Answer the following questions. The answers can be found in Part VI.

1. In the circle below with center O, what is the area of the circle? What is the circumference?

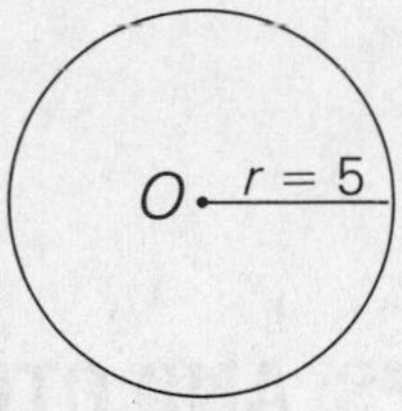

2. If the area of a circle is 36π, what is the circumference?

3. In the circle below with center O, if the arc RT is equal to $\frac{1}{6}$ of the circumference, what is the value of x?

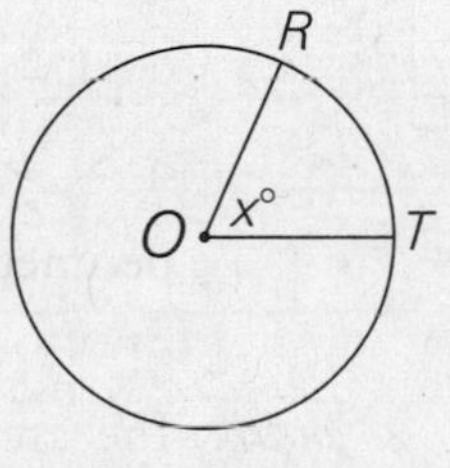

A real GMAT circle problem might look like this:

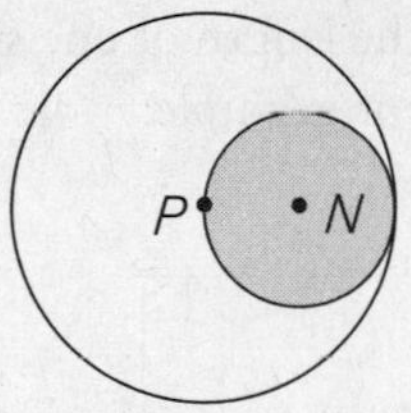

4. In the figure above, P is the center of the larger circle, and N is the center of the smaller, shaded circle. If the radius of the smaller circle is 5, what is the area of the unshaded region?

- 100π
- 75π
- 25π
- 20π
- 10π

You might see a Data Sufficiency problem like this on the GMAT:

5. What is the area of circle P?

(1) The diameter of circle Q is 6.

(2) The radius of circle Q is twice the radius of circle P.

RECTANGLES, SQUARES, AND OTHER FOUR-SIDED OBJECTS

A four-sided figure is called a **quadrilateral**. The perimeter of any four-sided object is the sum of the lengths of its sides. A **rectangle** is a quadrilateral whose four interior angles are each equal to 90 degrees. Opposite sides of a rectangle are always equal.

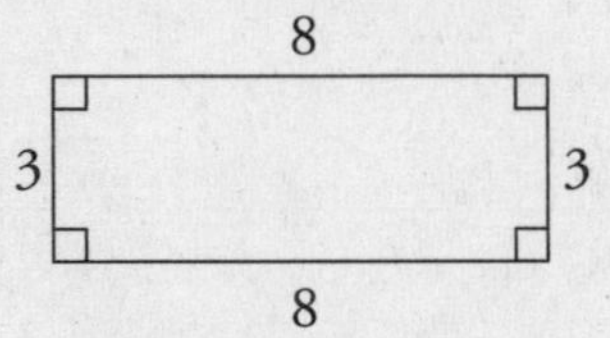

perimeter = 22

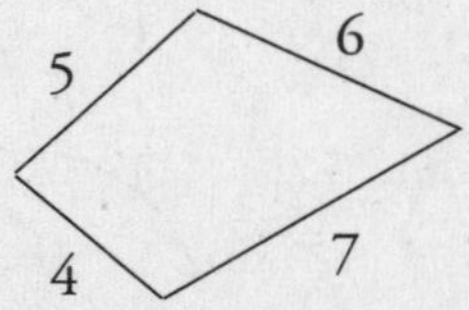

perimeter = 22

The area of a rectangle is *length* × *width*. The area of the rectangle above is therefore 3 × 8, or 24.

A **square** is a rectangle whose four sides are all equal in length. The *perimeter* of a square is therefore just four times the length of one side. The *area* of a square is the *length* of one of its sides squared. For example:

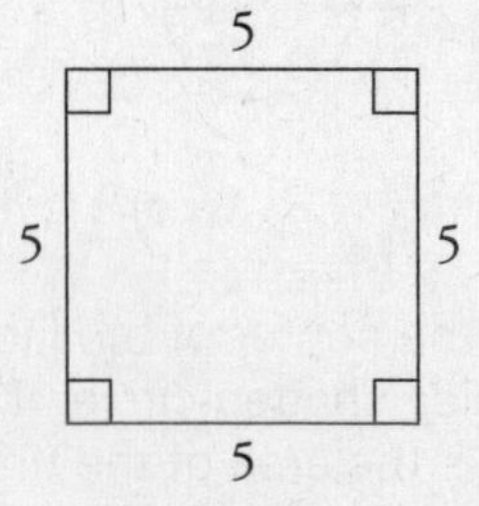

perimeter = 4 × 5 = 20

area = 5 × 5 = 25

A **parallelogram** is a quadrilateral in which the two pairs of opposite sides are parallel to each other and equal to each other, and in which opposite angles are equal to each other. A rectangle is obviously a parallelogram, but so is a figure like this:

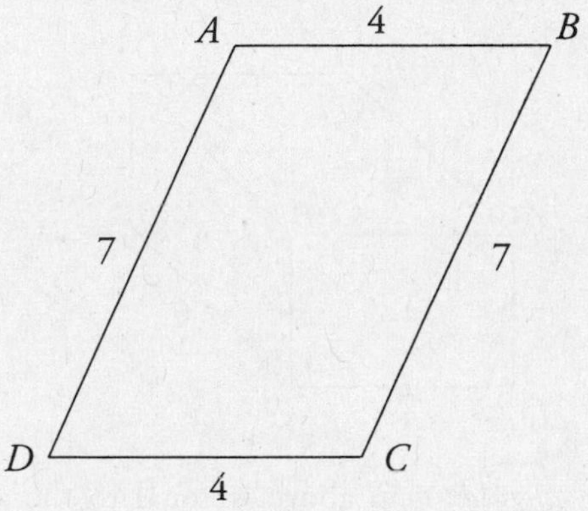

Angle ADC = angle ABC, and angle DAB = angle DCB.

The area of a parallelogram equals *base* × *height*.

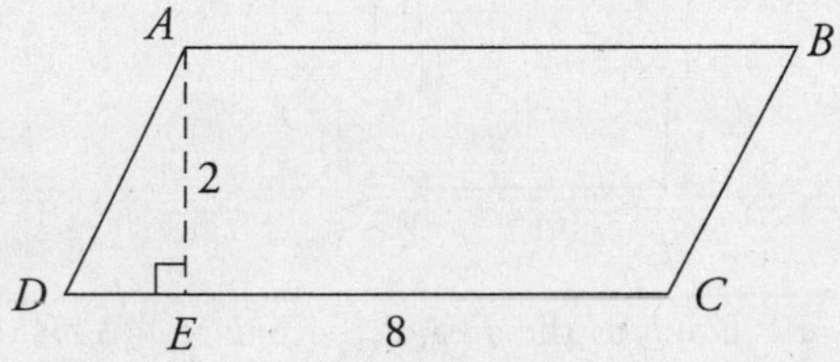

The area of parallelogram $ABCD = 8 \times 2 = 16$. (If you are having trouble picturing this, imagine cutting off the triangular region ADE and sticking it onto the other end of the figure. What you get is a rectangle with dimensions 8 by 2.)

SOLIDS, VOLUME, AND SURFACE AREA

Advance!
With GMAT geometry, just get going. Wade in there and do something. With each piece you add to the puzzle, the next piece to look for becomes evident.

The GMAT will occasionally ask you to find the *volume* or *surface area* of a three-dimensional object.

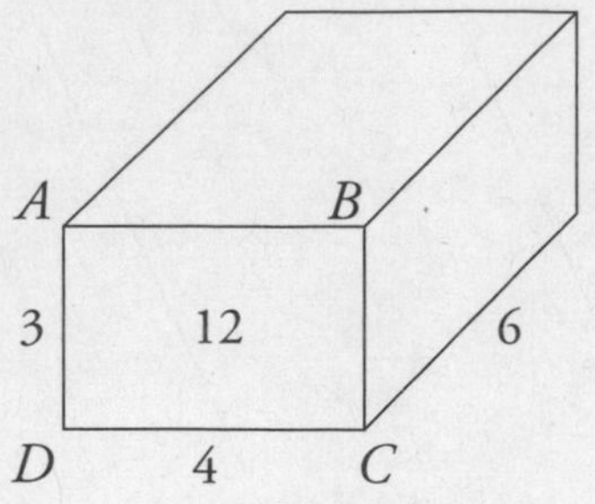

The volume of the *rectangular solid* above is equal to the area of the rectangle *ABCD* times the depth of the solid—in this case, 12 × 6, or 72. Another way to think of it is *length* × *width* × *depth* = 3 × 4 × 6, or 72.

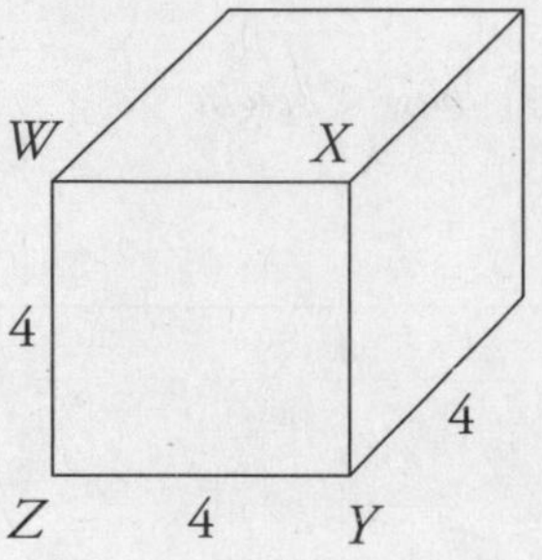

The volume of a *cube* is equal to the area of the square *WXYZ* times the depth of the cube, or again, *length* × *width* × *depth*. In the case of a cube, the length, width, and depth are all the same, so the volume of a cube is always the length of any side, cubed. The volume of this cube is 4 × 4 × 4, or 64.

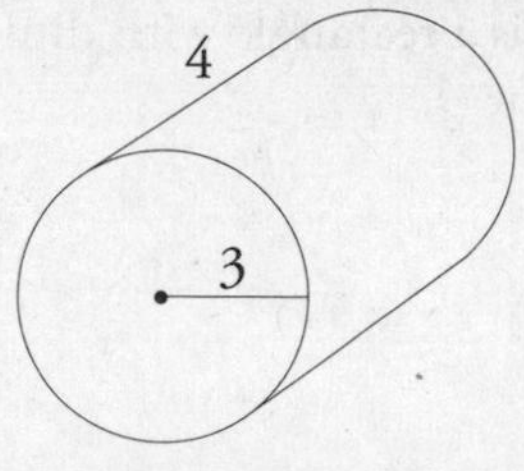

The volume of a *cylinder* is equal to the *area* of the circular base times the *depth*. The area of this circle is 9π. Thus the volume of the cylinder is 36π.

You may need to find the surface area of a solid. Surface area is just the sum of the areas of all the two-dimensional outer surfaces of the object. So, for example, the surface area of a rectangular solid is the sum of the areas of the solid's six faces. Take a look at how you'd calculate the surface area of the rectangular solid:

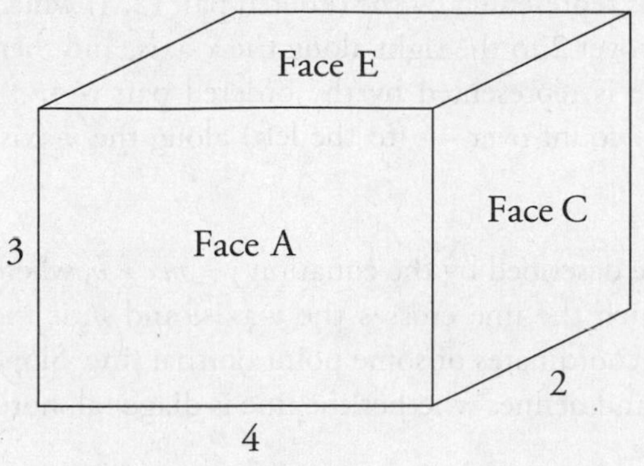

Face A: $3 \times 4 = 12$

Face B: $3 \times 4 = 12$
(opposite Face A)

Face C: $3 \times 2 = 6$

Face D: $3 \times 2 = 6$
(opposite Face C)

Face E: $4 \times 2 = 8$

Face F: $4 \times 2 = 8$
(opposite Face E)

Surface Area: $= 52$

COORDINATE GEOMETRY

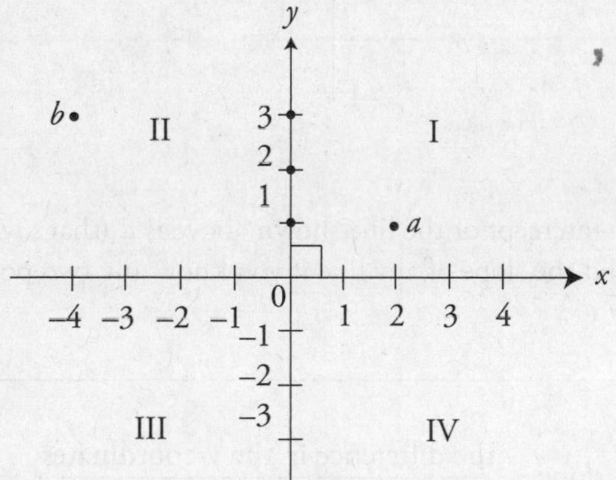

A coordinate plane, like the one above, lets you plot out lines and objects in two-dimensions. If you played the game Battleship as a child, this should feel very familiar—even if you don't remember learning about it in high school. The horizontal line is called the *x*-axis. The vertical line is called the *y*-axis. The axes divide the plane into four quadrants as shown above.

Every point on the plane has an ordered pair of numbers (x, y) that describes it. For example, in the plane above, point a is represented by the ordered pair (2, 1) which simply means starting from 0, count over 2 to the right along the x-axis, and then up 1 along the y-axis. Point b above is represented by the ordered pair (–4, 3), which simply means starting from 0, count over –4 (to the left) along the x-axis, and up 3 along the y-axis.

Any straight line on this plane can be described by the equation $y = mx + b$, where b is the y-intercept (the point at which the line crosses the y-axis) and m is the slope of the line, and x and y are the coordinates of some point on that line. Slope is the measure of steepness of a line, and defines whether the line is diagonal, horizontal, or vertical, and to what degree.

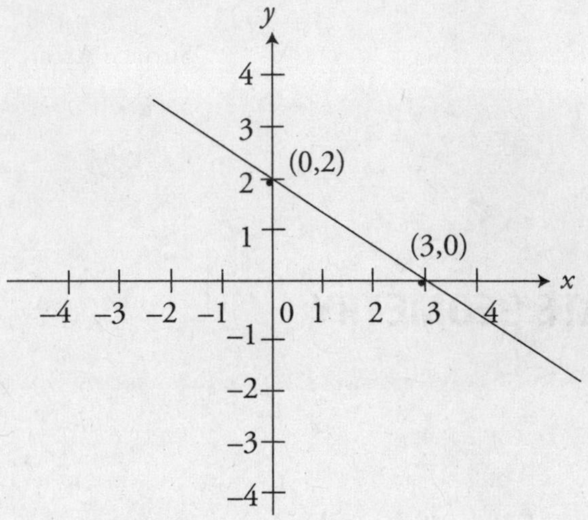

For example, the y-intercept of the line shown above is 2 (that's where it crosses the y-axis). You can find the slope of any line if you know any two points on that line:

$$\text{slope} = \frac{\text{the difference in the } y\text{-coordinates}}{\text{the difference in the } x\text{-coordinates}}$$

For example, the slope of the line above is

$$\frac{2-0}{0-3} \text{ or } \frac{2}{-3}$$

So the equation of this line can be written as $y = \frac{2}{-3}x + 2$.

Let's see how this might show up in a fairly tough GMAT problem:

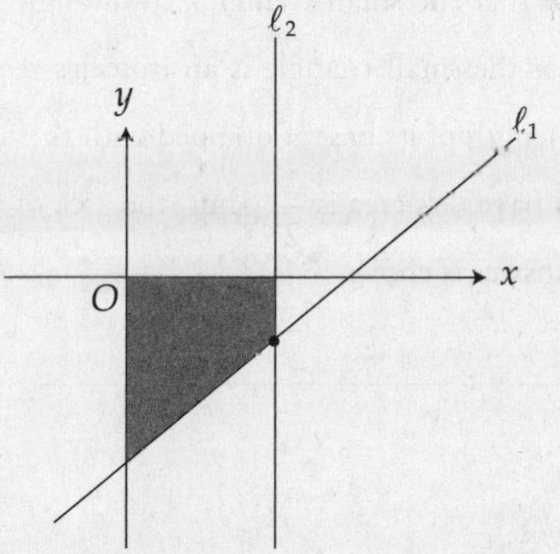

In the coordinate plane above, if the equation of ℓ_1 is $y = x - 3$ and the equation of ℓ_2 is $x = 2$, then what is the area of the shaded region?

(A) 3
(B) 4
(C) $3\sqrt{2}$
(D) 4.5
(E) 5

Here's How to Crack It

First, draw your own coordinate axes. The equation for ℓ_1 is $y = x - 3$, which means that the y-intercept is –3 and the slope is 1. That means the bottommost point of the large triangle is point (0, –3), and the rightmost point of the large triangle is (3, 0). What we have here is an upside-down right triangle with base 3 and height 3. The area of this entire triangle is $\frac{b \times h}{2}$ or $\frac{9}{2}$, which is choice D, but we aren't done yet. Now we have to find the area of the small triangle, and subtract it from the large triangle. What remains will be the shaded region.

The equation for ℓ_2 is $x = 2$, which means that ℓ_2 is a vertical line running parallel to the y-axis. The small triangle therefore must also be an upside-down right triangle. Its base is 1 (from point (2, 0) to point (3, 0)). Eyeballing it, you might decide that its height is 1, too. The way to know for sure is to realize that these two right triangles (the small one and the large one) share an angle formed by the x-axis and ℓ_1. The large triangle is isosceles, so its angles must measure 90-45-45. And since the small triangle shares one of the large triangle's 45-degree angles, we know that the small triangle's third angle must be 45 degrees as well. That means that the small triangle is an isosceles triangle, too, and that its height equals 1, the length of its base. Equipped with this information, we can calculate that the small triangle's area is $\frac{1}{2}$. Thus, the area of the shaded region is $\frac{9}{2} - \frac{1}{2}$, or 4. The best answer is choice B.

GMAT GEOMETRY: ADVANCED PRINCIPLES

All geometry problems (even easy ones) involve more than one step. Remember the first problem we looked at in this chapter?

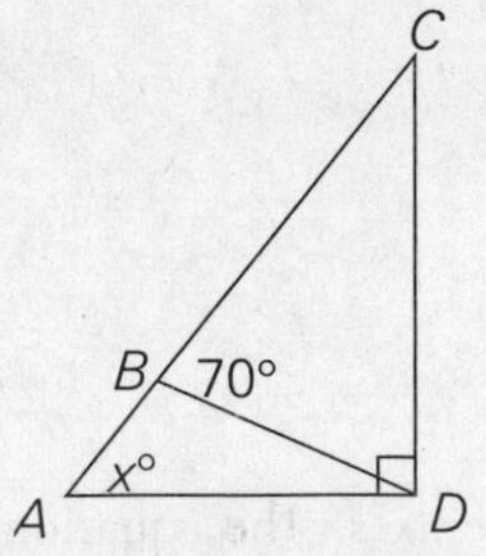

In the figure above, if $BC = CD$ and angle $ADC = 90$ degrees, then what is the value of x?

- 45
- 50
- 70
- 75
- 100

Here's How to Crack It

Just by looking at the figure, we were able to eliminate answer choices C, D, and E. Now let's solve the problem using geometry. The figure includes two—actually three—different triangles: *ABD, BCD*, and *ACD*. The test writers want even this easy problem to be a little challenging; there must be more than one step involved. To find angle *x*, which is part of triangles *ABD* and *ACD*, we must first work on triangle *BCD*.

What do we know about triangle *BCD*? The problem itself tells us that *BC* = *CD*. This is an isosceles triangle. Because angle *DBC* equals 70, so does angle *BDC*. Angle *BCD* must therefore equal 180 minus the other two angles. Angle *BCD* = 40.

Now look at the larger triangle, *ACD*. We know that angle *ACD* = 40, and that angle *ADC* = 90. What does angle *x* equal? Angle *x* equals 180 minus the other two angles, or 50 degrees. The answer is choice B.

Walking and Chewing Gum at the Same Time

Most GMAT geometry problems involve more than one geometric concept. A problem might require you to use both the properties of a triangle and the properties of a rectangle, or you might need to know the formula for the volume of a cube in order to find the dimensions of a cube's surface area. The difficult geometry problems do not test more complicated concepts—they just pile up easier concepts.

Bite-Sized Pieces

With GMAT geometry, you shouldn't expect to see every step a problem involves before you start solving it. Often, arriving at the right answer involves saying, "I have no idea how to get the answer, but because the problem says that *BC=CD*, let me start by figuring out the other angle of that triangle. Now what can I do?" At some point the answer usually becomes obvious. The main point is not to stare at a geometry problem looking for a complete solution. Just wade in there and start, one bite-sized piece at a time.

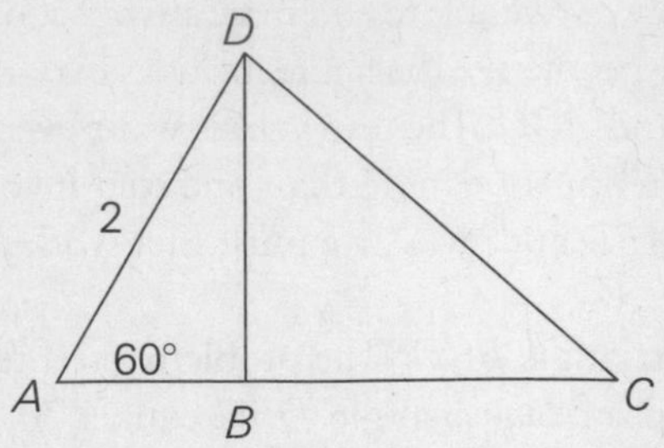

In the figure above, if a line segment connecting points B and D is perpendicular to AC, and the area of triangle ADC is $\frac{3\sqrt{3}}{2}$, then BC =

- $\sqrt{2}$
- $\sqrt{3}$
- 2
- $3\sqrt{3}$
- 6

Here's How to Crack It

You may remember that earlier in this chapter, we already got an approximate answer to this question by measuring; now let's solve it using geometry. If we draw in the line BD (which is perpendicular to line AC), we form a 30-60-90 triangle on the left side of the diagram (triangle ADB). The hypotenuse of this triangle is 2. Using the rules we've learned about 30-60-90 triangles, we can conclude that the measurements of triangle ADB are as follows:

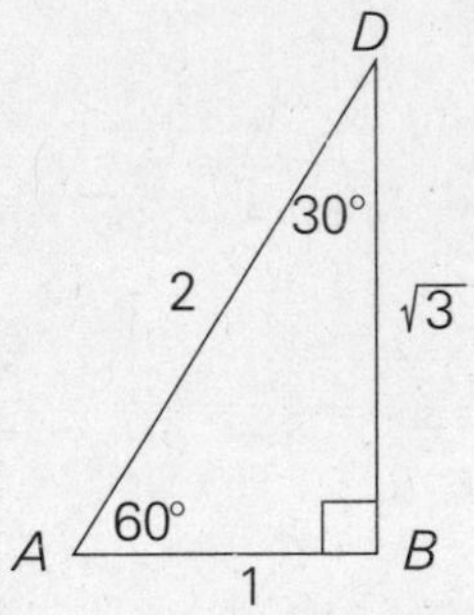

Thus $BD = \sqrt{3}$. At first you might think we're no closer to the solution, but don't despair. Just look for somewhere else to start. The problem tells us that the area of triangle ADC is $\frac{3\sqrt{3}}{2}$. The area of a triangle is $\frac{\text{base} \times \text{height}}{2}$. BD is the height. Let's find out what the base is. In other words, $\frac{\text{base} \times \sqrt{3}}{2} = \frac{3\sqrt{3}}{2}$, so the base equals 3. We know from the 30-60-90 triangle that AB = 1. What is BC? 2. The answer is choice C.

Plugging In on Geometry?

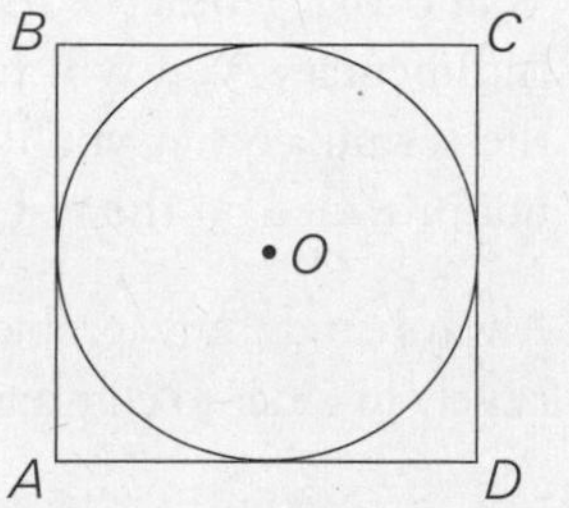

In the figure above, circle *O* is inscribed inside square *ABCD* as shown. What is the ratio of the area of circle *O* to the area of square *ABCD*?

- $\frac{\pi}{2}$
- $\frac{4}{\pi}$
- $\frac{\pi}{3}$
- $\frac{\pi}{4}$
- $\frac{\pi}{5}$

Here's How to Crack It

We already saw this problem in the first half of the chapter when we discussed eliminating crazy answers. As you recall, we were able to eliminate answer choices A, B, and C because we determined that the correct answer had to be the ratio of a smaller number to a bigger number.

Now let's solve this problem completely. You may have noticed that the answer choices do not contain *specific numbers* for the areas of the two figures—all we have here are *ratios* in the answer choices. Sound familiar? That's right! This is just another Plugging In problem.

To find the area of the circle, we need a radius. Let's just pick one—3. If the radius is 3, the area of the circle is 9π. Now let's tackle the square. The circle is inscribed inside the square, which means that the diameter of the circle is also the length of a side of the square. Because the radius of the circle is 3, the diameter is 6. Therefore the side of the square is 6, and the area is 36.

The problem asks for the ratio of the area of the circle to the area of the square:

$$\frac{9\pi}{36} = \frac{\pi}{4}$$

The answer is choice D.

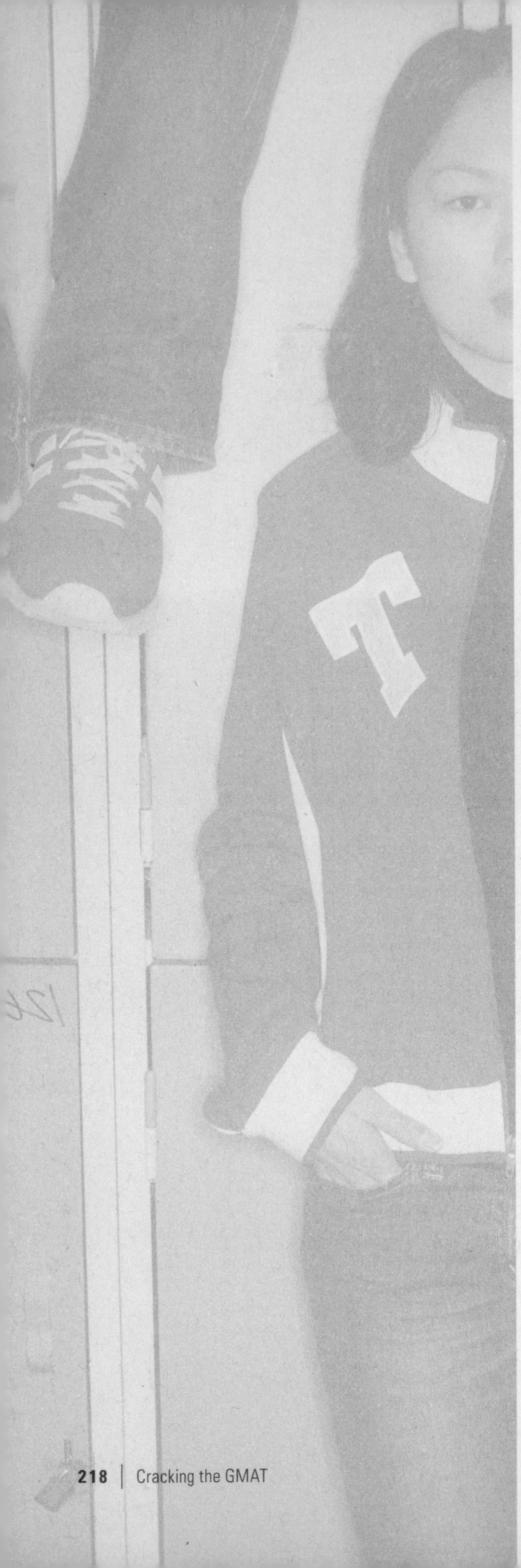

Summary

- While the geometry found on the GMAT is rudimentary, you will have to memorize all of the formulas that you'll need because they are not provided on the test.
- Always study any problem drawn to scale very closely in order to eliminate crazy answer choices.
- You must know the following approximate values: $\pi \approx 3$, $\sqrt{2} \approx 1.4$, and $\sqrt{3} \approx 1.7$.
- You must be familiar with the size of certain common angles:

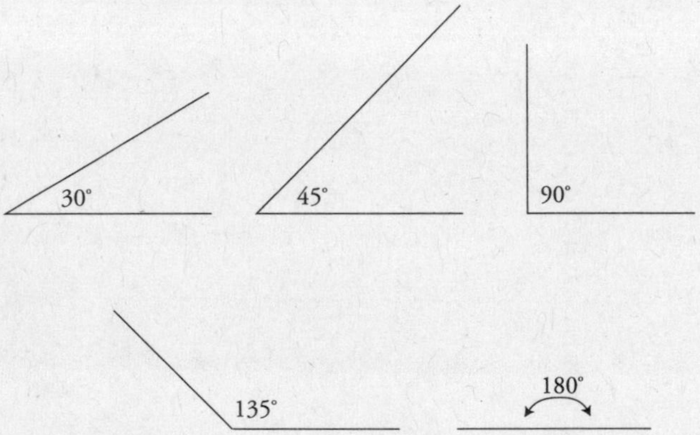

- You can estimate Problem Solving diagrams drawn to scale very precisely by using the marker that comes with your scratch booklet.
- When no diagram is provided, draw your own, and make it to scale.
- When the diagram is not drawn to scale, redraw it.

- Degrees and angles:
    - A circle contains 360 degrees.
    - When you think about angles, remember circles.
    - A line is a 180-degree angle.
    - When two lines intersect, four angles are formed, but in reality there are only two pairs of identical angles.
    - When two parallel lines are cut by a third line, eight angles are formed, but in reality there are only two sets of identical angles: a set of big ones and a set of little ones.

- Triangles:
    - Every triangle contains 180 degrees.
    - An equilateral triangle has three equal sides and three equal angles, each of which measures 60 degrees.
    - An isosceles triangle has two equal sides, and the angles opposite those sides are also equal.
    - A right triangle contains one 90-degree angle.
    - The perimeter of a triangle is the sum of the lengths of its sides.
    - The area of a triangle is $\frac{height \times base}{2}$.
    - In a right triangle, the Pythagorean theorem states that the square of the hypotenuse equals the sum of the squares of the other two sides, or $a^2 + b^2 = c^2$.
    - Some common right triangles are 3-4-5 triangles and multiples of 3-4-5 triangles, 5-12-13 triangles, and 7-24-25 triangles.
    - Two other triangles that often appear on the GMAT are the right isosceles triangle and the 30-60-90 triangle. Memorize the formulas for these two triangles.
    - The longest side of a triangle is opposite the largest angle; the shortest side is opposite the smallest angle.
    - One side of a triangle can never be as large as the sum of the two remaining sides, nor can it ever be as small as the difference of the two remaining sides.

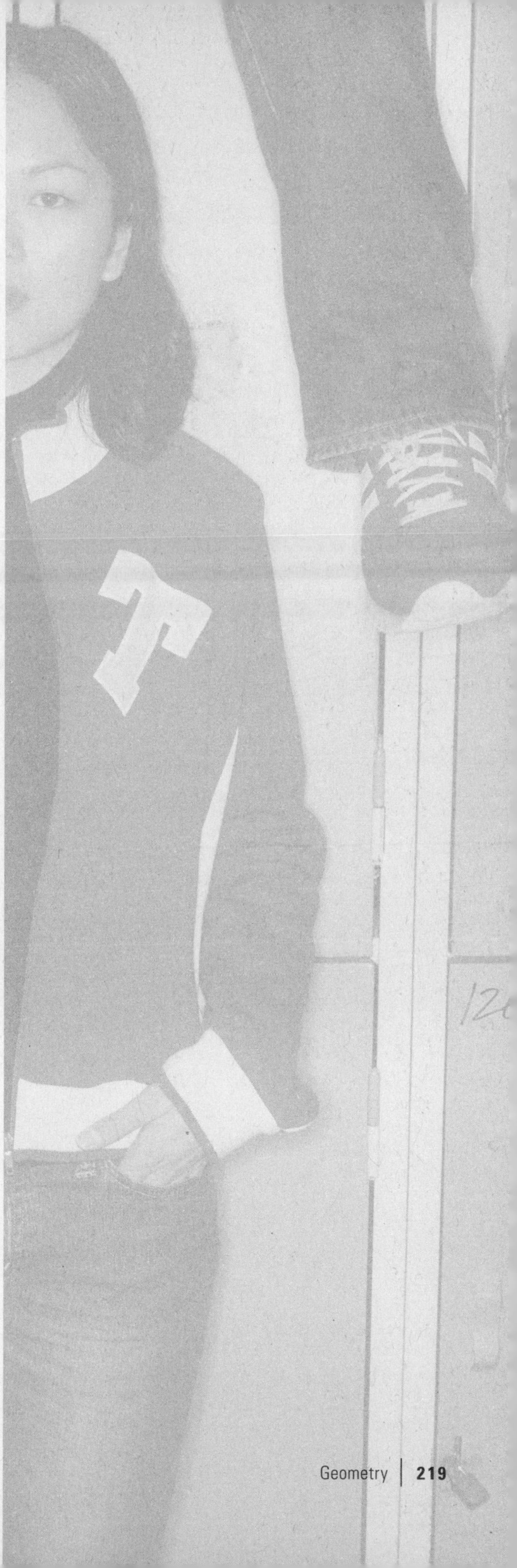

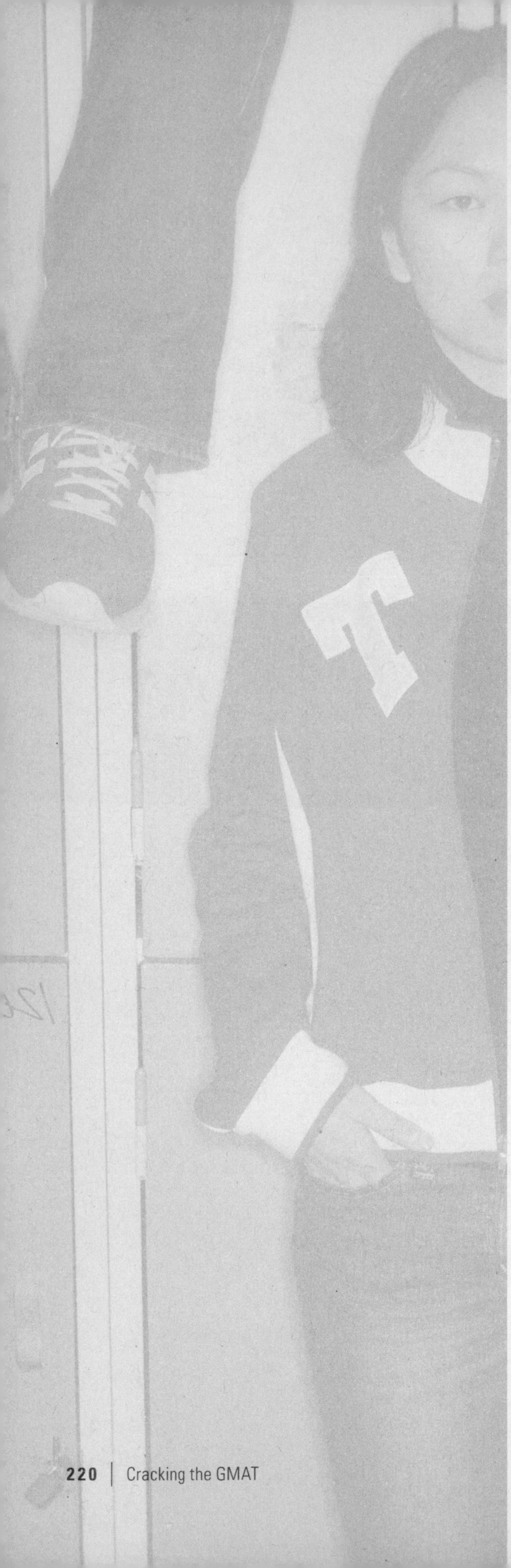

- Circles:
  - The circumference of a circle is $2\pi r$ or πd, where r is the radius of the circle and d is the diameter.
  - The area of a circle is πr^2, where r is the radius of the circle.
- Rectangles, squares, and other four-sided objects:
  - Any four-sided object is called a quadrilateral.
  - The perimeter of a quadrilateral is the sum of the lengths of the four sides.
  - The area of a rectangle, or of a square, is equal to *length* × *width*.
  - The area of a parallelogram is equal to *height* × *base*.
- Solids and volume:
  - The volume of most objects is equal to their two-dimensional *area* × their *depth*.
  - The volume of a rectangular solid is equal to *length* × *width* × *depth*.
  - The volume of a cylinder is equal to the *area* of the circular base × *depth*.
- GMAT geometry problems always involve more than one step, and difficult GMAT geometry problems may layer several concepts. Don't be intimidated if you don't see the entire process that's necessary to solve the problem. Start somewhere. You'll be amazed at how often you arrive at the answer.

Chapter 14 Advanced Data Sufficiency

In this chapter, we'll show you how to master Data Sufficiency problems, how to decipher the intermediate and advanced math hidden beneath the unfamiliar format, and how to use POE to eliminate tempting traps.

Now that you've reviewed all the important math concepts covered on the GMAT, it's time to take a second look at how these concepts are used in Data Sufficiency questions.

First, a quick review:

Every Data Sufficiency problem consists of a question followed by two statements:

What is x?

(1) $x^2 = 4$.

(2) x is negative.

You have to decide NOT what the answer is, but WHETHER the question can be answered based on the information in the two statements. There are five possible answer choices:

- ○ Statement (1) ALONE is sufficient, but statement (2) alone is not sufficient.
- ○ Statement (2) ALONE is sufficient, but statement (1) alone is not sufficient.
- ○ BOTH statements TOGETHER are sufficient, but NEITHER statement ALONE is sufficient.
- ○ EACH statement ALONE is sufficient.
- ○ Statements (1) and (2) TOGETHER are not sufficient

The best way to answer Data Sufficiency problems is to look at one statement at a time—so ignore Statement (2), and look only at Statement (1). Based on Statement (1), $x^2 = 4$, can we answer the question, "What is x?"

At first glance, you might think so. If $x^2 = 4$, then $x = 2$, right?

Well, not necessarily; x could also equal –2. And since Statement (1) gives us two different possible answers to this question, Statement (1) is NOT sufficient to answer the question. Choices A and D are out of the question; we are down to B, C, or E.

Now, ignore Statement (1) and look ONLY at Statement (2). Based on Statement (2), "x is negative," can we answer the question, "What is x?"

Nope, x could be any negative number. We are now down to C or E.

Look at both statements together. If $x^2 = 4$ and x is negative, can we answer the question, "What is x?"

AD or BCE

Just by looking at Statement (1) we have already eliminated several answer choices:

If Statement (1) is sufficient, we are down to A or D.

If Statement (2) is NOT sufficient, we are down to B, C, or E.

AD or BCE. Memorize it; these are always your options. And it makes sense to write it down this way in your scratch book.

Yup! Now there is only one unique number in the world that x could be: –2. The correct answer is C.

Here's a flowchart that walks you through each step of solving a Data Sufficiency question. If you need more information about how to use the chart or the basic strategy for solving a Data Sufficiency question, check out Chapter 9.

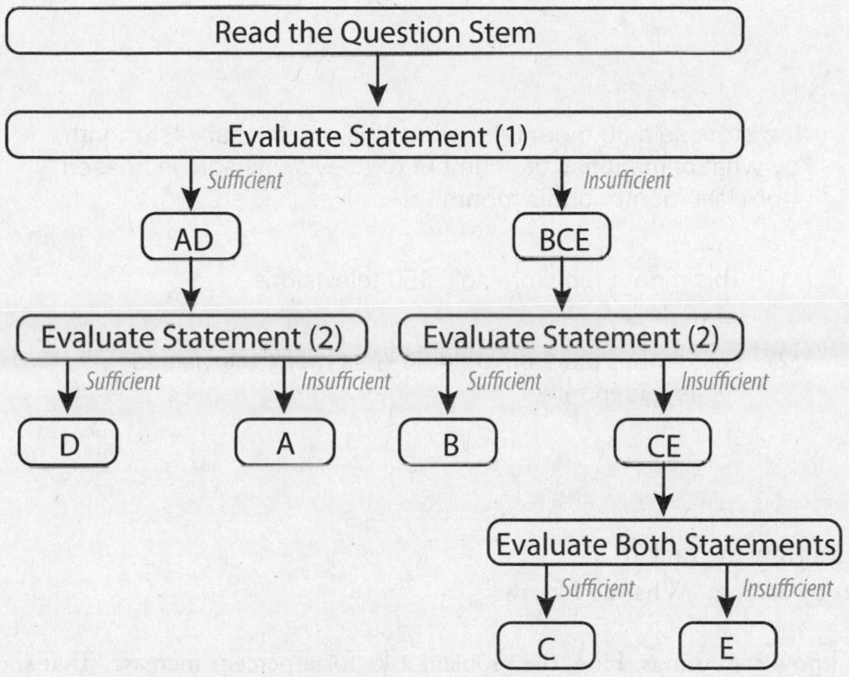

DATA SUFFICIENCY: PIECES OF THE PUZZLE

In terms of mathematical content, Data Sufficiency questions test the same kinds of topics tested by Problem Solving questions (as we told you in Chapter 9). You'll find problems involving integers, percents, averages, ratios, algebra, and geometry. Only the format is different.

Your familiarity with the math content, however, can give you an advantage when working a Data Sufficiency question. Most people read the question and then immediately read the statements. But that's not how you would normally work a math problem. Normally, you would read the problem and then ask yourself, "What do I already know?" and "What do I need?"

You should always attempt to do the same thing when working a Data Sufficiency question. Before proceeding to the statements, take stock of the information that you already know. Then, see if you can determine what sort of information the statements need to provide so that you could solve the problem.

We call this approach Pieces of the Puzzle. In a sense, Data Sufficiency questions are just like jigsaw puzzles. When you work a jigsaw puzzle, you know what piece you are looking for based on the shapes of the pieces that fit around it. In a Data Sufficiency question, you'll often know what sort of information you need from the statements based on what you already know from the question stem.

Here's an example:

If a store sold 30 more televisions this month than last month, by what percent has the number of televisions sold increased from last month to this month?

(1) This month the store sold 150 televisions.

(2) Last month the store sold 80% as many televisions as this month.

Here's How to Crack It

Start by asking, "What do I know?"

You know two things. First, the problem asks for a percent increase. That should get you thinking about the formula for percent change:

$$\% \text{ change} = \frac{\text{difference}}{\text{original}} \times 100$$

Pieces of the Puzzle

What do you know?

The difference is 30.

What do you need?

The sales for last month, the original.

Next, notice that you already know the change, since the question states that the store sold 30 more televisions this month than last month. So, you can plug the difference into the formula to get:

$$\% \text{ change} = \frac{30}{\text{original}} \times 100$$

Now, it's time to ask yourself, "What do I need?" By looking at the formula, you can see that you'll be able to answer the question if the statements give you a way to determine the original. So, as soon as you know how many televisions the store sold last month, you have sufficient information.

Now, remember to read only Statement (1). If the store sold 150 televisions this month and that represents an increase of 30 televisions, you know that the store sold 120 televisions last month. So, write down AD.

Now, forget about Statement (1) and read Statement (2). This statement is a little trickier than the first. If last month's sales were 80% of this month's sales, you know that the additional 30 televisions that were sold this month represent 20% of the total. Now, you set up a part-to-whole relationship:

$$\frac{\text{part}}{\text{whole}} = \frac{20}{100} = \frac{30}{x}$$

Can you find the value of x from this equation? Of course. Therefore, Statement (2) is also sufficient and the answer to this question is D.

Let's try the approach again on a difficult question.

What is the average (arithmetic mean) of a list of 6 consecutive two-digit integers?

(1) The remainder when the fourth integer is divided by 5 is 3.

(2) The ratio of the largest integer to the smallest integer is 5:4.

Here's How to Crack It

As before, apply the Pieces of the Puzzle approach by asking, "What do I know?"

Since the question asks you to find the average, you should remember that you can find an average if you have the sum of the items being averaged and the number of those items. In this case, you know that there are six integers. You also know that the integers are consecutive. Finally, since the question states that the integers are two digit, you know that each integer is between 9 and 100.

Now, it's time to ask, "What do I need?" There are lots of possibilities. The statements could give you the sum of the six numbers. Or, the statements could give you the value of one of the integers and its position in the list. For example, if you know that the second integer is 12, you could certainly find the average.

Now, read and evaluate only Statement (1). It's best to think about the information in this statement by plugging in some possible numbers. For example, the fourth integer could be 18 because the remainder when 18 is divided by 5 is 3.

If the fourth integer is 18, the first integer is 15. The complete list would be 15, 16, 17, 18, 19, 20 and their average is 17.5. However, the fourth integer could also be 33, making the first integer 30 and the average of the six integers 32.5.

So, Statement (1) does not provide sufficient information to find the average of the six integers. Write down BCE.

Now, forget what you know from the first statement and evaluate only Statement (2). At first, Statement (2) may not seem like much help either. After all, if you are going too quickly, you may be tempted to think that the largest integer could be 15 and the smallest 12 or the largest could be 20 and the smallest 16.

However, here's where you need to remember the puzzle piece that you already have—there are *six* consecutive integers on the list. So, while 12 and 15 may seem to fit the ratio provided in the second statement, those numbers really don't satisfy the statement and the problem because there wouldn't be six numbers for the list.

The only way to satisfy the information in the second statement and in the problem is to make the smallest number 20 and the largest number 25.

Therefore, the answer to this difficult question is B.

DRILL 9 (Data Sufficiency Parts and Wholes)

The answers can be found in Part VI.

1. If only people who paid deposits attended the Rose Seminar, how many people attended this year?

   (1) 70 people sent in deposits to attend the Rose Seminar this year.

   (2) 60% of the people who sent deposits to attend the Rose Seminar this year actually went.

   - Statement (1) ALONE is sufficient, but statement (2) alone is not sufficient.
   - Statement (2) ALONE is sufficient, but statement (1) alone is not sufficient.
   - BOTH statements TOGETHER are sufficient, but NEITHER statement ALONE is sufficient.
   - EACH statement ALONE is sufficient.
   - Statements (1) and (2) TOGETHER are not sufficient.

2. Luxo paint contains only alcohol and pigment. What is the ratio of alcohol to pigment in Luxo paint?

(1) Exactly 7 ounces of pigment are contained in a 12-ounce can of Luxo paint.

(2) Exactly 5 ounces of alcohol are contained in a 12-ounce can of Luxo paint.

- ◯ Statement (1) ALONE is sufficient, but statement (2) alone is not sufficient.
- ◯ Statement (2) ALONE is sufficient, but statement (1) alone is not sufficient.
- ◯ BOTH statements TOGETHER are sufficient, but NEITHER statement ALONE is sufficient.
- ◯ EACH statement ALONE is sufficient.
- ◯ Statements (1) and (2) TOGETHER are not sufficient.

3. A car drives along a straight road from Smithville to Laredo, going through Ferristown along the way. What is the total distance by car from Smithville to Laredo?

(1) The distance from Smithville to Ferristown is $\frac{3}{5}$ of the distance from Smithville to Laredo.

(2) The distance from Ferristown to Laredo is 12 miles.

- ◯ Statement (1) ALONE is sufficient, but statement (2) alone is not sufficient.
- ◯ Statement (2) ALONE is sufficient, but statement (1) alone is not sufficient.
- ◯ BOTH statements TOGETHER are sufficient, but NEITHER statement ALONE is sufficient.
- ◯ EACH statement ALONE is sufficient.
- ◯ Statements (1) and (2) TOGETHER are not sufficient.

Data Sufficiency and Geometry

For Problem Solving questions, the figures are generally drawn to scale. Chapter 13 discussed how you can ballpark by using the figure so long as it isn't marked "not drawn to scale."

For Data Sufficiency questions, however, you should be very careful when using the figure. The figures are drawn so that they represent the information in the question stem, but they need not accurately represent the information in the statements. So, you should base your conclusions about whether you have sufficient information on the statements rather than any figures provided with a Data Sufficiency question.

When Data Sufficiency questions are about geometry, however, you can often make very effective use of the Pieces of the Puzzle approach. The Pieces of the Puzzle approach works very well in situations in which you can use formulas and take stock of facts.

Here's an example of a medium question to illustrate:

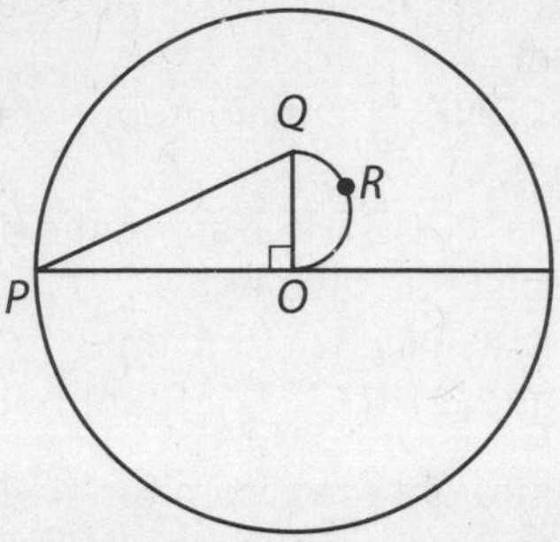

In the figure above, arc *QRO* is a semicircle. What is the area of the circle with center *O*?

(1) The area of triangle *PQO* is 30.

(2) The length of *QRO* is 2.5π.

Here's How to Crack It

Apply the Pieces of the Puzzle approach by asking, "What do I know?"

Pieces of the Puzzle
What do you know?

QRO is a semicircle. The triangle is a right triangle. The formulas for the area of a triangle, the circumference of a circle, and the area of a circle.

What do you need?

The length of *PO*, the radius of the circle.

For this problem, you actually know a lot. You know that arc *QRO* is half a circle and that its diameter is one side of a right triangle. Of course, you also know that triangle *PQO* is a right triangle, so the Pythagorean theorem applies.

Now, ask, "What do I need?" The question asks for the area of the circle. Since the formula for the area of a circle is $A = \pi r^2$, you'll need a way to find the radius of the circle. If the statements provide either the length of *PO* or a way to find that length, you'll have sufficient information.

You're ready to look at Statement (1). The formula for the area of a triangle is $A = \frac{base \times height}{2}$. You know the area but neither the base nor the height, so you have insufficient information. Write down BCE.

Next, look only at Statement (2). Now, it's time to remember that *QRO* is a semicircle. The statement gives you half of the circumference of a circle. You can use the circumference formula to find the diameter, *QO*. In this case, you actually have half the circumference, so use $2C = \pi d$ or $2(2.5\pi) = \pi d$ and $d = 5$. So, now you know the length of *QO*, but you still don't have the radius of the circle. (You may think that you recognize a 5:12:13 right triangle, but remember that you need two sides of the triangle to use the Pythagorean theorem.) Cross off B.

Finally, put the statements together. Now, you know both the area of the triangle and its height, so you can plug those values into the formula for the area of a triangle to get $-30 = \frac{1}{2}(b)(5)$. Can you use this formula to find *PO*? Yes. So, the answer to the problem is C.

Data Sufficiency and the Strange Powers of Powers

The Data Sufficiency question type is particularly well suited to testing your knowledge of the rules of equations and the strange powers of powers. Let's review this important information:

1. When working with equations, you generally need as many equations as there are variables in those equations.
   - A single equation with two variables cannot be solved,
   - but two distinct equations with the same two variables *can* be solved, using simultaneous equations, as you learned in Chapter 11.

   For example, $x = y + 1$ cannot be solved, but $x = y + 1$ and $2x = -y - 6$ can be added together, eliminating one variable so the other may be solved.

2. Just because there is only one variable doesn't mean that an equation has just one solution.
   - Generally, equations have as many solutions as the greatest exponent in the equation. So, an equation with a squared term will typically have two solutions.
   - Simple equations with a variable raised to an odd power may have only one solution.

   For example, if $x^2 = 4$, then x could equal either 2 or -2. If $x^3 = 8$, then x can only equal 2.

3. But sometimes, it's possible to get an answer even if there is only a single equation with two variables—IF the problem asks for an expression that contains both variables.

4. Sometimes you can also get an answer if there is only a single equation with two variables if both of those variables can only take on integer values.

Let's look at some problems that use these rules.

Mr. Jones spends $25 on movie tickets for a party of adults and children. How many children's tickets did he buy?

(1) Adult movie tickets cost $3 each and children's tickets cost $2 each.

(2) Mr. Jones buys a total of 11 tickets.

Here's How to Crack It

Start by asking, "What do I know?" In this case, you know that Mr. Jones spends $25 and that there are two variables—adult tickets and children's tickets.

Next, ask, "What do I need?" It's time to start thinking "two equations, two unknowns."

Now, evaluate Statement (1). From this statement, you get $3x + 2y = 25$. That's only one equation but two variables, so you do not have sufficient information. So, write down BCE.

Next, evaluate Statement (2), from which you can get the equation $x + y = 11$. Again, there's only one equation and two variables, so cross off B.

When the statements are combined, you have two distinct equations with two variables, which means that you can solve. So, the answer is C.

Here's a harder example. This example would be an upper-medium problem.

What is the value of $\frac{a}{b}$?

(1) $7a - 3b = 0$

(2) $b = 5$

- Statement (1) ALONE is sufficient, but statement (2) alone is not sufficient.
- Statement (2) ALONE is sufficient, but statement (1) alone is not sufficient.
- BOTH statements TOGETHER are sufficient, but NEITHER statement ALONE is sufficient.
- EACH statement ALONE is sufficient.
- Statements (1) and (2) TOGETHER are not sufficient.

Here's How to Crack It

You're not going to get much mileage out of the Pieces of the Puzzle approach for this question. All you really know is that there are two variables involved.

So, ignore Statement (2). Based on Statement (1) ALONE, can you answer this question? At first glance, you might think not—because there are two variables in one equation. But the question is not asking you to solve for a and for b, but for $\frac{a}{b}$. If you add $3b$ to both sides of the equation in Statement (1), you get $7a - 3b$. If you then divide both sides of the equation by b, you get $\frac{7a}{b}=\frac{3b}{b}$, which reduces to $\frac{7a}{b}=3$. By dividing both sides by 7, you get $\frac{a}{b}=\frac{3}{7}$, which answers the question. Statement (1) is sufficient, and you are down to AD. Looking at Statement (2) alone, of course, you can't answer the question, so the correct answer to the problem is choice A.

The problem we just solved made use of the third rule in our review. Notice that C was a trap answer for this problem. Sure, you could find the value of a and b by combining the statements. However, answer C states that you need to put the statements together *because* neither statement provides sufficient information by itself. So, you'll want to remember that it's possible to know the value of an expression without knowing the values of the variables that make up that expression.

Here's one more example. This one doesn't sound that bad, but it's actually a very difficult problem.

Mr. Jones spends \$76 on movie tickets for a group of adults and children. How many children's tickets did he purchase?

(1) Adult movie tickets cost \$11 each and children's movie tickets cost \$7 each.

(2) Mr. Jones bought two more adult tickets than children's tickets.

Here's How to Crack It

As always, start by asking, "What do I know?" In this case, Mr. Jones spends \$76 on movie tickets, and there are two variables. But, notice that there is actually one more thing that you know—movie tickets must be bought in integer quantities.

Next, ask, "What do I need?" You'll probably need two equations, but the fact that the variables can only take on integer values may change things.

Now, it's time to look at Statement (1), which gives you the equation $11x + 7y = 76$. Before dismissing this single equation with two variables as insufficient, remember that both x and y must be integers. Also, notice that the coefficients, 11 and 7, are large enough to limit the possibilities. Mr. Jones must buy fewer than 7 adult tickets. It's probably worthwhile to investigate how many of those integer values for x produce an integer value for y. As it happens, y is an integer only when $x = 5$. So, Mr. Jones bought 5 adult tickets and 3 children's tickets. So, write down AD.

Statement (2), however, does not provide sufficient information by itself. Remember that you don't even know how much the tickets cost based only on the second statement. So, the answer is A.

So, how was this problem different from the first problem in which Mr. Jones bought movie tickets? Why didn't we need to worry about the integer quantities on the first problem? Well, actually, we did. However, for the first problem, the first statement gave us the equation $3x + 2y = 25$. Had we taken some time to investigate this equation, we would have quickly discovered that there are several sets of integer solutions. For example, Mr. Jones could have bought 3 adult tickets and 8 children's tickets, or he could have bought 5 adult tickets and 5 children's tickets.

So, how do you know when to look for a single integer solution? Well, first make sure that the variables can only be integers! Since you can't buy half a movie ticket, that was part of the tip-off. Next, if there is going to be only one integer solution, it is likely that at least one of the coefficients will be a larger prime number like 11 or 17 or 29.

Finally, think about your current scoring level. A problem like that last one would show up only in one of the GMAT's most difficult question bins—because the test writers think so few people will get it right. You aren't likely to encounter this problem on your computer-adaptive section of the GMAT unless you are scoring in the mid to high 40s on your practice math tests.

DRILL 10 (Strange Powers of Powers)

The answers can be found in Part VI.

1. What is the value of x?

   (1) $x^2 = 4$

   (2) $x < 0$

   - Statement (1) ALONE is sufficient, but statement (2) alone is not sufficient.
   - Statement (2) ALONE is sufficient, but statement (1) alone is not sufficient.
   - BOTH statements TOGETHER are sufficient, but NEITHER statement ALONE is sufficient.
   - EACH statement ALONE is sufficient.
   - Statements (1) and (2) TOGETHER are not sufficient.

2. What is the value of xy?

   (1) $x^2 = 4$

   (2) $y = 0$

   - Statement (1) ALONE is sufficient, but statement (2) alone is not sufficient.
   - Statement (2) ALONE is sufficient, but statement (1) alone is not sufficient.
   - BOTH statements TOGETHER are sufficient, but NEITHER statement ALONE is sufficient.
   - EACH statement ALONE is sufficient.
   - Statements (1) and (2) TOGETHER are not sufficient.

Equation Tricks and Traps

Some equations are not distinct, such as when one equation can be multiplied to equal the other equation.

For example:

$x + y = 4$

$4x + 4y = 16$

These are not distinct equations. There is not enough data yet to solve for x or y.

3. What is the value of xy?

 (1) $x^2 = 4$

 (2) $y^2 = 9$

 ◯ Statement (1) ALONE is sufficient, but statement (2) alone
 is not sufficient.
 ◯ Statement (2) ALONE is sufficient, but statement (1) alone
 is not sufficient.
 ◯ BOTH statements TOGETHER are sufficient, but NEITHER
 statement ALONE is sufficient.
 ◯ EACH statement ALONE is sufficient.
 ◯ Statements (1) and (2) TOGETHER are not sufficient.

YES/NO DATA SUFFICIENCY

We covered the basics of Yes/No Data Sufficiency in Chapter 9.

First, let's do a quick review by looking at a problem.

_____◯_____

Is integer x prime?

 (1) $47 < x < 53$

 (2) $x > 0$

Here's How to Crack It

Notice that this question is phrased so that you would need to respond by saying "yes," "no," or "maybe" rather than by giving a numerical answer. That's why this is a yes/no question.

So, start by evaluating only Statement (1). There are 5 integers between 47 and 53—48, 49, 50, 51, and 52. Are any of these integers prime? No. But, notice that means that you can answer the question. Is x prime? No, it isn't. So, you have sufficient information. (Remember that a statement can be sufficient for a yes/no question if it allows you to answer the question in either the affirmative or the negative.) So, write down AD.

Now, look only at Statement (2). Based on Statement (2), you don't know whether x is prime. If x is 3, for example, the answer to the question is yes. However, if x is 4, the answer to the question is no. The best answer you could give to the question "Is x prime?" based on Statement (2) is "maybe." So, the answer to the problem is A.

Plugging In on Yes/No Questions

Because as many as half of the Data Sufficiency problems you'll see on the GMAT will be yes/no questions, it's a good idea to have a strategy for these questions. When yes/no questions involve variables, you can plug into the statement and use those numbers to see if you always get the same answer to the question.

In the problem we just looked at, we plugged into the second statement. Because we were able to find examples of numbers that satisfied the statement but that gave different answers to the question, we knew that Statement (2) wasn't sufficient.

Now, let's look at another example.

Is x an integer?

(1) $5x$ is a positive integer.

(2) $5x = 1$

Statements Must Be True
You can only plug in numbers that make the statement true. The answer to the QUESTION can be "yes" or "no," but the statements themselves must always be true. So, for example, if Statement (1) says "$5x$ is a positive integer," then you can't plug −2 in for x. It would make the statement UNTRUE.

Here's How to Crack It

As always, ignore Statement (2) and look only at Statement (1). Since this question is phrased as a yes/no question and there are variables involved, let's plug in.

When you plug in on a yes/no Data Sufficiency question, you start by picking a number that satisfies the statement. For example, we can start with a nice, simple number such as $x = 2$. Notice that we can use $x = 2$ because $5 \times 2 = 10$ and 10 is a positive integer.

Now that we've found a number that satisfies the first statement, it's time to use that number to answer the question. Be sure that you use the value that you picked for x, not the result of the statement. So, the question becomes "Is 2 a positive integer?" and the answer is, of course, yes. Careful! Don't write down AD yet!

All we've done is find one example of a number that satisfies the first statement and used that number to answer the question. Now that we have an answer of yes, we actually want to see if it's possible to get an answer of no to the question based on a number that satisfies the first statement.

What if we make $x = \frac{1}{5}$? We've satisfied the statement because $5 \times \frac{1}{5} = 1$ and 1 is a positive integer. However, now we need to use our number to get an answer to the question.

Is $\frac{1}{5}$ a positive integer? No.

So, some numbers that satisfy the first statement produce an answer of yes to the question, while other numbers that satisfy the statement produce an answer of no. Therefore, we don't have sufficient information to answer the question, "Is x an integer?" Write down BCE.

Now it's time to look at the second statement. In this case, we have an equation that we can solve to find that $x = \frac{1}{5}$. So, we ask, "Is $\frac{1}{5}$ an integer?" and give a definite answer of no.

The answer to the problem is B.

Plugging In is your most important strategy for handling yes/no data sufficiency questions.

To see how effective Plugging In can be, let's try it on a more difficult question.

Is $3^n > 2^k$?

(1) $k = n + 1$

(2) n is a positive integer.

Here's How to Crack It

This is a yes/no question involving variables, so Plugging In is a good idea.

Start by evaluating Statement (1) alone. Pick an easy number for n. If $n = 2$, then $k = 3$. The numbers satisfy the statement, so it's time to use them to answer the question. Is $3^2 > 2^3$? Yes.

Remember, however, that you can't properly evaluate the statement based on the results from only one set of numbers. Suppose we tried something a little weirder for n? If $n = -1$, then $k = 0$. Is $3^{-1} > 2^0$? No. (Remember that negative exponents are just another way of writing a reciprocal and that any nonzero number raised to 0 is 1.)

So, we don't actually know what the answer to the question is based only on Statement (1). It looks as though the answer depends on the numbers we choose. Write down BCE.

For Statement (2), we can also plug in. Notice that the statement doesn't tell us anything about k, however. So, we could say that $n = 2$ and $k = 1$ to get an answer of yes to the question. But, we could also say that $n = 2$ and $k = 4$ to get an answer of no. Cross off B.

When we combine the statements, we can still use $n = 2$ and $k = 3$, which, as we saw when we looked at Statement (1), gives us an answer of yes to the question. However, we could also use $n = 1$ and $k = 2$ to satisfy the combined statements. Is $3^1 > 2^2$? No. So, the answer to this problem is E.

Don't Do the Work in Your Head

To remember that you need to plug in at least twice for each statement, write down the numbers you plugged in and the answers you get to the questions on your scratch pad.

Yes or No Plugging In Checklist

- First, try plugging in a normal number for your variable. The number you pick must satisfy the statement itself. If it doesn't, plug in another number. The number will yield an answer to the question—either yes or no. But you're not done yet.
- Now, try plugging in a different number for your variable. This time, you might try one of the "weird" numbers, such as 0, 1, a negative number, or a fraction. If the number still answers the question the same way, then you can begin to suspect that the statement yields a consistent answer, and that you're down to AD.
- If you plug in a different number and get a different answer this time (a "yes" after getting a "no," or a "no" after getting a "yes"), then the statement does NOT definitively answer the question, and you're down to BCE.
- Now, repeat this checklist with Statement (2).

DRILL 11 (Yes or No)

The answers can be found in Part VI.

1. If x is a positive number, is $x < 1$?

   (1) $2x < 1$

   (2) $2x \leq 2$

   ◯ Statement (1) ALONE is sufficient, but statement (2) alone is not sufficient.
   ◯ Statement (2) ALONE is sufficient, but statement (1) alone is not sufficient.
   ◯ BOTH statements TOGETHER are sufficient, but NEITHER statement ALONE is sufficient.
   ◯ EACH statement ALONE is sufficient.
   ◯ Statements (1) and (2) TOGETHER are not sufficient.

2. Is x positive?

(1) $xy = 6$

(2) $x(y^2) = 12$

- Statement (1) ALONE is sufficient, but statement (2) alone is not sufficient.
- Statement (2) ALONE is sufficient, but statement (1) alone is not sufficient.
- BOTH statements TOGETHER are sufficient, but NEITHER statement ALONE is sufficient.
- EACH statement ALONE is sufficient.
- Statements (1) and (2) TOGETHER are not sufficient.

3. Are x and y integers?

(1) The product xy is an integer.

(2) $x + y$ is an integer.

- Statement (1) ALONE is sufficient, but statement (2) alone is not sufficient.
- Statement (2) ALONE is sufficient, but statement (1) alone is not sufficient.
- BOTH statements TOGETHER are sufficient, but NEITHER statement ALONE is sufficient.
- EACH statement ALONE is sufficient.
- Statements (1) and (2) TOGETHER are not sufficient.

More Ways to Plug In

As you have just seen, Plugging In can be a very helpful tool to evaluate whether the statements provide sufficient information to answer the question on yes/no Data Sufficiency question. Sometimes, however, Plugging In can also help you discover what the question is asking.

Often, test writers make a question harder by writing the question stem in a way that hides the concept being tested. After all, if you're having a hard time understanding the question, you'll almost certainly have a hard time answering the question. You should remember, however, that no matter how confusing the question stem appears when you first read it, GMAT questions really test only fairly straightforward math concepts. Plugging In can help you decipher the question stem.

Here's an example of how the test writers might ask a difficult question:

If l_1 and l_2 are distinct lines in the xy coordinate system such that the equation for l_1 is $y = ax + b$ and the equation for l_2 is $y = cx + d$, is $ac = a^2$?

(1) $d = b + 2$

(2) For each point (x, y) on l_1, there is a corresponding point $(x, y + k)$ on l_2 for some constant x.

Here's How to Crack It

One of the hardest things about this question is understanding the question stem. It's going to be impossible to evaluate the information in the statements before we understand what we're being asked.

Let's try applying the Pieces of the Puzzle approach by first asking, "What do we know?" We know there are two lines. And, since the question tells us that the lines are distinct, we know that they are different. We also sort of have the equations for each line, but we recognize that the equations we're given are really just the general equation for any line—$y = mx + b$.

At this point, it might be a good idea to take stock of what we know about lines. In the equation $y = mx + b$, m is the slope and b is the y-intercept. For our two lines in question, a and c represent the slopes and b and d represent the y-intercepts.

Okay, now we're getting somewhere. The question is asking us something about the slopes of the lines, since a and c represent the slopes. Now, let's plug in. If we let $a = 2$ and $b = 3$, then $(2)(3) \neq (2)(2)$. How could $ac = a^2$? That could only happen if $a = c$.

Now we've got it. If $a = c$, the slopes of the lines are equal. If the slopes of two lines are equal, the lines are parallel. This question is really just asking, "Is l_1 parallel to l_2?" If the test writers had asked the question this way, the difficulty of the question would have dropped.

Let's check out the statements. If we look only at Statement (1), all we know is that the y-intercept of l_2 is 2 more than the y-intercept of l_1. In that case, the slopes could be the same—producing an answer of yes to the question—or the slopes could be different—producing an answer of no. So, Statement (1) is insufficient. Write down BCE.

Now, let's look at Statement (2). Plugging In is a good way to evaluate this statement. Start by picking a value of k, which must be a constant. We'll let $k = 2$. Let's say that points (2,6) and (3,8) are on line l_1, which would mean that (2,8) and (3,10) are on l_2. Using those points, we can calculate that the slope of each line is 2. Since the slopes are the same, the lines are parallel. We have an answer of yes to the question.

Of course, when you plug in on yes/no data sufficiency, you shouldn't stop after plugging in just one set of numbers. This time, let $k = 3$. Let's also say that (2,8) and (3,11) are on l_1, which would mean that (2,11) and (3,14) are on l_2. Once again, we can calculate the slope of each line. In this case, both slopes turn out to be 3. Again, since the slopes are the same, the lines are parallel. (Don't be thrown by the fact that the slopes are different for each plug in. We're only trying to see if the slopes of the lines are the same each time we plug in.)

If you remain unconvinced, you could try Plugging In again, but you'll again find that the slopes of the lines are equal. In effect, the second statement tells us that for each point on l_1 there is a corresponding point on l_2 that is a distance of k units away. That can only happen if the lines are parallel. So, the answer is B.

If that question left you shaking your head, you're not alone. It's a very difficult question. Only a handful of test takers will wind up getting it right. In effect, the test writers pulled out every trick in their book to make this question difficult. Understanding the various ways that the GMAT test writers make questions difficult can help you improve your score dramatically.

POE PRINCIPLES FOR DATA SUFFICIENCY

Data Sufficiency questions that you find difficult and confusing are a distinct possibility when you take the GMAT, so you need to be prepared for them. After all, if the computer is doing its job properly—and you can pretty much count on that—it will keep feeding you progressively harder questions during the computer-adaptive section, in the hopes that it will find one that you don't know how to do.

In other words, almost every GMAT test taker hits a wall at some point. You've just gotten a string of questions right and suddenly there's a question on your screen that you find confusing. You need to answer it to move on to the next question, but you'd like to do better than a blind guess. In fact, if you narrow your available choices, you may just guess correctly, dodge the bullet, get the next couple of questions right, and wind up with a higher score than if you didn't have a plan for handling those tough, confusing questions. Good test takers always have a good guessing plan in hand.

Part of the key to using a guessing strategy effectively is to know your current GMAT math score. If your current score indicates that you are answering mostly easy questions (a score up to roughly 25), continue to concentrate on mastering the principles that we've already covered. As you master those principles, you'll start to see more questions on practice tests that will make use of the traps that we'll discuss in a minute. To make further improvements, you'll need to learn how to spot and avoid the test writers' favorite traps.

If your score is above 25, you're already seeing Data Sufficiency questions on your practice tests that contain the traps we're about to discuss. The first step to avoiding the traps is to learn to spot them. Learning to avoid the traps can be a very effective way to improve your GMAT score.

Work With What You Know

We've already been using Process of Elimination (POE) throughout this section. On Data Sufficiency questions, a little knowledge can go a long way. Suppose you saw the following Data Sufficiency question:

What is the area of square *ABCD*?

(1) The length of the side of square *ABCD* is 2.

(2) For square *EFGH*, which has sides that are 6 longer than those of square *ABCD*, the ratio of the perimeter to the area is the reciprocal of the corresponding ratio for square *ABCD*.

When we don't know something about a problem, our first impulse is to just skip the whole thing. Or to assume that there's no way to solve it. However, you can't skip questions on the GMAT, and you may not get your best score possible if you assume that everything that looks hard can't be solved.

Obviously, the second statement of this problem is wordy and confusing. You may not be sure what it says or whether it provides sufficient information to answer the question, but that doesn't mean you need to make a random guess.

Let's focus on what you DO know. To find the area of a square, you need to know the length of the side of the square—exactly what the first statement provides. Since the first statement is sufficient, your possible answers are A or D.

In other words, you have a fifty-fifty chance of getting the question right. And you get there even if you find the second statement confusing.

As long as you know *something* about a Data Sufficiency question, you can do some shrewd guessing. Take a look at this variation of the problem we've been discussing:

What is the area of square *ABCD*?

(1) The length of the side of square *ABCD* is greater than 1.

(2) For square *EFGH*, which has sides that are 6 longer than those of square *ABCD*, the ratio of the perimeter to the area is the reciprocal of the corresponding ratio for square *ABCD*.

You still know that you need the length of the side of the square to find its area. However, now the first statement does not provide that length. If the first statement is insufficient, your can narrow your choices down to B, C, or E.

This time, you have a 1 in 3 chance of getting the question right. As before, you didn't need to tackle the second statement to better your odds of getting the question right.

The Joe Bloggs Impulse and Data Sufficiency

Joe can help you avoid several types of traps on Data Sufficiency questions. The single most important thing to remember about Joe is that he tends to choose his answers very quickly. Any time that you are tempted to answer a Data Sufficiency question in only a few seconds, you may be about to fall for a Joe Bloggs answer. That's not to say that you aren't about to pick the correct answer. However, you should take a few more seconds just to make sure that you aren't missing anything.

There are several common traps that Joe falls for. Let's take a look at them.

Trap #1) Joe Thinks Answer E Means "I Don't Know"

Let's revisit that hard question from the More Ways to Plug In section to see how Joe might approach it.

If l_1 and l_2 are distinct lines in the *xy* coordinate system such that the equation for l_1 is $y = ax + b$ and the equation for l_2 is $y = cx + d$, is $ac = a^2$?

(1) $d = b + 2$

(2) For each point (x, y) on l_1, there is a corresponding point $(x, y + k)$ on l_2 for some constant x.

This question really confuses Joe. He has no idea what the question is asking. As a result, he has no idea how he's supposed to evaluate the information in the statements. But Joe doesn't want to admit that he doesn't know what to do. Joe's not alone in feeling that way—most people don't like to admit that they don't know how to solve a problem.

Joe tends to pick E on questions that he doesn't understand. That's because Joe thinks that answer E means "I don't know how to do this problem." Of course, answer E really means "I know exactly how to do the problem and that's how I know that the statements don't provide sufficient information."

If you want to pick E on a question that you find confusing, make sure that you can explain why you don't have enough information. Otherwise, you may be equating answer E with "I don't know how to do this problem."

Trap #2) Joe Thinks the Statements Are Missing Information

Sometimes Joe picks answer E because he's convinced that the statements need to provide more information. Of course, Joe arrived at his conclusion pretty quickly, so it's likely that he may have missed some way to use the information provided.

Consider this example:

What is the value of $r^2 + s$?

(1) $t - u = 8$

(2) $r^2t - su + st - r^2u = 24$

Here's How to Crack It

Joe's first impulse is to pick E on this question. He sees two variables in the question stem but 4 variables in the statements. He doesn't know what t and u have to do with finding the values of r^2 and s. With four variables, Joe thinks that he needs more equations to find the values of r and s so that he can answer the question. Joe is convinced that he's missing necessary information. So, he goes with E.

Joe's answer is not correct, however. He's fallen for the trap.

Statement (1) is obviously insufficient. There's no way to determine anything about r and s from information about t and u. So, write down BCE.

Now, let's take a good look at Statement (2). The equation provided does contain the two variables we're interested in. Let's try grouping the expressions differently:

$$r^2t - su + st - r^2u = 24$$

$$(r^2t + st) - (r^2u + su) = 24$$

$$t(r^2 + s) - u(r^2 + s) = 24$$

$$(r^2 + s)(t - u) = 24$$

So, Statement (2) is insufficient. Cross off B.

However, if the statements are combined, we can see that the value of $r^2 + s$ is 3. The correct answer is C.

To Joe's credit, he did try to think about what information he needed to solve this question. However, Joe didn't really try to evaluate the second statement. He just saw all those variables and concluded that he needed a lot more information and went for E.

How can you avoid Joe's mistake? Make sure that you take the time to fairly evaluate the information in each statement. You may need to do a little algebraic manipulation or plug in some numbers to see what's going on.

Trap #3) Joe Thinks That Confusing Statements Are Not Sufficient

As previously mentioned, Joe doesn't like to admit that he doesn't understand something. So, sometimes the test writers will match up a fairly easy statement with one that is difficult to understand. Let's see how Joe responds.

What is the volume of a certain rectangular solid?

(1) The solid can be cut into 16 cubes, each of which has a volume of 1.

(2) The base of the rectangular solid is a square, which has a diagonal length of $2\sqrt{2}$, and the ratio of the height of the solid to its length is 2:1.

Here's How to Crack It

Joe understands Statement (1), and he knows that it tells him that the volume of the rectangular solid is 16. He doesn't know what to make of the second statement, however. He's read it a couple of times and finds it pretty confusing. So, Joe—reluctant as he is to pick anything that he doesn't understand—quickly picks A for this question and moves on to the next problem.

Obviously, the first statement is sufficient, so write down AD. We'll need to take a better look at that second statement, however.

If the base of the rectangular solid is a square, the diagonal divides the square into two 45-45-90 triangles. For a 45-45-90 triangle, the hypotenuse is $s\sqrt{2}$. In this case, the side of the square turns out to be 2. So, for the rectangular solid, we now know both its length and width. The statement tells us that the ratio of the height of the solid to its length is 2:1, which means that the height of the solid is 4. So, we now know all three dimensions of the solid. Since the second statement was also sufficient, the correct answer is D.

How can you avoid Joe's mistake? This question had a very particular format. An easy to understand statement was matched with a statement that was much harder to understand. Joe didn't want to say that the statement he didn't understand was sufficient, so he went with A. Typically, however, when the test writers match an easy statement with a statement that is wordy and confusing, the harder statement is also sufficient. If the hard statement didn't work, the question would be an easy problem.

Obviously, you need to be careful in employing this guessing strategy. The easy statement needs to be so easy that very few people will evaluate it incorrectly. If that's the case, ask yourself why you're tempted to say that the more confusing statement is insufficient. Do you know what information it doesn't supply? Or are you saying, "I really am not sure what this statement says"? If your reason boils down to not fully understanding the statement, your better bet is to say that the confusing statement probably does supply sufficient information.

Trap #4) Joe Thinks Too Many Problems Are Easy

Joe thinks that many of the hard problems he sees are actually pretty easy. That's how he winds up with an average score. Every time he starts to do well and the computer feeds him harder questions, Joe gets a lot of those harder questions wrong.

What was the average (arithmetic mean) attendance for baseball games played at Memorial Stadium during the months of June and July?

(1) The average numbers of people attending baseball games at Memorial Stadium for June and July were 23,100 and 25,200, respectively.

(2) There were 20 baseball games played in June at the stadium and 22 games played in July.

Here's How to Crack It

Joe thinks this question is pretty easy. Statement (1) gives us the average attendance for June and the average attendance for July. Joe thinks he has all the information he needs because he thinks that he can get the average for the two months by averaging the two averages. (You—having completed our chapter on arithmetic—know better.) Joe looks at Statement (2) and doesn't see any attendance figures at all. He quickly picks answer choice A.

But, of course, Joe is wrong. The answer to this question is C. An average is the total sum of values divided by the *total* number of values. We need to know the number of games in each month in order to find out the total number of people attending.

How can you avoid Joe's mistake? First, slow down! Joe goes too fast and that causes him to make a lot of mistakes. Second, remember that Data Sufficiency questions most likely are not as easy as they seem.

Trap #5) Joe Makes Bad Assumptions

Data Sufficiency questions try to get test takers to make bad assumptions. The test writers know how most people think about math, and they often write the questions to take advantage of the assumptions that people routinely make.

For example, consider the following medium question:

What is the value of x?

(1) $x > 8$

(2) $x < 10$

Here's How to Crack It
Joe assumed that numbers are always integers and chose C. As always, Joe chooses his answer very quickly.

Of course, numbers are not always integers. Statement (1) is insufficient, so write down BCE. Statement (2) is also insufficient, so cross off B. Combining the statements only tells us that x is any number between 8 and 10—x could be 9, but it could also be 8.5. The answer is E.

How can you avoid Joe's mistake? Again, slow down! When a problem seems too easy, go back and reread the information. Are you, for example, assuming anything about the types of numbers that fit the statements?

Trap #6) Joe Remembers Statement (1) When Evaluating Statement (2)

Joe sometimes tries to use information that he learned in Statement (1) while evaluating Statement (2).

At a business dinner, people were offered coffee or tea. If all the diners had either coffee or tea, how many of the diners had tea?

(1) Of the 60 people at the dinner, 10% had tea.

(2) Fifty-four people had coffee.

Here's How to Crack It

Joe likes D for this question. He thinks the first statement is pretty easy. Joe has correctly determined that the first statement tells him that 6 people had tea. When Joe looks at the second statement, however, he thinks "54 people had coffee so that means that 6 had tea. Yeah, that works." So, he selects D.

There's only one small problem with Joe's reasoning—the second statement does not tell us the number of diners. So, based on the second statement, we have no idea how many people had tea. The correct answer is A.

How can you avoid Joe's mistake? *Always evaluate the statements independently.* Use the AD/BCE approach.

You should also be careful when the statements seem to agree. If the second statement had said "two people had coffee," it would have been easy to conclude that the second statement was not sufficient. By choosing a number that agreed with the information from the first statement, the test writers made it much easier to fall for the trap. So, remember that just because one statement seems to agree with the other, that doesn't mean that they say the same thing.

Putting It All Together

Joe's biggest problem always boils down to going too fast. While we have run through a list of common ways that Joe gets questions wrong, in all cases, Joe's first mistake was thinking that it's okay to answer Data Sufficiency questions quickly. Just because you don't need to compute an answer to a Data Sufficiency question, however, doesn't mean that you can race through the question.

Recognizing the types of errors that Joe makes on Data Sufficiency questions can sometimes help you guess your way to the right answer. That can be helpful if you find a question confusing or if you are running short on time close to the end of the section.

Let's look at one last example.

If the perimeter of right triangle ABC above is $3+3\sqrt{3}$, what is the area of the triangle?

(1) $AC \neq AB$

(2) angle $ABC = 30°$

Here's How to Crack It

The area of a triangle is $\frac{base \times height}{2}$. Joe looks at Statements (1) and (2) and sees neither the base nor the height of the triangle. So, he quickly concludes that the answer is E because he doesn't see any way to get the area of the triangle from the information in the statements.

Let's see how close we can get to the answer using Process of Elimination. Ignore Statement (2). The first statement only tells us that the base and height have different lengths. Even with the value for the perimeter, there's no way we're going to get the values of the base or height. So, cross off AD.

We're down to B, C, or E. We know that E, Joe's answer, is very unlikely, so let's cross that off. The remaining choices are B or C. Now, let's look at that second statement. From it, we can conclude that this triangle is a 30-60-90 triangle. If the triangle is 30-60-90, that would also mean that the base and the height of the triangle are different—exactly what the first statement told us. It doesn't sound like combining the statements adds anything that we don't know from just the second statement. So, C is unlikely. It seems very likely that the correct answer is B.

And the correct answer is B. If you were running out of time or not exactly sure how to solve this question, you can get to the right answer just by knowing how Joe would respond and employing a little deductive reasoning.

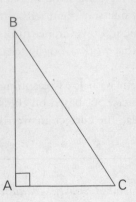

Here's How GMAC Wants You to Crack It

Statement (2) tells us that the right triangle is a 30-60-90 triangle. If you have already read our chapter on geometry, you know that the dimensions of a 30-60-90 triangle are always in the same proportion: x: $x\sqrt{3}:2x$. (Remember that the x in the proportion is the side opposite the 30-degree angle.) Since you can find the perimeter of any figure by adding up the sides, the perimeter of a 30-60-90 triangle is $3x + x\sqrt{3}$. And we can use what we know from the question stem to solve for the short side of the triangle:

$$3x + x\sqrt{3} = 3 + 3\sqrt{3}$$

Remember that you don't need to solve. You just need to know that you can solve, since this is a Data Sufficiency problem. (Just in case you're curious, $x = \sqrt{3}$). Once you've got the length of the base, you can find the height and then find the area of the triangle.

So, Statement (2) is sufficient and the answer is B.

That Was a Lot of Work

This question was very difficult and very time-consuming if you tried to solve it as the test writers wanted you to. Almost every test taker battles the clock on the GMAT. Knowing how to use Process of Elimination and what Joe would choose can help you make informed guesses when you are stuck on a problem and starting to run out of time.

Our guessing strategies are not infallible. However, if you must guess, it's better to make an informed guess than a random guess.

Need More Practice?
Math Workout for the New GMAT contains tons of drills with detailed answer explanations.

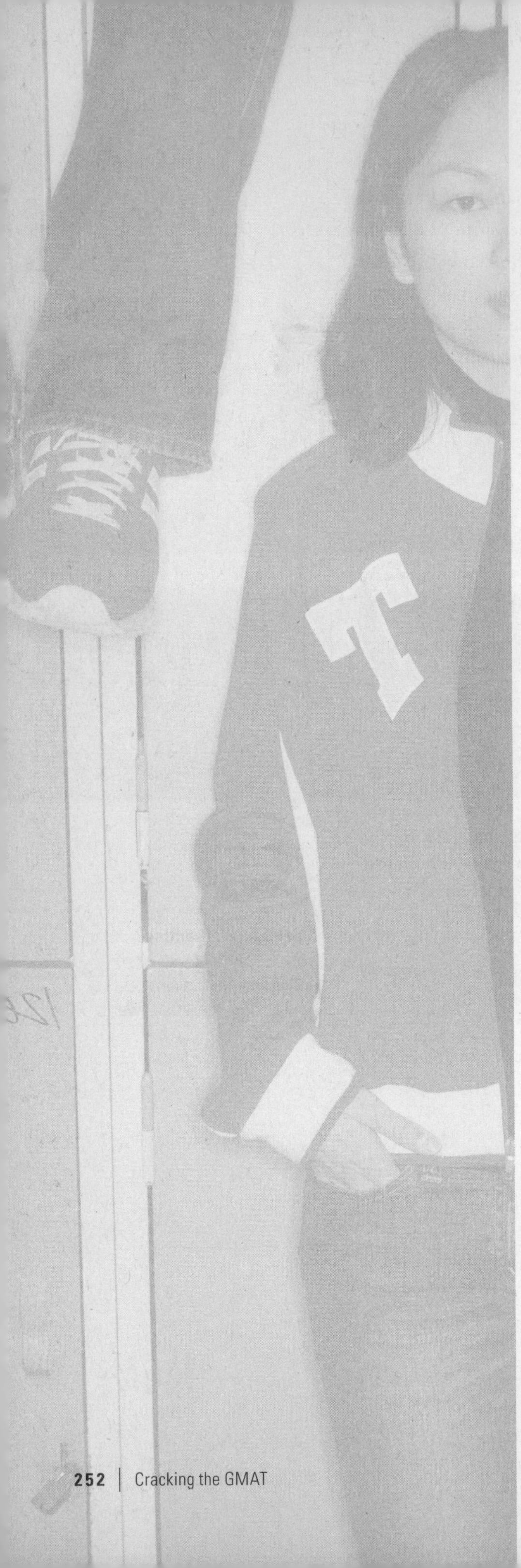

Summary

- The instructions for Data Sufficiency questions are very complicated. Memorize them now. Here is a pared-down checklist:
  - The first statement ALONE answers the question.
  - The second statement ALONE answers the question.
  - You need both statements TOGETHER to answer the question.
  - Both statements SEPARATELY answer the question.
  - Neither statement together or separately answers the question.
- To aid in scratch booklet eliminations, think of these answer choices as A, B, C, D, and E.
- Use POE to narrow down the field. If you know that Statement (1) is sufficient, you are already down to a fifty-fifty guess: A or D. If you know that Statement (1) is not sufficient, you are already down to a one-in-three guess: B, C, or E.
- If you are stuck on Statement (1), skip it and look at Statement (2). POE will be just as helpful.
- If Statement (2) is sufficient, you will be down to B or D. If Statement (2) is not sufficient, you will be down to A, C, or E.
- The math content of the Data Sufficiency questions is exactly the same as it is on the regular math questions.
- As you would in the regular math problems, look for the clues that tell you how to solve Data Sufficiency problems.
- When a problem asks a yes-or-no question, remember that the answer can be no.
- In yes-or-no questions, a statement is sufficient if it always gives us the *same* answer: always yes or always no. If the answer is sometimes yes and sometimes no, the statement is insufficient.

- In Data Sufficiency questions, look for opportunities to simplify or restate the question. If a question asks, "Did the foreman reject 40% of the 12,000 computers manufactured?" you could simplify that to ask, "Did the foreman reject 4,800 computers?"
- In intermediate and difficult Data Sufficiency problems, you must be on guard against careless assumptions.
- In *difficult* Data Sufficiency problems:
    - If Joe Bloggs *thinks* the problem is difficult, his favorite answers are choices E ("there isn't enough information"), or C ("this problem needs all the information it can get").
    - If Joe Bloggs thinks the problem is easy, he will be drawn to choices A, B, or D.
- On difficult Data Sufficiency problems, Joe's answer is always wrong.

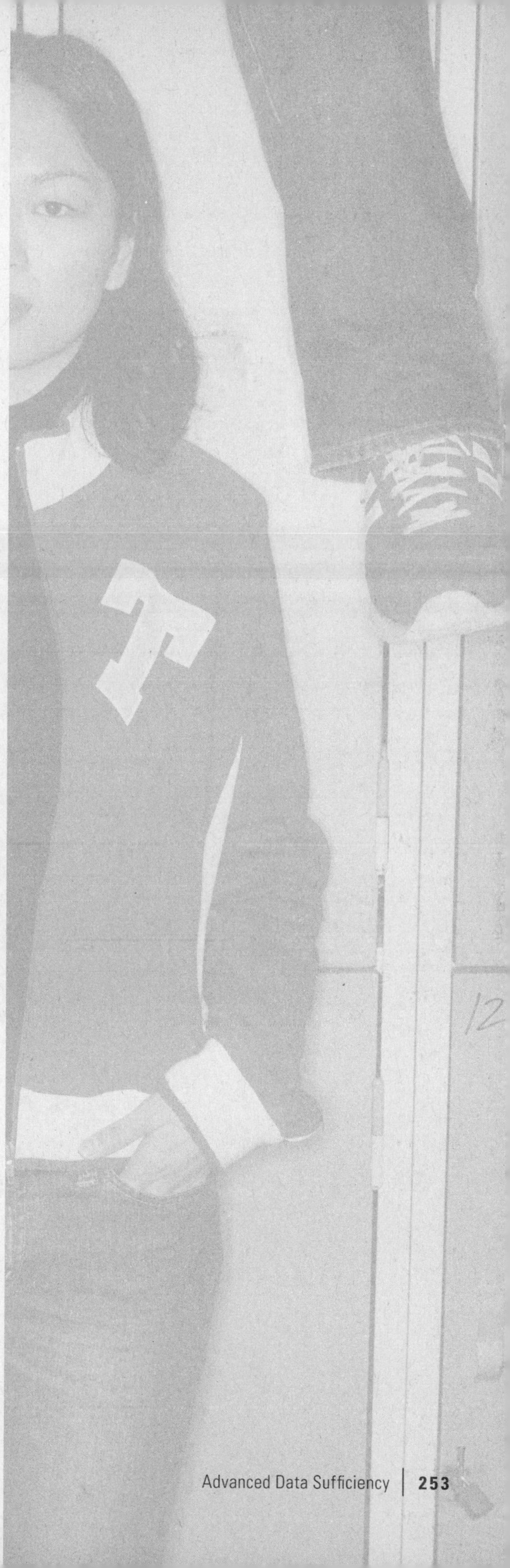

Part III
How to Crack the Verbal GMAT

Chapter 15
Sentence Correction

GMAT Sentence Correction involves finding a grammatical mistake (if there is one) in the original sentence and then finding the answer choice that fixes it. This chapter will begin with a review of grammar as it is tested on the GMAT and then move on to show you how to *recognize* the key errors the test writers like to test. Then you'll learn how to use the answer choices as clues to find the correct answer.

Sentence Corrections make up a little more than one-third of the 41 questions on the Verbal portion of the GMAT—approximately 16 questions that will be interspersed throughout the test. A Sentence Correction question consists of one long sentence that is either partially or completely underlined. You have to decide whether the sentence is grammatically correct as it's written, or if it is not, which of the answer choices best replaces the underlined portion.

B-School Lingo

finheads: finance heads (see *Sharks*)

four Ps: elements of marketing strategy—Price, Promotion, Place, Product

fume date: the date a company will run out of cash

Source: *The Best Business Schools*

Before we begin, take a moment to read the following instructions. They are a close approximation of the instructions you'll see on the real GMAT. Be sure you know and understand these instructions before you take the GMAT. If you learn them ahead of time, you won't have to waste valuable seconds reading them on the day of the test.

> Sentence Correction Directions: Each of the sentence correction questions presents a sentence, part or all of which is underlined. Beneath the sentence you will find five ways of phrasing the underlined part. The first of these repeats the original; the other four are different. Follow the requirements of standard written English to choose your answer, paying attention to grammar, word choice, and sentence construction. Select the answer that produces the most effective sentence; your answer should make the sentence clear, exact, and free of grammatical errors. It should also minimize awkwardness, ambiguity, and redundancy.

The Bad News

It's important to understand the fine print of the instructions you've just read. The test writers ask you to choose the "best" answer, by which they mean the answer that they think is right. The bad news is that some of the "correct" answer choices for the GMAT's Sentence Correction questions will probably not sound correct to you. The rules of English as interpreted by the GMAT are very different from the rules of English that govern what we read in newspapers, hear on television, or speak in our everyday lives.

How many times have you heard your boss, or a television anchorperson, or a president of the United States, make the following statement?

"Hopefully, we will know the answer to that question, tomorrow."

While you probably don't want to make a habit of correcting people's grammar, you should know that this sentence is not technically correct. According to the arbiters of grammar at GMAC, the president was supposed to say, "We hope that we will know the answer to that question tomorrow." It may be of some comfort to you that your boss, the television anchorperson, and a president of the United States would all get a question like this wrong if they took the GMAT.

GMAT English

GMAT English should be studied the same way you would approach any other foreign language. It has its own rules and its own internal logic. GMAT English has much in common with American English, but if you rely solely on your ear, you may get into trouble.

Confronted with a poorly constructed sentence, most of us could find *a* way to fix it. Most of the time we would probably break the sentence into two separate sentences (GMAT sentences are often too long and unwieldy). Unfortunately, on this test we are forced to find *the* way to fix the sentence; that is to say, GMAC's way to fix it.

To do well on Sentence Corrections, you will have to learn GMAT English.

The Good News

The people who write the GMAT try to stick to the basics. If they tested a controversial point of grammar, they might be proven wrong. They don't want to have to change their minds after a test is given and mail 20,000 letters explaining why they're changing the answer key (something that has happened from time to time in the past). The easiest way to avoid trouble is to test a handful of the rules of standard written English.

There are huge books devoted exclusively to the correct use of English. You could spend the next six weeks just studying grammar and never even scratch the surface of the subject. The good news is that this won't be necessary. Although there are hundreds of rules of standard written English that could be tested, the GMAT concentrates on only a few.

In other words, GMAT English is fairly easy to learn.

SENTENCE CORRECTION: CRACKING THE SYSTEM

In this chapter, we'll show you the most common types of errors that are tested in GMAT sentences and how to spot them. We'll show you how the test writers choose the four incorrect choices for each question, and we'll show you how to use Process of Elimination to make your life a lot easier.

To forestall the objections of the expert grammarians out there, let us say at the outset that this discussion is not designed to be an all-inclusive discussion of English grammar. You are reading this chapter to do well on Sentence Correction *as it appears on the GMAT.* Thus, if we seem to oversimplify a point or ignore an arcane exception to a rule, it is because we do not feel that any more detail is warranted. Remember, this isn't English; it's GMAT English.

Order of Difficulty

The Verbal section of the GMAT is computer-adaptive, meaning that the GMAT chooses questions for you from a large pool, based on your responses to previous questions. Theoretically, the computer knows which questions in its pool are easy and which are difficult. However, when it comes to Sentence Corrections, most of our students find that they can't tell the difference; "easy" questions often seem as poorly worded as "difficult" questions. You will discover that The Princeton Review techniques make the relative difficulty of Sentence Correction questions pretty meaningless.

Process of Elimination

Most people approach Sentence Correction questions the same way. They read the original sentence and then read the entire sentence again, substituting the first answer choice for the underlined part. Then they go back and do the same thing for the second, third, and fourth answer choices. This approach is both laborious and confusing. It's hard to keep five different versions of the same sentence straight, especially when all five of them are awkward.

The Princeton Review approach uses Process of Elimination to narrow down the choices before you have to start reading the answers carefully. Because there are relatively few types of errors that appear in Sentence Correction questions, we will focus on teaching you how to spot these errors. Once you've spotted the error in a sentence, you'll be able to go through the answer choices and eliminate any that also contain that error. Then you can decide among the remaining choices.

Write It Down

Effective use of POE on the GMAT always involves your scratch booklet and *always* involves thinking of the answer choices as A, B, C, D, and E, even though they are not labeled that way onscreen. As you eliminate answer choices, you should cross them off in your scratch booklet.

Basic Principles

Let's look at a Sentence Correction question that's written in a way that you will unfortunately never see on the real GMAT—with only the correct answer listed:

> Registered brokerage firms have been required to record details of all computerized program trades made in the past year so that government agencies <u>will be able to decide whether they should be banned</u>.
>
> ○
> ○
> ○
> ○
> ○ will be able to decide whether program trades should be banned

Piece of cake, right? It gets a little harder when they throw in the other four answer choices. Don't worry if you aren't sure why the last answer choice—what we call answer choice E—is better than the original sentence. We will cover how to spot this type of error (pronoun reference) a little later in the chapter. For now, it's enough to know that the "they" in the underlined portion of the sentence was ambiguous. It wasn't clear whether "they" referred to "registered brokerage firms," "details," or the "computerized program trades."

Don't bother saying it was perfectly obvious that "they" referred to the program trades. This is GMAT English, remember? It doesn't matter if you knew what the sentence meant. The sentence had to be clear to the GMAT test writer who wrote it.

Zen and the Art of Test Writing

Let's put ourselves in the place of the GMAT test writer who wrote this question. He has just finished his sentence and he has his correct answer, but he isn't finished yet. He still has to write four other answer choices. It's actually kind of difficult to come up with four answer choices that seem plausible but are wrong. If the test writer makes the incorrect choices too obviously wrong, Joe Bloggs might be able to pick the correct answer without having really understood the rule of grammar involved. If the test writer makes the incorrect answer choices too subtle, Joe won't find one that seems right to him, and therefore might guess at random. The test writer does not want Joe to guess at random. If Joe guesses at random, he might actually pick the right answer.

One Down, Four to Go

Coming up with the correct answer is easy for our test writer—after all, he wrote the question. He will probably spend much more time on the incorrect answer choices.

Answer Choice A

Composing the first wrong answer choice is also easy for our test writer; the first of the answer choices (what we call answer choice A) is always a repeat of the underlined part of the original sentence. Obviously, this is the choice to select if you think that the sentence is correct as it's written. Two down, three to go.

If You Can't Sell a Lemon, Repackage It

To see whether Joe has spotted the error in the sentence, the GMAT test writer will include the same error in at least one, and usually two, of the other answer choices. If Joe didn't like the error in the original sentence, maybe he'll like it better surrounded by different words. Look at the same sentence again, this time with two incorrect answer choices that include the error found in the original sentence:

> Registered brokerage firms have been required to record details of all computerized program trades made in the past year so that government agencies <u>will be able to decide whether they should be banned</u>.
>
> ◯ will be able to decide whether they should be banned
> ◯ should be able to decide whether they should be banned
> ◯ should be able to decide whether they can be banned
> ◯
> ◯ will be able to decide whether program trades should be banned

Joe Bloggs has no idea what point of grammar is tested in this question. He picks answers because they sound good. Our test writer hopes that one of these answer choices will sound better to Joe than the correct answer. Both choices change the sentence, but both also still contain the ambiguous word "they," so both are still wrong.

Almost Right

Our test writer has one more kind of trap to insert into a question. This time the trap isn't for Joe Bloggs; it's for the person who has spotted the error in the sentence but isn't in too big a hurry to make fine distinctions.

Usually one of the incorrect answer choices will actually fix the original error—*but will create some new error in the process.*

Spotting the original error is all well and good, but our test writer wants to make sure you really "deserve" to get this one right, so he includes an answer choice that's almost right. It will be a close variation of the "best" answer; it will correct the mistake in the original sentence, but it will be *wrong.*

Here's the same sentence with an answer choice that fixes the original mistake but creates a new one:

Registered brokerage firms have been required to record details of all computerized program trades made in the past year so that government agencies will be able to decide whether they should be banned.

○ will be able to decide whether they should be banned
○ should be able to decide whether they should be banned
○ should be able to decide whether they can be banned
○ will be able to decide whether program trades should be able to be banned
○ will be able to decide whether program trades should be banned

Answer choice D fixes the original problem; there is no longer an ambiguous "they" in the sentence. Our test writer is hoping that anyone who has spotted the original error will read just far enough to see that answer choice D fixes it, but not far enough to see that there is something else wrong. What's wrong? On the GMAT, only animate objects are "able" to do anything.

Three Down, Two to Go

Let's look at the entire problem, now that our test writer has finished it, and count our blessings.

Registered brokerage firms have been required to record details of all computerized program trades made in the past year so that government agencies will be able to decide whether they should be banned.

○ will be able to decide whether they should be banned
○ should be able to decide whether they should be banned
○ should be able to decide whether they can be banned
○ will be able to decide whether program trades should be able to be banned
○ will be able to decide whether program trades should be banned

Here's How to Crack It

By spotting what was wrong in the original sentence, we could have eliminated three of the five answer choices. Choice A merely repeats the original sentence word for word. Choices B and C contain the same error that was found in the original sentence.

We're down to choice D or E. Both fix the original error. What's the difference between them? Three words. If you don't see why one is correct and the other isn't, don't soul-search. Just click on one answer and move on. The correct answer is choice E.

Our Basic Approach

To use POE, you must be able to spot the errors in the original sentences. Fortunately, as we said before, GMAC leans heavily on only a few major types of errors. Just recognizing these errors should enable you to answer many of the Sentence Correction problems. There are two ways to do this.

Plan A

The first step in your Sentence Correction strategy should be to read the original sentence, looking for the very specific errors that the test writers like to test. As soon as you spot an error, you can eliminate any answer choices that repeat this error. Then, having gotten rid of several choices, you can actually read the remaining choices carefully to see which is best.

But what happens if you finish the sentence without spotting one of these errors? Unfortunately, you can't skip the question and come back to it later. So what do you do?

Plan B

If you don't spot the error as you read the original sentence, then the second step in your Sentence Correction strategy is to go straight to the answer choices to look for clues. Here are the answer choices to a real GMAT problem:

- ◯ gentleman of the eighteenth century protected their clothing while having their wig powdered by poking their head
- ◯ gentleman of the eighteenth century protected his clothing while having his wig powdered by poking his head
- ◯ gentleman of the eighteenth century protected their clothing while having their wigs powdered by poking their heads
- ◯ gentlemen of the eighteenth century protected his clothing while having his wig powdered by poking his head
- ◯ gentlemen of the eighteenth century protected their clothing while having his wig powdered by poking his head

Forget about the original sentence entirely for a moment (pretty easy, because we didn't give it to you). Just look at the first word of each of the choices. Does anything strike you?

The differences in the answer choices are excellent hints as to what kind of error you might be looking for in the original sentence. For example, in the answers above, the test writer is offering you a choice of the singular noun "gentleman" or the plural noun "gentlemen." A further fast scan of the answer choices reveals a choice of pronouns referring back to the nouns. What type of error might be involved if we're seeing singular and plural nouns, along with singular and plural pronouns? Aha—pronoun reference.

Even if the answer choices do not provide a clue, all is not lost. Remember how our GMAT test writer constructs wrong answer choices: The test writer likes to throw in one or more answer choices that fix the original error but create new errors in the process. You may not have been able to spot the original error, but you'll probably see the *new* errors in the bogus answer choices.

As you read the remaining answer choices, look for differences. Sometimes the realization that one answer choice is exactly the same as another with the exception of a couple of words will enable you to choose between them.

When you've eliminated everything you can, guess and move on.

The combination of Plan A and Plan B should allow you to get most of the Sentence Correction questions right—once you've learned one other important concept...

The Most Common Error Is *No* Error

While we are going to teach you to spot the eight most common errors used by the GMAT test writers, you should know that about one-fifth of the Sentence Correction sentences are fine just the way they are. If a sentence is correct as-is, the "best" answer is the first answer choice (what we call choice A), which repeats the original sentence. According to the law of averages, two or three of the Sentence Correction questions you will see on the GMAT will contain no error.

How do you tell when there is nothing wrong with a sentence?

You can tell that a sentence is correct by the *absence* of any of the other types of errors that we're going to show you how to spot. Try not to use your ear—at least not at first. As you're reading each sentence, you'll mark off a mental checklist of likely errors. If you come to the end of the list without having found a specific error, go to Plan B and look for differences in the answer choices. If you still haven't found an error in the original sentence, chances are very good that there isn't one.

We'll come back to answer choice A later in the chapter, after you've learned how to spot the major errors.

Before We Start, Some Basic Terminology

You won't be asked to name the parts of speech on the GMAT. However, an acquaintance with some of these terms is necessary to understand the techniques we're about to show you.

- A *noun* is a word that's used to name a person, place, thing, or idea.
- A *verb* is a word that expresses action.

Here is a very basic sentence:

Sue opened the box.

In this sentence, *Sue* and *box* are both nouns, and *opened* is a verb. *Sue* is considered the subject of this sentence because it is the person, place, or thing doing the verb. *Box* is considered the object of the sentence because it receives the action of the verb.

- An *adjective* is a word that modifies a noun.
- An *adverb* is a word that modifies a verb, adjective, or another adverb.
- A *preposition* is a word that notes the relation of a noun to an action or a thing.
- A *phrase* is a group of words acting as a single part of speech. A phrase is missing either a subject or a verb or both.
- A *prepositional phrase* is a group of words beginning with a preposition and containing its object and any of the object's modifiers.

Here's a more complicated version of the same sentence:

Sue quickly opened the big box of chocolates.

B-School Lingo
net net: end result
Source: *The Best Business Schools*

In this sentence, *quickly* is an adverb modifying the verb *opened*. *Big* is an adjective modifying the noun *box*. *Of* is a preposition because it shows a relation between *box* and *chocolates*. *Of chocolates* is a prepositional phrase that acts like an adjective by modifying *box*.

- A *pronoun* is a word that takes the place of a noun.
- A *clause* is a group of words that contains a subject and a verb.

Here's an even more complicated version of the same sentence:

Because she was famished, Sue quickly opened the big box of chocolates.

There are two clauses in this sentence. *Sue quickly opened the big box of chocolates* is considered an *independent clause* because it contains the main idea of the sentence and could stand by itself. *Because she was famished* is also a clause (it contains a subject and a verb), but it cannot stand by itself. This is known as a *dependent clause*. The word *she* is a pronoun referring to the noun *Sue*.

THE MAJOR ERRORS OF GMAT ENGLISH

1. Pronoun Errors

There are two main types of pronoun errors. The first is called *pronoun reference.* You saw an example of this in the sentence about program trading. Take a look at a simple example:

> *Samantha and Jane went shopping, but she couldn't find anything she liked.*

This type of mistake used to drive Harold Ross, the founding editor of *The New Yorker*, crazy. He was famous for scrawling *Who he*? in the margins of writers' manuscripts. It is supposed to be absolutely clear who is being referred to by a pronoun. In the example above, the pronoun *she* could refer to either Samantha or Jane. The pronoun is ambiguous and must be fixed. It can be fixed in three different ways:

> *Samantha and Jane went shopping, but Samantha couldn't find anything she liked.*

> *Samantha and Jane went shopping, but Jane couldn't find anything she liked.*

> *Samantha and Jane went shopping, but they couldn't find anything they liked.*

The second type of pronoun error is called *pronoun number* (singular or plural). Here is a simple example:

> *The average male moviegoer expects to see at least one scene of violence per film, and they are seldom disappointed.*

In this case, the pronoun *they* clearly refers to the average male moviegoer, so there is no ambiguity of reference. However, *the average male moviegoer* is singular. *They* cannot take the place of a singular noun. There is really only one way to fix this sentence.

> *The average male moviegoer expects to see at least one scene of violence per film, and he is seldom disappointed.*

The people who write the GMAT are very fond of both of these types of errors and routinely make use of them. By the way, as we mentioned earlier, you don't have to memorize any of the terminology we use. You simply have to recognize a GMAT English error when you see it.

Admissions Insight No. 7: The Interview

- Always accept an interview opportunity if it is offered.
- Be on time, and dress appropriately.
- Prepare ahead of time—literally practice your responses out loud.
- Put together several points from your essays, and find a way to make these points during the interview.
- If there are any suspicious holes in your resume, or embarrassing incidents in your past, find a way to bring them up yourself, and have a great explanation.
- When they ask—and they will—about your biggest setback, or your greatest challenge, be prepared to give them a positive spin on a challenging situation that you were able to overcome and learn from.

How Do You Spot a Pronoun Error?

That's easy. Look for pronouns.

A pronoun is a word that replaces a noun. Here's a list of common pronouns. (You don't need to memorize these—just be able to recognize them.)

Singular	Plural	Can Be Singular or Plural Depending on Context
I, me	we, us	some
he, him	they, them	none
she, her	both	ours
it	these	you
each	those	who
another		which
one		what
other		that
mine		
yours		
his, hers		
this		
either		
neither		
each		
everyone		
nobody		
no one		

Every single time you spot a pronoun, you should immediately ask yourself the following two questions:

- Is it completely clear, not just to me but to a pedantic GMAT test writer, who or what the pronoun is referring to?
- Does the pronoun agree in number with the noun it is referring to?

Let's look at an example.

While Brussels has smashed all Western European tourism revenue records this year, they still lag well behind in exports.

- ◯ this year, they still lag well behind in exports
- ◯ in the past year, they still lag well behind in exports
- ◯ in the past year, it lags still well behind in exports
- ◯ this year, they lag still well behind in exports
- ◯ this year, it still lags well behind in exports

Here's How to Crack It

Plan A: As you read the sentence for the first time, look to see if there is a pronoun. There is: *they*. Let's make sure the pronoun is used correctly. Who is the *they* supposed to refer to? *Brussels*. Is *Brussels* plural? No, it's the name of a city.

Now that you've spotted the problem, go through the answer choices. Any answer choice with the pronoun *they* in it has to be wrong. You can cross off answer choices A, B, and D. You're down to answer choices C and E.

Both of the remaining answer choices solve the original problem. Read them carefully. If you aren't sure, take a guess. If you said answer choice E, you were right. The adverb *still* in answer choice C should go in front of the verb.

Plan B: Now, what if Plan A lets you down, and you don't spot the error as you read the sentence in the first place? There is always Plan B. Go straight to the answer choices and ask yourself how they are different. Obviously, they differ in several ways—but one huge difference is that some answer choices use the pronoun they, while others use the pronoun it. This is a clue that will remind you to check pronoun reference and number.

Admissions Insight No. 8: Full Time or Part Time

Most students find that the experience of attending business school full time is generally more fulfilling than attending part time, because it allows students to build relationships and devote themselves completely to their studies. However, there can be compelling reasons to go part time: for example, if you simply can't afford to take two years off without pay, or if your company is willing to pay all or part of your tuition costs.

2. Misplaced Modifiers

Misplaced modifiers come in several forms, but the test writers' favorite looks like this:

Coming out of the department store, John's wallet was stolen.

When a sentence begins with a *participial phrase* (just a fancy term for a phrase that starts with a verb ending in *-ing*), that phrase is supposed to modify the noun or pronoun immediately following it.

Was the *wallet* coming out of the department store? No.

There are two ways to fix this sentence. First, we could change the second half of the sentence so that the noun or pronoun that comes after the participial phrase is actually what the phrase is supposed to refer to:

Coming out of the department store, John was robbed of his wallet.

Or, we could change the first half of the sentence into an adverbial clause (which contains its own subject) so that it is no longer necessary for the first half of the sentence to modify the noun that follows it:

As John was coming out of the department store, his wallet was stolen.

Other forms of misplaced modifiers include:

A. participial phrases preceded by a preposition:
On leaving the department store, John's wallet was stolen.

(**Correct:** *On leaving the department store, John was robbed of his wallet.*)

B. adjectives:
Frail and weak, the heavy wagon could not be budged by the old horse.

(**Correct:** *Frail and weak, the old horse could not budge the heavy wagon.*)

C. adjectival phrases:
An organization long devoted to the cause of justice, the mayor awarded a medal to the American Civil Liberties Union.

(**Correct:** *An organization long devoted to the cause of justice, the American Civil Liberties Union was awarded a medal by the mayor.*)

In each of these examples, the modifying phrase modified the wrong noun or pronoun.

How Do You Spot a Misplaced Modifier?

That's easy. Whenever a sentence begins with a modifying phrase that's followed by a comma, the noun or pronoun right after the comma should be what the phrase is referring to. Every single time you see a sentence that begins with a modifying phrase, check to make sure that it modifies the right noun or pronoun. If it doesn't, you've spotted the error in the sentence.

The correct answer choice will either change the noun that follows the modifying phrase (the preferred method) or change the phrase itself into an adverbial clause so that it no longer needs to modify the noun.

Let's look at two examples:

Written in 1961, Joseph Heller scored a literary hit with his comedic first novel, *Catch-22*.

- Written in 1961, Joseph Heller scored a literary hit with his comedic first novel, *Catch-22*.
- Written in 1961, Joseph Heller scored a literary hit with *Catch-22*, his comedic first novel.
- Written in 1961, *Catch-22,* the comedic first novel by Joseph Heller, was a literary hit.
- *Catch-22,* which was written in 1961 by Joseph Heller, scored a literary hit with his comedic first novel.
- *Catch-22,* the comedic first novel, scored a literary hit for Joseph Heller by its being written in 1961.

Here's How to Crack It

Plan A: As you read the sentence for the first time, go through your checklist. Is there a pronoun error in the sentence? No. Does the sentence begin with a modifying phrase? Yes. Now we're getting somewhere. Let's check to see if the modifying phrase actually modifies what it is *supposed to.* Does it? No. "Joseph Heller" is not what was written in 1961. This is a misplaced modifier.

Now that you've spotted the error, look through the other answer choices and eliminate any that contain the same error. Choice B contains the same error. Get rid of it. You're down to choices C, D, and E.

Now, there are really only two ways to fix this kind of error, as you know. Do any of the answer choices change the noun that follows the modifying phrase? Yes, answer choice C. This is probably the right answer. Read through the other two choices just to make sure there's nothing better. Choices D and E contain awkward constructions. Choice C is the "best" answer.

Plan B: If you don't spot the error as you read the sentence for the first time, you have a second chance to spot it by looking for differences in the answer choices. Several contain a participial phrase followed by the noun the phrase is supposed to modify. But in one of those choices, the noun following the phrase is different. Hmmm. Could this sentence be a case of a misplaced modifier?

Although not quite as liquid an investment as a money-market account, financial experts recommend a certificate of deposit for its high yield.

- ◯ Although not quite as liquid an investment as
- ◯ Although it is not quite as liquid an investment as
- ◯ While not being quite as liquid an investment as
- ◯ While it is not quite as liquid as an investment
- ◯ Although not quite liquid an investment as

Here's How to Crack It

Plan A: Go through your checklist. Is there a pronoun in this sentence? Yes, the third to last word of the sentence is a pronoun, but it clearly refers back to the certificate of deposit. False alarm. Does the sentence begin with a modifying phrase? Yes. Now we're getting warmer. Check to see whether the modifying phrase modifies what it's supposed to modify. Does *although not quite as liquid an investment...* refer to financial experts? No. This is a misplaced modifier.

The clearest way to fix this sentence would be to change the noun that follows the modifying phrase:

> *Although not quite as liquid an investment as a money-market account, a* certificate of deposit *is recommended by financial experts for its high yield.*

Q: What is a tip-off to a misplaced modifier?
Turn the page for the answer.

However, you can't fix *this* sentence that way for the very good reason that only the first phrase of the sentence was underlined. This time, you'll have to find a way to fix the modifying phrase itself. Look for an answer choice that changes the modifying phrase into an adverbial clause with its own subject and verb.

Choices A, C, and E do not have subjects and therefore can be eliminated immediately. Choices B and D each have a subject—in both cases, the word *it* turns the modifying phrase into an adverbial clause. However, choice D contains a new error: The word *as* has been moved, leaving *money-market* stranded in the middle of the sentence with no function. While it may sound atrocious, choice B is the "best" answer.

Plan B: Again, if you didn't spot the error as you read the original sentence, the answer choices were there to provide you with a clue. Of the five answer choices, two turned the beginning phrase into a clause by means of the pronoun it. By noticing this, you might be reminded to check for a misplaced modifier.

A close relative of a misplaced modifier is a *dangling modifier*. You can spot the two errors in the same way. Here's a simple example:

> *Before designing a park, the public must be considered.*

Again, this sentence starts with a modifying phrase followed by a comma. The noun following the comma is what the modifying phrase is supposed to modify. Does it? No! *The public* didn't design the park. So who did? A dangling modifier differs from a misplaced modifier in that a dangling modifier doesn't just modify the wrong word—it doesn't modify any word.

> **Be Careful Though!**
> While modifying *phrases* need to refer to the word they are modifying, modifying *clauses* (which have a subject and a verb) are a different story: "Before an architect designs a park, the public must be considered" is perfectly correct.

To fix this sentence, we would have to insert whoever is designing the park into the sentence:

> *Before designing a park,* the architect *must consider the public.*

3. Parallel Construction

There are two kinds of GMAT sentences that test parallel construction. The first is a sentence that contains a list or has a series of actions set off from one another by commas. Here's an example:

> *Among the reasons cited for the city councilwoman's decision not to run for reelection were the high cost of a campaign, the lack of support from her party, and desiring to spend more time with her family.*

When a main verb controls several phrases that follow it, each of those phrases has to be set up in the same way. In the sentence above, three reasons were listed. The three reasons *were* (main verb):

> the high cost of a campaign,
> the lack of support from her party,
> and
> desiring to spend more time with her family.

The construction of each of the three reasons is supposed to be parallel. The first two items on the list are phrases that are essentially functioning as nouns: the high *cost* (of a campaign); the *lack* (of support from her party). However, the third item on the list seems more like a verb than a noun. How could we change the word *desiring* to a noun? If you said, "the desire," you were absolutely correct. It should read:

> the high cost of a campaign,
> the lack of support from her party,
> and
> *the desire* to spend more time with her family.

The second kind of GMAT sentence that tests parallel construction is a sentence that's divided into two parts. Here's an example:

> *To say that the song patterns of the common robin are less complex than those of the indigo bunting is doing a great disservice to both birds.*

If the first half of a sentence is constructed in a particular way, the second half must be constructed in the same way. The first half of this sentence begins, "To…"; therefore; the second half has to begin the same way:

> *To say that the song patterns of the common robin are less complex than those of the indigo bunting is* to do *a great disservice to both birds.*

How Do You Spot Parallel Construction?

A: A modifying phrase followed by a comma. To correct it, make sure that what comes after the comma is modified by what comes before it.

That's easy. Every time you read a Sentence Correction problem, look to see if you can find a series of actions, a list of several things, or a sentence that is divided into two parts.

Here's an example:

In a recent survey, the Gallup poll discovered that the average American speaks 1.3 languages, buys a new car every 5.2 years, <u>drinks 14 gallons of alcoholic beverages every year, and forgot to pay at least one bill per quarter</u>.

- ◯ drinks 14 gallons of alcoholic beverages every year, and forgot to pay at least one bill per quarter
- ◯ drinks 14 gallons of alcoholic beverages every year, and forgets to pay at least one bill per quarter
- ◯ can drink 14 gallons of alcoholic beverages every quarter and forgot to pay at least one bill per quarter
- ◯ drinks 14 gallons of alcoholic beverages every year, and forgets at least to pay one bill per quarter
- ◯ drank 14 gallons of alcoholic beverages every year, and forgets to pay at least one bill per quarter

Here's How to Crack It

Plan A: As you read the sentence for the first time, run through your checklist: Is there a pronoun? No. Does the sentence begin with a modifying phrase? Yes, but the word after the phrase is what is supposed to be modified, so this is not a misplaced modifier. Is there a series or list of three things or a series of actions? Yes. Let's see if all the actions are parallel. The average American…

> speaks (1.3 languages)
> buys (a new car…)
> drinks (14 gallons…)
> and
> forgot (to pay…)

The first three verbs are all in the present tense, but the fourth one is in the past tense. The problem in this sentence is a lack of parallel construction.

Now that you know what the error is, go through the answer choices. Any choice that contains the word *forgot* is wrong. We can eliminate choices A and C. Choice E, even though it fixes the parallel construction of the fourth verb, changes the construction of the third verb. Eliminate it.

Choices B and D have perfect parallel construction. If you aren't sure which one is correct, guess and move on. If you picked choice B, you were right. In choice D, the adjectival phrase *at least* had to be in front of *one bill.*

Plan B: The error on which this question hinges is easy to spot if you use Plan B. Clearly, what is at issue is the verb that begins the underlined portion of the sentence. Why would the test writers change around the form of this verb? Aha! They do it in order to create a parallel construction problem.

4. Parallel Comparison

Another form of parallel construction error that appears on the GMAT is what we call faulty comparison sentences. Here's a simple example:

> *The people in my office are smarter than other offices.*

Taken literally, this sentence compares *the people in my office* with *other offices*. Therefore, it's an example of faulty comparison—it compares two dissimilar things (in this case, *people* and *offices*). To fix this sentence, we need to make the comparison clear or parallel. There are two ways to do this:

> *The people in my office are smarter than* the people *in other offices.*
>
> or
>
> *The people in my office are smarter than* those *in other offices.*

We hope that you recognized *those* as a pronoun that takes the place of *the people*. The correct answer to a parallel comparison question on the GMAT almost invariably involves the use of a pronoun (*that* or *those*) rather than a repetition of the noun.

Parallel comparison problems also come up when you compare two actions:

> *Synthetic oils burn less efficiently than natural oils.*

In this case, what is compared is not the two types of oil, but how well each type of oil *burns*. You could fix this by changing the sentence to read,

> *Synthetic oils burn less efficiently than natural oils* burn.

However, the GMAT test writers would rather that you fix it by replacing the second verb (in this case, *burn*) with a replacement verb (*do* or *does*.) Here is how GMAC would like to see this sentence rewritten:

> *Synthetic oils burn less efficiently than* do *natural oils.*

How Do You Spot Parallel Comparison?

Look for sentences that make comparisons. These sentences often include words such as *than*, *as*, *similar to*, and *like*. When you find one of these comparison words, check to see whether the two things compared are really comparable.

Q: What is an indication of a parallel comparison error?
Turn the page for the answer.

Let's look at an example:

Doctors sometimes have difficulty diagnosing viral pneumonia because the early symptoms of this potentially deadly illness <u>are often quite similar to the common cold</u>.

- ◯ are often quite similar to the common cold
- ◯ often resemble that of the common cold
- ◯ are often quite similar to those of the common cold
- ◯ are often quite similar to the common cold's symptom
- ◯ quite often are, like the common cold, similar

Here's How to Crack It

Plan A: Go through your checklist: Do you see any suspicious pronouns, misplaced modifiers, or unparallel constructions? Good. There aren't any. Do you see any comparison words? Yes, the sentence uses "are" and "similar to." Let's see exactly what is being compared. The symptoms of one illness are being compared directly to…another illness. Aha! This is a parallel comparison error. To make this sentence correct, we need to compare the "symptoms" of one illness to the "symptoms" of the other, and the way GMAC would prefer that we do it is by using a replacement pronoun.

If we look at the answer choices, we can eliminate choices A and E because neither makes any attempt to compare symptoms to symptoms. Choice B looks promising because it uses the replacement pronoun "that"; however, "symptoms" is plural and therefore can't be replaced by the singular "that." Choice D seems promising because it looks like it's trying to compare symptoms to symptoms—but if you look more closely, you'll notice that the last word of choice D is "symptom," which is singular. The correct answer is choice C.

Plan B: There are often clues to parallel comparison questions in the answer choices as well. Just as you should be on the lookout for words like similar to in the sentences themselves, you can also often spot faulty comparison problems by looking for replacement nouns such as that of and those of, or replacement verbs such as than do and than does in the answer choices.

A: A comparison! Check that the two things being compared are really comparable.

5. Tense

On the GMAT, tense problems are often just a matter of parallel construction. In general, if a sentence starts out in one tense, it should probably stay there. Let's look at an example:

> *When he was younger, he walked three miles every day and has lifted weights, too.*

The clause *when he was younger* puts the entire sentence firmly in the past. Thus, the two verbs that follow should be in the past tense as well. You may not have known the technical term for *has lifted* (the present perfect tense), but you probably noticed that it was inconsistent with *walked* (the simple past tense). The sentence should read:

> *When he was younger, he walked three miles every day and* lifted *weights, too.*

Here are the tenses that come up on the GMAT:

Tense	**Example**
present	He *walks* three miles a day.
simple past	When he was younger, he *walked* three miles a day.
present perfect	He *has walked* three miles a day for the last several years.
past perfect	He *had walked* three miles a day until he bought his motorcycle.
future	He *will walk* three miles a day, starting tomorrow.

It isn't important that you know the names of these tenses as long as you understand how they're used. As we said before, a sentence that begins in one tense should generally stay in that tense. For example, a sentence that begins in the present perfect (which describes an action that has happened in the past, but is potentially going on in the present as well) should stay in the present perfect.

> *He has walked three miles a day for the last several years and has never complained.*

One exception to this rule is a sentence that contains the past perfect (in which one action in the past happened before another action in the past). By definition, any action set in the past perfect must have another action that comes after it, set in the simple past.

He had ridden his motorcycle for two hours when it ran out of gas.

The only other exceptions to this rule come up when one action in a sentence clearly precedes another.

The dinosaurs are extinct now, but they were once present on the earth in large numbers.

In this case, the sentence clearly refers to two different time periods: *now*, which requires the present tense, and a period long ago, which requires the past tense.

How Do You Spot Tense Errors?

By now, you probably have a pretty good sense of what to do. Using Plan A, look for changes in verb tense in the sentence. Or, using Plan B, look for changes in verb tense in the answer choices. If the answer choices give you several versions of a particular verb themselves, then you should be looking to see which one is correct. Here's an example:

A doctor at the Amsterdam Clinic maintains that if children eat a diet high in vitamins and took vitamin supplements, they will be less likely to catch the common cold.

- took vitamin supplements, they will be less likely to catch
- took vitamin supplements, they are less likely to catch
- take vitamin supplements, they were less likely of catching
- take vitamin supplements, they will be less likely of catching
- take vitamin supplements, they are less likely to catch

Here's How to Crack It

Plan A: As you read the sentence, go through your checklist. There is one pronoun (*they*) in the sentence, but in this case it clearly refers only to the children. Is there a modifying phrase? No. Is there a list of things or a series of actions? Not really. Are the verb tenses inconsistent? Hmm. Now we're getting somewhere. The first verb, "maintains," is in the present tense. So is the verb "eat." But the third verb, "took," which is supposed to be a parallel action with "eat," is in the past tense.

Look at the dependent clause that is partially underlined.

...that if children eat *a diet high in vitamins and* took *vitamin supplements...*

B-School Lingo
OOC: out of cash

opportunity cost: the cost of pursuing an opportunity, e.g., b-school tuition and the forfeiture of two years' income

Obviously, the two verbs are inconsistent with each other, and because only one of them is underlined, that's the one that must be wrong. The correct sentence must have a *take* in it, so we can eliminate choices A and B. Choice C puts the rest of the sentence in the past tense, so scratch C. Choice D puts the rest of the sentence in the future tense. This *might* be acceptable, but the choice also uses the incorrect idiomatic expression *likely of catching.* We'll talk more about idioms in a moment. The correct answer to this question is E, which keeps the entire sentence in the present tense.

Plan B: If you don't spot the error as you read the original sentence, look at the answer choices. Aha! Choices A and B offer us *took,* while D and E offer us *take.* One of these two alternatives must be right. Why would the test writers be offering us this choice of present- and past-tense verbs? Clearly, this is a tense question.

6. Subject-Verb Agreement Errors

A verb is supposed to agree with its subject. Let's look at an example:

The number of arrests of drunken drivers are increasing every year.

GMAT test writers like to separate the subject of a sentence from its verb with several prepositional phrases, so that by the time you get to the verb you've forgotten whether the subject was singular or plural.

On Objects and Subjects

The object of a preposition can never be the subject of a sentence. "Of arrests" is a prepositional phrase modifying "number," with arrests being the object of the preposition "of." Any word following a preposition cannot be the subject of the sentence.

The subject of the sentence above is *number,* which is singular. The phrase *of arrests of drunken drivers* modifies the subject. The verb of this sentence is *are,* which is plural. If we set off the prepositional phrase with parentheses, this is what the sentence looks like:

The number (of arrests of drunken drivers) are…

To fix this sentence we need to make the verb agree with the subject.

The number (of arrests of drunken drivers) is *increasing every year.*

Singular or Plural?
"The number of…" is singular.
"A number of…" is plural.

How to Spot Subject-Verb Agreement Errors

Cover up the prepositional phrases between the subject and the verb of each clause of the sentence so you can see whether there is an agreement problem. You should also be on the lookout for nouns that sound plural but are in fact singular.

Nouns That Sound Plural (But Aren't)

- The Netherlands (the name of any city, state, or country)
- Tom or John (any two singular nouns connected by *or*)
- the family
- the audience
- politics
- measles
- the number
- the amount

You are already on the lookout for pronouns because they're first on your checklist. Sometimes pronouns can be the subject of a sentence, in which case the verb has to agree with the pronoun. There are some pronouns that people tend to think are plural when they are in fact singular:

Q: A parallel construction error can be recognized by what giveaways?
Turn the page for the answer.

Pronouns That Sound Plural (But Aren't)

everyone	no one	anyone	none
everybody	nobody	anybody	each
everything	nothing	anything	

Let's look at an example of a subject-verb error as it might appear on the GMAT:

Many political insiders now believe that the dissension in Congress over health issues <u>decrease the likelihood for significant action being</u> taken this year to combat the rising costs of healthcare.

- ◯ decrease the likelihood for significant action being
- ◯ decrease the likelihood that significant action will be
- ◯ decrease the likelihood of significant action to be
- ◯ decreases the likelihood for significant action being
- ◯ decreases the likelihood that significant action will be

Here's How to Crack It

Plan A: As you read the sentence for the first time, run through your mental checklist. Is there a pronoun, a modifying phrase, a list of several things, a series of parallel actions, or a change in tense? Not this time. Let's check for subject-verb agreement. The subject of the independent clause is "insiders" and the correct verb, "believe," follows almost immediately, so there's no problem in the main clause.

However, let's look at the dependent clause that follows: "that the dissension in Congress over health issues decrease the likelihood…"

In this clause, the subject is "dissension," not "health issues." Remember to imagine that there are parentheses around any prepositional phrases, as if the clause looked like this:

> …the dissension (in Congress over health issues) decrease…

Is this correct? No, the singular "dissension" needs the singular verb "decreases." Looking at the answers, we can immediately eliminate choices A, B, and C. Now let's examine choices D and E. Both fix the subject-verb error, but choice D uses the unidiomatic expression "likelihood for," and it also uses "being" instead of "will be." The correct answer is choice E.

A: A list or a series of actions set off by commas. Every item in the list or series should take the same form.

Plan B: If you don't spot the error as you read the sentence the first time, it takes only a second to look at the answer choices and see that one big difference in the answer choices is the form of the verb "decrease," which means this is a subject-verb issue.

7. Idiom

GMAC likes to test certain idiomatic expressions. Here's an easy example:

> *There is little doubt that large corporations are indebted for the small companies that broke new ground in laser optics.*

It is incorrect to say you are indebted *for* someone.

> *There is little doubt that large corporations are indebted* to *the small companies that broke new ground in laser optics.*

Idiomatic errors are difficult to spot because there is no one problem to look for. In fact, there are really no rules. Each idiom has its own particular usage. There is no real reason an idiomatic expression is correct. It is simply a matter of custom.

However, you haven't been speaking English for the past 20 years for nothing. The main similarity between GMAT English and American English is that they both use the same idiomatic expressions.

You probably already know them.

How Do You Spot Idiomatic Errors?

If you've gone through the first six items on your checklist—pronouns, misplaced modifiers, parallel construction, faulty comparison, tense, and subject-verb agreement—and still haven't found an error, try pulling any idiomatic expressions out of the sentence so that you can see whether they're correct.

Then make up your own sentence using the suspect idiom:

I am indebted for my parents for offering to help pay for graduate school.

Does that sound right? Of course not. I am indebted *to* my parents. Usually, if you take the expression out of the long and awkward sentence and use it in an everyday sentence, the error (if there is one) will be obvious. Here's what an idiom question might look like on the GMAT:

The administration of a small daily dose of aspirin has not only been shown to lower the risk of heart attack, <u>and it has also been shown to help</u> relieve the suffering of arthritis.

- ◯ and it has also been shown to help
- ◯ and it has also been shown helpful to
- ◯ but it has also been shown to help
- ◯ but it has been shown helpful in addition for
- ◯ in addition it has also been shown helping

Here's How to Crack It

Plan A: As always, run through your checklist. Is there a pronoun in the sentence? Yes, but if you check the answer choices, you'll discover that the same pronoun appears in each one. Obviously, pronoun error is *not* what is tested this time. Is there a modifying phrase? No. So much for misplaced modifiers. Is there a list of things or a series of actions? No. To be sure that there really is no parallel construction problem, we should look at the two halves of the sentence as well. The first half, "…has been shown," matches the second half, "…has also been shown," and both are in the same tense, so there is no problem with either parallel construction or tense. There are no comparison words either, so we don't have to worry about faulty comparison. Could there be something wrong with an idiomatic expression in the original sentence? Let's try a sentence of our own.

Not only is he nasty…

Q: What is the rule when looking for tense errors?
Turn the page for the answer.

How would you finish this sentence? If you said something like "…but he is also disgusting," you would be absolutely correct. In GMAT English, "not only…" is always followed somewhere in the same sentence by "but also…." Let's look at the answer choices to see which can be eliminated. A, B, and E all use some other conjunction instead of "but," which means that the only possible answers are C and D. Choice D uses "in addition" instead of "also." This *might* not be fatal, but then keep reading after the underlining: "helpful in addition for relieve the suffering of arthritis." If the word "for" seems to stick out, it is because we need to form the infinitive case of "relieve" by using "to." Thus, the correct answer is C.

Plan B: If you didn't spot the idiomatic error in the sentence itself, the first word of each of the answer choices gives you a clue. Does the sentence need an "and," a "but," or an "in addition"? In this case, you need to follow the "not only" in the portion of the sentence that isn't underlined with "but also". The only answer that does that is C.

The Idioms Most Commonly Tested on the GMAT

There are, of course, thousands of idiomatic expressions that could be tested on the GMAT. But here are a handful that seem to come up all the time.

not only…but also…
not so much…as…
defined as
regard as
neither…nor…
modeled after
based on
a result of
to result in
a debate over
a dispute over
a responsibility to
responsible for
different from
a consequence of
so…as to be…
so (adjective) that
depicted as
define as
as great as
as good as, or better than
credited with
according to
agree with
appear to
because of
choose from
conclude that
contribute to
depend on
due to
in order to
instead of
rather than
subject to
worry about
think of…as
see…as
target…as
prohibit from
distinguish between…and…
distinguish…from…
attributed to

THE MINOR ERRORS OF GMAT ENGLISH

The seven errors you've just learned to spot will enable you to answer most of the Sentence Correction problems that come up on the GMAT. However, there is one more error that shows up often enough that you will probably want to be looking out for it.

8. Quantity Words

GMAC likes to see if you know how to indicate quantity. Here's an example:

> *On the flight to Los Angeles, Nancy had to choose among two dinner entrees.*

If there were more than two items being compared, then "among" would be correct. However, if there are only two choices available, the correct quantity word would be "between."

> *On the flight to Los Angeles, Nancy had to choose* between *two dinner entrees.*

Below are the comparison quantity words that come up on the GMAT most frequently:

If two items	If more than two items
between	among
more	most
better	best
less	least

Another type of quantity word that shows up on the GMAT from time to time involves things that can be counted as opposed to things that can't. For example, if you were standing in line at a buffet, and you didn't want as big a serving of soup as the person in front of you received, which of the following would be correct?

> *Could I have* fewer *soup, please?*
>
> or
>
> *Could I have* less *soup, please?*

If an item can't be counted, the correct adjective would be "less." However, if we were talking about french fries (which can be counted), the correct adjective would be "fewer."

A: Keep the same tense throughout the sentence.

Countable items	Uncountable items
fewer	less
number	amount, quantity
many	much

How Do You Spot Quantity Word Errors?

That's easy. Look for quantity words. Whenever you see a "between," check to see if there are only two items discussed in the sentence. (If there are more, you'll need an "among.") Whenever you see an "amount," make sure that whatever is discussed cannot be counted. (If the sentence is talking about the "amount" of people, then you'll need to change it to "number.")

Here's what a "between–among" quantity word error might look like on the GMAT:

Of the many decisions facing the energy commission as it meets to decide on new directions for the next several decades, the question of the future of nuclear energy <u>is for certain the more perplexing</u>.

- ○ is for certain the more perplexing
- ○ is certainly the most perplexing
- ○ it seems certain, is the most perplexed
- ○ is certainly the more perplexing
- ○ it seems certain, is perplexing the most

Admissions Insight No. 9: Taking the GMAT
Limiting your GMAT attempts to two is best, but don't take the test more than once if you don't expect a good increase. Three tries are okay if there were unusual circumstances or if you really need another shot at it. If you take it more than three times, the admissions committee will think you have an unhealthy obsession.
Source: *The Best Business Schools*

Here's How to Crack It

Plan A: If your checklist includes quantity words, the word "more" will set off red flags as you read the sentence. If there were two decisions facing the energy commission, then "the more perplexing" would be correct. However, the sentence says there are "many" decisions. Therefore the sentence must read, "the most perplexing."

This allows us to eliminate choices A and D immediately. Choice C gives the impression that it is the *question* that is perplexed. Eliminate it. Choice E incorrectly positions "the most" after the word it is supposed to modify. The correct answer is choice B.

Plan B: If you don't notice the quantity word in the question itself, you'll probably notice the series of different quantity words ("more" and "most") in the answer choices.

One Last Example

The foresight that was evident in the court's selection of an independent trustee to oversee the provisions of the agreement will probably go unremarked by the press.

- that was evident in the court's selection of an independent trustee
- that was evident by the court's selection of an independent trustee
- evidenced with the court's selection of an independent trustee
- evidenced of the court's selection of an independent trustee
- that was evident of the court's selection of an independent trustee

Here's How to Crack It

Plan A: As you read the sentence, go through your checklist. Is there a pronoun? No. Does the sentence begin with a modifying phrase? No. Is there a list of several things or a series of actions? No. Is there a tense error? No. Is there a subject-verb problem? No. Is there a comparison word such as "similar" or "than"? No. Are there any quantity words to check? No. Do any expressions in the sentence seem suspicious? No.

We have checked off all of the items on our list. Maybe nothing is wrong with this sentence. The "best" answer to this question is choice A.

Plan B: In cases like this in which there is nothing wrong, you want to be careful not to go off on a wild goose chase. The idea behind Plan B is to look for clues that will lead you to spot one of the major errors that the test writers like to test. If all you're doing is trying out each of the answers in turn to see which one sounds better, you aren't really using Plan B. If you can't spot one of the major errors in the sentence or in the answer choices, you have to start considering that the sentence might be correct as written.

If You're Really Gung Ho

You can expand your checklist to include as many types of errors as you like. Obviously, the more types of errors you can identify, the better prepared you'll be to take the test. But you should bear in mind that while there are other types of errors that we haven't discussed, these errors don't come up very often on the GMAT. Some of the errors to consider: redundant words, misuse of the subjunctive mood, and the use of the passive voice when the active voice is possible. If you're seriously gunning to get every Sentence Correction question correct, you should dig out your old grammar book from high school and study it carefully. You should also do as many of the real GMAT Sentence Correction questions in *The Official Guide for GMAT Review* as you can; pay special attention to the idiomatic expressions that come up in these sections, because these are sometimes repeated.

Summary

- GMAT English is different from American English, and you have to learn the rules of GMAT English to do well on the test.
- Fortunately, Sentence Correction questions test only a handful of rules. Once you learn them, you will be able to score quite well on this type of question.
- There are two Princeton Review techniques that together will help you to ace Sentence Correction: Plan A, in which you look for specific errors as you read the sentence, and Plan B, in which you treat differences among the answer choices as clues that will help you spot the error.
- Make a checklist of errors to look for when you read a Sentence Correction question. The most common are:
    - **Pronouns:** If a sentence contains a pronoun, check to see whether it clearly refers to the noun it is replacing; also check to see whether the pronoun agrees in number with the noun to which it refers.
    - **Misplaced modifiers:** If the sentence begins with a modifying phrase, check to make sure that the noun it modifies comes directly after the modifying phrase.
    - **Parallel construction:** If a sentence contains a list of things, or actions, or is broken up into two halves, check to make sure the parts of the sentence are parallel.
    - **Parallel comparison:** When a sentence makes a comparison, check to see whether the two things compared are really comparable.
    - **Tense:** If the answer choices contain different verb tenses, make sure that the tense of the verb or verbs in the original sentence is correct. For the most part, verb tense should be consistent throughout a sentence.

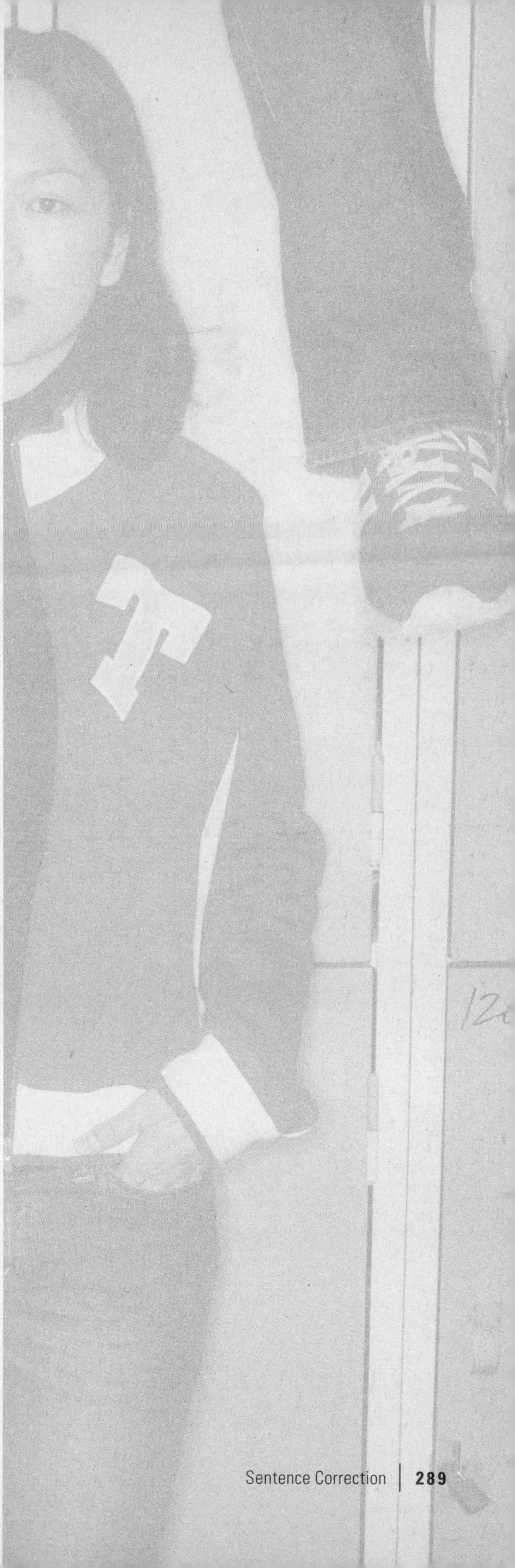

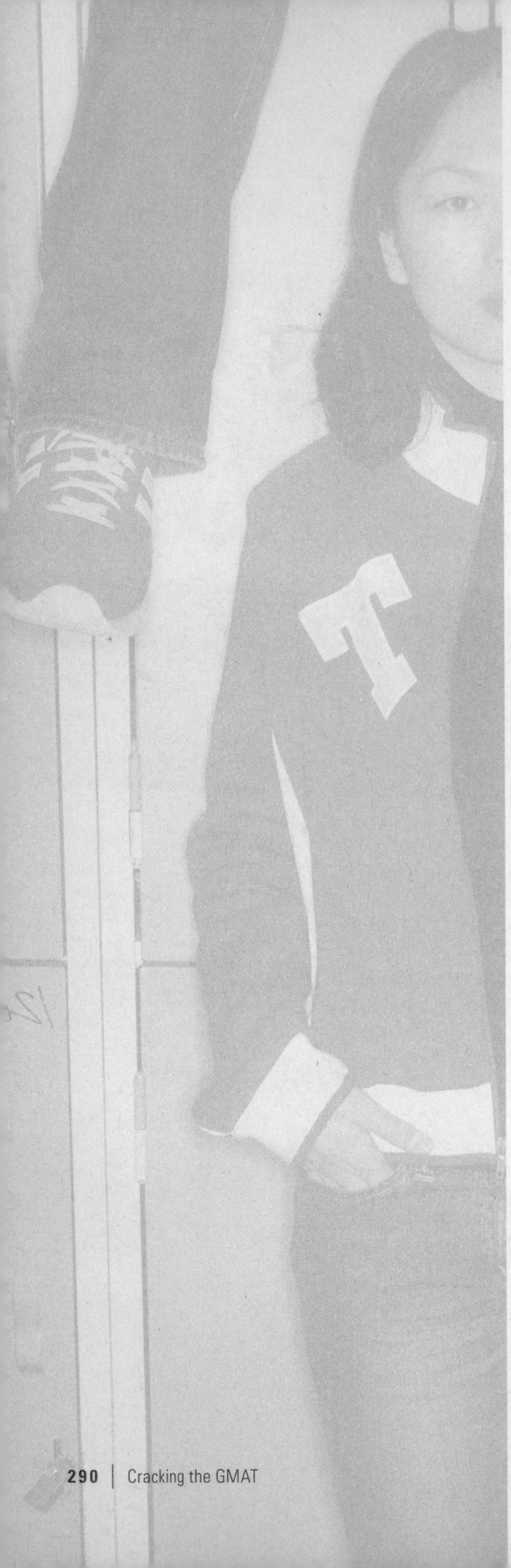

    - **Subject-verb agreement:** GMAT test writers sometimes put extraneous prepositional phrases between the subject and the verb. Cover up or ignore these phrases so that you can see whether the subject and the verb of each clause in the sentence agree with each other.
    - **Idiom:** If a sentence contains an idiomatic expression that seems wrong to you, try taking the expression out of the sentence and creating a sentence of your own with the suspect expression.
    - **Quantity words:** Whenever you see a quantity word (countable vs. uncountable; two vs. three or more), check to see if it is used correctly.

- If you've spotted the error, go through the answer choices and eliminate any that contain the same error. Then look at the remaining answer choices and find the one that fixes the sentence.

- If you can't find the error, look to the answer choices for clues. Then consider the possibility that there might not be an error.

- About one-fifth of the sentences are correct as they are. When a sentence is correct, the answer is choice A, which simply repeats the sentence word for word.

- Once you've gained confidence in your ability to spot the major errors, you should expand your checklist to include other types of errors.

Chapter 16 Reading Comprehension

Each GMAT Reading Comprehension passage contains a host of information—most of which is never tested by the three or four questions you will be asked. In this chapter, you'll learn how to read passages for what is actually important and how to go back for the specific facts to quickly answer individual questions.

Reading Comprehension questions make up roughly one-third of the 41 questions on the Verbal section of the GMAT—approximately 14 questions. Unlike the other questions on the test, Reading Comprehension questions come in clumps of three or four, and are based on reading passages that range from 200 to 350 words in length. Most test takers report seeing four reading passages in all.

Before we begin, take a moment to read the following instructions, which are a close approximation of the instructions you will find on the real GMAT.

> Reading Comprehension Directions: Each of the reading comprehension questions is based on the content of a passage. After reading the passage, answer all questions pertaining to it on the basis of what is stated or implied in the passage. For each question, select the best answer of the choices given.

Be sure you know and understand these instructions before you take the GMAT. If you learn them ahead of time, you won't have to waste valuable seconds reading them on the day you take the test.

GMAT READING COMPREHENSION: CRACKING THE SYSTEM

It's important to know the instructions for Reading Comprehension questions on the GMAT, but it's much more important to understand what these instructions mean; they don't tell you everything you need to know about GMAT Reading Comprehension questions. The rest of this chapter will teach you what you do need to know.

Our techniques will enable you to:

1. Read quickly in a way that will allow you to understand the main idea of the passage.
2. Eliminate answer choices that could not possibly be correct.
3. Take advantage of outside knowledge.
4. Take advantage of inside information (about the way the test writers think).
5. Find answers in some cases *without reading the passage.*

Basic Passage Types

There are only three types of passages on the GMAT:

1. **The social science passage:** This usually concerns a social or historical issue. For example, you might see a passage about world food shortages or the history of a civil rights movement.
2. **The science passage:** This might describe a scientific phenomenon, such as gravitation or plate tectonics.
3. **The business passage:** This usually discusses a business-related topic. For example, you might see a passage about the privatization of state-owned industries or the causes of inflation.

The subject matter for one of the passages on each test may concern a minority group. There are certain useful techniques that can be used on this passage. We'll tell you more about that later in the chapter.

Order of Difficulty

The level of difficulty of the passages you see will depend on how you are doing on the exam, but unlike all the other verbal questions on the GMAT, the three to four Reading Comprehension questions based on each passage are *not* arranged in order of difficulty. You will see the same questions based on this passage, regardless of how you answer them. The test writers found it too hard to create lots of different questions based on such brief passages.

Sentence Correction Review

Q: How do you find quantity word mistakes?

Turn the page for the answer.

What You Will See on Your Screen

The reading passage appears on the left side of the screen. The questions appear one at a time on the right side of the screen, so you can always refer back to the passage. You can't see the next question until you answer the one before, and as always, you can't go back to a previous question once you've moved on.

Sentence Correction Review
A: Look for quantity words and know whether the noun they modify is countable or not.

When you are working on a Reading Comprehension question, your screen will look a lot like this:

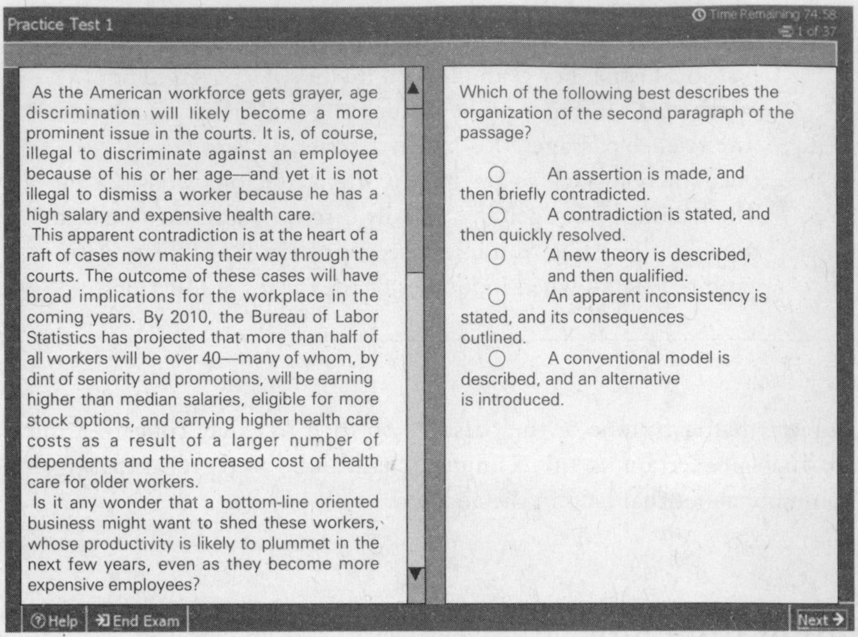

The reading passages come in two lengths—the shorter passages usually fit completely on the computer screen, but the longer passages will require you to use the scroll bar to read them entirely.

Is This Like Normal Reading?

GMAT reading has nothing to do with normal reading. For one thing, no one in her right mind would ever read one of these passages of her own free will. They are almost always boring.

Is This Like Business Reading?

GMAT reading has even less to do with business reading. If your boss asked you to analyze a quarterly report and make a presentation of all the points it raised, you would go home and spend hours going over it. You would look for important information, anticipate questions, and memorize statistics. In short, business reading is a careful, painstaking process. Reading on the GMAT is different.

How to Succeed on the GMAT

If you try to read GMAT passages the way you read quarterly reports, you'll never have time for the questions. Worse, you'll have spent a lot of time absorbing information that you don't need to know.

Sentence Correction Review

Q: How do you spot an idiom error?

Turn the page for the answer.

Reading Comprehension Questions Cover Only a Tiny Fraction of the Material in the Passage

Each reading passage is followed by three or four questions. You probably assume that to answer these questions correctly you need to know all of the information in the passage, but that's not true. The questions cover only a small portion of the passage. We're going to teach you how to identify the important parts and ignore most of the rest. The less time you spend reading the passage, the more time you'll have for earning points.

There are two types of questions in Reading Comprehension and neither requires you to memorize specific information:

1. **General questions:** To answer these, you need to have an understanding of the main idea and, perhaps, the *structure* of the passage.
2. **Specific questions:** Because you'll be asked about only a few specific pieces of information, it's silly to try to remember all of the specific information contained in a passage. It makes much more sense to have a vague idea of where specific information is located in the passage. That way you'll know where to look for it if you need it.

GMAT READING: THE PRINCETON REVIEW METHOD

Think of a GMAT reading passage as a house. The main idea of the passage is like the overall plan of the house; the main idea of each paragraph is like the plan of each room. Reading the passage is like walking quickly through the house. You don't want to waste time memorizing every detail of every room; you want to develop a general sense of the layout of the house.

Later, when you're asked what was sitting on the table beside the chair in the master bedroom, you won't know the answer off the top of your head, but you will know exactly where to look for it. And you'll be able to answer more questions in less time than someone who has tried to memorize every detail.

STEP ONE: READ FOR THE MAIN IDEA

Take a look at the first paragraph of a sample GMAT passage:

> Biologists have long known that some types of electromagnetic radiation such as X rays and gamma rays can be dangerous to human beings. Operating at a frequency of 10^{18} through 10^{22} MHz, these rays, which are well above the visible light spectrum, were first detected in the early years of the twentieth century.

Here's How to Crack It

You should always read the first sentence of a paragraph carefully because it is often the key to understanding the entire paragraph. The first sentence of the paragraph you just read is no exception: It tells you that the paragraph is about two types of radiation and their danger to humans. When you've identified the main idea, it's a good idea to jot down a couple of key words to encapsulate it.

Once you know what the paragraph is about, it isn't necessary to pay a lot of attention to the other sentences in the paragraph. For example, you probably noticed that while the second sentence included some specific facts, it added nothing to our understanding of the main point of the paragraph. Later, if GMAC asks you a specific question about this radiation, you can go back and find the answer; it will still be there.

Taking Notes

As you make your fast read, you'll probably want to write a one- or two-word summary of each paragraph in your scratch booklet. This is partly to make yourself articulate what the main idea of each paragraph is, but it is also to help you remember them. Have you ever had the experience of reading an entire passage, getting to the end, and then saying, "I have no idea what I just read"?

Most GMAT passages inspire exactly that thought.

Think of This as *Variable* Speed Reading

Until you know what the main idea of a paragraph is, you want to read very carefully. However, as soon as you've got a handle on what's going on, you can speed up. Let your eyes glaze over when you get to the small details. Until GMAC asks you about them, who cares?

The goal is to spend no more than a minute or two "reading" the entire passage. Impossible? Sure, if you're going to insist on reading the way you normally do. Just remember that you don't get any points for reading the passages; when you take the real GMAT the proctor will *not* be walking around the test room awarding extra points for great reading technique. You get points for *answering questions.*

Sentence Correction Review

A: Become familiar with the list of idioms most commonly tested on the GMAT on page 284.

Try reading the second paragraph in the way we've suggested above:

> However, until now, no one has ever suggested that microwave radiation might also be harmful. In preliminary laboratory results, Cleary and Milham have found elevated growth rates in cancer cells exposed to low doses of microwaves. Cleary exposed cancer cells to levels of radiation that are commonly found in microwave ovens and found that the abnormal cells grew 30 percent faster than did unexposed cells. Milham's study focused on ham radio operators who are commonly exposed to levels of radiation slightly higher than those emitted by cellular telephones. He discovered elevated levels of myeloid leukemia.

Here's How to Crack It

Reading the first sentence carefully, we realize that this paragraph is going off on a tangent thought. In fact, the passage is *not* going to be about the dangers of X rays or gamma rays; it is going to be about the possible dangers of microwaves. Now that we have the main idea, we can afford to skim or skip over the rest of the paragraph. If the test writers ask us later about Cleary or Milham, we'll know where to find them, but until then, we can let this part of the passage pass in a blur.

Now try reading the last paragraph of the passage:

> The methodology of Cleary and Milham has been questioned by other scientists in the field. However, no one seriously disputes that their preliminary findings must be taken seriously or that new studies should be set up to try to duplicate their results. Although federal guidelines for how much electromagnetic energy can be allowed to enter the work and home environment have been made more stringent since they were first implemented in 1982, the recent studies pose troubling questions about the safety of microwaves.

Here's How to Crack It

The first word of the second sentence ("however") lets us know that the author was going to come back to the original point: Microwaves may be dangerous. Was this a conclusion? You bet.

In retrospect, the organization of the passage is pretty clear.

- The **first** paragraph states the known dangers of electromagnetic radiation.
- The **second** paragraph talks about the possible dangers of microwaves as shown by two studies.
- The **third** questions the two studies but decides that, on balance, microwaves may indeed be dangerous.

STEP TWO: AS YOU READ, LOOK FOR STRUCTURAL SIGNPOSTS

Certain words instantly tell you a lot about the structure of a passage. For example, if you were reading a paragraph that began, *There are three reasons the Grand Canyon should be strip-mined*, at some point in the paragraph you would expect to find three reasons listed. If a sentence begins, *On the one hand*, you would expect to find an *on the other hand* later in the sentence. These structural signposts show an alert reader what's going to happen later in a passage. Here are some structural signposts to look out for on the GMAT.

Trigger Words

The second paragraph you just read began with a word that probably automatically clued you in to the fact that a change was on its way: The word was "however."

Trigger words (such as "however" and "but") always signal a change in the direction of a passage. Here's a simple example:

First paragraph:	Most economists believe that the budget deficit will take years to remedy…
Second paragraph:	HOWEVER (trigger word), some economists believe there may be a fast solution to the problem.

In this example, the trigger word signals that the second paragraph will modify or qualify what has gone before. A trigger word at the beginning of any paragraph is a sure sign that this paragraph will disagree with what was stated in the preceding one.

Trigger words are important even if they do not appear at the beginning of a paragraph; they always signal a change of meaning, even if it is only within a sentence.

Here are the trigger words that often appear on the GMAT:

but	nonetheless
although (even though)	notwithstanding
however	except
yet	while
despite (in spite of)	unless
nevertheless	on the other hand

Continuing-the-Same-Train-of-Thought Words

Some structural signposts let you know that there will be no contradiction, no change in path. If you see a *first of all,* it stands to reason that there will be a *second of all* and perhaps a *third*. Other signs of continuation:

in addition
by the same token
likewise
similarly
this (implies a reference to preceding sentence)
thus (implies a conclusion)

One other continuing structural element that appears on the GMAT is not a word. Sentences or fragments that appear inside *parentheses* often contain information you'll need to answer a question. You should make a mental note of any sentence or fragment that is enclosed in parentheses.

A Day in the Life of a B-School Student

7:00 A.M.: Review notes for first class.
7:30 A.M.: Eat some high-energy flake cereal; read *The Wall Street Journal* (professors like to discuss news items that relate to the class topics).
8:00 A.M.: Read review for quantitative methods exam; do practice problems; reread case on control systems for organizational behavior class.
9:00 A.M.: Arrive at school. Go to "reading room" to hang out with everyone. Check student mailbox for invitations to recruiter events.
9:30 A.M.: Integrative Management Class: Guest speaker from case study discusses how the company approached problems.
10:45 A.M.: Hang out.
11:00 A.M.: Organizational Behavior Class: Get in a couple of good comments; debate the effectiveness of a management decision with another student in class.
12:15 P.M.: Grab some lunch and sit with friends. Talk about the lousy cafeteria food and who's dating whom.
2:00 P.M.: Microeconomics Class: Listen to lecture on monopolistic competition.
3:15 P.M.: Arrive at home, change into workout clothes. Go running, lift weights, relax.
6:00 P.M.: Eat dinner; watch the news. Read the next day's case study.
7:45 P.M.: Meet up for a group study session; help each other with homework problems on interpreting regression statistics; discuss how to account for capital leases versus operating leases.
10:00 P.M.: Back at home. Review more cases, read next class assignment in textbook.
Midnight: Watch Letterman 'til asleep. Boardroom dreams.

Yin-Yang Words

One of the test writers' all-time favorite types of passage contrasts two opposing viewpoints, and certain words immediately give this away. See if you can supply the second half of the following sentences:

> The traditional view *of the causes of global warming focuses on the burning of fossil fuel...*

(Second half: However, the *new* view is that there is some other cause.)

> Until recently, *it was thought that the Mayan civilization was destroyed as a result of drought...*

(Second half: However, *now* we believe that it was destroyed by space invaders.)

> The classical *model of laissez-faire capitalism does not even admit the possibility of government intervention...*

(Second half: But the *rock'n'roll* version of laissez-faire capitalism says, "Let me just get my checkbook.")

> Before 1960, *it was commonly assumed that the atom was the smallest particle in the universe...*

(Second half: However, *after 1960* scientists began to suspect that there was something even smaller.)

Sentence Correction Review: Quantity Comparison Words
Comparing two items
between
more
better
less
Comparing more than two items
among
most
best
least

Whenever you spot a "yin" word, you should realize that there is a "yang" on the way. Some other yin-yang words:

Yin	**Yang**
generally	(however, this time...)
the old view	(however, the new view...)
the widespread belief	(but the in-crowd believes...)
most scientists think	(but Doctor Spleegle thinks...)
on the one hand	(on the other hand...)

Getting Through the Passage Faster

Structural elements like these can help you understand a passage more quickly, with less "reading" and less wear and tear on your brain. When you spot one of these signposts, make a mental note. If it actually starts a paragraph, you might begin your three-word synopsis of the paragraph with a big "but." A structural signpost is usually more important to your understanding of a passage than any individual fact within that passage.

STEP THREE: ATTACK THE QUESTIONS

Once you've grasped the main ideas of the paragraphs, you can attack the questions aggressively. As we noted earlier, each passage is followed by up to four questions of varying levels of difficulty. These questions *generally* follow the organization of the passage. In other words, a question about the first paragraph will probably come before a question about the second paragraph.

General Questions

- "What is the primary purpose of this passage?"
- "What is the author's tone?"
- "Which of the following best describes the structure of the passage?"

Each of the questions above is a general question. A two-minute "read" using the techniques we've shown you over the last few pages should be all that you need to answer the general questions—without going back to the passage. Always try to answer a general question in your own words *before* you look at the answer choices.

Using POE to Eliminate Wrong Answers on General Questions

Once you have your *own* idea of what the answer should be, it's time to use POE to zero in on GMAC's answer. In the chapter on Sentence Correction, you learned that it's often easier to eliminate incorrect answers than to select the correct answers. The Process of Elimination is just as useful on Reading Comprehension questions. How can you use POE to eliminate wrong answers to general questions?

General questions have general answers. Thus, we can eliminate any answer to a general question that focuses on only one part of the passage or is too specific in some other way. We can also eliminate answers that cite information that's not in the passage at all. For example, here's a question based on the passage you have already read:

The main topic of the passage is

- ⬭ the health hazards of X rays and gamma rays on humans
- ⬭ the overly severe federal guidelines on radiation
- ⬭ the potential dangers of microwaves
- ⬭ to compare and contrast the work of Cleary and Milham
- ⬭ the limits of study methodology in science

Here's How to Crack It

In spite of the fact that X rays and gamma rays were mentioned in the first sentence, we know that this was just an introductory thought to get to the real idea of the passage—the danger of microwaves. So eliminate choice A. The federal guidelines in choice B were mentioned in the passage, but only at the very end. Could this be the main idea of the entire passage? No way. Choice C is the best answer and exactly what we should be expecting from our fast "read." Although Cleary and Milham are discussed several times, they are never compared, so we can eliminate choice D. And even though the passage mentions that the methodologies of the two scientists have been questioned, choice E goes much further than that to question the methodology of *all* science.

Specific Questions

- "The passage suggests which of the following about the laboratory results on microwaves mentioned in the highlighted section?"
- "According to the passage, a study of ham radio operators might be expected to find which of the following?"

Each of the questions above is a specific question. Specific questions have specific answers which you'll now need to find. Naturally, your two-minute "read" has not equipped you with the answers to these questions, but every specific question gives you a clue about where to look for the answer.

Line References

Sentence Correction Review: Countability

Different words are used depending on whether you are talking about things that you can count (french fries) or things that are not countable (water).

Countable
fewer
number
many
Not countable
less
amount, quantity
much

Some questions refer to a highlighted portion of the passage. The highlighting will be visible only when you're working on the question that it pertains to. In this book, we'll use line numbers instead of highlighting, so you don't have to look at the highlighting when you're trying to answer other questions.

So, how do you find the answer to the following question?

> The passage suggests which of the following about the federal guidelines on microwaves mentioned in line 12?

That's easy: It has a line reference. All you have to do is go back to the cited (or, on the GMAT, the highlighted) line or lines. You should start reading a little above them until you come to the answer to the question.

Lead Words

How do you find the answer to *this* question?

> "According to the passage, a study of ham radio operators might be expected to find which of the following?"

When a question seems to be specific but is not highlighted, look for a catchy word or phrase in the question. For example, in this question, there's a very clear specific reference: "ham radio operators." We call this a **lead** phrase. Now that you know what you're looking for, run your finger down the passage on the screen as you scroll until you see your lead word or phrase. When you find it, you will have almost certainly found your answer.

Try this technique out right now by running your finger down the passage below until you find "ham radio operators." Don't read; just look:

> Biologists have long known that some types of electromagnetic radiation such as X rays and gamma rays can be dangerous to human beings. Operating at a frequency of 10^{18} through 10^{22} MHz, these rays, which are well above the visible light spectrum, were first detected in the early years of the twentieth century.
>
> However, until now, no one has ever suggested that microwave radiation might also be harmful. In preliminary laboratory results, Cleary and Milham have found elevated growth rates in cancer cells exposed to low doses of microwaves. Cleary exposed cancer cells to levels of radiation that are commonly found in microwave ovens and found that the abnormal cells grew 30 percent faster than did unexposed cells. Milham's study focused on ham radio operators who are commonly exposed to levels of radiation slightly higher than those emitted by cellular telephones. He discovered elevated levels of myeloid leukemia.
>
> The methodology of Cleary and Milham has been questioned by other scientists in the field. However, no one seriously disputes that their preliminary findings must be taken seriously or that new studies should be set up to try to duplicate their results. Although federal guidelines for how much electromagnetic energy can be allowed to enter the work and home environment have been made more stringent since they were first implemented in 1982, the recent studies pose troubling questions about the safety of microwaves.

Using POE to Eliminate Wrong Answers on Specific Questions

Specific questions have very specific answers. Before you even go to the answer choices, you should usually be able to point to the exact spot in the passage where the answer to the question is to be found.

General or Specific?
When you read a Reading Comprehension question, determine whether it is general or specific. To answer general questions, you need to have an understanding of the main idea and the structure of the passage. To answer specific questions, you need to have a vague sense of where to find the information based on your knowledge of the passage's structure.

Once you go to the answer choices, you'll probably be able to eliminate several right away. However, if you are down to two possibilities, don't try to prove one of the answers right. Look for something in the passage that will make one of the answers *wrong*. It's often easier to find the flaw in an incorrect answer. For example, here's a question (complete with answer choices) based on the passage you have already read:

According to the passage, a study of ham radio operators might be expected to find which of the following?

- ⬭ The presence of X rays and gamma rays
- ⬭ Unusual cells growing 30% faster than normal
- ⬭ A level of radiation exposure similar to that found in users of microwave ovens
- ⬭ Higher levels of a particular type of leukemia
- ⬭ Levels of radiation identical to those emitted by cellular phones

Here's How to Crack It

The lead words "ham radio operators" led us to the second half of the second paragraph. If you haven't already, read the relevant sentences and get an idea of what you might expect the answer to be.

Now, go to the answer choices. Would a study of ham radio operators find the presence of X rays and gamma rays? Well, neither are mentioned in *this* paragraph. The *first* paragraph did mention these rays—but only to introduce the dangers of microwaves. So much for choice A.

Both choices B and C were mentioned in this paragraph, but only in connection with *Cleary's* work—which had nothing to do with ham radio operators.

You might have been torn between choices D and E because both come from the right place in the passage. Don't try to decide which is best. Look for a reason one of them is *wrong*. Let's attack choice E. It says that ham operators were exposed to levels of radiation identical to those emitted by cellular phones. Is that *exactly* what the passage said? Well, no. According to the passage, ham radio operators were exposed to slightly *higher* levels. Choice E is history. The correct answer must be choice D.

Inference Questions

> Which of the following can be inferred from the passage about the level of radiation from cellular telephones?

Q: What is the purpose of skimming the passage?
Turn the page for the answer.

Although this question asks you to draw an inference, you'll find that GMAC's idea of an inference will be much more timid than yours. GMAT inferences go at most a *tiny* bit further than the passage itself. If your thoughts about this type of question becomes too subtle, you'll get it wrong. Here's an example:

> Which of the following can be inferred from the passage about the studies conducted by Cleary and Milham?
>
> ◯ Cleary's results were better documented than Milham's.
> ◯ Neither study is scientifically valid.
> ◯ Both studies indicated that microwaves were more harmful than X rays.
> ◯ The final results were not in at the time the article was written.
> ◯ The results of both studies were based on the same scientific data.

Here's How to Crack It

The passage never said that one study was better than the other, so eliminate answer choice A. While both studies were questioned in the third paragraph, it would be inferring far too much to say that neither was scientifically valid. Eliminate choice B. The passage never said that microwaves were more harmful than X rays. It seems likely that they are less harmful. Eliminate choice C. The results of both studies were called "preliminary" in paragraph two. Thus, choice D seems so obvious that you might almost hesitate to call it an inference. This is exactly the kind of inference that the GMAT test writers feel comfortable making. Not only was choice E not stated, but it is likely to be false. Cleary concentrated on cancerous cells exposed to levels of radiation equivalent to microwave ovens. Milham studied ham radio operators. The best answer is D.

A: To gain basic familiarity with the topic and to sum up each paragraph. Devote only about two minutes to skimming; do not get caught up in details or difficult concepts. Remember, you get points for answering the questions, not reading the passage.

Advanced POE: Attacking Disputable Answer Choices

Say you've eliminated two answer choices on a Reading Comprehension question, but you can't decide which of the remaining three choices is best. All three seem to say the same thing. How do you choose among them? The test writers and GMAC want their correct answers to be indisputable so that no one will ever be able to complain

Here are three statements. Which of them is indisputable?

- ⬭ Shaw was the greatest dramatist of his time.
- ⬭ Shaw's genius was never understood.
- ⬭ Shaw was a great dramatist, although some critics disagree.

Shaw's status as a playwright will always be a matter of opinion. If GMAC made the first statement the correct answer to a Reading Comprehension question, people who got the question wrong might argue that not everyone considers Shaw the greatest dramatist of his time.

If GMAC made the second statement the best answer to a Reading Comprehension question, people who got the question wrong could argue that someone, somewhere in the world, must have understood poor old Shaw.

The third statement, by contrast, is indisputable. Most critics would agree that Shaw was *a* great dramatist. If there are any critics who do not, the test writers cover themselves with a little disclaimer: "although some critics disagree." The third statement is so vague that no one could possibly argue with it.

In general, an answer choice that is highly specific and unequivocal is *disputable* and is therefore usually not the best answer.

> An answer choice that is general and vague is *indisputable* and is therefore often the correct answer.

How to *Pick* an Indisputable Answer Choice

Certain words make a statement so vague that it is almost impossible to dispute. Here are some of these words:

usually	can
sometimes	some
may	most

If a statement says that Shaw is *sometimes* considered the greatest dramatist ever, who can dispute that?

How to *Avoid* a Disputable Answer Choice

Certain words make a statement so *absolute* that it's easy to dispute. Here are some of these words:

always	all
must	complete
everybody	never

If a statement says that Shaw is *always* considered the greatest dramatist ever, who couldn't dispute that?

Respect for Professionals

GMAC has tremendous respect for all professionals—doctors, scientists, economists, writers, and artists. It is very unlikely that the test writers would create a right answer that implies anything negative about a professional.

By the same token, it would be unusual to find a best answer choice that took any but the lightest digs at America. Our country is pretty much beyond GMAC's reproach.

Moderate Emotion

The test writers avoid using passages that convey strong emotions on the GMAT. The author's tone might be "slightly critical," but it will not be "scornful and envious." The author's tone might be "admiring," but it will never be "overly enthusiastic." If you see strong words like these in an answer choice, it's probably wrong and can be eliminated.

Reading Comprehension

Trigger words that signal a change in meaning:

but
although (even though)
however
yet
despite (in spite of)
nevertheless
nonetheless
notwithstanding
except
while
unless
on the other hand

The Diversity Passage

For many years, minority groups have complained—justifiably—that standardized tests like the GMAT discriminate against them. GMAC responded to this criticism by adding a diversity passage to many of its tests. One of the reading passages on the GMAT you take will almost certainly be about some marginalized group—African Americans, Mexican Americans, women.

Designed to answer charges that the GMAT is biased, the diversity passage is invariably positive in tone. This doesn't make the test any fairer to minorities, but it does sometimes make the test easier to beat. Any answer choice that expresses negative views of the marginalized group in question is almost certainly wrong. Try the following example:

The author considers women's literature to be

- ⬭ derivative
- ⬭ lacking in imagination
- ⬭ full of promise and hope
- ⬭ much better than the literature being written by men today
- ⬭ uninteresting

Here's How to Crack It

You don't need to see the passage to answer this question. The whole purpose of the diversity passage is to illustrate to everyone how broad-minded and unbiased the GMAT really is. "Derivative," "lacking in imagination," and "uninteresting" all express negative opinions of literature written by (what the test writers consider to be) a minority group.

Answer choice D goes too far in the other direction. As far as the test writers are concerned, women's literature is just as good as, but no better than, anyone else's. The answer must be choice C.

Putting All This to Work

Now that you know something about how to tackle GMAT passages and what to look for in them, try the sample passage below. Find the main idea of each paragraph (and if you like, jot down a few key words about each one); look for structural signposts along the way.

Try to spend no more than two minutes "reading." Remember, you only get points for answering questions. (At the end of this chapter, you will find the notes that one of our teachers made when she "read" the passage.)

Remember, on the GMAT, you'll have no more than four questions per passage. We've included a few extra questions just for practice.

Until recently, corporate ideology in the United States has held that bigger is better. This traditional view of the primacy of big, centralized companies is now being challenged as some of the giants of American business are being outperformed by a new generation of smaller, streamlined businesses. If it was the industrial revolution that spawned the era of massive industrialized companies, then perhaps it was the information revolution of the 1990s that spawned the era we're now in—the era of the small company.

For most of the 20th century, big companies dominated an American business scene that seemed to thrive on its own grandness of scale. The expansion westward, the growth of the railroad and steel industries, an almost limitless supply of cheap raw materials, plus a population boom that provided an ever-increasing demand for new products (although not a cheap source of labor) all coincided to encourage the growth of large companies.

But rapid developments in the marketplace have begun to change the accepted rules of business and have underscored the need for fast reaction times. Small companies, without huge overhead and inventory, can respond quickly to a technologically advanced age in which new products and technologies can become outmoded within a year of their being brought to market.

Of course, successful emerging small companies face a potential dilemma in that their very success will tend to turn them into copies of the large corporate dinosaurs they are now supplanting. To avoid this trap, small companies may look to the example of several CEOs of large corporations who have broken down their sprawling organizations into small, semi-independent divisions capable of surviving in today's marketplace.

Attacking the Questions

1. The primary purpose of the passage is to

- ○ present evidence that resolves a contradiction in business theory
- ○ discuss reasons an accepted business pattern is changing
- ○ describe a theoretical model and a method whereby that model can be tested
- ○ argue that a traditional ideology deserves new attention
- ○ resolve two conflicting explanations for a phenomenon

Here's How to Crack It

Sentence Structure
While you skim a passage, be aware of its structure. Is one theory presented and then discounted? Are there lists of items? Does it provide two schools of thought? Trigger words, which act as structural signposts, can help you uncover a passage's structure.

This is a general question, and general questions always reflect the structure of the passage. The first words of the passage were "until recently." We hope you recognized right away that this was "yin-yang" terminology, as was "this traditional view." Obviously, this passage is about to present a *new* view.

The old view, according to the passage, was that in America, large companies were always better off than small companies. Of course, the new view is that smaller companies are now doing better than big companies. This was probably enough for you to answer all the general questions in this section, but let's look quickly at the rest of the passage: Paragraph two gives historical reasons why bigger used to be better; paragraph three explains why this is no longer true today; and paragraph four concludes by talking about how small companies can stay successful as they inevitably get bigger. Let's analyze the answer choices:

(A) In yin-yang passages, new is virtually always better than old. There is really no contradiction here. Also, GMAT passages hardly ever "resolve" anything definitively. How could they in only 250 words? Eliminate this answer.

(B) This is the best answer. It mirrors the yin-yang structure of the passage—the accepted pattern of almost a century is now changing.

(C) If you picked this one, you were thinking too hard. Perhaps you thought the primacy of the small company was the new theoretical model, about to be tested. However, the passage seems to imply that the decline of large companies and the ascendancy of small companies started before anyone even realized what was happening, let alone came up with some smart theory about it.

(D) Was the author arguing that in fact the traditional view that "bigger is better" is actually correct after all? Nope. Eliminate it.

(E) Again, GMAT passages rarely "resolve" anything. Also, while there are two conflicting elements in this passage, they are not conflicting explanations for a single phenomenon.

2. According to the passage, all of the following are examples of developments that helped promote the growth of large companies in the last century EXCEPT

- ⬭ the growth of the railroad industry
- ⬭ America's westward expansion
- ⬭ an almost inexhaustible source of raw materials
- ⬭ the existence of an inexpensive source of labor
- ⬭ the development of an industry to produce steel

Here's How to Crack It

This is a specific question without a line number, but you probably knew just where to look. Which paragraph gives historical background on the growth of large companies? If you said paragraph two, you are absolutely correct.

The first time you "read" this passage, you may have skipped over the specifics in this paragraph because they weren't necessary to understand the purpose of the paragraph. Now, of course, you are interested. But even if you had spent 20 minutes (you didn't really have) memorizing the entire passage, wouldn't you still have wanted to peek back at this paragraph just to make sure you remembered it correctly? Because you were going to have to look back anyway, it made sense to skip over the details the first time around. Remember, there was no guarantee that there would even be a question about this information. It is not unusual to find GMAT passages whose questions completely ignore whole paragraphs at a time.

This is an "except" question, which means that every answer choice is correct but one. The answer to this question was buried inside the parentheses in line 18: ("although not a cheap source of labor"). The answer to this question is choice D.

B-School Lingo

poets: mathematically challenged students with little quantitative skill or experience

power naps: brief in-class unconsciousness that revives sleep-deprived students

power tool: someone who does all the reading and homework and sits in the front of the class with his hand up

Source: *The Best Business Schools*

3. The author's attitude toward the traditional view expressed in lines 1–6 can best be described as

- scornful and denunciatory
- dispirited and morose
- critical but respectful
- admiring and deferential
- uncertain but interested

Here's How to Crack It

You could eliminate two of these answer choices without even reading the passage. GMAC would never include a passage in which the author's attitude toward companies like General Motors is "scornful and denunciatory" or "dispirited and morose." Both choices A and B are so strong and out in left field that we can safely eliminate them. As far as the passage is concerned, the traditional ideology no longer works, so we can pretty much rule out choice D, "admiring and deferential." Choice E is a little too vague. The only possible answer is choice C.

4. It can be inferred from the passage that which of the following actions would be most consistent with the traditional ideology described in the passage?

- Splitting a manufacturing company into several smaller divisions
- Bringing a new product to market within a year
- Creating a department to utilize new emerging technologies
- Expanding an existing company in anticipation of growing demand
- Cutting inventory and decreasing overhead

Here's How to Crack It

The trick in inference questions is to infer as little as possible. The traditional ideology is that bigger is better. Which of the answer choices shows a situation getting bigger? The best answer is choice D. Choices A and E both illustrate the process of downsizing as described in the passage. Choices B and C illustrate the lean-and-mean tactics attributed in the passage to small companies.

5. According to the passage, to avoid the trap posed by "a potential dilemma," mentioned in line 29, emerging successful small companies will have to do which of the following?

- ⬭ Turn for advice to the industry analysts who earlier predicted the problems of large companies
- ⬭ Avoid taking paths that will make them too successful
- ⬭ Learn to embrace the traditional ideology of large corporations
- ⬭ Create small interconnected divisions rather than expanding in traditional ways
- ⬭ Hire successful CEOs from other firms

Here's How to Crack It

Whenever you see a specific question with a line reference (indicated on the test by highlighting, or in this book by line numbers), always remember to read a little above and a little below the referenced line. In this case, we are not interested so much in the "dilemma" as we are in avoiding the trap posed by the dilemma. The answer to this question is in the last three lines of the passage.

Let's analyze the answer choices:

(A) This is an interesting idea, but it is not said in the passage, so we can eliminate it.

(B) The right idea, but takes it too far. It is practically un-American to think that a company would try not to become too successful.

(C) The traditional ideology is what got the big companies into trouble. Eliminate it.

(D) This is the best answer and a nice paraphrase of what was said in the last three lines of the passage.

(E) The passage suggests that small companies could learn from these CEOs, but does not suggest that the small companies *hire* the CEOs.

Another Day in the Life of a B-School Student

6:45 A.M.: Get dressed while listening to CNN and pick up *The Wall Street Journal* on way to school.
8:00 A.M.: Arrive at school. Bargaining and Negotiations class. Perform role play on conflict resolution.
10:15 A.M.: Hang out, grab a bagel.
10:30 A.M.: Intermediate Accounting Class—discussion on cash flow statements—nothing exciting.
12:45 P.M.: Arrive at admissions office to review résumé of applicant to b-school.
1:00 P.M.: Conduct interview of applicant.
1:45 P.M.: Write evaluation of candidate. Hand in to admissions secretary.
2:00 P.M.: Attend quality advisory board meeting; discuss creation of corporate survey.
3:30 P.M.: Competitive Strategy class. Lecture on barriers to entry.
5:45 P.M.: Attend recruiter event. Tell the recruiter how interested I am in the industry (I know nothing about it).
7:45 P.M.: Over to the health club for aerobics.
8:45 P.M.: Drive home, eat dinner, and finally read *The Wall Street Journal*—of course, it's not news by now.
9:30 P.M.: Study class notes, prepare next day's case studies.
11:45 P.M.: Quality phone time.
12:30 A.M.: Boardroom dreams.

6. Which of the following best describes the organization of the first paragraph of the passage?

- ⬭ A conventional model is described and an alternative is introduced.
- ⬭ An assertion is made and a general supporting example is given.
- ⬭ Two contradictory points of view are presented and evaluated.
- ⬭ A historical overview is given to explain a phenomenon.
- ⬭ A new theory is described and then qualified.

Here's How to Crack It

This is a structure question, pure and simple. Let's interpret the answers:

(A) correctly describes this yin-yang paragraph
(B) ignores the structure of the passage
(C) is close, but fails to show that one point of view is considered superior to the other
(D) describes paragraph two instead of paragraph one
(E) The word "qualified" means "limited." The author seems to like the idea of the small company and certainly doesn't qualify it in the first paragraph.

B-School Lingo

pre-enrollment courses: commonly known as MBA summer camp; quantitative courses offered in the summer before first year for the mathematically challenged

pro forma: financial presentation of hypothetical events; for example, how much debt would a company have to acquire if it grows ten percent per year?

run the numbers: analyze quantitatively

Source: *The Best Business Schools*

7. It can be inferred from the passage that small companies are better able to adapt to the new business climate due to which of the following factors?

I. low overhead and inventory
II. the ability to predict when new products will become outmoded
III. the capacity to change quickly to meet new challenges

- ⬭ I only
- ⬭ II only
- ⬭ III only
- ⬭ I and III only
- ⬭ I, II, and III

Here's How to Crack It

I, II, III–type questions are nasty because you have to answer three questions in order to get one right. Where in the passage were small companies actually described? If you said paragraph three, you were absolutely correct. Because this is an inference question, we need to make sure we don't infer too far. Let's look at Statement I. Can we infer that small companies are better able to adapt because of low inventory? Sure. In lines 23–24 the passage reads, "Small companies, without huge overhead and inventory…"

Because we know that Statement I works, we can cross off choices B and C; why? Because neither includes Statement I. Let's look at Statement II. While it seems likely that the ability to predict ahead of time which products are going to become outmoded would help small companies adapt faster, there is no indication in the passage that anyone has the ability to predict ahead. If you aren't sure about Statement II, you can skip it and go on to Statement III. This statement is definitely true. It is a paraphrase of lines 23–24. The best answer is choice D.

Here's What Your Notes Should Look Like After You've Finished Reading This Passage

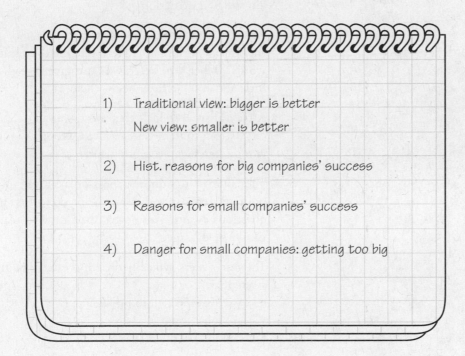

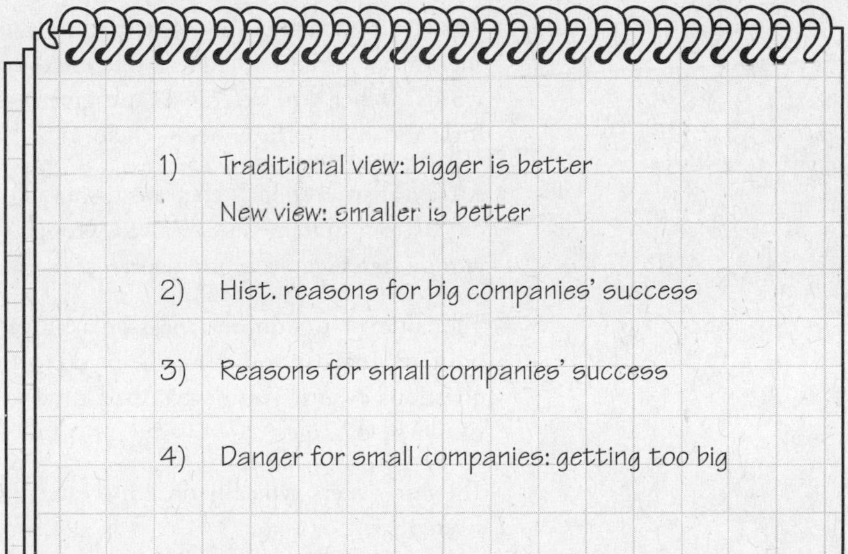

1) Traditional view: bigger is better
New view: smaller is better
2) Hist. reasons for big companies' success
3) Reasons for small companies' success
4) Danger for small companies: getting too big

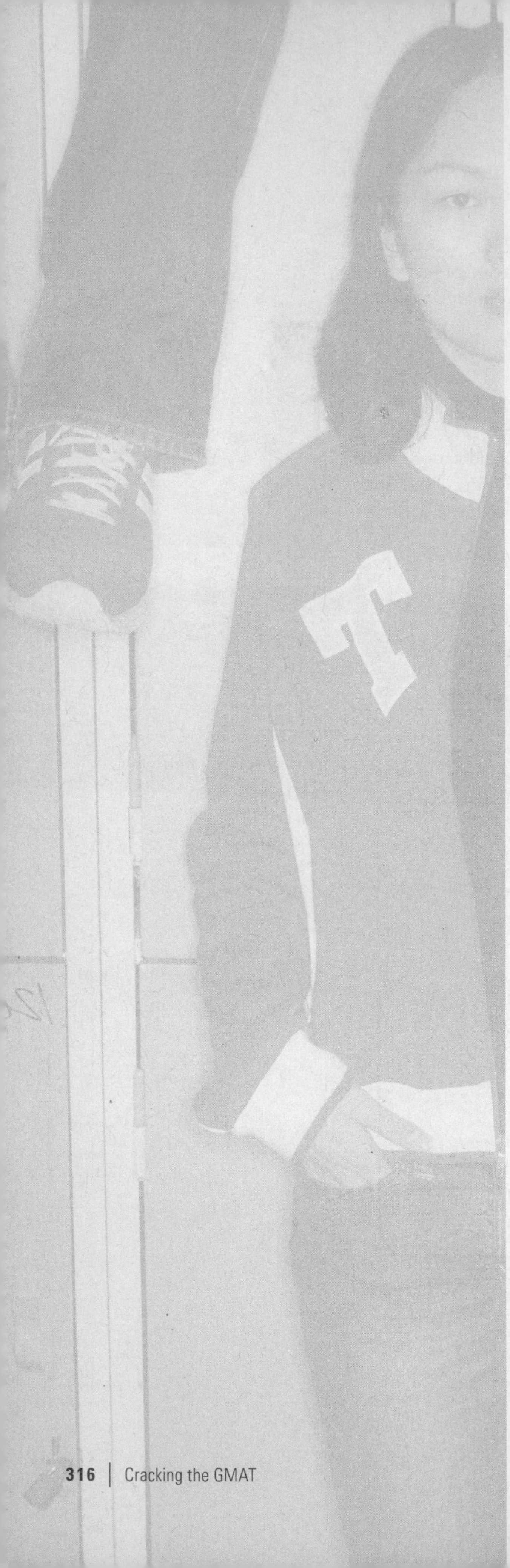

Summary

- Reading Comprehension questions make up roughly one-third of the 41 questions on the Verbal section of the GMAT—approximately 13 questions. The three types of passages that may appear on the test are social science, science, and business.
- Reading Comprehension questions are not presented in any order of difficulty, though the level of difficulty of the passages you see will depend on how well you are doing on the exam.
- Read a passage for its main idea. This will enable you to answer the general questions, and give you a good idea of where to look for the answers to specific questions. When you read, jot down a few words summarizing each paragraph.
- Structural signposts can help you see how a passage is organized. Look for trigger words, continuing-the-same-train-of-thought words, and yin-yang constructions.
- Answers to specific questions can be found either through highlighted **line references** or **lead words**. When line references are given, read a little above and a little below them.
- Attack answer choices that are disputable. Specific, strong statements are often wrong. Vague, wimpy statements are often correct.
- The tone of a minority passage is invariably positive. This can sometimes help you to answer questions even if you haven't had time to read the entire passage.
- The test writers typically do not create right answers that:
    - are disrespectful to professionals
    - are too strong
    - condone prejudicial attitudes
- I, II, III–type questions are best tackled by POE.

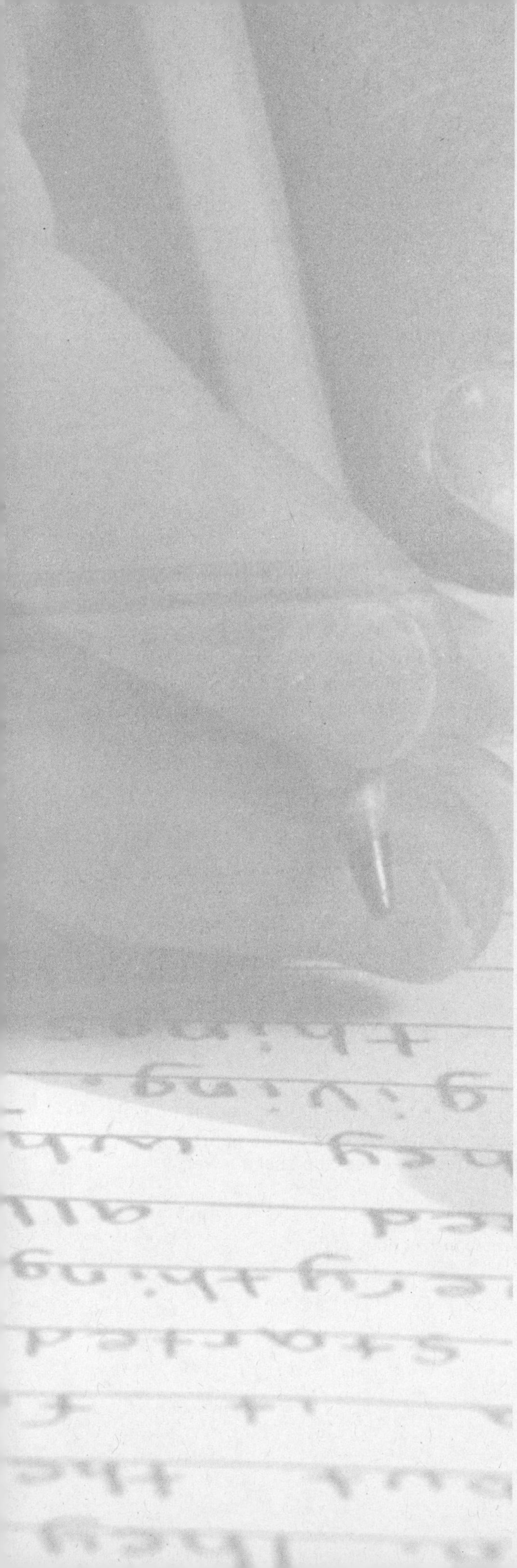

Chapter 17
Critical Reasoning

To understand Critical Reasoning passages, you need to know a bit about formal logic, how arguments are constructed, and how to weaken and strengthen an argument. In this chapter, we will break down arguments into their three parts and show you how to recognize—and ace—the 8 major types of arguments that show up on the GMAT.

Critical Reasoning questions make up a little less than one-third of the 41 questions on the Verbal section of the GMAT—approximately 11 questions. They consist of very short reading passages (typically 20 to 100 words). Each of these passages is followed by one or two questions, which are supposed to test your ability to think clearly. When this section was first introduced, the test writers said that "no knowledge of the terminology and of the conventions of formal logic is presupposed." Nevertheless, you'll find that while it may not be presupposed, some knowledge of the rudiments of formal logic—as applied by The Princeton Review—can substantially increase your score.

THE HISTORY OF CRITICAL REASONING

Over the years, the test writers have tried several different formats in an attempt to test reasoning ability.

The original GMAT contained a section called "Best Arguments." In 1961, this section was replaced with something called "Organization of Ideas." In 1966, this section was also phased out, and for six years reasoning ability went unmeasured. In 1972, GMAC tried again, with a section called "Analysis of Situations." Finally, on the October 1988 version of the GMAT, the test writers unveiled Critical Reasoning for the first time.

Well, Not Exactly the *First* Time

In fact, Critical Reasoning looks a lot like Best Arguments. Test writers have used this type of question for years on the LSAT (Law School Admission Test) and, until recently, on the GRE (Graduate Record Exam).

Before we begin, take a moment to read a close approximation of the instructions for Critical Reasoning questions:

> Critical Reasoning Directions: Each of the critical reasoning questions is based on a short argument, a set of statements, or a plan of action. For each question, select the best answer of the choices given.

Obviously you won't need to read these instructions again.

How to Attack the Critical Reasoning Questions

The terseness of these instructions implies that all you need on these questions is common sense. Common sense will certainly help, but you should also understand a bit about the formal logic on which Critical Reasoning is based.

Like the other types of questions found on the GMAT, Critical Reasoning questions tend to be predictable. There are only a few question types, and as you learn how the test writers use their smattering of formal logic to write Critical Reasoning questions, you'll be able to anticipate the answers to certain of those questions. In this chapter we'll teach you how to:

1. Use clues in the questions to anticipate the kind of answer you're looking for in a passage.
2. Analyze and attack the passages in an organized fashion.
3. Understand the basic structure of the passages.
4. Use Process of Elimination to eliminate wrong choices.

Reading Comprehension Review

Q: What should you keep in mind with Reading Comprehension inference questions?

Turn the page for the answer.

A Word About GMAT Logic

GMAT logic is different from the formal logic you may have studied in college. Our review of GMAT logic is not intended to be representative of logic as a whole. We don't intend to teach you logic; we're going to teach you *GMAT* logic.

The Passage

Most Critical Reasoning passages are in the form of *arguments* in which the writer tries to convince the reader of something. Here's an example:

> In the past 10 years, advertising revenues for the magazine *True Investor* have fallen by 30%. The magazine has failed to attract new subscribers, and newsstand sales are down to an all-time low. Thus, sweeping editorial changes will be necessary if the magazine is to survive.

There are three main parts to an argument:

- **Conclusion:** This is what the author is trying to persuade us to accept.
- **Premises:** These are the pieces of evidence the author gives to support the conclusion.
- **Assumptions:** These are unstated ideas or evidence without which the entire conclusion might be invalid.

In the passage above, the author's *conclusion* is found in the last line:

> Thus, sweeping editorial changes will be necessary if the magazine is to survive.

To support this, the author gives three pieces of evidence, or *premises*: Advertising revenue is down; there are no new subscribers; and very few people are buying the newspaper at the newsstand.

Are there any *assumptions* here? Well, not in the passage itself. Assumptions are never stated by the author. They are parts of the argument that have been left out. Even the best-thought-out argument has assumptions. In this case, one important assumption the author seems to make is that it was the old editorial policy that caused the problems the magazine is now encountering. Another assumption is that editorial changes alone will be enough to restore the magazine's financial health.

A Critical Reasoning passage is not necessarily made up of only these three parts. The passage might contain other information as well—extraneous ideas, perhaps, or statements of an opposing point of view. This is why it's so important to find and identify the conclusion and the premises (as well as the argument's underlying assumptions).

- Look for conclusions at the beginning and end of a passage. Most arguments follow one of two common structures:

premise, premise, premise, conclusion

or

conclusion, premise, premise, premise

Therefore, the conclusion can often be found in the first or last sentence of the passage.

A: Do not infer too much! Stick to the passage as closely as possible.

- Look for the same kinds of structural signposts we showed you in the Reading Comprehension chapter (Chapter 16). Words like the following often signal that a conclusion is about to be made:

therefore	hence
thus	implies
so	indicates that

- Look for a statement that cannot stand alone; in other words, a statement that needs to be supported by premises.
- If you can't find the conclusion, look for the premises instead. These are the parts of the argument that support the conclusion.

Premises are often preceded by another kind of signpost. Words like the following signal that evidence is about to be given to support a conclusion:

because	in view of
since	given that

This Is Not Like Reading Comprehension

Reading Comprehension passages are long and filled with useless facts. By now you've gotten used to reading these passages for their structure, letting your eyes skip over factual data you probably won't be tested on anyway.

By contrast, Critical Reasoning passages are quite short, and every single word should be considered carefully; shades of meaning are very important. Because the passages are relatively short, you will probably never have to use the scroll bar to see them on your screen in their entirety.

The Question

Immediately after the passage, there will be a question. There is usually only one question per passage—which means it is essential that you *always read the question first.*

The question contains important clues that will tell you what to look for as you read the passage.

There Are Eight Question Types

Here are examples of the eight major question types you'll see (we'll go into much greater detail later in the chapter):

1. The passage above assumes that...

We call these **assumption questions.** As you read the passage in question, you will be looking for an unstated premise upon which the argument depends.

2. Which of the following, if true, would most strengthen the conclusion drawn above?

We call these **strengthen-the-argument questions.** This type of question is like an assumption question in that it asks you to find an unstated premise upon which the argument depends, and then bolster it.

Reading Comprehension Review
Trigger words that signal a conclusion:
therefore
thus
so
hence
implies
indicates

3. Which of the following, if true, would most seriously weaken the conclusion of the passage above?

We call these **weaken-the-argument questions**. This type of question, like an assumption question, asks you to find an unstated premise of the argument and poke holes in it.

4. Which of the following can best be inferred from the passage above?

We call these **inference questions**. This question, like inference Reading Comprehension questions, is at most asking you to go a tiny bit further than the passage does.

5. Which of the following best resolves the apparent contradiction in the passage above?

We call these **resolve/explain questions**. This type of question asks you to pick an answer choice that explains an inconsistency between two incompatible facts.

6. Which of the following would be most useful in evaluating the logic of the argument above?

We call these **evaluate-the-argument questions**. This type of question asks you to pick an answer choice that would help to "assess" or "evaluate" part of an argument.

7. The bolded phrase plays which of the following roles in the argument above?

We call these **identify-the-reasoning questions**. This type of question asks you to identify the method or technique the author is using.

8. Which of the following most resembles the method used by the author to make the point above?

We call these **parallel-the-reasoning questions**. This type of question asks you to find a new argument among the answer choices that mimics the original argument.

While the wording of the questions may vary, these are the question types you'll see—there are only eight. Each type of question has its own strategy, as we'll show you.

Scope

As you read through this chapter you will notice that certain sentences keep coming up again and again in our discussions of how to eliminate wrong answers.

The ones you'll see most often are:

> "This answer choice goes too far."
>
> "That choice is outside of the scope of the argument."

Why do these sentences appear so frequently? Because scope is one of the test writers' favorite topics for Critical Reasoning questions. It takes a little practice to figure out how scope works. We'll give you an introduction to the concept here, but you'll need to work through the entire chapter (and practice on the questions in our online tests or in *The Official Guide for GMAT Review*) to understand it completely.

Here's an example:

> In an effort to save money, a country's government is considering reducing its military spending. However, without military contracts, crucial industries in that country face bankruptcy, which could disrupt the economy. Thus, the same government that is reducing its military spending will eventually have to provide these industries with money for peacetime research and development.
>
> Which of the following states the conclusion of the passage above?
>
> ◯ The necessity of providing money to keep crucial industries from going bankrupt will discourage the government from reducing its military budget.
>
> ◯ If the government decreases its military budget, it will eventually be forced to increase its military budget to its former level.
>
> ◯ The industries that receive research and development money will be successful in their efforts to convert to peacetime manufacturing.
>
> ◯ In the event of war, this country would be unprepared for military conflict.
>
> ◯ Reducing military spending to save money will result in some increases in other types of spending.

We will discuss how to do this type of question (inference) shortly, but for now, we're going to summarize the argument and skip right to the answer choices in order to illustrate how to use scope as an elimination technique. The argument states that a country wants to save money by decreasing its military budget; however, in order to keep the industries that depend on military contracts from collapsing, the country will have to *spend* some additional money as well.

The GMAT Rewards Narrow Minds

Critical Reasoning Step 1

Q: What is the very first thing you should do when starting a Critical Reasoning passage?

Turn the page for the answer.

In the Critical Reasoning section, it is easy to think too much. The first answer choice (what we call answer choice A) might look very tempting at first, because it seems to take the argument to its logical conclusion: "Hey, if cutting military spending is going to end up *costing* the country money, they may as well not do it." But the test writers consider answer choice A to be outside the scope of this argument. In fact, if you think about it, we have no idea whether or not the government will be discouraged, or even whether the costs of supplying research and development money will be greater than the savings in military spending. This answer goes much further than the argument itself.

Choice B goes too far as well. Perhaps cutting military spending will turn out to be a bad idea, but even if that is true, how do we know that the country will then eventually decide to increase military spending? What might happen in the future is well outside the scope of this argument.

We can eliminate choice C for the same reason, because it merely goes off on a tangent to speculate as to the ultimate fate of the industries mentioned in the passage. Whether these industries succeed in making the transition to peacetime manufacturing is not crucial to this argument.

If you are tempted by choice D, you're still thinking too much. When a country reduces its military spending, you could argue that it might be less prepared for war—but that is way outside the scope of this passage. Be careful not to impose your own value judgments or thought processes on these questions.

Keeping Track of POE

As you eliminate answer choices, it's vital that you physically cross them off in your scratch booklet. This will prevent you from wasting time rereading answer choices you've already eliminated.

Choice E may have seemed simplistic when you first read it, but simple is exactly what we want here. Rather than asking us to make assumptions, inferences, or explanations, this question simply asks for the conclusion of the passage—nothing more. Choice E stays within the scope of the argument.

Now let's look at the eight types of critical reading questions.

1. ASSUMPTION QUESTIONS

An assumption question asks you to identify an *unstated* premise of the passage from among the answer choices. As you read the passage, what you will be looking for is a gap in the underlying logic of the argument—a gap that can be closed only by specifically stating what is now only being assumed. There are many different kinds of assumptions the GMAT test writers can use, but let's get you started by identifying three: causal assumptions, statistical assumptions, and analogy assumptions.

Causal Assumptions

The test writers are extremely fond of these and make use of them several times on every GMAT. Causal assumptions take an effect and suggest a cause for it. Take a look at the simplified example below.

Every time I wear my green suit, people like me. Therefore, it is my green suit that makes people like me.

The author's conclusion (it is the green suit that makes people like him) is based on the premise that every time he wears it, he has observed that people like him. But this argument relies on the assumption that there is no other possible cause for people liking him. Perhaps he always wears a red tie with his green suit, and it's really the tie that people like.

Whenever you spot a cause being suggested for an effect, ask yourself if the cause is truly the reason for the effect, or if there might be an alternate cause.

Analogy Assumptions

An argument by analogy compares one situation to another, ignoring the question of whether the two situations are comparable.

Use of this product causes cancer in laboratory animals. Therefore, you should stop using this product.

The author's conclusion (you should stop using the product) is based on the premise that the product causes cancer in laboratory animals. This argument is not really complete. It relies on the assumption that because this product causes cancer in laboratory animals, it will also cause cancer in humans.

Whenever you see a comparison in a Critical Reasoning passage, you should ask yourself: Are these two situations really comparable?

Statistical Assumptions

A statistical argument uses statistics to "prove" its point. Remember what Mark Twain said: "There are lies, damned lies, and statistics."

Four out of five doctors agree: The pain reliever in Sinutol is the most effective analgesic on the market today. You should try Sinutol.

Critical Reasoning Step 1

A: Read the question! This will allow you to focus on what the question is asking when you read the passage.

The conclusion (you should try Sinutol) is based on the premise that four out of five doctors found the pain reliever in Sinutol to be the most effective. However, a literal reading of the passage tells us that the statistic that the author uses in support of his conclusion is based only on the opinions of five doctors (all of whom may be on the board of directors of Sinutol). The author's conclusion is based on the *assumption* that four out of *every* five doctors will find Sinutol to be wonderful. This may be correct, but we do not know for sure. Therefore, the most we can say about the conclusion is that it may be true.

Whenever you see statistics in an argument, always be sure to ask yourself the following question: Are the statistics representative?

Neither analogy nor statistical arguments are as prevalent on the GMAT as causal arguments.

How to Recognize an Assumption Question

Assumption questions generally contain one of the following wordings:

- Which of the following is an assumption on which the argument depends?
- The argument above assumes which of the following?
- The claim above rests on the questionable presupposition that...

How to Attack the Answer Choices on an Assumption Question

Assumptions plug holes in the argument and help make a conclusion true. Here are some guidelines for spotting assumptions among the answer choices:

- Assumptions are never stated in the passage. If you see an answer choice that comes straight from the passage, it is **not** correct.
- Assumptions support the conclusion of the passage. Find the conclusion in the passage, then try out each answer choice to see whether it makes the conclusion stronger.
- Assumptions frequently turn on the gaps of logic we've just discussed. If the argument proposes a cause for an effect, you should ask yourself whether there might be some other cause. If the argument uses statistics, you should probably ask yourself whether the statistics involved are representative. If the argument offers an analogy, you should ask yourself whether the two situations are analogous.

Now Let's Try the Passage

Many people believe that gold and platinum are the most valuable commodities. To the true entrepreneur, however, gold and platinum are less valuable than opportunities that can enable him to further enrich himself. Therefore, in the world of high finance, information is the most valuable commodity.

The author of the passage above makes which of the following assumptions?

- ⬭ Gold and platinum are not the most valuable commodities.
- ⬭ Entrepreneurs are not like most people.
- ⬭ The value of information is incalculably high.
- ⬭ Information about business opportunities is accurate and will lead to increased wealth.
- ⬭ Only entrepreneurs feel that information is the most valuable commodity.

Critical Reasoning Step-By-Step

1. Read the question first, looking for clues as to which type of argument this might be.
2. Read the passage carefully (no skimming), looking for the conclusion, the premises, and—most importantly—the assumptions.
3. Begin eliminating answer choices based on POE.

Here's How to Crack It

The question tells you that you are looking for an assumption, which means that as you read, you'll be looking for a hole in the argument.

Because an assumption supports the conclusion, it's a good idea to know what the conclusion is. Can you identify it? It was in the last sentence, preceded by "therefore": "In the world of high finance, information is the most valuable commodity."

As you read the passage, keep your eyes open for potential holes in the argument. For example, as you read, it might occur to you that the author is assuming that there is no such thing as bad information. Anyone who has ever taken a stock tip knows the error in that assumption.

Don't be upset if you can't find a hole in the argument as you read. The answer choices will give you a clue.

Let's attack the answer choices:

⬭ Gold and platinum are not the most valuable commodities.

Does this support the conclusion? In a way, it does. If information is supposed to be the most valuable commodity, it might help to know that gold and platinum are not the most valuable commodities.

Assumption Guidelines

1) Assumptions are never stated in the passage.
2) An assumption must support the conclusion; eliminate answer choices that do not strengthen the conclusion.
3) Assumptions frequently work to fill in gaps in the reasoning of the argument.
4) Look to see if the assumption, whether it is statistical, analogical, or causal, links the evidence to the conclusion.

Q: Most arguments can be divided into what three parts?
Turn the page for the answer.

However, saying that gold and platinum are *not* the most valuable commodities does not necessarily mean that information *is* the most valuable commodity.

⬭ Entrepreneurs are not like most people.

If most people find gold and platinum to be the most valuable commodities, while entrepreneurs prefer information, then it *could* be inferred that entrepreneurs are not like most people. Does this support the conclusion, though? Not really. Remember, the GMAT rewards narrow thinking.

⬭ The value of information is incalculably high.

This answer merely restates the conclusion. Remember, we're looking for an assumption, which is an *unstated* premise. In addition, this answer goes beyond the scope of the argument. To say that information is valuable does not mean that its value is "incalculable."

⬭ Information about business opportunities is accurate and will lead to increased wealth.

This is the best answer. If the business information is not accurate, it could not possibly be valuable. Therefore, this statement supports the conclusion by plugging a dangerous hole in the argument.

⬭ Only entrepreneurs feel that information is the most valuable commodity.

Does this statement strengthen the conclusion? Actually, it might weaken it. The conclusion states that "in the world of high finance, information is the most valuable commodity." Presumably the world of high finance is not composed exclusively of entrepreneurs. If only entrepreneurs believed information to be the most valuable commodity, then not everyone in the world of high finance would feel the same way.

2. STRENGTHEN-THE-ARGUMENT QUESTIONS

If a question asks you to strengthen an argument, it is saying that the argument can be strengthened; in other words, again, you're going to be dealing with an argument that has a gap in its logic.

Like assumption questions, strengthen-the-argument questions are really asking you to find this gap and then fix it with additional information. Here are some guidelines for spotting strengthen-the-argument statements among the answer choices:

- The best answer will strengthen the argument with *new* information. If you see an answer choice that comes straight from the passage, it's wrong.
- The new information you're looking for will support the conclusion of the passage. Find the conclusion in the passage, then try out each answer choice to see whether it makes the conclusion stronger.

- Strengthen-the-argument questions frequently turn on the gaps of logic we've already discussed. If the argument proposes a cause for an effect, you should ask yourself whether there might be some other cause. If the argument uses statistics, you should probably ask yourself whether the statistics involved are representative. If the argument offers an analogy, you should ask yourself whether the two situations are analogous.

How to Recognize a Strengthen-the-Argument Question

Strengthen-the-argument questions are generally worded in one of two ways:

- Which of the following, if true, most strengthens the author's argument?
- Which of the following, if true, most strongly supports the author's hypothesis?

Now Let's Try the Passage

It has recently been proposed that we adopt an all-volunteer army. This policy was tried on a limited basis several years ago and was a miserable failure. The level of education of the volunteers was unacceptably low, while levels of drug use and crime soared among army personnel. Can we trust our national defense to a volunteer army? The answer is clearly "No."

Which of the following statements, if true, most strengthens the author's claim that an all-volunteer army should not be implemented?

- ◯ The general level of education has risen since the first time an all-volunteer army was tried.
- ◯ The proposal was made by an organization called Citizens for Peace.
- ◯ The first attempt to create a volunteer army was carried out according to the same plan now under proposal and under the same conditions as those that exist today.
- ◯ A volunteer army would be less expensive than an army that relies on the draft.
- ◯ The size of the army needed today is smaller than that needed when a volunteer army was first tried.

Conclusion Is Key

The easiest way to strengthen an argument is to strengthen the conclusion. You can do this by presenting new evidence that strengthens the underlying assumptions. Any answer choice that comes from the passage will probably be wrong. New evidence or assumptions, whether statistical, analogical, or causal, must support the conclusion.

Here's How to Crack It

You know from reading the question first that you're expected to fix a flaw in the argument. Even better, the question itself tells you the conclusion of the passage: "An all-volunteer army should not be implemented."

Because the reasoning in a strengthen-the-argument question is going to contain gaps, it pays to see whether the argument is statistical, causal, or analogous. You may have noticed that the argument does, in fact, use an analogy. The author bases his conclusion on the results of one previous experience. In effect he says, "The idea didn't work then, so it won't work now." This is the potential flaw in the argument.

If you didn't spot the argument by analogy, don't worry. You would probably have seen it when you started attacking the answer choices:

◯ The general level of education has risen since the first time an all-volunteer army was tried.

Does this support the author's conclusion? Actually, it may weaken the conclusion. If the general level of education has risen, it could be argued that the level of education of army volunteers is also higher. This would remove one of the author's objections to a volunteer army. Eliminate it.

◯ The proposal was made by an organization called Citizens for Peace.

This is irrelevant to the author's conclusion. You might have wondered whether a group called "Citizens for Peace" was the right organization to make suggestions about the army. Attacking the reputation of a person in order to cast doubt on that person's ideas is a very old pastime. There's even a name for it: an *ad hominem fallacy*. An ad hominem statement does not strengthen an argument. Eliminate it.

◯ The first attempt to create a volunteer army was carried out according to the same plan now under proposal and under the same conditions as those that exist today.

A: Conclusion, premises (evidence), and assumptions (evidence not stated).

This is the best answer. The passage as it stands is potentially flawed because we cannot know that a new attempt to institute an all-volunteer army would turn out the same way it did before. This answer choice provides new information that suggests that the two situations *are* analogous.

◯ A volunteer army would be less expensive than an army that relies on the draft.

Does this support the conclusion? No. In fact, it makes a case *for* a volunteer army. Eliminate it.

◯ The size of the army needed today is smaller than that needed when a volunteer army was first tried.

Like answer choice D, this answer contradicts the conclusion of the passage. If we need a smaller army today, maybe we would be able to find enough smart and honest volunteers to make a volunteer army work. Eliminate it.

3. WEAKEN-THE-ARGUMENT QUESTIONS

If a question asks you to weaken an argument, it implies that the argument can be weakened; in other words, once again, you're going to be dealing with unstated premises and a logical gap.

Like assumption questions and strengthen-the-argument questions, weaken-the-argument questions really ask you to find a hole in the argument. This time, however, you don't need to fix the hole. All you have to do is expose it. Here are some guidelines for finding weaken-the-argument statements among the answer choices:

- The statement you'll look for should weaken the *conclusion* of the passage. Find the conclusion in the passage, then try out each answer choice to see whether it makes the conclusion less tenable.
- Weaken-the-argument questions frequently trade on the gaps of logic that we've already discussed. If the argument proposes a cause for an effect, ask yourself whether there might be some other cause. If the argument uses statistics, ask yourself whether the statistics involved are representative. If the argument offers an analogy, ask yourself whether the two situations are analogous.

How to Recognize a Weaken-the-Argument Question

Weaken-the-argument questions are usually worded in one of the following ways:

- Which of the following, if true, most seriously weakens the conclusion drawn in the passage?
- Which of the following indicates a flaw in the reasoning above?
- Which of the following, if true, would cast the most serious doubt on the argument above?

Where, Oh Where, Is the Conclusion?

Q: What are some helpful approaches to finding the conclusion?

Turn the page for the answer.

Now Let's Try the Passage

The recent turnaround of the LEX Corporation is a splendid example of how an astute chief executive officer can rechannel a company's assets toward profitability. With the new CEO at the helm, LEX has gone, in only three business quarters, from a 10 million dollar operating loss to a 22 million dollar operating gain.

A major flaw in the reasoning of the passage above is that

- ◯ the passage assumes that the new CEO was the only factor that affected the corporation's recent success
- ◯ the recent success of the corporation may be only temporary
- ◯ the chief executive officer may be drawing a salary and bonus that will set a damaging precedent for this and other corporations
- ◯ the author does not define "profitability"
- ◯ rechanneling assets is only a short-term solution

Here's How to Crack It

You know from reading the question that you'll need to find a flaw in the reasoning of the argument. As you read the passage, look for the conclusion. The correct answer choice will weaken this conclusion. In this passage, the conclusion is in the first sentence: "The recent turnaround of the LEX Corporation is a splendid example of how an astute chief executive officer can rechannel a company's assets toward profitability."

Because this is a weaken-the-argument question that will almost certainly contain a gap in its reasoning, you should look to see whether the argument is causal, statistical, or analogical. In this case, the argument is causal. The passage implies that the sole cause of the LEX Corporation's turnaround is the new CEO. While this *may* be true, it is also possible that there are other causes. If you didn't spot the causal argument, don't worry. You would probably have seen it when you attacked the answer choices. Let's do that now:

- ◯ the passage assumes that the new CEO was the only factor that affected the corporation's recent success

This is the best answer. The new chief executive officer may not have been the cause of the turnaround—there may have been some other cause we don't know about.

- ◯ the recent success of the corporation may be only temporary

It may be hasty to crown LEX with laurels after only three economic quarters, but this statement doesn't point out a flaw in the *reasoning* of the passage. Eliminate it.

◯ the chief executive officer may be drawing a salary and bonus that will set a damaging precedent for this and other corporations

This answer choice may seem tempting because it's not in favor of the new CEO. But this alone doesn't represent a major flaw in the reasoning of the passage. Eliminate it.

◯ the author does not define "profitability"

An author can't define every word he uses. Profitability seems a common enough word, and a change in the balance sheet from minus 10 million to plus 22 million seems to qualify. Eliminate it.

◯ rechanneling assets is only a short-term solution

Like the second answer choice, this statement implies that all the votes aren't in yet. This does not affect the reasoning of the argument, however. Eliminate it.

Weaken-the-Argument Questions Come in Different Flavors

GMAT test writers use a variety of different wordings to ask the same question. One variation on the weaken-the-argument question might look like this:

A telephone poll conducted over two states asked respondents whether their homes were ever cold during the winter months. 99% of respondents said they were never cold during the winter months. The pollsters published their findings, concluding that 99% of all homes in the United States have adequate heating.

Which of the following most accurately describes what might be a questionable technique employed by the pollsters in drawing their conclusion?

◯ The poll wrongly ascribes the underlying causes of the problem.
◯ The poll assumes conditions in the two states are representative of the entire country.
◯ The pollsters conducted the poll by telephone, thus relying on the veracity of the subjects they spoke to.
◯ The pollsters did not go to the houses in person, thus precluding the actual measurement of temperatures in the subjects' homes.
◯ The pollsters never defined the term "cold" in terms of a specific temperature.

Where, Oh Where, Is the Conclusion?

A: Look at the beginning or end of the passage and be familiar with conclusion flag words.

Popular GMAT Assumptions

Q: What kind of assumptions crop up the most on the GMAT?

Turn the page for the answer.

Here's How to Crack It

Whether a question contains the words "weakens the argument," or "undermines the conclusion," or even "describes a questionable technique," what it is really asking you to do is find a hole in the logic of the argument. And, as usual, there are three types of holes that the GMAT test writers are very fond of: statistical, causal, and analogical. Did you spot one of these as you read the passage? Whenever you see an actual statistic in an argument (in this case, 99 percent), you should examine it closely: The pollsters are basing a statistic for the entire country on a poll conducted in only two states. If you didn't spot this as you read the passage, don't worry; you'll spot it as you read the answer choices.

◯ The poll wrongly ascribes the underlying causes of the problem.

This answer choice says there might be an alternate cause for the conclusion—but does this feel like a causal argument? Let's hold onto this and keep reading.

◯ The poll assumes conditions in the two states are representative of the entire country.

Aha! This choice is saying there is a statistical flaw in the argument. What if the two states were located in the southern part of the United States? If the residents of Florida were warm in January, would that be representative of the rest of the country who might be freezing? This seems like it must be the best answer, but let's keep reading to make sure.

◯ The pollsters conducted the poll by telephone, thus relying on the veracity of the subjects they spoke to.

Popular GMAT Assumptions

A: Causal assumptions. If an argument states that one event caused another, always ask yourself if there could have been an alternate cause.

While this might represent a weakness in their interviewing technique, the question to ask yourself is whether this is an inherent weakness in the way the pollsters *drew their conclusion*. It is not; eliminate it.

◯ The pollsters did not go to the houses in person, thus precluding the actual measurement of temperatures in the subjects' homes.

Again, if the pollsters had measured the temperature in each of the houses they went to, their information would probably have been more accurate, but does this constitute a flaw in the way the conclusion was drawn? Nope. Cross this one off.

◯ The pollsters never defined the term "cold" in terms of a specific temperature.

This choice is nitpicking. While it might have been better if the pollsters had asked the respondents what temperature they considered cold, this wouldn't really weaken the conclusion. The best answer is the second one.

4. INFERENCE QUESTIONS

Like inference questions in Reading Comprehension, Critical Reasoning inference questions do not really ask you to make an inference. In fact, you will often find that the answer to a Critical Reasoning inference question is so basic that you won't believe it could be correct the first time you read it. Inference questions often have little to do with the conclusion of the passage; instead they might ask you to make inferences about one or more of the premises.

How to Recognize an Inference Question

Inference questions are typically worded in one of the following ways:

- Which of the following can be inferred from the information above?
- Which of the following must be true on the basis of the statements above?
- Which of the following conclusions is best supported by the passage?
- Which of the following conclusions could most properly be drawn from the information above?

You'll note that the last two questions seem to ask about the conclusion—but, as you'll see, they in fact ask for an inference.

Let's try an example:

In film and videotape, it is possible to induce viewers to project their feelings onto characters on the screen. In one study, when a camera shot of a woman's face was preceded by a shot of a baby in a crib, the audience thought the woman's face was registering happiness. When the same shot of the woman's face was preceded by a shot of a lion running toward the camera, the audience thought the woman's face was registering fear. Television news teams must be careful to avoid such manipulation of their viewers.

Which of the following can be inferred from the passage?

- ◯ Television news teams have abused their position of trust in the past.
- ◯ The expression on the woman's face was, in actuality, blank.
- ◯ A camera shot of a baby in a crib provoked feelings of happiness in the audience.
- ◯ Audiences should strive to be less gullible.
- ◯ The technique for manipulating audiences described in the passage would also work with photo slide shows.

B-School Lingo

sharks: aggressive students who smell blood and move in for the kill

shark comment: comment designed to gore a fellow student in class discussion

slice and dice: running all kinds of quantitative analysis on a set of numbers

soft courses: touchy-feely courses such as human resources and organizational behavior

soft skills: conflict resolution, teamwork, negotiation, and oral and written communication

Source: *The Best Business Schools*

Here's How to Crack It

This is an inference question. The test writers are probably not interested in the conclusion of the passage. You'll look for a statement that seems so obvious that it almost doesn't need saying. Let's attack the answer choices:

◯ Television news teams have abused their position of trust in the past.

If you chose this answer, you inferred too much. The passage doesn't say that news teams have ever abused their position of trust. Eliminate it.

◯ The expression on the woman's face was, in actuality, blank.

The audience had no idea what the expression on the woman's face was, and neither do we. It would make sense for the woman's face to be blank, but we don't know whether this is so. This answer goes too far.

◯ A camera shot of a baby in a crib provoked feelings of happiness in the audience.

This is the best answer. The passage says that the audience projects its own feelings onto characters on the screen. If the audience believes the woman's face reflects happiness, then that must have been its own reaction.

⬭ Audiences should strive to be less gullible.

This statement goes way beyond the intent of the passage. Eliminate it.

⬭ The technique for manipulating audiences described in the passage would also work with photo slide shows.

Again, this statement goes too far to be the correct answer to an inference question. Just because you know the technique works with film and videotape, that doesn't mean it will work for other visual formats. Eliminate it.

Another Type of Inference Question

Inference questions come in one other form—and as you read them, you might think you are being asked to supply a conclusion rather than an inference. Almost invariably, the question asks you to find a "conclusion that is best supported by the passage above." But, in fact, this is really nothing more than an inference question. And again, the key is not going too far.

Here's an example.

Fewer elected officials are supporting environmental legislation this year than at any time in the last decade. In a study of 30 elected officials, only five were actively campaigning for new environmental legislation. This comes at a time when the public's concern for the environment is growing by leaps and bounds.

Which of the following conclusions is best supported by the passage above?

⬭ More elected officials are needed to support environmental legislation.
⬭ Elected officials have lost touch with the concerns of the public.
⬭ The five elected officials who actively campaigned for new environmental legislation should be congratulated.
⬭ If the environment is to be saved, elected officials must support environmental legislation.
⬭ If elected officials are truly to represent their constituents, many of them must increase their support of environmental legislation.

Reading Comprehension Review
"Yin-Yang" Words:
Yin
generally...
the old view...
the widespread belief...
most scientists think...
on the one hand...
Yang
however, this time...
however, the new view...
but the in-crowd believes...
but Doctor Spleegle thinks...
on the other hand...

Here's How to Crack It

Because you read the question first, you know that this is really just an inference question—and, as always with inference questions, the main thing is not to go too far. Be wary of answer choices that go further than the scope of the original argument. For example, if the passage has given you several noncontroversial facts about advertising, do not select an answer choice that says advertising is a waste of time.

Let's attack the answer choices:

> ◯ More elected officials are needed to support environmental legislation.

This statement ignores the last premise of the passage—that the public is becoming more and more concerned about the environment. Eliminate it.

> ◯ Elected officials have lost touch with the concerns of the public.

This clearly goes beyond the scope of the argument and ignores parts of the first two premises that relate to the environment.

> ◯ The five elected officials who actively campaigned for new environmental legislation should be congratulated.

This statement, while consistent with the sentiments of the author, again does not deal with the last premise, relating to the concerns of the public.

> ◯ If the environment is to be saved, elected officials must support environmental legislation.

This answer choice again ignores the last premise in the passage and goes too far. Eliminate it.

> ◯ If elected officials are truly to represent their constituents, many of them must increase their support of environmental legislation.

Bingo. This answer is supported by all the premises, and it does not go beyond the scope of the argument.

FOUR DOWN—FOUR TO GO

As you begin working through the practice questions in this book or in *The Official Guide to GMAT Review,* you will quickly realize that most Critical Reasoning questions turn out to be one of the four major question types you have just learned: assumption, strengthen-the-argument, weaken-the-argument, or inference. The four remaining question types appear much less often. However, because of the somewhat random nature of the CAT, one of these less frequently asked questions could easily be the first one you see on the Verbal portion of the GMAT; therefore, it is just as important to be familiar with all eight.

5. RESOLVE/EXPLAIN QUESTIONS

Some GMAT questions ask you to resolve an apparent paradox or explain a possible discrepancy. In these questions, the passage will present you with two seemingly contradictory facts. Your job is to find the answer choice that allows both of the facts from the passage to be true.

How to Recognize a Resolve/Explain Question

Resolve/Explain questions are usually worded in one of the following ways:

- Which of the following, if true, resolves the apparent contradiction presented in the passage above?
- Which of the following, if true, best explains the discrepancy described above?
- Which of the following, if true, forms a partial explanation for the paradox described above?

Here's an example:

In 1994, TipTop Airlines reported an increase in the total number of passengers it carried from the year before, but a *decrease* in total revenues—even though prices for its tickets on all routes remained unchanged during the two-year period.

Which of the following, if true, best reconciles the apparent paradox described above?

- ⬭ TipTop Airlines was a victim of a mild recession in 1994.
- ⬭ Total passenger miles were up in 1994.
- ⬭ Fuel costs remained constant during the two-year period.
- ⬭ Passengers traveled shorter (and thus less expensive) distances in 1994.
- ⬭ TipTop did not buy any new airplanes or equipment in 1994.

Q: What is key when eliminating choices from an assumption question?
Turn the page for the answer.

A: Scope! If something is out of scope—if it is not closely tied to what's said in the passage—then you should eliminate it.

Here's How to Crack It

First, restate the contradiction in your own words.

"TipTop's revenues went down even though they flew more passengers."

Now, let's see which of the answer choices makes both of the facts in the argument true.

◯ TipTop Airlines was a victim of a mild recession in 1994.

If TipTop was affected by a recession, that might explain a loss of revenues. But because ticket prices remained the same, it would not explain how the number of passengers could have increased at the same time. Eliminate it.

◯ Total passenger miles were up in 1994.

If total passenger miles were up, and prices remained the same, there is no way that there could have been a loss of revenues. We can eliminate this choice as well.

◯ Fuel costs remained constant during the two-year period.

If fuel costs had *not* remained constant, the company's profits might have fallen. An increase in fuel prices could have increased its costs and cut into profits. But it would not have cut into total *revenues*, which is what we are concerned with in this passage. Of course, because choice C told us that the costs remained constant, this choice has no bearing on the argument at all. Eliminate it.

◯ Passengers traveled shorter (and thus less expensive) distances in 1994.

Bingo! If passengers traveled on short, inexpensive flights, then they paid less money. In spite of the increase in number of passengers, the money they paid could have added up to less than that of the year before. This is the best answer, but always remember to read all the choices anyway.

◯ TipTop did not buy any new airplanes or equipment in 1994.

This answer is much like the third choice, which we call choice C. If TipTop *had* bought new planes, it might have cut into its profits, but it would not have had any bearing on revenues. Of course, because this choice told us that TipTop did not buy any planes, there is no relevance at all. Eliminate it.

6. EVALUATE-THE-ARGUMENT QUESTIONS

A few GMAT Critical Reasoning questions will ask you to pick an answer choice that would help to "evaluate" or "assess" part of an argument. Like assumption questions, evaluate-the-argument questions revolve around understanding the unspoken gap in the logic of an argument.

How to Recognize an Evaluate-the-Argument Question

Evaluate-the-argument questions are generally worded in one of the following ways:

- The answer to which of the following questions would be most useful in evaluating the significance of the author's claims?
- Which of the following pieces of information would be most useful in assessing the logic of the argument presented above?

Take a look at the following example:

Following a period of lingering malaise after a recent remarkable economic upturn in the solar-powered energy sector, Company X, a major maker of solar-powered generators, claimed that its rapid upturn resulted from the inventory still on hand in its warehouse.

Which of the following, if it could be carried out, would be most useful in evaluating the company's hypothesis as to the causes of its rapid economic upturn?

- ◯ Comparing the length of the economic downturn experienced by Company X to the length of the upturn later experienced by Company X
- ◯ Comparing the rapidity of the economic upturn for Company X to that of other major makers of solar-powered generators, which did not have inventory on hand
- ◯ Calculating the average sales increases within the individual business units of Company X
- ◯ Comparing the total number of solar-powered generator sales by Company X just before the economic upturn to the total number of solar-powered generator sales by Company X just after the economic upturn
- ◯ Using economic theory to predict the most likely date of the next economic upturn for Company X

Q: How would you approach a strengthening- or weakening-the-argument question?
Turn the page for the answer.

Here's How to Crack It

As always, you should begin by reading the question first—and the key word that should jump out at you in this question is "evaluate." In this particular passage, the conclusion is in the second half of the argument: Company X claims that its economic upturn was particularly fast-moving because the company already had existing inventory on hand.

This is an evaluate-the-argument question and will almost certainly contain a gap in its reasoning. You should, as always, look to see whether the argument is causal, statistical, or analogical. Take a moment before you keep reading, and look at the passage again to see if you can spot which type of argument this is.

In this case, the argument was causal. Company X says the cause of its rapid turnaround was the inventory it had in its warehouses—which presumably let the company immediately take advantage of the new demand for its product. The company implies that the sole cause of the rapidity of its economic upturn was its inventory. While this may be true, it is also possible that there are other causes. If you didn't spot the causal argument, don't worry. You would probably have seen it when you attacked the answer choices. Let's look at them now:

⬭ Comparing the length of the economic downturn experienced by Company X to the length of the upturn later experienced by Company X

The length of the economic downturn that preceded the upturn seems like it would be outside the scope of this argument, and, in any case, would not have much to do with whether the speed of Company X's upturn had anything to do with the inventory it had on hand once the upturn began. If you were thinking that the length of time would matter because the inventory might be out of date, you overthought the problem. Eliminate it.

⬭ Comparing the rapidity of the economic upturn for Company X to that of other major makers of solar-powered generators, which did not have inventory on hand

If Company X's competitors, which did not have inventory on hand, did just as well or better during the economic upturn, then Company X's explanation for its speedy upturn might be incorrect. In other words, there might be some other cause. Would this comparison be useful in evaluating Company X's argument? This seems like it would be very useful, but let's hold onto it while we look at the other answer choices.

⬭ Calculating the average sales increases within the individual business units of Company X

This answer choice might help us to understand in more detail the extent of the upturn at Company X, but it gives us no insights into the causes behind the rapidity of their economic upturn. Let this one go.

- ○ Comparing the total number of solar-powered generator sales by Company X just before the economic upturn to the total number of solar-powered generator sales by Company X just after the economic upturn

Like the comparison in the previous answer choice, this comparison would no doubt detail exactly the extent of the rapid economic upturn for Company X, but not explain the cause of the rapid upturn. Eliminate it.

- ○ Using economic theory to predict the most likely date of the next economic upturn for Company X

A future economic upturn (presumably preceded by a downturn) is surely well beyond the scope of this question. We are concerned only with evaluating the reason that Company X believes is the cause of its speedy economic upturn. Eliminate it.

Given the fact that we've eliminated all the other possible answers, choice B looks even better.

7. IDENTIFY-THE-REASONING QUESTIONS

Occasionally, a Critical Reasoning question will ask you to identify a method, technique, or strategy used in the passage, or to identify the role of a bolded phrase or sentence in the passage. Either way, the best technique for answering this rare question type is to do what you would do to answer any of the other question types: identify the conclusion and the premise and think about how they are related.

To check out which b-schools have the "Best Professors," check out the Business School Ranking lists at PrincetonReview.com.

How to Recognize an Identify-the-Reasoning Question

Identify-the-reasoning questions are generally worded in one of the following ways:

- The bolded phrase plays which of the following roles in the argument above?
- The argument uses which of the following methods of reasoning?

Here's a typical example:

Although measuring the productivity of outside consultants is a complex endeavor, **Company K, which relies heavily on consultants for long-term projects, must find ways to assess the performance of these workers.** The risks to a company that does not review the productivity of its human resources are simply too great. **Last year, Company L was forced into receivership after its productivity declined for the third straight quarter.**

The bolded sentences play which of the following roles in the argument above?

- ○ The first sentence states the author's conclusion, and the second sentence refutes that conclusion.
- ○ The first sentence states an assumption of the argument, and the second sentence provides evidence to undermine that position.
- ○ The first sentence states one of the author's premises, and the second sentence provides the argument's conclusion.
- ○ The first sentence states a position, and the second sentence refutes that position.
- ○ The first sentence states the conclusion, and the second sentence supports the conclusion with an analogy.

A: Expose the assumption and build it up to strengthen the argument or tear it down to weaken the argument.

Here's How to Crack It

As you read the question, the first things that should jump out at you are the words "bolded sentences," which signal that this is an identify-the-reasoning question. And the first thing to do in an identify-the-reasoning question is to find the conclusion. Where is it? If you said "in the second half of the first sentence," then you are doing just fine. Company K, according to the argument, should find a way to measure the productivity of its consultants. The second sentence merely reiterates the first, and the third sentence supports the conclusion with what appears to be an analogous situation.

As you look at the answer choices, look for an answer that correctly explains the purpose of the two bolded sentences. Now, let's look at the answer choices:

- ○ The first sentence states the author's conclusion, and the second sentence refutes that conclusion.

The first bolded sentence is, in fact, the conclusion of the passage; so far, so good. But does the second sentence refute that conclusion? Not at all. In fact, it seems to be supporting it. Eliminate it.

◯ The first sentence states an assumption of the argument, and the second sentence provides evidence to undermine that position.

We've already determined that the first bolded sentence is the conclusion of the argument—but even if we weren't sure of that, we could rule out this answer choice because an assumption is never stated in the passage. Even if you missed that, you would probably be able to eliminate this answer choice because the second bolded sentence seems to be supporting the first sentence, not undermining it. Eliminate it.

◯ The first sentence states one of the author's premises, and the second sentence provides the argument's conclusion.

A premise is evidence in support of a conclusion. The first bolded sentence (about Company K) seems less a piece of evidence than the conclusion itself. The second bolded sentence is about another company entirely and seems to be offered in support of the first sentence; in other words, it is not likely to be the conclusion of the argument. Eliminate it.

◯ The first sentence states a position, and the second sentence refutes that position.

Like answer choices A and B, this says the second bolded sentence refutes the first. Because this is clearly not so, we can forget about this answer choice as well. Eliminate it.

◯ The first sentence states the conclusion, and the second sentence supports the conclusion with an analogy.

Because we have eliminated all the other possibilities, you should feel hopeful that this is the best answer, but never skip the final step and assume that choice E must be right without reading it. Does the first bolded sentence state the conclusion of the argument? Yes, it does. Does the second sentence support the conclusion with an analogy? Yes, in fact it does. The argument compares Company K's situation to that of Company L. If this were a weaken-the-argument question, you would need to be asking yourself if these two companies were actually analogous. However, in this case, all we have to do is pick answer choice E and move on.

Need More Practice?
Verbal Workout for the New GMAT contains tons of drills with detailed answer explanations.

8. PARALLEL-THE-REASONING QUESTIONS

Parallel-the-reasoning questions ask you to recognize the reasoning in a passage and follow the same line of reasoning in one of the answer choices. The best way to understand the passage associated with a reasoning question is to simplify the terms. Here's an example: "If it rains, I will stay home today." We could simplify this by saying, "If A, then B."

How to Recognize a Parallel-the-Reasoning Question

Parallel-the-reasoning questions are usually worded in one of the following ways:

- Which of the following most closely parallels the reasoning used in the argument above?
- Which of the following supports its conclusion in the same manner as the argument above?
- Which of the following is most like the argument above in its logical structure?

Here's an example:

World-class marathon runners do not run more than six miles per day when they are training. Therefore, if you run more than six miles per day, you are not world-class.

Which of the following statements supports its conclusion in the same manner as the argument above?

- ⬭ Sprinters always run in the morning. If it is morning, and you see someone running, it will not be a sprinter.
- ⬭ Paint never dries in less than three hours. If it dries in less than three hours, it is not paint.
- ⬭ Little League games are more fun for the parents than for the children who actually play. Therefore, the parents should be made to play.
- ⬭ If a car starts in the morning, chances are it will start again that evening. Our car always starts in the morning, and it always starts in the evening as well.
- ⬭ If you sleep less than four hours per night, you may be doing yourself a disservice. Studies have shown that the most valuable sleep occurs in the fifth hour.

Here's How to Crack It

First, simplify the argument in the passage. World-class marathon runners do not run more than six miles per day when they are training. (If A, then B.) Therefore, if you run more than six miles per day, you are not world-class. (If not B, then not A.)

Now let's attack the answer choices:

- ◯ Sprinters always run in the morning. If it is morning, and you see someone running, it will not be a sprinter.

Just because this answer choice is also about running doesn't mean the reasoning will be the same. In fact, it is unlikely that the test writers would use the same subject matter for the correct answer. If we simplify this argument, we get: If A, then B. If B, then not A. Is this the same reasoning used in the passage? No. Eliminate it.

- ◯ Paint never dries in less than three hours. If it dries in less than three hours, it is not paint.

If we simplify this argument, we get: If A, then B. If not B, then not A. This is the best answer.

- ◯ Little League games are more fun for the parents than for the children who actually play. Therefore, the parents should be made to play.

Simplifying this argument, we get…not much. The reasoning here is totally different. Also, note that the subject matter here is still about sports. Eliminate it.

- ◯ If a car starts in the morning, chances are it will start again that evening. Our car always starts in the morning, and it always starts in the evening as well.

If we simplify this argument, we get: If A, then B. If always A, then always B. That doesn't sound right. Eliminate it.

- ◯ If you sleep less than four hours per night, you may be doing yourself a disservice. Studies have shown that the most valuable sleep occurs in the fifth hour.

Simplifying this argument, we get…again, not much. The reasoning in this answer choice is very different from the reasoning in the passage. Eliminate it.

Putting It All Together

Now that you know how to spot and how to approach each of the eight question types, the best way to proceed is to practice. As you do each Critical Reasoning question, force yourself to decide what type of question it is before you start reading the passage. Once identified, a Critical Reasoning question isn't a mystery anymore—it will adhere to the conventions you've learned, and you will have a much easier time choosing the best answer.

To get you started, here's a drill to see how you are doing at spotting the different Critical Reasoning question types.

DRILL 12 (Spotting Critical Reasoning Question Types)

The answers can be found in Part VI.

For each of the questions below, decide which question type it belongs to. For extra credit, list what you should look for in the passage that would normally precede the question.

1. Which of the following, if true, gives the most support to the recommendations above?
2. If the statements above are true, which of the following can properly be inferred on the basis of them?
3. The answer to which of the following questions would be most useful in evaluating the significance of the counter-claimant's charge?
4. The argument in the passage depends on which of the following assumptions?
5. Which of the following statements, if true, provides the best evidence that the CEO's reasoning is flawed?
6. Which of the following, if true, best reconciles the seeming discrepancy described above?
7. The bolded phrase plays which of the following roles in the argument?
8. Which of the following most closely parallels the reasoning used in the argument above?

Summary

- Critical Reasoning is made up of short passages. Each of these passages is followed by one or two questions, for a total of roughly 11 questions.
- The test writers have said that no formal logic is required to answer these questions, but in fact some knowledge of the rudiments of GMAT logic *will* increase your score.
- There are three parts to an argument.
    - Conclusion
    - Premises
    - Assumptions
- Critical Reasoning is **not** like Reading Comprehension.
    - You should never skim; each word is important.
    - Most of the Reading Comprehension techniques we have shown you are inappropriate for Critical Reasoning.
- Always read the question first because it will contain clues that will help you to find the answer as you read the passage. As you eliminate answer choices, cross them off in your scratch booklet.
- In Critical Reasoning, the most important POE technique is eliminating answers that are outside the scope of the argument.
- There are eight question types. Each type has its own strategy.
    - **Assumption questions**
      Assumptions are unstated premises that support the conclusion. Look for a flaw in the argument that is fixed by the assumption.
    - **Strengthen-the-argument questions**
      Look for an answer choice with information that supports the conclusion.
    - **Weaken-the-argument questions**
      These questions ask you to find the answer choice that points out flaws in the reasoning of passages.

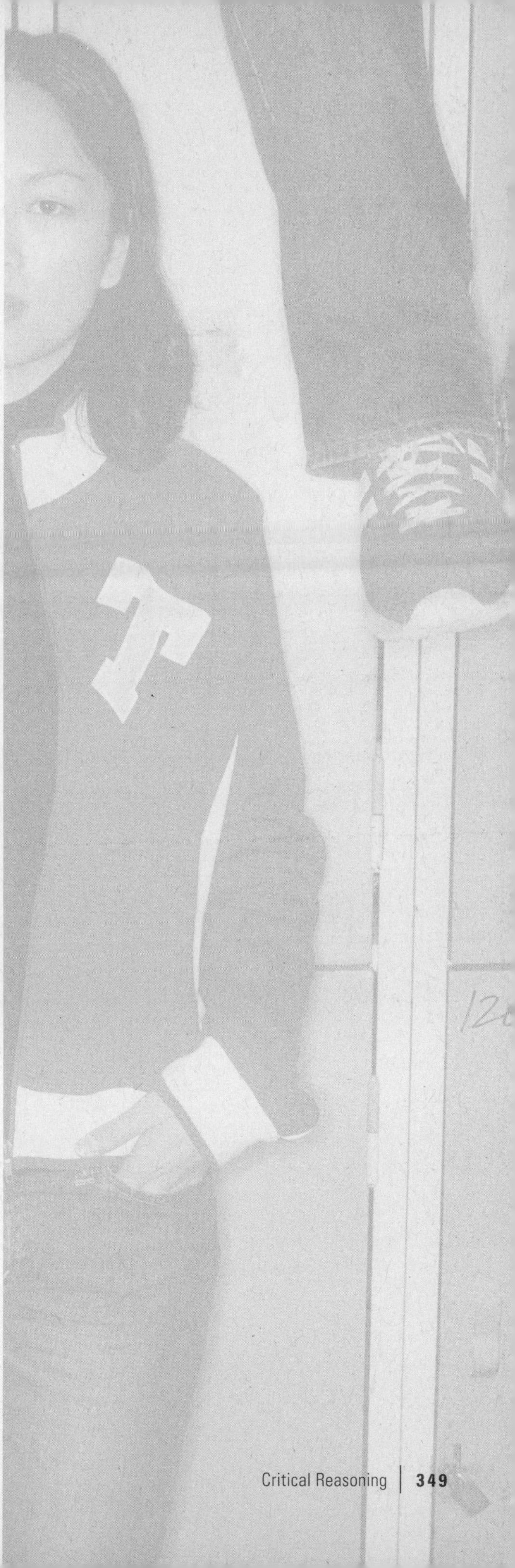

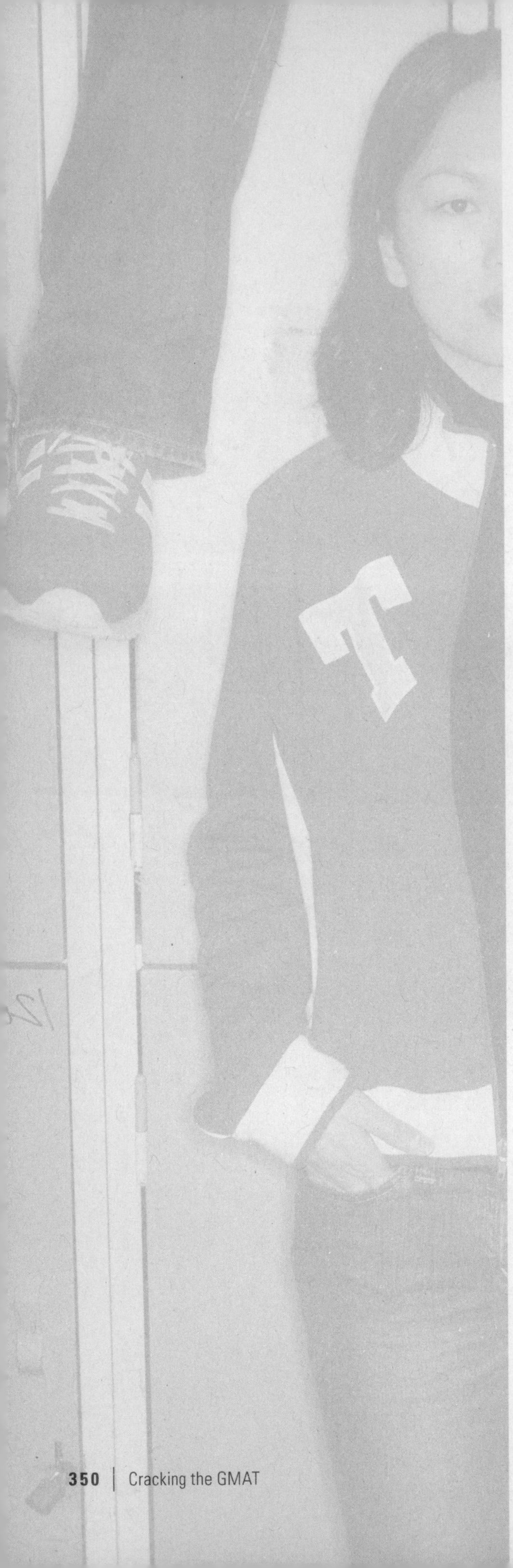

- **Inference questions**
  Like Reading Comprehension inference questions, these questions do not actually want you to infer. Unlike most Critical Reasoning questions, these questions typically concern the *premises,* not the conclusion.

- **Resolve/explain questions**
  This type of question asks you to pick an answer choice that explains an apparent contradiction between two incompatible facts.

- **Evaluate-the-argument questions**
  This type of question asks you to pick an answer choice that would help to evaluate an unspoken assumption about the argument.

- **Identify-the-reasoning questions**
  This type of question asks you to pick an answer choice that identifies the purpose of a word or phrase or the type of reasoning used in an argument.

- **Parallel-the-reasoning questions**
  This type of question asks you to find an argument in one of the answer choices that mimics the method of reasoning used in the original argument. Most of these questions can be answered by simplifying (if A, then B).

o In assumption questions, weaken-the-argument questions, and strengthen-the-argument questions, there are three types of assumptions for which you should be on the lookout. These are (in order of frequency):
  - Causal assumptions—Ask yourself whether there might be an alternate cause.
  - Assumptions of analogy—Ask yourself whether the two situations are analogous.
  - Statistical assumptions—Ask yourself whether the statistics are representative.

Part IV
How to Crack the Integrated Reasoning GMAT

Chapter 18 Integrated Reasoning: Basics

GMAC introduced the Integrated Reasoning section to the GMAT in June of 2012. This chapter provides an overview of the section. The following chapter provides some specific strategies. We have also included some practice questions to help you prepare.

In 2012, the GMAT gained a new section called Integrated Reasoning. This chapter reviews the basics of the new section, including a run down on all four new question types. We've also included a chapter that explains some strategies that will help you handle these questions. Finally, this book includes two complete Integrated Reasoning sections with explanations so that you can practice.

MEET THE INTEGRATED REASONING SECTION

The Integrated Reasoning section is 30 minutes long. You'll see it as the second section of your test. Officially, there are only 12 questions, which sounds pretty great. However, most of those questions have multiple parts. So, for example, a Table Analysis question—one of the new question types we'll discuss—usually has three statements that you need to evaluate. So, your answer to the question really consists of three separate responses. For the entire section, you'll actually need to select approximately 28 different responses.

Integrated Reasoning Is Not Adaptive

Unlike the Quantitative and Verbal sections, the Integrated Reasoning section is not adaptive. So, you won't see harder questions if you keep answering questions correctly. That's good news because it means that you'll more easily be able to focus your attention on the current question rather than worrying whether you got the previous question right!

Test writers refer to non-adaptive sections as linear. Pacing for a linear section is different from the pacing that we reviewed for the adaptive Quantitative and Verbal sections.

For Integrated Reasoning, pacing is motivated by two general principles.

Pacing Guidelines

1. Work the easier parts of each question first. As you'll see, many Integrated Reasoning questions call for more than one response per question. Work the easier parts of each question first.

2. Don't get stubborn. With so many questions to answer in only 30 minutes, the Integrated Reasoning section can seem very fast paced. Spending too much time on one question means that you may not get to see all of the questions. Sometimes it's best to guess and move on.

Integrated Reasoning Scores

The Integrated Reasoning section is scored on a scale from 1 to 8 in one point increments. While GMAC has not released too many details about the way in which they calculate the score for this section of the test, there are two key facts to keep in mind.

- **Scoring is all or nothing.** Most Integrated Reasoning questions include multiple parts. To get credit for the question, you must select the correct response for each part. For example, Table Analysis questions generally include three statements that you must evaluate. If you select the wrong response for even one of these statements, you get no credit for the entire question.
- **There are experimental questions.** GMAC has stated that the Integrated Reasoning section contains experimental questions that do not count toward your score. They have not, however, stated how many experimental questions there are in the section. It's likely that two or three of the twelve questions in the section are experimental. If you find a question particularly difficult or time-consuming, it is worthwhile to remember that the question could be experimental.

To score the section, GMAC first calculates a raw score. You get one point for each non-experimental question that you get completely correct. Then, your raw score is converted to the 1 to 8 Integrated Reasoning scaled score.

There's a Calculator

There's an onscreen calculator available for the Integrated Reasoning section. The calculator is not available, however, for the Quantitative section. For the Quantitative section, you still need to perform any necessary calculations by hand.

The calculator for the Integrated Reasoning section is relatively basic. There are buttons to perform the four standard operations: addition, subtraction, multiplication, and division. In addition, buttons to take a square root, find a percent, and take a reciprocal round out the available functions. There are also buttons to store and recall a value in the calculator's memory.

To use the calculator, you'll need to open it by clicking on the 'calculator' button in the upper left corner of your screen. The calculator will generally open in the middle of your screen but you can move it around so that you can see the text of the problem or the numbers on any charts or graphs that are part of the question. The calculator is available for all Integrated Reasoning questions. You can enter a number into the calculator either by clicking on the onscreen number buttons or by typing the number using the keyboard.

Here's what the calculator looks like:

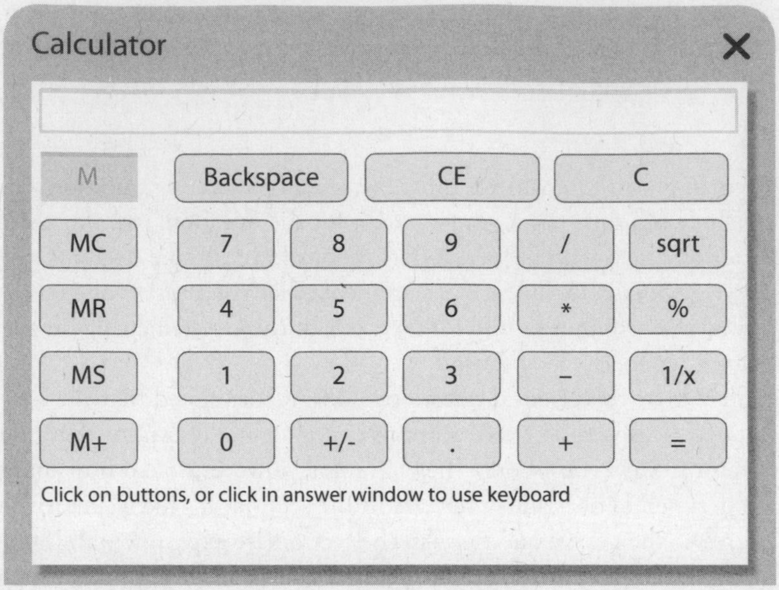

For the most part, the keys on the onscreen calculator work as you might expect. However, a few keys may not work as expected. Oddly enough, that's particularly true if you are used to using a more sophisticated calculator. So, here are few tips about using some of the calculator keys:

MC is the memory clear key. Use this key to wipe out any values that you have stored in the calculator's memory.

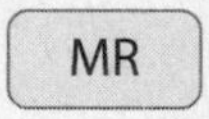

MR is the memory recall key. Use this key to return any value that you have stored in the memory to the calculation area. For example, if you want to divide the number currently on your screen by the number in the memory, you would enter the key sequence / MR =.

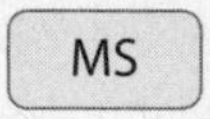

MS is the memory store key. Use this key to store the number currently on the screen in the calculator's memory.

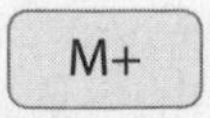

M+ is the memory addition key. Use this key to add the current onscreen number to the number in the calculator's memory. For example, if 2 is stored in the calculator's memory and 3 is on screen, then clicking M+ will result in 5 being stored in the calculator's memory.

Backspace is used to clear the last digit entered. Use this key to correct mistakes when entering numbers without clearing the entire number. For example, if you entered 23 but meant to enter 25, click backspace then enter 5.

CE

CE is the clear entry button. Use this button to correct a mistake when entering a longer calculation without starting over. For example, suppose you entered 2*3+5 but you meant to enter 2*3+9. If you click on CE right after you enter 5, your screen will show 6, the result of 2*3, and you can now enter +9= to finish your intended calculation.

C

C is the clear key. Use this key when you want to start a calculation over. In our previous example, if you click C after you enter 5, the intermediate result, 6, is not retained.

sqrt

sqrt is the square root key. Click this key after you enter the number for which you want to take the square root. For example, if you enter 4 sqrt, the result 2 will display on your screen.

%

% is the key used to take a percentage without entering a decimal. For example, if you want to take 20% of 400, enter 400*20%. The result 80 will now show on your screen. Note that you do not need to enter = after you click %.

1/x

1/x is used to take a reciprocal. Click this key after you enter the number for which you want to take the reciprocal. For example, the keystrokes 2 followed by 1/x produces the result 0.5 on your screen. Again, note that you do not need to enter = after you click 1/x.

Calculator Practice Tip
When you practice for the Integrated Reasoning section, use a calculator similar to the calculator provided by GMAC. If you are doing online practice, use the onscreen calculator. If you are working problems from this book, use a basic calculator rather than that fancy calculator that you might still have from your high school or college math classes.

Be sure that you thoroughly understand the way the keys for the onscreen calculator work so as to avoid errors and wasted time when you take your GMAT.

THE QUESTION TYPES

There are four question types in the Integrated Reasoning section. While some of these questions test Critical Reasoning skills similar to those tested on the Verbal section, these question types are also used to test the same type of content that is tested in the Quantitative section. So, expect to calculate percents and averages. You'll also be asked to make a lot of inferences based on the data presented in the various charts, graphs, and tables that accompany the questions. So, the format of these questions may take some getting used to but the content will probably seem familiar.

Let's take a more detailed look at each of the new question types.

Table Analysis

Table Analysis questions present data in a table. If you've ever seen a spreadsheet—and really, who hasn't?—you'll feel right at home. Most tables have 5 to 10 columns and anywhere from 6 to 25 rows. You'll be able to sort the data in the table by each column heading. The sort function is fairly basic, however. If you're used to being able to sort first by a column such as state and then a column such as city to produce an alphabetical list of cities by state, you can't do that sort of sorting for these questions. You can sort only one column at a time.

Answers for this Question

We'll discuss how you can solve this Table Analysis question—including which strategies you can apply—in our second chapter devoted to the Integrated Reasoning section.

Here's what a Table Analysis question looks like:

Sort By [Select... ▼] (1)

National Park		Visitors			Area	
Name	State	Number	% change	Rank	Acres	Rank
Grand Canyon	AZ	4,388,386	0.9	2	1,217,403	11
Yosemite	CA	3,901,408	4.4	3	791,266	16
Yellowstone	WY	3,640,185	10.5	4	2,219,791	8
Rocky Mtn.	CO	2,955,821	4.7	5	265,828	26
Zion	UT	2,665,972	-2.5	8	145,598	35
Acadia	ME	2,504,208	12.4	9	47,390	47
Bryce	UT	1,285,492	5.7	15	35,835	50
Arches	UT	1,014,405	1.8	19	76,519	42
Badlands	SD	977,778	4.7	22	242,756	28
Mesa Verde	CO	559,712	1.7	30	52,122	46
Canyonlands	UT	435,908	-0.1	36	337,598	23

The table above gives information for 2010 on total visitors and total acreage for 11 US National Parks. In addition to the numbers of total visitors and total acreage for each National Park, the table also provides the percent increase or decrease over the total visitors for 2009 and the rank of the National Park for total visitors and total acreage in 2010. (4)

Each column of the table can be sorted in ascending order by clicking on the word "Select" above the table and choosing, from the drop-down menu, the heading of the column on which you want the table to be sorted. (2)

Consider each of the following statements about these National Parks. For each statement indicate whether the statement is true or false, based on the information provided in the table. (3)

True False (5)

○ ○ The park that experienced the greatest percent increase in visitors from 2009 to 2010 also had the least total acreage.

○ ○ The park with the median rank by the number of visitors is larger than only one other park by acreage.

○ ○ The total number of visitors at Arches in 2009 was less than 1,000,000.

One thing you won't see on your screen when you take the Integrated Reasoning section are the circled numbers. We've added those so we can talk about different parts of a Table Analysis question. Here's what each circled number represents:

(1) This is the Sort By drop-down box. When opened, you'll see all the different ways that you can sort the data in the table. In this table, for example, the possibilities are National Park Name, National Park State, Visitors Number, Visitors % change, Visitors Rank, Area Acreage, and Area Rank. You can always sort by every column.

2 These are the standard directions for a Table Analysis question. These directions are the same for every Table Analysis question. So, once you've read these directions once, you don't really need to bother reading them again.

3 These lines are additional directions. These additional directions are slightly tailored to the question. However, they'll always tell you to base your answers on the information in the table. They always tell you which type of evaluation you are to make for each statement: true / false, yes /no, agree / disagree, etc. Again, you can probably get by without reading these most of the time.

4 These lines explain the table. Mostly, this information will recap the column headings from the table. Occasionally, you can learn some additional information by reading this explanatory text. For example, the explanatory text for this table states that the Visitors Number column is for 2010 and that % change column shows the change from 2009 to 2010.

5 These statements are the questions. Typically, there are four statements and you need to evaluate and select an answer for each. The good news is that you can answer these in any order. However, if you try to move to the next question without selecting a response for one or more statements, a pop up window opens to inform you that you have not selected an answer for all statements. You cannot leave any part of the question blank.

Read What You Need When You Need It
You may not need to read the explanatory information about the table (number 4) to evaluate the statements. You should study the column headings first. If you understand those, go straight to the statements. You can always go back and read the explanatory information if you need to.

If you've read through the statements, you may have noticed that the questions asked you to do things such as calculate a percentage or find a median. That's typical for Table Analysis questions. You've probably also realized just how helpful the sorting function can be in answering some questions.

Graphics Interpretation

Graphics Interpretation questions give you one chart, graph, or image and ask you to answer two questions based on that information. The questions are statements that include one drop-down box. You select your answer from the drop-down box to complete the statement.

Here's an example of a Graphics Interpretation question:

1

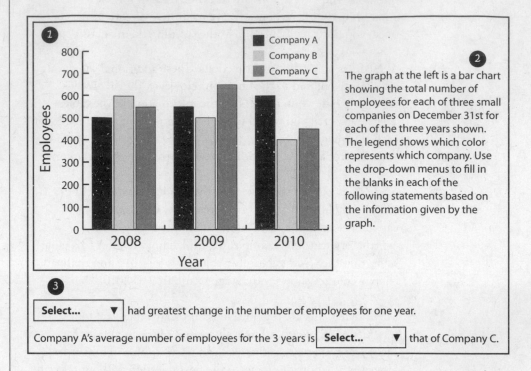

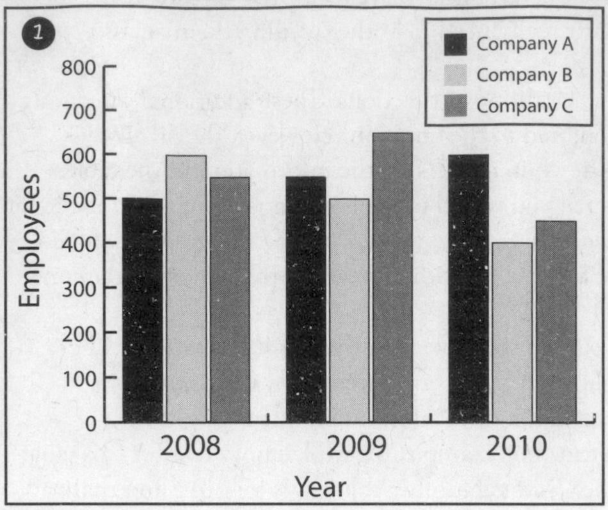

2

The graph at the left is a bar chart showing the total number of employees for each of three small companies on December 31st for each of the three years shown. The legend shows which color represents which company. Use the drop-down menus to fill in the blanks in each of the following statements based on the information given by the graph.

3

Select... ▼ had greatest change in the number of employees for one year.

Company A's average number of employees for the 3 years is **Select...** ▼ that of Company C.

Want to See What's in the Drop-Downs?
We'll be discussing how to answer this question in the strategy chapter. We'll expand the drop-down boxes there!

As with the Table Analysis questions, we've added the circled numbers so we can point out the different things that you'll see on your screen for a Graphics Interpretation question. Here's what each circled number represents:

1. The chart, graph, or image is always in the upper left of the screen. As shown here, the chart will take up a good deal of the screen. It will certainly be large enough that you can clearly extract information from it. You can expect to see a variety of different types of charts or graphs including scatter plots, bar charts, line graphs, and circle (or pie) charts. For the most part, you'll see fairly standard types of graphs, however. Be sure to check out any labels on the axes as well as any sort of included legend.

2. These lines provide an explanation of the graph or chart. Mostly, you'll be told what the chart represents as well as what the individual lines, bars, or sectors may represent. Sometimes, you'll be given some additional information such as when measurements were made. For example, here you are told that the bars show the numbers of employees for each firm on December 31st of the year in question. This information is typically extraneous to answering the questions. The explanatory information always ends with the same line about selecting your answers from the drop-down menu.

❸ These are the questions. Graphics Interpretation questions typically include two statements. You don't have to answer them in order, but you must answer them both to move on to the next question. Each statement is typically a single sentence with one drop-down menu. Each drop-down menu typically includes three to five answer choices. Choose that answer choice that makes the statement true.

Graphics Analysis questions mostly ask you to find relationships and trends for the data. You can also be asked to calculate percentage increases or decreases, averages, and medians.

Two-Part Analysis

Next up is the Two-Part Analysis question. In many ways, the Two-Part Analysis question is most similar to a standard math question. You'll typically be presented with a word problem that essentially has two variables in it. You'll need to pick an answer for each variable that makes some condition in the problem true.

Here's an example of a Two-Part Analysis question:

> Two families buy new refrigerators using installment plans. Family A makes an initial payment of $750. Family B makes an initial payment of $1200. Both families make five additional payments to pay off the balance. Both families pay the same amount for their refrigerators including all taxes, fees and finance charges. ❶
>
> In the table below, identify a monthly payment, in dollars, for Family A and a monthly payment, in dollars, for Family B that are consistent with the installment plan described above. Make only one selection in each column. ❷

Family A	Family B	Monthly payment (in dollars)
○	○	50
○	○	80
○	○	120 ❸
○	○	160
○	○	250
○	○	300

What's the Answer?
Be sure to read our second chapter on the Integrated Reasoning section to find out!

As you might have surmised, we have once again added the circled numbers so we can described the different parts of the question. Here's what each circled number represents:

❶ This first block of text is the actual problem. Here, you'll find the description of the two variables in the problem. You'll also find the condition that needs to be made true. As with any word problem, make sure that you read the information carefully. For these problems, you'll also want to make sure that you are clear about which information goes with the first variable and which information goes with the second.

2. This part of the problem tells you how to pick your answers. Mostly this part tells you to pick a value for column A and a value for column B based on the conditions of the problem. This part is mostly boilerplate text that varies slightly from problem to problem.

3. These are the answer choices. Two-Part Analysis questions generally have five or six answer choices. You choose only one answer choice for each column. It is possible that the same number is the answer for both columns. So, if that's what your calculations indicate, go ahead and choose the same number for both columns.

Most Two-Part Analysis questions can be solved using math that is no more sophisticated than simple arithmetic. There is one exception to that, however. While most Two-Part Analysis questions are math problems, you may see one that looks like a Critical Reasoning question. For these, you'll be give an argument and you'll need to do something like pick one answer that strengthens and one answer that weakens the argument. For these questions, just use the methods from our Critical Reasoning Chapter.

Multi-Source Reasoning

Finally, we come to the Multi-Source Reasoning question. Multi-Source Reasoning questions present information on tabs. The information can be text, charts, graphs, or a combination. In other words, GMAC can put almost anything on the tabs! The layout looks a little bit like Reading Comprehension because the tabbed information is on the left side of your screen while the right side shows the questions.

Here's an example of a Multi-Source Reasoning question:

1

Text #1 | Graph #1 | Graph #2

The graph below shows the CO_2 emissions per capita for five selected countries from 1980 to 2005.

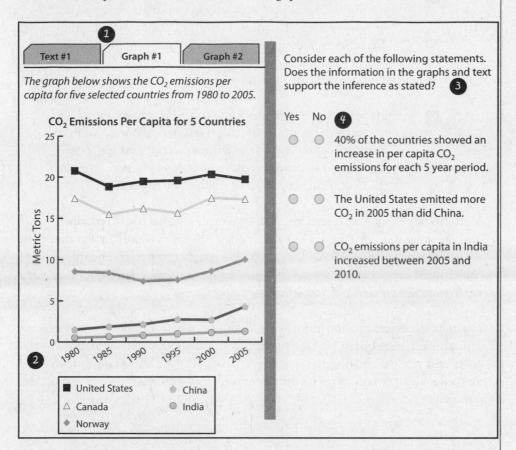

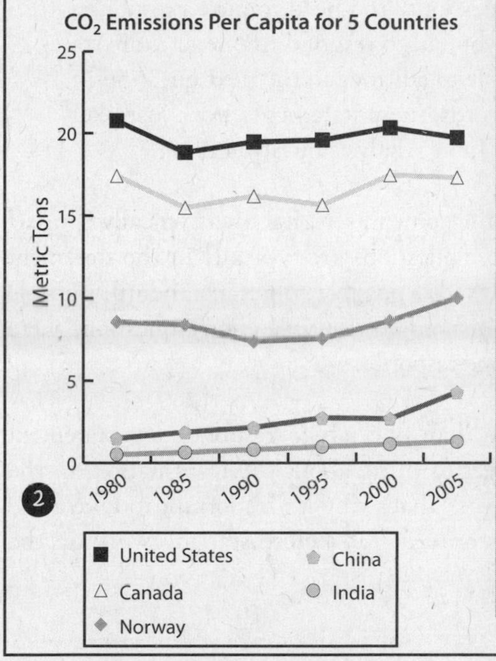

Consider each of the following statements. Does the information in the graphs and text support the inference as stated? 3

Yes No 4

- 40% of the countries showed an increase in per capita CO_2 emissions for each 5 year period.
- The United States emitted more CO_2 in 2005 than did China.
- CO_2 emissions per capita in India increased between 2005 and 2010.

Again, we've added circled numbers to indicate the different parts of the question. Here's what each circled number represents:

1. The tabs appear across the top left of the screen. Some questions have two tabs and some, as in this example, have three. The tabs typically give you some sort of indication about what's on the tab. The currently selected tab is white while the unselected tabs are grey. GMAC can put almost anything on each tab including graphs, tables, charts, text, or some combination. It's a good idea to take a few seconds and get your bearings before attempting the questions. Make sure you know what is on each tab and how the information on one tab relates to information on the other tab or tabs.

2. The information for each tab appears on the left of the screen. In this case, the information is a graph. When you see a chart or graph, be sure to check out the axes. You'll also want to look for a legend or other information to help explain the information shown by the graph or chart. For tables, check out the column headings so as to better understand the table. Finally, don't neglect to read any supplied headings for the chart, graph, or table. Sometimes, that's all you need for the chart to make sense.

What's on those Other Tabs?

We'll show you the other tabs and the answers to these questions in our other chapter on the Integrated Reasoning section.

3. These are the basic instructions for how to respond to the statements. These instructions help to explain how you need to evaluate each statement. Here, for example, you need to determine whether the statements are valid inferences. In other cases, you may be asked to evaluate the statements for a different choice such as true or false.

4. These are the actual questions. You need to pick a response for each statement. If you fail to respond to one or more statements, you won't be able to advance to the next question in the section. In other words, these statements work just like the statements for the Table Analysis question type.

Multi-Source Reasoning questions usually come in sets. Each set typically consists of three separate questions. Two of those questions are typically in the statement style as shown in the example above. It's also possible to get a standard multiple choice question as part of the set. For a standard multiple choice question, there are five answer choices and you select one response.

You may need information from more than one tab to respond to a statement or multiple choice question. Don't forget to think about the information on the other tabs while evaluating the statements. That's why it's important to take a few moments and get familiar with what's on each tab before starting work on the questions.

Strategies and More Questions

Now, that you understand the basics of the new question types, it's time to start thinking about the best ways to solve these questions. You can find strategies and more practice questions in Chapters 19 and 20.

Summary

- The Integrated Reasoning section is 30 minutes long and contains 12 questions, each with multiple parts. This section is not adaptive and you may use an onscreen calculator.
- Work the easier questions first, then tackle the tougher ones. Sometimes your best bet is simply to guess and move along.
- There are four question types. Be sure that you familiarize yourself with these:
  - Table Analysis
  - Graphics Interpretation
  - Two-Part Analysis
  - Multi-Source Reasoning
- Check out these new question types on www.mba.com and practice with the full-length practice GMAT exams available to you once you've registered your book at **PrincetonReview.com.**

Chapter 19
Integrated Reasoning: Strategies

GMAC has devised four question types for the Integrated Reasoning section. As with any section on a standardized test, doing well requires a blend of content knowledge and strategy. Test takers who approach the Integrated Reasoning section with a firm grasp of strategy will do better than those who haven't thought about strategies for the section.

We'll be looking at two types of strategies in this chapter. Some strategies apply to most or all of the question types that you'll see. Other strategies apply to specific questions types. We'll start by reviewing strategies and pointers for the entire section and then move on to examine some methods for the individual question types.

GENERAL STRATEGIES

Some strategies apply to the entire section and you'll use these methods on almost every question. The more consistently you apply these pointers, the better you'll do and the more efficiently you'll use your time.

Get Your Bearings

Before you can use a chart, graph, or table to answer questions, you need to understand the information on it. So, before you evaluate any statements or answer any questions, take a few moments to review the charts, graphs, and tables.

What Do the Questions Look Like?
If you aren't sure what the Integrated Reasoning questions look like, you should read Chapter 18, Integrated Reasoning: Basics. We introduce the four new question types there.

For charts and graphs, make sure you look at the axes. You'll want to take note of what each axis measures and the units used to make the measurements. You'll also want to read any headings or titles because those can provide valuable insight into the purpose of the graph. There may be a legend. If there is, take a moment to identify the different items that the chart or graph compares. For tables, make sure that you look at each column heading. This sort of review is essential before you start working on evaluating the statements or answering the questions that go with Table Analysis and Graphics Interpretation questions.

For Multi-Source Reasoning questions, you need to review the information that is on each tab. It's also a good idea to look for connections between the charts on one tab and those on the others. One way that you can do so is to think about what quantities you'd be able to calculate if you used the information from two charts. For example, if one chart shows the number of cars per day that several factories produce and another chart shows the number of days those factories were active in a year, you know that you could calculate the total number of cars each factory produced that year.

Read What You Need When You Need

Both Table Analysis and Graphics Interpretation questions include a blurb of text that explains the table or chart. While GMAC includes this information to help you to understand the table or chart, you may not need to take the time to read it.

Most of the charts and tables are understandable without the explanatory text. So, if your review of the chart or table doesn't turn up any unusual quantities or units that need further explanation, you're most likely ready to get to work on the actual questions. You can also be guided by the questions. If something about the question or statement isn't making sense, then you can always go back and read the explanatory information.

Valid Inferences

Both Table Analysis and Multi-Source Reasoning items include statement style questions. (Reread Chapter 18 to see examples of statement style questions.) In some cases, you'll be asked to decide whether the statement is true or false. In other cases, you'll be asked whether the information supplied supports the inference as stated and asked to respond yes or no. That's a little different from asking whether the statement is true or false. After all, there's the possibility that there is insufficient information to conclude whether the statement is true or false. If that's the case, you need to pick "no" as your answer.

What's an Inference?
An inference is a statement that you can prove true using supplied facts or other evidence.

It's also important to remember that a valid inference is something that you know to be true. You know something is true if you can support it with evidence. GMAC knows, however, that most people start thinking "interpret" or "read into" when they see the word "infer." So, some statements provided on Table Analysis and Multi-Source Reasoning questions attempt to get you to read too much into the information on the chart or table to come up with a conclusion. For example, there may be a clear trend on a chart showing that a company has increased its sales for every year between 2000 and 2008. The statement may try to get you to conclude that the company also increased its sales in 2009 even though 2009 is not shown on the chart. That's not a valid inference! Be careful that you don't mix up "true" and "very likely" when evaluating what can be inferred from the data.

TABLE ANALYSIS

Table Analysis questions always include one table to display data. You'll be asked to evaluate four statements. You may be asked whether the statements are true or false based on the data in the table. You may also be asked whether the statements represent valid inferences based on the table.

While you won't be called upon to provide numerical answers as part of Table Analysis questions, you may need to perform some calculations to evaluate the statements. For example, you may be asked to verify that a certain percentage of the items in the table have a certain characteristic.

The Sort Function

The sort function allows you to sort the data in the table by any column. However, the sort function will sort only one column at a time. So, forget all those fancy multiple column sorts that you can do with Excel.

To see how the sort function works for Table Analysis questions, let's look at a very simple table. This table is really too simple for a GMAT question but it will help us to illustrate how the sort function works.

When you first see the table, it is typically sorted by one key statistic from the table. All numerical sorts are always smallest to largest. This table, for example, is sorted by Median Income (2009) and represents the original sort for this table.

City	State	Median Income (2009)
Rochester	NY	$30,553
Philadelphia	PA	$37,045
Salt Lake City	UT	$45,754
New York	NY	$50,033

Now, here's what you'll see if you sort by state.

City	State	Median Income (2009)
Rochester	NY	$30,553
New York	NY	$50,033
Philadelphia	PA	$37,045
Salt Lake City	UT	$45,754

If you sort next by City, you might expect that Rochester and New York would exchange positions. That's particularly true if you are used to the way that Excel lets you sort by multiple columns.

However, what you'll really get is an alphabetical listing by City. Here's what the sort by City looks like.

City	State	Median Income (2009)
New York	NY	$50,033
Philadelphia	PA	$37,045
Rochester	NY	$30,553
Salt Lake City	UT	$45,754

Question Order
In general, you should just evaluate the statements in order for Table Analysis questions. Of course, if you get stuck on one statement, skip over it, evaluate the other statements and come back to the one that gave you trouble.

To Sort or Not To Sort

While the sort feature can be a huge help when answering some questions, you may not need to use it to answer every question. In some cases, you may need to find only one piece of information on the table. In other cases, the table may not have that many rows. Table Analysis questions can have as few as six rows of data. It may be faster to simply scan the table for the information that you need.

On the other hand, remember that sorting the table takes only a few seconds. If you think sorting will help, do it! One thing you shouldn't do, however, is spend time trying to organize the statements so that you do as little sorting as possible. You're actually likely to waste more time trying to come up with the perfect order in which to evaluate the statements than you would if you wind up sorting the same way twice in evaluating the statements.

Let's look at a sample Table Analysis question. Here's the question that we discussed in Chapter 18.

Get Your Bearings
Step one for any Table Analysis question is to review the information presented by the table.

Sort By [Select... ▼]

National Park		Visitors			Area	
Name	State	Number	% change	Rank	Acres	Rank
Grand Canyon	AZ	4,388,386	0.9	2	1,217,403	11
Yosemite	CA	3,901,408	4.4	3	791,266	16
Yellowstone	WY	3,640,185	10.5	4	2,219,791	8
Rocky Mtn.	CO	2,955,821	4.7	5	265,828	26
Zion	UT	2,665,972	-2.5	8	145,598	35
Acadia	ME	2,504,208	12.4	9	47,390	47
Bryce	UT	1,285,492	5.7	15	35,835	50
Arches	UT	1,014,405	1.8	19	76,519	42
Badlands	SD	977,778	4.7	22	242,756	28
Mesa Verde	CO	559,712	1.7	30	52,122	46
Canyonlands	UT	435,908	-0.1	36	337,598	23

The table above gives information for 2010 on total visitors and total acreage for 11 US National Parks. In addition to the numbers of total visitors and total acreage for each National Park, the table also provides the percent increase or decrease over the total visitors for 2009 and the rank of the National Park for total visitors and total acreage in 2010.

Each column of the table can be sorted in ascending order by clicking on the word "Select" above the table and choosing, from the drop-down menu, the heading of the column on which you want the table to be sorted.

Consider each of the following statements about these National Parks. For each statement indicate whether the statement is true or false, based on the information provided in the table.

True	False	
○	○	The park that experienced the greatest percent increase in visitors from 2009 to 2010 also had the least total acreage.
○	○	The park with the median rank by the number of visitors is larger than only one other park by acreage.
○	○	The total number of visitors at Arches in 2009 was fewer than 1,000,000.

Here's How To Crack It:

As with any Table Analysis question, the first step is to make sure that you take a moment to understand the information presented by the table. While it might be tempting to jump straight to the statements, you'll be able to evaluate the statements more efficiently when you first take a moment to understand the information on the table. Looking at the column headings can also help you to decide whether you need to read the explanatory information under the table.

The first two columns of this table—National Park Name and National Park State—are self-explanatory. More importantly, however, the first column—National Park Name—tells you that this table provides information about national parks. Next, you get information about visitors to the national parks included in the table. The third column heading—Visitors Number—is pretty clear. However, you don't know the time period for the visitation numbers. The next column—Visitors % Change—shows increases or decreases from some previous time period. Again, you don't know the time period just by looking at the table. Do the time periods matter? Probably not. You'll probably learn the time period from the statements. If the statements seem to indicate that the time periods matter, you can read the explanatory text at that time.

The next column—Visitors Rank—is potentially more confusing, however. Does the rank refer to the number of visitors or the percent change? That's an important distinction for understanding the information in the table. There are two ways to figure out what's being ranked. You could scan the table looking for evidence. Of course, that could be time consuming. Or, you could scan the explanatory text beneath the table. *If you don't understand one of the column headings shown in the table, that's when you want to read the explanatory text.* The explanation indicates that the rank refers to the total number of visitors. As a bonus, you now also know that the visitation numbers are for 2010.

Step 2
Decide the best way to sort the table. For some statements, you may be able to sort in more than one way. Sort by the column with the larger numbers or more complex data.

The last two column headings—Area Acres and Area Rank—are also pretty clear. Note that the inclusion of Area Rank means that you won't need to deal with the larger number in the Area Acres column if all you need to do is compare the size of one park to another. The same is also true of the inclusion of the Visitors Rank column. The inclusion of these columns makes it much easier to make some types of comparisons about the parks in the table. That's definitely something to make note of as you finish reviewing the information presented by the chart.

We'll just evaluate the statements in order. First, we'll evaluate:

> The park that experienced the greatest percent increase in visitors from 2009 to 2010 also had the least total acreage.

This statement is typical of the sorts of statements that you are called upon to evaluate for Table Analysis questions. Note that there are two possible sorts that you could perform to evaluate this question. First, you could sort by Visitors % Change. But, you could also sort by Area Acres. So, what's the best? Sort by only one of those columns? Sort by both? Sort by neither?

With 11 rows of data, you'll probably find it safer to sort by at least one of the columns. But, which one? Well, note that the table provides you with ranking information for the areas of the parks. The smaller numbers used to rank the parks by area make it easier to identify the smallest park by area without sorting.

However, you might reasonably be worried about missing which park had the greatest percent increase by visitors. So, sort by Visitors % Change.

Here's what the sorted table looks like:

National Park		Visitors			Area	
Name	State	Number	% Change	Rank	Acres	Rank
Zion	UT	2,556,972	-2.5	8	145,598	35
Canyonlands	UT	435,908	-0.1	36	337,598	23
Grand Canyon	AZ	4,388,386	0.9	2	1,217,403	11
Mesa Verde	CO	559,712	1.7	30	52,122	46
Arches	UT	1,014,405	1.8	19	76,519	42
Yosemite	CA	3,901,408	4.4	3	791,266	16
Rocky Mtn.	CO	2,955,821	4.7	5	265,828	26
Badlands	SD	977,778	4.7	22	242,756	28
Bryce	UT	1,285,492	5.7	15	35,835	50
Yellowstone	WY	3,640,185	10.5	4	2,219,791	8
Acadia	ME	2,504,208	12.4	9	47,390	47

Now, it's clear that Acadia had the greatest percent increase in the number of visitors from 2009 to 2010. Acadia was ranked 47th in terms of overall acreage. You could sort the chart by Area Acres or by Area Rank at this point to finish evaluating the statement. However, since you know Acadia's rank for acreage, it's probably slightly faster to simply scan to see if any park had a higher rank for area. In this case, Bryce was ranked 50th, so this first statement is false.

Medians, Modes, Percents
Medians, modes, and percents are all frequently used in Integrated Reasoning questions. If you need a review, be sure to read through Chapters 10 and 12.

Now, let's take a look at the second statement, which states:

> The park with the median rank by the number of visitors is larger than only one other park by acreage.

Again, you may be considering several different ways to sort the chart. So, start by asking yourself "What's hardest to see right now?" Remember that your chart will still be sorted as shown above, which is the sort that you did to evaluate the first statement. This sort makes it pretty hard to see which park had the median rank for visitors, so it makes sense to sort by Visitors Rank.

Here's what the sorted chart looks like:

National Park		Visitors			Area	
Name	State	Number	% Change	Rank	Acres	Rank
Grand Canyon	AZ	4,388,386	0.9	2	1,217,403	11
Yosemite	CA	3,901,408	4.4	3	791,266	16
Yellowstone	WY	3,640,185	10.5	4	2,219,791	8
Rocky Mtn.	CO	2,955,821	4.7	5	265,828	26
Zion	UT	2,665,972	-2.5	8	145,598	35
Acadia	ME	2,504,208	12.4	9	47,390	47
Bryce	UT	1,285,492	5.7	15	35,835	50
Arches	UT	1,014,405	1.8	19	76,519	42
Badlands	SD	977,778	4.7	22	242,756	28
Mesa Verde	CO	559,712	1.7	30	52,122	46
Canyonlands	UT	435,908	-0.1	36	337,598	23

With the table sorted by Visitors Rank, it's now fairly easy to find the park with the median rank. To find a median, you start by putting the items on a list into numerical order, which we just did by sorting the list. Then, you can just choose the middle number. In this case, Acadia is the park in the middle position since there are 5 parks ranked before it and 5 parks ranked after it.

Use Your Noteboards
For more complicated statements, you may want to make a list of the items that satisfy a condition in the statement.

Note that you could have also sorted the list by Visitors Number. Since data is always sorted from least to greatest, Canyonlands would have been the first row of the table and Grand Canyon would have been the last row. But, Acadia still would have been in the middle. We chose to sort by Visitors Rank because that term was mentioned in the question and it's easier to work with smaller numbers.

Having identified Acadia as the park with the median rank, you now need to decide whether to sort the table again. Since the table provides ranks for the total acreage of the parks on the list, you likely don't need to sort again. Acadia is 47th by acreage. One park, Bryce with a rank of 50, is smaller. So, Acadia, the median park by visitation, is larger than only one other park on the list. The second statement is true.

Note, however, that if the table had not provided ranks for the parks by total area, then you most likely would have wanted to sort by Area Acres. After all, it's a lot easier to see that only one number is greater than 47 than to see that only one number is less than 47,390. Remember that sorting takes only a few seconds and you should sort whenever you think doing so will help you to accurately find what you need on the table.

Now, it's time to finish the question by evaluating the third statement. The third statement claims:

The total number of visitors at Arches in 2009 was fewer than 1,000,000.

Because this statement involves only a single data point, you don't really need to worry about doing any sorting. Even the most involved GMAT tables will have fewer than 30 rows of data. So, it will never be an issue to quickly scan the table, no matter how it is currently sorted, to find one data point. Just use the current sort which has Arches in the 8th row.

Next, you need some information about Arches to evaluate the statement. The table shows that Arches had 1,014,405 visitors in 2010. The table also shows that the number of visitors in 2010 was 1.8% greater than it was in 2009.. To find the number of visitors in 2009, use the percent change formula:

Calculations Required
Expect to do some calculations such as computing an average or a percent change to evaluate one or two of the statements in a Table Analysis question.

$$\% \text{ change} = \frac{\text{difference}}{\text{original}} \times 100$$

Next, put the numbers that you know into the formula to get:

$$1.8 = \frac{(1{,}014{,}405 - x)}{x} \times 100$$

Calculator Time!
Don't forget that you can use the onscreen calculator to perform messy calculations such as dividing through by 101.8!

We've called the 2009 number that we're trying to find x. A little rearranging gives:

$$101.8x = 101{,}440{,}500$$

Finally, just divide through by 101.8 to find that x, the 2009 visitation at Arches, was 996,469 rounded to the nearest integer. So, statement four is true.

Here's what your answers should look like just before you click next to move onto the next question in the Integrated Reasoning section:

Sort By [Select... ▼]

National Park		Visitors			Area	
Name	State	Number	% change	Rank	Acres	Rank
Grand Canyon	AZ	4,388,386	0.9	2	1,217,403	11
Yosemite	CA	3,901,408	4.4	3	791,266	16
Yellowstone	WY	3,640,185	10.5	4	2,219,791	8
Rocky Mtn.	CO	2,955,821	4.7	5	265,828	26
Zion	UT	2,665,972	-2.5	8	145,598	35
Acadia	ME	2,504,208	12.4	9	47,390	47
Bryce	UT	1,285,492	5.7	15	35,835	50
Arches	UT	1,014,405	1.8	19	76,519	42
Badlands	SD	977,778	4.7	22	242,756	28
Mesa Verde	CO	559,712	1.7	30	52,122	46
Canyonlands	UT	435,908	-0.1	36	337,598	23

The table above gives information for 2010 on total visitors and total acreage for 11 US National Parks. In addition to the numbers of total visitors and total acreage for each National Park, the table also provides the percent increase or decrease over the total visitors for 2009 and the rank of the National Park for total visitors and total acreage in 2010.

Each column of the table can be sorted in ascending order by clicking on the word "Select" above the table and choosing, from the drop-down menu, the heading of the column on which you want the table to be sorted.

Consider each of the following statements about these National Parks. For each statement indicate whether the statement is true or false, based on the information provided in the table.

True	False	
○	◉	The park that experienced the greatest percent increase in visitors from 2009 to 2010 also had the least total acreage.
◉	○	The park with the median rank by the number of visitors is larger than only one other park by acreage.
◉	○	The total number of visitors at Arches in 2009 was fewer than 1,000,000.

GRAPHICS INTERPRETATION

Graphics Interpretation questions provide you with one chart, graph, or image. Each chart is followed by two statements. The statements each contain one drop-down list from which you choose one answer. Your job is to pick the answer that makes the statement true. Each drop-down list typically contains between three to five answer choices.

You'll find a few sentences of explanatory text to the right of the chart or graph. As with Table Analysis questions, you may not need to read this explanatory information. Just as with Table Analysis questions, you can be guided by how well you understand the chart or graph. If you understand the chart or graph, then you probably don't need to read the explanatory text.

So, what should you look for when you review the chart or graph? Start by looking at any labels on the axes. Are quantities being measured in common, easily understood units? You should also look to see if the chart or graph has any titles that help to explain the data it shows. Finally, see if there's any sort of legend that helps to differentiate different types of data.

Let's take a look at the sample Graphics Interpretation question that we discussed in Chapter 18.

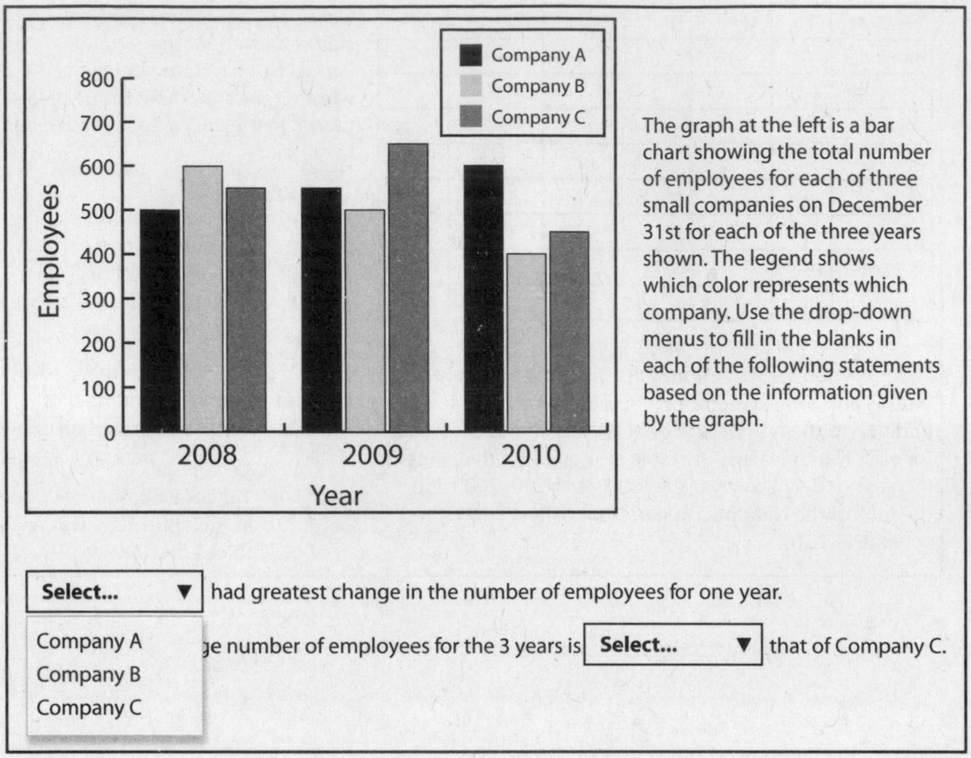
Company A
Company B
Company C
800
700
600
500
400
300
200
100
0
Employees
2008
2009
2010
Year
The graph at the left is a bar chart showing the total number of employees for each of three small companies on December 31st for each of the three years shown. The legend shows which color represents which company. Use the drop-down menus to fill in the blanks in each of the following statements based on the information given by the graph.
Select... ▼ had greatest change in the number of employees for one year.
Company A
Company B
Company C
ge number of employees for the 3 years is Select... ▼ that of Company C.

Here's How To Crack It:

Before we get started discussing this question, note that we've expanded the drop down list for the first statement. When the question first appears on the screen, none of the drop-downs are expanded. Here, we just wanted to show what the expanded drop-downs look like in the context of a question.

The first step in answering any Graphics Interpretation question is to review the chart or graph. In this case, there's a bar chart. The vertical axis shows employees in hundreds, which seems fairly easy to understand. The horizontal axis shows results for three years. The different colored bars are explained by the legend—there are three companies. So, this chart seems fairly straightforward. It shows the number of employees for three companies for three different years.

With everything on the chart so clearly marked, there's little reason to read the explanatory text to the right of the chart. Note that the only piece of information that the explanatory text really adds is that the number of employees for each company was tallied on December 31 of each year. That's the sort of detail that often turns out to be irrelevant in answering the questions. Remember that you can always go back and read the explanatory text if it seems like you need to know something that wasn't clearly reflected on the chart or graph.

Let's take a look at the questions. As with Table Analysis questions, it's best to just evaluate the statements in order. If one of them gives you trouble or seems particularly time-consuming, you can always skip over it and evaluate the other statements first. Of course, you'll need to pick an answer for all three statements before you can move to the next question in the Integrated Reasoning section.

Here's the first statement again:

Select... ▼ had greatest change in the number of employees for one year.

- Company A
- Company B
- Company C

For this statement, the task is to determine which company had the greatest overall changes in employees in any one year period. You'll probably find it helpful to write down the changes on your noteboard. You may even want to construct a rough table to keep track of the changes. In that way, you can easily spot the largest overall change.

Avoid Common Errors

Be careful when you read the chart. Are you looking at the right item? It's also a good idea to write down the data before performing any calculations with the data.

Here's a table that shows the changes for each company:

	2008 to 2009	2009 to 2010
Company A	50	50
Company B	–100	–100
Company C	100	–200

For this statement, it's important to note that the question asked for the greatest change. So, you need to include overall decreases in looking for the greatest change. Employment at Company C declined by 200 between 2009 and 2010. The correct answer to statement one is "Company C".

Here's the second statement showing the possible answers:

Company A's average number of employees for the 3 years is **Select...** ▼ that of Company C.

- greater than
- less than
- the same as

To evaluate this statement, you need to calculate the average number of employees for Companies A and C. Questions that ask you to perform calculations such as finding an average are fairly common for Graphics Interpretation questions. Just be sure to read the information from the chart carefully. Common errors for questions such as this one usually involve reading the information for the wrong company or mixing the information for two companies.

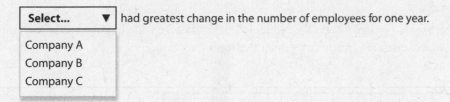

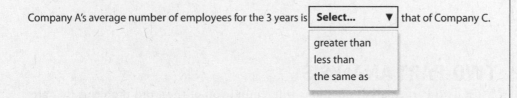

Calculator Required?
While using the calculator is fine, you may be able to do the calculations for some questions faster without the calculator. Make sure you need the calculator before you use it!

For Company A, the total number of employees for each year was 500, 550, and 600. To find the average, take the sum of the three numbers to get 1,650. Now, just divide by 3 because you want the average over three years. So, the average number of employees for Company A is 550.

For Company C, the total number of employees for each year was 550, 650, and 450. The average number of employees per year for Company C is also 550. So, the correct answer for the second statement is 'the same as'.

Here's what your answers should look like just before you click next to move on to the next question in the Integrated Reasoning section:

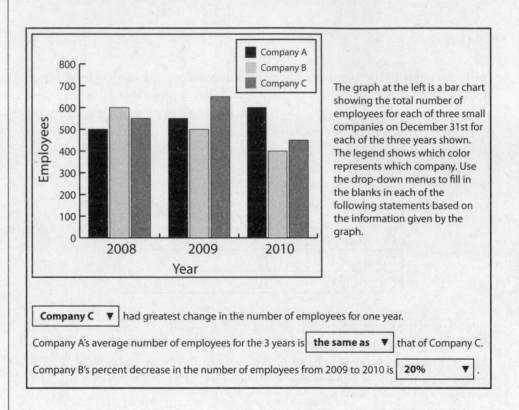

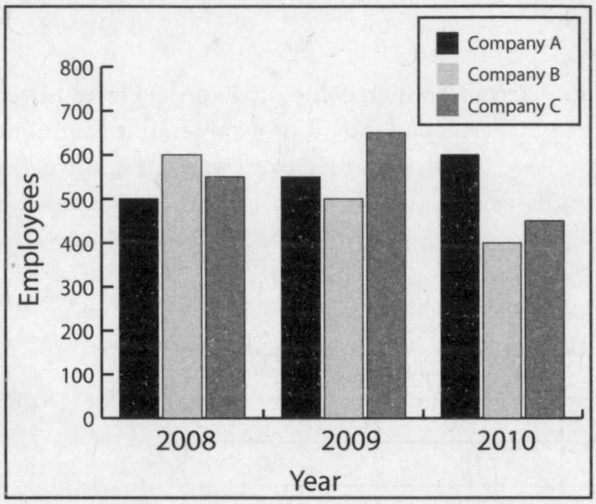

The graph at the left is a bar chart showing the total number of employees for each of three small companies on December 31st for each of the three years shown. The legend shows which color represents which company. Use the drop-down menus to fill in the blanks in each of the following statements based on the information given by the graph.

Company C ▼ had greatest change in the number of employees for one year.

Company A's average number of employees for the 3 years is **the same as** ▼ that of Company C.

Company B's percent decrease in the number of employees from 2009 to 2010 is **20%** ▼.

TWO-PART ANALYSIS

Most Two-Part Analysis questions will remind you of the word problems that are part of the Quantitative section of the GMAT. The only difference is that you'll need to pick two answers rather than one! It's likely that you'll need to do some calculations to solve most Two-Part Analysis questions. For the most part, the math you'll need to do will be fairly straightforward arithmetic. You may find that it's faster to do the calculations without the calculator. However, remember that the calculator is available. Just remember to set up your calculations before entering them into the calculator.

For most Two-Part Analysis questions, the two answers that you need to pick are related or linked in some way. When that's the case, you may be able to identify one part as easier to solve than the other. If so, do the easier part first. It's also important to remember that working with the answer choices is often easier for these questions. While some Two-Part Analysis questions can be solved algebraically, it's very often faster to just test out the answer choices. In other words, you'll be able to use a form of PITA (Plugging In the Answers, discussed in our Algebra Chapter) to solve most of these questions. Let's take a look at how to solve the question we saw in Chapter 18.

Two families buy new refrigerators using installment plans. Family A makes an initial payment of \$750. Family B makes an initial payment of \$1200. Both families make five additional payments to pay off the balance. Both families pay the same amount for their refrigerators including all taxes, fees and finance charges.

In the table below, identify a monthly payment, in dollars, for Family A and a monthly payment, in dollars, for Family B that are consistent with the installment plan described above. Make only one selection in each column.

Family A	Family B	Monthly payment (in dollars)
○	○	50
○	○	80
○	○	120
○	○	160
○	○	250
○	○	300

Here's How to Crack It

For this problem, one of the first things to notice is that there is a connection between the payments that each family makes. Since Family B's initial payment is \$450 more than that of Family A, Family A's monthly payment is larger than that of Family B. That can help when you start testing the answer choices. Moreover, you can also see that the answer for Family A cannot be either \$50 or \$80. If Family A's monthly payment were \$80, then they would have paid only an additional \$400 after 5 months. That's not even enough to make Family A's total payment equal to Family B's initial payment. Of course, Family B makes monthly payments, too.

The other thing to notice in this question is that there is a crucial piece of information missing: the cost of the refrigerator. In this case, Plugging In the Answers will enable us to verify that the cost of that fridge is the same for both families. You can set the problem up just like you would a PITA question with one change. So that you can keep track of your process of elimination, write the answer choices down twice leaving some space between the answers to show any quantities that you needed to calculate. Of course, you'll label your answer choices just as you would with any other PITA question. For this problem, you can label your columns of numbers as "A's payment" and "B's payment." Here's what your initial setup should look like:

A's payment		B's payment	
~~50~~		50	
~~80~~		80	
120		120	
160		160	
250		250	
300		300	

Note that we've already crossed off 50 and 80 as possible payments for Family A. As discussed, these answers are too small for A's payment. As with any other PITA question, it makes sense to start with a number in the middle. We'll start with $160 for Family A's payment.

If Family A's payment is $160, what can you find? The problem states that Family A makes 5 payments, so the total of those 5 payments is $800. Moreover, the problem also states that Family A made an initial payment of $750. So, if Family A made payments of $160, then the refrigerator cost $750 + $800 = $1,550. That's what goes into the next column for Family A.

What about Family B? If Family A makes payments of $160, then Family B's payments must be less than that amount. So, Family B could make payments of $50, $80 or $120. For each of those numbers, calculate how much Family B would have paid for the refrigerator. Here's what your table should look like at this step:

A's payment	A's Total	B's payment	B's Total
~~50~~		50	$1450
~~80~~		80	$1600
120		120	$1800
160	$1550	160	
250		250	
300		300	

So, how do you know if you've found the correct answers? Remember that the problem states that both families pay the same amount for their refrigerators.

Since Family B cannot pay $1,550 for their refrigerator, you can eliminate 160 as an answer for Family A.

It's not that clear whether Family A's payment needs to be larger or smaller. So, just pick a direction and try it. Let's try $250 for Family A's payment. If Family A's payment is $250, then their refrigerator costs $750 + (5 × $250) = $2,000. For Family B, none of the answers we've already worked out make their refrigerator cost $2,000. However, we can also check what happens if Family B makes monthly payments of $160. In that case, Family B's refrigerator costs $1,200 + (5 × $160) = $2,000. So, the answers are 250 for Family A and 160 for Family B.

Here's what your completed table looks like:

A's payment	A's Total	B's payment	B's Total
~~50~~		50	$1,450
~~80~~		80	$1,600
120		120	$1,800
~~160~~	$1,550	160	$2,000
250	$2,000	250	
300		300	

Here's what your answers should look like just before you click next to move on to the next question in the Integrated Reasoning section:

Two families buy new refrigerators using installment plans. Family A makes an initial payment of $750. Family B makes an initial payment of $1200. Both families make five additional payments to pay off the balance. Both families pay the same amount for their refrigerators including all taxes, fees and finance charges.

In the table below, identify a monthly payment, in dollars, for Family A and a monthly payment, in dollars, for Family B that are consistent with the installment plan described above. Make only one selection in each column.

Family A	Family B	Monthly payment (in dollars)
○	○	50
○	○	80
○	○	120
○	◉	160
◉	○	250
○	○	300

Check Your Answers

Always double check your answers for a Two-Part Analysis question. Flipping your answers is a very common mistake for these questions. Make sure you have the correct answer for each column.

We used a form of Plugging In the Answers (PITA) to solve the previous question. You can use that approach for most of the Two-Part Analysis questions that you see. Here's a recap of the steps.

PITA for Two-Part Analysis Questions

1. Write down the answer choices on your noteboard. Make two columns leaving some space between.
2. Decide which variable is easier to work with. For example, you might be able to eliminate some answers for one variable because those answers are too big or too small.
3. Write a label over each column of numbers. Label the first column as the easier variable to work with.
4. Starting with an answer in the middle for the first column, work the steps of the problem. For the second column, remember that you may need to test only the answers that are bigger or smaller than the number you worked with in the first column.
5. Check for a match between the first and second column that makes a condition in the problem true.

For some Two-Part Analysis questions, however, you won't be able to use PITA. For the problem we just discussed, the two monthly payments were linked because both families needed to pay the same amount for a refrigerator. For some Two-Part Analysis questions, however, the variables are either unlinked or, at least, less linked.

Let's look at an example:

Jack divides $30,000 between two investments. He invests 35% of the money in Investment A which pays 4% simple interest annually for 5 years. He invests the remainder of the money in Investment B which pays 2% interest compounded semiannually for 4 years.

In the table below, identify the total interest earned, in dollars, for Investment A and the total interest earned, rounded to the nearest dollar, for Investment B that are consistent with the investments described above. Make only one selection in each column.

Investment A	Investment B	Interest Earned (in dollars)
○	○	392
○	○	870
○	○	1560
○	○	1616
○	○	2100
○	○	3347

Here's How to Crack It

For this question, note that there's no common condition that needs to be satisfied. Rather, there are two independent calculations. That's how you know that you can't use PITA to solve this question.

The solution to this question starts with calculating how Jack divides the $30,000 between the two investments. Start by calculating 35% of $30,000. Remember that you can just use the onscreen calculator: 30,000 × 0.35 = 10,500. So, $10,500 is invested in Investment A and the rest, or $19,500, is invested in Investment B.

Next, it's time to calculate the interest earned on each investment. Investment A earns simple interest at a rate of 4% per year for 5 years. To find simple interest, you multiply the principal amount, $10,500, by the interest rate, 0.04, by the time period, 5 years. Here's what the calculation looks like:

$$\$10{,}500 \times 0.04 \times 5 = \$2{,}100$$

The onscreen calculator makes doing the calculation an easy, one-step operation. Just make sure that you use the right numbers from the problem!

For Investment B, the interest is compounded semiannually. That means that every six months the interest is added to the principle so that interest can be earned on the combined amount. There are several ways to calculate compound interest. One of the easiest is to divide the yearly interest rate by the compounding period. For this problem, the investment pays 2% per year but the interest is compounded twice per year.

So, that's 1% every six months. In four years, there are 8 compounding periods. So, to find the account balance at the end of 4 years, you'd calculate the interest for the first six months by multiplying by 0.01. Then, you'd add that amount to the principal and repeat the calculation. Keep calculating until you've done all 8 compounding periods. Of course, since you are multiplying each time, there's a shorter way. Here's what the overall calculation looks like.

$$\$19{,}500 \times (1.01)^8 = \$21{,}115.71$$

Now, to find the interest just subtract $19,500 from the account balance. The interest earned is $1,616 rounded to the nearest dollar.

Here's what your answers should look like just before you click next to move onto the next question in the Integrated Reasoning section:

Jack divides $30,000 between two investments. He invests 35% of the money in Investment A which pays 4% simple interest annually for 5 years. He invests the remainder of the money in Investment B which pays 2% interest compounded semiannually for 4 years.

In the table below, identify the total interest earned, in dollars, for Investment A and the total interest earned, rounded to the nearest dollar, for Investment B that are consistent with the investments described above. Make only one selection in each column.

Investment A	Investment B	Interest Earned (in dollars)
○	○	392
○	○	870
○	○	1560
○	◉	1616
◉	○	2100
○	○	3347

MULTI-SOURCE REASONING

For Multi-Source Reasoning questions, you'll be given a variety of information that can include text, charts, tables, and graphs. The information is arranged on 2 or 3 tabs. Multi-Source Reasoning questions typically come in sets. So, you'll probably get two sets of statement style questions and perhaps one standard multiple choice question.

When a new Multi-Source question appears on your screen, you should take a minute to review the information on each tab. As usual, you'll want to check out things like the axes on graphs and any headings for the charts. But, for Multi-Source Reasoning questions, you also want to see how the information on one tab relates to the information on the other tabs.

Let's look at the example that we saw in the previous Integrated Reasoning chapter. This time, we'll take a look at the information on all three tabs. We'll also discuss how to evaluate statements and answer questions.

Text #1 | Graph #1 | Graph #2

The population of a country affects its ability to compete in the global economy. On the one hand, a large population can be a source of inexpensive labor that can attract investment. On the other hand, large populations can also create resource allocation problems, especially for items such as food, clean water and health care.

Increased wealth sometimes results in reduced population growth. The table below compares the 2005 populations and 2005 population growth rates for the United States, Canada, Norway, India and China.

Country	Population	Rate of Growth
United States	295,753,000	0.9%
Canada	32,312,000	1.0%
Norway	4,623,000	0.7%
India	1,095,000,000	1.4%
China	1,304,000,000	0.6%

Consider each of the following statements. Does the information in the graphs and text support the inference as stated?

Yes	No	
○	○	40% of the countries showed an increase in per capita CO_2 emissions for each 5 year period.
○	○	The United States emitted more CO_2 in 2005 than did China.
○	○	CO_2 emissions per capita in India increased between 2005 and 2010.

Here's How to Crack It

We'll review the information one tab at a time before we start evaluating the statements. The first tab, Text #1, provides some background information about the ways in which a country's population can affect its participation in the global economy. This tab also presents a table with population and growth rates for five countries. Notice that you need to read the included information on this tab to determine that the table displays data from 2005. Unlike the other question types that we've discussed, you should always read any text that's included on a tab in a Multi-Source Reasoning question.

Make Connections
As you review the information on each tab, try to find ways that it relates to the information on the other tabs.

Now, here's the information for the second tab:

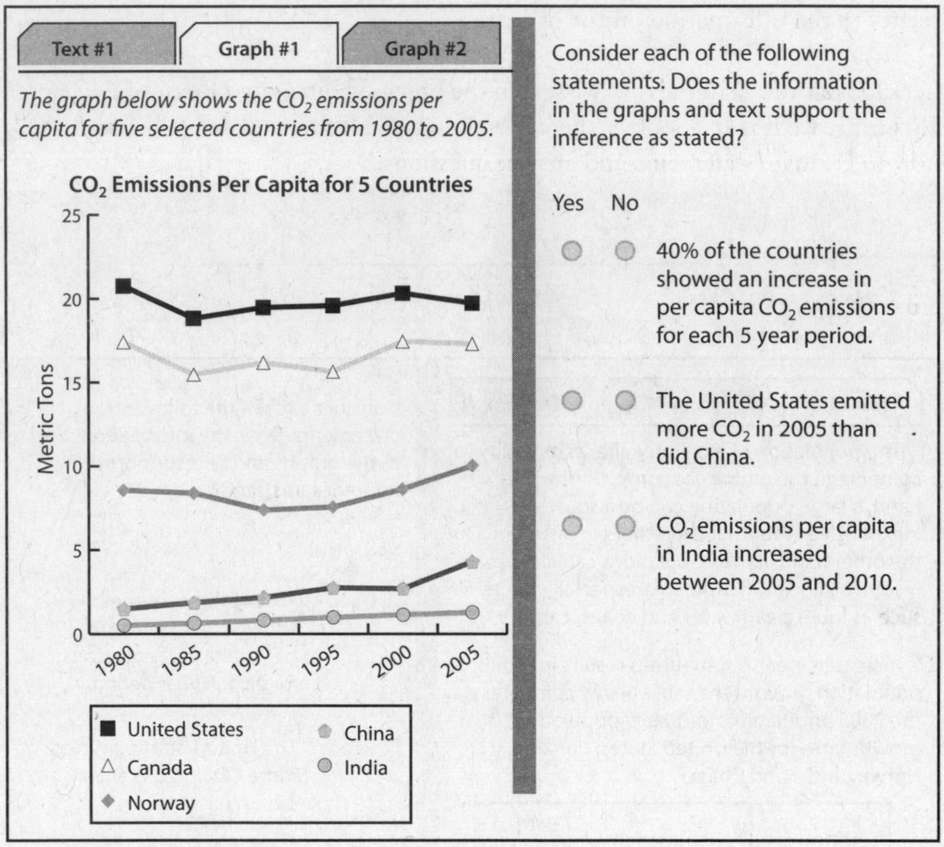

This tab shows CO_2 emissions for five countries over a 25 year period. Notice that the countries on this tab are the same as the countries on the first tab. It's also important to note that the CO_2 emissions on this tab are per capita emissions. Since the first tab provided information about populations for 2005, it would be possible to calculate approximate total CO_2 emissions for these five countries for 2005. While you don't necessarily need to consider all the calculations you could perform, thinking about what you could calculate is an excellent way to notice connections between the data provided on the tabs.

Next, let's take a look at the information on the third tab:

Text #1 | Graph #1 | Graph #2

The graph below shows the Gross Domestic Product per Capita for India and China from 1990 to 2005.

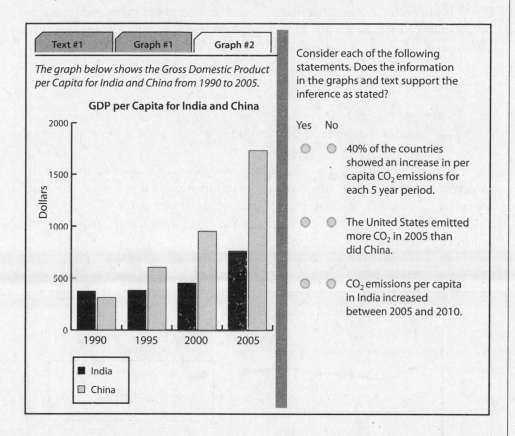

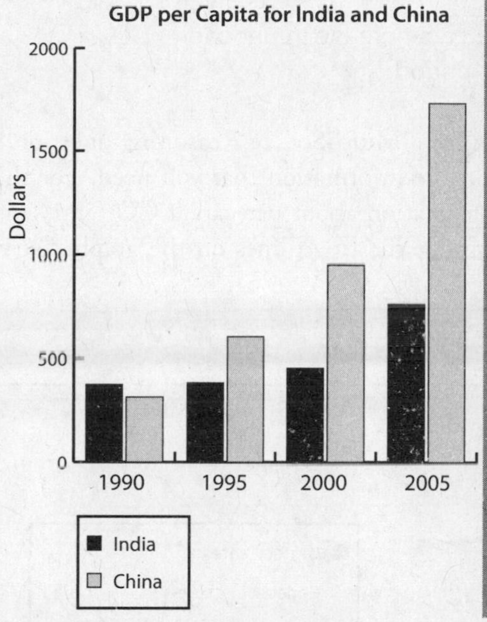

Consider each of the following statements. Does the information in the graphs and text support the inference as stated?

Yes	No	
○	○	40% of the countries showed an increase in per capita CO_2 emissions for each 5 year period.
○	○	The United States emitted more CO_2 in 2005 than did China.
○	○	CO_2 emissions per capita in India increased between 2005 and 2010.

This tab provides GDP information about two of the countries, India and China, discussed on the first two tabs. The information on this tab is provided for a subset of the timespan from the second tab. The second tab showed the 25 year range from 1980 to 2005 while this information is only for the 15 year timespan from 1990 to 2005. The GDP information is provided as per capita information. Again, that means that the information on the first tab could be used to calculate the overall GDP for India and China. Of course, that calculation can be completed only for 2005.

Now, that we've reviewed the information on each tab, it's time to start evaluating the statements. But first, we need to consider the directions carefully. The directions state that you are supposed to consider "Does the information in the graphs and text support the inference as stated?" Remember our discussion of valid inferences. An inference is a statement that you know to be true because you can back it up with proof.

There are really three cases to consider when evaluating these statements. If the graphs and other information on the tabs are sufficient to show that the statement is true, answer "yes." If the graphs and other information on the tabs are sufficient to show that the statement is false, answer "no". But, what if there is simply insufficient information to conclusively show that the statement is either true or false? In that case, you answer "no" because the information did not support the inference. In other words, the task here is a little different than simply evaluating whether the statements are true or false. After all, GMAC could have made the answer choices True and False rather than Yes and No.

Remember, however, that most GMAC statements won't try to trick you that way. But, it is important to remember that you need proof to claim that something can be inferred. You will see statements that try to get you to read into or interpret the information. Such activities do not lead to valid inferences!

Let's take a look at the first statement:

> 40% of the countries showed an increase in per capita CO_2 emissions for each five year period.

The first step in evaluating a statement for a Multi-Source Reasoning question is to determine which tab or tabs contain the information that you need. For this statement, the second tab contains information about per capita CO_2 emissions so select that tab. Next, start checking out the trend lines on the graph. We've reprinted the chart from the second tab below.

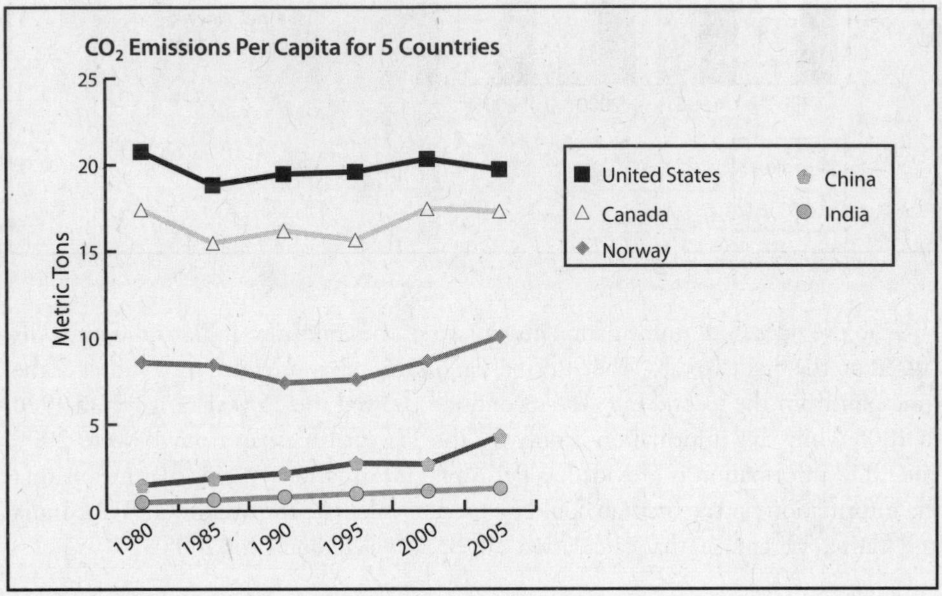

The trend lines for the United States, Canada, and Norway clearly show both increases and decreases between five year periods. So, none of those countries fit the requirements of the statement. The trend line for China needs to be examined carefully. China's CO_2 emissions per capita increase for four out of the five five-year periods shown. However, China's emissions decreased slightly between 1995 and 2000. So, China also does not fit the requirements of the statement. Only India's trend line shows an increase for every five-year period depicted on the graph. But, that means that only 1 out of 5 or 20% of the countries showed an increase in CO_2 emissions for each five year period. So, the answer to the first statement is no.

Next, let's take a look at the second statement:

> The United States emitted more CO_2 in 2005 than did China.

Evaluating this statement is a little trickier than evaluating the first statement. First, be careful of the wording. The statement is about total CO_2 emissions rather than the per capita emissions that are shown by the chart on the second tab. So, while the emissions chart does show that per capita emissions for the US were greater than those for China in 2005, you cannot base your answer only on that piece of information. Remember that the test writers will try to get you to make hasty conclusions so always check out the wording of the statement carefully.

Since none of the provided charts allows you to simply look up the information for this statement, you need to determine if you have sufficient information to evaluate the statement. To go from per capita CO_2 emissions in 2005 to total CO_2 emissions in 2005, you need to know the populations for China and the United States in 2005. That information is provided by the table on the first tab. As discussed above, if there had been insufficient information, you could have clicked "no" right away for your answer.

Since there is sufficient information, however, you'll need to calculate the total 2005 CO_2 emissions for both China and the United States. To do so, multiply the per capita emissions for each country from the chart on the second tab by the population for that country from the table on the first tab. We've duplicated the relevant information from the first two tabs below.

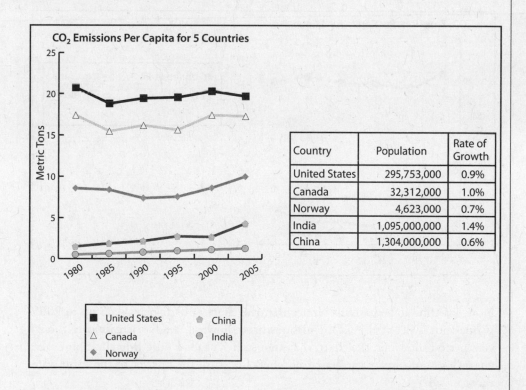

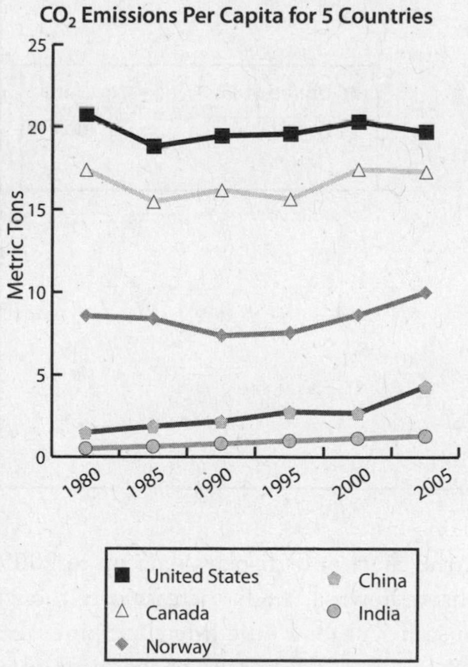

Country	Population	Rate of Growth
United States	295,753,000	0.9%
Canada	32,312,000	1.0%
Norway	4,623,000	0.7%
India	1,095,000,000	1.4%
China	1,304,000,000	0.6%

Of course, you won't be able to split the view on your computer screen this way. So, you'll need to write down some of the relevant information on your noteboards. You should use your noteboards to take notes whenever you need information from two different tabs. Simply trying to remember the numbers can cause errors and waste time. For example, to evaluate this statement, you might jot down the 2005 per capita CO_2 emissions for the United States and China. Then, go to the first tab to get the population numbers for each country.

Use Your Noteboards
If the information you need is on two different tabs, use your noteboards to keep track of the information from one of the tabs.

For the US, per capita CO_2 emissions in 2005 were approximately 20 metric tons. The US population in 2005 was 295,753,000. So, the total 2005 CO_2 emissions for the United States was 20 × 295,753,3000 = 5,915,060,000 metric tons. For China, the per capita CO_2 emissions are approximately 4.8 and the population was 1,304,000,000. So, China's total CO_2 emissions for 2005 were 4.8 × 1,304,000,000 = 6,259,200,000, greater than those of the United States. Therefore, the answer to the second statement is no.

It's time to tackle the third statement:

> CO_2 emissions per capita in India increased between 2005 and 2010.

In contrast with the second statement, evaluating this statement is certainly less time consuming. However, as we'll see, you'll need to remember what is necessary for a valid inference. The necessary information is displayed on the graph on the second tab. Again, we've duplicated the necessary information below.

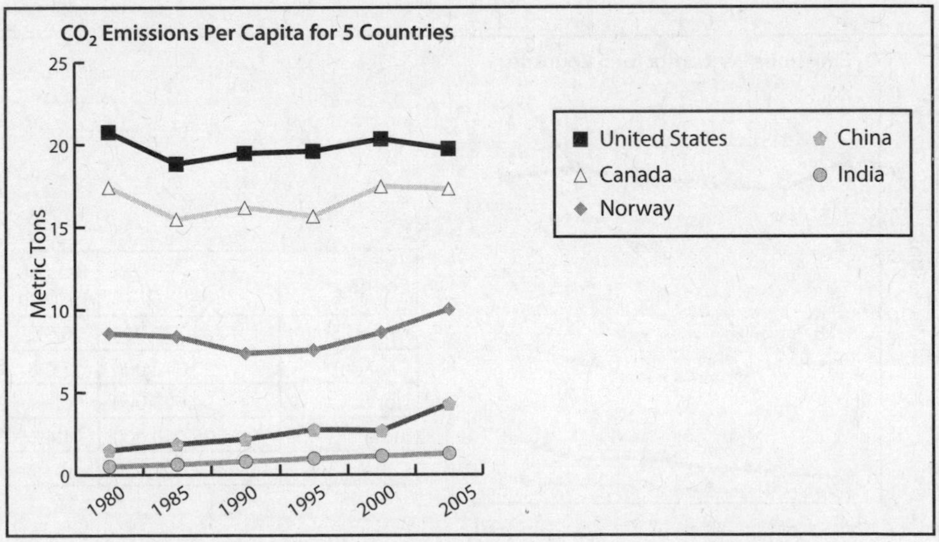

Now, it's time to be careful. Notice that the chart only displays data up to 2005. While India's per capita CO_2 emissions have shown a steady increase over the 25 year period shown on the chart, that's not sufficient for a valid inference. Since the chart does not display the actual numbers for 2010, the answer to the third statement is "no."

Here's what your answers should look like just before you click next to move on to the next question in the Integrated Reasoning section:

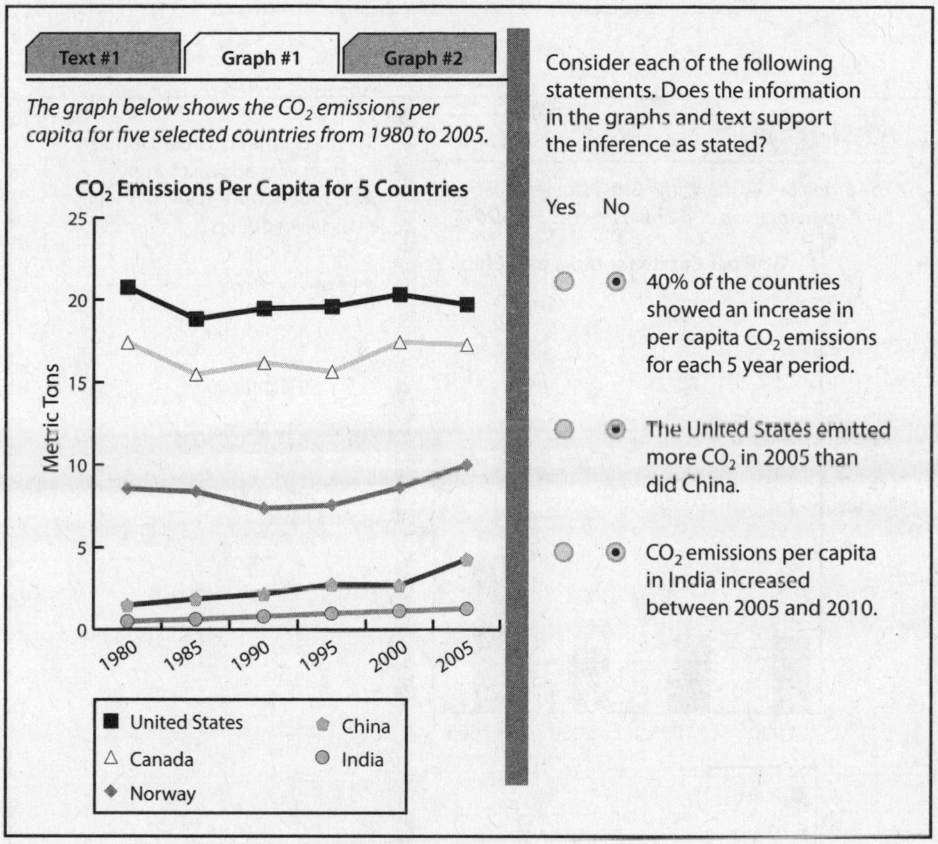

As mentioned, Multi-Source Reasoning questions usually come in sets. Typically, you'll get two statement style questions and one multiple choice style question. The questions on the right change but the tabbed information on the left stays the same.

Let's take a look at a multiple choice question for the tabbed information that we just used to evaluate a statement style question.

Text #1 | Graph #1 | Graph #2

The graph below shows the Gross Domestic Product per Capita for India and China from 1990 to 2005.

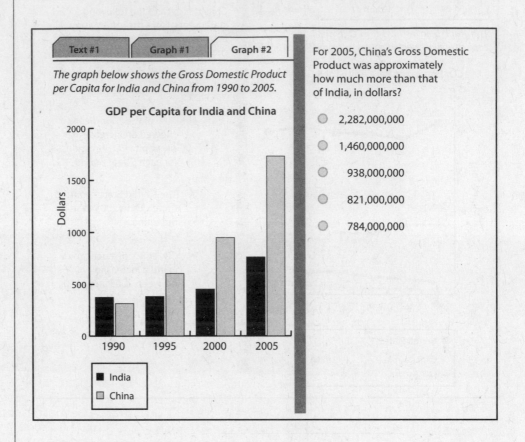

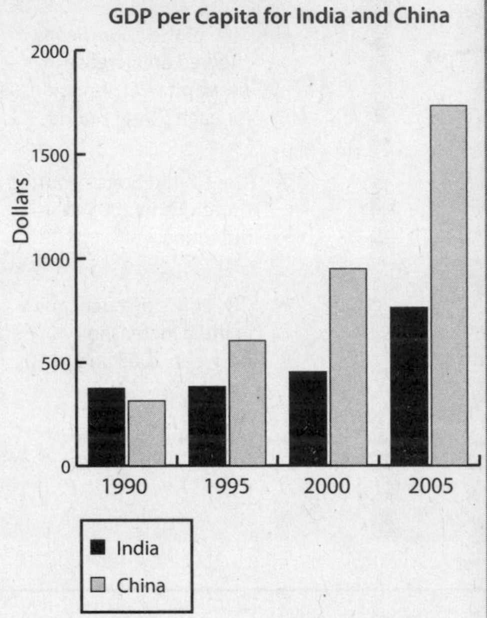

For 2005, China's Gross Domestic Product was approximately how much more than that of India, in dollars?

- 2,282,000,000
- 1,460,000,000
- 938,000,000
- 821,000,000
- 784,000,000

Here's How to Crack It

As with any other Multi-Source Reasoning question, your first step is to determine which chart or charts contain the relevant data. For this question, you certainly need the bar chart on the third tab because that chart shows information about GDP. The bar chart is shown above. However, the bar chart displays data about GDP per capita and the question asks about overall Gross Domestic Product. So, you'll also need the 2005 population numbers from the table on tab one. We've reproduced the relevant table below.

Country	Population	Rate of Growth
United States	295,753,000	0.9%
Canada	32,312,000	1.0%
Norway	4,623,000	0.7%
India	1,095,000,000	1.4%
China	1,304,000,000	0.6%

To answer the question, you need to multiply each countries GDP per capita from 2005 by its population from 2005. Then, subtract India's GDP from that of China.

Based on the bar chart, China's 2005 per capita GDP was approximately $1,750. Since China's population in 2005 was 1,304,000,000, China's 2005 GDP was approximately $1,750 × 1,304,000,000 = $2,282,000,000,000. (Remember that you can use the onscreen calculator to perform the calculation.) For India, the 2005 per capita GDP was approximately $750 while India's population was 1,095,000,000. That means that India's GDP was approximately $750 × 1,095,000,000 = $821,250,000,000. Now, just subtract to find that China's 2005 GDP was approximately $1,460,750,000 more than that of India. That's closest to Answer Choice B.

Need More Practice?
Check out *1,037 Practice Questions for the New GMAT* for access to 100 more Integrated Reasoning questions!

Complex Calculations and the Memory Keys

The problem just discussed featured several longer calculations. Your calculator at home probably has parentheses which makes entering such a calculation a one step operation. Is there a way to do this calculation in one step using the onscreen GMAT calculator which doesn't have parentheses? Sure, use the memory keys!

Enter the following keystrokes:

1750 * 1304000000 = [MS]

750 * 1095000000 = [+/-] [M+] [MR]

These keystrokes will minimize the number of times you need to enter the large numbers which helps to avoid errors.

Summary

- Before you jump into the Integrated Reasoning questions, get your bearings and peruse each tab or piece of information.
- On Table Analysis questions, know that you can sort only by one column at a time. If you think that sorting will help, go for it. But don't waste time devising the perfect order to evaluate statements.
- On Graphics Interpretation questions, start by looking for labels on the axes and finding the legend if there is one.
- On Two-Part Analysis questions, do some algebra or PITA to get to the right answer. Careful that you select the right button in the right column when answering these questions.
- On Multi-Source Reasoning questions, take a minute to review the information on each tab before you jump in. Think about how the information on one tab relates to the information on other tabs.

Chapter 20 Integrated Reasoning: Drills

PRACTICE INTEGRATED REASONING: SECTION 1

12 Items

Time limit: 30 minutes

This section is a full practice Integrated Reasoning section. Please note that some questions are laid out slightly differently in this book versus what you'll see on the GMAT. Many of the new question formats are interactive. Hence, only approximations can be printed. Specifically,

- Table Analysis questions are shown with a main sort and several alternate sorts. You may not need every sort.
- Graphics Interpretation questions include drop down boxes. In this book, the box is shown as a fill-in blank and the answers printed below the blank.
- For Multi-Source Reasoning questions, we've printed what's on each tab consecutively on the page.
- For some questions, you'll see (A), (B), (C), etc. next to answer choices. These are included only to make it easier to check your work. These do not appear on the real GMAT.

We've included answers to this section starting on page 459.

Item 1:

Subway Station	Riders	% Change	Connecting Subway Lines
Times Square/42nd St.	58,422,597	0.6%	11
Grand Central/42nd St.	41,903,210	–0.2%	5
34th St./Herald Square	37,769,752	2.2%	7
14th St./Union Square	34,730,692	1.4%	7
34th St./Penn Station (Red Lines)	26,892,243	–1.1%	3
34th St./Penn Station (Blue Lines)	24,265,016	0.3%	3
59th St/Columbus Circle	20,711,058	1.4%	5
Lexington Ave/59th St	19,553,597	3.3%	6
86th St. (Green Lines)	19,147,021	1.4%	3

The table above gives information on the ridership in 9 subway stations in New York City for the year 2010. The subway stations were chosen for inclusion in the table because they were the busiest stations in 2010, based on the number of passengers entering the station. In addition to annual ridership (number of passengers) for each station in 2010, the table also gives the percent increase or decrease in ridership from 2009 to 2010 and the number of subway lines that connect to the station.

Each column of the table can be sorted in ascending order by clicking on the word "Select" above the table and choosing, from the drop-down menu, the heading of the column on which you want the table to be sorted.

Alternate Sort 1: *% Change*

Subway Station	Riders	% Change	Connecting Subway Lines
34th St./Penn Station (Red Lines)	26,892,243	–1.1%	3
Grand Central/42nd St.	41,903,210	–0.2%	5
34th St./Penn Station (Blue Lines)	24,265,016	0.3%	3
Times Square/42nd St	58,422,597	0.6%	11
14th St./Union Square	34,730,692	1.4%	7
59th St/Columbus Circle	20,711,058	1.4%	5
86th St. (Green Lines)	19,147,021	1.4%	3
34th St./Herald Square	37,769,752	2.2%	7
Lexington Ave/59th St	19,553,597	3.3%	6

Alternate Sort 2: *Connecting Subway Lines*

Subway Station	Riders	% Change	Connecting Subway Lines
34th St./Penn Station (Red Lines)	26,892,243	–1.1%	3
34th St./Penn Station (Blue Lines)	24,265,016	0.3%	3
86th St. (Green Lines)	19,147,021	1.4%	3
Grand Central/42nd St.	41,903,210	–0.2%	5
59th St/Columbus Circle	20,711,058	1.4%	5
Lexington Ave/59th St	19,553,597	3.3%	6
14th St./Union Square	34,730,692	1.4%	7
34th St./Herald Square	37,769,752	2.2%	7
Times Square/42nd St	58,422,597	0.6%	11

Consider each of the following statements about the subway stations. For each statement indicate whether the statement is true or false, based on the information provided in the table.

	True	False	
Question 1-1	O	O	The station with the median rank based on annual ridership is also the station with the greatest decrease in annual ridership from 2009 to 2010.
Question 1-2	O	O	The ratio of the average (arithmetic mean) number of riders in 2010 for those subway stations having 5 connecting lines to those having 3 connecting lines is approximately 4:3.
Question 1-3	O	O	The station with the greatest percent increase in riders from 2009 to 2010 had the least annual ridership in 2010.

Item 2:

Frank researched the 45 doctors in his local area and found that 8 of them graduated from medical school with honors, but that the services of only 3 of those 8 doctors are covered by his medical plan. He also found that 27 doctors whose services are covered by his medical plan graduated from medical school without honors.

In the table below, for the doctors in Frank's local area, identify the total number of doctors whose services are not covered by Frank's medical plan, and identify the number of doctors who both graduated from medical school without honors and whose services are not covered by Frank's health plan. Make only one selection in each column.

	Services Not Covered by Medical Plan	Graduated Without Honors and Services Not Covered by Medical Plan	Total Number
(A)	○	○	10
(B)	○	○	15
(C)	○	○	18
(D)	○	○	30
(E)	○	○	37
(F)	○	○	40

Item 3:

A flower market sells orchids for $1.35 and dahlias for $1.80. Faustino spends $18.00 on orchids and dahlias.

In the table below, choose the number of orchids and the number of dahlias that are consistent with the amount spent by Faustino. Make only one selection in each column.

Orchids	Dahlias	Number Purchased
(A) ○	○	0
(B) ○	○	2
(C) ○	○	4
(D) ○	○	5
(E) ○	○	6
(F) ○	○	8

Item 4:

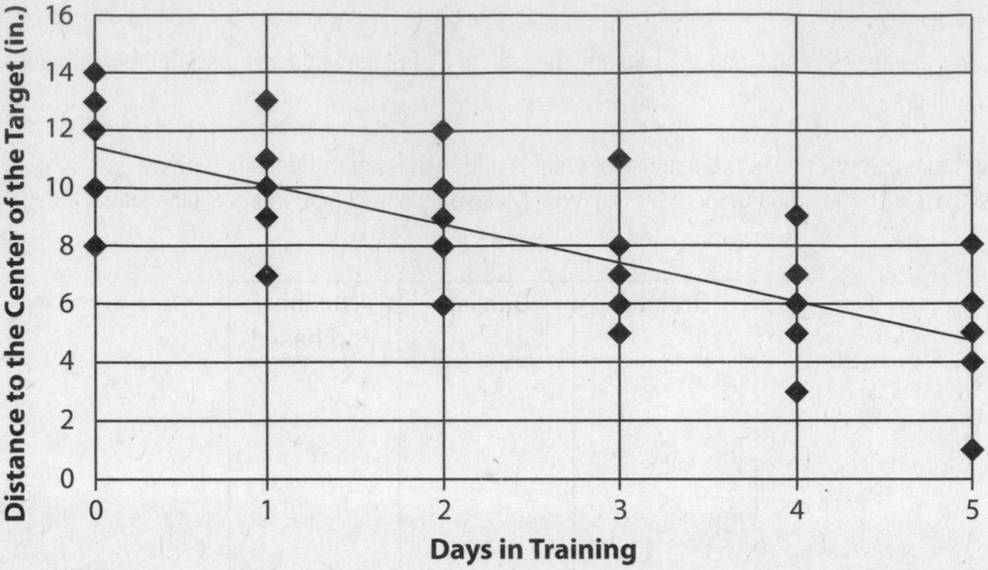

At a certain archery school, each of five students shot a single arrow at the end of each day of training, as well as one arrow before the first day of training. The graph above is a scatterplot, in which each of the 30 points represents the distance from the center of the target to each student's arrow and the number of days the student had been in training at the time the arrow was shot. The solid line is the regression line. Use the drop-down menus to fill in the blanks in each of the following statements based on the information given by the graph.

Question 4-1:

The slope of the regression line is closest to ________.

(A) –2.6
(B) –1.4
(C) –0.8
(D) 1.2
(E) 2.9

Question 4-2:

The number of students within 11 inches of the center of the target is ________ after day 2 of training than before any training.

(A) 50% less
(B) 25% less
(C) 50% greater
(D) 100% greater
(E) 200% greater

Item 5:

The earliest known evidence of seafaring by human ancestors dates to approximately 130,000 years ago. However, in 2010, archaeologists discovered stone tools on the coast of a Mediterranean island that date to the Paleolithic age (about 2.6 million years ago). Because more than 40 miles of open sea separate the island from Greece, the archaeologists theorized that some human ancestors developed nautical skills millions of years earlier than previously discovered.

Question 5-1:

In the table below, identify which statement, if true, most strengthens the argument above, and which statement, if true, most seriously weakens the argument above.

	Strengthen	Weaken	Statement
(A)	○	○	In the same area of the island, archaeologists discovered pieces of ancient harpoons and spears used for fishing.
(B)	○	○	The stone tools resemble those made and used by *Homo erectus* and *Homo heidelbergensis*, human ancestors in the Paleolithic era who lived on the mainland of Greece.
(C)	○	○	The stone tools were probably used primarily for skinning animals.
(D)	○	○	It would be impossible to construct a seaworthy boat solely from the tools discovered by the archaeologists.
(E)	○	○	Approximately 5 million years ago, during the Messinian Salinity Crisis of the late Miocene era, the Mediterranean Sea dried up.
(F)	○	○	The stone tools were likely used for purposes other than construction of boats or rafts.

There is no testing material on this page.

Data for Items 6, 7, and 8:

CD Offerings | **Memo**

This table provides the standard interest rates offered by Central Bank for CDs, listed according to term offering and purchase amount. The interest rates listed are annual rates, compounded yearly, to be paid when the CD comes to term. No bonuses or other adjustments are included.

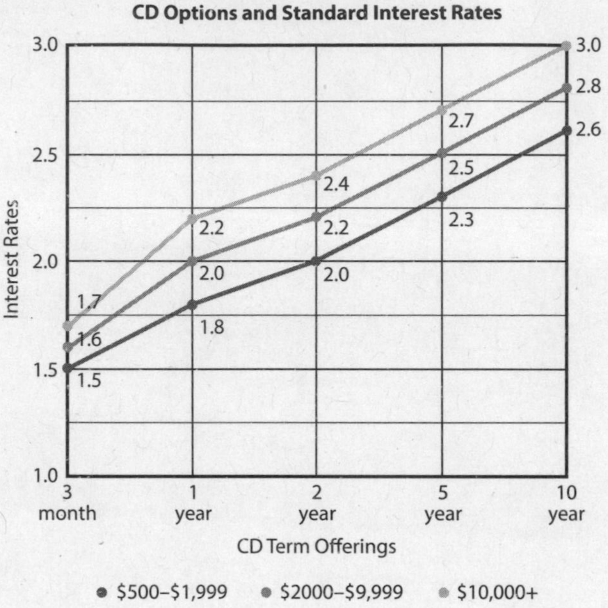

CD Offerings | Memo

General memo to employees of Central Bank:

January 15th

In order to improve and stabilize our bank's investment opportunities, we are seeking to shift the balance of our customers' CD accounts towards those with longer maturity terms. We have begun testing two incentive programs. All CDs purchased with terms of at least 5 years now receive, as a bonus, an additional 0.1% interest during the first year to be added to the standard rate. Moreover, preferred customers (those who have previously bought CDs of any term length in amounts of $10,000 or more) will receive a bonus of 0.2% during the first year when they purchase a CD with a term of 5 or 10 years in the amount of at least $10,000. Other CDs continue at the standard rates.

We have also revised the schedule of penalties for early withdrawal and made these applicable to all new CDs. The penalties are as follows: For any CD, early withdrawal less than a year after the CD is purchased results in a loss of all interest. For 2-year CDs, early withdrawal after the first year results in the loss of one year of interest. For 5-year and 10-year CDs, withdrawal after the first year results in the loss of two years of interest and of any accrued bonus interest.

Item 6:

Determine whether each of the following investments will earn at least $250 of interest in its first year.

	Yes	No	
Question 6-1	○	○	$11,000 invested by a new customer in a 1-year CD
Question 6-2	○	○	$9,500 invested by a preferred customer in a 5-year CD
Question 6-3	○	○	$9,500 invested by a new customer in a 10-year CD

Item 7:

Determine whether each of these transactions will, according to the new rules and rates described, yield a total interest payment of between $500 and $600.

	Yes	No	
Question 7-1	○	○	A new customer's $20,000 1-year CD held for the complete term.
Question 7-2	○	○	A new customer's $4,000 5-year CD held for the complete term.
Question 7-3	○	○	A preferred customer's $10,000 2-year CD held for the complete term.

Item 8:

Consider each of the following statements. Does the information in the memo and the table support the inference as stated?

	Yes	No	
Question 8-1	○	○	Prior to the policy changes described, there were no penalties for early CD withdrawals.
Question 8-2	○	○	Certain bank policies are designed to reward preferred customers for their loyalty.
Question 8-3	○	○	If the bank accomplishes its stated intentions, it will likely pay a higher average (arithmetic mean) interest rate to customers than if it does not.

Item 9:

Year of Election	President	Political Party	Popular Vote (millions)	% of Popular Vote	Electoral Vote	% of Electoral Vote
1960	John Kennedy	Democratic	34.2	49.72%	303	56.40%
1964	Lyndon Johnson	Democratic	43.1	61.05%	486	90.30%
1968	Richard Nixon	Republican	31.8	43.42%	301	55.90%
1972	Richard Nixon	Republican	47.2	60.67%	520	96.70%
1976	James Carter	Democratic	40.8	50.08%	297	55.20%
1980	Ronald Reagan	Republican	43.9	50.75%	489	90.90%
1984	Ronald Reagan	Republican	54.5	58.77%	525	97.60%
1988	George Bush	Republican	48.9	53.37%	426	79.20%
1992	William Clinton	Democratic	44.9	43.01%	370	68.80%
1996	William Clinton	Democratic	47.4	49.23%	379	70.40%
2000	George W. Bush	Republican	50.5	47.87%	271	50.40%
2004	George W. Bush	Republican	62.0	50.73%	286	53.20%
2008	Barack Obama	Democratic	69.5	52.87%	365	67.80%

The table above gives information about the voting patterns in United States presidential elections from 1960 to 2008. In addition to giving the name and the political party of the President elected in each year, the table provides the total popular vote and electoral vote that the winner received in that election, as well as the percentage of the total vote that each figure represents.

Each column of the table can be sorted in ascending order by clicking on the word "Select" above the table and choosing, from the drop-down menu, the heading of the column on which you want the table to be sorted.

Alternate Sort 1: *Electoral Vote*

Year of Election	President	Political Party	Popular Vote (millions)	% of Popular Vote	Electoral Vote	% of Electoral Vote
2000	George W. Bush	Republican	50.5	47.87%	271	50.40%
2004	George W. Bush	Republican	62.0	50.73%	286	53.20%
1976	James Carter	Democratic	40.8	50.08%	297	55.20%
1968	Richard Nixon	Republican	31.8	43.42%	301	55.90%
1960	John Kennedy	Democratic	34.2	49.72%	303	56.40%
2008	Barack Obama	Democratic	69.5	52.87%	365	67.80%
1992	William Clinton	Democratic	44.9	43.01%	370	68.80%
1996	William Clinton	Democratic	47.4	49.23%	379	70.40%
1988	George Bush	Republican	48.9	53.37%	426	79.20%
1964	Lyndon Johnson	Democratic	43.1	61.05%	486	90.30%
1980	Ronald Reagan	Republican	43.9	50.75%	489	90.90%
1972	Richard Nixon	Republican	47.2	60.67%	520	96.70%
1984	Ronald Reagan	Republican	54.4	58.77%	525	97.60%

Alternate Sort 2: *Percent of Popular Vote*

Year of Election	President	Political Party	Popular Vote (millions)	% of Popular Vote	Electoral Vote	% of Electoral Vote
1992	William Clinton	Democratic	44.9	43.01%	370	68.80%
1968	Richard Nixon	Republican	31.8	43.42%	301	55.90%
2000	George W. Bush	Republican	50.5	47.87%	271	50.40%
1996	William Clinton	Democratic	47.4	49.23%	379	70.40%
1960	John Kennedy	Democratic	34.2	49.72%	303	56.40%
1976	James Carter	Democratic	40.8	50.08%	297	55.20%
2004	George W. Bush	Republican	62.0	50.73%	286	53.20%
1980	Ronald Reagan	Republican	43.9	50.75%	489	90.90%
2008	Barack Obama	Democratic	69.5	52.87%	365	67.80%
1988	George Bush	Republican	48.9	53.37%	426	79.20%
1984	Ronald Reagan	Republican	54.4	58.77%	525	97.60%
1972	Richard Nixon	Republican	47.2	60.67%	520	96.70%
1964	Lyndon Johnson	Democratic	43.1	61.05%	486	90.30%

Consider each of the following statements about the Presidential election data. For each statement indicate whether the statement is true or false, based on the information provided in the table.

	True	False	
Question 9-1	○	○	Of those Presidents elected for two terms, William Clinton had the smallest percent increase in popular vote between the two years.
Question 9-2	○	○	The average (arithmetic mean) number of electoral votes received by Democratic presidents was greater than the average number of electoral votes received by Republican presidents.
Question 9-3	○	○	The same President was elected in the two election years in which the winner's percentage of the popular vote and percentage of the electoral vote were most nearly equal.

Data for Items 10, 11, and 12:

Memo #1 | **Memo #2** | **Email #1**

MEMORANDUM
To: Regional Office Managers
From: Chief Operations Officer
RE: Travel planning

Once again, our annual management retreat will be held in Bloomsbury. In preparation for this year's retreat, all Regional Office Managers (ROMs) will be responsible for arranging the travel reservations for all Level 2 managers within his or her Region. You may delegate that task should you wish.

ROMs will receive a research memorandum from the Logistics Division providing the average (arithmetic mean) airfare from the 6 Regions to Bloomsbury. While ROMs should use that average airfare as a guide, we anticipate that there may be some variation in ticket prices based upon the specifics of travel arrangements. As such, Regional offices will be reimbursed for the full cost of any plane ticket priced within 1 (one) standard deviation of the average airfare from its region to Bloomsbury, inclusive. For any ticket priced more than 1 (one) standard deviation above the mean, regional offices will be reimbursed up to the average airfare from your region to Bloomsbury. For any ticket priced more than 1 (one) standard deviation below the average, in addition to full reimbursement of the ticket cost, regional offices will receive a "Budget Bonus" of 50% of the difference between the ticket price and the average airfare from your region to Bloomsbury.

Memo #1 | **Memo #2** | **Email #1**

MEMORANDUM
To: Regional Office Managers
From: Logistics Division
RE: Airfare Research

The attached chart lists the average (arithmetic mean) airfare from the listed Regions to Bloomsbury. The mean airfare was calculated based upon taking a normally distributed sample of airfares. The standard deviation and size of each sample is also listed in the chart.

Research Summary on Airfare

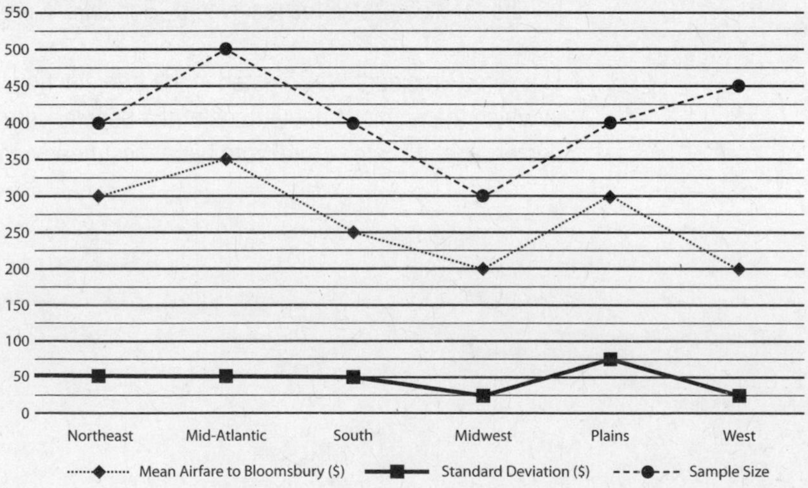

(See the next page for additional information)

Memo #1 | Memo #2 | Email #1

Email from Marco Roland, Human Resources Manager, West Region to Marisa Cortland, Regional Office Manager, West Region

Dear Marisa,

Tickets have been purchased for all of the Level 2 Managers in the West Region. Below is a summary:

Airfare	Number of Tickets Purchased
$150	18
$210	4
$230	8

Best,

Marco

Item 10:

Consider each of the following statements. Select *Yes* if the information contained in the two memoranda and the email support the inference as stated. Otherwise, select *No.*

	Yes	No	
Question 10-1	O	O	No region had a lower average (arithmetic mean) airfare to Bloomsbury than the Midwest
Question 10-2	O	O	Only Level 2 managers will attend the management retreat.
Question 10-3	O	O	The Regional Office Manager need not make the reservations personally.

Item 11:

Consider each of the following statements. Based upon the information contained in the two memoranda and the email, determine whether each statement is true or false as stated.

	True	False	
Question 11-1	O	O	The West Region will receive a "Budget Bonus" of $450.
Question 11-2	O	O	In the Mid-Atlantic sample, more than 20 tickets were priced over $450.
Question 11-3	O	O	In the Northeast sample, more than 50 tickets were priced under $250.

Item 12:

If one of the tickets purchased by the West Region's Level 2 managers were selected at random, what is the probability that it is eligible to be fully reimbursed?

(A) $\frac{4}{15}$

(B) $\frac{9}{15}$

(C) $\frac{11}{15}$

(D) $\frac{12}{15}$

(E) $\frac{14}{15}$

PRACTICE INTEGRATED REASONING: SECTION 2

12 Items

Time limit: 30 minutes

This section is a full practice Integrated Reasoning section. Please note that some questions are laid out slightly differently in this book versus what you'll see on the GMAT. Many of the new question formats are interactive. Hence, only approximations can be printed. Specifically,

- Table Analysis questions are shown with a main sort and several alternate sorts. You may not need every sort.
- Graphics Interpretation questions include drop down boxes. In this book, the box is shown as a fill-in blank and the answers printed below the blank.
- For Multi-Source Reasoning questions, we've printed what's on each tab consecutively on the page.
- For some questions, you'll see (A), (B), (C), etc. next answer choices. These are included only to make it easier to check your work. These do not appear on the real GMAT.

We've included answers to this section starting on page 466.

Item 1:

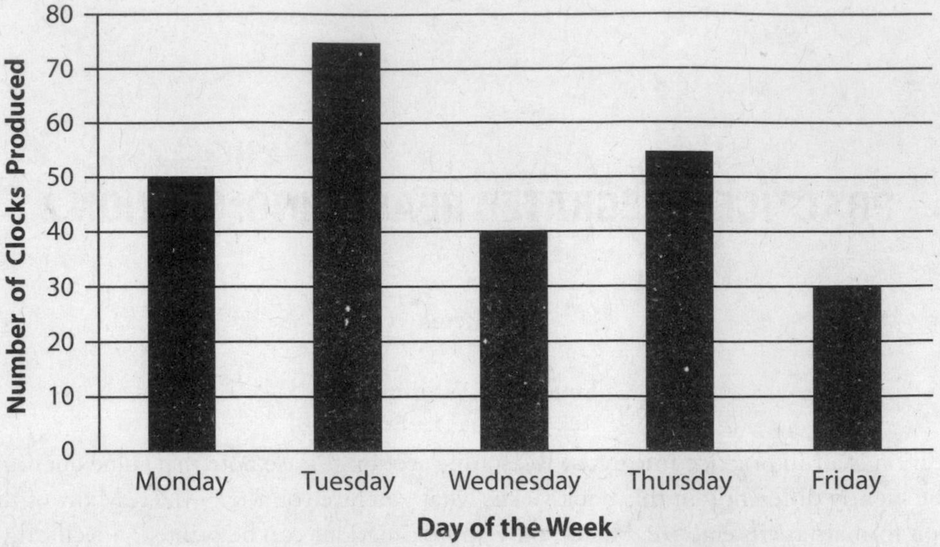

The graph above gives the daily output for five days at a certain clock factory. Use the drop-down menus to fill in the blanks in each of the following statements based on the information given by the graph.

Question 1-1:

The ratio of the number of clocks produced on Tuesday to those produced on Wednesday is approximately _________.

(A) 15 to 8
(B) 12 to 7
(C) 10 to 9
(D) 8 to 11
(E) 5 to 13

Question 1-2:

The total number of clocks produced on Monday and Wednesday is approximately _________ of the number of clocks produced for all five days.

(A) 16%
(B) 20%
(C) 28%
(D) 36%
(E) 45%

Item 2:

Company X: Our company's computer technology is out of date. We will be unable to compete effectively in the modern economy if we are not using current computer technology. We have decided to purchase new computers that run Portals 8, the newest version of the world's best-selling operating system, throughout the entire company.

Technology Consultant: We agree that Company X needs to purchase new computers, but instead of installing Portals 8, Company X should purchase GreenCap, our consulting firm's proprietary operating system. The initial purchase of a GreenCap operating system costs substantially less than does Portals 8, and it provides the same functionality with current computer technology. With the money saved, Company X will be better able to compete effectively in the modern economy.

In the table below, identify which statement, if true, most weakens Company X's argument, and which statement, if true, most weakens the Technology Consultant's argument.

Weakens Company X	Weakens Technology Consultant	Statement
(A) ○	○	GreenCap makes more efficient use of computer resources than does Portals 8.
(B) ○	○	GreenCap is not the most cutting-edge software available on the market.
(C) ○	○	Although Portals 8 was released this year, GreenCap has been available for three years.
(D) ○	○	GreenCap requires purchase of an annual maintenance agreement, making it more expensive overall than Portals 8.
(E) ○	○	Portals 8 is available in several different versions with different price levels, depending on the proposed use of the operating system.
(F) ○	○	Portals 8, which was newly released, contains bugs and design flaws that will impair Company X's ability to compete in the modern economy.

There is no testing material on this page.

Item 3:

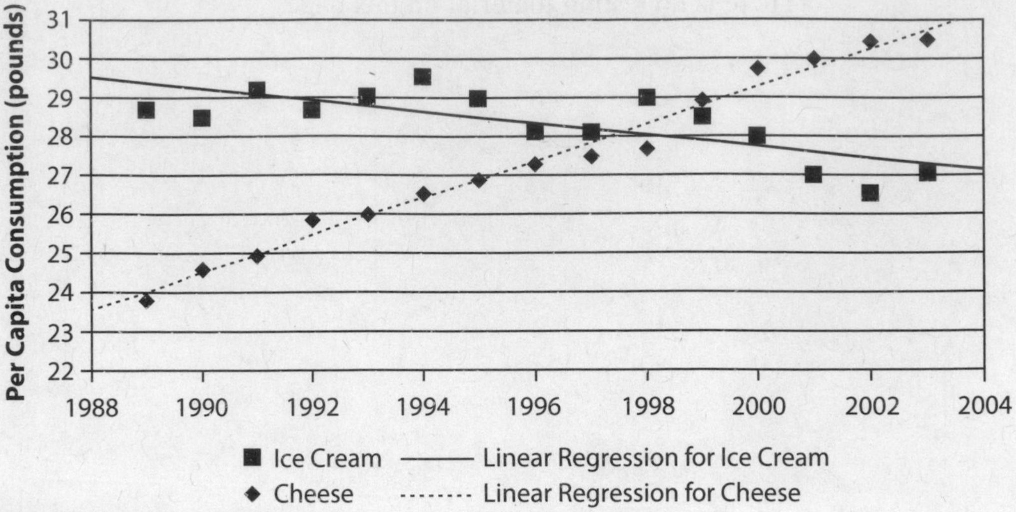

The graph above is a scatter plot with 30 points, each representing the per capita consumption, in pounds, of of ice cream and cheese for the years 1989 through 2003 in the United States. The solid line is a regression line for the points representing the per capita consumption of ice cream. The dashed line is a regression line for the points representing the per capita consumption of cheese. Use the drop-down menus to fill in the blanks in each of the following statements based on the information given by the graph.

Question 3-1:

For the year with the lowest total per capita consumption of both ice cream and cheese combined, the ratio of per capita ice cream consumption to per capita cheese consumption is approximately ________ .

(A) 2 to 3
(B) 3 to 2
(C) 6 to 5
(D) 5 to 6

Question 3-2:

The slope of the regression line for ice cream is ________ the slope of the regression line for cheese.

(A) greater than
(B) less than
(C) equal to

Item 4:

XM Representative: Your federal committee thoroughly reviews all of the geo-engineering industry's planned projects and approves only those that meet your guidelines for safety and environmental impact. Since less than two percent of XM projects have ever been rejected, the costly and time-consuming review should be waived so that our latest project can be passed and implemented quickly.

Committee Member: Your request fails to consider that the decisions of our board affect not only the corporation involved, but also the entire field. If we fail to review your project, we also fail to observe innovations in geo-engineering that may need guidelines drafted for the safety of subsequent projects throughout the industry.

In the table below, please identify the additional evidence that most strengthens and the additional evidence that most weakens the committee member's response to the XM representative.

Strengthens Committee Member's Response	Weakens Committee Member's Response	Additional Evidence
(A) ○	○	XM's latest project is nearly identical to a previous project by XM that had successfully passed the committee review process
(B) ○	○	The geo-engineering corporation CL, which is XM's biggest competitor, has had less than one percent of its projects rejected by the committee
(C) ○	○	Once a geo-engineering innovation has been passed by the committee, the same innovation is automatically approved in all subsequent projects, without further review.
(D) ○	○	Many of XM's geo-engineering projects are peer-reviewed within the industry before they are submitted to the federal committee.
(E) ○	○	Geo-engineering is a hazardous field that deserves careful monitoring.
(F) ○	○	The federal committee has had to reverse some of its decisions on past projects.

Item 5:

A group of entomologists estimates that the population of Insect Species X is decreasing at a constant rate of 10% per year, while the population of Insect Species Y is decreasing at a constant rate of 15% per year. Based on these estimates, in four years, the two species will have equal populations, rounded to the nearest million.

In the table below, identify a number for the current population of Insect Species X, in millions, and a number for the current population of Insect Species Y, in millions, that is consistent with the entomologists' estimates.

Insect Species X	Insect Species Y	Current Populations (in millions)
(A) ○	○	450
(B) ○	○	525
(C) ○	○	565
(D) ○	○	600
(E) ○	○	625
(F) ○	○	770

Data for Items 6, 7 and 8:

Email #1 | **Email #2** | **Memo #1**

Email from Marketing Director to Marketing Researcher on October 4, 2011.

As you know, our revenues have declined for each of the past three quarters. To address this issue, I suggest that we initiate a massive advertising buy. On three separate occasions, in 1978, 1987, and 1993, we responded to revenue decreases by increasing our advertising expenditures by 30%. On all three occasions, our revenues began to increase again within one quarter. Therefore, if we increase the number of advertisements targeted at our top consumers by 30%, we will once again increase our revenues.

Since our top consumers are females aged 15–25, determine the top two television programs watched by that group. Also, research the prices for a 30-second commercial for each television program.

Email #1 | **Email #2** | **Memo #1**

Email from Marketing Researcher to Marketing Director on October 10, 2011.

We've hit a slight complication in our research. While we've had no problem determining the top two programs and advertising prices for each, we've realized that there is a fair amount of overlap between the viewers of the two programs. We've found that 80% of the viewers who are females aged 15–25 for *Hart Attack* also watch *Blonde Fury*.

I'll send you the chart summarizing the audience size and advertising prices tomorrow.

Email #1 | **Email #2** | **Memo #1**

MEMORANDUM
TO: Marketing Director
FROM: Marketing Researcher
DATE: October 11, 2011
RE: Market Research Results

The attached chart presents the results from our research on the top 2 television programs watched by females aged 15–25.

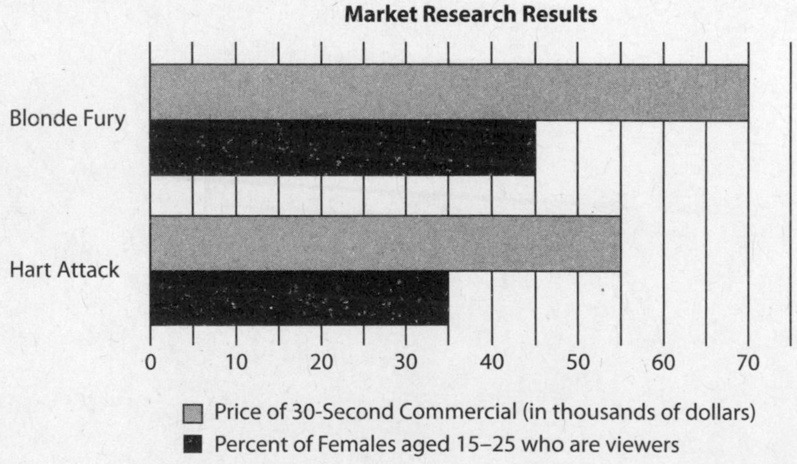

Item 6:

Consider each of the following statements. Select *Yes* if the information contained in the two emails and the memorandum support the inference as stated. Otherwise, select *No.*

	Yes	No	
Question 6-1	O	O	No age and gender group watches Blonde Fury more frequently than does females aged 15–25.
Question 6-2	O	O	Thirty second advertisements are more expensive for programs with larger audiences.
Question 6-3	O	O	The ratio of female viewers aged 15 to 25 to dollars spent on advertising for *Hart Attack* is greater than that for *Blonde Fury.*

Item 7:

If there are 20,000,000 females aged 15–25, then how many females aged 15–25 (in millions) watch neither *Blonde Fury* nor *Hart Attack*?

(A) 1.4
(B) 4.0
(C) 5.6
(D) 9.6
(E) 11.2

Item 8:

Consider each of the following statements. Based on the information contained in the two emails and the memoranda, select *Yes* if the statements is an assumption made by the Marketing Director. Otherwise, select *No.*

	Yes	No	
Question 8-1	O	O	It is possible for a strategy that succeeded in the past to succeed again.
Question 8-2	O	O	The previous increases in revenues were attributable at least in part to the effect of increased advertising
Question 8-3	O	O	Increasing the number of advertisements has a similar effect on revenues as increasing the amount of money spent on advertising expenditures.

Item 9:

Name	Population 2010	Population 2050	% of Population Foreign-Born
Andorra	84,000	75,000	77.25
Australia	22,729,000	29,013,000	19.93
Barbados	273,000	282,000	9.31
Brazil	190,733,000	260,692,000	0.34
Canada	34,611,000	41,136,000	18.76
China	1,399,725,000	1,303,723,000	0.29
Egypt	80,942,000	137,873,000	0.22
France	65,822,000	69,768,000	10.18
India	1,210,193,000	1,656,554,000	0.52
Indonesia	237,556,000	313,021,000	0.07
Kazakhstan	16,518,000	15,100,000	16.88
Laos	6,230,000	10,069,000	0.42
Nauru	10,000	12,000	38.45
Portugal	10,637,000	9,933,000	7.2
Republic of the Congo	4,043,000	9,599,000	7.2
Russia	142,914,000	109,187,000	8.48
Suriname	525,000	617,000	1.11
United Kingdom	62,436,000	71,154,000	8.98
United States	312,399,000	439,010,000	21.81

The table above gives 2010 populations based on UN estimates and 2050 populations based on UN projections for 19 selected countries. The table also gives the UN estimates of the percentage of the population that is foreign-born for each country in 2010.

Each column of the table can be sorted in ascending order by clicking on the word "Select" above the table and choosing, from the drop-down menu, the heading of the column on which you want the table to be sorted.

Alternate Sort 1: *Population 2010*

Name	Population 2010	Projected Population 2050	% of Population Foreign-Born
Nauru	10,000	12,000	38.45
Andorra	84,000	75,000	77.25
Barbados	273,000	282,000	9.31
Suriname	525,000	617,000	1.11
Republic of the Congo	4,043,000	9,599,000	7.2
Laos	6,230,000	10,069,000	0.42
Portugal	10,637,000	9,993,000	7.2
Kazakhstan	16,518,000	15,100,000	16.88
Australia	22,729,000	29,013,000	19.93
Canada	34,611,000	41,136,000	18.76
United Kingdom	62,436,000	71,154,000	8.98
France	65,822,000	69,768,000	10.18
Egypt	80,942,000	137,873,000	0.22
Russia	142,914,000	109,187,000	8.48
Brazil	190,733,000	260,692,000	0.34
Indonesia	237,556,000	313,021,000	0.07
United States	312,399,000	439,010,000	21.81
India	1,210,193,000	1,656,554,000	0.52
China	1,399,725,000	1,303,723,000	0.29

Consider each of the following statements about these countries. For each statement indicate whether the statement is supported based on the information provided in the table.

	Supported	Unsupported	
Question 9-1	○	○	Of the countries with a population greater than 150 million in 2010, the country with the median number of foreign-born inhabitants is China.
Question 9-2	○	○	The total population of Laos is projected to be about 8 million in 2030.
Question 9-3	○	○	Andorra's rank for the number of foreign born inhabitants is greater than that for all other countries listed.

Data for Items 10, 11 and 12:

The following emails come from the Public Relations division of a large non-profit organization.

Email #1 | **Email #2**

Hello Gloria!

We have to choose a caterer for our upcoming gala. Two caterers under consideration are DoxySource and BrightRight. Although DoxySource has delivered satisfactory service in the past, our First Annual Sponsors Gala promises to be the largest event we have ever hosted, and BrightRight is known for large event planning and production. However, I'd like more information before switching from a tried and true contractor. Also, I'd like to consider how to justify any over-budget costs from using BrightRight, if that comes up. I am committed to using only one provider. Please work up a comparison of costs of services and rentals for BrightRight and DoxySource. We require: tables, audio, food, and a punch fountain or fountains (a dessert fountain would be a lovely addition). Our budget is $6,000.00, and we plan for a maximum of 400 people.

Thanks!

Evelyn Schott

Gala Coordinator

Email #1 | **Email #2**

Hello Evelyn,

I've broken out the data in the following chart:

	DoxySource		BrightRight	
	Description	Price	Description	Price
AUDIO	200 Watt P.A. System (up to 40 people)	$65.00	Party Sound System	$650.00
	500 Watt P.A. System (up to 120 people)	$90.00	Marquee Sound System	$850.00
CATERING	Choice of appetizers (shrimp or spring roll)	$2.00 per piece	The Classic Western BBQ	$14.00 per person
	Choice of entree (chicken or beef w/ rice)	$6.25 per piece	The Greek Feast	$17.50 per person
	Choice of dessert (cupcakes or lemon bars)	$3.40 per piece	The Far East Extravaganza	$19.50 per person
TABLES	Trestle Table (seats 8)	$15.50 each	Classroom (seats 8)	$20.00 each
	Circular Table (seats 7)	$17.00 each	Bistro/Hightop (seats 6)	$22.00 each
FOUNTAINS	Chocolate Fountain (supplies not included)	$105.00	Chocolate Fountain (supplies included)	$500.00
	Punch Fountain (7 gallons, provided, serves approx. 70)	$47.00	Punch Fountain, waterfall tier (40 gallons, provided)	$350.00

BrightRight offers packages that are generally more elegant and comprehensive, and more expensive. For instance, we can choose a single full meal set, such as "The Greek Feast," for the entire gala. Using Doxy Source, while more economical and flexible in the catering, does mean more hands-on involvement on our end.

The biggest price difference comes in the audio systems. BrightRight, which consistently hosts events with attendance of several hundreds, offers complex systems that include lights and sound effects, in addition to high-definition audio reproduction. DoxySource offers two standard, large public address systems. I am not sure whether the Gala will need all the flash and sizzle of the high-end sound system; but the projected attendance is above the recommended usage for DoxySource's P.A. systems. Due to electrical concerns, we can only have one P.A. system at the gala.

Gloria Welch

Administrative Assistant, Public Relations

Item 10:

If the maximum number of guests attend the gala, determine if each of the statements is true or false based on the information in the two emails.

	True	False	
Question 10-1	O	O	If the coordinator uses DoxySource and orders one appetizer, one entrée and one dessert per person, then the least amount that can be spent on tables to seat all guests is approximately 16.6% of the cost of food.
Question 10-2	O	O	If the large punch fountain from BrightRight is sufficient for 400 guests, then using smaller fountains from DoxySource to serve the same number of guests would cost at least 20% less per gallon.
Question 10-3	O	O	If BrightRight is used, the project will go over its present budget by at least 15%.

Item 11:

Suppose the Gala Coordinator uses DoxySource, for the maximum number of guests. If she wants to use at least one of each type of table, what is the least possible cost for the tables?

(A) $775.00
(B) $778.44
(C) $792.00
(D) $873.21
(E) $971.43

Item 12:

Based on the information in the messages between the Gala Coordinator and the Administrative Assistant, select *Yes* if the statement can be inferred. Otherwise, select *No*.

	Yes	No	
Question 12-1	O	O	The Gala Coordinator is willing to ask for a budgetary increase, if necessary.
Question 12-2	O	O	According to the Administrative Assistant, audio costs are not the only determining factor in choosing one event planning service over another.
Question 12-3	O	O	Fountains are an optional element of the gala.

Part V
How to Crack the Analytical Writing Assessment

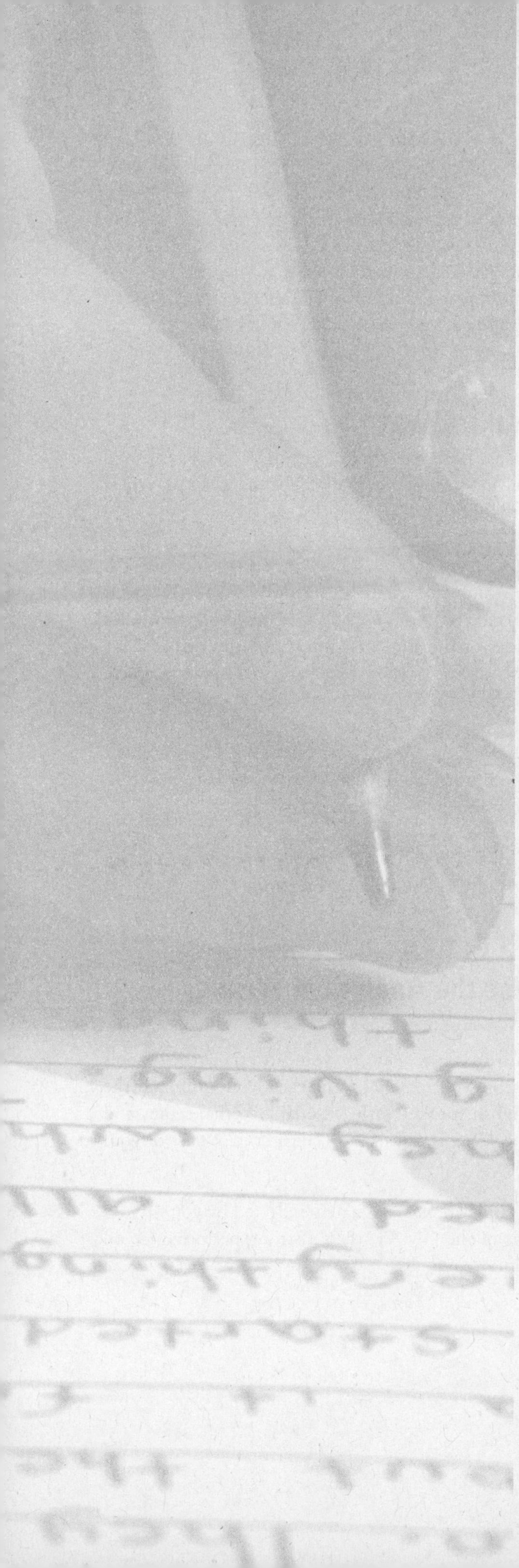

Chapter 21
Analytical Writing Assessment

Writing a coherent essay in 30 minutes might seem daunting, but in this chapter, you will learn techniques of pre-construction and pre-structuring that will make the process easy. You will also learn how the essay is scored and the *key factor* the readers are told to look for. (*Hint*: It isn't originality.)

The very first thing you will be asked to do on the GMAT is to write an essay using a word-processing program. You will have 30 minutes for your essay. You will not be given the essay topic in advance, nor will you be given a choice of topics. However, there is a complete list of all the possible writing assessment topics available for you to review on the GMAC website. Simply go to **www.mba.com/us/the-gmat-exam/gmat-exam-format-timing**, select the link for the Analytical Writing Assessment section, and follow the directions to download a list of current topics. Oh, and just in case you are wondering, it's free!

Practice writing an essay when you take a full-length GMAT at **PrincetonReview.com**. You'll have the option of selecting free LiveGrader™ essay scoring.

Why Have an Essay on the GMAT?

The business schools themselves asked for the essay. Recent studies have indicated that success in business (and in business school) actually depends more on verbal skills than has been traditionally thought.

The business schools have also had to contend with a huge increase in the number of applicants from overseas. Admissions officers at the business schools were finding that the application essays they received from outside the United States did not always accurately reflect the abilities of the students who were supposed to have written them. To put it more bluntly, some of these applicants were paying native English speakers to write their essays for them.

The GMAT Analytical Writing Assessment (AWA) is thus at least partly a check on the writing ability of foreign applicants who now make up more than one-third of all applicants to American business schools.

At the business schools' request, all schools to which you apply now receive, in addition to your AWA score, a copy of the actual essay you wrote.

How Do the Schools Use the Analytical Writing Assessment?

If you are a citizen of a non-English-speaking country, you can expect the schools to look quite closely at both the score you receive on the essay you write and the essay itself. If you are a native English speaker with reasonable Verbal scores and English grades in college, then the AWA is not likely to be a crucial part of your package.

On the other hand, if your verbal skills are *not* adequately reflected by your grades in college, or in the other sections of the GMAT, then a strong performance on the AWA could be extremely helpful.

How Is the Essay Scored?

When you get your GMAT score back from GMAC, you will also receive a separate score for the AWA. Your essay is read by two readers, each of whom will assign your writing a grade from 0 to 6, in half-point increments (6 being the highest score possible). If the two scores are within a point of each other, they will be averaged. If there is more than a one-point spread, the essay will be read by a third reader, and scores will be adjusted to reflect the third scorer's evaluation.

The essay readers use the "holistic" scoring method to grade essays; your writing will be judged not on small details but rather on its overall impact. The readers are supposed to ignore small errors of grammar and spelling. Considering that these readers are going to have to plow through more than 600,000 essays each year, this is probably just as well.

Who Are These Readers Anyway?

We'll put this in the form of a multiple-choice question:

Your essay will be read by:

(A) captains of industry
(B) leading business school professors
(C) college TAs working part time

If you guessed C, you're doing just fine. Each essay will be read by part-time employees of the testing company, mostly culled from graduate school programs.

Admissions Insight No. 10: Financial Aid, Part 1

The perception is that there is no financial aid available for business school. While this is generally true in the case of grants (money you don't have to pay back), it is not true about government-subsidized student loans. Right now, about 70 percent of graduate students receive some form of aid.

How Much Time Do They Devote to Each Essay?

The graders get two minutes, tops. They work in eight-hour marathon sessions (nine to five, with an hour off for lunch), and are each required to read 30 essays per hour. Obviously, these poor graders do not have time for an in-depth reading of your essay. They probably aren't going to notice how carefully you thought out your ideas or how clever your analysis was. Under pressure to meet their quota, they are simply going to be giving it a fast skim. By the time your reader gets to your essay, she will probably have already seen more than a hundred essays—and no matter how ingenious you were in coming up with original ideas, she's already seen them.

So How Do You Score High on the AWA Essays?

On the face of it, you might think it would be pretty difficult to impress these jaded readers, but it turns out that there are some very specific ways to persuade them of your superior writing skills.

What GMAC Doesn't Want You to Know

In a 1982 internal study, two researchers from one of the big testing companies analyzed a group of essays written by actual test takers and the grades that those essays received. The most successful essays had one thing in common. Which of the following characteristics do you think it was?

- o good organization
- o proper diction
- o noteworthy ideas
- o good vocabulary
- o sentence variety
- o length
- o number of paragraphs

What Your Essay Needs in Order to Look Like a Successful Essay

Those researchers discovered that the essays that received the highest grades from the essay graders had one single factor in common: length.

To ace the AWA, you need to take one simple step: *Write as much as you possibly can*. Each essay should include at least four indented paragraphs.

Admissions Insight No. 11: Financial Aid, Part 2

The best kind of student loans: low-cost Stafford loans (which don't have to be repaid until the student has graduated or left the program and which generally have much lower rates than regular, unsecured loans). If necessary, borrow the rest through private educational loans.

How Does the Word-Processing Program Work?

The test makers have created a simple word-processing program to allow students to compose their essays on the screen.

Here's what your screen will look like during the essay portion of the test:

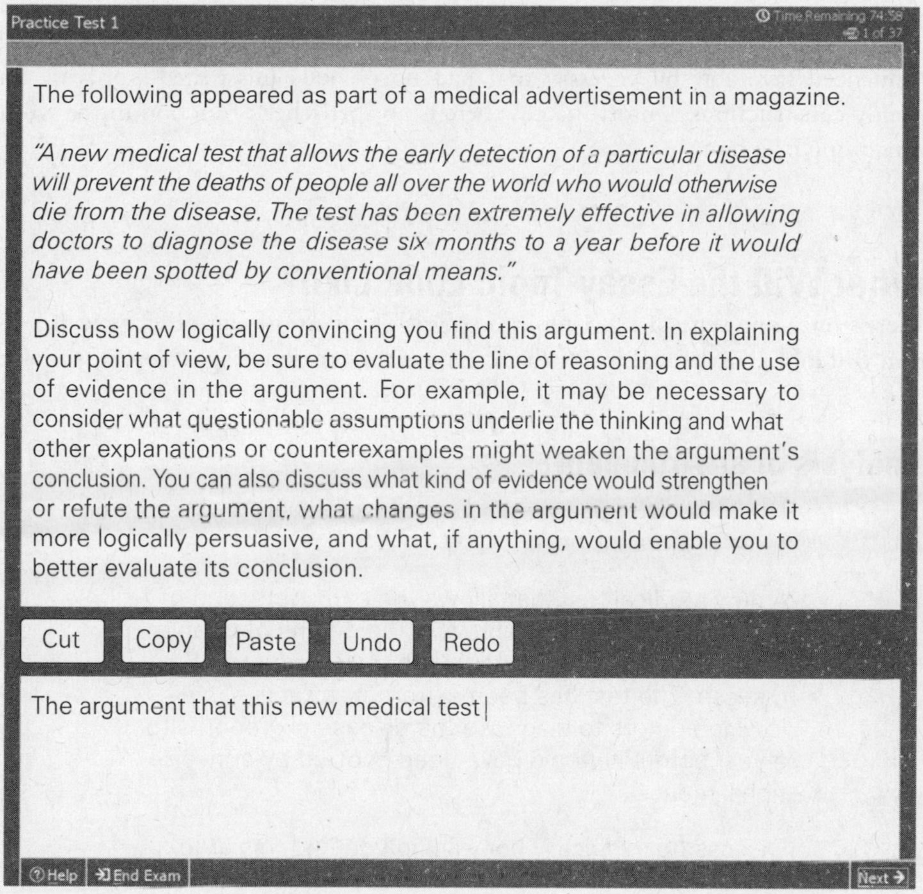

The question always appears at the top of your screen. Below it, in a box, will be your writing area (where you can see a partially completed sentence). When you click inside the box with your mouse, a winking cursor will appear, indicating that you can begin typing. The program supports the use of many of the normal computer keys, plus the following shortcuts:

Cut: Ctrl + X and Alt + T
Copy: Ctrl + C and Alt + C
Paste: Ctrl + V and Alt + A
Undo: Ctrl + Z and Alt + U
Redo: Ctrl + Y and Alt + R

You can also use the icons above the writing area to copy and paste words, sentences, or paragraphs and to undo and redo actions.

Obviously, this small box is not big enough to display your entire essay. However, you can see your entire essay by using the scroll bar, the up and down arrows, or the Page Up and Page Down keys.

Does Spelling Count?

Officially, no. Essay readers are supposed to ignore minor errors of spelling and grammar. However, the readers wouldn't be human (so to speak) if they weren't influenced favorably by an essay that had no obvious misspelled words or unwieldy constructions. Unfortunately, there is no spell-check function in the word-processing program.

What Will the Essay Topic Look Like?

There's only one type of essay topic: Analysis of an Argument. The typical question will look like the text inside the screen on the previous page. Here it is again:

Analysis of an Argument

The following appeared as part of a medical advertisement in a magazine.

"A new medical test that allows the early detection of a particular disease will prevent the deaths of people all over the world who would otherwise die from the disease. The test has been extremely effective in allowing doctors to diagnose the disease six months to a year before it would have been spotted by conventional means."

Discuss how logically convincing you find this argument. In explaining your point of view, be sure to evaluate the line of reasoning and the use of evidence in the argument. For example, it may be necessary to consider what questionable assumptions underlie the thinking and what other explanations or counterexamples might weaken the argument's conclusion. You can also discuss what kind of evidence would strengthen or refute the argument, what changes in the argument would make it more logically persuasive, and what, if anything, would enable you to better evaluate its conclusion.

THE AWA: BASIC PRINCIPLES

You might think that there is really no way to prepare for the AWA (other than by practicing writing over a long period of time and by practicing your typing skills). After all, you won't find out the topic of the essay they'll ask you to write until you get there, and there is no way to plan your essay in advance.

However, it turns out there are some very specific ways to prepare for the GMAT essay. Let's take a look.

Create a Template

When a builder builds a house, the first thing he does is construct a frame. The frame supports the entire house. After the frame is completed, he can nail the walls and windows to the frame. We're going to show you how to build the frame for the perfect GMAT essay. Of course, you won't know the exact topic of the essay until you get there (just as the builder may not know what color his client is going to paint the living room), but you will have an all-purpose frame on which to construct a great essay no matter what the topic is.

We call this frame the *template.*

Preconstruction

Just as a builder can construct the windows of a house in his workshop weeks before he arrives to install them, so too can you pre-build certain elements of your essay.

We call this *preconstruction*.

In the rest of this chapter, we'll show you how to prepare *ahead of time* to write essays on two topics you won't see until they appear on your screen.

Admissions Insight No. 12: Financial Aid, Part 3
To get student loans, you will probably have to fill out both the FAFSA form (available at **www.fafsa.ed.gov**) and the PROFILE form (available at **student.collegeboard.org/css-financial-aid-profile**). For simple and straightforward advice about making your way through all of that financial aid paperwork, visit **PrincetonReview.com**.

ANALYSIS OF AN ARGUMENT

The Analysis of an Argument essay must initially be approached just like a logical argument in the Critical Reasoning section.

An Analysis of an Argument topic requires the following steps:

Step 1: Read the topic and separate out the conclusion from the premises.
Step 2: Because they're asking you to critique (i.e., weaken) the argument, concentrate on identifying its assumptions.
Brainstorm as many different assumptions as you can think of. It helps to write or type these out.
Step 3: Look at the premises. Do they actually help to prove the conclusion?
Step 4: Choose a template that allows you to attack the assumptions and premises in an organized way.
Step 5: At the end of the essay, take a moment to illustrate how these same assumptions could be used to make the argument more compelling.
Step 6: Read over the essay and do some editing.

Opinions Vs. Arguments
The most common mistake our students make is offer an opinion on the topic presented in the argument. For the Analysis of an Argument essay, you need to analyze the reasoning rather than explain why you agree or disagree.

What the Readers Look For

An Analysis of an Argument topic presents you with an argument. Your job is to critique the argument's line of reasoning and the evidence supporting it and suggest ways in which the argument could be strengthened. You aren't required to know more about the subject than would any normal person—but you must be able to spot logical weaknesses. This should start to remind you of Critical Reasoning.

The essay readers will look for four things as they skim through your Analysis of an Argument essay at the speed of light. According to GMAC, "an outstanding argument essay...

- clearly identifies and insightfully analyzes important features of the argument;
- develops ideas cogently, organizes them logically, and connects them smoothly with clear transitions;
- effectively supports the main points of the critique; and
- demonstrates superior control of language, including diction, syntactic variety, and the conventions of standard written English. There may be minor flaws."

To put it more simply, the readers look for good organization, good analysis based on a cursory understanding of the rules of logic, and reasonable use of the English language.

Critical Reasoning in Essay Form

In any GMAT argument, the first thing to do is to separate the conclusion from the premises.

Let's see how this works with an actual essay topic. Check out the Analysis of an Argument topic you saw before.

Topic:

The following appeared as part of a medical advertisement in a magazine.

"A new medical test that allows the early detection of a particular disease will prevent the deaths of people all over the world who would otherwise die from the disease. The test has been extremely effective in allowing doctors to diagnose the disease six months to a year before it would have been spotted by conventional means."

Discuss how logically convincing you find this argument. In explaining your point of view, be sure to evaluate the line of reasoning and the use of evidence in the argument. For example, it may be necessary to consider what questionable assumptions underlie the thinking and what other explanations or counterexamples might weaken the argument's conclusion. You can also discuss what kind of evidence would strengthen or refute the argument, what changes in the argument would make it more logically persuasive, and what, if anything, would enable you to better evaluate its conclusion.

The conclusion in this argument comes in the first line:

A new medical test that allows the early detection of a particular disease will prevent the deaths of people all over the world who would otherwise die from that disease.

The premises are the evidence in support of this conclusion.

The test has been extremely effective in allowing doctors to diagnose the disease six months to a year before it would have been spotted by conventional means.

The assumptions are the *unspoken* premises of the argument—without which the argument would fall apart. Remember that assumptions are often causal, analogical, or statistical. What are some assumptions of *this* argument? Let's brainstorm.

Brainstorming for Assumptions

You can often find assumptions by looking for a gap in the reasoning:

Medical test → early detection: According to the conclusion, the medical test leads to the early detection of the disease. There doesn't seem to be a gap here.

Early detection → nonfatal: In turn, the early detection of the disease allows patients to survive the disease. Well, hold on a minute. Is this necessarily true? Let's brainstorm:

1. First of all, do we know that early detection will necessarily lead to survival? We don't even know if this disease is *curable*. Early detection of an incurable disease is not going to help someone survive it.
2. Second, will the test be widely available and cheap enough for general use? If the test is expensive or available only in certain parts of the world, people will continue to die from the disease.
3. Will doctors and patients interpret the tests correctly? The test may be fine, but if doctors misinterpret the results or if patients ignore the need for treatment, then the test will not save lives.

The Use of the Evidence

Okay, we've uncovered some assumptions. Now, the essay graders also want to know what we thought of the argument's "use of evidence." In other words, did the premises help to prove the conclusion? Well, in fact, no, they didn't. The premise here (the fact that the test can *spot* the disease six months to a year earlier than conventional tests) does not really help to prove the conclusion that the test will save *lives*.

B-School Lingo

three Cs: the primary forces considered in marketing—Customer, Competition, Company

Source: *The Best Business Schools*

Organizing the Analysis of an Argument Essay

We're ready to put this into a ready-made template. In any Analysis of an Argument essay, the template structure will be pretty straightforward: You're simply going to reiterate the argument, attack the argument in three different ways (one to a paragraph), summarize what you've said, and mention how the argument could be strengthened. From an organizational standpoint, this is pretty easy. Try to minimize your use of the word "I." *Your* opinion is not really the point in an Analysis of an Argument essay.

A Sample Template

Of course, you will want to develop your *own* template for the Analysis of an Argument essay, but to get you started, here's one possible structure:

The argument that ___(restatement of the conclusion)___ is not entirely logically convincing, because it ignores certain crucial assumptions.

First, the argument assumes that ______________________________

____.

Second, the argument never addresses ______________________________

____.

Finally, the argument omits ______________________________

____.

Thus, the argument is not completely sound. The evidence in support of the conclusion ____.

Ultimately, the argument might have been strengthened by ______________

____.

The Analysis of an Argument Essay in Six Steps

Step 1: Read the topic. Isolate the conclusion and premises.

Step 2: Identify its assumptions. Brainstorm for five minutes.

Step 3: Look at the assumptions. Do they help to prove the conclusion?

Step 4: Choose a template that allows you to attack the assumptions in an organized way.

Step 5: Illustrate how these same assumptions could be used to make the argument more compelling.

Step 6: Do some editing to correct spelling or grammar mistakes.

How Would Our Brainstorming Fit Into the Template?

Here's how the assumptions we came up with for this argument would have fit into the template:

The argument that the new medical test will prevent deaths that would have occurred in the past is not entirely logically persuasive, because it ignores certain crucial assumptions.

First, the argument assumes that early detection of the disease will lead to a reduced mortality rate. There are a number of reasons this might not be true. For example, the disease might be incurable [etc.].

Second, the argument never addresses the point that the existence of this new test, even if totally effective, is not the same as the widespread use of the test [etc.].

Finally, even supposing the ability of early detection to save lives and the widespread use of the test, the argument still depends on the doctors' correct interpretation of the test and the patients' willingness to undergo treatment. [etc.]

Thus, the argument is not completely sound. The evidence in support of the conclusion (further information about the test itself) does little to prove the conclusion— that the test will save lives— because it does not address the assumptions already raised. Ultimately, the argument might have been strengthened by making it plain that the disease responds to early treatment, that the test will be widely available around the world, and that doctors and patients will make proper use of the test.

Customizing Your Analysis of an Argument Template

Your organizational structure may vary in some ways, but it will always include the following elements:

- The *first paragraph* should sum up the argument's conclusion.
- In the *second, third, and fourth paragraphs*, you should attack the argument and the supporting evidence.
- In the *last* paragraph, you should summarize what you've said and state how the argument could be strengthened. Here are some alternate ways of organizing your essay.

Variation 1:

1st paragraph:	Restate the argument.
2nd paragraph:	Discuss the link (or lack of one) between the conclusion and the evidence presented in support of it.
3rd paragraph:	Show three holes in the reasoning of the argument.
4th paragraph:	Show how each of the three holes could be plugged up by explicitly stating the missing assumptions.

Variation 2:

1st paragraph:	Restate the argument and say it has three flaws.
2nd paragraph:	Point out a flaw and show how it could be plugged up by explicitly stating the missing assumption.
3rd paragraph:	Point out a second flaw and show how it could be plugged up by explicitly stating the missing assumption.
4th paragraph:	Point out a third flaw and show how it could be plugged up by explicitly stating the missing assumption.
5th paragraph:	Summarize and conclude that because of these three flaws, the argument is weak.

Q: What are the most important aspects of writing a good Analysis of an Argument essay?
Turn the page for the answer.

Analysis of an Argument: Final Thoughts

You've separated the conclusion from the premises. You've brainstormed for the gaps that weaken the argument. You've noted how the premises support (or don't support) the conclusion. Now it's time to write your essay. Start typing, indenting each of the four or five paragraphs. Use all the tools you've learned in this chapter. Remember to keep an eye on the time.

If you have a minute at the end, read over your essay and do any editing that's necessary.

PRECONSTRUCTION

The readers will look for evidence of your facility with standard written English. This is where preconstruction comes in. It's amazing how a little elementary preparation can enhance an essay. We'll look at three tricks that almost instantly improve the appearance of a person's writing:

- structure words
- sentence variety
- the impressive book reference

Structure Words

In our Reading Comprehension chapter, we brought up a problem that most students encounter when they get to the Reading Comprehension section: There isn't enough time to read the passages carefully and answer all the questions. To get around this problem, we showed you some ways to spot the overall organization of a dense reading passage in order to understand the main idea and to find specific points quickly.

When you think about it, the essay readers face almost the identical problem: They have less than two minutes to read your essay and figure out if it's any good. There's no time to appreciate the finer points of your argument. All they want to know is whether it's well organized and reasonably lucid—and to find out, they will look for the *same* structural clues you have learned to look for in the Reading Comprehension passages. Let's mention them again:

- If you have three points to make in a paragraph, it helps to point this out ahead of time:

  There are three reasons why I believe that the Grand Canyon should be preserved for all eternity. First...Second...Third...

- If you want to clue the reader in to the fact that you are about to support the main idea with examples or illustrations, the following words are useful:

  for example
  to illustrate
  for instance
  because

- To add yet another example or argument in support of your main idea, you can use one of the following words to indicate your intention:

  furthermore
  in addition
  similarly
  just as
  also
  moreover

- To indicate that the idea you're about to bring up is important, special, or surprising in some way, you can use one of these words:

  surely
  truly
  undoubtedly
  clearly
  certainly
  indeed
  as a matter of fact
  in fact
  most important

- To signal that you're about to reach a conclusion, you might use one of these words:

  therefore
  in summary
  consequently
  hence
  in conclusion
  in short

Key to Analysis of an Argument
Critique the weaknesses in the argument clearly.

A: Write at least four or five well-organized paragraphs (an introduction, in which you state that you will analyze the reasoning of the topic; a middle, to pick apart the argument by exposing assumptions; and a conclusion in which you state how the argument could be strengthened and sum up your position). Remember, this essay uses the same skills and approach you developed for the Critical Reasoning section of the test.

The Appearance of Depth

You may have noticed that much of the structure we have discussed thus far has involved contrasting viewpoints. Nothing will give your writing the *appearance* of depth faster than learning to use this technique. The idea is to set up your main idea by first introducing its opposite.

It is a favorite ploy of incoming presidents to blame the federal bureaucracy for the high cost of government, but I believe that bureaucratic waste is only a small part of the problem.

You may have noticed that this sentence contained a "trigger word." In this case, the trigger word *but* tells us that what was expressed in the first half of the sentence is going to be contradicted in the second half. We discussed trigger words in the Reading Comprehension chapter of this book. Here they are again:

but	*however*
on the contrary	*although*
yet	*while*
despite	*in spite of*
rather	*nevertheless*
instead	

By using these words, you can instantly give your writing the appearance of depth.

Example:

Main thought: *I believe that television programs should be censored.*

While many people believe in the sanctity of free speech, I believe that television programs should be censored.

Most people believe in the sanctity of free speech, but I believe that television programs should be censored.

How It Works

Here's a paragraph that consists of a main point and two supporting arguments:

I believe he is wrong. He doesn't know the facts. He isn't thinking clearly.

Watch how a few structure words can make this paragraph classier and clearer at the same time:

I believe he is wrong. ***For one thing****, he doesn't know the facts.* ***For another****, he isn't thinking clearly.*

I believe he is wrong. ***Obviously****, he doesn't know the facts.* ***Moreover****, he isn't thinking clearly.*

I believe he is wrong ***because, first****, he doesn't know the facts, and* ***second****, he isn't thinking clearly.*

Certainly*, he doesn't know the facts, and he isn't thinking clearly* ***either****.* ***Consequently****, I believe he is wrong.*

In addition to trigger words, here are a few other words or phrases you can use to introduce the view you are eventually going to decide *against*:

admittedly	*true*
certainly	*granted*
obviously	*of course*
undoubtedly	*to be sure*
one cannot deny that	*it could be argued that*

Also, don't forget about yin-yang words, which can be used to point directly to two contrasting ideas:

on the one hand/on the other hand

the traditional view/the new view

Contrasting Paragraphs

Trigger words can be used to signal the opposing viewpoints of entire paragraphs. Suppose you saw an essay that began:

Many people believe that youth is wasted on the young. They point out that young people never seem to enjoy, or even think about, the great gifts they have been given but will not always have: Physical dexterity, good hearing, good vision. However...

What do you think is going to happen in the second paragraph? That's right, the author is now going to disagree with the *many people* of the first paragraph.

Setting up one paragraph in opposition to another lets the reader know what's going on right away. The organization of the essay is immediately evident.

Sentence Variety

Many people think good writing is a mysterious talent that you either have or don't have, like good rhythm. In fact, good writing has a kind of rhythm to it, but there is nothing mysterious about it. Good writing is a matter of mixing up the different kinds of raw materials that you have available to you—phrases, dependent and independent clauses—to build sentences that don't all sound the same.

The graders won't have time to savor your essay, but they will look for variety in your writing. Here's an example of a passage in which all the sentences sound alike:

Movies cost too much. Everyone agrees about that. Studios need to cut costs. No one is sure exactly how to do it. I have two simple solutions. They can cut costs by paying stars less. They can also cut costs by reducing overhead.

Why do all the sentences sound alike? Well, for one thing, they are all about the same length. For another thing, the sentences are all made up of independent clauses with the same exact setup: Subject, verb, and sometimes object. There are no dependent clauses, almost no phrases, no structure words, and, frankly, no variety at all.

Now let's take a look at the same passage, with some minor modifications.

Everyone agrees that movies cost too much. Clearly, studios need to cut costs, but no one is sure exactly how to do it. I have two simple solutions: They can cut costs by paying stars less and by reducing overhead.

In this version of the passage, we've combined some clauses and used conjunctions. This helped to add variety in both sentence structure and sentence length. We also threw in a few structure words as well. As you can see, simple techniques like these can make your writing appear stronger and more polished.

The AWA

Few people are rejected by a business school based on their writing score, so don't bother feeling intimidated. Think of it this way: The essays represent an *opportunity* if your Verbal score is low, or if English is your second language. For the rest of you, the essay is as good a way as any to warm up (and wake up) before the sections that count.

Summary

- The GMAT AWA section consists of one essay, written in 30 minutes, using a basic word-processing program and the computer keyboard. The essay will be given scores that range from 0 to 6 in half-point increments.
- Each essay will be evaluated by at least two underpaid, overworked college teaching assistants.
- To score high on the AWA:
  - Write as many words as possible.
  - Use a prebuilt template to organize your thoughts.
  - Use structure words, and vary your sentence structure and length to give the appearance of depth to your writing.
  - If possible, refer to a well-known work of literature or nonfiction.
- For the Analysis of an Argument topic:

  Step 1: Read the topic and separate out the conclusion from the premises.

  Step 2: Because they ask you to critique (i.e., weaken) the argument, concentrate on identifying its assumptions. Brainstorm as many different assumptions as you can think of and write them down.

  Step 3: Look at the premises. Do they actually help to prove the conclusion?

  Step 4: Choose a template that allows you to attack the assumptions and premises in an organized way.

  Step 5: At the end of the essay, take a moment to illustrate how these same assumptions could be used to make the argument more compelling.

  Step 6: Read over the essay and edit your work.

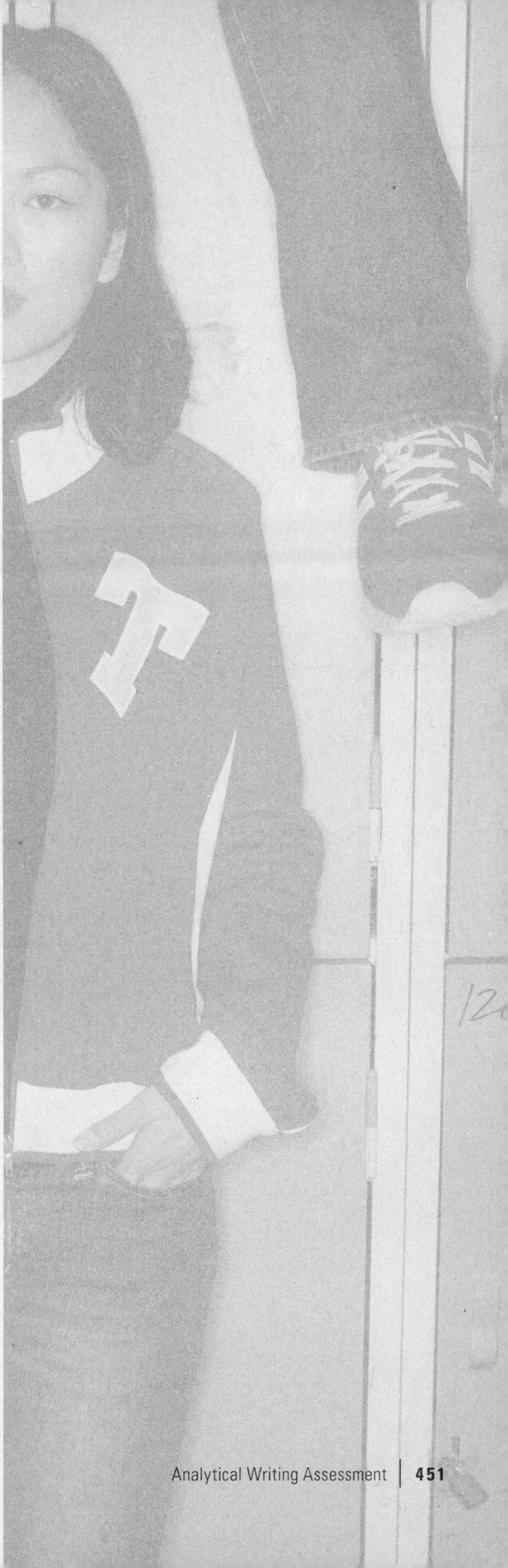

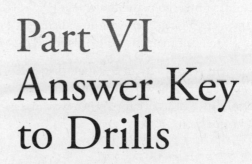

Part VI
Answer Key to Drills

DRILL 1 (AD/BCE)

1. BCE. From Statement (1) all we know is a value for y. There is no telling what the value of x will be.
2. BCE. From Statement (1) we know that $2y$ is an integer, but does that mean y must be an integer? Not necessarily. What if y were $\frac{1}{2}$?
3. AD. If we know from the question that there are 12 children in a room and Statement (1) tells us there are 3 girls, then we know there are 9 boys, and we can answer the question.
4. AD. Statement (1) gives us an equation that we *could* solve to get the value of x (not that we need to). If we can solve for x, then we can answer the question.

DRILL 2

1. 77
2. 79
3. 10
4. 16
5. choice B
6. Statement (1) gives us one unique value for x: $x = 2$. We're down to AD. Statement (2) on the other hand gives us two possible values for x: 2 or –2. The correct answer is choice A.

DRILL 3

1. $80 + 40 = 120$
2. $55 \times 100 = 5{,}500$
3. $ab + ac - ad$
4. $c(ab + xy)$
5. $\frac{12y - 6y}{y} = \frac{y(6)}{y} = 6$, choice B
6. Statement (1) gives us a value for x, but we need $x + y + d$. Statement (1) is not sufficient. We're down to BCE. Statement (2) might not have seemed much more helpful, BUT using the distributive property, we can rewrite the original equation to read $a(x + y + z) = 15$. If a is 5, then $x + y + z$ must equal 3. The correct answer is choice B.

DRILL 4

1. $\frac{145}{24}$ or $6\frac{1}{24}$
2. $\frac{1}{5}$
3. $\frac{29}{3}$
4. 18
5. choice C

DRILL 5

1. 33.30
2. 266.175
3. 6.09
4. 800
5. choice C
6. You were probably very tempted by choice C since Statement (1) gives us a value for x and Statement (2) gives us a value for y. However, if x and y are reciprocals (meaning that when multiplied together, their product must equal 1), then Statement (1) not only gives us a value for x ($\frac{2}{10}$ or $\frac{1}{5}$), but it also gives us a value for y: the reciprocal of $\frac{1}{5}$, which is 5.0. We're down to AD. Statement (2) does exactly the same thing in reverse. The correct answer is choice D.

DRILL 6 (Angles and Lengths)

1. $x = 110°$
2. $x = 50°$ $y = 130°$ $z = 130°$
3. $x = 60°$ $y = 120°$ $z = 120°$
4. $\frac{3}{4}$
5. choice D
6. Statement (1) by itself gives us a mystery angle y not related to angle x, so we're down to BCE. Statement (2) by itself relates angles x and y: together, they add up to 180 degrees. But by itself, Statement (2) is still not sufficient because we don't have either individual angles. We're down to C or E. However, when we put both statements together, we can answer the question: if $x + y = 180$, and $y = 40$, then x must equal 140. The correct answer is choice C.

DRILL 7 (Triangles)

1. $x = 8$

2. $x = 60$

3. $x = 5$

4. x must be less than 11 and greater than 3

5. $3\sqrt{2}$

6. $2\sqrt{3}$

7. choice B

8. Choice C. Statement (1) tell us that $y = 80$. Remember, however, that figures in Data Sufficiency problems are not necessarily drawn to scale. So, don't assume that angles x and y are equal! We are down to BCE. Statement (2) tells us that sides AB and BC are equal, so angles x and y are also equal. However, we don't know the degree measure of those angles, so cross off B. Combining the statements, we know that x and y are equal and that $y = 80$. So, $x = 80$. The correct answer is choice C.

DRILL 8 (Circles)

1. area = 25π, circumference = 10π

2. circumference = 12π

3. 60°

4. Choice B. You get the answer by subtracting the area of the small circle (25π) from the area of the large circle (100π) to get 75π.

5. Statement (1) by itself would allow you to find the area of circle Q, but that's not what the question is asking; we want circle P. We're down to BCE. Statement (2) by itself gives us a way to compare the two circles, but gives us no specific dimension. We're down to C or E. Combining the statements gives us both a specific dimension and a way to compare the circles. The correct answer is choice C.

DRILL 9 (Data Sufficiency Parts and Wholes)

1. Choice C. Statement (1) tells us only how many people paid a deposit. This is not sufficient to answer the question, and we are down to BCE. Statement (2) tells us only what percent of the people who paid deposits actually showed up. Again, by itself, this does not give us the number of people who attended, so we can eliminate B. But if we put the two statements together, we now know how many people paid deposits (70), and what percentage of those people actually attended (60%), which means we can figure out how many people attended.

2. Choice D. You might think you need both statements together, but in fact, either is sufficient by itself. Statement (1) tells us there are 7 ounces of pigment in a 12-ounce can. Because there are only two ingredients, this means the other ingredient must make up the rest, or 5 ounces. This is sufficient to figure out the ratio (7 : 5) and we are down to a fifty-fifty choice: A or D. Similarly, Statement (2) tells us there are 5 ounces of alcohol in a 12-ounce can. Because there are only two ingredients, this means the other ingredient must make up the rest, or 7 ounces. Again, this is sufficient to figure out the ratio, so the answer must be D.

3. Choice C. To answer this question, we need the total number of miles. Statement (1) does not give us any concrete figures—just a fraction, so it is not sufficient, and that narrows our options down to BCE. Statement (2) gives us a concrete number, but it is only for part of the distance, so we can eliminate B. However, if we combine the two statements, we learn that those 12 miles must make up the remaining $\frac{2}{5}$ of the entire trip. From this we can learn the entire distance of the trip by setting up the equation $\frac{2}{5} = \frac{12}{x}$. The correct answer is C.

DRILL 10 (Strange Powers of Powers)

1. Choice C. Statement (1) might *seem* to be sufficient, but remember, if $x^2 = 4$, then x could be either 2 or –2. The question asks for the one and only value of x. Statement (1) is not sufficient. Statement (2) by itself is not sufficient either, because the question is asking for the one and only value of x. But together, the two statements are sufficient because Statement (1) gets us down to two possibilities, 2 and –2, and Statement (2) eliminates the positive number.

2. Choice B. If $x^2 = 4$, then x could be either 2 or –2, so Statement (1) is not sufficient. You might not think Statement (2) is sufficient by itself, because it gives us a value only for y, not for x. However, the question is asking for the value of x times y. If $y = 0$, then we know the value of xy. Zero times any number equals zero.

3. Choice E. If $x^2 = 4$, then x could be either 2 or –2, so Statement (1) is not sufficient. If $y^2 = 9$, then y could be either 3 or –3. The question is asking for the one and only value of x, so Statement (2) is not sufficient by itself either. You might think that putting the two statements together would help us arrive at an answer, but in fact, we don't know. If $x = 2$ and $y = 3$, then $xy = 6$, but what if either x or y was negative? Then xy could also equal –6.

DRILL 11 (Yes or No)

1. Choice A. To answer this yes-or-no question, plug values into the statements. The only condition of the question itself is that x is positive. The only positive numbers that will make Statement (1) true are positive fractions less than $\frac{1}{2}$. This means Statement (1) always answers this question "yes" and we are down to AD. Plugging positive numbers into Statement (2), we could have $\frac{1}{2}$, which gives us a "yes," or 1, which gives us a "no." Therefore, the answer must be choice A.

2. Choice B. When we plug normal numbers 3 and 2 into Statement (1), x is positive. But if we plug in –3 and –2, x is negative, so we are down to BCE. Now, when we plug normal numbers 3 and 2 into Statement (2), we get a "yes." But when we try to plug weird numbers into Statement (2), we realize that (y^2) must always be positive—which means that x must always be positive as well, giving us a definitive "yes."

3. Choice E. To answer this yes-no question, plug in. Start by choosing two numbers that satisfy Statement (1). For example, $x = 2$ and $y = 3$ satisfy Statement (1) because $2 \times 3 = 6$, which is an integer. The answer to the question "Are x and y integers?" is "yes" for these numbers. Next, pick new numbers that satisfy the statement, but try to get an answe of "no" to the question. If $x = -\sqrt{2}$ and $y = \sqrt{2}$, Statement (1) is satisfied because the product of x and y is –2, an integer. However, the answer to the question is now "no." Since it's possible to get both an answer of "yes" and an answer of "no" with numbers that satisfy the statement, Statement (1) is insufficient and the possible answers are B, C, and E. Next, pick numbers that satisfy Statement (2). Both sets of numbers that satisfied Statement (1) also satisfy Statement (2). So it's possible to find numbers that produce both an answer of "yes" and an answer of "no" for Statement (2). Hence, Statement (2) is insufficient, so eliminate choice B. Since these numbers satisfy both statements, it also means that the combined statements are insufficient. The answer is choice E.

DRILL 12 (Spotting Critical Reasoning Question Types)

1. Strengthen-the-argument question. To find the correct answer, look for the gap in the argument, and try to close it.

2. Inference question. To find the correct answer, use scope and POE to rule out any answer choice that goes too far.

3. Evaluate-the-argument question. To find the correct answer, look for the unspoken assumptions in the passage.

4. Assumption question. To find the correct answer, look for the gap in the argument.

5. Weaken-the-argument question. To find the correct answer, look for the gap in the argument and try to widen it.

6. Resolve/explain question. To find the correct answer, look for the answer choice that allows both of the facts from the passage to be true at the same time.

7. Identify-the-reasoning question. To find the correct answer, identify the conclusion and the premises, and see how they relate to each other.

8. Parallel-the-reasoning question. To find the correct answer, simplify the argument (if A, then B), and look for an answer choice that matches.

How to Score Your Integrated Reasoning Section

Integrated Reasoning sections are scored on a scale from 1 to 8. GMAC has released only a few details about how they score this section. Use the chart below to approximate your score.

Please note that Integrated Reasoning items are scored all or nothing. For example, Table Analysis items have three parts. You must have picked the correct answer for each part to count the item as correct.

Please also note that Integrated Reasoning sections on the GMAT contain experimental questions that do not count toward your score. The chart below has been adjusted to compensate for the fact that these sections do not contain experimental questions.

Number Correct	Approximate Score
0–1	1
2	2
3–4	3
5–6	4
7–8	5
9–10	6
11	7
12	8

INTEGRATED REASONING DRILLS: Section 1

Item 1:

1-1. True

This question asks about the median, so first list the data in order of *Riders* and note the median (fifth) in the list: *34th St/Penn Station (Red Lines)*. Next, to find the station with the greatest decrease in passengers from 2009 to 2010, sort the data by *% Change* and note that the same station shows a percentage decrease of 1.1%, the greatest percentage decrease in the list.

The question, however, asks if the station had the greatest decrease in passengers, which is different from the greatest percent decrease in passengers. Confirm that the actual decrease in passengers was the greatest; since the only other station with a decrease from 2009 was *Grand Central/42nd St*, calculate the actual decrease for each station and compare them.

The 2010 ridership for *34th St/Penn Station (Red Lines)* is 26,892,243, which you can round to 27 million for this purpose. Since the decrease from 2009 to 2010 was 1.1%, the 2010 value is equal to 98.9% (100% – 1.1%) of the 2009 value. So, to solve for the 2009 value, the formula would be $\frac{98.9}{100}x = 27{,}000{,}000$.

Solving for x gives a 2009 ridership at *34th St/Penn Station (Red Lines)* of about 27.3 million for an actual decrease of about 300,000 riders. Calculating the actual decrease for *Grand Central/42nd St* in the same manner gives a decrease of less than 100,000 riders, and so *34th St/Penn Station (Red Lines)* had the greatest decrease in riders, and the statement is true.

1-2. True

Sorting the table by *Connecting Subway Lines* will make it easy to see which stations have 3 connecting lines and which have 5 connecting lines. The onscreen calculator can be used to find that the average *Riders* of the two stations with 5 connecting subway lines is 31,307,134; that the average *Riders* of the three stations with 3 connecting subway lines is 23,434,760; and that the ratio between those two numbers is 1.33. Presented as a fraction, 1.33 is approximately $\frac{4}{3}$, so the statement is true.

1-3. False

Sorting the table by *% Change* will make it easy to identify the station with the highest percent increase in riders from 2009 to 2010: *Lexington Ave/59th Street*. However, when the table is sorted by *Riders, Lexington Ave/59th Street* is 8th, not 9th (last), in annual ridership, and so the statement is false.

Item 2:

Services Not Covered by Medical Plan: B, 15

The problem divides the doctors into two categories: those whose services are, or are not, covered by Frank's medical plan, and those who graduated from medical school with, or without, honors. The information can be summarized in a group grid as follows:

	Services Covered by Medical Plans	Services Not Covered by Medical Plan	Total
Graduated with Honors	3		8
Graduated Without Honors	27		
Total			45

The remaining data in the table can be completed by solving for the missing data elements. The total number of doctors whose services are covered by the medical plan is 27 + 3, or 30, and so the number of doctors whose services are not covered by the medical plan is 45 – 30, or 15. Here's the group grid with that data filled in:

	Services Covered by Medical Plans	Services Not Covered by Medical Plan	Total
Graduated with Honors	3		8
Graduated Without Honors	27		
Total	30	15	45

Graduated Without Honors and Services Not Covered by Medical Plan: A, 10

To find the number of doctors who graduated with honors and whose services are not covered by Frank's medical plan, continue the work from the first part of the question by solving for additional missing elements in the group grid.

In this case, the total number of doctors who graduated without honors is 45 – 8, or 37. The number of doctors, then, who graduated without honors and whose services are not covered by Frank's medical plan is 37 – 27, or 10.

Here's the completely filled-in group grid:

	Services Covered by Medical Plans	Services Not Covered by Medical Plan	Total
Graduated with Honors	3	5	8
Graduated Without Honors	27	10	37
Total	30	15	45

Item 3:

Orchids: Choice F, 8

Dahlias: Choice C, 4

The word problem can be expressed in the form of an equation in terms of the price of each flower: 1.35*o* + 1.8*d* = 18. Generally, two distinct equations are required in order to solve for two different variables. However, the number of orchids and dahlias must be integers. This restriction makes it possible to solve this equation although there still may be more than one solution.

Since the number of orchids and the number of dahlias must both be integers, Plug In the Answers (PITA). Plug in each answer choice into the equation as the number of orchids and solve the equation for the number of dahlias, looking to see whether the result is also an answer choice.

Start with choice A: 0, giving the equation 1.35(0) + 1.8*d* = 18, which simplifies to 1.8*d* = 18, and *d* = 10. Since 10 is not an available answer choice, 0 is not the correct answer for orchids.

Plugging in choice B (2) for the number of orchids results in a solution of 8.5 dahlias. Since a whole number of dahlias is required, 2 is not the correct answer for orchids. Using choice C (4), the solution to the equation is 7 dahlias, but again, 7 is not an available answer choice, so 4 is not the correct answer for orchids.

Plugging in choice F, 8 orchids, to the equation gives 1.35(8) + 1.8*d* = 18, which can be simplified to 1.8*d* = 7.2, and when solved, *d* = 4. Since 4 is also an available response, 8 is the correct number of orchids and 4 is the correct number of dahlias, and no further testing of the answer choices is necessary.

Item 4:

4-1. Choice B, –1.4

The regression line comes close to the points (0,12) and (5,5). Therefore, the approximate slope is $\frac{y_2 - y_1}{x_2 - x_1} = \frac{12-5}{0-5} = \frac{7}{-5} = -1.4$. Even if you weren't sure exactly how to do this, you could have eliminated choices D and E because the slope (running from top right to lower left) surely had to be negative.

4-2. Choice D, 100% greater

After 0 days of training, only two students were able to get within 11 inches of the center of the target. After two days of training, there were four students who were able to get with 11 inches of the center of the target. Since there was clearly an increase, eliminate A and B. Now, to get the percent increase, use the percent change formula:

$$\frac{diff}{orig} \times 100 = \frac{4-2}{2} \times 100 = \frac{2}{2} \times 100 = 100.$$

Even if you weren't sure how to do this, you could have eliminated choices A and B because the students' aim was clearly improving with practice.

Item 5:

Strengthen: Choice B
The stone tools resemble those made and used by *Homo erectus* and *Homo heidelbergensis*, human ancestors in the Paleolithic era who lived on the mainland of Greece.

Weaken: Choice E
Approximately 5 million years ago, during the Messinian Salinity Crisis of the late Miocene era, the Mediterranean Sea dried up.

Conclusion:
"*...some human ancestors developed nautical skills millions of years earlier than previously discovered.*"

Premises:
"...earliest... evidence of seafaring by human ancestors dates to... 130,000 years ago... Archaeologists discovered stone tools on... a Mediterranean island that date to... 2.6 million years ago..." and "40 miles of open sea separate the island from Greece."

Assumption:
The only way the stone tools could have gotten to the island is if the human ancestors developed nautical skills and migrated to the island by boat or raft.

Based on the discovery of stone tools on an island that date to 2.6 million years ago, archaeologists hypothesize that human ancestors must have developed nautical skills and migrated to the island by boat. The argument assumes that the evidence is sufficient to support their hypothesis; that there is no alternative explanation that is supported by the data.

The answer that most strengthens the argument will strengthen the link between the premise (finding stone tools on the island) and the conclusion (the human ancestors developed nautical skills and migrated there), or will eliminate alternate explanations supported by the data.

Choice A is out of scope because the fact that tools *used for fishing* were found in the same area does not directly relate to whether the human ancestors had developed *nautical skills*; they could have fished from land or from the sea.

Choice B strengthens the argument by confirming that the stone tools were the same as those used by the human ancestors who lived on the other side of the water, and therefore increases the likelihood that they must have migrated there by boat or raft.

Choice C is irrelevant, because the argument is not concerned with the uses of the stone tools.

Choice D is irrelevant, because the argument is not concerned with whether the stone tools were used to construct boats.

Choice E weakens the argument by providing an alternate explanation of the migration that does not involve nautical skills: the human ancestors could have migrated to the island while the Mediterranean Sea was dry.

Choice F is irrelevant, because the argument is not concerned with whether the stone tools were used to construct boats.

Item 6:

6-1. No
No 1-year CDs qualify for bonuses, so this $11,000 CD earns an interest rate of 2.2%. Use your calculator. 2.2% of $11,000 is (0.022 × 11,000) $242. Therefore this 1-year CD does not earn at least $250.

6-2. No
All 5-year CDs qualify for a 0.1% bonus, so this $9,500 CD will earn 2.6% interest in its first year. Use your calculator. 2.6% of $9,500 is $247, so this CD does not earn at least $250 in its first year.

6-3. Yes
All 10-year CDs qualify for a 0.1% bonus, so this $9,500 CD will earn a 2.9% interest rate in its first year. Use your calculator. 2.9% of the $9,500 is $275.50. So this CD does earn more than $250 in its first year.

Item 7:

7-1. No
Since the CD has a term of 1 year, no bonus applies. The interest rate is 2.2%. So the interest is 2.2% of $20,000, which is $440. The interest is therefore less than $500.

7-2. Yes
Since the CD has a term of 5 years, there is a 0.1% interest bonus. So the interest rate is 2.6%. The interest for the first year is 2.6% of $4,000, which is $104. The interest for each succeeding year will increase by around $2 (2.6% of $104). So the total interest will be a bit more than $520, but certainly less than $600.

7-3. No
Since the CD has a term of 2 years, there are no bonuses to consider (even though the customer is "preferred"). The rate for a 2-year CD is therefore 2.4%. The interest from the first year will be $240 and the interest from the second year will be 2.4% of $10,240, which is about $246. So the total interest is $486, less than $500.

Item 8:

8-1. No
The memo refers to a revised schedule of penalties for early withdrawal. There must have been a schedule in place previously to revise.

8-2. No
It is true that the stated policy offers a bonus available to preferred customers but not to new customers. There is no reference however to this being a reward for loyalty. Rather, the stated purpose is to increase the overall stability of the bank's portfolio. This statement introduces outside information.

8-3. Yes
The stated intention is to shift the CD investments towards those with longer maturation periods. For each type of CD, this means paying higher interest rates to customers. So if the bank succeeds in making this shift, it will pay higher overall average interest rates than it will if a greater proportion of investments remain in shorter term CDs. This statement is well-supported by the evidence.

Item 9:

9-1. True

First sort the chart by *Year of Election* to more easily see which Presidents won two terms. They are George W. Bush, Richard Nixon, Ronald Reagan, and William Clinton. Now look at the *Popular Vote* column (not the *% of Popular Vote* column) for each candidate, comparing the results for the two years in which each candidate was elected. Use the percent change formula $\left(\frac{difference}{original}\right)$ to compare the percent increases in popular vote, rounding to the nearest integer. You should get Bush: $\frac{12}{50}$; Nixon: $\frac{16}{31}$; Reagan: $\frac{11}{43}$; Clinton: $\frac{3}{45}$. Clinton's percentage increase is less than (10%), far lower than the other three. So, of the two-term Presidents, Clinton does have the smallest percent increase in popular vote.

9-2. False

There are six Democrats and seven Republicans. To find the average electoral vote for each party, add the electoral votes of the Presidents in that party with your calculator and divide by the number of Presidents. The six Democrats add up to 2,200, which gives an average or about 367. The seven Republicans add up to 2,818, which gives an average of about 403. So the Democratic Presidents do not have the higher average.

9-3. True

Sort the chart by *% of Popular Vote* to make it easy to scan down the list. Now compare the *% of Popular Vote* and the *% of Electoral Vote* columns for each line in the table. Look for those lines in which the two values are closest together. There are three elections, 2000, 1976, and 2004, in which the two values are within about 5 points of each other. In 1976, the difference was slightly greater than 5, but in 2000 and 2004 it was closer to 3 points difference, (48.87% vs. 50.4% in 2000 and 50.73% to 53.2% in 2004). So 2000 and 2004 are the two years in which the percentages differ the least. Since George W. Bush was elected both years, it is true that the same President was elected in the two years in which the percentages were the closest.

Item 10:

10-1. Yes

Memo #2 lists the regions and their respective average airfares. At $200 the Midwest and the West are tied for the lowest. This means that no region has lower average airfares than the Midwest.

10-2. No

Memo #1 states that Regional Office Managers will be responsible for the travel reservations for Level 2 managers, but we don't know that they will be the only persons in attendance. Therefore we cannot infer this to be true.

10-3. Yes

Memo #1 states that Regional Office Managers may *delegate that task*, meaning that they do not have to do it themselves.

Item 11:

11-1. True

Memo #1 states that regions will receive a *"Budget Bonus" of 50% of the difference between the ticket price and the average airfare* for tickets priced more than 1 standard deviation below the mean. Memo #2 states that the mean for the West is \$200 and the standard deviation is \$25. Thus the West will get a bonus for all tickets priced less than \$175. Since there are 18 tickets priced at \$150, the West will get a bonus of 50% of (18)(200 – 150) = 50% of 900 = \$450.

11-2. False

Memo #2 states that the sample size for the Mid-Atlantic was 500. Since the standard deviation is \$50, \$450 is two standard deviations from the mean of \$350. In a normally distributed sample, approximately 2% of the data points are more than two standard deviations from the mean. 2% of 500 is 10, which is half of 20.

11-3. True

Memo #2 states that the sample size for the Northeast was 400. Since the standard deviation is \$50, \$250 is one standard deviation below the mean of \$300. In a normally distributed sample, approximately 16% of the data points are more than one standard deviation below the mean. 16% of 400 is 64, which is more than 50.

Item 12:

Choice C, $\frac{11}{15}$

Memo #1 states that tickets will be fully reimbursed if it either falls within 1 standard deviation or below 1 standard deviation of the mean. Since the mean is \$200 and the standard deviation is \$25, 4 tickets fall within 1 standard deviation and 18 fall below 1 standard deviation. Thus 22 tickets out of 30 will be fully reimbursed, which gives a probability of $\frac{11}{15}$.

INTEGRATED REASONING DRILLS: Section 2

Item 1:

1-1. Choice A, 15 to 8

The number of clocks produced on Tuesday is 75 and the number of clocks produced on Wednesday is 40. Therefore, the ratio of these two numbers is 75 to 40. Since both numbers are multiples of 5, you can reduce by a factor of 5 to get an equivalent ratio of 15 to 8.

1-2. Choice D, 36%

To get the percentage, you need to calculate $\frac{part}{whole} \times 100$. The part is the sum of the combined clocks produced on Monday and the clocks produced on Wednesday, which is 50 + 40 = 90. Now, you need the total number produced during the entire week. This is 50 + 75 + 40 + 55 + 30 = 250. Therefore, the percentage is $\frac{part}{whole} \times 100 = \frac{90}{250} \times 100 = \frac{9}{25} \times \frac{100}{1} = \frac{9}{1} \times \frac{4}{1} = 36.$

Item 2:

Weakens A's Argument: Choice F Company X: Portals 8, which was just released, contains bugs and design flaws that will impair Company X's ability to compete in the modern economy.

Conclusion:
"We have decided to purchase new computers that run Portals 8, the newest version of the world's best selling operating system, throughout the entire company."

Premise:
"Our company's computer technology is out of date. We will be unable to compete effectively in the modern economy if we are not using current computer technology."

Assumption:
The plan to purchase new computers running Portals 8 will allow Company X to compete effectively in the modern economy.

Company X's argument uses a planning structure; it describes a problem (the company's computer technology is out of date, and the company needs current technology to be able to compete effectively), and then proposes a plan to solve that problem (buy new computers running Portals 8).

In a planning argument, the assumption is always that there are no problems with the proposed plan. In this case, Company X assumes that the new computers with Portals 8 will actually help the company to compete effectively in the modern economy.

Because this is a weaken question, the answer will likely suggest a potential problem with the proposed plan (i.e., that the plan will NOT allow the company to compete effectively in the modern economy).

Choice A is out of scope, because the argument is not concerned with *efficient use of computer resources.*

Choice B is irrelevant because the argument is concerned with whether the plan will allow the company to compete in the modern economy, not whether GreenCap is *the most cutting-edge software.*

Choice C does not explain in what way the amount of time GreenCap *has been available* would affect the company's ability to compete in the modern economy.

Choice D weakens the Technology Consultant's argument, because it provides a reason why the consulting firm's plan may not work, but it has no effect on Company X's argument.

Choice E is out of scope, because the fact that Portals 8 *is available in several different versions* has no impact on the plan.

Choice F weakens Company X's argument by providing a potential problem with Company X's proposed plan (because Portals 8 *contains a number of bugs and design flaws that would impair Company X's ability to compete*).

Weaken B's Argument: Choice D Technology Consultant: GreenCap requires purchase of an annual maintenance agreement, making it more expensive overall than Portals 8.

Conclusion:
"Company X should purchase GreenCap."

Premise:
"GreenCap costs substantially less than Portals 8, and it provides the same functionality with current computer technology. With the money saved, Company X will be better able to compete effectively in the modern economy."

Assumption:
Purchasing GreenCap will actually end up saving money for Company X.

The Technology Consultant observes that GreenCap is substantially cheaper than Portals 8, while providing the same functionality, and that if Company X saves money, it will be better able to compete economically. Based on these premises, the consultant concludes that Company X should purchase GreenCap.

The argument assumes that Company X will actually save money by purchasing GreenCap. Since this is a weaken question, the answer will likely provide a potential problem with the proposed plan (for example, a reason purchasing GreenCap would NOT end up saving money for Company X).

Choice A is out of scope, because the argument is not concerned with *efficient use of computer resources.*

Choice B is irrelevant because the argument is concerned with whether Company X will actually save money, not whether the GreenCap is *the most cutting-edge software.*

Choice C is out of scope, because the amount of time GreenCap *has been available* does not affect whether Company X would save money by purchasing GreenCap.

Choice D weakens the Technology Consultant's argument, because it provides a reason why purchasing GreenCap will not save money for Company X (because it requires a costly *annual maintenance agreement* that would eliminate the savings and end up costing more).

Choice E is out of scope, because the fact that Portals 8 *is available in several different versions* has no impact on the plan.

Choice F weakens Company X's argument by providing a potential problem with Company X's proposed plan (because Portals 8 *contains a number of bugs and design flaws* that would *impair Company X's ability to compete*).

Item 3:

3-1. Choice C, 6 to 5

This question requires two steps to solve: first, which year had the lowest total per capita consumption of both ice cream and cheese, and second, what was the ratio of ice cream consumption to cheese consumption in that year?

By examining the data points for each year, you can identify that in 1989, the total consumption of ice cream and cheese was less than 53 pounds (because the ice cream consumption was less than 29 pounds, and the cheese consumption was less than 24 pounds.) Testing other years, such as 1990, confirms that 1989 had the lowest total consumption. (In 1990, the total consumption was approximately 53 pounds, based on the data points of approximately 28.5 pounds of ice cream and 24.5 pounds of cheese.)

To calculate the ratio of per capita ice cream consumption to per capita cheese consumption for 1989, divide the data point for ice cream (approximately 29) by the data point for cheese (approximately 24) for a ratio of approximately 1.2 (or, in fractional terms, $\frac{6}{5}$).

3-2. Choice B, less than

The regression line for ice cream slopes down, while the line for cheese slopes up; per capita ice cream consumption is reducing over time, while per capita cheese consumption is increasing over time. Thus, the slope of the ice cream line is negative, and is less than the slope of the cheese line, which is positive.

Item 4:

Strengthens: Choice C

Once a geo-engineering innovation has been passed by the committee, the same innovation is automatically approved in all subsequent projects, without further review.

In disagreeing with the XM representative, the federal committee member has based her rebuttal on the statement that *if we fail to review your project, we also fail to observe innovations in geo-engineering that may need guidelines drafted for the safety of subsequent projects throughout the industry.* Setting a precedent for future projects is therefore the central concern of the committee member. To strengthen her argument, you need additional evidence that supports this assertion. Answer C states that once an innovation has been passed, the same innovation in subsequent projects is passed without further review. Including this additional evidence undermines the XM representative's claim that the project should be passed without review and thus supports the committee member's rebuttal.

Weakens: Choice A

XM's latest project is nearly identical to a previous project by XM that had successfully passed the committee review process.

The XM representative claims that *the costly and time-consuming review should be waived so that our latest project can be quickly passed and implemented.* The federal committee member disagrees because doing what the representative suggests could mean the committee would *also fail to observe innovations in geo-engineering that may need guidelines drafted for the safety of subsequent projects throughout the industry.* To weaken the committee member's argument, you need evidence that suggests that no such failure to observe innovations will occur in this case. If XM's latest project is identical to a previous project by XM that had successfully passed the committee review process, as answer choice A states, then there are no innovations to consider. This weakens the federal committee member's argument, and provides additional support for the XM representative's request.

Item 5:

Insect Species X: Choice A, 450

Insect Species Y: Choice C, 565

First, note that, if the populations are to become equal in four years, at a 10% and a 15% rate of decrease, respectively, then the two populations are not currently equal. Additionally, the current population of Insect Species Y must be more than the current population of Insect Species X, in order for their totals to converge, at these independent rates of decrease, in four years. Therefore, the current population of Insect Species X cannot be 770, and the current population of Insect Species Y cannot be 450.

The problem requires working with two unknowns: the current population of Insect Species X and the current population of Insect Species Y. Therefore, Plug In the Answers to determine which will satisfy the conditions of the question. To approach the problem most efficiently, recognize that a 10% decrease is the same as taking 90% of the original number. Suppose that the current population of Insect Species X is 450. A 10% decrease from 450 is equivalent to 90% of 450, or (0.9)(450), which is 405. That's the decrease for one year. To find the decrease for the next year, begin with the adjusted population and decrease from there: a 10% decrease from 405 is equivalent to (0.9)(405), which is 364.5. So, to find the decreased population after two years of 10% decreases from a starting population of 450 is equivalent to calculating (0.9)(0.9)(450) = 364.5. Similarly, to find the decreased population after four years of 10% decreases from a starting population of 450 is equivalent to calculating (0.9)(0.9)(0.9)(0.9)(450) = (0.6561)(450) = 295.245. So, to find the decreased population of Insect Species X after four years of yearly 10% decreases, calculate (0.6561)(current population X).

A 15% decrease is the same as taking 85% of the original number, so to find the decreased population of Insect Species Y after four years of yearly 15% decreases, calculate (0.85)(0.85)(0.85)(0.85)(current population Y), or approximately (0.522)(current population Y).

To determine which starting populations are equal (rounded to the nearest million) after four years, you are looking for values that satisfy the equation (0.6561)(current population X) = (0.522)(current population Y). Now you can simply calculate with each value provided to see what the future populations are:

Insect Species X: 10% decrease, for four years	Insect Species Y: 15% decrease, for four years
450 (0.6561) = 295.245	Y must be larger than X; 450 is not possible
525 (0.6561) = 344.4525	525 (0.522) = 274.05
565 (0.6561) = 370.6965	565 (0.522) = 294.93
600 (0.6561) = 393.66	600 (0.522) = 313.2
625 (0.6561) = 410.0625	625 (0.522) = 326.25
X must be smaller than Y; 770 is not possible	770 (0.522) = 401.94

Rounded to the nearest million, the values that satisfy the equation (0.6561)(current population X) = (0.522)(current population Y) are 450 for the current population of Insect Species X and 565 for the current population of Insect Species Y, which both decrease to approximately 295 million, at their independent rates of decrease, after four years.

Item 6:

6-1. No
Email #1 asked for the top rated shows among females aged 15–25 and *Memo #1* states that *Blonde Fury* is the most watched program for that group. However, it is still possible that another group watches this show as much or more than do females aged 15–25.

6-2. No
Careful. While this is certainly true in the real world, there is not enough information to make that inference here. The emails describe only two programs, thus you can make inferences about only those two.

6-3. Yes
Blonde Fury has a ratio of female viewers aged 15–25 to advertising dollars of 45% of viewers to $70,000 or 45/70, which is 9/14, or about 0.643. *Hart Attack* has a ratio of 35% to $55K or 35/55, or 7/11, or about 0.636, which is less.

Item 7:

Choice D, 9.6
Email #2 states that "80% of the viewers who are females aged 15–25 for *Hart Attack* also watch *Blonde Fury*." If there are 20 million females 15-25, and 35% watch *Hart Attack*, then 7 million females 15-25 watch *Hart Attack*. Since 80% of *Hart Attack* viewers who are females aged 15–25 also watch *Blonde Fury*, that's 80% of 7 million, which is 5.6 million. If 45% of 20 million watch *Blonde Fury*, that's 45% of 20 million = 9 million. Using the Group Equation, Total = Group 1 + Group 2 – Both + Neither, we get 20 = 7 + 9 – 5.6 + Neither. This gives Neither = 9.6 million. The answer is choice D.

Item 8:

8-1. Yes
In *Email #1*, the Marketing Director states that the company previously was able in increase revenues by buying advertisement. In stating that if the company increased its advertising expenditures, then *we will once again increase our revenues*, the Marketing Director assumes that this can work again.

8-2. Yes
Memo #1 states that, since increased revenues followed increased advertising, increasing advertising will increase revenues. Therefore, it must be true that the Marketing Director thinks that some of the increased revenues were caused by the increased advertising, and thus assumes that advertising has some effect upon revenues.

8-3. Yes
In *Email #1*, the Marketing Director states that the company previously had increased advertisement expenditures and now plans to increase the number of advertisements. This assumes that the effects are similar.

Item 9:

9-1. Supported
Sort the countries by population in 2010. There are five countries with populations above 150 million: China, India, United States, Indonesia, and Brazil. If China were to have the median foreign-born population, there would be two countries with a higher foreign-born population and two countries with a lower foreign born population. First, estimate China's foreign-born population. According to the table 0.29% of China's population of 1,399,725,000 is foreign-born. This is close to 0.3% of 1.4 billion. Multiply 0.003 by 1,400 million: China has 4.2 million foreign-born inhabitants. Now, estimate the foreign-born population of the other four countries. India's foreign-born population is about 0.5% of 1.2 billion, or is 6 million, which is greater than China's foreign born population. The foreign-born population of the United States is about 20% of 312 million, about 62 million. This is greater than China's foreign-born population. Indonesia's foreign-born population is less than 1% of about 238 million. 1% of 238 million is about 2 million. Therefore, Indonesia's foreign-born population is less than 2 million and less than China's. Brazil's foreign-born population is less than 1% of about 190 million. Since 1% of 190 million is about 1.9 million, Brazil's foreign-born population is less than 1.9 million. Therefore, Brazil's foreign-born population is less than China's. Since two of the countries have a higher foreign born population than China and two of the countries have a lower foreign-born population than China, China's foreign born population is the median.

9-2. Unsupported
This might appear to be a reasonable conclusion, since 8 million is approximately the average of the population in 2010 and the projected population for 2050. However, there is no information in the table which allows you to assume a uniform population increase from 2010 to 2050. Therefore, this conclusion is unsupported.

9-3. Unsupported
Although Andorra has the highest percentage of its population that is foreign born, this does not mean it has the great number of immigrants. About 20% of Australia's population of about 20 million is made up of immigrants. Therefore, Australia has about 4 million immigrants. Since this is greater than the entire population of Andorra, the statement is unsupported.

Item 10:

10-1. True

The chart on the second tab lists two types of tables for DoxySource, and the first tab mentions the maximum number attending: 400. The cost of the food is (appetizer + entrée + dessert)(400) or ($2.00 + $6.25 + $3.40)(400) = ($11.65)(400) = $4,660.

If the less expensive tables (seating eight) are used, 50 tables are required at $15.50 each, for a total of $775. So, the cost of the tables ($775) is approximately 16.6% of the cost of the food ($4,660). However, if the more expensive tables are used, the table cost rises to $986, which is approximately 21% of the cost of the food ($4,660).

10-2. True

The chart on the first tab shows that the punch fountain from BrightRight comes with 40 gallons of punch. To acquire the same amount from DoxySource, the Gala Coordinator would have to order six of the smaller fountains, providing seven gallons of punch each. Thus, the cost per gallon for the BrightRight fountain is $350 ÷ 40, or $8.75 per gallon. The cost per gallon for the Doxy-Source fountains is (6)($47) ÷ 42 gallons = 6.71 per gallon. Since the question states percent less, you figure the percent decrease by calculating the difference over the original: $\frac{8.75-6.71}{8.75}=\frac{2.04}{8.75}=0.233$, which is approximately 23%.

10-3. True

The first tab states that the present budget is $6,000 and the maximum number of guests is 400. Assume the Gala Coordinator wants to use BrightRight, but to stay within the present budget. The costs are listed on the chart on the second tab. The least expensive food costs for BrightRight is The Classic Western BBQ option, which is $14.00 per person, so total food costs are (400)($14.00) = $5,600.00. Adding in the least expensive costs for the audio ($650) and the punch fountain ($350) brings the cost to $6,600. Lastly, calculate the least expensive table cost: 400 guests at eight guests per table requires 50 tables; (50)($20) = $1,000, and so the total cost is now $7,600, $1,600 over the current budget of $6,000. The percent over budget is $\frac{1600}{6000}=0.266$ or approximately 27%.

Item 11:

Choice C, $792.00
This question asks about the least possible cost for the tables, using DoxySource. In the chart on the second tab, there are two prices listed for DoxySource tables: $15.50 for a table that seats eight (less expensive), or $17.00 for a table that seats seven (more expensive). The lowest cost way to use at least one of each table is for the Gala Coordinator to use only one of the more expensive tables, and use the less expensive tables for the remaining guests.

Using one of the more expensive tables seats 7 guests, leaving 393 guests who need to be seated at the remaining less expensive tables. Calculate the number of tables needed: 393 ÷ 8= 49.125, meaning that 50 more tables are required, since you can't have fractions of tables. So, there is one table at $17.00 and 50 tables at $15.50:$17.00 + (50)($15.50) = $792.00.

Item 12:

12-1. Yes
Referring to the first email from the Gala Coordinator, the message states *Also, I'd like to consider how to justify any over-budget costs from using BrightRight.* The Gala Coordinator is considering how to justify any over-budget costs: therefore, she is willing to ask for a budgetary increase.

12-2. Yes
Referring to the second tab, the Administrative Assistant mentions both *more flexibility in the catering and more hands-on involvement on our end* as factors to consider when weighing the benefits of one event planning service against another.

12-3. No
On the first tab, the Gala Coordinator states *We require: tables, audio, food, and a punch fountain or fountains*, meaning that a punch fountain is required. Although she goes on to state a *dessert fountain would be a lovely addition*, this refers only to a dessert fountain; the punch fountains are necessary.

Part VII
The Princeton Review GMAT Math and Verbal Warm-Up Test and Explanations

Chapter 22 GMAT Math and Verbal Warm-Up Test

The purpose of this 60-minute test is to get a rough idea of your current scoring range on the Math and Verbal sections of the GMAT and rough percentiles. Using these scores as a guide, you can then select from the bins of practice questions that follow to improve your performance.

According to the test makers, the computer-adaptive sections of the GMAT hones in on your approximate scoring level after only a few questions. You then spend the rest of the test time answering questions from around that level of difficulty, chosen by the computer from bins of potential questions.

To further refine your assessment of where you are right now, we recommend that you take one of The Princeton Review computer-adaptive tests (available free online). See the So Much More... section at the beginning of this book for details. We also highly recommend that you take an actual computer-adaptive GMAT, downloadable for free from the GMAT website at **www.mba.com**.

Math Test
Time—30 Minutes
20 Questions

This test is composed of both problem solving questions and data sufficiency questions.

Problem Solving Directions: Solve each problem and choose the best of the answer choices provided.

Data Sufficiency Directions: Each data sufficiency problem consists of a question and two statements, labeled (1) and (2), which contain certain data. Using these data and your knowledge of mathematics and everyday facts (such as the number of days in July or the meaning of *counterclockwise*), decide whether the data given are sufficient for answering the question and then indicate one of the following answer choices:

(A) Statement (1) ALONE is sufficient, but statement (2) alone is not sufficient.

(B) Statement (2) ALONE is sufficient, but statement (1) alone is not sufficient.

(C) BOTH statements TOGETHER are sufficient, but NEITHER statement ALONE is sufficient.

(D) EACH statement ALONE is sufficient.

(E) Statements (1) and (2) TOGETHER are not sufficient.

---

1. If $(16)(3)^2 = x(2^3)$, then $x =$

(A) 81
(B) 72
(C) 18
(D) 16
(E) 8

2. By how many dollars is the price of a certain portable tape recorder reduced during a sale?

(1) The price of the portable tape recorder is reduced by 25% during the sale.

(2) The sale price of the portable tape recorder is $36.

(A) Statement (1) ALONE is sufficient, but statement (2) alone is not sufficient.
(B) Statement (2) ALONE is sufficient, but statement (1) alone is not sufficient.
(C) BOTH statements TOGETHER are sufficient, but NEITHER statement ALONE is sufficient.
(D) EACH statement ALONE is sufficient.
(E) Statements (1) and (2) TOGETHER are not sufficient.

GO ON TO THE NEXT PAGE.

3. Of the 720 players who participated in a softball tournament, 65 percent traveled more than 200 miles to play. What is the difference between the number of participants who traveled more than 200 miles and the number of participants who traveled 200 miles or less?

(A) 108
(B) 216
(C) 252
(D) 468
(E) 655

4. If $r - s = 240$, does $r = 320$?

(1) $r = 4s$

(2) $s = 80$

(A) Statement (1) ALONE is sufficient, but statement (2) alone is not sufficient.
(B) Statement (2) ALONE is sufficient, but statement (1) alone is not sufficient.
(C) BOTH statements TOGETHER are sufficient, but NEITHER statement ALONE is sufficient.
(D) EACH statement ALONE is sufficient.
(E) Statements (1) and (2) TOGETHER are not sufficient.

5. If a heavy-load trailer travels 7 miles in 1 hour and 10 minutes, what is its speed in miles per hour?

(A) 6
(B) 6.5
(C) 8
(D) 8.5
(E) 10

6. If Bob purchases 18 cans of soda, how many of the cans do not contain diet soda?

(1) The number of cans Bob purchases that contain diet soda is equal to the number that do not contain diet soda.

(2) Bob purchases an odd number of cans of diet soda.

(A) Statement (1) ALONE is sufficient, but statement (2) alone is not sufficient.
(B) Statement (2) ALONE is sufficient, but statement (1) alone is not sufficient.
(C) BOTH statements TOGETHER are sufficient, but NEITHER statement ALONE is sufficient.
(D) EACH statement ALONE is sufficient.
(E) Statements (1) and (2) TOGETHER are not sufficient.

GO ON TO THE NEXT PAGE.

7. If y is an odd integer, which of the following must be an even integer?

(A) $y + 2$
(B) $y + 6$
(C) $2y - 1$
(D) $3y$
(E) $3y + 1$

8. At Perry High School, the ratio of students who participate in either the band program or the choral program to students who participate in neither program is 3 to 8. If 220 students attend Perry High School, how many of them participate in neither program?

(A) 40
(B) 60
(C) 100
(D) 160
(E) 180

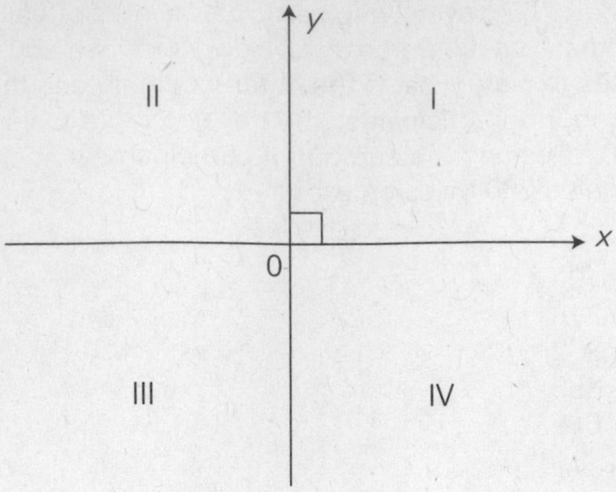

9. If $wxyz \neq 0$, in which quadrant of the rectangular coordinate system shown above does point (x, y) lie?

(1) Point (x, z) lies in quadrant I.

(2) Point (w, y) lies in quadrant III.

(A) Statement (1) ALONE is sufficient, but statement (2) alone is not sufficient.
(B) Statement (2) ALONE is sufficient, but statement (1) alone is not sufficient.
(C) BOTH statements TOGETHER are sufficient, but NEITHER statement ALONE is sufficient.
(D) EACH statement ALONE is sufficient.
(E) Statements (1) and (2) TOGETHER are not sufficient.

GO ON TO THE NEXT PAGE.

10. Laura borrowed $240, interest free, from her parents to pay for a college textbook. If she pays back $2\frac{1}{2}$ percent of this amount quarterly, how many months will it take for her to pay back $42.00 ?

(A) 6
(B) 7
(C) 19
(D) 21
(E) 24

11. If x and y are positive integers, is x a factor of 12 ?

(1) xy is a factor of 12

(2) $y = 3$

(A) Statement (1) ALONE is sufficient, but statement (2) alone is not sufficient.
(B) Statement (2) ALONE is sufficient, but statement (1) alone is not sufficient.
(C) BOTH statements TOGETHER are sufficient, but NEITHER statement ALONE is sufficient.
(D) EACH statement ALONE is sufficient.
(E) Statements (1) and (2) TOGETHER are not sufficient.

12. If a zebra can only get water from either a stream or a pond, which of the two sources of water is closer to the zebra's current position?

(1) Moving at a constant rate from its current position, the zebra reaches the stream in 2 hours.

(2) Moving at a constant rate from the stream, the zebra takes 2 hours to reach the pond.

(A) Statement (1) ALONE is sufficient, but statement (2) alone is not sufficient.
(B) Statement (2) ALONE is sufficient, but statement (1) alone is not sufficient.
(C) BOTH statements TOGETHER are sufficient, but NEITHER statement ALONE is sufficient.
(D) EACH statement ALONE is sufficient.
(E) Statements (1) and (2) TOGETHER are not sufficient.

13. What is the value of $x^2 - y^2$?

(1) $x - y = 0$

(2) $x + y = 4$

(A) Statement (1) ALONE is sufficient, but statement (2) alone is not sufficient.
(B) Statement (2) ALONE is sufficient, but statement (1) alone is not sufficient.
(C) BOTH statements TOGETHER are sufficient, but NEITHER statement ALONE is sufficient.
(D) EACH statement ALONE is sufficient.
(E) Statements (1) and (2) TOGETHER are not sufficient.

GO ON TO THE NEXT PAGE.

14. If the remainder when a certain integer x is divided by 5 is 2, then each of the following could also be an integer, EXCEPT

(A) $\frac{x}{17}$

(B) $\frac{x}{11}$

(C) $\frac{x}{10}$

(D) $\frac{x}{6}$

(E) $\frac{x}{3}$

15. A mixture of ground meat consists of 2 pounds of veal that costs x dollars per pound, and 5 pounds of beef that costs y dollars per pound. What is the cost of the mixture in dollars per pound?

(A) $2x + 5y$

(B) $\frac{2x+5y}{xy}$

(C) $5(2x + 5y)$

(D) $x + y$

(E) $\frac{2x+5y}{7}$

16. Is $0 < y < 1$?

(1) $0 < \sqrt{y} < 1$

(2) $y^2 = \frac{1}{4}$

(A) Statement (1) ALONE is sufficient, but statement (2) alone is not sufficient.
(B) Statement (2) ALONE is sufficient, but statement (1) alone is not sufficient.
(C) BOTH statements TOGETHER are sufficient, but NEITHER statement ALONE is sufficient.
(D) EACH statement ALONE is sufficient.
(E) Statements (1) and (2) TOGETHER are not sufficient.

17. If a and b are positive integers, is ab odd?

(1) $b = 3$

(2) a and b are consecutive integers.

(A) Statement (1) ALONE is sufficient, but statement (2) alone is not sufficient.
(B) Statement (2) ALONE is sufficient, but statement (1) alone is not sufficient.
(C) BOTH statements TOGETHER are sufficient, but NEITHER statement ALONE is sufficient.
(D) EACH statement ALONE is sufficient.
(E) Statements (1) and (2) TOGETHER are not sufficient.

GO ON TO THE NEXT PAGE.

18. Last year, an appliance store sold an average (arithmetic mean) of 42 microwave ovens per month. In the first 10 months of this year, the store sold an average of only 20 microwaves per month. What is the average number of microwaves sold per month for the entire 22-month period?

(A) 21
(B) 30
(C) 31
(D) 32
(E) 44

19. If AB is the diameter of the circle with center X and C is a point on the circle such that $AC = AX = 3$, what is the perimeter of triangle ABC ?

(A) $\frac{9\sqrt{3}}{2}$
(B) 9
(C) $6 + 3\sqrt{3}$
(D) $9 + 3\sqrt{3}$
(E) $9\sqrt{3}$

ADVANCED PURCHASE DISCOUNTS FOR AIRLINE TRAVEL	
Days Prior to Departure	**Percentage Discount**
0–6 days	0%
7–13 days	10%
14–29 days	25%
30 days or more	40%

20. The table above shows the discount structure for advanced purchase of tickets at a particular airline. A passenger bought a ticket at this airline for $1,050. Had she purchased the ticket one day later, she would have paid $210 more. How many days before her departure did she purchase her ticket?

(A) 6 days
(B) 7 days
(C) 13 days
(D) 14 days
(E) 29 days

GO ON TO THE NEXT PAGE.

Verbal Test
Time—30 Minutes
20 Questions

This test is made up of sentence correction, critical reasoning, and reading comprehension questions.

Sentence Correction Directions: Each of the sentence correction questions presents a sentence, part or all of which is underlined. Beneath the sentence you will find five ways of phrasing the underlined part. The first of these repeats the original; the other four are different. Follow the requirements of standard written English to choose your answer, paying attention to grammar, word choice, and sentence construction. Select the answer that produces the most effective sentence; your answer should make the sentence clear, exact, and free of grammatical errors. It should also minimize awkwardness, ambiguity, and redundancy.

Reading Comprehension Directions: Each of the reading comprehension questions is based on the content of a passage. After reading the passage, answer all questions pertaining to it on the basis of what is stated or implied in the passage. For each question, select the best answer of the choices given.

Critical Reasoning Directions: Each of the critical reasoning questions is based on a short argument, a set of statements, or a plan of action. For each question, select the best answer of the choices given.

---

21. Unseasonable weather in the months before a wine harvest can cool vineyards in the Bordeaux region enough to affect the overall size of the grapes themselves, create unwanted moisture that can cause mold in some grape varieties and deterioration in others.

(A) to affect the overall size of the grapes themselves, create
(B) to affect the overall size of the grapes themselves, and create
(C) that the overall size of the grapes themselves are affected, create
(D) that it affects the overall size of the grapes themselves, creates
(E) that the size of the grapes are affected and creates

22. It is posited by some scientists that the near extinction of the sap-eating gray bat of northwestern America was caused by government-sponsored logging operations in the early 1920s that greatly reduced the species' habitat.

Which of the following, if true, most strongly weakens the scientists' claims?

(A) Logging operations in the 1920s are widely held responsible for the near extinction of other species that lived in the same area.
(B) A boom in new home construction in the early 1920s led congress to open federal lands to logging operations.
(C) A 5-year drought in the early 1920s severely reduced the output of sap in trees in northwestern America.
(D) Numbers of sightings of sap-eating gray bats fell to their lowest numbers in 1926.
(E) Sightings of sap-eating gray bats in Europe stayed roughly the same during the same period.

GO ON TO THE NEXT PAGE.

23. Upset by the recent downturn in production numbers during the first half of the year, <u>the possibility of adding worker incentives was raised by the board of directors at its quarterly meeting</u>.

(A) the possibility of adding worker incentives was raised by the board of directors at its quarterly meeting
(B) the addition of worker incentives was raised as a possibility by the board of directors at its quarterly meeting
(C) added worker incentives was raised by the board of directors at its quarterly meeting as a possibility
(D) the board of directors raised at its quarterly meeting the possibility of worker incentives being added
(E) the board of directors, at its quarterly meeting, raised the possibility of adding worker incentives

24. Whenever a major airplane accident occurs, there is a dramatic increase in the number of airplane mishaps reported in the media, a phenomenon that may last for as long as a few months after the accident. Airline officials assert that the publicity given the gruesomeness of major airplane accidents focuses media attention on the airline industry, and the increase in the number of reported accidents is caused by an increase in the number of news sources covering airline accidents, not by an increase in the number of accidents.

Which of the following, if true, would seriously weaken the assertions of the airline officials?

(A) The publicity surrounding airline accidents is largely limited to the country in which the crash occurred.
(B) Airline accidents tend to occur far more often during certain peak travel months.
(C) Media organizations do not have any guidelines to help them decide how severe an accident must be for it to receive coverage.
(D) Airplane accidents receive coverage by news sources only when the news sources find it advantageous to do so.
(E) Studies by government regulators show that the number of airplane flight miles remains relatively constant from month to month.

GO ON TO THE NEXT PAGE.

Questions 25–28 are based on the following passage:

The function of strategic planning is to position a company for long-term growth and expansion in a variety of markets by analyzing its strengths and weaknesses and examining current and potential opportunities. Based on this information, the company develops a strategy for itself. That strategy becomes the basis for supporting strategies for the company's various departments.

This implementation strategy is where all too many strategic plans go astray. Recent business management surveys show that most CEOs who have a strategic plan are concerned with the potential breakdown in the implementation of the plan. Unlike corporations in the 1980s that blindly followed their 5-year plans, even when they were misguided, today's corporations tend to second-guess their long-term plans.

Outsiders can help facilitate the process, but in the final analysis, if the company does not make the plan, the company will not follow the plan. This was one of the problems with strategic planning in the 1980s. In that era, strategic planning was an abstract, top-down process involving only a few top corporate officers and hired guns. Number crunching experts came into a company and generated tome-like volumes filled with a mixture of abstruse facts and grand theories which had little to do with the day-to-day realities of the company. Key middle managers were left out of planning sessions, resulting in lost opportunities and ruffled feelings.

However, more hands-on strategic planning can produce startling results. A recent survey queried more than a thousand small-to-medium sized businesses to compare companies with a strategic plan to companies without one. The survey found that companies with strategic plans had annual revenue growth of 6.2 percent as opposed to 3.8 percent for the other companies.

Perhaps most important, a strategic plan helps companies anticipate—and survive— change. New technology and the mobility of capital means that markets can shift faster than ever before. Some financial analysts wonder why companies should bother planning two years ahead when market dynamics might be transformed by next quarter. However, it is this pace of change that makes planning so crucial. Now, more than ever, companies have to stay alert to the marketplace. In an environment of continual and rapid change, long-range planning expands options and organizational flexibility.

25. The primary purpose of the passage is to

(A) refute the idea that change is bad for a corporation's long-term health
(B) describe how long-term planning, despite some potential pitfalls, can help a corporation to grow
(C) compare and contrast two styles of corporate planning
(D) evaluate the strategic planning goals of corporate America today
(E) defend a methodology that has come under sharp attack

26. It can be inferred from the passage that strategic planning during the 1980s had all of the following shortcomings EXCEPT

(A) a reliance on outside consultants who did not necessarily understand the nuts and bolts of the business
(B) a dependence on theoretical models that did not always perfectly describe the workings of the company
(C) an inherent weakness in the company's own ability to implement the strategic plan
(D) an excess of information and data that made it difficult to get to key concepts
(E) the lack of a forum for middle managers to express their ideas

GO ON TO THE NEXT PAGE.

27. The author most likely mentions the results of the survey of 1,000 companies in order to

(A) put forth an opposing view on strategic plans which is later refuted
(B) illustrate that when strategic planning is "hands-on," it produces uninspiring results
(C) give a concrete example of why strategic planning did not work during the 1980s
(D) support the contention that strategic planning can be very successful when done correctly
(E) give supporting data to prove that many companies have implemented strategic plans

28. The passage suggests which of the following about the "financial analysts" mentioned in lines 44–47 ?

(A) They believe that strategic planning is the key to weathering the rapid changes of the marketplace.
(B) They are working to understand and anticipate market developments that are two years ahead.
(C) Their study of market dynamics has led them to question the reliability of short-term planning strategies.
(D) They might not agree with the author that one way to survive rapidly changing conditions comes from long-range planning.
(E) They consider the mobility of capital to be a necessary condition for the growth of new technology.

29. The Internal Revenue Service has directed that taxpayers who generate no self-employment income can no longer deduct home offices, home office expenses, <u>or nothing that was already</u> depreciated as a business expense the previous year.

(A) or nothing that was already
(B) or that was already
(C) or anything that was already
(D) and anything
(E) and nothing that already was

30. Informed people generally assimilate information from several divergent sources before coming to an opinion. However, most popular news organizations view foreign affairs solely through the eyes of our State Department. In reporting the political crisis in a foreign country, news organizations must endeavor to find alternative sources of information.

Which of the following inferences can be drawn from the argument above?

(A) To the degree that a news source gives an account of another country that mirrors that of our State Department, that reporting is suspect.
(B) To protect their integrity, news media should avoid the influence of State Department releases in their coverage of foreign affairs.
(C) Reporting that is not influenced by the State Department is usually more accurate than are other accounts.
(D) The alternative sources of information mentioned in the passage might not share the same views as the State Department.
(E) A report cannot be seen as influenced by the State Department if it accurately depicts the events in a foreign country.

GO ON TO THE NEXT PAGE.

31. When automatic teller machines were first installed in the 1980s, bank officials promised they would be faster, more reliable, and less prone to make errors than their human counterparts.

(A) they would be faster, more reliable, and less prone to make errors
(B) they would be faster, more reliable, and that they would be less prone for making errors
(C) the machines would be faster, more reliable, and less prone to errors
(D) the machines were faster, more reliable, and errors would occur much less
(E) faster, more reliable machines, and that errors would be less prone

32. With its plan to create a wildlife sanctuary out of previously unused landfill, Sweden is but one of a number of industrialized nations that is accepting its responsibility to protect endangered species and promote conservation.

(A) is accepting its responsibility to protect endangered species and promote
(B) is accepting its responsibility for protecting endangered species and promoting
(C) are accepting its responsibility to protect endangered species and promoting
(D) are accepting of their responsibility to protect endangered species and to promote
(E) are accepting their responsibility to protect endangered species and promote

33. A decade after a logging operation in India began cutting down trees in a territory that serves as a sanctuary for Bengal tigers, the incidence of tigers attacking humans in nearby villages has increased by 300 percent. Because the logging operation has reduced the number of acres of woodland per tiger on average from 15 acres to approximately 12 acres, scientists have theorized that tigers must need a minimum number of acres of woodland in order to remain content.

Which of the following statements, if true, would most strengthen the scientists' hypothesis?

(A) In other wildlife areas in India where the number of acres of woodland per tiger remains at least 15 acres, there has been no increase in the number of tiger attacks on humans.
(B) Before the logging operation began, there were many fewer humans living in the area.
(C) The largest number of acres per tiger before the logging operation began was 32 acres per tiger in one area of the sanctuary, whereas the smallest number of acres per tiger after the logging operation was 9 acres.
(D) Other species of wild animals have begun competing with the Bengal tigers for the dwindling food supply.
(E) The Bengal tiger has become completely extinct in other areas of Asia.

GO ON TO THE NEXT PAGE.

34. The machine press union and company management were not able to communicate effectively, and it was a major cause of the 1999 strike in Seattle.

(A) The machine press union and company management were not able to communicate effectively, and it
(B) Communications between the machine press union and company management were not effective, and it
(C) For the machine press union and company management, to be unable to communicate effectively
(D) The inability of the machine press union and company management to communicate effectively
(E) The machine press union, being unable to communicate effectively with company management,

35. A greater number of fresh vegetables are sold in City *X* than in City *Y*. Therefore, the people in City *X* have better nutritional habits than those in City *Y*.

Each of the following, if true, weakens the conclusion above EXCEPT:

(A) City *X* has more people living in it than City *Y*.
(B) Most of the people in City *Y* work in City *X* and buy their vegetables there.
(C) The people in City *X* buy many of their vegetables as decorations, not to eat.
(D) The per capita consumption of junk food in City *X* is three times that of City *Y*.
(E) The average price per pound of vegetables in City *Y* is lower than the average price per pound of vegetables in City *X*.

36. Heavy metals, toxic waste by-products that can cause tumors in fish, are generally found in the waters off industrial shorelines, but have been discovered in trace amounts even in the relatively pristine waters of the South Pacific.

(A) are generally found in the waters off industrial shorelines, but have been discovered in trace amounts even
(B) are generally to be found in the waters off industrial shorelines, and have even been discovered in trace amounts
(C) can, in general, be found in the waters off industrial shorelines, and have been discovered in trace amounts even
(D) had generally been found in the waters off industrial shorelines, but have even been discovered in trace amounts
(E) are found generally in the waters off industrial shorelines, but have been discovered in a trace amount even

GO ON TO THE NEXT PAGE.

Questions 37–40 are based on the following passage:

In Roman times, defeated enemies were generally put to death as criminals for having offended the emperor of Rome. In the Middle Ages, however, the practice of ransoming, or returning prisoners in exchange for money, became common. Though some saw this custom as a step toward a more humane society, the primary reasons behind it were economic rather than humanitarian.

In those times, rulers had only a limited ability to raise taxes. They could neither force their subjects to fight nor pay them to do so. The promise of material compensation in the form of goods and ransom was therefore the only way of inducing combatants to participate in a war. In the Middle Ages, the predominant incentive for the individual soldier was the expectation of spoils. Although collecting ransom clearly brought financial gain, keeping a prisoner and arranging for his exchange had its costs. Consequently, procedures were devised to reduce transaction costs.

One such device was a rule asserting that the prisoner had to assess his own value. This compelled the prisoner to establish a value without too much distortion; indicating too low a value would increase the captive's chances of being killed, while indicating too high a value would either ruin him financially or create a prohibitively expensive ransom that would also result in death.

37. The primary purpose of the passage is to

(A) discuss the economic basis of the medieval practice of exchanging prisoners for ransom
(B) examine the history of the treatment of prisoners of war
(C) emphasize the importance of a warrior's code of honor during the Middle Ages
(D) explore a way of reducing the costs of ransom
(E) demonstrate why warriors of the Middle Ages looked forward to battles

38. It can be inferred from the passage that a medieval soldier

(A) was less likely to kill captured members of opposing armies than was a soldier of the Roman Empire
(B) operated on a basically independent level and was motivated solely by economic incentives
(C) had few economic options and chose to fight because it was the only way to earn an adequate living
(D) was motivated to spare prisoners' lives by humanitarian rather than economic ideals
(E) had no respect for his captured enemies since captives were typically regarded as weak

GO ON TO THE NEXT PAGE.

39. Which of the following best describes the change in policy from executing prisoners in Roman times to ransoming prisoners in the Middle Ages?

(A) The emperors of Rome demanded more respect than did medieval rulers, and thus Roman subjects went to greater lengths to defend their nation.
(B) It was a reflection of the lesser degree of direct control medieval rulers had over their subjects.
(C) It became a show of strength and honor for warriors of the Middle Ages to be able to capture and return their enemies.
(D) Medieval soldiers were not as humanitarian as their ransoming practices might have indicated.
(E) Medieval soldiers demonstrated more concern about economic policy than did their Roman counterparts.

40. The author uses the phrase "without too much distortion" (lines 24–25) in order to

(A) indicate that prisoners would fairly assess their worth
(B) emphasize the important role medieval prisoners played in determining whether they should be ransomed
(C) explain how prisoners often paid more than an appropriate ransom in order to increase their chances for survival
(D) suggest that captors and captives often had understanding relationships
(E) show that when in prison a soldier's view could become distorted

END OF WARM-UP TEST

Chapter 23
GMAT Math and Verbal Warm-Up Test Scoring Guide

GMAT WARM-UP TEST SCORING GUIDE

Detailed explanations to these answers can be found in the next chapter.

ANSWER KEY

MATH		VERBAL	
1.	C	21.	B
2.	C	22.	C
3.	B	23.	E
4.	D	24.	B
5.	A	25.	B
6.	A	26.	C
7.	E	27.	D
8.	D	28.	D
9.	C	29.	C
10.	D	30.	D
11.	A	31.	C
12.	E	32.	E
13.	A	33.	A
14.	C	34.	D
15.	E	35.	E
16.	A	36.	A
17.	B	37.	A
18.	D	38.	A
19.	D	39.	B
20.	D	40.	A

The Math Score

If you got 6 or fewer math questions correct: Your percentile rank is in the lower one-third of the testing group and you should begin by practicing the problems in Math Bin 1. Once you've mastered the material in Math Bin 1, you should move on to the questions in Math Bin 2 of our practice test.

If you got between 6 and 13 math questions correct: Your percentile rank is in the middle one-third of the testing group and you should begin by practicing the problems in Math Bin 2 of our practice test. Once you've mastered the material in Math Bin 2, you should move on to the questions in Math Bin 3.

If you got 14 or more math questions correct: Your percentile rank is in the top one-third of the testing group and you should begin by practicing the problems in Math Bins 3 and 4 of our practice test.

The Verbal Score

If you got 6 or fewer verbal questions correct: Your percentile rank is in the lower one-third of the testing group and you should begin by practicing the problems in Verbal Bin 1 of our practice test. Once you've mastered the material in Verbal Bin 1, you should move on to the questions in Verbal Bin 2.

If you got between 6 and 13 verbal questions correct: Your percentile rank is in the middle one-third of the testing group and you should begin by practicing the problems in Verbal Bin 2 of our practice test. Once you've mastered the material in Verbal Bin 2, you should move on to the questions in Verbal Bin 3 of our practice test.

If you got 14 or more verbal questions correct: Your percentile rank is in the top one-third of the testing group and you should begin by practicing the problems in Verbal Bin 3 of our practice test.

(If you want additional practice for either the Math or the Verbal section, you may find it helpful to do the problems in a bin with a lower number than the one suggested. So if your math diagnostic score indicates that you should do the questions in Math Bin 2, you might want to do the questions in Math Bin 1 as well.)

The Combined Score

If you got 12 or fewer of the 40 total questions correct: Your combined score at the moment is less than 450.

If you got between 12 and 31 of the 40 total questions correct: Your combined score at the moment is between 450 and 550.

If you got 32 or more of the 40 total questions correct: Your combined score at the moment is more than 550.

Chapter 24 GMAT Math and Verbal Warm-Up Test: Answers and Explanations

QUESTIONS

1. If $(16)(3)^2 = x(2^3)$, then $x =$

(A) 81
(B) 72
(C) 18
(D) 16
(E) 8

2. By how many dollars is the price of a certain portable tape recorder reduced during a sale?

(1) The price of the portable tape recorder is reduced by 25% during the sale.

(2) The sale price of the portable tape recorder is $36.

(A) Statement (1) ALONE is sufficient, but statement (2) alone is not sufficient.
(B) Statement (2) ALONE is sufficient, but statement (1) alone is not sufficient.
(C) BOTH statements TOGETHER are sufficient, but NEITHER statement ALONE is sufficient.
(D) EACH statement ALONE is sufficient.
(E) Statements (1) and (2) TOGETHER are not sufficient.

3. Of the 720 players who participated in a softball tournament, 65 percent traveled more than 200 miles to play. What is the difference between the number of participants who traveled more than 200 miles and the number of participants who traveled 200 miles or less?

(A) 108
(B) 216
(C) 252
(D) 468
(E) 655

MATH EXPLANATIONS

1. **C** Rather than multiply out each side of the equation, let's simplify. We can rewrite 16 as 2^4. If we cancel 2^3 from each side of the equation, we are left with $2(3)^2 = x$. The correct answer is C, 18.

2. **C** Statement (1) tells us the reduction as a percentage, but without a dollar figure we don't know the exact amount of the reduction. We are left with B, C, and E.

Looking at Statement (2), we now know the dollar amount after the reduction, but without knowing either the original amount, or the percentage of the reduction, we don't know enough to answer the question. Eliminate B and only C and E remain.

However, when we put the two statements together, we have enough information to write an equation: $0.75x = \$36$, where x is the original amount. Once we subtract the price after the reduction, we'll have answered the question. But remember, for Data Sufficiency questions, we don't need to get the actual answer to the question; we just need to know that we can. The correct answer is choice C.

3. **B** This is a percent problem, so let's start by finding the number of players who traveled more than 200 miles: 65% of 720 is 468. The number of players who traveled 200 miles or less, then, is $720 - 468 = 252$ (or, alternatively, 35% of 720 is 252). Although both 468 and 252 are answer choices, the question asks for the difference between the two types of participants: $468 - 252 = 216$.

If you'd prefer, you can also deal with the difference of the percentages rather than that of the actual numbers of people: $65\% - 35\% = 30\%$ and 30% of 720 is 216.

QUESTIONS

4. If $r - s = 240$, does $r = 320$?

(1) $r = 4s$

(2) $s = 80$

(A) Statement (1) ALONE is sufficient, but statement (2) alone is not sufficient.
(B) Statement (2) ALONE is sufficient, but statement (1) alone is not sufficient.
(C) BOTH statements TOGETHER are sufficient, but NEITHER statement ALONE is sufficient.
(D) EACH statement ALONE is sufficient.
(E) Statements (1) and (2) TOGETHER are not sufficient.

5. If a heavy-load trailer travels 7 miles in 1 hour and 10 minutes, what is its speed in miles per hour?

(A) 6
(B) 6.5
(C) 8
(D) 8.5
(E) 10

6. If Bob purchases 18 cans of soda, how many of the cans do not contain diet soda?

(1) The number of cans Bob purchases that contain diet soda is equal to the number that do not contain diet soda.

(2) Bob purchases an odd number of cans of diet soda.

(A) Statement (1) ALONE is sufficient, but statement (2) alone is not sufficient.
(B) Statement (2) ALONE is sufficient, but statement (1) alone is not sufficient.
(C) BOTH statements TOGETHER are sufficient, but NEITHER statement ALONE is sufficient.
(D) EACH statement ALONE is sufficient.
(E) Statements (1) and (2) TOGETHER are not sufficient.

MATH EXPLANATIONS

4. **D** Joe Bloggs might be tempted by B on this yes-or-no Data Sufficiency problem, because Statement (2) certainly does answer the question. But take another look at Statement (1). If $r = 4s$, then we can substitute $4s$ for r in the first equation, making it $4s - s = 240$, or $3s = 240$, which means s equals 80, and r equals 320.

5. **A** Any problem with terms like "speed" or "miles per hour" can typically be solved with the formula: *distance* = *rate* × *time*. This problem asks for the speed, or rate, which means *distance* divided by *time*. 7 divided by $1\frac{1}{6}$, which is 1 hour and 10 minutes written as a mixed number, equals 6.

6. **A** The question tells us that Bob purchases a total of 18 cans of soda. Statement (1) tells us there is an equal number of diet and non-diet cans. This answers the question so our choices left are A and D.

Statement (2) may seem to *agree* with Statement (1) because we may have noticed that the number of diet cans supplied by the information in Statement (1) happens to be odd. However, there are lots of odd numbers. The correct answer is A.

QUESTIONS

7. If y is an odd integer, which of the following must be an even integer?

(A) $y + 2$
(B) $y + 6$
(C) $2y - 1$
(D) $3y$
(E) $3y + 1$

8. At Perry High School, the ratio of students who participate in either the band program or the choral program to students who participate in neither program is 3 to 8. If 220 students attend Perry High School, how many of them participate in neither program?

(A) 40
(B) 60
(C) 100
(D) 160
(E) 180

MATH EXPLANATIONS

7. E The variables in the answer choices indicate this is a Plugging In problem, but the word "must" means you may have to plug in *twice* to be sure you have the correct answer. Because y must be an odd integer, let's use 3. Now, all we have to do is plug 3 into each of the answer choices. Any choice that does *not* yield an even integer can be crossed off immediately. If more than one of the choices yields an even integer, we will have to plug in a second number for y to see which choice *always* yields an even integer. Using 3 as our value for y, we find that choices A, B, C, and D all yield odd integers, and E produces an even integer. Therefore, the correct answer is E.

8. D This is a ratio problem, so set up the ratio box. We need to add the "parts" of our ratio to get the "whole" required to form a fraction. Since our parts are 3 and 8, our whole is 11; the total number of students is 220, so 220 divided by 11 is 20, which means we need to multiply all the numbers by 20. 8 students participate in neither program, so 8 multiplied by 20 is 160. The correct answer is D.

Be careful not to choose B, the number of students who do participate in one of the programs, or C, the difference between the number of students who participate and the number who don't. Judicious use of POE might have eliminated both answers, though, along with A: Since we know that more than half of the students do not participate in either program, we can eliminate any answer less than 110.

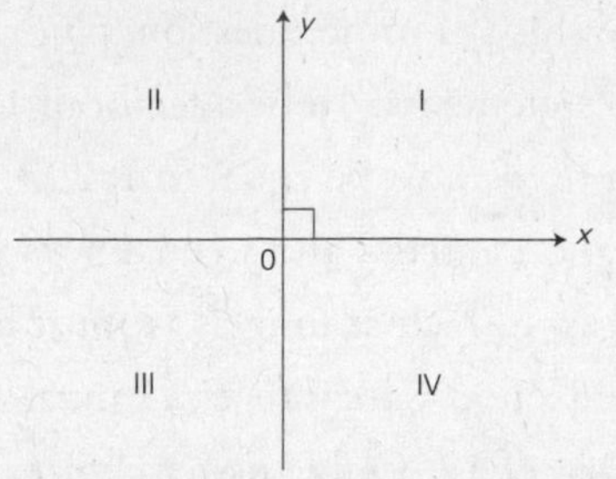

9. If $wxyz \neq 0$, in which quadrant of the rectangular coordinate system shown above does point (x, y) lie?

(1) Point (x, z) lies in quadrant I.

(2) Point (w, y) lies in quadrant III.

(A) Statement (1) ALONE is sufficient, but statement (2) alone is not sufficient.
(B) Statement (2) ALONE is sufficient, but statement (1) alone is not sufficient.
(C) BOTH statements TOGETHER are sufficient, but NEITHER statement ALONE is sufficient.
(D) EACH statement ALONE is sufficient.
(E) Statements (1) and (2) TOGETHER are not sufficient.

9. **C** To help understand this question, try plugging in some values. Statement (1) tells us that point (x, z) lies in quadrant I, which means that x and z must both be positive. For example, let's say (x, z) is (3, 4). We know x is positive, but does this tell us anything about y? Nope, so only answer choices B, C, and E remain.
Statement (2) tells us that point (w, y) lies in quadrant III, which means that w and y must both be negative. For example, let's say (w, y) is (–2, –5). In this case, we know y must be negative, but does this tell us anything about x? Nope, so we are left with answer choices C or E.
If we put the two statements together, we know x must be positive and we know y must be negative—for example, using the points we plugged in, (x, y) is (3, –5)—which means point (x, y) must be in quadrant IV. The answer is C.

10. Laura borrowed $240, interest free, from her parents to pay for a college textbook. If she pays back $2\frac{1}{2}$ percent of this amount quarterly, how many months will it take for her to pay back $42.00 ?

(A) 6
(B) 7
(C) 19
(D) 21
(E) 24

10. **D** Laura pays back 2.5 percent of the loan each quarter of the year. 2.5% of $240 is $6.00. If she has already paid $42.00, that means she has paid that $6.00 for seven quarters. To pay back $42.00 requires 7 quarterly payments. How many months is that? Each quarter of the year is 3 months. The correct answer is D.

QUESTIONS

11. If x and y are positive integers, is x a factor of 12 ?

(1) xy is a factor of 12

(2) $y = 3$

(A) Statement (1) ALONE is sufficient, but statement (2) alone is not sufficient.
(B) Statement (2) ALONE is sufficient, but statement (1) alone is not sufficient.
(C) BOTH statements TOGETHER are sufficient, but NEITHER statement ALONE is sufficient.
(D) EACH statement ALONE is sufficient.
(E) Statements (1) and (2) TOGETHER are not sufficient.

12. If a zebra can only get water from either a stream or a pond, which of the two sources of water is closer to the zebra's current position?

(1) Moving at a constant rate from its current position, the zebra reaches the stream in 2 hours.

(2) Moving at a constant rate from the stream, the zebra takes 2 hours to reach the pond.

(A) Statement (1) ALONE is sufficient, but statement (2) alone is not sufficient.
(B) Statement (2) ALONE is sufficient, but statement (1) alone is not sufficient.
(C) BOTH statements TOGETHER are sufficient, but NEITHER statement ALONE is sufficient.
(D) EACH statement ALONE is sufficient.
(E) Statements (1) and (2) TOGETHER are not sufficient.

MATH EXPLANATIONS

11. A To solve this yes-or-no question, plug values into the two statements. To be a factor of 12, the product of xy must be equal to 1, 2, 3, 4, 6, or 12. Let's make x equal 2 and y equal 3. Is x a factor of 12? Yes. In fact, as long as xy must be a factor of 12 and x and y are integers, x must ALWAYS be a factor of 12. Only answer choices A and D remain.

Now, let's look at Statement (2). The fact that $y = 3$ does not help us to know whether x is a factor of 12. The answer is A. Joe Bloggs might have been tempted by C because he'd have a definitive value for x.

12. E Statement (1) tells us only the time it takes the zebra to reach the stream from its current position; since it gives us no information about the time required to reach the pond, Statement (1) is insufficient alone, and we're down to B, C, or E.

Similarly, since Statement (2) only tells us the time it takes the zebra to get from the pond to the stream—and doesn't mention the zebra's current position—Statement (2) is insufficient alone, and we're down to C or E.

Be careful when you combine the two statements: Although it may be tempting to simply add our travel time and calculate that it takes the zebra 4 hours to go from its current position to the pond, this is true only if all 3 locations were in a straight line, so that the pond would be directly on the other side of the stream. We, of course, can't assume that to be the case. For instance, if the zebra travels 2 hours due west from its current position to the stream, and then travels 2 hours due east from the stream to the pond, the zebra's current location would be *at* the pond! The correct answer to this question is E.

QUESTIONS

MATH EXPLANATIONS

13. What is the value of $x^2 - y^2$?

(1) $x - y = 0$

(2) $x + y = 4$

(A) Statement (1) ALONE is sufficient, but statement (2) alone is not sufficient.
(B) Statement (2) ALONE is sufficient, but statement (1) alone is not sufficient.
(C) BOTH statements TOGETHER are sufficient, but NEITHER statement ALONE is sufficient.
(D) EACH statement ALONE is sufficient.
(E) Statements (1) and (2) TOGETHER are not sufficient.

13. **A** Joe Bloggs wants to pick answer C because he knows that $x^2 - y^2 = (x + y)(x - y)$ and he figures he will need both statements to give him the answer. But if $(x - y) = 0$, then what $(x + y)$ equals is irrelevant because zero times any number equals zero.

14. If the remainder when a certain integer x is divided by 5 is 2, then each of the following could also be an integer, EXCEPT

(A) $\frac{x}{17}$

(B) $\frac{x}{11}$

(C) $\frac{x}{10}$

(D) $\frac{x}{6}$

(E) $\frac{x}{3}$

14. **C** As always, when there are variables in the answer choices, the easiest thing to do is plug in. If you always get a remainder of 2 when you divide x by 5, then x is some multiple of 5 plus 2 more. In other words, x could be 7 or 12 or 17 or 22, etc. Now, we have to go through the answer choices Plugging in numbers for x that allow them to be integers as well. For example, in A, if we plugged in 17 for x, that gives us $\frac{17}{17}$, which is an integer. Cross off choice A. In choice B, if we plugged in 22, we get $\frac{22}{11}$ which is an integer. Cross off B. In D and E, Plugging In the number 12 makes both choices integers. Only choice C is never an integer as long as x divided by 5 has a remainder of 2. The correct answer is C.

QUESTIONS

15. A mixture of ground meat consists of 2 pounds of veal that costs x dollars per pound, and 5 pounds of beef that costs y dollars per pound. What is the cost of the mixture in dollars per pound?

(A) $2x + 5y$

(B) $\frac{2x+5y}{xy}$

(C) $5(2x + 5y)$

(D) $x + y$

(E) $\frac{2x+5y}{7}$

16. Is $0 < y < 1$?

(1) $0 < \sqrt{y} < 1$

(2) $y^2 = \frac{1}{4}$

(A) Statement (1) ALONE is sufficient, but statement (2) alone is not sufficient.
(B) Statement (2) ALONE is sufficient, but statement (1) alone is not sufficient.
(C) BOTH statements TOGETHER are sufficient, but NEITHER statement ALONE is sufficient.
(D) EACH statement ALONE is sufficient.
(E) Statements (1) and (2) TOGETHER are not sufficient.

MATH EXPLANATIONS

15. **E** When you see variables in the answer choices, the best way to solve the problem is to plug in. Because the total number of pounds of meat is 7, it makes sense to choose numbers that are divisible by 7. Choosing \$14 for x and \$7 for y, we end up with \$9 per pound for the mixture. Plugging our values for x and y into the answer choices, only one gives us \$9: E.

16. **A** To solve this yes-or-no question, plug values into the two statements. Joe Bloggs liked Statement (2) because he forgot that y could equal $-\frac{1}{2}$. However, only Statement (1) answered the question. Square roots are always positive. The correct answer is A.

QUESTIONS

17. If a and b are positive integers, is ab odd?

(1) $b = 3$

(2) a and b are consecutive integers.

(A) Statement (1) ALONE is sufficient, but statement (2) alone is not sufficient.
(B) Statement (2) ALONE is sufficient, but statement (1) alone is not sufficient.
(C) BOTH statements TOGETHER are sufficient, but NEITHER statement ALONE is sufficient.
(D) EACH statement ALONE is sufficient.
(E) Statements (1) and (2) TOGETHER are not sufficient.

18. Last year, an appliance store sold an average (arithmetic mean) of 42 microwave ovens per month. In the first 10 months of this year, the store sold an average of only 20 microwaves per month. What is the average number of microwaves sold per month for the entire 22-month period?

(A) 21
(B) 30
(C) 31
(D) 32
(E) 44

MATH EXPLANATIONS

17. **B** To solve this yes-or-no question, try plugging values into the statements. Looking first at Statement (1), we know that $b = 3$. If we plug in 2 for a, we get a "no" answer to the question "is the product ab odd." If we plug in 5 for a, we get a "yes" answer, so we are left with B, C, and E as the potential answer choices.

Now, Plugging In for Statement (2), we eventually realize that if a and b are consecutive integers, one of them must always be even, and the other odd. And the product of even times odd is always even. So Statement (2) answers this yes-or-no question with a resounding "No." Joe Bloggs was probably tempted by C, but if you plug in enough in this question, you will notice that Statement (2) is sufficient.

18. **D** To find this average, draw an average pie and realize you have to divide the total number of sales by the total number of months. The total sales for the first year were 12 times 42 or 504. The total sales for the first 10 months of this year were 10 times 20 or 200. So the average number of sales per month is found by dividing the total number of sales, 704, by the total number of months, 22. The answer is 32. Note that A and E are completely out of the ballpark. Because there were more months for which the sales averaged 42 than for which they averaged 20, the correct answer is bound to be a *little* more than the average of the two averages, 31. Choice C, 31, is the Joe Bloggs answer; Joe loves to take an average of two averages.

QUESTIONS

19. If AB is the diameter of the circle with center X and C is a point on the circle such that $AC = AX = 3$, what is the perimeter of triangle ABC ?

(A) $\frac{9\sqrt{3}}{2}$

(B) 9

(C) $6 + 3\sqrt{3}$

(D) $9 + 3\sqrt{3}$

(E) $9\sqrt{3}$

MATH EXPLANATIONS

19. D First, draw the picture. It looks something like this:

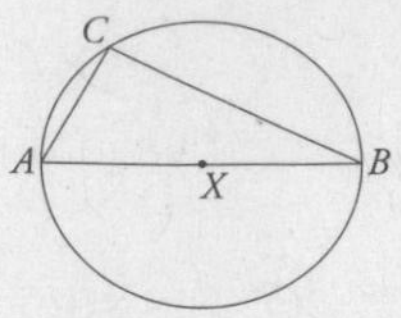

The problem states that AB is the diameter of the circle and that X is center of the circle. Note that point C lies closer to point A than to point B but if you miss that subtlety, you can still get the problem correct. ABC is the triangle that connects the 3 points. AC and AX can be labeled 3—as can BX, since, like AX, it's a radius.

We already have 2 of the 3 sides we need to find the perimeter of the triangle! To find the 3rd side, we'll need to know a geometry fact that is only infrequently tested by the GMAT: Triangle ABC, because it's inscribed in a semicircle, is a right triangle, with the right angle being at point C. Now we can use the Pythagorean theorem—or, even better, recognize ABC as a 30–60–90 triangle—to determine that BC is $3\sqrt{3}$. Our perimeter is thus $6 + 3 + 3\sqrt{3}$, or $9 + 3\sqrt{3}$. The correct answer is D.

Be careful not to fall for any trap answers: A is the *area* of triangle ABC; B and C are the perimeters of the 2 smaller triangles.

QUESTIONS

ADVANCED PURCHASE DISCOUNTS FOR AIRLINE TRAVEL	
Days Prior to Departure	**Percentage Discount**
0–6 days	0%
7–13 days	10%
14–29 days	25%
30 days or more	40%

20. The table above shows the discount structure for advanced purchase of tickets at a particular airline. A passenger bought a ticket at this airline for $1,050. Had she purchased the ticket one day later, she would have paid $210 more. How many days before her departure did she purchase her ticket?

(A) 6 days
(B) 7 days
(C) 13 days
(D) 14 days
(E) 29 days

MATH EXPLANATIONS

20. **D** If we add up what this passenger actually paid, $1,050, plus the $210 she saved, we get what the purchase price would have been the following day, or $1,260. Now, according to the table, if she had purchased her ticket 6 days before the flight, she would not have saved any money at all, so we can eliminate A. If she bought the ticket 7 days before, she would have saved 10%. Does 10% of $1,260 equal $210? No, so eliminate B. If she purchased her ticket 13 days before the flight, she would not have saved any more money than if she had bought it the next day (12 days before the flight) so we can eliminate choice C. Let's assume she bought the ticket 14 days in advance of the flight for $1,050, which is a $210 saving from what the ticket would have cost her the day after. That means the ticket would have cost $1,260 from days 13 through 7, and $1,400 on day 14. $1,050 is 75% of $1,400, which is the amount of the discount if the ticket had been purchased 14 days in advance, so choice D is correct.

QUESTIONS

21. Unseasonable weather in the months before a wine harvest can cool vineyards in the Bordeaux region enough to affect the overall size of the grapes themselves, create unwanted moisture that can cause mold in some grape varieties and deterioration in others.

(A) to affect the overall size of the grapes themselves, create
(B) to affect the overall size of the grapes themselves, and create
(C) that the overall size of the grapes themselves are affected, create
(D) that it affects the overall size of the grapes themselves, creates
(E) that the size of the grapes are affected and creates

22. It is posited by some scientists that the near extinction of the sap-eating gray bat of northwestern America was caused by government-sponsored logging operations in the early 1920s that greatly reduced the species' habitat.

Which of the following, if true, most strongly weakens the scientists' claims?

(A) Logging operations in the 1920s are widely held responsible for the near extinction of other species that lived in the same area.
(B) A boom in new home construction in the early 1920s led congress to open federal lands to logging operations.
(C) A 5-year drought in the early 1920s severely reduced the output of sap in trees in northwestern America.
(D) Numbers of sightings of sap-eating gray bats fell to their lowest numbers in 1926.
(E) Sightings of sap-eating gray bats in Europe stayed roughly the same during the same period.

VERBAL EXPLANATIONS

21. **B** Go through your checklist of potential errors. Is there a misplaced modifier here? No. Is there a pronoun problem? No. Is there a parallel construction problem? Yes! At first it seems as if this sentence contains a list of three actions: to affect... create...and deteriorate—but wait! The third action is not an action, it's a noun: deterioration. However, since *deterioration* is not underlined, we can't fix this. Going back to the original sentence, it becomes clear that, in fact, there are only two main actions: to affect the overall size of the grapes and (to) create unwanted moisture. To correctly use this compound verb, the original sentence would need an "and" between the verbs. Only choice B gives you this option. Choices C, D, and E use the idiomatic expression "enough that" which is not necessarily wrong, but which would require the word "creating."

22. **C** This is a causal argument. The scientists claim that the bat's near extinction was caused by logging. How do we weaken this argument? By presenting an alternate cause—another reason why the bat almost became extinct. Choices A and B actually strengthen the argument. Choice A says that other species were also threatened with extinction by logging, and choice B gives us a reason the government might have been tempted to agree to logging on federal lands. Choice D is outside the scope of the argument since "sightings" are irrelevant. Choice E also goes outside the scope of the argument by telling us about the bat population on another continent. But choice C gives us an alternate cause for the near extinction of these bats: the sap they depended on for nourishment was severely reduced at the time in question by a five-year drought.

QUESTIONS

23. Upset by the recent downturn in production numbers during the first half of the year, the possibility of adding worker incentives was raised by the board of directors at its quarterly meeting.

(A) the possibility of adding worker incentives was raised by the board of directors at its quarterly meeting
(B) the addition of worker incentives was raised as a possibility by the board of directors at its quarterly meeting
(C) added worker incentives was raised by the board of directors at its quarterly meeting as a possibility
(D) the board of directors raised at its quarterly meeting the possibility of worker incentives being added
(E) the board of directors, at its quarterly meeting, raised the possibility of adding worker incentives

24. Whenever a major airplane accident occurs, there is a dramatic increase in the number of airplane mishaps reported in the media, a phenomenon that may last for as long as a few months after the accident. Airline officials assert that the publicity given the gruesomeness of major airplane accidents focuses media attention on the airline industry, and the increase in the number of reported accidents is caused by an increase in the number of news sources covering airline accidents, not by an increase in the number of accidents.

Which of the following, if true, would seriously weaken the assertions of the airline officials?

(A) The publicity surrounding airline accidents is largely limited to the country in which the crash occurred.
(B) Airline accidents tend to occur far more often during certain peak travel months.
(C) News organizations do not have any guidelines to help them decide how severe an accident must be for it to receive coverage.
(D) Airplane accidents receive coverage by news sources only when the news sources find it advantageous to do so.
(E) Studies by government regulators show that the number of airplane flight miles remains relatively constant from month to month.

VERBAL EXPLANATIONS

23. E This is a misplaced modifier question. Who was "upset by the recent downturn"? It was the board of directors. This eliminates choices A, B, and C. Choice E correctly positions the prepositional phrase "at its quarterly meeting" and avoids the passive phrase "being added" in D.

24. B This is a statistical argument. The officials assert that there is in fact no increase in actual mishaps during the months after an accident, but an increase in the number of news sources *reporting* the mishaps—in other words, they argue that the statistics are not representative. To weaken this assertion, we would have to show that the statistics are in fact representative. B does this by implying that certain months are more likely to have more frequent accidents due to high volume of flights. A is outside the scope of the argument. C, D, and E would all *strengthen* the assertions of the officials.

Questions 25–28 are based on the following passage:

The function of strategic planning is to position a company for long-term growth and expansion in a variety of markets by analyzing its strengths and weaknesses and examining current and potential opportunities. Based on this information, the company develops a strategy for itself. That strategy becomes the basis for supporting strategies for the company's various departments.

This implementation stage is where all too many strategic plans go astray. Recent business management surveys show that most CEOs who have a strategic plan are concerned with the potential breakdown in the implementation of the plan. Unlike corporations in the 1980s that blindly followed their 5-year plans, even when they were misguided, today's corporations tend to second-guess its long-term plans.

Outsiders can help facilitate the process, but in the final analysis, if the company does not make the plan, the company will not follow the plan. This was one of the problems with strategic planning in the 1980s. In that era, strategic planning was an abstract, top-down process involving only a few top corporate officers and hired guns. Number crunching experts came into a company and generated tome-like volumes filled with a mixture of abstruse facts and grand theories which had little to do with the day-to-day realities of the company. Key middle managers were left out of planning sessions, resulting in lost opportunities and ruffled feelings.

However, more hands-on strategic planning can produce startling results. A recent survey queried more than a thousand small-to-medium sized businesses to compare companies with a strategic plan to companies without one. The survey found that companies with strategic plans had annual revenue growth of 6.2 percent as opposed to 3.8 percent for the other companies.

Perhaps most important, a strategic plan helps companies anticipate—and survive—change. New technology and the mobility of capital means that markets can shift faster than ever before. Some financial analysts wonder why companies should bother planning two years ahead when market dynamics might be transformed by next quarter. However, it is this pace of change that makes planning so crucial. Now, more than ever, companies have to stay alert to the marketplace. In an environment of continual and rapid change, long-range planning expands options and organizational flexibility.

QUESTIONS

25. The primary purpose of the passage is to

(A) refute the idea that change is bad for a corporation's long-term health
(B) describe how long-term planning, despite some potential pitfalls, can help a corporation to grow
(C) compare and contrast two styles of corporate planning
(D) evaluate the strategic planning goals of corporate America today
(E) defend a methodology that has come under sharp attack

26. It can be inferred from the passage that strategic planning during the 1980s had all of the following shortcomings EXCEPT

(A) a reliance on outside consultants who did not necessarily understand the nuts and bolts of the business
(B) a dependence on theoretical models that did not always perfectly describe the workings of the company
(C) an inherent weakness in the company's own ability to implement the strategic plan
(D) an excess of information and data that made it difficult to get to key concepts
(E) the lack of a forum for middle managers to express their ideas

VERBAL EXPLANATIONS

25. **B** Most Reading Comprehension passages ask some form of this question characterized by the phrase "primary purpose." Choice B best summarizes the main idea of the passage: that despite some potential problems, strategic planning can allow a company to expand and grow.

26. **C** According to the passage, the difficulty in implementation of strategic plans is a more modern phenomenon, not related to the weaknesses of the 1980s.

QUESTIONS

27. The author most likely mentions the results of the survey of 1,000 companies in order to

(A) put forth an opposing view on strategic plans which is later refuted
(B) illustrate that when strategic planning is "hands-on," it produces uninspiring results
(C) give a concrete example of why strategic planning did not work during the 1980s
(D) support the contention that strategic planning can be very successful when done correctly
(E) give supporting data to prove that many companies have implemented strategic plans

28. The passage suggests which of the following about the "financial analysts" mentioned in lines 44–47 ?

(A) They believe that strategic planning is the key to weathering the rapid changes of the marketplace.
(B) They are working to understand and anticipate market developments that are two years ahead.
(C) Their study of market dynamics has led them to question the reliability of short-term planning strategies.
(D) They might not agree with the author that one way to survive rapidly changing conditions comes from long-range planning.
(E) They consider the mobility of capital to be a necessary condition for the growth of new technology.

VERBAL EXPLANATIONS

27. **D** Skim the passage quickly to find the survey, then read that portion carefully. According to the passage, the survey shows that companies with strategic plans outperformed companies without strategic plans.

28. **D** It's always a good idea to read a few lines above and below the cited lines, just to make sure you understand the context. The financial analysts mentioned in the passage seem to say that it is not worth trying to plan when the market is changing so rapidly. The author mentions their views in order to refute them.

QUESTIONS

29. The Internal Revenue Service has directed that taxpayers who generate no self-employment income can no longer deduct home offices, home office expenses, <u>or nothing that was already</u> depreciated as a business expense the previous year.

(A) or nothing that was already
(B) or that was already
(C) or anything that was already
(D) and anything
(E) and nothing that already was

30. Informed people generally assimilate information from several divergent sources before coming to an opinion. However, most popular news organizations view foreign affairs solely through the eyes of our State Department. In reporting the political crisis in a foreign country, news organizations must endeavor to find alternative sources of information.

Which of the following inferences can be drawn from the argument above?

(A) To the degree that a news source gives an account of another country that mirrors that of our State Department, that reporting is suspect.
(B) To protect their integrity, news media should avoid the influence of State Department releases in their coverage of foreign affairs.
(C) Reporting that is not influenced by the State Department is usually more accurate than are other accounts.
(D) The alternative sources of information mentioned in the passage might not share the same views as the State Department.
(E) A report cannot be seen as influenced by the State Department if it accurately depicts the events in a foreign country.

VERBAL EXPLANATIONS

29. **C** After running down your checklist of potential errors without encountering an ambiguous pronoun, a misplaced modifier, a tense problem, or a subject-verb disagreement, you should begin thinking about the possibility of an idiomatic error. Try making your own sentence: "I no longer deduct…nothing on my taxes." Does that seem right? In fact, it is incorrect: a double negative. Scanning the answer choices can give you a clue as well: You have a choice of "nothing" or "anything." Which is better? If you said "anything," you were absolutely correct. Choice D includes "anything" but begins with the conjunction "and."

30. **D** To get an inference question correct, just look for an answer that you know to be true. Choice A implies that the State Department's views are always likely to diverge from other news sources, which is an extreme answer, and extreme answers are almost always incorrect. B implies that the State Department should never be used as a news source, which is also extreme. Choice C is never mentioned; therefore, it is out of scope. E is wrong because the answer is too extreme. Choice D is the credited answer because the argument makes it clear that the "alternative" sources of information would provide the "divergent" opinions mentioned in the first sentence.

QUESTIONS

31. When automatic teller machines were first installed in the 1980s, bank officials promised they would be faster, more reliable, and less prone to make errors than their human counterparts.

(A) they would be faster, more reliable, and less prone to make errors
(B) they would be faster, more reliable, and that they would be less prone for making errors
(C) the machines would be faster, more reliable, and less prone to errors
(D) the machines were faster, more reliable, and errors would occur much less
(E) faster, more reliable machines, and that errors would be less prone

32. With its plan to create a wildlife sanctuary out of previously unused landfill, Sweden is but one of a number of industrialized nations that is accepting its responsibility to protect endangered species and promote conservation.

(A) is accepting its responsibility to protect endangered species and promote
(B) is accepting its responsibility for protecting endangered species and promoting
(C) are accepting its responsibility to protect endangered species and promoting
(D) are accepting of their responsibility to protect endangered species and to promote
(E) are accepting their responsibility to protect endangered species and promote

VERBAL EXPLANATIONS

31. **C** Go through your checklist of potential errors. Is there a misplaced modifier here? No. Is there a pronoun problem? There certainly is a pronoun here, so be sure to check it out. Is it possible that the "they" could be ambiguous? As a matter of fact, "they" is obviously supposed to refer to the automatic teller machines, but it also could refer to the bank officials. Replacing "they" with "the machines" clarifies the sentence, which means we are down to C, D, or E, but C is correct because D and E are not parallel.

32. **E** This is a subject-verb question. The verb *is* in the underlined portion seems to agree with the subject of the sentence, *Sweden*, but in fact, the noun *is* must agree with *nations*, which is plural. We're down to C, D, or E. C keeps the singular pronoun *its,* so we can eliminate that. Choice D contains the unidiomatic *accepting of,* making E the credited answer.

QUESTIONS

33. A decade after a logging operation in India began cutting down trees in a territory that serves as a sanctuary for Bengal tigers, the incidence of tigers attacking humans in nearby villages has increased by 300 percent. Because the logging operation has reduced the number of acres of woodland per tiger on average from 15 acres to approximately 12 acres, scientists have theorized that tigers must need a minimum number of acres of woodland in order to remain content.

Which of the following statements, if true, would most strengthen the scientists' hypothesis?

(A) In other wildlife areas in India where the number of acres of woodland per tiger remains at least 15 acres, there has been no increase in the number of tiger attacks on humans.
(B) Before the logging operation began, there were many fewer humans living in the area.
(C) The largest number of acres per tiger before the logging operation began was 32 acres per tiger in one area of the sanctuary, whereas the smallest number of acres per tiger after the logging operation was 9 acres.
(D) Other species of wild animals have begun competing with the Bengal tigers for the dwindling food supply.
(E) The Bengal tiger has become completely extinct in other areas of Asia.

VERBAL EXPLANATIONS

33. **A** In this causal argument, the decrease in the number of acres of woodland per tiger is said to cause the increasing number of tiger attacks on humans. To strengthen this argument, it would help if the Bengal tigers in areas with a normal number of acres of woodland per tiger have NOT increased their attacks on humans. That's what A tells us. B gives us an alternate cause for the increase in tiger attacks—in other words, it weakens the argument instead of strengthening it. Choice C adds details without really strengthening the argument. Choice D weakens the scientists' hypothesis by presenting a possible alternate cause for the tigers' attacks on humans. Choice E emphasizes the seriousness of the problem without shedding light on its cause.

34. The machine press union and company management were not able to communicate effectively, and it was a major cause of the 1999 strike in Seattle.

(A) The machine press union and company management were not able to communicate effectively, and it
(B) Communications between the machine press union and company management were not effective, and it
(C) For the machine press union and company management, to be unable to communicate effectively
(D) The inability of the machine press union and company management to communicate effectively
(E) The machine press union, being unable to communicate effectively with company management,

34. D The tip-off here is the pronoun *it*. To what does *it* refer? Not the union nor the management. Really what *it* seems to refer to is the inability of the two sides to communicate. We can eliminate A and B for that reason. C seems to indicate that it was effective communication that led to the strike. E is both awkward and unidiomatic. Choice D is the correct response.

35. A greater number of fresh vegetables are sold in City *X* than in City *Y*. Therefore, the people in City *X* have better nutritional habits than those in City *Y*.

Each of the following, if true, weakens the conclusion above EXCEPT:

(A) City *X* has more people living in it than City *Y*.
(B) Most of the people in City *Y* work in City *X* and buy their vegetables there.
(C) The people in City *X* buy many of their vegetables as decorations, not to eat.
(D) The per capita consumption of junk food in City *X* is three times that of City *Y*.
(E) The average price per pound of vegetables in City *Y* is lower than the average price per pound of vegetables in City *X*.

35. E We are looking for an answer that does NOT weaken the argument. You might think that means the correct answer would *strengthen* the argument, but while that COULD be the case, it doesn't have to be. The correct answer might simply be irrelevant to the argument. In this causal argument, more fresh vegetable sales in City *X* are said to mean that City *X* has better nutritional habits than City *Y*. Each of the answer choices pokes holes in that argument, except for E. It suggests that if vegetables are cheaper in City *Y*, and yet more vegetables are being sold in City *X*, then the argument that *X* has better nutritional habits might be right.

QUESTIONS

36. Heavy metals, toxic waste by-products that can cause tumors in fish, are generally found in the waters off industrial shorelines, but have been discovered in trace amounts even in the relatively pristine waters of the South Pacific.

(A) are generally found in the waters off industrial shorelines, but have been discovered in trace amounts even
(B) are generally to be found in the waters off industrial shorelines, and have even been discovered in trace amounts
(C) can, in general, be found in the waters off industrial shorelines, and have been discovered in trace amounts even
(D) had generally been found in the waters off industrial shorelines, but have even been discovered in trace amounts
(E) are found generally in the waters off industrial shorelines, but have been discovered in a trace amount even

VERBAL EXPLANATIONS

36. **A** In both B and C, the conjunction *and* wrongly gives the impression that the second half of the sentence is merely an added thought, instead of a new and dangerous development that goes beyond what *generally* happens. D needlessly changes the verb tense. E's *in a trace amount* does not agree with the plural *heavy metals*.

Questions 37–40 are based on the following passage:

In Roman times, defeated enemies were generally put to death as criminals for having offended the emperor of Rome. In the Middle Ages, however, the practice of ransoming, or returning prisoners in exchange for money, became common. Though some saw this custom as a step toward a more humane society, the primary reasons behind it were economic rather than humanitarian.

In those times, rulers had only a limited ability to raise taxes. They could neither force their subjects to fight nor pay them to do so. The promise of material compensation in the form of goods and ransom was therefore the only way of inducing combatants to participate in a war. In the Middle Ages, the predominant incentive for the individual soldier was the expectation of spoils. Although collecting ransom clearly brought financial gain, keeping a prisoner and arranging for his exchange had its costs. Consequently, procedures were devised to reduce transaction costs.

One such device was a rule asserting that the prisoner had to assess his own value. This compelled the prisoner to establish a value without too much distortion; indicating too low a value would increase the captive's chances of being killed, while indicating too high a value would either ruin him financially or create a prohibitively expensive ransom that would also result in death.

37. The primary purpose of the passage is to

(A) discuss the economic basis of the medieval practice of exchanging prisoners for ransom
(B) examine the history of the treatment of prisoners of war
(C) emphasize the importance of a warrior's code of honor during the Middle Ages
(D) explore a way of reducing the costs of ransom
(E) demonstrate why warriors of the Middle Ages looked forward to battles

37. A Choice A best summarizes the main idea of the first paragraph. While D reflects a part of the passage, it does not encompass the main idea of the passage.

QUESTIONS

38. It can be inferred from the passage that a medieval soldier

    (A) was less likely to kill captured members of opposing armies than was a soldier of the Roman Empire
    (B) operated on a basically independent level and was motivated solely by economic incentives
    (C) had few economic options and chose to fight because it was the only way to earn an adequate living
    (D) was motivated to spare prisoners' lives by humanitarian rather than economic ideals
    (E) had no respect for his captured enemies since captives were typically regarded as weak

39. Which of the following best describes the change in policy from executing prisoners in Roman times to ransoming prisoners in the Middle Ages?

    (A) The emperors of Rome demanded more respect than did medieval rulers, and thus Roman subjects went to greater lengths to defend their nation.
    (B) It was a reflection of the lesser degree of direct control medieval rulers had over their subjects.
    (C) It became a show of strength and honor for warriors of the Middle Ages to be able to capture and return their enemies.
    (D) Medieval soldiers were not as humanitarian as their ransoming practices might have indicated.
    (E) Medieval soldiers demonstrated more concern about economic policy than did their Roman counterparts.

VERBAL EXPLANATIONS

38. **A** The first paragraph gives us the information to answer this question. Note the trigger word *however* that underscores the difference between the Roman era and the Middle Ages.

39. **B** The best answer can be found in the first line of the second paragraph. Ransom was one of the few ways a ruler could give his subjects what they wanted to get them to do something *he* wanted.

QUESTIONS

40. The author uses the phrase "without too much distortion" (lines 24–25) in order to

(A) indicate that prisoners would fairly assess their worth
(B) emphasize the important role medieval prisoners played in determining whether they should be ransomed
(C) explain how prisoners often paid more than an appropriate ransom in order to increase their chances for survival
(D) suggest that captors and captives often had understanding relationships
(E) show that when in prison a soldier's view could become distorted

VERBAL EXPLANATIONS

40. **A** To get the answer, we have to understand the meaning of the quoted words, but it also helps to read the rest of the paragraph. The paragraph describes a ransom value that was neither too low nor too high, therefore making A the best answer choice.

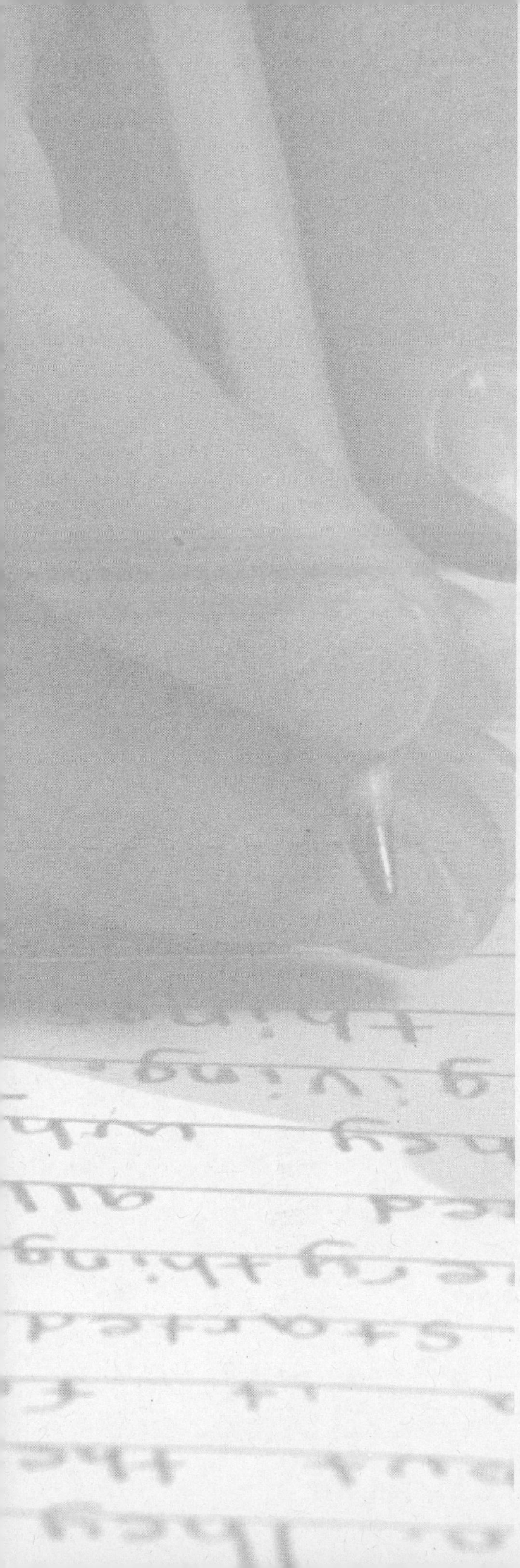

Part VIII The Princeton Review GMAT Math and Verbal Practice Bins and Explanations

Chapter 25 GMAT Math and Verbal Practice Bins

Once you know your current scoring level from taking the Warm-Up Test, use the "bins" in the following pages to improve your performance.

If you got six or fewer math questions correct on the Warm-Up Test, start by practicing with the problems in Math Bin 1. If you got 6–13 math questions correct on the Warm-Up Test, start by practicing with the problems in Math Bin 2. If you got 14 or more math questions correct, practice with the problems in Math Bins 3 and 4.

If you got six or fewer verbal questions correct on the Warm-up Test, start by practicing with the problems in Verbal Bin 1. If you got 6–13 verbal questions correct on the Warm-Up Test, start by practicing with the problems in Verbal Bin 2. If you got 14 or more verbal questions correct, practice with the problems in Verbal Bin 3.

Math Test
Bin 1—Easier Questions
26 Questions

This test is composed of both problem solving questions and data sufficiency questions.

Problem Solving Directions: Solve each problem and choose the best of the answer choices provided.

Data Sufficiency Directions: Each data sufficiency problem consists of a question and two statements, labeled (1) and (2), which contain certain data. Using these data and your knowledge of mathematics and everyday facts (such as the number of days in July or the meaning of *counterclockwise*), decide whether the data given are sufficient for answering the question and then indicate one of the following answer choices:

(A) Statement (1) ALONE is sufficient, but statement (2) alone is not sufficient.

(B) Statement (2) ALONE is sufficient, but statement (1) alone is not sufficient.

(C) BOTH statements TOGETHER are sufficient, but NEITHER statement ALONE is sufficient.

(D) EACH statement ALONE is sufficient.

(E) Statements (1) and (2) TOGETHER are not sufficient.

---

1. What percent of 112 is 14 ?

(A) 0.125%
(B) 8%
(C) 12.5%
(D) 125%
(E) 800%

2. The number of flights leaving a certain airport doubles during every one-hour period between 9 A.M. and noon; after noon, the number of flights leaving from the airport doubles during every two-hour period. If 4 flights left from the airport between 9 and 10 A.M., how many flights left the airport between 2 and 4 P.M.?

(A) 32
(B) 48
(C) 64
(D) 128
(E) 256

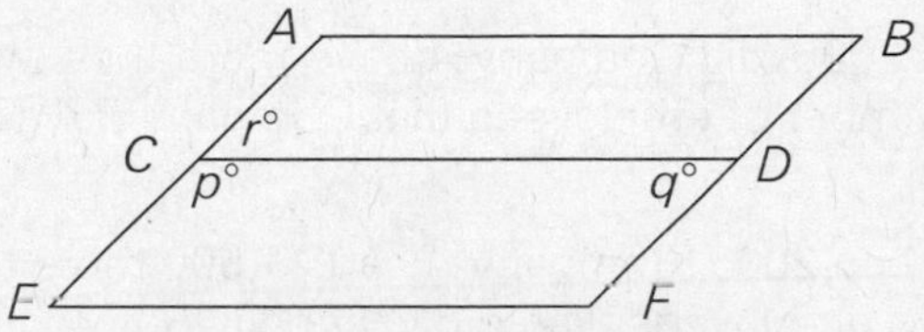

3. If both *ABDC* and *CDFE* are parallelograms, what is $q + r$?

(1) $r = 70$

(2) $p = 110$

(A) Statement (1) ALONE is sufficient, but statement (2) alone is not sufficient.
(B) Statement (2) ALONE is sufficient, but statement (1) alone is not sufficient.
(C) BOTH statements TOGETHER are sufficient, but NEITHER statement ALONE is sufficient.
(D) EACH statement ALONE is sufficient.
(E) Statements (1) and (2) TOGETHER are not sufficient.

GO ON TO THE NEXT PAGE.

4. Chris's convertible gets gas mileage that is 40 percent greater than that of Stan's SUV. If Harry's hatchback gets gas mileage that is 15 percent greater than that of Chris's convertible, then Harry's hatchback gets gas mileage that is what percent greater than that of Stan's SUV?

(A) 25%
(B) 46%
(C) 55%
(D) 61%
(E) 66%

5. If x is equal to 1 more than the product of 3 and z, and y is equal to 1 less than the product of 2 and z, then $2x$ is how much greater than $3y$ when z is 4 ?

(A) 1
(B) 2
(C) 3
(D) 5
(E) 6

6. In 2005, did Company *A* have more than twice the number of employees that Company *B* did?

(1) In 2005, Company *A* had 11,500 more employees than did Company *B*.

(2) In 2005, the 3,000 employees with advanced degrees at Company *A* made up 12.5 percent of that company's total number employees, and the 2,500 employees with advanced degrees at Company *B* made up 20 percent of that company's total number of employees.

(A) Statement (1) ALONE is sufficient, but statement (2) alone is not sufficient.
(B) Statement (2) ALONE is sufficient, but statement (1) alone is not sufficient.
(C) BOTH statements TOGETHER are sufficient, but NEITHER statement ALONE is sufficient.
(D) EACH statement ALONE is sufficient.
(E) Statements (1) and (2) TOGETHER are not sufficient.

7. Is x^3 equal to 125 ?

(1) $x > 4$

(2) $x < 6$

(A) Statement (1) ALONE is sufficient, but statement (2) alone is not sufficient.
(B) Statement (2) ALONE is sufficient, but statement (1) alone is not sufficient.
(C) BOTH statements TOGETHER are sufficient, but NEITHER statement ALONE is sufficient.
(D) EACH statement ALONE is sufficient.
(E) Statements (1) and (2) TOGETHER are not sufficient.

8. Bob leaves point *A* and drives due west to point *B*. From point *B*, he drives due south to point *C*. How far is Bob from his original location?

(1) Point *A* is 24 miles from point *B*.

(2) Point *B* is 18 miles from point *C*.

(A) Statement (1) ALONE is sufficient, but statement (2) alone is not sufficient.
(B) Statement (2) ALONE is sufficient, but statement (1) alone is not sufficient.
(C) BOTH statements TOGETHER are sufficient, but NEITHER statement ALONE is sufficient.
(D) EACH statement ALONE is sufficient.
(E) Statements (1) and (2) TOGETHER are not sufficient.

GO ON TO THE NEXT PAGE.

9. The formula $M = \sqrt{l^2 + w^2 + d^2}$ describes the relationship between the length of M, which is the longest line that can be drawn in a rectangular solid, and the length, l, width, w, and depth, d, of that rectangular solid. The longest line that can be drawn in a rectangular solid with a length of 12, a width of 4, and a depth of 3 is how much longer than the longest line that can drawn in a rectangular solid with a length of 6, a width of 3, and a depth of 2 ?

(A) 5
(B) 6
(C) 7
(D) 9
(E) 13

10. Is the average (arithmetic mean) of a, b, and c equal to 8 ?

(1) Three times the sum of a, b, and c is equal to 72.

(2) The sum of $2a$, $2b$, and $2c$ is equal to 48.

(A) Statement (1) ALONE is sufficient, but statement (2) alone is not sufficient.
(B) Statement (2) ALONE is sufficient, but statement (1) alone is not sufficient.
(C) BOTH statements TOGETHER are sufficient, but NEITHER statement ALONE is sufficient.
(D) EACH statement ALONE is sufficient.
(E) Statements (1) and (2) TOGETHER are not sufficient.

11. $\sqrt{\sqrt{\left(1 + \frac{17}{64}\right)}} =$

(A) $\frac{\sqrt{34}}{8}$

(B) $\frac{3\sqrt{2}}{4}$

(C) $\frac{9}{8}$

(D) $\frac{\sqrt{68}}{4}$

(E) $\frac{3\sqrt{2}}{2}$

12. A certain stadium is currently full to $\frac{13}{16}$ of its maximum seating capacity. What is the maximum seating capacity of the stadium?

(1) If 1,250 people were to enter the stadium, the stadium would be full to $\frac{15}{16}$ of its maximum seating capacity.

(2) If 2,500 people were to leave the stadium, the stadium would be full to $\frac{9}{16}$ of its maximum seating capacity.

(A) Statement (1) ALONE is sufficient, but statement (2) alone is not sufficient.
(B) Statement (2) ALONE is sufficient, but statement (1) alone is not sufficient.
(C) BOTH statements TOGETHER are sufficient, but NEITHER statement ALONE is sufficient.
(D) EACH statement ALONE is sufficient.
(E) Statements (1) and (2) TOGETHER are not sufficient.

GO ON TO THE NEXT PAGE.

13. Andre has already saved $\frac{3}{7}$ of the cost of a new car, and he has calculated that he will be able to save $\frac{2}{5}$ of the remaining amount before the end of the summer. What fraction of the cost of the new car will he still need to save after the end of the summer?

(A) $\frac{6}{35}$

(B) $\frac{8}{35}$

(C) $\frac{12}{35}$

(D) $\frac{23}{35}$

(E) $\frac{29}{35}$

$\{1, 4, 6, y\}$

14. If the average (arithmetic mean) of the set of numbers above is 6, then what is the median?

(A) 5
(B) 6
(C) 7
(D) 13
(E) 24

15. A store sells a six-pack of soda for $2.70. If this represents a savings of 10 percent of the individual price of cans of soda, then what is the price of a single can of soda?

(A) $ 0.35
(B) $ 0.40
(C) $ 0.45
(D) $ 0.50
(E) $ 0.55

16. If Beth spent $400 of her earnings last month on rent, how much did Beth earn last month?

(1) Beth saved $\frac{1}{3}$ of her earnings last month and spent half of the remainder on rent.

(2) Beth earned twice as much this month as last month.

(A) Statement (1) ALONE is sufficient, but statement (2) alone is not sufficient.
(B) Statement (2) ALONE is sufficient, but statement (1) alone is not sufficient.
(C) BOTH statements TOGETHER are sufficient, but NEITHER statement ALONE is sufficient.
(D) EACH statement ALONE is sufficient.
(E) Statements (1) and (2) TOGETHER are not sufficient.

17. If n is an integer, is n even?

(1) $2n$ is an even integer.

(2) $n - 1$ is an odd integer.

(A) Statement (1) ALONE is sufficient, but statement (2) alone is not sufficient.
(B) Statement (2) ALONE is sufficient, but statement (1) alone is not sufficient.
(C) BOTH statements TOGETHER are sufficient, but NEITHER statement ALONE is sufficient.
(D) EACH statement ALONE is sufficient.
(E) Statements (1) and (2) TOGETHER are not sufficient.

GO ON TO THE NEXT PAGE.

18. At apartment complex Z, 30 percent of the residents are men over the age of 18, and 40 percent are women over the age of 18. If there are 24 children living in the complex, how many total residents live in apartment complex Z?

(A) 32
(B) 80
(C) 94
(D) 112
(E) 124

19. Over the course of a soccer season, 30 percent of the players on a team scored goals. What is the ratio of players on the team who scored goals to those who did not?

(A) 3 to 10
(B) 1 to 3
(C) 3 to 7
(D) 1 to 1
(E) 3 to 1

20. At a restaurant, Luis left a tip for his waiter equal to 20 percent of his entire dinner check, including tax. What was the amount of the dinner check?

(1) The sum of the dinner check and the tip was $16.80.

(2) Luis's tip consisted of two bills and four coins.

(A) Statement (1) ALONE is sufficient, but statement (2) alone is not sufficient.
(B) Statement (2) ALONE is sufficient, but statement (1) alone is not sufficient.
(C) BOTH statements TOGETHER are sufficient, but NEITHER statement ALONE is sufficient.
(D) EACH statement ALONE is sufficient.
(E) Statements (1) and (2) TOGETHER are not sufficient.

21. Which sport utility vehicle has a higher list price, the Touristo or the Leisure?

(1) The list price of the Leisure is $\frac{5}{6}$ the list price of the Touristo.

(2) The list price of the Touristo is 1.2 times the list price of the Leisure.

(A) Statement (1) ALONE is sufficient, but statement (2) alone is not sufficient.
(B) Statement (2) ALONE is sufficient, but statement (1) alone is not sufficient.
(C) BOTH statements TOGETHER are sufficient, but NEITHER statement ALONE is sufficient.
(D) EACH statement ALONE is sufficient.
(E) Statements (1) and (2) TOGETHER are not sufficient.

GO ON TO THE NEXT PAGE.

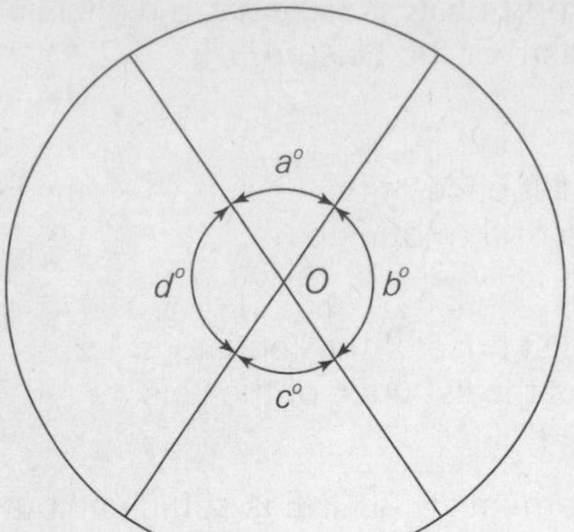

22. In the circle above, center O is intersected by 2 straight lines, and $3a = b$. What is the value of $b - a$?

(A) 2
(B) 30
(C) 45
(D) 90
(E) 135

23. What is the value of integer w ?

(1) w is a multiple of 3.

(2) $420 < w < 425$

(A) Statement (1) ALONE is sufficient, but statement (2) alone is not sufficient.
(B) Statement (2) ALONE is sufficient, but statement (1) alone is not sufficient.
(C) BOTH statements TOGETHER are sufficient, but NEITHER statement ALONE is sufficient.
(D) EACH statement ALONE is sufficient.
(E) Statements (1) and (2) TOGETHER are not sufficient.

24. What is the quotient when 0.25% of 600 is divided by 0.25 of 600 ?

(A) 10
(B) 1
(C) 0.1
(D) 0.01
(E) 0.001

25. A certain town's economic development council has 21 members. If the number of females on the council is 3 less than 3 times the number of males on the council, then the town's economic development council has how many male members?

(A) 5
(B) 6
(C) 7
(D) 9
(E) 15

26. Roger can chop down 4 trees in an hour. How long does it take Vincent to chop down 4 trees?

(1) Vincent spends 6 hours per day chopping down trees.

(2) Vincent takes twice as long as Roger to chop down trees.

(A) Statement (1) ALONE is sufficient, but statement (2) alone is not sufficient.
(B) Statement (2) ALONE is sufficient, but statement (1) alone is not sufficient.
(C) BOTH statements TOGETHER are sufficient, but NEITHER statement ALONE is sufficient.
(D) EACH statement ALONE is sufficient.
(E) Statements (1) and (2) TOGETHER are not sufficient.

GO ON TO THE NEXT PAGE.

Math Test
Bin 2—Medium Questions
27 Questions

This test is composed of both problem solving questions and data sufficiency questions.

Problem Solving Directions: Solve each problem and choose the best of the answer choices provided.

Data Sufficiency Directions: Each data sufficiency problem consists of a question and two statements, labeled (1) and (2), which contain certain data. Using these data and your knowledge of mathematics and everyday facts (such as the number of days in July or the meaning of *counterclockwise*), decide whether the data given are sufficient for answering the question and then indicate one of the following answer choices:

(A) Statement (1) ALONE is sufficient, but statement (2) alone is not sufficient.

(B) Statement (2) ALONE is sufficient, but statement (1) alone is not sufficient.

(C) BOTH statements TOGETHER are sufficient, but NEITHER statement ALONE is sufficient.

(D) EACH statement ALONE is sufficient.

(E) Statements (1) and (2) TOGETHER are not sufficient.

---

1. If $x = \dfrac{\frac{5}{9}+\frac{15}{27}+\frac{45}{81}}{3}$, then $\sqrt{1-x} =$

(A) $\dfrac{\sqrt{5}}{9}$

(B) $\dfrac{5}{9}$

(C) $\dfrac{2}{3}$

(D) $\dfrac{\sqrt{5}}{3}$

(E) $\dfrac{15}{9}$

2. Steven has run a certain number of laps around a track at an average (arithmetic mean) time per lap of 51 seconds. If he runs one additional lap in 39 seconds and reduces his average time per lap to 49 seconds, how many laps did he run at an average time per lap of 51 seconds?

(A) 2
(B) 5
(C) 6
(D) 10
(E) 12

3. $200^2 - 2(200)(199) + 199^2 =$

(A) −79,201
(B) −200
(C) 1
(D) 200
(E) 79,999

GO ON TO THE NEXT PAGE.

4. If $x \neq \frac{1}{2}$, then $\frac{6x^2+11x-7}{2x-1} =$

(A) $3x + 7$
(B) $3x - 7$
(C) $3x + 1$
(D) $x + 7$
(E) $x - 7$

5. If Amy drove the distance from her home to the beach in less than 2 hours, was her average speed greater than 60 miles per hour?

(1) The distance that Amy drove from her home to the beach was less than 125 miles.

(2) The distance that Amy drove from her home to the beach was greater than 122 miles.

(A) Statement (1) ALONE is sufficient, but statement (2) alone is not sufficient.
(B) Statement (2) ALONE is sufficient, but statement (1) alone is not sufficient.
(C) BOTH statements TOGETHER are sufficient, but NEITHER statement ALONE is sufficient.
(D) EACH statement ALONE is sufficient.
(E) Statements (1) and (2) TOGETHER are not sufficient.

6. If $x = m - 1$, which of the following is true when $m = \frac{1}{2}$?

(A) $x^0 > x^2 > x^3 > x^1$
(B) $x^0 > x^2 > x^1 > x^3$
(C) $x^0 > x^1 > x^2 > x^3$
(D) $x^2 > x^0 > x^3 > x^1$
(E) $x^3 > x^2 > x^1 > x^0$

7. If a comedian plays two shows and twice as many tickets are available for the evening show as for the afternoon show, what percentage of the total number of tickets available for both shows have been sold?

(1) A total of 450 tickets are available for both shows.

(2) Exactly $\frac{3}{5}$ of the tickets available for the afternoon show have been sold, and exactly $\frac{1}{5}$ of the tickets available for the evening show have been sold.

(A) Statement (1) ALONE is sufficient, but statement (2) alone is not sufficient.
(B) Statement (2) ALONE is sufficient, but statement (1) alone is not sufficient.
(C) BOTH statements TOGETHER are sufficient, but NEITHER statement ALONE is sufficient.
(D) EACH statement ALONE is sufficient.
(E) Statements (1) and (2) TOGETHER are not sufficient.

8. If $\frac{1}{y} = 2\frac{2}{3}$, then $\left(\frac{1}{y+1}\right)^2 =$

(A) $\frac{9}{64}$
(B) $\frac{3}{8}$
(C) $\frac{64}{121}$
(D) $\frac{121}{64}$
(E) $\frac{64}{9}$

GO ON TO THE NEXT PAGE.

9. An operation $\sim$ is defined by $a \sim b = \dfrac{a+b}{(ab)^2}$ for all numbers a and b such that $ab \neq 0$. If $c \neq 0$ and $a \sim c = 0$, then $c =$

(A) $-a$

(B) 0

(C) $\sqrt{a}$

(D) a

(E) a^2

10. If x is a positive integer, is the greatest common factor of 150 and x a prime number?

(1) x is a prime number.

(2) $x < 4$

(A) Statement (1) ALONE is sufficient, but statement (2) alone is not sufficient.
(B) Statement (2) ALONE is sufficient, but statement (1) alone is not sufficient.
(C) BOTH statements TOGETHER are sufficient, but NEITHER statement ALONE is sufficient.
(D) EACH statement ALONE is sufficient.
(E) Statements (1) and (2) TOGETHER are not sufficient.

$X = \{9, 10, 11, 12\}$

$Y = \{2, 3, 4, 5\}$

11. If one number is chosen at random from each of the sets above and the number from Set X is divided by the number from Set Y, what is the probability that the result is an integer?

(A) $\dfrac{1}{16}$

(B) $\dfrac{3}{8}$

(C) $\dfrac{1}{2}$

(D) $\dfrac{3}{4}$

(E) $\dfrac{15}{16}$

12. If p and q are integers, is $\dfrac{p+q}{2}$ an integer?

(1) $p < 17$

(2) $p = q$

(A) Statement (1) ALONE is sufficient, but statement (2) alone is not sufficient.
(B) Statement (2) ALONE is sufficient, but statement (1) alone is not sufficient.
(C) BOTH statements TOGETHER are sufficient, but NEITHER statement ALONE is sufficient.
(D) EACH statement ALONE is sufficient.
(E) Statements (1) and (2) TOGETHER are not sufficient.

GO ON TO THE NEXT PAGE.

13. A perfectly spherical satellite with a radius of 4 feet is being packed for shipment to its launch site. If the inside dimensions of the rectangular crates available for shipment, when measured in feet, are consecutive even integers, then what is the volume of the smallest available crate that can be used? (Note: the volume of a sphere is given by the equation $V = \frac{4}{3}\pi r^3$.)

(A) 48
(B) 192
(C) 480
(D) 960
(E) 1,680

14. Richard is 6 years older than David, and David is 8 years older than Scott. In 8 years, if Richard will be twice as old as Scott, then how old was David 4 years ago?

(A) 8
(B) 10
(C) 12
(D) 14
(E) 16

15. What is the value of x?

(1) $x^2 - 5x + 4 = 0$

(2) x is not prime.

(A) Statement (1) ALONE is sufficient, but statement (2) alone is not sufficient.
(B) Statement (2) ALONE is sufficient, but statement (1) alone is not sufficient.
(C) BOTH statements TOGETHER are sufficient, but NEITHER statement ALONE is sufficient.
(D) EACH statement ALONE is sufficient.
(E) Statements (1) and (2) TOGETHER are not sufficient.

16. Sam and Jessica are invited to a dance. If there are 7 men and 7 women in total at the dance, and one woman and one man are chosen to lead the dance, what is the probability that Sam and Jessica will NOT be the pair chosen to lead the dance?

(A) $\frac{1}{49}$

(B) $\frac{1}{7}$

(C) $\frac{6}{7}$

(D) $\frac{47}{49}$

(E) $\frac{48}{49}$

17. What is the surface area of rectangular solid Y ?

(1) The dimensions of one face of rectangular solid Y are 2 by 3.

(2) The volume of rectangular solid Y is 12.

(A) Statement (1) ALONE is sufficient, but statement (2) alone is not sufficient.
(B) Statement (2) ALONE is sufficient, but statement (1) alone is not sufficient.
(C) BOTH statements TOGETHER are sufficient, but NEITHER statement ALONE is sufficient.
(D) EACH statement ALONE is sufficient.
(E) Statements (1) and (2) TOGETHER are not sufficient.

GO ON TO THE NEXT PAGE.

18. A six-sided die with faces numbered one through six is rolled three times. What is the probability that the face with the number 6 on it will NOT be facing upward on all three rolls?

(A) $\frac{1}{216}$
(B) $\frac{1}{6}$
(C) $\frac{2}{3}$
(D) $\frac{17}{18}$
(E) $\frac{215}{216}$

19. What is the sum of x, y, and z?

(1) $2x + y + 3z = 45$

(2) $x + 2y = 30$

(A) Statement (1) ALONE is sufficient, but statement (2) alone is not sufficient.
(B) Statement (2) ALONE is sufficient, but statement (1) alone is not sufficient.
(C) BOTH statements TOGETHER are sufficient, but NEITHER statement ALONE is sufficient.
(D) EACH statement ALONE is sufficient.
(E) Statements (1) and (2) TOGETHER are not sufficient.

20. A department store receives a shipment of 1,000 shirts, for which it pays $9,000. The store sells the shirts at a price 80 percent above cost for one month, after which it reduces the price of the shirts to 20 percent above cost. The store sells 75 percent of the shirts during the first month and 50 percent of the remaining shirts afterward. How much gross income did sales of the shirts generate?

(A) $10,000
(B) $10,800
(C) $12,150
(D) $13,500
(E) $16,200

21. David has three credit cards: a Passport card, an EverywhereCard, and an American Local card. He owes balances on all three cards. Does he owe the greatest balance on the EverywhereCard?

(1) The sum of the balances on his EverywhereCard and American Local card is $1,350, which is three times the balance on his Passport card.

(2) The balance on his EverywhereCard is $\frac{4}{3}$ of the balance on his Passport card and $\frac{4}{5}$ of the balance on his American Local card.

(A) Statement (1) ALONE is sufficient, but statement (2) alone is not sufficient.
(B) Statement (2) ALONE is sufficient, but statement (1) alone is not sufficient.
(C) BOTH statements TOGETHER are sufficient, but NEITHER statement ALONE is sufficient.
(D) EACH statement ALONE is sufficient.
(E) Statements (1) and (2) TOGETHER are not sufficient.

GO ON TO THE NEXT PAGE.

22. Automobile *A* is traveling at two-thirds the speed that Automobile *B* is traveling. At what speed is Automobile *A* traveling?

(1) If both automobiles increased their speed by 10 miles per hour, Automobile *A* would be traveling at three-quarters the speed that Automobile *B* would be traveling.

(2) If both automobiles decreased their speed by 10 miles per hour, Automobile *A* would be traveling at half the speed that Automobile *B* would be traveling.

(A) Statement (1) ALONE is sufficient, but statement (2) alone is not sufficient.
(B) Statement (2) ALONE is sufficient, but statement (1) alone is not sufficient.
(C) BOTH statements TOGETHER are sufficient, but NEITHER statement ALONE is sufficient.
(D) EACH statement ALONE is sufficient.
(E) Statements (1) and (2) TOGETHER are not sufficient.

23. a and b are nonzero integers such that $0.35a = 0.2b$. What is the value of b in terms of a ?

(A) $0.07a$
(B) $0.57a$
(C) $0.7a$
(D) $1.75a$
(E) $17.5a$

24. The Binary Ice Cream Shoppe sells two flavors of cones, vanilla and chocolate. On Friday, the ratio of vanilla cones sold to chocolate cones sold was 2 to 3. If the store sold 4 more vanilla cones, the ratio of vanilla cones sold to chocolate cones sold would have been 3 to 4. How many vanilla cones did the store sell on Friday?

(A) 32
(B) 35
(C) 42
(D) 48
(E) 54

25. Is integer a a prime number?

(1) $2a$ has exactly three factors.

(2) a is an even number.

(A) Statement (1) ALONE is sufficient, but statement (2) alone is not sufficient.
(B) Statement (2) ALONE is sufficient, but statement (1) alone is not sufficient.
(C) BOTH statements TOGETHER are sufficient, but NEITHER statement ALONE is sufficient.
(D) EACH statement ALONE is sufficient.
(E) Statements (1) and (2) TOGETHER are not sufficient.

26. Renee rides her bicycle 20 miles in m minutes. If she rides x miles in 10 minutes at the same rate, which of the following is an expression for x, in terms of m ?

(A) $\frac{m}{200}$

(B) $\frac{m}{20}$

(C) $\frac{m}{2}$

(D) $2m$

(E) $\frac{200}{m}$

27. If s and w are integers, is $\frac{w}{5}$ an integer?

(1) $4s + 2$ is divisible by 5.

(2) $w + 3 = 4s$

(A) Statement (1) ALONE is sufficient, but statement (2) alone is not sufficient.
(B) Statement (2) ALONE is sufficient, but statement (1) alone is not sufficient.
(C) BOTH statements TOGETHER are sufficient, but NEITHER statement ALONE is sufficient.
(D) EACH statement ALONE is sufficient.
(E) Statements (1) and (2) TOGETHER are not sufficient.

Math Test
Bin 3—Medium-Hard Questions
26 Questions

This test is composed of both problem solving questions and data sufficiency questions.

Problem Solving Directions: Solve each problem and choose the best of the answer choices provided.

Data Sufficiency Directions: Each data sufficiency problem consists of a question and two statements, labeled (1) and (2), which contain certain data. Using these data and your knowledge of mathematics and everyday facts (such as the number of days in July or the meaning of *counterclockwise*), decide whether the data given are sufficient for answering the question and then indicate one of the following answer choices:

(A) Statement (1) ALONE is sufficient, but statement (2) alone is not sufficient.

(B) Statement (2) ALONE is sufficient, but statement (1) alone is not sufficient.

(C) BOTH statements TOGETHER are sufficient, but NEITHER statement ALONE is sufficient.

(D) EACH statement ALONE is sufficient.

(E) Statements (1) and (2) TOGETHER are not sufficient.

---

1. An electronics store normally sells all its merchandise at a 10 percent to 30 percent discount from the suggested retail price. During a sale, if the store were to deduct an additional 20 percent from the discounted price, what is the lowest price possible for an item with a suggested retail price of $260 ?

(A) $130.00
(B) $145.60
(C) $163.80
(D) $182.00
(E) $210.00

2. A certain gas station discounts the price per gallon of all gasoline purchased after the first 10 gallons by 10 percent. The total per gallon discount for 25 gallons of gas purchased at this station is what percent of the total per gallon discount for 20 gallons of gas?

(A) 80%
(B) 100%
(C) 116.7%
(D) 120%
(E) 140%

GO ON TO THE NEXT PAGE.

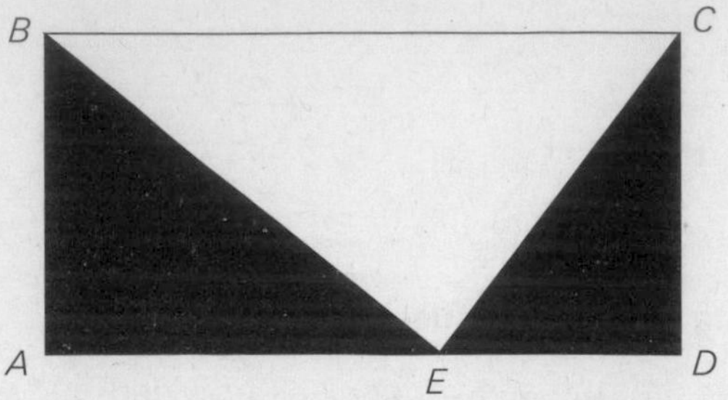

3. What is the area of the shaded region in the figure shown above?

(1) The area of rectangle *ABCD* is 54.

(2) $AE = 2ED$

(A) Statement (1) ALONE is sufficient, but statement (2) alone is not sufficient.
(B) Statement (2) ALONE is sufficient, but statement (1) alone is not sufficient.
(C) BOTH statements TOGETHER are sufficient, but NEITHER statement ALONE is sufficient.
(D) EACH statement ALONE is sufficient.
(E) Statements (1) and (2) TOGETHER are not sufficient.

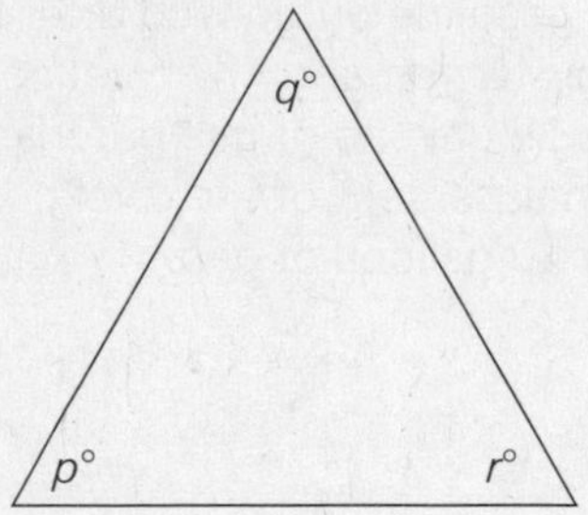

4. For the triangle shown above, does $p = q = 60$?

(1) $r = 180 - (p + r)$

(2) $p = 60$

(A) Statement (1) ALONE is sufficient, but statement (2) alone is not sufficient.
(B) Statement (2) ALONE is sufficient, but statement (1) alone is not sufficient.
(C) BOTH statements TOGETHER are sufficient, but NEITHER statement ALONE is sufficient.
(D) EACH statement ALONE is sufficient.
(E) Statements (1) and (2) TOGETHER are not sufficient.

5. During a certain two week period, a video rental store rented only comedies, dramas, and action movies. If 70 percent of the movies rented were comedies, and of the remaining movies rented, 5 times as many dramas as action movies were rented and A action movies were rented, then, in terms of A, how many of the movies rented were comedies?

(A) $\frac{A}{14}$

(B) $\frac{5A}{7}$

(C) $\frac{7A}{5}$

(D) $14A$

(E) $35A$

6. x, y, and z are consecutive positive integers such that $x < y < z$. If the units digit of x^2 is 6 and the units digit of y^2 is 9, what is the units digit of z^2 ?

(A) 0
(B) 1
(C) 2
(D) 4
(E) 5

GO ON TO THE NEXT PAGE.

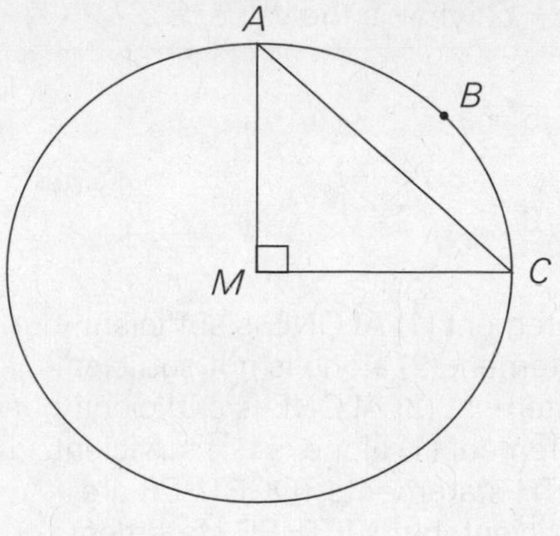

7. What is the area of the circle with center M shown above?

(1) The length of AC is $8\sqrt{2}$.

(2) The length of arc ABC is 4π.

(A) Statement (1) ALONE is sufficient, but statement (2) alone is not sufficient.
(B) Statement (2) ALONE is sufficient, but statement (1) alone is not sufficient.
(C) BOTH statements TOGETHER are sufficient, but NEITHER statement ALONE is sufficient.
(D) EACH statement ALONE is sufficient.
(E) Statements (1) and (2) TOGETHER are not sufficient.

8. If 70 percent of the female and 90 percent of the male students in the senior class at a certain school are going on the senior trip and the senior class is 60 percent female, what percent of the senior class is going on the senior trip?

(A) 82%
(B) 80%
(C) 78%
(D) 76%
(E) 72%

9. If P is a set of integers and 3 is in P, is every positive multiple of 3 in P?

(1) For any integer in P, the sum of 3 and that integer is also in P.

(2) For any integer in P, that integer minus 3 is also in P.

(A) Statement (1) ALONE is sufficient, but statement (2) alone is not sufficient.
(B) Statement (2) ALONE is sufficient, but statement (1) alone is not sufficient.
(C) BOTH statements TOGETHER are sufficient, but NEITHER statement ALONE is sufficient.
(D) EACH statement ALONE is sufficient.
(E) Statements (1) and (2) TOGETHER are not sufficient.

10. A certain seafood restaurant gets a delivery of fresh seafood every day of the week. If the delivery company charges d dollars per delivery and c cents per delivered item and the restaurant has an average (arithmetic mean) of x items delivered per day, then which of the following is an expression for the total cost, in dollars, of one week's deliveries?

(A) $\frac{7cdx}{100}$

(B) $d+\frac{7cx}{100}$

(C) $7d+\frac{xc}{100}$

(D) $7d+\frac{7xc}{100}$

(E) $7cdx$

GO ON TO THE NEXT PAGE.

11. Which of the following contains the interval two standard deviations from the mean of a set of data with an arithmetic mean of 46 and a standard deviation of 4 ?

(A) 38 to 46
(B) 38 to 54
(C) 42 to 50
(D) 44 to 48
(E) 46 to 50

12. If a and b are positive integers, is a a multiple of b ?

(1) Every distinct prime factor of b is also a distinct prime factor of a.

(2) Every factor of b is also a factor of a.

(A) Statement (1) ALONE is sufficient, but statement (2) alone is not sufficient.
(B) Statement (2) ALONE is sufficient, but statement (1) alone is not sufficient.
(C) BOTH statements TOGETHER are sufficient, but NEITHER statement alone is sufficient.
(D) EACH statement ALONE is sufficient.
(E) Statements (1) and (2) TOGETHER are NOT sufficient.

13. If Set X contains 10 consecutive integers and the sum of the 5 least members of the set is 265, then what is the sum of the 5 greatest members of the set?

(A) 290
(B) 285
(C) 280
(D) 275
(E) 270

14. If $a - b = c$, what is the value of b ?

(1) $c + 6 = a$

(2) $a = 6$

(A) Statement (1) ALONE is sufficient, but statement (2) alone is not sufficient.
(B) Statement (2) ALONE is sufficient, but statement (1) alone is not sufficient.
(C) BOTH statements TOGETHER are sufficient, but NEITHER statement ALONE is sufficient.
(D) EACH statement ALONE is sufficient.
(E) Statements (1) and (2) TOGETHER are not sufficient.

$$\{3, 5, 9, 13, y\}$$

15. If the average (arithmetic mean) and the median of the set of numbers shown above are equal, then what is the value of y ?

(A) 7
(B) 8
(C) 10
(D) 15
(E) 17

16. For a certain foot race, how many different arrangements of medal winners are possible?

(1) Medals will be given for 1st, 2nd, and 3rd place.

(2) There are 10 runners in the race.

(A) Statement (1) ALONE is sufficient, but statement (2) alone is not sufficient.
(B) Statement (2) ALONE is sufficient, but statement (1) alone is not sufficient.
(C) BOTH statements TOGETHER are sufficient, but NEITHER statement ALONE is sufficient.
(D) EACH statement ALONE is sufficient.
(E) Statements (1) and (2) TOGETHER are not sufficient.

GO ON TO THE NEXT PAGE.

17. For the set of measurements 3, x_2, x_3, what is the value of x_3 ?

(1) The range of the set of measurements is 0.

(2) The standard deviation of the set of measurements is 0.

(A) Statement (1) ALONE is sufficient, but statement (2) alone is not sufficient.
(B) Statement (2) ALONE is sufficient, but statement (1) alone is not sufficient.
(C) BOTH statements TOGETHER are sufficient, but NEITHER statement ALONE is sufficient.
(D) EACH statement ALONE is sufficient.
(E) Statements (1) and (2) TOGETHER are not sufficient.

18. An employer has 6 applicants for a programming position and 4 applicants for a manager position. If the employer must hire 3 programmers and 2 managers, what is the total number of ways the employer can make the selection?

(A) 1,490
(B) 132
(C) 120
(D) 60
(E) 23

19. On Monday, an animal shelter housed 55 cats and dogs and by Friday, exactly $\frac{1}{5}$ of the cats and $\frac{1}{4}$ of the dogs had been adopted. If no new cats or dogs were brought to the shelter during this period, what is the greatest possible number of pets that could have been adopted from the animal shelter between Monday and Friday?

(A) 11
(B) 12
(C) 13
(D) 14
(E) 20

20. If x is an integer, then which of the following statements about $x^2 - x - 1$ is true?

(A) It is always odd.
(B) It is always even.
(C) It is always positive.
(D) It is even when x is even and odd when x is odd.
(E) It is even when x is odd and odd when x is even.

21. During a five-day period, Monday through Friday, the average (arithmetic mean) high temperature was 86 degrees Fahrenheit. What was the high temperature on Friday?

(1) The average high temperature for Monday through Thursday was 87 degrees Fahrenheit.

(2) The high temperature on Friday reduced the average high temperature for the five-day period by 1 degree Fahrenheit.

(A) Statement (1) ALONE is sufficient, but statement (2) alone is not sufficient.
(B) Statement (2) ALONE is sufficient, but statement (1) alone is not sufficient.
(C) BOTH statements TOGETHER are sufficient, but NEITHER statement ALONE is sufficient.
(D) EACH statement ALONE is sufficient.
(E) Statements (1) and (2) TOGETHER are not sufficient.

GO ON TO THE NEXT PAGE.

22. What is the value of $x^2 - y^2$?

(1) $x + y = 0$

(2) $x - y = 2$

(A) Statement (1) ALONE is sufficient, but statement (2) alone is not sufficient.
(B) Statement (2) ALONE is sufficient, but statement (1) alone is not sufficient.
(C) BOTH statements TOGETHER are sufficient, but NEITHER statement ALONE is sufficient.
(D) EACH statement ALONE is sufficient.
(E) Statements (1) and (2) TOGETHER are not sufficient.

23. If P is the perimeter of an equilateral triangle, which of the following represents the height of the triangle?

(A) $\frac{P}{3}$

(B) $\frac{P\sqrt{3}}{3}$

(C) $\frac{P}{4}$

(D) $\frac{P\sqrt{3}}{6}$

(E) $\frac{P}{6}$

24. If 75 percent of all Americans own an automobile, 15 percent of all Americans own a bicycle, and 20 percent of all Americans own neither an automobile nor a bicycle, then what percent of Americans own *both* an automobile and a bicycle?

(A) 0%
(B) 1.33%
(C) 3.75%
(D) 5%
(E) 10%

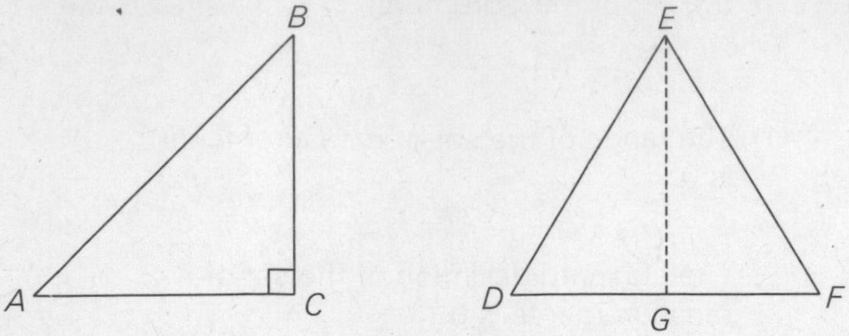

25. Triangle ABC above is an isosceles right triangle and triangle DEF above is an equilateral triangle with height EG. What is the ratio of the area of ABC to the area of DEF?

(1) The ratio of BC to EG is 1:1.

(2) The ratio of AC to DF is $\sqrt{3}:2$.

(A) Statement (1) ALONE is sufficient, but statement (2) alone is not sufficient.
(B) Statement (2) ALONE is sufficient, but statement (1) alone is not sufficient.
(C) BOTH statements TOGETHER are sufficient, but NEITHER statement ALONE is sufficient.
(D) EACH statement ALONE is sufficient.
(E) Statements (1) and (2) TOGETHER are not sufficient.

26. What is the value of integer x?

(1) $\sqrt[x]{64} = 4$

(2) $x^2 = x + 6$

(A) Statement (1) ALONE is sufficient, but statement (2) alone is not sufficient.
(B) Statement (2) ALONE is sufficient, but statement (1) alone is not sufficient.
(C) BOTH statements TOGETHER are sufficient, but NEITHER statement ALONE is sufficient.
(D) EACH statement ALONE is sufficient.
(E) Statements (1) and (2) TOGETHER are not sufficient.

GO ON TO THE NEXT PAGE.

Math Test
Bin 4—Hard Questions
25 Questions

This test is composed of both problem solving questions and data sufficiency questions.

Problem Solving Directions: Solve each problem and choose the best of the answer choices provided.

Data Sufficiency Directions: Each data sufficiency problem consists of a question and two statements, labeled (1) and (2), which contain certain data. Using these data and your knowledge of mathematics and everyday facts (such as the number of days in July or the meaning of *counterclockwise*), decide whether the data given are sufficient for answering the question and then indicate one of the following answer choices:

(A) Statement (1) ALONE is sufficient, but statement (2) alone is not sufficient.

(B) Statement (2) ALONE is sufficient, but statement (1) alone is not sufficient.

(C) BOTH statements TOGETHER are sufficient, but NEITHER statement ALONE is sufficient.

(D) EACH statement ALONE is sufficient.

(E) Statements (1) and (2) TOGETHER are not sufficient.

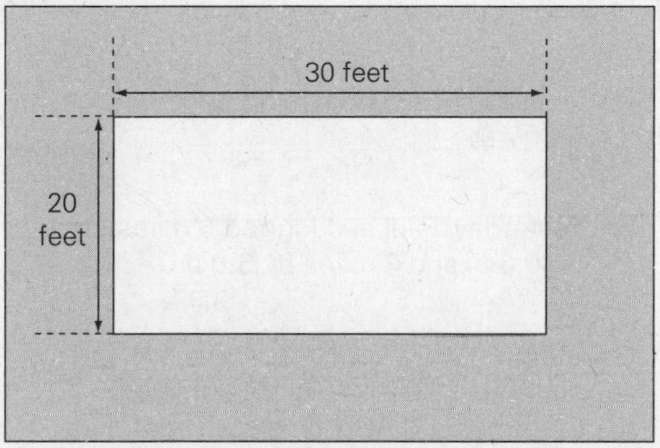

1. A rectangular garden with dimensions 20 feet by 30 feet is surrounded by a rectangular brick walkway of uniform width as shown by the figure above. If the area of the walkway equals the area of the garden, what is the width of the walkway?

(A) 1 foot
(B) 3 feet
(C) 5 feet
(D) 8 feet
(E) 10 feet

2. If a fair two-sided coin is flipped 6 times, what is the probability that tails is the result at least twice but at most 5 times?

(A) $\frac{5}{8}$

(B) $\frac{3}{4}$

(C) $\frac{7}{8}$

(D) $\frac{57}{64}$

(E) $\frac{15}{16}$

GO ON TO THE NEXT PAGE.

3. The new recruits of a military organization who score in the bottom 16 percent on their physical conditioning tests are required to retest. If the test scores are normally distributed and have an arithmetic mean of 72, what is the score at or below which the recruits are required to retest?

(1) There are 500 new recruits.

(2) 10 new recruits scored at least 82 on the physical conditioning test.

(A) Statement (1) ALONE is sufficient, but statement (2) alone is not sufficient.
(B) Statement (2) ALONE is sufficient, but statement (1) alone is not sufficient.
(C) BOTH statements TOGETHER are sufficient, but NEITHER statement ALONE is sufficient.
(D) EACH statement ALONE is sufficient.
(E) Statements (1) and (2) TOGETHER are not sufficient.

4. Each of the integers from 1 to 20 is written on a separate index card and placed in a box. If the cards are drawn from the box at random without replacement, how many cards must be drawn to ensure that the product of all the integers drawn is even?

(A) 19
(B) 12
(C) 11
(D) 10
(E) 3

5. The average (arithmetic mean) of integers r, s, t, u, and v is 100. Are exactly two of the integers greater than 100 ?

(1) Three of the integers are less than 50.

(2) None of the integers is equal to 100.

(A) Statement (1) ALONE is sufficient, but statement (2) alone is not sufficient.
(B) Statement (2) ALONE is sufficient, but statement (1) alone is not sufficient.
(C) BOTH statements TOGETHER are sufficient, but NEITHER statement ALONE is sufficient.
(D) EACH statement ALONE is sufficient.
(E) Statements (1) and (2) TOGETHER are not sufficient.

6. Paul jogs along the same route every day at a constant rate for 80 minutes. What distance does he jog?

(1) Yesterday, Paul began jogging at 5:00 P.M.

(2) Yesterday, Paul had jogged 5 miles by 5:40 P.M. and 8 miles by 6:04 P.M.

(A) Statement (1) ALONE is sufficient, but statement (2) alone is not sufficient.
(B) Statement (2) ALONE is sufficient, but statement (1) alone is not sufficient.
(C) BOTH statements TOGETHER are sufficient, but NEITHER statement ALONE is sufficient.
(D) EACH statement ALONE is sufficient.
(E) Statements (1) and (2) TOGETHER are not sufficient.

GO ON TO THE NEXT PAGE.

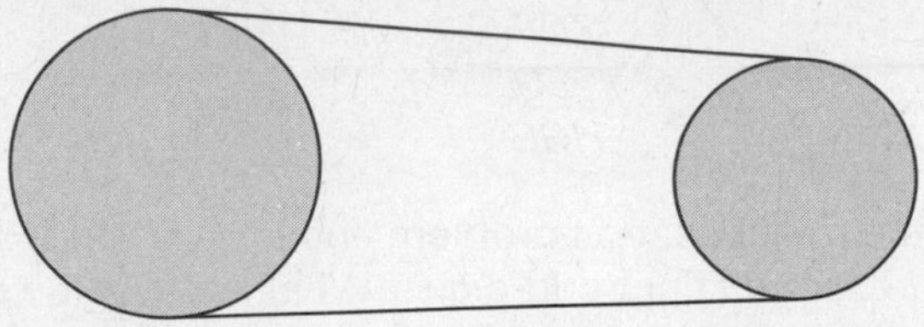

7. The diagram above shows two wheels that drive a conveyor belt. The larger wheel has a diameter of 40 centimeters, and the smaller wheel has a diameter of 32 centimeters. If each wheel must rotate the exact same number of centimeters per minute, and the larger wheel makes *r* revolutions per minute, then, in terms of *r*, how many revolutions does the smaller wheel make per hour?

(A) $\frac{1,280\pi}{3}$

(B) $75r$

(C) $48r$

(D) $24r$

(E) $\frac{64\pi}{3}$

8. An automobile dealership sells only sedans and coupes. It sells each in only two colors: red and blue. Last year, the dealership sold 9,000 vehicles, half of which were red. How many coupes did the dealership sell last year?

(1) The dealership sold three times as many blue coupes as red sedans last year.

(2) The dealership sold half as many blue sedans as blue coupes last year.

(A) Statement (1) ALONE is sufficient, but statement (2) alone is not sufficient.
(B) Statement (2) ALONE is sufficient, but statement (1) alone is not sufficient.
(C) BOTH statements TOGETHER are sufficient, but NEITHER statement ALONE is sufficient.
(D) EACH statement ALONE is sufficient.
(E) Statements (1) and (2) TOGETHER are not sufficient.

9. At a college football game, $\frac{4}{5}$ of the seats in the lower deck of the stadium were sold. If $\frac{1}{4}$ of all the seats in the stadium are located in the lower deck, and if $\frac{2}{3}$ of all the seats in the stadium were sold, what fraction of the unsold seats in the stadium are in the lower deck?

(A) $\frac{3}{20}$

(B) $\frac{1}{6}$

(C) $\frac{1}{5}$

(D) $\frac{1}{3}$

(E) $\frac{7}{15}$

10. At Company *R*, the average (arithmetic mean) age of executive employees is 54 years old and the average age of non-executive employees is 34 years old. What is the average age of all the employees at Company *R* ?

(1) There are 10 executive employees at Company *R*.

(2) The number of non-executive employees at Company *R* is four times the number of executive employees at Company *R*.

(A) Statement (1) ALONE is sufficient, but statement (2) alone is not sufficient.
(B) Statement (2) ALONE is sufficient, but statement (1) alone is not sufficient.
(C) BOTH statements TOGETHER are sufficient, but NEITHER statement ALONE is sufficient.
(D) EACH statement ALONE is sufficient.
(E) Statements (1) and (2) TOGETHER are not sufficient.

GO ON TO THE NEXT PAGE.

11. If a, b, c, d, and x are all nonzero integers, is the product $ax \cdot (bx)^2 \cdot (cx)^2 \cdot (dx)^2$ negative?

(1) $a < c < x < 0$

(2) $b < d < x < 0$

(A) Statement (1) ALONE is sufficient, but statement (2) alone is not sufficient.
(B) Statement (2) ALONE is sufficient, but statement (1) alone is not sufficient.
(C) BOTH statements TOGETHER are sufficient, but NEITHER statement ALONE is sufficient.
(D) EACH statement ALONE is sufficient.
(E) Statements (1) and (2) TOGETHER are not sufficient.

12. A four character password consists of one letter from the English alphabet and three different digits from 0 to 9. If the letter is the second or third character of the password, how many different passwords are possible?

(A) 5,040
(B) 18,720
(C) 26,000
(D) 37,440
(E) 52,000

13. If x is a positive integer, is x divisible by 48 ?

(1) x is divisible by 8.

(2) x is divisible by 6.

(A) Statement (1) ALONE is sufficient, but statement (2) alone is not sufficient.
(B) Statement (2) ALONE is sufficient, but statement (1) alone is not sufficient.
(C) BOTH statements TOGETHER are sufficient, but NEITHER statement ALONE is sufficient.
(D) EACH statement ALONE is sufficient.
(E) Statements (1) and (2) TOGETHER are not sufficient.

$$\begin{array}{r} FGF \\ \times\ G \\ \hline HGG \end{array}$$

14. In the multiplication problem above, F, G, and H represent distinct odd digits. What is the value of the three-digit number FGF ?

(A) 151
(B) 161
(C) 171
(D) 313
(E) 353

15. A group of 20 friends formed an investment club, with each member contributing an equal amount to the general fund. The club then invested the entire fund, which amounted to d dollars, in Stock X. The value of the stock subsequently increased 40 percent, at which point the stock was sold and the proceeds divided evenly among the members. In terms of d, how much money did each member of the club receive from the sale? (Assume that transaction fees and other associated costs were negligible.)

(A) $800d$

(B) $\frac{7d}{5}$

(C) $\frac{d}{20}+40$

(D) $\frac{d}{2}$

(E) $\frac{7d}{100}$

GO ON TO THE NEXT PAGE.

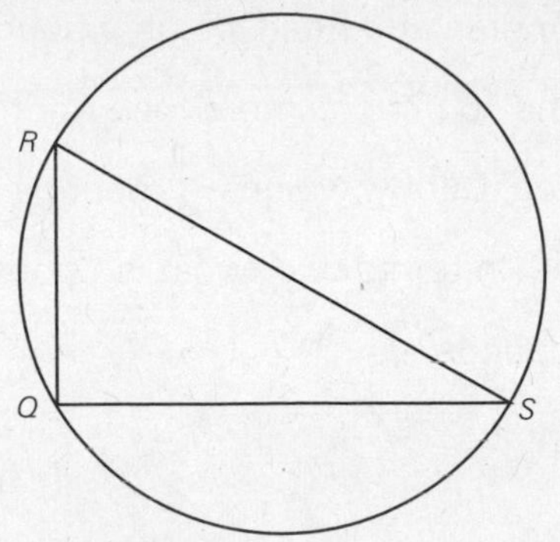

16. Triangle QRS is inscribed in a circle as shown above. Is QRS a right triangle?

(1) RS is a diameter of the circle.

(2) $QR = 3$ and $RS = 5$

(A) Statement (1) ALONE is sufficient, but statement (2) alone is not sufficient.
(B) Statement (2) ALONE is sufficient, but statement (1) alone is not sufficient.
(C) BOTH statements TOGETHER are sufficient, but NEITHER statement ALONE is sufficient.
(D) EACH statement ALONE is sufficient.
(E) Statements (1) and (2) TOGETHER are not sufficient.

17. Square G has sides of length 4 inches. Is the area of Square H exactly one half the area of Square G ?

(1) The length of the diagonal of Square H equals the length of one side of Square G.

(2) The perimeter of Square H is twice the length of the diagonal of Square G.

(A) Statement (1) ALONE is sufficient, but statement (2) alone is not sufficient.
(B) Statement (2) ALONE is sufficient, but statement (1) alone is not sufficient.
(C) BOTH statements TOGETHER are sufficient, but NEITHER statement ALONE is sufficient.
(D) EACH statement ALONE is sufficient.
(E) Statements (1) and (2) TOGETHER are not sufficient.

18. In a certain state, 70 percent of the counties received some rain on Monday, and 65 percent of the counties received some rain on Tuesday. No rain fell either day in 25 percent of the counties in the state. What percent of the counties received some rain on Monday and Tuesday?

(A) 12.5%
(B) 40%
(C) 50%
(D) 60%
(E) 67.5%

GO ON TO THE NEXT PAGE.

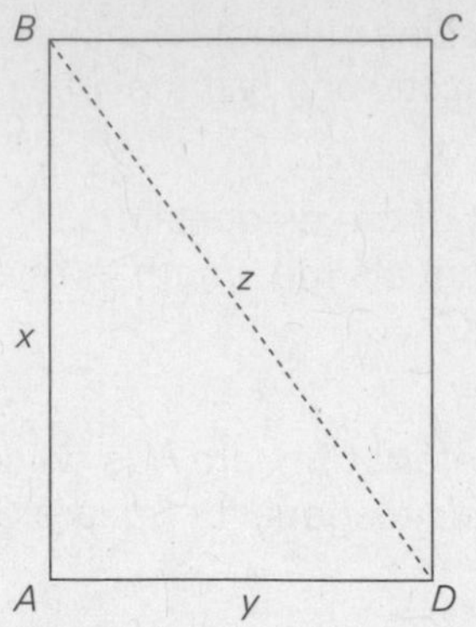

19. *ABCD* is a rectangle with sides of length *x* centimeters and width *y* centimeters, and a diagonal of length *z* centimeters. What is the perimeter, in centimeters, of *ABCD* ?

(1) $x - y = 7$

(2) $z = 13$

(A) Statement (1) ALONE is sufficient, but statement (2) alone is not sufficient.
(B) Statement (2) ALONE is sufficient, but statement (1) alone is not sufficient.
(C) BOTH statements TOGETHER are sufficient, but NEITHER statement ALONE is sufficient.
(D) EACH statement ALONE is sufficient.
(E) Statements (1) and (2) TOGETHER are not sufficient.

20. Together, Andrea and Brian weigh *p* pounds. Brian weighs 10 pounds more than Andrea and Andrea's dog, Cubby, weighs $\frac{p}{4}$ pounds more than Andrea. In terms of *p*, what is Cubby's weight in pounds?

(A) $\frac{p}{2} - 10$

(B) $\frac{3p}{4} - 5$

(C) $\frac{3p}{2} - 5$

(D) $\frac{5p}{4} - 10$

(E) $5p - 5$

21. A first-grade teacher uses ten flash cards, numbered 1 through 10, to teach her students to order numbers correctly. She has students choose four flash cards at random, then arrange the cards in ascending order. If she removes the cards numbered 2 and 4, how many different correctly ordered arrangements of the four selected cards are possible?

(A) 70
(B) 210
(C) 336
(D) 840
(E) 1,680

GO ON TO THE NEXT PAGE.

22. If A and B are two-digit integers that share the same digits, except in reverse order, then what is the sum of A and B?

(1) $A - B = 45$

(2) The difference between the two digits in each number is 5.

(A) Statement (1) ALONE is sufficient, but statement (2) alone is not sufficient.
(B) Statement (2) ALONE is sufficient, but statement (1) alone is not sufficient.
(C) BOTH statements TOGETHER are sufficient, but NEITHER statement ALONE is sufficient.
(D) EACH statement ALONE is sufficient.
(E) Statements (1) and (2) TOGETHER are not sufficient.

23. A university awarded grants in the amount of either $7,000 or $10,000 to selected incoming freshmen. If the total amount of all such awards is $2,300,000, did the university award more $7,000 grants than $10,000 grants to the selected incoming freshmen?

(1) A total of 275 freshmen received grants in one of the two amounts.

(2) The amount of money awarded in $10,000 grants was $200,000 more than the amount of money awarded in $7,000 grants.

(A) Statement (1) ALONE is sufficient, but statement (2) alone is not sufficient.
(B) Statement (2) ALONE is sufficient, but statement (1) alone is not sufficient.
(C) BOTH statements TOGETHER are sufficient, but NEITHER statement ALONE is sufficient.
(D) EACH statement ALONE is sufficient.
(E) Statements (1) and (2) TOGETHER are not sufficient.

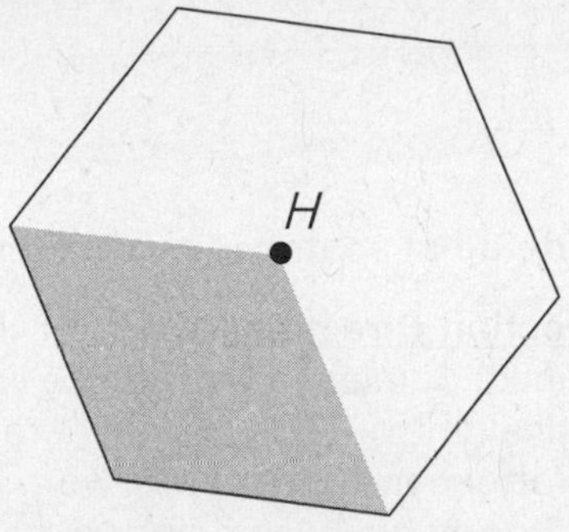

24. The figure shown above is a regular hexagon with center H. The shaded area is a parallelogram that shares three vertices with the hexagon and its fourth vertex is the center of the hexagon. If the length of one side of the hexagon is 8 centimeters, what is the area of the unshaded region?

(A) $16\sqrt{3}$ cm^2
(B) 96 cm^2
(C) $64\sqrt{3}$ cm^2
(D) $96\sqrt{3}$ cm^2
(E) 256 cm^2

25. A fish tank contains a number of fish, including 5 Fantails. If two fish are selected from the tank at random, what is the probability that both will be Fantails?

(1) The probability that the first fish chosen is a Fantail is $\frac{1}{2}$.

(2) The probability that the second fish chosen is a Fantail is $\frac{4}{9}$.

(A) Statement (1) ALONE is sufficient, but statement (2) alone is not sufficient.
(B) Statement (2) ALONE is sufficient, but statement (1) alone is not sufficient.
(C) BOTH statements TOGETHER are sufficient, but NEITHER statement ALONE is sufficient.
(D) EACH statement ALONE is sufficient.
(E) Statements (1) and (2) TOGETHER are not sufficient.

GO ON TO THE NEXT PAGE.

Verbal Test
Bin 1—Easy Questions
25 Questions

This test is made up of sentence correction, critical reasoning, and reading comprehension questions.

Sentence Correction Directions: Each of the sentence correction questions presents a sentence, part or all of which is underlined. Beneath the sentence you will find five ways of phrasing the underlined part. The first of these repeats the original; the other four are different. Follow the requirements of standard written English to choose your answer, paying attention to grammar, word choice, and sentence construction. Select the answer that produces the most effective sentence; your answer should make the sentence clear, exact, and free of grammatical errors. It should also minimize awkwardness, ambiguity, and redundancy.

Reading Comprehension Directions: Each of the reading comprehension questions is based on the content of a passage. After reading the passage, answer all questions pertaining to it on the basis of what is stated or implied in the passage. For each question, select the best answer of the choices given.

Critical Reasoning Directions: Each of the critical reasoning questions is based on a short argument, a set of statements, or a plan of action. For each question, select the best answer of the choices given.

---

1. As its reputation for making acquisitions of important masterpieces has grown, the museum has increasingly turned down gifts of lesser-known paintings they would in the past have accepted gratefully.

(A) they would in the past have accepted gratefully
(B) they would have accepted gratefully in the past
(C) it would in the past have accepted gratefully
(D) it previously would have accepted gratefully in the past
(E) that previously would have been accepted in the past

2. Over the past few decades, despite periodic attempts to reign in spending, currencies in South America are devalued by rampant inflation.

(A) are devalued
(B) are becoming more devalued
(C) which have lost value
(D) have become devalued
(E) have since become devalued

3. A fashion designer's fall line for women utilizing new soft fabrics broke all sales records last year. To capitalize on her success, the designer plans to launch a line of clothing for men this year that makes use of the same new soft fabrics.

The designer's plan assumes that

(A) other designers are not planning to introduce new lines for men utilizing the same soft fabrics
(B) men will be as interested in the new soft fabrics as women were the year before
(C) the designer will have time to develop new lines for both men and women
(D) the line for men will be considered innovative and daring because of its use of fabrics
(E) women who bought the new line last year will continue to buy it this year

GO ON TO THE NEXT PAGE.

4. The standard lamp is becoming outmoded, and so too is the incandescent light bulb, it is Edison's miraculous invention to use so much more energy than the new low-wattage halogen bulbs.

(A) so too is the incandescent light bulb, it is Edison's miraculous invention to use
(B) so too is the incandescent light bulb, Edison's miraculous invention that uses
(C) so too the incandescent light bulb, Edison's miraculous invention using
(D) also the incandescent light bulb, it is Edison's miraculous invention that uses
(E) also the incandescent light bulb, which is Edison's miraculous invention to use

5. Over the last 20 years, the growth of information technology has been more rapid than any other business field, but has recently begun to lag behind as newly emerging fields seem more enticing to new graduates.

(A) the growth of information technology has been more rapid than any other business field
(B) the growth of information technology has been more rapid than any other fields of business
(C) information technology's growth has been more rapid than any other fields of business
(D) the growing of information technology has been more rapid than that of any other business field
(E) the growth of information technology has been more rapid than that of any other business field

6. According to mutual fund sales experts, a successful year for a stock fund should result not only in increased investor dollars flowing into the fund, but also in increased investor dollars flowing into other mutual stock funds offered by the same company. However, while last year the Grafton Mutual Company's "Growth Stock Fund" beat average market returns by a factor of two and recorded substantial new investment, the other stock funds offered by Grafton did not report any increase whatsoever.

Which of the following conclusions can properly be drawn from the statements above?

(A) When one of the mutual funds offered by a company beats average market returns, the other mutual funds offered by that company will beat average market returns.
(B) The mutual fund sales experts neglected to consider bond funds in formulating their theory.
(C) The performance of the Grafton "Growth Stock Fund" was a result of a wave of mergers and acquisitions that year.
(D) Investors currently dislike all stock mutual funds because of market volatility.
(E) The success of one mutual fund is not the only factor affecting whether investors will invest in other mutual funds run by the same company.

7. With less than thirty thousand dollars in advance ticket sales and fewer acceptances by guest speakers than expected, the one-day symposium on art and religion was canceled for lack of interest.

(A) less than thirty thousand dollars in advance ticket sales and fewer
(B) fewer than thirty thousand dollars in advance ticket sales and less
(C) fewer than thirty thousand dollars in advance ticket sales and fewer
(D) lesser than thirty thousand dollars in advance ticket sales and fewer
(E) less than thirty thousand dollars in advance ticket sales and as few

GO ON TO THE NEXT PAGE.

8. New technology now makes it feasible for computer call-in help desk services to route calls they receive to almost anywhere, theoretically allowing employees to work from home, without the need for a daily commute.

   The adoption of this policy would be most likely to increase productivity if employees did not ____________.

   (A) commute from a distance of fewer than
   10 miles
   (B) commute by car as opposed to by rail
   (C) live in areas with dependable phone service
   (D) need to consult frequently with each other to solve callers' problems
   (E) have more than one telephone line

9. The port cities of England in the 19th century saw a renaissance of ship construction, with some innovative designs breaking new ground, stretching the limits of ship-building theory, and <u>received</u> acclaim from around the world.

   (A) received
   (B) it received
   (C) receiving
   (D) would receive
   (E) it had received

10. According to a consumer research group survey, the majority of kitchen appliances purchased in the United States are purchased by men. This appears to belie the myth that women spend more time in the kitchen than men.

    The argument is flawed primarily because the author ____________.

    (A) fails to differentiate between buying and using
    (B) does not provide information about the types of kitchen appliances surveyed
    (C) depends on the results of one survey
    (D) does not give exact statistics to back up his case
    (E) does not provide information on other appliances such as washers and dryers

11. <u>A contribution to a favorite charity being sent instead</u> of flowers when a colleague dies is becoming more the rule than the exception when it comes to funeral etiquette.

    (A) A contribution to a favorite charity being sent instead
    (B) A contribution being sent to a favorite charity as opposed
    (C) To send a contribution for a favorite charity instead
    (D) Sending a contribution to a favorite charity instead
    (E) Sending a contribution to a favorite charity as opposed

GO ON TO THE NEXT PAGE.

Questions 12–15 are based on the following passage:

As a business model, the world of publishing has always been a somewhat sleepy enclave, but now all that seems poised to change. Several companies have moved aggressively into a new business endeavor whose genesis comes from the question: Who owns the great works of literature?

Text-on-demand is not a completely new idea, of course. In the 1990s, the Gutenberg project sought volunteers to type literary classics that had expired copyrights into word processing files so that scholars would have searchable databases for their research. Most of the works of Shakespeare, Cervantes, Proust, and Molière were to be found free online by as early as 1995.

However, now large-scale companies have moved into the market, with scanners and business plans, and are looking for bargain basement content. These companies are striking deals with libraries, and some publishers, to be able to provide their content, for a price, to individual buyers over the Internet.

At stake are the rights to an estimated store of 30 million books, most of which are now out of print. Many of these books are now also in the public domain, giving any company the right to sell them online. Still, a good portion of the books a general audience might actually want to buy is still under copyright. The urgent question: Who owns those copyrights? In the case of all too many books put out more than 20 years ago by now-defunct publishing companies, the answer is unclear—a situation the new text-on-demand companies are eager to exploit. An association of publishers has sued, claiming massive copyright infringement. The case is several years away from trial.

12. The primary purpose of the passage is to

(A) present the results of a statistical analysis and propose further study
(B) explain a recent development and explore its consequences
(C) identify the reasons for a trend and recommend measures to address it
(D) outline several theories about a phenomenon and advocate one of them
(E) describe the potential consequences of implementing a new policy and argue in favor of that policy

13. It can be inferred from the passage that the works of Shakespeare, Cervantes, and Molière

(A) are some of the most popular works of literature
(B) are no longer copyrighted
(C) are among the works for which the association of publishers is suing text-on-demand companies
(D) do not currently exist as searchable databases
(E) were owned by now-defunct publishing companies

14. Which of the following is an example of a book that a text-on-demand company would not have to acquire the rights to?

(A) a book still under copyright
(B) a book more than 20 years old
(C) a book in the public domain
(D) a book a general audience might want to buy
(E) a book not already owned by publishers the company has a deal with

15. It can be inferred from the passage that text-on-demand companies are

(A) using scanners to find books they want to acquire
(B) creating business plans well before they have any actual business
(C) buying content at premium prices
(D) acquiring the rights to books for as little as possible
(E) attempting to supplant the role of traditional publishers

GO ON TO THE NEXT PAGE.

16. Exit polls, conducted by an independent organization among voters at five polling locations during a recent election, suggested that the incumbent mayor—a Democrat—was going to lose the election by a wide margin. But, in fact, by the time the final results were tabulated, the incumbent had won the election by a narrow margin.

    Which of the following, if true, would explain the apparent contradiction in the results of the exit polls?

    (A) The people chosen at random to be polled by the independent organization happened to be Democrats.
    (B) The exit poll locations chosen by the independent organization were in predominantly Republican districts.
    (C) The exit polls were conducted during the afternoon, when most of the districts' younger voters, who did not support the incumbent mayor, were at work.
    (D) The incumbent mayor ran on a platform that promised to lower taxes if elected.
    (E) An earlier poll, conducted the week before the election, had predicted that the incumbent mayor would win.

17. The spread of Avian flu from animals to humans has been well-documented, but less understood is the mechanism by which it is spread from one bird species to another. **In order to avoid a worldwide epidemic of Avian flu, scientists must make that study a first priority.** To solely tackle the human dimension of this possible pandemic is to miss half of the problem: its spread from one hemisphere to another.

    The bolded phrase plays which of the following roles in the argument above?

    (A) The bolded phrase states a premise of the argument.
    (B) The bolded phrase contradicts the author's main point.
    (C) The bolded phrase makes a statement that the author is about to contradict.
    (D) The bolded phrase states the author's conclusion.
    (E) The bolded phrase states an assumption the author is making.

18. Successful business leaders not only anticipate potential problems and have contingency plans <u>ready, instead proceeding as if they are likely to occur at any time</u>.

    (A) ready, instead proceeding as if they are likely to occur at any time
    (B) ready, but also proceed as if such problems are likely to occur at any time
    (C) ready, but also proceeding as if the occurrence of them is at any time likely
    (D) ready; they instead proceed as if their occurrence is likely at any time
    (E) ready; such problems are likely to occur at any time, is how they proceed

19. An artist who sells her paintings for a fixed price decides that she must increase her income. Because she does not believe that customers will pay more for her paintings, she decides to cut costs by using cheaper paints and canvases. She expects that, by cutting costs, she will increase her profit margin per painting and thus increase her annual net income.

    Which of the following, if true, most weakens the argument above?

    (A) Other area artists charge more for their paintings than the artist charges for hers.
    (B) The artist has failed to consider other options, such as renting cheaper studio space.
    (C) The artist's plan will result in the production of inferior paintings which, in turn, will cause a reduction in sales.
    (D) If the economy were to enter a period of inflation, the artist's projected increase in income could be wiped out by increases in the price of art supplies.
    (E) The artist considered trying to complete paintings more quickly and thus increase production, but concluded that it would be impossible.

GO ON TO THE NEXT PAGE.

20. Although tapirs reared in captivity are generally docile and have even been kept as pets by South American villagers, <u>it is nonetheless a volatile creature</u> prone to unpredictable and dangerous temper tantrums.

(A) it is nonetheless a volatile creature
(B) it is nonetheless volatile creatures
(C) being nonetheless volatile creatures
(D) they are nonetheless a volatile creature
(E) they are nonetheless volatile creatures

21. According to a recent report, the original tires supplied with the Impressivo, a new sedan-class automobile, wore much more quickly than tires conventionally wear. The report suggested two possible causes: (1) defects in the tires, and (2) improper wheel alignment of the automobile.

Which of the following would best help the authors of the report determine which of the two causes identified was responsible for the extra wear?

(A) a study in which the rate of tire wear in the Impressivo is compared to the rate of tire wear in all automobiles in the same class
(B) a study in which a second set of tires, manufactured by a different company from the one that made the first set, is installed on all Impressivos and the rate of wear is measured
(C) a study in which the level of satisfaction of workers in the Impressivo manufacturing plant is measured and compared to that of workers at other automobile manufacturing plants
(D) a study that determines how often improper wheel alignment results in major problems for manufacturers of other automobiles in the Impressivo's class
(E) a study that determines the degree to which faulty driving techniques employed by Impressivo drivers contributed to tire wear

<u>Questions 22–25</u> are based on the following passage:

Founded at the dawn of the modern industrial era, the nearly forgotten Women's Trade Union League (WTUL) played an instrumental role in advancing the cause of working women throughout the early part of the twentieth century. In the face of considerable adversity, the WTUL made a contribution far greater than did most historical footnotes.

The organization's successes did not come easily; conflict beset the WTUL in many forms. During those early days of American unions, organized labor was aggressively opposed by both industry and government. The WTUL, which represented a largely unskilled labor force, had little leverage against these powerful opponents. Also, because of the skill level of its workers as well as inherent societal gender bias, the WTUL had great difficulty finding allies among other unions. Even the large and powerful American Federation of Labor (AFL), which nominally took the WTUL under its wing, kept it at a distance. Because the AFL's power stemmed from its highly skilled labor force, the organization saw little economic benefit in working with the WTUL. The affiliation provided the AFL with political cover, allowing it to claim support for women workers; in return, the WTUL gained a potent but largely absent ally.

The WTUL also had to overcome internal discord. While the majority of the group's members were working women, a sizeable and powerful minority consisted of middle- and upper-class social reformers whose goals extended beyond labor reform. While workers argued that the WTUL should focus its efforts on collective bargaining and working conditions, the reformers looked beyond the workplace, seeking state and national legislation aimed at education reform and urban poverty relief as well as workplace issues.

Despite these obstacles, the WTUL accomplished a great deal. The organization was instrumental in the passage of state laws mandating an eight-hour workday, a minimum wage for women, and a ban on child labor. It provided seed money to women who organized workers in specific plants and industries, and also established strike funds and soup kitchens to support striking unionists. After the tragic Triangle Shirtwaist Company fire of 1911, the WTUL launched a four-year investigation whose

GO ON TO THE NEXT PAGE.

conclusions formed the basis of much subsequent workplace safety legislation. The organization also offered a political base for all reform-minded women, and thus helped develop the next generation of American leaders. Eleanor Roosevelt was one of many prominent figures to emerge from the WTUL.

The organization began a slow death in the late 1920s, when the Great Depression choked off its funding. The organization limped through the 1940s; the death knell eventually rang in 1950, at the onset of the McCarthy era. A turn-of-the-century labor organization dedicated to social reform, one that during its heyday was regarded by many as "radical," stood little chance of weathering that storm. This humble ending, however, does nothing to diminish the accomplishments of an organization that is yet to receive its historical due.

22. The primary purpose of this passage is to

(A) describe the barriers confronting women in the contemporary workplace
(B) compare and contrast the methods of two labor unions of the early industrial era
(C) critique the methods employed by an important labor union
(D) rebuke historians for failing to cover the women's labor movement adequately
(E) call readers' attention to an overlooked contributor to American history

23. Which of the following best characterizes the American Federation of Labor's view of the Women's Trade Union League, as it is presented in the passage?

(A) The WTUL was an important component of the AFL's multifront assault on industry and its treatment of workers.
(B) Because of Eleanor Roosevelt's affiliation with the organization, the WTUL was a vehicle through which the AFL could gain access to the White House.
(C) The WTUL was to be avoided because the radical element within it attracted unwanted government scrutiny.
(D) The WTUL offered the AFL some political capital but little that would assist it in labor negotiations.
(E) The WTUL was weakened by its hesitance in pursuing widespread social reform beyond the workplace.

24. Each of the following is cited in the passage as an accomplishment of the Women's Trade Union League EXCEPT

(A) It organized a highly skilled workforce to increase its bargaining power.
(B) It contributed to the development of a group of leaders in America.
(C) It provided essential support to striking women.
(D) It helped fund start-up unions for women.
(E) It contributed to the passage of important social and labor reform legislation.

GO ON TO THE NEXT PAGE.

25. The passage suggests which of the following about the "middle- and upper-class social reformers" mentioned in lines 32–33?

(A) They did not understand, nor were they sympathetic to, the plight of poor women workers.
(B) Their naive interest in Communism was ultimately detrimental to the Women's Trade Union League.
(C) It was because of their social and political power that the Women's Trade Union League was able to form an alliance with the American Federation of Labor.
(D) They represented only an insignificant fraction of the leadership of Women's Trade Union League.
(E) They sought to advance a broad political agenda of societal improvement.

GO ON TO THE NEXT PAGE.

Verbal Test
Bin 2—Medium Questions
27 Questions

This test is made up of sentence correction, critical reasoning, and reading comprehension questions.

Sentence Correction Directions: Each of the sentence correction questions presents a sentence, part or all of which is underlined. Beneath the sentence you will find five ways of phrasing the underlined part. The first of these repeats the original; the other four are different. Follow the requirements of standard written English to choose your answer, paying attention to grammar, word choice, and sentence construction. Select the answer that produces the most effective sentence; your answer should make the sentence clear, exact, and free of grammatical errors. It should also minimize awkwardness, ambiguity, and redundancy.

Reading Comprehension Directions: Each of the reading comprehension questions is based on the content of a passage. After reading the passage, answer all questions pertaining to it on the basis of what is stated or implied in the passage. For each question, select the best answer of the choices given.

Critical Reasoning Directions: Each of the critical reasoning questions is based on a short argument, a set of statements, or a plan of action. For each question, select the best answer of the choices given.

---

1. As its performance has risen on all the stock indexes, the bio-tech start-up has branched out into new markets to look for opportunities they would previously have had to ignore.

    (A) they would previously have had to ignore
    (B) they would have had to ignore previously
    (C) that previously they would have had to ignore
    (D) it previously would have had to ignore in past years
    (E) it would previously have had to ignore

2. Scientists wishing to understand the kinetic movements of ancient dinosaurs are today studying the movements of modern day birds, which many scientists believe are descended from dinosaurs. A flaw in this strategy is that birds, although once genetically linked to dinosaurs, have evolved so far that any comparison is effectively meaningless.

    Which of the following, if true, would most weaken the criticism made above of the scientists' strategy?

    (A) Birds and dinosaurs have a number of important features in common that exist in no other living species.
    (B) Birds are separated from dinosaurs by 65 million years of evolution.
    (C) Our theories of dinosaur movements have recently undergone a radical reappraisal.
    (D) The study of kinetic movement is a relatively new discipline.
    (E) Many bird experts do not study dinosaurs to draw inferences about birds.

GO ON TO THE NEXT PAGE.

3. A factory in China has two options to improve efficiency: adding robotic assembly lines and subcontracting out certain small production goals that could be done more efficiently elsewhere. Adding robotic assembly lines will improve efficiency more than subcontracting some small production goals. Therefore, by adding robotic assembly lines, the factory will be doing the most that can be done to improve efficiency.

   Which of the following is an assumption on which the argument depends?

   (A) Adding robotic assembly lines will be more expensive than subcontracting some small production goals.
   (B) The factory has a choice of robotic assembly lines, some of which might be better suited to this factory than others.
   (C) The factory may or may not decide to choose either alternative.
   (D) Efficiency cannot be improved more by using both methods together than by adding robotic assembly lines alone.
   (E) This particular factory is already the third most efficient factory in China.

4. <u>Just as the early NASA space explorers attempted on each flight to push the frontiers of our knowledge, so too</u> are the new private-consortium space explorers seeking to add to man's general understanding of the cosmos.

   (A) Just as the early NASA space explorers attempted on each flight to push the frontiers of our knowledge, so too
   (B) The early NASA space explorers attempted on each flight to push the frontiers of our knowledge, and in the same way
   (C) Like the case of the early NASA space explorers who attempted on each flight to push the frontiers of our knowledge, so too
   (D) As in the early NASA space explorers' attempts on each flight to push the frontiers of our knowledge, so too
   (E) Similar to the early NASA space explorers attempted on each flight to push the frontiers of our knowledge, so too

5. A proposal for a new building fire safety code requires that fire-retardant insulation no longer be sprayed on steel girders in the factory, but be sprayed on once the girders have arrived at the building site. This will eliminate the dislodging of the insulation in transit and reduce fatalities in catastrophic fires by an estimated 20%.

   Which of the following, if true, represents the strongest challenge to the new proposal?

   (A) The fire-retardant insulation will also be required to be one inch thicker than in the past.
   (B) Studies have shown that most dislodgement of insulation occurs after the girders arrive on site.
   (C) Catastrophic fires represent only 4% of the fires reported nationally.
   (D) The proposed safety code will add considerably to the cost of new construction.
   (E) In most of Europe, spraying fire-retardant insulation onto steel girders at the building site has been required for the past ten years.

6. An effort <u>to control the crippling effects of poverty in Brazil's interior cities, begun almost thirty years ago,</u> has been partially successful, despite the setback of a major drought and the interruption of aid during an extended economic crisis.

   (A) to control the crippling effects of poverty in Brazil's interior cities, begun almost thirty years ago,
   (B) begun almost thirty years ago for controlling the crippling effects of poverty in Brazil's interior cities,
   (C) begun for controlling the crippling effects of poverty in Brazil's interior cities almost thirty years ago,
   (D) at controlling the crippling effects of poverty in Brazil's interior cities begun almost thirty years ago,
   (E) that has begun almost thirty years ago to control the crippling effects of poverty in Brazil's interior cities,

GO ON TO THE NEXT PAGE.

7. A newly discovered disease is thought to be caused by a certain bacterium. However, recently released data note that the bacterium thrives in the presence of a certain virus, implying that it is actually the virus that causes the new disease.

Which of the following pieces of evidence would most support the data's implication?

(A) In the absence of the virus, the disease has been observed to follow infection by the bacterium.
(B) The virus has been shown to aid the growth of bacteria, a process which often leads to the onset of the disease.
(C) The virus alone has been observed in many cases of the disease.
(D) In cases where the disease does not develop, infection by the bacterium is usually preceded by infection by the virus.
(E) Onset of the disease usually follows infection by both the virus and the bacterium.

8. The company was not even publicly traded until 1968, when the owner and founder sold it to David P. Markham, a private investor, who took the company public and established a long and generous policy of stock options for valued employees.

(A) who took the company public and established a long and generous policy of stock options for
(B) who, taking the company public, established a long and generous policy of stock options to
(C) who, when he took the company public, established a long and generous policy of stock options to
(D) who had taken the company public, establishing a long and generous policy of stock options as
(E) taking the company public and establishing a long and generous policy of stock options for

9. Because of a quality control problem, a supplier of flu vaccines will not be able to ship any supplies of the vaccine for the upcoming flu season. This will create a shortage of flu vaccines and result in a loss of productivity as workers call in sick.

Which of the following, if true, most seriously weakens the argument above?

(A) The quality control problem of the supplier is not as severe as some experts had initially predicted.
(B) Other suppliers of flu vaccine have not been affected by the quality control problem.
(C) Last year there was also a shortage of flu vaccine available.
(D) The price of flu vaccines is expected to fall in the next ten years.
(E) The flu season is expected to last longer than usual this year.

10. Never before had the navy defeated so many foes at once as it had in the battle of Trafalgar in 1805.

(A) so many foes at once as it had in
(B) at once as many foes as
(C) at once as many foes that there were in
(D) as many foes at once as it did in
(E) so many foes at once as that it defeated in

11. The changes that may be part of a general global warming trend include an increase in the frequency and severity of hurricanes, a gradual rise in sea level, depleting the ozone layer, and raising the temperature of the earth.

(A) depleting the ozone layer, and raising the temperature of the earth
(B) depleting the ozone layer, and a rise in the earth's temperature
(C) a depletion of the ozone layer, and raising the earth's temperature
(D) a depletion of the ozone layer, and a raise of the temperature of the earth
(E) a depletion of the ozone layer, and a rise in the temperature of the earth

GO ON TO THE NEXT PAGE.

Questions 12–16 are based on the following passage:

It has long been a tenet of business theory that the best decisions are made after careful review and consideration. Only after weighing all the options and studying projections, say most professors of business, can a practical decision be made.

Now, that model is being questioned by some business thinkers in the light of the theories of Malcolm Gladwell, who states that human beings often make better decisions in the blink of an eye.

It is, at first glance, a theory so counter-intuitive as to seem almost ludicrous. Behind any decision, Gladwell posits, there is a behind-the-scenes subconscious process in which the brain analyzes; ranks in order of importance; compares and contrasts vast amounts of information; and dismisses extraneous factors, seemingly almost instantaneously, often arriving at a conclusion in less than two seconds. Citing a multitude of studies and examples from life, Gladwell shows how that split-second decision is often better informed than a drawn-out examination.

Evanston and Cramer were the first to apply this theory to the business world. Evanston videotaped the job interviews of 400 applicants at different firms. He then played only 10 seconds of each videotape to independent human resources specialists. The specialists were able to pick out the applicants who were hired with an accuracy of over 90%.

Cramer took the experiment even further, using only five seconds of videotape, without sound. To his astonishment, the rate of accuracy with which the HR specialists were able to predict the successful applicants fell only to 82%.

Critics argue that these results illustrate a problem with stereotyping that impedes human resources specialists from hiring the best candidates even when they have the time to get below the surface: going for the candidate who "looks the part." Gladwell argues that, on the contrary, the human mind is able to make complicated decisions quickly, and that intuition often trumps an extended decision-making process.

12. The primary purpose of the passage is to

(A) discuss reasons an accepted business theory is being reexamined
(B) present evidence that resolves a contradiction in business theory
(C) describe a tenet of business practices and how that tenet can be tested in today's economic environment
(D) argue that a counter-intuitive new business idea is, in the final analysis, incorrect
(E) present evidence that invalidates a new business model

13. According to the passage, all of the following are examples of the subconscious processes by which the brain makes a decision EXCEPT

(A) analysis of information
(B) ranking of information
(C) comparison and contrast of information
(D) rejecting information that is not pertinent
(E) consulting a multitude of studies and examples

14. The author's attitude toward the long-held view that decisions should be made carefully over time expressed in lines 1–5 can best be described as

(A) dismissive and scornful
(B) respectful but questioning
(C) admiring and deferential
(D) uncertain but optimistic
(E) condescending and impatient

GO ON TO THE NEXT PAGE.

15. The author most likely mentions the results of Cramer's extension of Evanston's experiment in order to

(A) show that Cramer's hypothesis was correct while Evanston's hypothesis turned out to be incorrect
(B) show that Evanston's hypothesis was correct, while Cramer's hypothesis turned out to be incorrect
(C) demonstrate that while both experiments were scientifically rigorous, neither ended up being scientifically valid
(D) illustrate that the principle of subconscious decisions continues to work even when less information is available
(E) demonstrate that Cramer's experiment was 8% more accurate than Evanston's, even though his subjects had less information to work with

16. It can be inferred that the critics referred to in line 36 believed the excellent results of the two experiments had less to do with the innate decision-making of the subjects than with

(A) the excellent decision-making of Evanston and Cramer
(B) the expertise of Malcolm Gladwell, who originated the theory
(C) not choosing candidates who "looked the part"
(D) the use of videotape as a method of choosing candidates
(E) their unconscious use of visual stereotypes in making their selections

17. The women's volleyball team at a local college finished fifth in its division, prompting the college to fire the team's general manager. The manager responded by suing the college, saying that the team's performance put it among the top teams in the country.

Which of the following statements, if true, would support the claim of the team's manager, and resolve the apparent contradiction?

(A) The team won all of its "away" games during the season in question.
(B) Attendance at the volleyball team's games was up 35% from the year before.
(C) Of the starting team, three team members were unable to play for at least half the season because of injuries.
(D) There are 80 teams in this particular volleyball team's division.
(E) The team lost more games this year than it did the year before.

18. Country *A* recently broke off diplomatic relations with Country *B* when it was reported that Country *B* had been running a covert intelligence operation within the borders of Country *A*. While a spokesperson for Country *B* admitted the charge, the spokesperson said that it was common knowledge that all countries do this, and that Country *A* was no exception.

Which of the following inferences can be drawn from the argument above?

(A) Country *B* should apologize and dismantle its intelligence operation in Country *A*.
(B) The spokesperson for Country *B* claims that Country *A* engages in intelligence gathering too.
(C) Because all countries engage in this practice, Country *A*'s outrage was disingenuous.
(D) Relations between Country *A* and Country *B* will be strained for some time.
(E) Country *B* would be just as outraged if it was reported that Country *A* was running a covert intelligence operation with Country *B*'s borders.

GO ON TO THE NEXT PAGE.

19. Because cellular telephones emit signals that can interfere with cockpit-to-control-tower transmissions, airplane passengers' use of these instruments at all times that the airplane is in motion, even while on the ground, are prohibited.

(A) at all times that the airplane is in motion, even while on the ground, are
(B) at all times during which the airplane, even while on the ground, is in motion, are
(C) during airplane motion, even when it is on the ground, are
(D) during times of the airplane being in motion, even on the ground, is
(E) when the airplane is in motion, even while on the ground, is

20. In contrast to classical guitars, whose owners prefer the dulcet, rounded tones produced by nylon strings, folk guitar owners prefer the bright and brassy sound that only bronze or steel can create.

(A) folk guitar owners prefer the bright and brassy sound
(B) folk guitar owners prefer to get a sound that is bright and brassy
(C) with a folk guitar, the owner gets the preferably bright and brassy sound
(D) folk guitars produce a bright and brassy sound, which their owners prefer,
(E) folk guitars produce a preferred bright and brassy sound for their owners

Questions 21–22 are based on the following passage:

A system-wide county school anti-smoking education program was instituted last year. The program was clearly a success. Last year, the incidence of students smoking on school premises decreased by over 70 percent.

21. Which of the following assumptions underlies the argument in the passage?

(A) Cigarettes are detrimental to one's health; once people understand this, they will quit smoking.
(B) The doubling of the price of a pack of cigarettes last year was not the only cause of the students' altered smoking habits.
(C) The teachers chosen to lead the anti-smoking education program were the most effective teachers in the school system.
(D) The number of cigarettes smoked each day by those students who continued to smoke last year did not greatly increase.
(E) School policy enforcers were less vigilant in seeking out smokers last year than they were in previous years.

22. Which of the following, if true, would most seriously weaken the argument in the passage?

(A) The author of this statement is a school system official hoping to generate good publicity for the anti-smoking program.
(B) Most students who smoke stopped smoking on school premises last year continued to smoke when away from school.
(C) Last year, another policy change made it much easier for students to leave and return to school grounds during the school day.
(D) The school system spent more on anti-smoking education programs last year than it did in all previous years.
(E) The amount of time students spent in anti-smoking education programs last year resulted in a reduction of in-class hours devoted to academic subjects.

GO ON TO THE NEXT PAGE.

23. Mild exercise throughout pregnancy may reduce the discomfort associated with pregnancy and result in a speedier, easier birth, according to a recent study.

(A) may reduce the discomfort associated with pregnancy and result in
(B) may reduce the discomfort associated with pregnancy, with the result
(C) may cause a reduction in the discomfort associated with pregnancy and as a result
(D) might lead to a reduction in the discomfort associated with pregnancy and as a result
(E) might reduce the discomfort associated with pregnancy and resulting in

Questions 24–27 are based on the following passage:

What is it that keeps the developing world in an apparent state of perpetual poverty? Poor education, lack of basic medical care, and the absence of democratic structures all certainly contribute to these nations' plight. However, according to Peruvian economist Hernando de Soto, the overriding cause is the overwhelming prevalence of black market activity, well outside the formal economy, in these countries. The losses incurred from this condition are twofold. First, they deny the government tax revenues which could be used to improve education, medical treatment, and government efficiency. More important, however, they deny earners the chance to accumulate assets recognized by law and thus prevent them from leveraging those assets to borrow. Reforming these nations' legal systems in order to confer ownership through titling, De Soto argues, would help the poor there access the assets their work should be generating. These assets could then be used to buy homes and construct businesses, thus building a more stable and prosperous economy. De Soto estimates the value of these assets, which he terms "dead capital," at nearly $10 trillion worldwide.

De Soto is not the first to locate the developing world's problems in the domain of property rights. Others have tried property rights reform and failed. According to de Soto, this is because his predecessors attempted to model their plans on existing, successful property rights systems. In other words, they tried to transplant American and British property law to an inhospitable host. De Soto argues that within many of the extralegal markets of the developing world, mutually agreed upon rules for distributing assets and recognizing property rights already exist. Rather than force these markets to adjust to a new, foreign system of property titling, reformers should focus on codifying the existing systems wherever it is practical to do so. This would facilitate a quicker, more natural transition to an economy that builds wealth rather than squanders it.

GO ON TO THE NEXT PAGE.

24. The author's primary goal in the passage is to

(A) compare several failed attempts to address a problem
(B) respond to criticism of a new theory
(C) identify the problems inherent in a new economic theory
(D) describe a novel approach to an old problem
(E) compare different property rights systems in the industrial world

25. According to the passage, de Soto believes that the quickest way to address poverty in the developing world is to

(A) increase funding for education
(B) build the infrastructure to support lending
(C) ensure medical care for all citizens
(D) aggressively root out corruption in government
(E) increase tax rates on all citizens in developing countries

26. The author's assertion that "reformers should focus on codifying the existing systems wherever it is practical to do so" (lines 39–41) suggests that

(A) in some instances, current systems are inadequate to meet the needs of a market economy
(B) these systems are already written down and need only be enacted as law
(C) where it is impractical to codify existing systems, countries should adopt American property law
(D) the existing systems are superior to those currently in use in modern industrialized countries
(E) improving education and medical care in these countries should take priority over reforming property laws

27. The term "dead capital" (line 24) refers to

(A) loans that are never repaid
(B) failed investments in new businesses
(C) cities ruined by over-industrialization
(D) the proceeds of extralegal commerce
(E) property passed from generation to generation

GO ON TO THE NEXT PAGE.

Verbal Test
Bin 3—Hard Questions
26 Questions

This test is made up of sentence correction, critical reasoning, and reading comprehension questions.

Sentence Correction Directions: Each of the sentence correction questions presents a sentence, part or all of which is underlined. Beneath the sentence you will find five ways of phrasing the underlined part. The first of these repeats the original; the other four are different. Follow the requirements of standard written English to choose your answer, paying attention to grammar, word choice, and sentence construction. Select the answer that produces the most effective sentence; your answer should make the sentence clear, exact, and free of grammatical errors. It should also minimize awkwardness, ambiguity, and redundancy.

Reading Comprehension Directions: Each of the reading comprehension questions is based on the content of a passage. After reading the passage, answer all questions pertaining to it on the basis of what is stated or implied in the passage. For each question, select the best answer of the choices given.

Critical Reasoning Directions: Each of the critical reasoning questions is based on a short argument, a set of statements, or a plan of action. For each question, select the best answer of the choices given.

---

1. Unlike Franklin D. Roosevelt's bootstrap program that helped to restart economic growth in the 1930s through public works, Ronald Reagan proposed a program of trickle-down economics to restart the economy.

(A) Franklin D. Roosevelt's bootstrap program that helped
(B) Franklin D. Roosevelt and his bootstrap program which helped
(C) Franklin D. Roosevelt, whose bootstrap program helped
(D) the bootstrap program of Franklin D. Roosevelt that has helped
(E) Franklin D. Roosevelt and his bootstrap program helping

2. In the 1970s, it became evident that writing about someone else's research was much easier for social scientists who wanted to make a quick name for themselves than it was to do their own research.

(A) that writing about someone else's research was much easier for social scientists who wanted to make a quick name for themselves
(B) that for social scientists who wanted to make a quick name for themselves, it was much easier to write about someone else's research
(C) that for social scientists wanting to make a quick name for themselves, writing about someone else's research was much easier
(D) for social scientists who wanted to make a quick name for themselves that writing about someone else's research was much easier
(E) for social scientists who wanted to make a quick name for themselves, writing about someone else's research was much easier

GO ON TO THE NEXT PAGE.

<u>Questions 3–4</u> are based on the following:

To improve the town's overcrowded school system, the town council has proposed an ambitious education plan to reduce classroom size and make capital improvements—a plan they intend to pay for with an increase in property taxes for homes valued over $500,000. Although the school system desperately needs improving, the town council's plan should be defeated because the majority of the people who would end up paying for the improvements receive no benefit from them.

3. Which of the following, if true, most strengthens the argument above?

(A) The town's school system is currently ranked among the worst in the state.
(B) Other towns nearby that have made similar capital improvements did not find that the improvements translated to a better quality of education.
(C) The town will need to spend additional money on architect's plans for the capital improvements.
(D) An examination of the tax rolls shows that most homeowners in this category no longer have school-age children.
(E) Some homeowners will delay home improvement projects in order to keep the value of their homes below $500,000.

4. Which of the following, if true, provides the town council with the strongest counter to the objection that its plan is unfair?

(A) Even with the proposed increase, property taxes in the town are well below the national average.
(B) Paying for the school system improvements using existing town funds will result in shortfalls that will force the town into arrears.
(C) The teachers in the town's school system receive some of the lowest salary packages in the immediate area, which is a major cause of attrition.
(D) Smaller class sizes and capital improvements in a school system tend to increase property values in the surrounding community.
(E) A feasibility study has shown that the cost of the improvements will likely be 20% higher than projected.

5. The rules of engagement under which a border patrol station can decide to use deadly force <u>includes responding to an invasionary incursion and the return of</u> hostile fire.

(A) includes responding to an invasionary incursion and the return of
(B) includes responding to an invasionary incursion and returning
(C) include responding to an invasionary incursion and the return of
(D) include a response to an invasionary incursion and the return of
(E) include a response to an invasionary incursion and returning

6. Although the word "phonetician" is popularly associated with Henry Higgins's task of improving the diction of Eliza Doolittle in *My Fair Lady*, in linguistics, <u>it is someone who studies</u> the formation of language.

(A) it is someone who studies
(B) it is a person studying
(C) it refers to someone who studies
(D) they are people who study
(E) it is in reference to people who study

GO ON TO THE NEXT PAGE.

7. Experts studying patterns of shark attacks on humans have noted that attacks tend to diminish when the water temperature drops below 65 degrees Fahrenheit. Until recently, researchers believed this was because sharks prefer warmer water, and thus are present in fewer numbers in colder water. However, new research shows that sharks are present in equal numbers in cold and warm water.

Which of the following, if true, best explains the apparent paradox?

(A) In general, humans prefer warm water.
(B) Sharks' keen sense of smell is enhanced in cold water.
(C) In the Pacific, shark attacks tend to occur more frequently in the daytime.
(D) Of the more than 200 types of sharks present in the ocean, only three attack humans.
(E) The average temperature of the earth's oceans is 55 degrees.

8. As a result of surging economic indicators, most analysts upgraded the company's stock to a strong "buy," ignoring the advice of the head of a watchdog organization <u>who warned that the company's product would prove not only dangerous but</u> ineffective in the long run.

(A) who warned that the company's product would prove not only dangerous but
(B) warning that the company's product would prove not only dangerous and also
(C) warning that the company's product would prove itself to be both dangerous and
(D) who warned that the company's product would prove to be both dangerous and
(E) who was warning that the company's product would prove not only dangerous but

9. Scientists today accept that the increased severity of hurricanes in the last 10 years has been a result of warmer water in the Caribbean, which "feeds" the storms as they pass over it by a mechanism not yet completely understood. Thus, these severe hurricanes are yet more evidence of global warming.

Which of the following, if true, would most strengthen the argument above?

(A) Accurate statistics on the warming of the earth do not go back more than 100 years.
(B) Scientists have now discovered a new undersea current, fueled by an undersea volcano, which could have funneled warmer water into the Caribbean.
(C) The arctic ice caps have been losing three feet of circumference each year for the past five years.
(D) A new modeling computer program projects that the severity of hurricanes will increase over the next 10 years.
(E) Some scientists believe they will soon prove that the mechanism by which a storm picks up energy from warm water is based on convection.

10. A new influx of unprecedented private investment should create a bright new future for manned space exploration, <u>making the possibility of commercial space tourism much more viable than 10 years ago</u>.

(A) making the possibility of commercial space tourism much more viable than 10 years ago
(B) and make the possibility of commercial space tourism much more viable than 10 years ago
(C) making the possibility of commercial space tourism much more viable than it was 10 years ago
(D) and make the possibility of commercial space tourism much more viable than it was 10 years in the past
(E) making the possibility of commercial space tourism much more viable than 10 years in the past

GO ON TO THE NEXT PAGE.

Questions 11–15 are based on the following passage:

As the American workforce gets grayer, age discrimination will likely become a more prominent issue in the courts. It is, of course, illegal to discriminate against an employee because of his or her age, and yet it is not illegal to dismiss a worker because he has a high salary and expensive health care.

This apparent contradiction is at the heart of a raft of cases now making their way through the courts. The outcome of these cases will have broad implications for the workplace in the coming years. By 2010, the Bureau of Labor Statistics has projected that more than half of all workers will be over 40—many of whom, by dint of seniority and promotions, will be earning higher than median salaries, eligible for more stock options, and carrying higher health care costs as a result of a larger number of dependents and the increased cost of health care for older workers.

Is it any wonder that a bottom-line oriented business might want to shed these workers, whose productivity is likely to plummet in the next few years, even as they become more expensive employees?

Still, the legal challenges of implementing this policy are daunting. Businesses have the right to rate workers on their productivity and to rank them against their peers. But they are not allowed to prejudge individuals based on their sex, race or age. Each worker must be treated on his or her own merits, rather than by how they fit into a larger profile of the group they belong to.

For companies looking to lay off these workers, the cost of making a mistake is high; while only one in three age discrimination suits are won by the plaintiff, the awards tend to be steep and the political fall-out harsh.

11. The primary purpose of the passage is to

(A) advocate on behalf of the older American worker who could soon face dismissal
(B) describe the origin of two theories of labor law and their effects on the workplace
(C) present an overview of the legal ramifications of a practice some call discriminatory
(D) describe the process by which America's workforce is getting older
(E) describe the methods by which a company could reduce its bottom line

12. Which of the following best describes the organization of the second paragraph of the passage?

(A) An assertion is made and then briefly contradicted.
(B) A contradiction is stated and then quickly resolved.
(C) A new theory is described and then qualified.
(D) An apparent inconsistency is stated and its consequences outlined.
(E) A conventional model is described and an alternative is introduced.

13. Which of the following, if true, would most effectively weaken the author's assertion that a "bottom-line oriented business" might want to fire older workers?

(A) A new study shows that, on average, younger workers earn less and have lower associated medical costs than older workers.
(B) Older workers have a higher rate of absenteeism than younger workers.
(C) A new study shows that older workers are in fact more productive and have fewer medical expenses compared to younger workers.
(D) A forecasted downturn in the economy will erode profits in may American businesses.
(E) A new bill scheduled to become law will make it easier for employers to employ illegal aliens.

GO ON TO THE NEXT PAGE.

14. It can be inferred from the passage that

(A) what is good for American companies is not necessarily good for older Americans
(B) American companies are prohibited by law from practices that discriminate based on gender, color of skin, or age
(C) large monetary judgments from age discrimination suits might prove more expensive than paying older employees' salaries
(D) by the year 2020, the percentage of older employees will be even higher than in the year 2010
(E) some older employees may well be more productive than some younger employees

15. The author mentions all of the following as driving up the cost to employers for employing workers over the age of 40 EXCEPT

(A) the cost of out-placement services
(B) a larger number of dependents
(C) increased cost of health care
(D) higher median salaries
(E) the cost of employee stock options

16. A pharmaceutical company claims that its new drug promotes learning in children. To back up its claims, the company points to a study of 300 children who were given the drug, along with a control group of 300 children who were given a placebo. The 300 children who were given the drug reported that they were able to retain new information much more easily.

Which of the following statements, if true, would most tend to weaken the claims of the pharmaceutical company?

(A) The 300 children in the control group also reported that they were able to retain new information much more easily.
(B) The drug has also been shown to prevent common skin rashes.
(C) The drug has been proven to have severe side-effects.
(D) The children in the study were not given any other medications during the study.
(E) The children who were given the drug did better on cognitive measurement tests after the drug therapy than before.

17. In order to understand the dangers of the current real-estate bubble in Country *Y*, one has only to look to the real-estate bubble of the last decade in Country *Z*. In that country, incautious investors used the inflated value of their real estate as collateral in risky margin loans. When the real-estate market collapsed, many investors went bankrupt, creating a major recession. Country *Y* is in real danger of a similar recession if more-stringent laws restricting margin loans are not enacted promptly.

The answer to which of the following questions would be most useful in evaluating the significance of the author's claims?

(A) Was the real estate in Country *Z* located principally in rural areas or was it located in more urban communities?
(B) Could the bankruptcies in Country *Z* have been prevented by a private bailout plan by the nation's banks?
(C) Does Country *Y* currently have any laws on its books regarding margin loans?
(D) Are there business ties and connections between Country *Y* and Country *Z*?
(E) Were there other factors in the case of Country *Y* that would make the comparison with Country *Z* less meaningful?

18. Rules governing participation in a new extreme sports fantasy camp require <u>that applicants should be physically fit enough to endure the demanding</u> activities in which they will be engaging.

(A) that applicants should be physically fit enough to endure the demanding
(B) that applicants be physically fit enough to endure the demanding
(C) applicants should have enough physical fitness to allow enduring the demands of
(D) applicants are physically fit enough as to endure the demands of
(E) physical fitness in applicants, enough for endurance of demanding

GO ON TO THE NEXT PAGE.

19. During the summer of 2002, the Outer Banks suffered a massive toad infestation, discouraging many vacationers from visiting the area.

(A) suffered a massive toad infestation, discouraging
(B) suffered from a massive toad infestation and discouraged
(C) suffered a massive infestation of toads, which discouraged
(D) was suffering a massive infestation of toads and discouraging
(E) had suffered from a massive toad infestation and this discouraged

20. A prolonged period of low mortgage rates resulted in a period of the most robust home sales ever. At the same time, the average sale price of resale homes actually dropped, when adjusted for inflation.

Which of the following, if true, would explain the apparent contradiction between the robust home sales and the drop in the average sale price of resale homes?

(A) The inflation rate during this period exceeded the increase in the average salary, thus preventing many buyers from securing mortgages.
(B) Resale homes represent the best value on the real estate market.
(C) Without the adjustment for inflation, the price of resale homes actually increased by a very slight amount.
(D) The decrease in mortgage rates was accompanied by a widening of the types of mortgages from which borrowers could choose.
(E) The increase in home sales was due entirely to an increase in the sale of new homes.

21. Luis is taller than Rei. Kiko is taller than Marcus. Therefore, Kiko is taller than Rei.

The conclusion drawn above is not supported by the argument; however, the addition of one additional piece of information would make the conclusion logically sound. All of the following could be that additional piece of information EXCEPT:

(A) Kiko is taller than Luis.
(B) Luis is taller than Marcus.
(C) Luis and Marcus are the same height.
(D) Marcus and Rei are the same height.
(E) Marcus is taller than Rei.

22. It has been estimated that an increase in average regional temperature of even 0.5 degrees Fahrenheit could cost the southern United States more than $10 billion in lost agricultural income annually.

(A) an increase in average regional temperature of even 0.5 degrees Fahrenheit could cost the southern United States more than $10 billion in lost agricultural income annually
(B) every year, $10 billion in agricultural income could be the cost to the southern United States as a result of an increase in the average temperature of the region of even 0.5 degrees Fahrenheit
(C) the cost to the southern United States could be more than $10 billion in income from agriculture that results from a regional increase in average temperature of even 0.5 degrees Fahrenheit annually
(D) annual income losses in agriculture of more than $10 billion could be the cost from increasing average temperatures in the southern United States of even 0.5 degrees Fahrenheit
(E) annual income losses to the southern United States from the increase in average regional temperature of even 0.5 percent costing more than $10 billion in agricultural income each year

GO ON TO THE NEXT PAGE.

23. Within the Green Party, an internal debate is raging among those who believe in compromising with mainstream politicians in order to achieve some goals with those who believe the party must not abandon any of its principles.

(A) among those who believe in compromising with mainstream politicians in order to achieve some goals with those who believe the party must not abandon any of its principles
(B) among those who believe that achieving some goals requires compromise with mainstream politicians and those believing that none of the party's principles must be abandoned
(C) between those believing in compromising with mainstream politicians in order to achieve some goals with those who believe the party must not abandon any of its principles
(D) between those who believe in compromising with mainstream politicians in order to achieve some goals and those who believe the party must not abandon any of its principles
(E) between those believing that achieving some goals means compromising with mainstream politicians and those who believe that the principles of the party must not be abandoned

24. In comparison to the drivers who live in Mountainview, a greater proportion of the drivers who live in Oak Valley exceed the speed limit regularly. This explains why there are more accidents each year in Oak Valley than in Mountainview.

All of the following statements, if true, weaken the conclusion drawn above EXCEPT:

(A) Oak Valley has a greater proportion of blind intersections and sharp turns than has Mountainview.
(B) There is a greater number of drivers in Oak Valley than in Mountainview.
(C) Drivers in Mountainview must travel to Oak Valley to shop and work.
(D) Per capita, there are fewer police officers monitoring traffic in Oak Valley than there are in Mountainview.
(E) The roads are icier for a greater portion of the year in Oak Valley than in Mountainview.

GO ON TO THE NEXT PAGE.

25. A study showed that only ten percent of American dog owners enroll their dogs in formal obedience training classes. More than twenty percent of these dog owners, the study also showed, participate in dog shows. Thus, it is obvious that people who train their dogs are more likely to participate in dog shows than are people who do not train their dogs.

The conclusion above is correct provided which of the following statements is also true?

(A) It is impossible for a dog to compete in a dog show if the dog has not completed at least one formal obedience training class.
(B) The proportion of dog owners who enroll their dogs in formal obedience training classes is representative of the proportion who train their dogs outside such classes.
(C) Dog owners who participate in dog shows only train their dogs by enrolling them in formal obedience training lessons.
(D) Participation in dog shows is a reliable indicator of how much attention a dog owner pays to his dog.
(E) Only purebred dogs can participate in dog shows, so many owners who enroll their dogs in formal obedience training classes are excluded from this activity.

26. A bullet train travels in excess of 150 miles per hour. Therefore, if a train travels slower than 150 miles per hour, it is not a bullet train.

Which of the following most closely parallels the reasoning used in the argument above?

(A) An orange ripens only on the vine. If it ripens on the vine, then it is not an orange.
(B) Newspapers are often read by more than one person. Therefore, magazines are also likely to be read by more than one person.
(C) An earthquake of 5.0 or above on the Richter scale causes massive damage. If there is not massive damage, then the earthquake did not attain a 5.0 or above.
(D) A supersonic plane travels at speeds in excess of Mach 1. If it is not supersonic, then it will travel at speeds below Mach 1.
(E) Fluoride generally prevents cavities. If there are no cavities, then there was no fluoride used.

END OF EXAMINATION

ANSWER KEY

MATH				VERBAL		
Bin 1	**Bin 2**	**Bin 3**	**Bin 4**	**Bin 1**	**Bin 2**	**Bin 3**
1. C	1. C	1. B	1. C	1. C	1. E	1. C
2. C	2. B	2. D	2. C	2. D	2. A	2. B
3. D	3. C	3. A	3. C	3. B	3. D	3. D
4. D	4. A	4. C	4. C	4. B	4. A	4. D
5. D	5. B	5. D	5. E	5. E	5. B	5. D
6. B	6. A	6. D	6. B	6. E	6. A	6. C
7. E	7. B	7. D	7. B	7. A	7. C	7. A
8. C	8. C	8. C	8. C	8. D	8. A	8. D
9. B	9. A	9. A	9. A	9. C	9. B	9. B
10. D	10. C	10. D	10. B	10. A	10. D	10. C
11. B	11. B	11. B	11. A	11. D	11. E	11. C
12. D	12. B	12. B	12. D	12. B	12. A	12. D
13. C	13. D	13. A	13. E	13. B	13. E	13. C
14. A	14. B	14. A	14. A	14. C	14. B	14. B
15. D	15. E	15. D	15. E	15. D	15. D	15. A
16. A	16. E	16. C	16. A	16. B	16. E	16. A
17. B	17. C	17. D	17. D	17. D	17. D	17. E
18. B	18. E	18. C	18. D	18. B	18. B	18. B
19. C	19. C	19. C	19. C	19. C	19. E	19. C
20. A	20. D	20. A	20. B	20. E	20. D	20. E
21. D	21. B	21. D	21. A	21. B	21. B	21. B
22. D	22. D	22. A	22. E	22. E	22. C	22. A
23. C	23. D	23. D	23. D	23. D	23. A	23. D
24. D	24. A	24. E	24. C	24. A	24. D	24. D
25. B	25. A	25. D	25. D	25. E	25. B	25. B
26. B	26. E	26. A			26. A	26. C
	27. C				27. D	

Chapter 26
GMAT Math and Verbal Practice Bins: Answers and Explanations

If you really want to improve your score, then you should read *all* the explanations for *all* the questions on the pages that follow, not just the ones you got wrong. It's important to make sure you're getting questions correct for the right reasons and even more important that you are recognizing opportunities to use The Princeton Review techniques, which can save you time and eliminate the possibility of careless errors.

MATH BIN 1

QUESTIONS

1. What percent of 112 is 14 ?

(A) 0.125%
(B) 8%
(C) 12.5%
(D) 125%
(E) 800%

EXPLANATIONS

1. **C** Since this is a percent problem, you can solve it by thinking in terms of $\frac{part}{whole}$. In this case, $\frac{part}{whole} = \frac{14}{112} = \frac{x}{100}$; cross-multiply to get $112x = 1{,}400$, so $x = \frac{1{,}400}{112}$, and $x = 12.5$.

Like most percent questions on the GMAT, you can also find the answer using POE. 14 is a little bigger than $\frac{1}{10}$, or 10%, of 112—11.2 is exactly 10%—so the answer can only be C.

2. The number of flights leaving a certain airport doubles during every one-hour period between 9 A.M. and noon; after noon, the number of flights leaving from the airport doubles during every two-hour period. If 4 flights left from the airport between 9 and 10 A.M., how many flights left the airport between 2 and 4 P.M.?

(A) 32
(B) 48
(C) 64
(D) 128
(E) 256

2. **C** Rather than try to rely on high school-style exponential growth formulas, let's just count this one out. If 4 flights left the airport between 9 and 10 A.M., then 8 left between 10 and 11 A.M., and 16 left between 11 A.M. and noon. Starting at noon, the flights begin to double every *two* hours, so 32 left between noon and 2 P.M., and 64 left between 2 P.M. and 4 P.M. The correct answer is C. If you chose E, you may have forgotten to account for the afternoon change in the rate of increase, and the test writers, of course, made sure that the answer you came up with was there waiting for you.

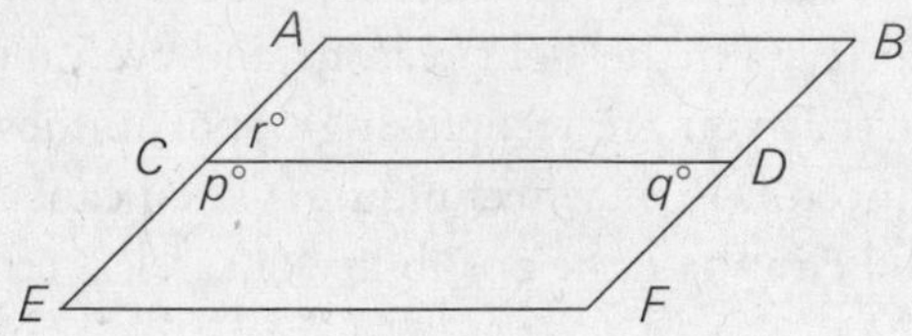

3. If both *ABDC* and *CDFE* are parallelograms, what is $q + r$?

(1) $r = 70$

(2) $p = 110$

(A) Statement (1) ALONE is sufficient, but statement (2) alone is not sufficient.
(B) Statement (2) ALONE is sufficient, but statement (1) alone is not sufficient.
(C) BOTH statements TOGETHER are sufficient, but NEITHER statement ALONE is sufficient.
(D) EACH statement ALONE is sufficient.
(E) Statements (1) and (2) TOGETHER are not sufficient.

3. **D** Since we have parallelograms, we really have only two angles, big ones and small ones, and we know that a big angle plus a small one equals 180. Statement (1) tells us the value of *r*; *q*, like *r*, is a small angle, so $q + r = 70 + 70$, or 140. We're down to A and D.
Statement (2) gives us the value of a big angle, which we can subtract from 180 to get the value of a small angle. We now have the same information we had in Statement (1) and our answer is D.

MATH BIN 1

QUESTIONS

4. Chris's convertible gets gas mileage that is 40% greater than that of Stan's SUV. If Harry's hatchback gets gas mileage that is 15% greater than that of Chris's convertible, then Harry's hatchback gets gas mileage that is what percent greater than that of Stan's SUV?

(A) 25%
(B) 46%
(C) 55%
(D) 61%
(E) 66%

5. If x is equal to 1 more than the product of 3 and z, and y is equal to 1 less than the product of 2 and z, then $2x$ is how much greater than $3y$ when z is 4 ?

(A) 1
(B) 2
(C) 3
(D) 5
(E) 6

6. In 2005, did Company *A* have more than twice the number of employees that Company *B* did?

(1) In 2005, Company *A* had 11,500 more employees than did Company *B*.

(2) In 2005, the 3,000 employees with advanced degrees at Company *A* made up 12.5% of that company's total number employees, and the 2,500 employees with advanced degrees at Company *B* made up 20% of that company's total number of employees.

(A) Statement (1) ALONE is sufficient, but statement (2) alone is not sufficient.
(B) Statement (2) ALONE is sufficient, but statement (1) alone is not sufficient.
(C) BOTH statements TOGETHER are sufficient, but NEITHER statement ALONE is sufficient.
(D) EACH statement ALONE is sufficient.
(E) Statements (1) and (2) TOGETHER are not sufficient.

EXPLANATIONS

4. **D** This is a Plugging In problem. Since it's a percent problem, too, and the question asks us to find a percentage greater than the mileage of Stan's SUV, let's make Stan's mileage 100. Chris's mileage is therefore 140; 15% of 140 is 21, so Harry's mileage is 161. 161 is 61% greater than 100, and the correct answer is D.
Answer choices A and C are both traps, since they're simple addition and subtraction, respectively, of the numbers in the problem. If you got B, you probably increased Chris's mileage by 15% of 40, rather than 15% of 140.

5. **D** Start by translating the two original equations: $x = 3z + 1$ and $y = 2z - 1$. If z is 4, then $x = 13$ and $y = 7$. $2x$ is thus 26 and $3y$ is 21. The difference between the two values is 5, so the correct answer is D.
If you chose A, you may have mistakenly added when the problem asked for a product. If you got E, you may have solved for $x - y$ when the problem asked for $2x - 3y$. And if you got C, you may have done both.

6. **B** Statement (1) tells us the difference between the numbers of employees at the two companies. Without the actual number of employees at either company, though, this information isn't sufficient to answer this yes-or-no question, so we're down to B, C, or E.
Statement (2), on the other hand, gives us the part-to-whole relationship we need to solve for the actual number of employees at each of the companies. We therefore know we can answer the question with a definitive "yes" or "no"—it doesn't matter which one is actually correct—so the answer is B.

(If you really want to crunch the numbers, that 12.5% at Company *A* is the same as $\frac{1}{8}$, and Company *A* had 24,000 employees; that 20% at Company *B* is the same as $\frac{1}{5}$, and Company *B* had 12,500 employees. The answer to the original question is "no"; Company *A* did not have more than twice the number of employees as did Company *B*.)

QUESTIONS

7. Is x^3 equal to 125 ?

(1) $x > 4$

(2) $x < 6$

(A) Statement (1) ALONE is sufficient, but statement (2) alone is not sufficient.
(B) Statement (2) ALONE is sufficient, but statement (1) alone is not sufficient.
(C) BOTH statements TOGETHER are sufficient, but NEITHER statement ALONE is sufficient.
(D) EACH statement ALONE is sufficient.
(E) Statements (1) and (2) TOGETHER are not sufficient.

8. Bob leaves point *A* and drives due west to point *B*. From point *B*, he drives due south to point *C*. How far is Bob from his original location?

(1) Point *A* is 24 miles from point *B*.

(2) Point *B* is 18 miles from point *C*.

(A) Statement (1) ALONE is sufficient, but statement (2) alone is not sufficient.
(B) Statement (2) ALONE is sufficient, but statement (1) alone is not sufficient.
(C) BOTH statements TOGETHER are sufficient, but NEITHER statement ALONE is sufficient.
(D) EACH statement ALONE is sufficient.
(E) Statements (1) and (2) TOGETHER are not sufficient.

EXPLANATIONS

7. **E** The question "Is x^3 equal to 125?" can be rewritten as "Is $x = 5$?" This is a yes-or-no question, and the best way to tackle it is to plug in twice. In Statement (1), we can plug in 5, in which case the answer to the question "Is x^3 equal to 125?" is "yes." Or, we can plug in 6, in which case the answer is "no." Thus, because we get two different answers depending on the numbers we plug in, Statement (1) is not sufficient. We're down to B, C, or E.
In Statement (2), we can plug in 5, in which case the answer is "yes," or 4, in which case the answer is "no." Eliminate B.
To see if the answer is C, we must choose a number that satisfies the conditions of both Statements (1) and (2) at the same time. We can plug in 5, in which case the answer is "yes." You might have been tempted to choose C at this point because no other integer will satisfy the two equations at the same time, but does this problem limit us to picking integers? Nope. What about 4.5? Or 5.2? In either of these cases, the answer is "no." Because we get two different answers depending on what numbers we plug in, the combination of Statements (1) and (2) is not sufficient either, and the correct answer is E.

8. **C** When a geometry problem comes without a diagram, always start by drawing one of your own. In this case, your diagram should look like this:

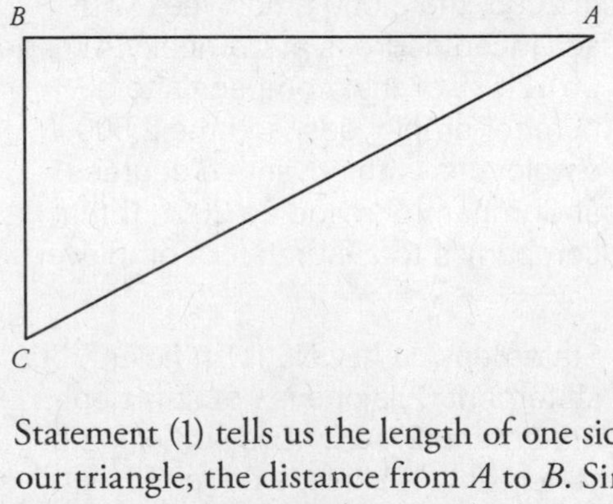

Statement (1) tells us the length of one side of our triangle, the distance from *A* to *B*. Since we know we have a right triangle (because Bob drove due west and due south), any two sides would be enough to find the remaining side. And *if* we knew that we had a "special" right triangle, one side might be enough. Neither of these cases applies, though, so we're down to B, C, or E.

QUESTIONS

EXPLANATIONS

Statement (2) gives us, again, a single side. Remember, though, that we can no longer consider the information from Statement (1), so this statement alone is also insufficient. We're down to C or E.

When we put the 2 statements together, we know we *could* solve for the remaining side using the Pythagorean theorem—although, since this is a Data Sufficiency question, there's no reason we would. The correct answer is C. Incidentally, if we did want to solve for the third side, we could save a lot of unnecessary calculation by recognizing this as a multiple of the old GMAT favorite, the 3-4-5 triangle. The two shorter sides of the triangle are multiplied by 6, so the remaining side must be 30.

9. The formula $M = \sqrt{l^2 + w^2 + d^2}$ describes the relationship between the length of *M*, which is the longest line that can be drawn in a rectangular solid, and the length, *l*, width, *w*, and depth, *d*, of that rectangular solid. The longest line that can be drawn in a rectangular solid with a length of 12, a width of 4, and a depth of 3 is how much longer than the longest line that can drawn in a rectangular solid with a length of 6, a width of 3, and a depth of 2 ?

(A) 5
(B) 6
(C) 7
(D) 9
(E) 13

9. **B** Although the relationship provided in the problem is based on geometry, this isn't really a geometry problem for us: We can simply plug the given numbers into the formula. Starting with the larger rectangular solid, $\sqrt{12^2 + 4^2 + 3^2}$ $= \sqrt{144 + 16 + 9} = \sqrt{169} = 13$. For the smaller rectangular solid, $\sqrt{6^2 + 3^2 + 2^2} = \sqrt{36 + 9 + 4} =$ $\sqrt{49} = 7$. Both 13 and 7 are, of course, answer choices, but the problem asked us for the *difference* between the two values, so the correct answer is 6, choice B.

QUESTIONS

10. Is the average (arithmetic mean) of *a*, *b*, and *c* equal to 8 ?

(1) Three times the sum of *a*, *b*, and *c* is equal to 72.

(2) The sum of 2*a*, 2*b*, and 2*c* is equal to 48.

(A) Statement (1) ALONE is sufficient, but statement (2) alone is not sufficient.
(B) Statement (2) ALONE is sufficient, but statement (1) alone is not sufficient.
(C) BOTH statements TOGETHER are sufficient, but NEITHER statement ALONE is sufficient.
(D) EACH statement ALONE is sufficient.
(E) Statements (1) and (2) TOGETHER are not sufficient.

EXPLANATIONS

10. **D** This is a yes-or-no question, and we need to recognize that it's not asking about the individual values of *a*, *b*, and *c*—it's asking only about the average of those values. Of course, we could easily find the average if we knew the individual values. But, we can also find the average if we know the sum of the values, since the average of any group of values is their sum divided by the number of values in the group. Therefore, the question is asking us whether $\frac{a+b+c}{3} = 8$. To simplify this equation, multiply both sides by 3 to get $a + b + c = 24$. If the sum is 24, then the average is 8.

Statement (1) tells us that $3(a + b + c) = 72$. We can divide both sides by 3 to find out that the sum is, indeed, 24; the average is 8; and the answer to the question is "yes." Since this is a Data Sufficiency problem, though, we can stop as soon as we know that we can find the sum of *a*, *b*, and *c*, and we're down to A and D.

Statement (2) tells us that $2a + 2b + 2c = 48$. If we factor a 2 out of the left side of the equation, we get $2(a + b + c) = 48$ and once again see that we can find the sum. The correct answer is D.

QUESTIONS

11. $\sqrt{\sqrt{\left(1+\frac{17}{64}\right)}} =$

(A) $\frac{\sqrt{34}}{8}$

(B) $\frac{3\sqrt{2}}{4}$

(C) $\frac{9}{8}$

(D) $\frac{\sqrt{68}}{4}$

(E) $\frac{3\sqrt{2}}{2}$

EXPLANATIONS

11. **B** Since we should always calculate things inside the parentheses first—don't forget PEMDAS!—start by adding 1 and $\frac{17}{64}$ to get $\frac{81}{64}$. Those are both perfect squares, so the inner root sign will be easy to handle: $\sqrt{\frac{81}{64}} = \frac{\sqrt{81}}{\sqrt{64}} = \frac{9}{8}$. Don't grab answer choice C, though—we still need to work the outer sign: $\sqrt{\frac{9}{8}} = \frac{\sqrt{9}}{\sqrt{8}} = \frac{3}{2\sqrt{2}}$. Like in high school, we can't leave a radical on the bottom of a fraction, so we'll need to multiply our answer by $\frac{\sqrt{2}}{\sqrt{2}}$ to get our final answer of B, $\frac{3\sqrt{2}}{4}$.

If you're comfortable estimating fractions and roots, you can apply POE to this question. $1 + \frac{17}{64}$ is a little greater than 1; the square root of something a little greater than 1 is also something a little greater than 1; and the square root of that number is, again, something a little greater than 1. Only B and C are a little greater than 1.

QUESTIONS

12. A certain stadium is currently full to $\frac{13}{16}$ of its maximum seating capacity. What is the maximum seating capacity of the stadium?

(1) If 1,250 people were to enter the stadium, the stadium would be full to $\frac{15}{16}$ of its maximum seating capacity.

(2) If 2,500 people were to leave the stadium, the stadium would be full to $\frac{9}{16}$ of its maximum seating capacity.

(A) Statement (1) ALONE is sufficient, but statement (2) alone is not sufficient.
(B) Statement (2) ALONE is sufficient, but statement (1) alone is not sufficient.
(C) BOTH statements TOGETHER are sufficient, but NEITHER statement ALONE is sufficient.
(D) EACH statement ALONE is sufficient.
(E) Statements (1) and (2) TOGETHER are not sufficient.

EXPLANATIONS

12. D This is a fraction problem, so the key is to convert fractions to actual numbers. Statement (1) tells us that 1,250 people will take the stadium from $\frac{13}{16}$ full to $\frac{15}{16}$ full; that's a difference of $\frac{2}{16}$, or $\frac{1}{8}$, so we know that 1,250 represents $\frac{1}{8}$ of the total seating capacity of the stadium. The stadium must, therefore, hold 8 × 1,250, or 10,000 people, and we're down to A or D. Statement (2) allows us to find a similar equivalence: a change of 2,500 represents the difference between $\frac{9}{16}$ and $\frac{13}{16}$, that is, $\frac{4}{16}$, or $\frac{1}{4}$ of the stadium's total seating capacity. So we know we can find the total seating capacity (4 × 2,500, or 10,000 people) with Statement (2) as well, making D the correct answer.

MATH BIN 1

QUESTIONS

13. Andre has already saved $\frac{3}{7}$ of the cost of a new car, and he has calculated that he will be able to save $\frac{2}{5}$ of the remaining amount before the end of the summer. What fraction of the cost of the new car will he still need to save after the end of the summer?

(A) $\frac{6}{35}$

(B) $\frac{8}{35}$

(C) $\frac{12}{35}$

(D) $\frac{23}{35}$

(E) $\frac{29}{35}$

$\{1, 4, 6, y\}$

14. If the average (arithmetic mean) of the set of numbers above is 6, then what is the median?

(A) 5
(B) 6
(C) 7
(D) 13
(E) 24

EXPLANATIONS

13. **C** Because there are fractions in the answer choices, and they're fractions of an unspecified amount, the quickest way to solve this problem is to plug in. Let's make the price of Andre's dream car \$35—the denominators of the fractions in the problem are 7 and 5 (both factors of 35) and, moreover, 35 is in the denominator of *all* of the answer choices.

If the car costs \$35, and Andre has already saved $\frac{3}{7}$ of that, or \$15, he currently has \$20 left to save. Before the end of the summer he'll be able to save $\frac{2}{5}$ of that remaining \$20, or \$8. That will give him a total of \$23 saved toward his car, leaving him \$12 to go. Expressed as a fraction of the cost of the car, that's $\frac{12}{35}$, and the correct answer is C.

As always, watch those trap answers. Choice D is the fraction of the cost that Andre will have saved by the end of the summer. Choice A is what you'd get if you calculated Andre's summer earnings as two-fifths of the total cost of the car instead of two-fifths of what Andre has left to save. Choice E is what you'd get if you made both mistakes.

14. **A** The average of all four numbers is 6, so the numbers must add up to 6 times 4, or 24. That means y must equal 13. And if y equals 13, the median must be 5—that is, the average of the two middle numbers in the set. Even if y is very large, the middle numbers will still be 4 and 6, so choices D and E are much too large.

QUESTIONS

15. A store sells a six-pack of soda for \$2.70. If this represents a savings of 10 percent of the individual price of cans of soda, then what is the price of a single can of soda?

(A) \$ 0.35
(B) \$ 0.40
(C) \$ 0.45
(D) \$ 0.50
(E) \$ 0.55

16. If Beth spent \$400 of her earnings last month on rent, how much did Beth earn last month?

(1) Beth saved $\frac{1}{3}$ of her earnings last month and spent half of the remainder on rent.

(2) Beth earned twice as much this month as last month.

(A) Statement (1) ALONE is sufficient, but statement (2) alone is not sufficient.
(B) Statement (2) ALONE is sufficient, but statement (1) alone is not sufficient.
(C) BOTH statements TOGETHER are sufficient, but NEITHER statement ALONE is sufficient.
(D) EACH statement ALONE is sufficient.
(E) Statements (1) and (2) TOGETHER are not sufficient.

17. If n is an integer, is n even?

(1) $2n$ is an even integer.

(2) $n - 1$ is an odd integer.

(A) Statement (1) ALONE is sufficient, but statement (2) alone is not sufficient.
(B) Statement (2) ALONE is sufficient, but statement (1) alone is not sufficient.
(C) BOTH statements TOGETHER are sufficient, but NEITHER statement ALONE is sufficient.
(D) EACH statement ALONE is sufficient.
(E) Statements (1) and (2) TOGETHER are not sufficient.

EXPLANATIONS

15. D If a six-pack sells for \$2.70, then each can costs 45 cents when purchased together. When purchased individually, the price is higher than 45 cents, so cross off Choices A, B, and C. Let's plug in Choice D. Choice D says the price of an individual can is 50 cents. 10% of 50 cents is 5 cents, so the price per can of a six-pack would be 50 – 5 = 45 cents. Therefore, choice D is correct.

16. A Covering up Statement (2) and looking only at Statement (1), we see that Beth saved one-third of her earnings and spent half of the two-thirds that remained on rent. Half of two-thirds is one-third. So we can set up the equation:

$$\frac{1}{3} = \frac{400}{x}$$

And x equals \$1,200. Note that we didn't actually need to find out how much Beth earned. We just needed to know that we *could* find out. We're down to A or D.
Now, looking at Statement (2) we see that it tells us how Beth did THIS month. But do we care? Nope. The question asks us about LAST month. The correct answer is choice A.

17. B To answer this yes-or-no question, you must plug in values that make the statements true. Starting with Statement (1), let's plug in 4 for n, which makes the statement "$2n$ is an even integer" true, and gives us a "yes" to our overall question. Now, let's plug in 3 for n, which still makes the statement true, but gives us a "no" to our overall question. Because the answer is sometimes yes and sometimes no, we're down to BCE.
Looking at Statement (2) only, let's plug in values that make the statement true. If $n = 2$, the statement is true, and the answer to our overall question is a tentative "yes." Now, if we can find even one case where we can plug a number into this statement that makes the statement true but

QUESTIONS

EXPLANATIONS

answers the question "no," then we'll be down to CE. But as you try different numbers, you'll realize that in order to make Statement (2) true, n has to be even. So the answer to this question is B.

18. At apartment complex Z, 30 percent of the residents are men over the age of 18, and 40 percent are women over the age of 18. If there are 24 children living in the complex, how many total residents live in apartment complex Z?

(A) 32
(B) 80
(C) 94
(D) 112
(E) 124

18. **B** Altogether, the percentages of men and women add up to 70%, so that means 30% of the residents at this complex are children. Just set up an equation:

$$\frac{30}{100} = \frac{24}{x}$$

Solving for x, the total number of residents is 80. The answer is B.

You could also Plug In the Answers. Choice C seems difficult, so why not start with choice B, which has an easy number to work with? 30% of 80 = 24. 40% of 80 = 32. So there are a total of 24 + 32 = 56 adults. If choice B is correct, there should be 24 kids. And guess what? That's just what the problem says.

19. Over the course of a soccer season, 30 percent of the players on a team scored goals. What is the ratio of players on the team who scored goals to those who did not?

(A) 3 to 10
(B) 1 to 3
(C) 3 to 7
(D) 1 to 1
(E) 3 to 1

19. **C** If 30% of the players on the soccer team scored goals during the season, then 70% did not score goals. The ratio of those who scored to those who did not is 30 to 70, which reduces to 3 to 7. Some will find that Plugging In is the easiest way to solve this problem. Plug in 10 for the number of players on the team (choose this number because it is easy to work with in a percentage problem). 30% of the 10 players—that is to say, 3 players—scored goals. The other 7, it then follows, did not score goals. The ratio of those who scored to those who did not is 3 to 7. The correct answer is C.

QUESTIONS

20. At a restaurant, Luis left a tip for his waiter equal to 20 percent of his entire dinner check, including tax. What was the amount of the dinner check?

 (1) The sum of the dinner check and the tip was $16.80.

 (2) Luis's tip consisted of two bills and four coins.

 (A) Statement (1) ALONE is sufficient, but statement (2) alone is not sufficient.
 (B) Statement (2) ALONE is sufficient, but statement (1) alone is not sufficient.
 (C) BOTH statements TOGETHER are sufficient, but NEITHER statement ALONE is sufficient.
 (D) EACH statement ALONE is sufficient.
 (E) Statements (1) and (2) TOGETHER are not sufficient.

21. Which sport utility vehicle has a higher list price, the Touristo or the Leisure?

 (1) The list price of the Leisure is $\frac{5}{6}$ the list price of the Touristo.

 (2) The list price of the Touristo is 1.2 times the list price of the Leisure.

 (A) Statement (1) ALONE is sufficient, but statement (2) alone is not sufficient.
 (B) Statement (2) ALONE is sufficient, but statement (1) alone is not sufficient.
 (C) BOTH statements TOGETHER are sufficient, but NEITHER statement ALONE is sufficient.
 (D) EACH statement ALONE is sufficient.
 (E) Statements (1) and (2) TOGETHER are not sufficient.

EXPLANATIONS

20. **A** Because Luis tipped the waiter 20%, we know that the sum of the check and tip equals 1.2 times the amount of the check. Thus, we can write the equation
$$1.2x = 16.80$$
and solve for x to determine both the amount of the check and the amount of Luis's tip. The answer must be A or D.
Statement (2) is insufficient because it does not identify either the bills or the coins. The correct answer is A.

21. **D** According to Statement (1), the list price of the Leisure is $\frac{5}{6}$ the list price of the Touristo. The list price of the Touristo is therefore greater than the list price of the Leisure. Statement (1) is sufficient; the answer must be A or D. Statement (2) tells you that the list price of the Touristo is 1.2 times the list price of the Leisure. So Statement (2) also tells you that the list price of the Touristo is greater than the list price of the Leisure. The correct answer is D.

QUESTIONS

EXPLANATIONS

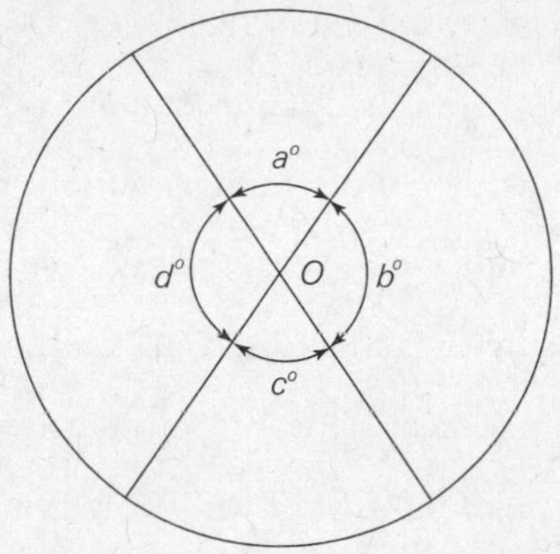

22. In the circle above, center *O* is intersected by 2 straight lines, and $3a = b$. What is the value of $b - a$?

(A) 2
(B) 30
(C) 45
(D) 90
(E) 135

22. **D** If you look carefully at the drawing, you should notice that *a* and *b* are supplementary angles; that is, together they make up a line. The sum of these angles, therefore, is 180°. Or, to put this in math-speak:

$$a + b = 180$$

Now, return to the equation in the question stem, $3a = b$. We can use this information to rewrite the equation $a + b = 180$ as

$$a + 3a = 180$$
$$4a = 180$$
$$a = 45$$

Because $a + b = 180$, and $a = 45$, *b* must equal 135, which is answer choice E. Wait, though, you're not done yet: The question asks for the solution $b - a$. Because $b - a - 135 - 45$, the answer to this question is 90. The correct answer is D.

23. What is the value of integer *w*?

(1) *w* is a multiple of 3.

(2) $420 < w < 425$

(A) Statement (1) ALONE is sufficient, but statement (2) alone is not sufficient.
(B) Statement (2) ALONE is sufficient, but statement (1) alone is not sufficient.
(C) BOTH statements TOGETHER are sufficient, but NEITHER statement ALONE is sufficient.
(D) EACH statement ALONE is sufficient.
(E) Statements (1) and (2) TOGETHER are not sufficient.

23. **C** Because there are an infinite number of multiples of 3, it is clear that Statement (1) is not sufficient to answer the question. The answer must be B, C, or E. Statement (2) narrows the range of possible answers to 421, 422, 423, or 424. However, because it does not narrow the answer to a single solution, it is not sufficient. Eliminate B.
When you put the two statements together, you know that *w* is a multiple of 3 that is either 421, 422, 423, or 424. Because only one of these values, 423, is a multiple of 3, the two statements together are sufficient. (A quick way to test whether an integer is divisible by 3 is to add its digits; if the sum of the digits is divisible by 3, then the number is divisible by 3.) The correct answer is C.

QUESTIONS

24. What is the quotient when 0.25% of 600 is divided by 0.25 of 600 ?

(A) 10
(B) 1
(C) 0.1
(D) 0.01
(E) 0.001

25. A certain town's economic development council has 21 members. If the number of females on the council is 3 less than 3 times the number of males on the council, then the town's economic development council has how many male members?

(A) 5
(B) 6
(C) 7
(D) 9
(E) 15

EXPLANATIONS

24. **D** Before we worry about the division, let's solve for the two values. The second one is easier, so let's start there: "of" means multiply, so $0.25 \times 600 = 150$. With the first value, we have to be sure to take into account both the decimal *and* the percent sign: 0.25% can be represented as $\frac{0.25}{100}$, or 0.0025. Either way, when you multiply by 600, the result is 1.5. The quotient is thus 1.5 divided by 150, or 0.01. The answer is D.

If you're really comfortable with manipulating fractions, you can save yourself a lot of math. The whole question translates into $\frac{\frac{0.25}{100} \times 600}{0.25 \times 600}$, which easily cancels down to $\frac{1}{100}$, or 0.01.

25. **B** Although you could solve this by writing a pair of algebraic equations ($f + m = 21$ and $f = m - 3$), it's simpler to Plug In the Answers. Start with answer choice C, 7 men. The number of women would be 3 less than 3 times that number, or $21 - 3 = 18$ women. That's a total of 25 council members altogether, and we're looking for 21. Now that we know that C is too big, we can eliminate answer choices C, D, and E. If we try answer choice B, 6 men, then we have $18 - 3 = 15$ women. This gives us our desired total of 21 council members, so the correct answer is B. If you got E, by the way, you solved for the number of *female* members on the board.

QUESTIONS

26. Roger can chop down 4 trees in an hour. How long does it take Vincent to chop down 4 trees?

(1) Vincent spends 6 hours per day chopping down trees.

(2) Vincent takes twice as long as Roger to chop down trees.

(A) Statement (1) ALONE is sufficient, but statement (2) alone is not sufficient.
(B) Statement (2) ALONE is sufficient, but statement (1) alone is not sufficient.
(C) BOTH statements TOGETHER are sufficient, but NEITHER statement ALONE is sufficient.
(D) EACH statement ALONE is sufficient.
(E) Statements (1) and (2) TOGETHER are not sufficient.

EXPLANATIONS

26. **B** Statement (1) tells you how many hours Vincent spends chopping down trees in a day, but it provides no data to help you determine how long it takes him to chop down 4 trees. This statement is clearly insufficient to answer the question. The answer must be B, C, or E.
Statement (2) tells you that Vincent takes twice as long as Roger to chop down trees. Because the question stem tells you that Roger chops down 4 trees per hour, you can deduce that Vincent chops down 4 trees every 2 hours. Thus, Statement (2) is sufficient to answer the question. The correct answer is B.

MATH BIN 2

QUESTIONS

1. If $x = \dfrac{\frac{5}{9} + \frac{15}{27} + \frac{45}{81}}{3}$, then $\sqrt{1-x} =$

(A) $\dfrac{\sqrt{5}}{9}$

(B) $\dfrac{5}{9}$

(C) $\dfrac{2}{3}$

(D) $\dfrac{\sqrt{5}}{3}$

(E) $\dfrac{15}{9}$

2. Steven has run a certain number of laps around a track at an average (arithmetic mean) time per lap of 51 seconds. If he runs one additional lap in 39 seconds and reduces his average time per lap to 49 seconds, how many laps did he run at an average time per lap of 51 seconds?

(A) 2
(B) 5
(C) 6
(D) 10
(E) 12

EXPLANATIONS

1. **C** You could start by converting all the fractions to their least common denominator of 81—an understandable temptation. However, in this case, it's quicker and simpler to reduce the fractions instead. They all reduce to $\frac{5}{9}$, so $x = \dfrac{\frac{5}{9} + \frac{5}{9} + \frac{5}{9}}{3}$, or $\dfrac{3\left(\frac{5}{9}\right)}{3}$ ...or $\frac{5}{9}$. Now that we know the value of x, we can solve for $\sqrt{(1-x)}$: $\sqrt{\left(1-\frac{5}{9}\right)} = \sqrt{\frac{4}{9}} = \frac{\sqrt{4}}{\sqrt{9}} = \frac{2}{3}$. The correct answer is C. Answer choice B, of course, is x itself, and answer choice D is $\sqrt{x}$.

2. **B** This is a multistep average problem involving an unknown quantity—in short, a perfect place to Plug In the Answers! Start with answer choice C: If Steven has already run 6 laps, then we know that he has run for a total of 6 × 51, or 306, seconds. One more lap in 39 seconds gives him a total of 7 laps in 345 seconds, and the average works out to be a little greater than 49 seconds ($49\frac{2}{7}$, to be exact). Close, but not quite. Fewer laps will reduce Steven's average speed, so answer choice B is the next logical choice to try. Five laps in 51 seconds means Steven has run 5 × 51, or 255, seconds so far, and the additional 39-second lap gives a total of 6 laps run in 294 seconds. The average is now $\frac{294}{6} = 49$ seconds, and B is the correct answer.

MATH BIN 2

QUESTIONS

3. $200^2 - 2(200)(199) + 199^2 =$

(A) −79,201
(B) −200
(C) 1
(D) 200
(E) 79,999

4. If $x \neq \frac{1}{2}$, then $\frac{6x^2 + 11x - 7}{2x - 1} =$

(A) $3x + 7$
(B) $3x - 7$
(C) $3x + 1$
(D) $x + 7$
(E) $x - 7$

EXPLANATIONS

3. **C** Although you could solve this problem with lots of tedious multiplication, it's much faster to recognize the common quadratic hidden in the numbers: $x^2 - 2xy + y^2 = (x - y)(x - y)$. That means this calculation can be rewritten as (200 – 199) (200 – 199), or (1)(1). The correct answer is C.

Since the answer choices vary so widely, you could have applied some POE to the most extreme answer choices, A and E. The product of 200 and 199, which we have to double, is not too different from either 200^2 or 199^2. Thus, the negative value in the equation is roughly equal to the sum of the two positive values in the equation. If you did the math, by the way, and *got* one of those answers, you must have reversed an addition or subtraction sign.

4. **A** Since this problem has variables in the answer choices, the simplest way to solve it is to plug in. If $x = 2$, the equation becomes $\frac{6(2)^2 + 11(2) - 7}{2(2) - 1} = \frac{24 + 22 - 7}{4 - 1} = \frac{39}{3} = 13$.

Now plug in 2 for x in the answer choices—only answer choice A gives us 13, so it must be the correct answer.

You could also try Plugging In the Answers. Try multiplying the answer choices by the expression in the denominator of the fraction and see which one yields the expression in the numerator. Only answer choice A does, so it is the correct answer.

MATH BIN 2

QUESTIONS

5. If Amy drove the distance from her home to the beach in less than 2 hours, was her average speed greater than 60 miles per hour?

(1) The distance that Amy drove from her home to the beach was less than 125 miles.

(2) The distance that Amy drove from her home to the beach was greater than 122 miles.

(A) Statement (1) ALONE is sufficient, but statement (2) alone is not sufficient.
(B) Statement (2) ALONE is sufficient, but statement (1) alone is not sufficient.
(C) BOTH statements TOGETHER are sufficient, but NEITHER statement ALONE is sufficient.
(D) EACH statement ALONE is sufficient.
(E) Statements (1) and (2) TOGETHER are not sufficient.

6. If $x = m - 1$, which of the following is true when $m = \frac{1}{2}$?

(A) $x^0 > x^2 > x^3 > x^1$
(B) $x^0 > x^2 > x^1 > x^3$
(C) $x^0 > x^1 > x^2 > x^3$
(D) $x^2 > x^0 > x^3 > x^1$
(E) $x^3 > x^2 > x^1 > x^0$

EXPLANATIONS

5. **B** Take a moment to translate what this question is really asking: Is the distance Amy drove greater than 120 miles? This rate problem is also a yes-or-no question, so we don't need to know Amy's exact speed, just whether her average speed was greater than 60 miles per hour. The simplest way to find out whether Statement (1) is sufficient is to try different possible times and distances. If her total driving time was, for instance, 1 hour, a distance of 61 miles yields an answer of "yes." Meanwhile, a distance of 59 miles yields an answer of "no." That means the possible answers are B, C, or E.
Regardless of what times and distances you plug in for Statement (2), you will always get an answer of "yes." Even if Amy were to have driven the *full* 2 hours and gone *only* 122 miles, she would be driving at a rate of 61 miles per hour; since she actually drove a greater distance in less time, her rate must be greater than 61. Since Statement (2) always gives us the same answer, it is sufficient, and the answer is B.

6. **A** Once you've solved for x, which equals $-\frac{1}{2}$, this question is just a matter of putting the four values in order. Even better, you already know two of them: $x = -\frac{1}{2}$ and $x^0 = 1$. With the other two values, be especially careful about the negative sign: $x^2 = \frac{1}{4}$ and $x^3 = -\frac{1}{8}$. The correct order is $x^0 > x^2 > x^3 > x^1$, and the answer is A.

MATH BIN 2

QUESTIONS

7. If a comedian plays two shows and twice as many tickets are available for the evening show as for the afternoon show, what percentage of the total number of tickets available for both shows have been sold?

   (1) A total of 450 tickets are available for both shows.

   (2) Exactly $\frac{3}{5}$ of the tickets available for the afternoon show have been sold, and exactly $\frac{1}{5}$ of the tickets available for the evening show have been sold.

   (A) Statement (1) ALONE is sufficient, but statement (2) alone is not sufficient.
   (B) Statement (2) ALONE is sufficient, but statement (1) alone is not sufficient.
   (C) BOTH statements TOGETHER are sufficient, but NEITHER statement ALONE is sufficient.
   (D) EACH statement ALONE is sufficient.
   (E) Statements (1) and (2) TOGETHER are not sufficient.

8. If $\frac{1}{y} = 2\frac{2}{3}$, then $\left(\frac{1}{y+1}\right)^2 =$

   (A) $\frac{9}{64}$

   (B) $\frac{3}{8}$

   (C) $\frac{64}{121}$

   (D) $\frac{121}{64}$

   (E) $\frac{64}{9}$

EXPLANATIONS

7. **B** The information in Statement (1), along with that in the question itself, is enough for us to find the number of tickets issued for each show. Without any information about the number of tickets that were sold, though, we can't answer the question, and we're down to B, C, or E.
Statement (2), along with the information in the question, is sufficient—even without the information in Statement (1). If we have the fraction of each type of ticket that was sold, and the ratio of one type of ticket to the other, we can figure out the overall percentage of tickets sold. The correct answer is B.
Want to prove it? Try Plugging In. In Statement (2), the denominator of both fractions is 5, so let's say that 25 tickets have been issued for the afternoon show and 50 have been issued for the evening show. That means 15 tickets have been sold for the afternoon show and 10 have been sold for the evening show, for a total of 25 tickets sold out of a total of 75 tickets issued. The answer is $\frac{1}{3}$, as it will always be if we meet the requirements of Statement (2) and the question itself.

8. **C** First, solve for *y*. Since $2\frac{2}{3} - \frac{8}{3}$, $\frac{1}{y} = \frac{8}{3}$ and thus $y = \frac{3}{8}$. Now plug the value for *y* into the expression:

$$\left(\frac{1}{\frac{3}{8}+1}\right)^2 = \left(\frac{1}{\left(\frac{11}{8}\right)}\right)^2 = \frac{1^2}{\left(\frac{11}{8}\right)^2} = \frac{1}{\frac{121}{64}} = \frac{64}{121}.$$

The correct answer is C.
Answer choice B, of course, is the value of *y*. Choice D is the reciprocal of the correct answer, which could indicate that you didn't do the last step of the calculation. If you chose A, you forgot to add 1 when you put the value for *y* into the expression. And if you chose E, you did both.

MATH BIN 2

QUESTIONS

9. An operation $\sim$ is defined by $a \sim b = \frac{a+b}{(ab)^2}$ for all numbers a and b such that $ab \neq 0$. If $c \neq 0$ and $a \sim c = 0$, then $c =$

(A) $-a$
(B) 0
(C) $\sqrt{a}$
(D) a
(E) a^2

10. If x is a positive integer, is the greatest common factor of 150 and x a prime number?

(1) x is a prime number.

(2) $x < 4$

(A) Statement (1) ALONE is sufficient, but statement (2) alone is not sufficient.
(B) Statement (2) ALONE is sufficient, but statement (1) alone is not sufficient.
(C) BOTH statements TOGETHER are sufficient, but NEITHER statement ALONE is sufficient.
(D) EACH statement ALONE is sufficient.
(E) Statements (1) and (2) TOGETHER are not sufficient.

EXPLANATIONS

9. A Answering a function problem on the GMAT is simply a matter of following the directions provided by the definition of the function. In this case, the operation signified by two numbers with the ~ between them is defined as the sum of the numbers on either side of the ~ sign divided by the square of the product of the two numbers. If $a \sim c = 0$, then $\frac{a+c}{(ac)^2} = 0$; since the numerator must be zero in order for the fraction itself to equal zero, we know that $a + c = 0$. Subtract a from both sides and $c = -a$. The answer is A.

10. C The easiest way to determine whether Statement (1) by itself is sufficient is to plug in different values for x. If $x = 2$, the greatest common factor is 2, and the answer to this yes-or-no question is "yes." If $x = 7$, on the other hand, the greatest common factor is 1, and since 1 is not prime, the answer is "no." The possible answers are B, C, or E.
Statement (2) by itself is also not sufficient. If x is equal to 1, 2, or 3, then the greatest common factor of x and 150 is x itself. But since 2 and 3 are prime, and 1 is not, the possible answers are C and E.
When we put the statements together, the only possible values for x are 2 and 3. With either one, the greatest common factor is equal to x itself and is, therefore, prime. The correct answer is C.

QUESTIONS

$X = \{9, 10, 11, 12\}$

$Y = \{2, 3, 4, 5\}$

11. If one number is chosen at random from each of the sets above and the number from Set X is divided by the number from Set Y, what is the probability that the result is an integer?

(A) $\frac{1}{16}$

(B) $\frac{3}{8}$

(C) $\frac{1}{2}$

(D) $\frac{3}{4}$

(E) $\frac{15}{16}$

EXPLANATIONS

11. B As with all probability problems, we'll have to find a fraction that has the total number of possibilities in the denominator and the number of those possibilities that meet a certain requirement in the numerator. The denominator is the easy part: Because there are 4 members of each set, there are $4 \times 4 - 16$ total possibilities for the quotient when one member of X is divided by one member of Y. Now we just have to figure out how many of those possibilitics mcct thc rcquirement.

The requirement, in this case, is that the quotient is an integer—in other words, that the member chosen from X is divisible by the member chosen from Y—and we can count out all of the combinations that meet that requirement quickly and easily. The first member of Set X, 9, is divisible by only one member of Set Y, 3, so that's one. Then, working through Set X: 10 is divisible by both 2 and 5, so there are another two possibilities; 11 is prime, and so it's not divisible by any members of Set Y; and 12 gives us another three possibilities, because it's divisible by 2, 3, and 4. Thus, 6 of our total of 16 possibilities meet our requirement, and our probability is $\frac{6}{16}$, or $\frac{3}{8}$. The answer is B.

QUESTIONS

12. If p and q are integers, is $\frac{p+q}{2}$ an integer?

(1) $p < 17$

(2) $p = q$

(A) Statement (1) ALONE is sufficient, but statement (2) alone is not sufficient.
(B) Statement (2) ALONE is sufficient, but statement (1) alone is not sufficient.
(C) BOTH statements TOGETHER are sufficient, but NEITHER statement ALONE is sufficient.
(D) EACH statement ALONE is sufficient.
(E) Statements (1) and (2) TOGETHER are not sufficient.

13. A perfectly spherical satellite with a radius of 4 feet is being packed for shipment to its launch site. If the inside dimensions of the rectangular crates available for shipment, when measured in feet, are consecutive even integers, then what is the volume of the smallest available crate that can be used? (The volume of a sphere is $V = \frac{4}{3}\pi r^3$.)

(A) 48
(B) 192
(C) 480
(D) 960
(E) 1,680

EXPLANATIONS

12. **B** Since Statement (1) doesn't tell us anything about the value of q, and very little about the value of p, it is, by itself, insufficient to answer this yes-or-no question. Statement (2), though, while it gives us no new specifics about the values of p or q, gives enough information to know the answer to the question. If $p = q$, then $\frac{p+q}{2} = \frac{p+p}{2} = \frac{2p}{2} = p$ since we know from the question that p is an integer, the answer to the question is "yes," and our answer is B. Of course, we can easily show the sufficiency of Statement (2) by plugging in values for p and q: as long as the values are equal integers, the answer is always "yes."

13. **D** Although this may seem like a volume question, it's really about being able to fit the diameter of the satellite inside the crate—we can entirely disregard the formula for the volume of a sphere. Let's start with what we know: Since the radius of the sphere is 4, the diameter is 8. Therefore, every dimension in our crate must be at least 8 and the smallest available crate will measure 8 × 10 × 12. The volume of that crate is 960, and the correct answer is D.

In fact, if we try to use the volume formula we can easily go astray. Using a rough value of 3 for π, we can approximate the value of the sphere to be a little greater than 250 (replacing π with 3 in the formula gives a value of 256, and the exact value is a little greater than 268). We might be tempted, therefore, to select answer choice C, but we can't: The only set of three consecutive integers that yields a volume of 480 is 6 × 8 × 10, and we can't put a spherical object with a diameter of 8 feet into a crate that's only 6 feet across in one direction.

MATH BIN 2

QUESTIONS

14. Richard is 6 years older than David, and David is 8 years older than Scott. In 8 years, if Richard will be twice as old as Scott, then how old was David 4 years ago?

(A) 8
(B) 10
(C) 12
(D) 14
(E) 16

15. What is the value of x ?

(1) $x^2 - 5x + 4 = 0$

(2) x is not prime.

(A) Statement (1) ALONE is sufficient, but statement (2) alone is not sufficient.
(B) Statement (2) ALONE is sufficient, but statement (1) alone is not sufficient.
(C) BOTH statements TOGETHER are sufficient, but NEITHER statement ALONE is sufficient.
(D) EACH statement ALONE is sufficient.
(E) Statements (1) and (2) TOGETHER are not sufficient.

16. Sam and Jessica are invited to a dance. If there are 7 men and 7 women in total at the dance, and one woman and one man are chosen to lead the dance, . what is the probability that Sam and Jessica will NOT be the pair chosen to lead the dance?

(A) $\frac{1}{49}$

(B) $\frac{1}{7}$

(C) $\frac{6}{7}$

(D) $\frac{47}{49}$

(E) $\frac{48}{49}$

EXPLANATIONS

14. **B** This problem could be an algebraic nightmare, so let's Plug In the Answers. We'll start with answer choice C, 12. If David was 12 years old 4 years ago, he's 16 now, and that means Richard is 22 and Scott is 8. In 8 years, then, Richard will be 30 and Scott will be 16; since Richard won't be twice as old as Scott at that point, this can't be the answer.

Now try answer choice B, 10, using the same process. If David was 10 years old 4 years ago, he's 14 now, so Richard is 20 and Scott is 6. In 8 years, then, Richard will be 28 and Scott will be 14; since Richard will then be twice as old as Scott, the answer is B.

15. **E** Statement (1) is a quadratic equation, so let's factor it and see what the options are for x: $x^2 - 5x + 4 = 0$ factors into $(x - 4)(x - 1) = 0$, so x could be 4 or 1. Since there's more than one value for x, Statement (1) alone is insufficient, and we're down to B, C, or E.

Statement (2) alone leaves us with the vast majority of all numbers— this statement is *definitely* not sufficient, so we're down to C or E.

When we combine the statements, they're still not sufficient. Be careful not to fall for one of the classic GMAT traps: 1 is *not* prime. Because 4 is also not prime, we're left with both values, and the correct answer is E.

16. **E** The probability that Sam will be chosen is $\frac{1}{7}$.

The probability that Jessica will be chosen is also $\frac{1}{7}$. The probability that they will both be chosen is $\frac{1}{7} \text{ x } \frac{1}{7} = \frac{1}{49}$ This is choice A, but we aren't done yet. The question asks for the probability that they will NOT both be chosen. The probability that an event does NOT happen can be expressed as 1 minus the probability that the event DOES happen. So $1 - \frac{1}{49} = \frac{48}{49}$, or choice E.

MATH BIN 2

QUESTIONS

17. What is the surface area of rectangular solid Y ?

    (1) The dimensions of one face of rectangular solid Y are 2 by 3.

    (2) The volume of rectangular solid Y is 12.

    (A) Statement (1) ALONE is sufficient, but statement (2) alone is not sufficient.
    (B) Statement (2) ALONE is sufficient, but statement (1) alone is not sufficient.
    (C) BOTH statements TOGETHER are sufficient, but NEITHER statement ALONE is sufficient.
    (D) EACH statement ALONE is sufficient.
    (E) Statements (1) and (2) TOGETHER are not sufficient.

18. A six-sided die with faces numbered 1 through 6 is rolled three times. What is the probability that the face with the number 6 on it will NOT face upward on all three rolls?

    (A) $\frac{1}{216}$

    (B) $\frac{1}{6}$

    (C) $\frac{2}{3}$

    (D) $\frac{17}{18}$

    (E) $\frac{215}{216}$

EXPLANATIONS

17. C Whenever you see a geometry problem without a diagram, it's a good idea to make one. Statement (1) tells us only two of the three dimensions we need to find the surface area. We're down to BCE.

Statement (2) tells us the the volume of the rectangular solid. By itself, the volume does not give us any of the three dimensions that we need to find the surface area, so we're down to C and E. Putting the two statements together, we have all three dimensions. Statement (1) tells us that two of the dimensions are 2 and 3. Since the formula for the volume of a rectangular solid is V = lwh, the third dimension of the solid is 2. With all three dimensions, the surface area can be calculated. The answer is C.

18. E Before you start calculating, it is always helpful to think about what is reasonable. The probability that the number 6 is going to come up three times in a row is pretty low, which is another way of saying that the probability that 6 is NOT going to come up three times in a row is pretty high. So we can eliminate choices A, B, and C. Now, let's figure out the problem. The probability that the first roll yields the number 6 is $\frac{1}{6}$. The probability that the second roll yields the number 6 is also $\frac{1}{6}$. The probability that the third roll yields the number 6? You guessed it: $\frac{1}{6}$. To find the probability of the series of these three events happening, you multiply the probabilities of each of the individual events: $\frac{1}{6} \times \frac{1}{6} \times \frac{1}{6} = \frac{1}{216}$. That's choice A, but we aren't done yet. $\frac{1}{216}$ is the probability that the number 6 WILL face up on all three rolls. The probability that an event does NOT

QUESTIONS

EXPLANATIONS

happen can be expressed as 1 minus the probability that the event DOES happen.

$1 - \frac{1}{216} = \frac{215}{216}$. The correct answer is choice E.

19. What is the sum of x, y, and z?

(1) $2x + y + 3z = 45$

(2) $x + 2y = 30$

(A) Statement (1) ALONE is sufficient, but statement (2) alone is not sufficient.
(B) Statement (2) ALONE is sufficient, but statement (1) alone is not sufficient.
(C) BOTH statements TOGETHER are sufficient, but NEITHER statement ALONE is sufficient.
(D) EACH statement ALONE is sufficient.
(E) Statements (1) and (2) TOGETHER are not sufficient.

19. C Gut instinct may lead to you select E on this one; after all, Statement (1) provides a three-variable equation, which does not have an unique solution. Statement (2) refers to only two of the three variables mentioned in the question stem, so clearly it cannot be sufficient. At first glance, it may be hard to imagine how the two statements together could be any more helpful than each is on its own.

Statement (1) is, in fact, insufficient on its own, for the reason stated above. The possible answers are B, C, or E. Statement (2) is also insufficient, again for the reason stated above. Eliminate B. The answer is C or E.

Now, add the two equations provided by Statements (1) and (2) to get $3x + 3y + 3z = 75$. Factor a 3 out of both sides of the equation and you end up with $x + y + z = 25$. Thus, the two statements together *are* sufficient to answer the question. The correct answer is C.

20. A department store receives a shipment of 1,000 shirts, for which it pays \$9,000. The store sells the shirts at a price 80 percent above cost for one month, after which it reduces the price of the shirts to 20 percent above cost. The store sells 75 percent of the shirts during the first month and 50 percent of the remaining shirts afterward. How much gross income did sales of the shirts generate?

(A) \$10,000
(B) \$10,800
(C) \$12,150
(D) \$13,500
(E) \$16,200

20. D To answer this question, break the problem down into small, manageable steps. The first job at hand is to determine the selling price of the shirt, both during the first month they were on sale and then during subsequent months. Because the store bought 1,000 shirts for \$9,000, the cost of each shirt was \$9.00. The store sold the shirts at an 80% markup during the first month. $1.8 \times \$9.00 = \$16.20$, so during the first month, the shirts sold for \$16.20 each. After the first month, the selling price was 20% above cost. $1.20 \times \$9.00 = \$10.80$, so that was the selling price after the first month.

The store sold 75% of the shirts during the first month. 75% of 1,000 is 750; the store sold 750 shirts at \$16.20 each. $750 \times \$16.20 = \$12{,}150$. Note that this partial answer is answer choice C. Test takers who only half-finish their work will choose

QUESTIONS

EXPLANATIONS

this incorrect answer. The store then sold 50% of its remaining stock at $10.80 per shirt. The remaining stock is 250 shirts (1,000 – 750), half of which is 125. The store, then, sold 125 shirts at $10.80 each. 125 × $10.80 = $1,350. The store's gross income from the sale of these shirts, then, is $12,150 + $1,350 = $13,500. The correct answer is D.

21. David has three credit cards: a Passport card, an EverywhereCard, and an American Local card. He owes balances on all three cards. Does he owe the greatest balance on the EverywhereCard?

(1) The sum of the balances on his EverywhereCard and American Local card is $1,350, which is three times the balance on his Passport card.

(2) The balance on his EverywhereCard is $\frac{4}{3}$ of the balance on his Passport card and $\frac{4}{5}$ of the balance on his American Local card.

(A) Statement (1) ALONE is sufficient, but statement (2) alone is not sufficient.
(B) Statement (2) ALONE is sufficient, but statement (1) alone is not sufficient.
(C) BOTH statements TOGETHER are sufficient, but NEITHER statement ALONE is sufficient.
(D) EACH statement ALONE is sufficient.
(E) Statements (1) and (2) TOGETHER are not sufficient.

21. **B** Statement (1) provides information only about the sum of the balances on David's EverywhereCard and his American Local card. Therefore, the statement is insufficient to determine whether the balance on David's EverywhereCard is his highest balance, because it does not provide any information that allows you to compare the balance on the EverywhereCard to the balances on the other two cards. The possible answers are B, C, or E.

Statement (2) tells you that the balance on David's EverywhereCard is greater than the balance on his Passport card and less than the balance on his American Local card. Thus, it provides enough information to answer the question. The correct answer is B.

There are a couple of places where you can go wrong on this question. The first involves the fact that Statement (2) answers the question this way: "No, he does not owe the greatest balance on the EverywhereCard." Some test takers get confused and use a "No" answer to decide that a statement is insufficient. Remember, it doesn't matter how you answer a yes-or-no question, just so long as you can answer it conclusively.

Some test takers might realize that Statements (1) and (2) together provide enough information to calculate the exact balance on each credit card, and thus may choose C. But because Statement (2) is sufficient on its own, C cannot be the correct answer to this question.

QUESTIONS

22. Automobile *A* is traveling at two-thirds the speed that Automobile *B* is traveling. At what speed is Automobile *A* traveling?

(1) If both automobiles increased their speed by 10 miles per hour, Automobile *A* would be traveling at three-quarters the speed that Automobile *B* would be traveling.

(2) If both automobiles decreased their speed by 10 miles per hour, Automobile *A* would be traveling at half the speed that Automobile *B* would be traveling.

(A) Statement (1) ALONE is sufficient, but statement (2) alone is not sufficient.
(B) Statement (2) ALONE is sufficient, but statement (1) alone is not sufficient.
(C) BOTH statements TOGETHER are sufficient, but NEITHER statement ALONE is sufficient.
(D) EACH statement ALONE is sufficient.
(E) Statements (1) and (2) TOGETHER are not sufficient.

23. *a* and *b* are nonzero integers such that $0.35a = 0.2b$. What is the value of *b* in terms of *a*?

(A) $0.07a$
(B) $0.57a$
(C) $0.7a$
(D) $1.75a$
(E) $17.5a$

EXPLANATIONS

22. **D** To solve this problem, we need to write some equations. Let's call Automobile *A*'s current speed *A* and Automobile *B*'s current speed *B*. The question stem tells us that $A = \frac{2}{3}B$. Statement (1) tells us that $A + 10 = \frac{3}{4}(B + 10)$. Thus, between the question stem and Statement (1), we have two distinct equations, which means we can solve for the two variables. The possible answers are A or D. Statement (2) tells us that $A - 10 = \frac{1}{2}(B - 10)$. Once again, we have two distinct equations and two variables. Statement (2) is sufficient, and the correct answer is D.

23. **D** What makes this problem tricky is the presence of decimals, so the best thing to do is to convert the decimals to integers. Multiply both sides of the equation by 100 to produce the equation $35a = 20b$. (If you don't multiply both sides carefully, you could end up with answer E.) Now, simply solve for *b* by dividing both sides by 20 to get $b = \frac{35}{20}a$. Convert the fraction to a decimal by dividing 35 by 20 to yield $b = 1.75a$. The correct answer is D.

QUESTIONS

24. The Binary Ice Cream Shoppe sells two flavors of cones, vanilla and chocolate. On Friday, the ratio of vanilla cones sold to chocolate cones sold was 2 to 3. If the store sold 4 more vanilla cones, the ratio of vanilla cones sold to chocolate cones sold would have been 3 to 4. How many vanilla cones did the store sell on Friday?

(A) 32
(B) 35
(C) 42
(D) 48
(E) 54

EXPLANATIONS

24. A Plug In the Answers! Start with answer C. If this is the correct answer, then the Binary Ice Cream Shoppe sold 42 vanilla cones on Friday. Because vanilla cones sold at a 2-to-3 ratio to chocolate cones, this means that the shop sold 63 chocolate cones $\left(\frac{2}{3}=\frac{42}{63}\right)$. If this is the correct answer, then the ratio of 46, the result of adding 4 to the number of vanilla cones sold, to 63 is 3 to 4. It is not, so this answer is incorrect.

You must decide next whether the correct answer is more or less than 42. Since the situation is complicated, you may not be sure which direction to go so just pick a direction; you'll find the correct answer soon enough. Note that the answer cannot be B because B is an odd number. Because it is not divisible by 2, it cannot be the number of vanilla cones sold. A is the correct answer. 32 to 48 is a 2-to-3 ratio; add 4 more vanilla cones to get a ratio of 36 to 48, which reduces to 3 to 4.

MATH BIN 2

QUESTIONS

25. Is integer *a* a prime number?

(1) 2*a* has exactly three factors.

(2) *a* is an even number.

(A) Statement (1) ALONE is sufficient, but statement (2) alone is not sufficient.
(B) Statement (2) ALONE is sufficient, but statement (1) alone is not sufficient.
(C) BOTH statements TOGETHER are sufficient, but NEITHER statement ALONE is sufficient.
(D) EACH statement ALONE is sufficient.
(E) Statements (1) and (2) TOGETHER are not sufficient.

26. Renee rides her bicycle 20 miles in *m* minutes. If she rides *x* miles in 10 minutes at the same rate, which of the following is an expression for *x*, in terms of *m*?

(A) $\frac{m}{200}$

(B) $\frac{m}{20}$

(C) $\frac{m}{2}$

(D) $2m$

(E) $\frac{200}{m}$

EXPLANATIONS

25. **A** In order to answer this yes-or-no question correctly, you must remember that 2 is a prime number. Statement (1) tells us that 2*a* has exactly 3 distinct factors. Let's plug in some numbers. If you choose 3 for *a*, then 2*a* = 6. What are the factors of 6? 1, 6, 2, and 3. In other words, there are 4 factors. Is there any number we can plug in for *a* that gives us only 3 factors for the number 2*a*? As a matter of fact, there is only one: 2. Only 2 times 2, or 4, has exactly three factors: 1, 2, and 4. This tells us that *a* is 2; any other multiple of 2 has at least 4 factors (itself, 1, 2, and the product of itself and 2.) So if *a* can only be 2, can we definitely answer this yes-or-no question? Yes, 2 is a prime number.
Statement (2) is tempting for several reasons. If you forgot that 2 is prime, you would incorrectly conclude that this statement alone is sufficient to answer the question "No." If you figured out that *a* = 2 from Statement (1), you may be tempted to choose this because it confirms the information given in Statement (1). However, because it is not sufficient to answer the question on its own, you must resist temptation. The correct answer is A.

26. **E** Solve this problem by Plugging In. Set *m* equal to a value that turns the question into an easy arithmetic problem. For example,
m = 40 is a good, easy value. It tells us that Renee can ride 1 mile every 2 minutes. How many miles, then, can she ride in 10 minutes? She can ride 5 miles in 10 minutes.
Now, plug in 40 for *m* in each of the answer choices. The correct answer will calculate to 5, the value of *x* when *m* = 40. Because E is the only answer that equals 5, E is the correct answer.

QUESTIONS

27. If s and w are integers, is $\frac{w}{5}$ an integer?

(1) $4s + 2$ is divisible by 5.

(2) $w + 3 = 4s$

(A) Statement (1) ALONE is sufficient, but statement (2) alone is not sufficient.
(B) Statement (2) ALONE is sufficient, but statement (1) alone is not sufficient.
(C) BOTH statements TOGETHER are sufficient, but NEITHER statement ALONE is sufficient.
(D) EACH statement ALONE is sufficient.
(E) Statements (1) and (2) TOGETHER are not sufficient.

EXPLANATIONS

27. C Since this question is a yes-no question, plug in to evaluate the statements. Note that Statement (1) does not provide any information about w. So, while we can say that $s = 2$ is a value that satisfies Statement (1), we can pick any value for w. If $s = 2$ and $w = 5$, the answer to the question is yes. However, if $s = 2$ and $w = 7$, the answer to the question is no. So, as we suspected, Statement (1) is insufficient. The possible answers are B, C, or E.

For Statement (2), $s = 2$ and $w = 5$ satisfy the statement and produce an answer of yes to the question. However, $s = 4$ and $w = 13$ also satisfy the statement and produce an answer of no to the question. The possible answers are C or E. Now, pick numbers that satisfy both statements. Start by using a pair that we've already used: $s = 2$ and $w = 5$. These numbers satisfy both statements and produce an answer of yes to the question. Now, try $s = 7$ and $w = 25$. These numbers also satisfy both statements and produce an answer of yes to the question. If you keep trying to pick numbers that satisfy both statements, you'll discover that you must pick values for w that are divisible by 5. The correct answer is C.

You might also note the algebraic reason the combined statements ensure that w is divisible by 5. Statement (2) provides an expression for $4s$ that can be substituted into the expression in Statement (1): $w + 3 + 2 = w + 5$ is divisible by 5. Both parts of this expression must be divisible by 5 for $w + 5$ to be divisible by 5. So, w is divisible by 5.

MATH BIN 3

QUESTIONS

1. An electronics store normally sells all its merchandise at a 10 percent to 30 percent discount from the suggested retail price. During a sale, if the store were to deduct an additional 20 percent from the discounted price, what is the lowest price possible for an item with a suggested retail price of $260 ?

(A) $130.00
(B) $145.60
(C) $163.80
(D) $182.00
(E) $210.00

2. A certain gas station discounts the price per gallon of all gasoline purchased after the first 10 gallons by 10 percent. The total per gallon discount for 25 gallons of gas purchased at this station is what percent of the total per gallon discount for 20 gallons of gas?

(A) 80%
(B) 100%
(C) 116.7%
(D) 120%
(E) 140%

EXPLANATIONS

1. **B** We don't need to worry about that range for the initial discount: Since we want the *lowest* possible price, we want the *greatest* possible discount. Thirty percent of 260 is 78, so the price after the initial discount is $260 – $78, or $182. The additional 20% discount amounts to $36.40—remember, the 20% discount is 20% of the already-discounted price. $182 – $36.40 = $145.60, and the correct answer is B.

2. **D** This problem never specifies the cost of a gallon of gas, so let's plug in $1. If the price per gallon is $1 for the first 10 gallons, then the price for every subsequent gallon is $0.90. Now calculate the per gallon discount for 20 gallons. First, calculate the total cost for 20 gallons. The cost is $10 for the first 10 gallons and 10 × $0.90 = $9 for the next 10 gallons, for a total of $19 and an average price per gallon of $0.95. So the per gallon discount is 5 cents. Repeat this process to calculate the per gallon discount for 25 gallons. The total price for 25 gallons is $23.50, for an average per gallon price of $0.94 and a discount of 6 cents. The question asks us to relate the per gallon discounts as a percentage, so 6 is 120% of 5 and the correct answer is D.

QUESTIONS

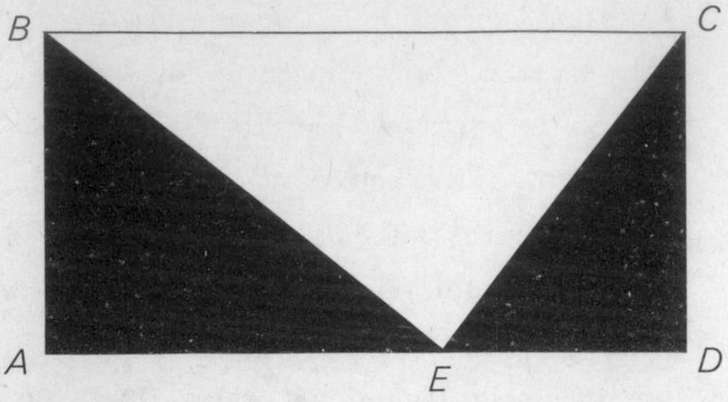

3. What is the area of the shaded region in the figure shown above?

(1) The area of rectangle *ABCD* is 54.

(2) $AE = 2ED$

(A) Statement (1) ALONE is sufficient, but statement (2) alone is not sufficient.
(B) Statement (2) ALONE is sufficient, but statement (1) alone is not sufficient.
(C) BOTH statements TOGETHER are sufficient, but NEITHER statement ALONE is sufficient.
(D) EACH statement ALONE is sufficient.
(E) Statements (1) and (2) TOGETHER are not sufficient.

EXPLANATIONS

3. A Statement (1) is sufficient, by itself, to answer the question. Although we can't determine, from Statement (1), the individual areas of the two triangular shaded regions, when combined they equal 27 (half of the total area of rectangle *ABCD*). The easiest way to see this is to draw a vertical line through point *E*, cutting the rectangle into two smaller ones. Now we have two rectangles that are divided by diagonals, and diagonals, by definition, cut rectangles in half. If half of the two smaller rectangles are shaded, then so is half of the larger rectangle. We're down to A and D.

Statement (2) gives us the relationship between the two smaller shaded regions, but it doesn't allow us to determine anything about their individual areas. Statement (2) is insufficient, and the correct answer is A.

MATH BIN 3

QUESTIONS

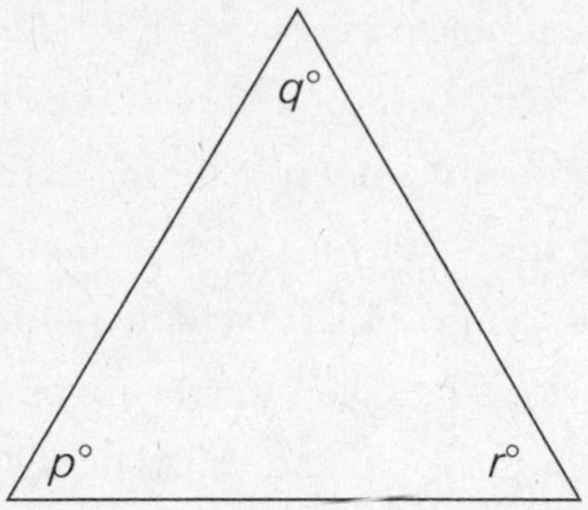

4. For the triangle shown above, does $p = q = 60$?

(1) $r = 180 - (p + r)$

(2) $p = 60$

(A) Statement (1) ALONE is sufficient, but statement (2) alone is not sufficient.
(B) Statement (2) ALONE is sufficient, but statement (1) alone is not sufficient.
(C) BOTH statements TOGETHER are sufficient, but NEITHER statement ALONE is sufficient.
(D) EACH statement ALONE is sufficient.
(E) Statements (1) and (2) TOGETHER are not sufficient.

EXPLANATIONS

4. C First, take a moment to rephrase the question. If $p = q = 60$, the triangle is equilateral. So, the question is equivalent to asking "Is the triangle equilateral?" Statement (1) is, by itself, insufficient to answer the question, although it does provide the very useful information that $r = q$. If you're comfortable working with triangles, you may have immediately read "180 minus the sum of p and r" as being equal to q. If not, you can prove this by doing some algebraic manipulation. Add $(p + r)$ to both sides to yield $r + p + r = 180$ but since 180 also equals $p + q + r$, you can combine the equations to get $r + p + r = p + q + r$. Subtract a p and a q from each side, and you're left with $r = q$. Nonetheless, this is still insufficient to answer the question. If r and q are both 60, the answer is "yes"; if they're both 45—remember, you can't trust the diagrams in Data Sufficiency—the answer is "no." We're down to B, C, or E.

Statement (2), by itself, is also insufficient to answer the question; the only thing it tells us about q and r is their sum, which equals 120. Eliminate B.

When we combine the statements, though, we can determine whether the triangle is equilateral. If r and q are equal and their sum is 120, then they, like p, equal 60. If all three angles equal 60, the triangle is equilateral, and the correct answer is C.

QUESTIONS

5. During a certain two week period, a video rental store rented only comedies, dramas, and action movies. If 70 percent of the movies rented were comedies, and of the remaining movies rented, 5 times as many dramas as action movies were rented and *A* action movies were rented, then, in terms of *A*, how many of the movies rented were comedies?

(A) $\frac{A}{14}$

(B) $\frac{5A}{7}$

(C) $\frac{7A}{5}$

(D) $14A$

(E) $35A$

6. x, y, and z are consecutive positive integers such that $x < y < z$. If the units digit of x^2 is 6 and the units digit of y^2 is 9, what is the units digit of z^2 ?

(A) 0
(B) 1
(C) 2
(D) 4
(E) 5

EXPLANATIONS

5. **D** Since the problem never specifies how many videos were rented during the two-week period, this is a good opportunity to plug in. Rather than plugging in a value for *A* and trying to determine the total number of videos rented—possible but problematic—let's plug in an easy number, such as 100, for the total, and calculate the rest of the numbers from there.

If a total of 100 videos were rented in the two-week period, then 70 were comedies. Of the remaining 30, there were 5 times as many dramas as action movies, so that means 25 dramas and 5 action movies. We now know both the value for *A*, 5, and the target answer, 70. Only answer choice D yields 70 when 5 is plugged in for A, so D is the correct answer.

6. **D** Because the units digit of x^2 is 6, the units digit of x must be either 4 or 6. Because x, y, and z are consecutive positive integers, the units digit of y is 5 if the units digit of x is 4. However, the units digit of y *can't* be 5 because the problem tells us that the units digit of y^2 is 9; if the units digit of y were 5, then the units digit of y^2 would also be 5. Therefore, the units digit of x is 6, the units digit of y is 7, and the units digit of z is 8. The units digit of z^2, then, is 4.

MATH BIN 3

QUESTIONS

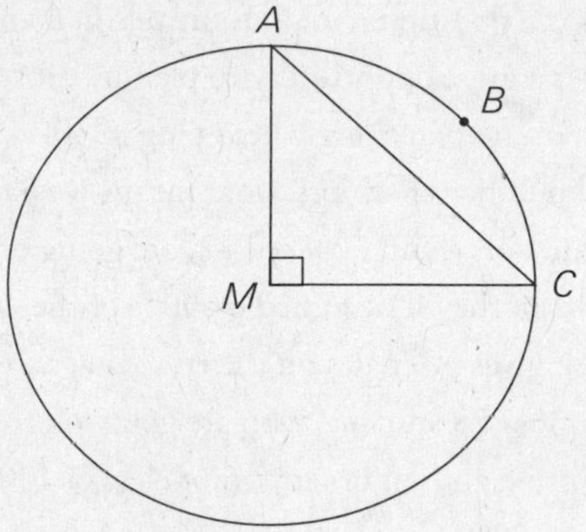

7. What is the area of the circle with center M shown above ?

   (1) The length of AC is $8\sqrt{2}$.

   (2) The length of arc ABC is 4π.

   (A) Statement (1) ALONE is sufficient, but statement (2) alone is not sufficient.
   (B) Statement (2) ALONE is sufficient, but statement (1) alone is not sufficient.
   (C) BOTH statements TOGETHER are sufficient, but NEITHER statement ALONE is sufficient.
   (D) EACH statement ALONE is sufficient.
   (E) Statements (1) and (2) TOGETHER are not sufficient.

EXPLANATIONS

7. **D** Statement (1) alone is sufficient to answer the question. Ordinarily, having one side of a right triangle isn't enough to solve for all three sides. However, since two of the sides of this triangle are also radii of the circle, this is no ordinary right triangle: It's an isosceles right triangle, also known as a 45-45-90 triangle. As such, knowing that the long side of the triangle is $8\sqrt{2}$ is enough to tell us that the short sides are both 8. Once we know the radius, we can solve for the area—64π, if you were wondering—and we're down to A or D.

Statement (2) alone is also sufficient to answer the question. Arc *ABC*, since it's subtended (or "cut out") by a 90° angle, must represent $\frac{90}{360}$, or $\frac{1}{4}$, of the entire circumference. That gives us an entire circumference of 16π; from the circumference, we can find the radius, 8, and from there the area. The correct answer is D.

QUESTIONS

8. If 70 percent of the female and 90 percent of the male students in the senior class at a certain school are going on the senior trip and the senior class is 60 percent female, what percent of the senior class is going on the senior trip?

(A) 82%
(B) 80%
(C) 78%
(D) 76%
(E) 72%

9. If *P* is a set of integers and 3 is in *P*, is every positive multiple of 3 in *P* ?

(1) For any integer in *P*, the sum of 3 and that integer is also in *P*.

(2) For any integer in *P*, that integer minus 3 is also in *P*.

(A) Statement (1) ALONE is sufficient, but statement (2) alone is not sufficient.
(B) Statement (2) ALONE is sufficient, but statement (1) alone is not sufficient.
(C) BOTH statements TOGETHER are sufficient, but NEITHER statement ALONE is sufficient.
(D) EACH statement ALONE is sufficient.
(E) Statements (1) and (2) TOGETHER are not sufficient.

EXPLANATIONS

8. C This is a question about an unspecified amount, so it is a great opportunity to plug in! Since the answers are percentages, let's plug in 100 for the total number of seniors. That means we have 60 females, of whom 70%, or 42, are going on the senior trip; they'll be joined by 90% of the 40 males, which gives 36 males on the trip. That's a total of 42 + 36 = 78 students who are going on the trip. Seventy-eight out of our senior class of 100 is, of course, 78%, so the correct answer is C.

9. A To find the answer to this yes-or-no question, try Plugging In to the two statements, starting with the one number that you know is in the set: 3. For Statement (1), if 3 is in the set, then 6 is in the set. If 6 is in the set, then 9 is also in the set. Using similar reasoning, it can be shown that every positive multiple of 3 is in the set. So, the answer to the question is yes and Statement (1) is sufficient. The possible answers are A or D. For Statement (2), it can be shown that 3, 0, –3, –6 are in the set. But the positive multiples of 3 can be in the set, in which case the answer is to the question is yes, or not in the set in which case the answer to the question is no. So, Statement (2) is not sufficient. The answer is A.

QUESTIONS

10. A certain seafood restaurant gets a delivery of fresh seafood every day of the week. If the delivery company charges d dollars per delivery and c cents per delivered item and the restaurant has an average (arithmetic mean) of x items delivered per day, then which of the following is an expression for the total cost, in dollars, of one week's deliveries?

(A) $\frac{7cdx}{100}$

(B) $d+\frac{7cx}{100}$

(C) $7d+\frac{xc}{100}$

(D) $7d+\frac{7xc}{100}$

(E) $7cdx$

EXPLANATIONS

10. D Since the answer choices contain variables, this is a good place to plug in. Let's make $d = 10$, $c = 200$ (a particularly helpful number, because it allows us to work the problem in whole dollar amounts), and $x = 5$. If the restaurant has an average of 5 items per day delivered, then it had a total of 35 items delivered for the week. Multiplied by the 200 cents (or $2) charge per item, that's a total of $70 in per-item charges. When we add that amount to the $70 total for the per-delivery charges—7 deliveries at $10 per delivery—we get a total of $140 for the week. Our target answer, then, is 140; only D gives us 140 when we plug our values into our answer choices, and, therefore, D is the correct answer.
If you got C, by the way, check your calculations for your target answer. You likely calculated the per-item charges as though x were the total, rather than the daily average, of the items delivered.

QUESTIONS

11. Which of the following contains the interval two standard deviations from the mean of a set of data with an arithmetic mean of 46 and a standard deviation of 4 ?

(A) 38 to 46
(B) 38 to 54
(C) 42 to 50
(D) 44 to 48
(E) 46 to 50

EXPLANATIONS

11. **B** Standard deviation is the measure of how greatly the individual elements in a data set vary from the arithmetic mean of the set. As a general rule, the more widely dispersed the data in a set, the greater the standard deviation.

For the GMAT, you mostly need to know that standard deviation is measured from the arithmetic mean of a data set. If a data set has an arithmetic mean of 10 and a standard deviation of 2, then 8 and 12 are the values that are exactly one standard deviation from the arithmetic mean of the set.

In this problem, the standard deviation is 4, and the question asks for an interval that covers two standard deviations from the arithmetic mean of 46. It's key here to remember that "two standard deviations" means two *in each direction*—that is, both above *and* below the mean. Thus, we need an interval that covers 2×4, or 8, from the mean in each direction: $46 - 8 = 38$, so the bottom end of the interval is 38, and $46 + 8 = 54$, so the top end of the interval is 54. The correct answer is B. If you chose A, by the way, you accounted for only the two standard deviations below the mean. If you chose E, you accounted only for the two standard deviations above the mean. And if you chose C, you forgot to take two standard deviations in each direction.

QUESTIONS

12. If a and b are positive integers, is a a multiple of b ?

(1) Every distinct prime factor of b is also a distinct prime factor of a.

(2) Every factor of b is also a factor of a.

(A) Statement (1) ALONE is sufficient, but statement (2) alone is not sufficient.
(B) Statement (2) ALONE is sufficient, but statement (1) alone is not sufficient.
(C) BOTH statements TOGETHER are sufficient, but NEITHER statement ALONE is sufficient.
(D) EACH statement ALONE is sufficient.
(E) Statements (1) and (2) TOGETHER are not sufficient.

EXPLANATIONS

12. **B** To solve this yes-or-no problem, your best bet is to plug in values that meet the requirements given in the statements to determine whether Plugging In always yields the same answer to the question.

For Statement (1), for example, we could plug in 4 for both a and b—that's one easy way to make sure that every prime factor of b is also a prime factor of a—and since every number is a multiple of itself, the answer to the question is "yes." However, if we leave $b = 4$ but make $a = 2$, we can still satisfy the requirement of Statement (1)—4 has only one prime factor, 2, which is also a prime factor of 2—but now our answer is "no." Since Statement (1) yields different answers, it's insufficient, and the possible answers are B, C, or E. Similar attempts in Statement (2), however, will always yield the answer "yes." We could, of course, again plug in 4 for both variables, and we have our first "yes." If we leave $b = 4$, though, we can't make $a = 2$, since 4 isn't a factor of 2; a is a number such as 4 (which we've already used), 12, 16, or some other number that has 1, 2, and 4 as factors. Whichever one we pick, though, our answer is "yes"; Statement (2) is therefore sufficient, and the answer to the problem is B.

MATH BIN 3

QUESTIONS

13. If Set X contains 10 consecutive integers and the sum of the 5 least members of the set is 265, then what is the sum of the 5 greatest members of the set?

(A) 290
(B) 285
(C) 280
(D) 275
(E) 270

14. If $a - b = c$, what is the value of b?

(1) $c + 6 = a$

(2) $a = 6$

(A) Statement (1) ALONE is sufficient, but statement (2) alone is not sufficient.
(B) Statement (2) ALONE is sufficient, but statement (1) alone is not sufficient.
(C) BOTH statements TOGETHER are sufficient, but NEITHER statement ALONE is sufficient.
(D) EACH statement ALONE is sufficient.
(E) Statements (1) and (2) TOGETHER are not sufficient.

EXPLANATIONS

13. **A** We *could* solve this problem algebraically, although it's a bit of a chore. If we assign x to represent the smallest integer in the set, then $x + (x + 1) + (x + 2) + (x + 3) + (x + 4) = 265$, so $5x + 10 = 265$, $5x = 255$, and $x = 51$. The five least consecutive integers are thus 51 through 55; we can now add the five greatest consecutive integers, which are 56 through 60. The total is 290, and the correct answer is A.

A much simpler way to solve the problem, though, is to recognize that the difference between the sums of *any* two adjacent sets of five consecutive integers is the same; we can, therefore, find this difference using much smaller, easier-to-work-with numbers, and then add this difference to the total given in the problem. The sum of the integers from 1 to 5 is 15, and the sum of the integers from 6 to 10 is 40; our difference, thus, is 25, and $265 + 25 = 290$.

14. **A** It can be a good idea to simplify before heading into the statements. If you have the equation $a - b = c$ and want b, then you could simply write it as $b = a - c$. Now, consider Statement (1) on its own. Statement (1) can be rewritten as $a - c = 6$. Since $a - c = b$ from the question stem, we know that $b = 6$. Statement (1) is sufficient, and the answer is A or D. Statement (2) provides information about only one of the three variables in the original equation, so it cannot be sufficient on its own. The correct answer is A.

QUESTIONS

{3, 5, 9, 13, y}

15. If the average (arithmetic mean) and the median of the set of numbers shown above are equal, then what is the value of y ?

(A) 7
(B) 8
(C) 10
(D) 15
(E) 17

16. For a certain foot race, how many different arrangements of medal winners are possible?

(1) Medals will be given for 1st, 2nd, and 3rd place.

(2) There are 10 runners in the race.

(A) Statement (1) ALONE is sufficient, but statement (2) alone is not sufficient.
(B) Statement (2) ALONE is sufficient, but statement (1) alone is not sufficient.
(C) BOTH statements TOGETHER are sufficient, but NEITHER statement ALONE is sufficient.
(D) EACH statement ALONE is sufficient.
(E) Statements (1) and (2) TOGETHER are not sufficient.

EXPLANATIONS

15. **D** This problem is a great opportunity to Plug In the Answers. Start with choice C and substitute 10 for y in the problem. The average of the numbers {3, 5, 9, 13, 10} is 8, but the median of those numbers is 9. Eliminate C. The value of y needs to be greater, so try choice D, 15. The average of the numbers {3, 5, 9, 13, 15} is 9, and the median of those numbers is also 9. We're done. The correct answer is choice D.

16. **C** This is a permutation problem. Looking at Statement (1), it might seem enough to know that medals will be awarded for 1st, 2nd, and 3rd place. While some test takers might be quick to assume that there are $3 \times 2 \times 1$ possible arrangements of medal winners, until we know the number of runners, we don't know enough. The possible answers are B, C, or E.

Statement (2) tells us the number of runners. Since we cannot use the information from Statement (1) while evaluating Statement (2), we now do not know how many medals are to be given. We're down to C or E.

Putting the two statements together, we can now find out how many different arrangements of medal winners there are: $10 \times 9 \times 8 = 720$. The correct answer is C.

QUESTIONS

17. For the set of measurements 3, x_2, x_3, what is the value of x_3 ?

(1) The range of the set of measurements is 0.

(2) The standard deviation of the set of measurements is 0.

(A) Statement (1) ALONE is sufficient, but statement (2) alone is not sufficient.
(B) Statement (2) ALONE is sufficient, but statement (1) alone is not sufficient.
(C) BOTH statements TOGETHER are sufficient, but NEITHER statement ALONE is sufficient.
(D) EACH statement ALONE is sufficient.
(E) Statements (1) and (2) TOGETHER are not sufficient.

18. An employer has 6 applicants for a programming position and 4 applicants for a manager position. If the employer must hire 3 programmers and 2 managers, what is the total number of ways the employer can make the selection?

(A) 1,490
(B) 132
(C) 120
(D) 60
(E) 23

EXPLANATIONS

17. **D** The range of any set of measurements is equal to the greatest item in the set minus the least. Statement (1) gives us a value for the range. If that value were anything other than 0, we would not be able to solve the problem based only on this statement. Because Statement (1) tells us that the range is 0, we actually know more than you might think about these three numbers. Because the problem tells us that the first measurement is 3, let's plug in values for x_2 and x_3, just to see what happens. For example, if x_2 and x_3 both equal 5, the range does not equal 0. When you start plugging in numbers, you realize that the only way for the range of these three numbers to be 0 is if each of the numbers is exactly the same. And because we know the first value is 3, that means both x_2 and x_3 equal 3 as well. The possible answers are A or D.
Statement (2) tells us that all the measurements correspond exactly to the arithmetic mean—which tells us that all three measurements are equal to 3. The correct answer is choice D.

18. **C** In this combination problem, the employer's choice of a programmer can be written as

$$\frac{6\times5\times4}{3\times2\times1} \text{ or } 20$$

The employer's choice of a manager can be written as

$$\frac{4\times3}{2\times1} \text{ or } 6$$

To find the total number of ways she could make her selection, multiply the respective number of possibilities. 6 × 20 = 120. The correct answer is choice C.

QUESTIONS

19. On Monday, an animal shelter housed 55 cats and dogs and by Friday, exactly $\frac{1}{5}$ of the cats and $\frac{1}{4}$ of the dogs had been adopted. If no new cats or dogs were brought to the shelter during this period, what is the greatest possible number of pets that could have been adopted from the animal shelter between Monday and Friday?

(A) 11
(B) 12
(C) 13
(D) 14
(E) 20

EXPLANATIONS

19. C The question asks you for the greatest number of animals that could have been adopted from the shelter within the parameters of the problem. Because a greater proportion of dogs than cats was adopted, you should seek a scenario that maximizes the number of dogs adopted. You must also satisfy the other conditions of the problem, however; the number of cats, for example, must be a multiple of 5, because that is the only way that $\frac{1}{5}$ of the cats can be adopted.

Because we want to maximize the number of dogs in the shelter, let's start by assuming the minimum possible number of cats, 5. This would leave 50 dogs in the shelter. This solution, unfortunately, is impossible; because 50 is not evenly divisible by 4, there cannot be 50 dogs in the shelter. Could there be 10 cats at the shelter? No, because this would leave 45 dogs, again making it impossible for exactly $\frac{1}{4}$ of the dogs to be adopted. 15 cats is the magic number, as it means there are 40 dogs. $\left(\frac{1}{5} \times 15\right) + \left(\frac{1}{4} \times 40\right) =$ $3 + 10 = 13$ animals. The correct answer is C.

QUESTIONS

20. If x is an integer, then which of the following statements about $x^2 - x - 1$ is true?

(A) It is always odd.
(B) It is always even.
(C) It is always positive.
(D) It is even when x is even and odd when x is odd.
(E) It is even when x is odd and odd when x is even.

21. During a five-day period, Monday through Friday, the average (arithmetic mean) high temperature was 86 degrees Fahrenheit. What was the high temperature on Friday?

(1) The average high temperature for Monday through Thursday was 87 degrees Fahrenheit.

(2) The high temperature on Friday reduced the average high temperature for the five-day period by 1 degree Fahrenheit.

(A) Statement (1) ALONE is sufficient, but statement (2) alone is not sufficient.
(B) Statement (2) ALONE is sufficient, but statement (1) alone is not sufficient.
(C) BOTH statements TOGETHER are sufficient, but NEITHER statement ALONE is sufficient.
(D) EACH statement ALONE is sufficient.
(E) Statements (1) and (2) TOGETHER are not sufficient.

EXPLANATIONS

20. A Because x is an integer, x must be either even or odd. If x is even, then $x^2 - x$ must also be even, and therefore $x^2 - x - 1$ is always odd. If x is odd, then $x^2 - x$ must be even, and again, $x^2 - x - 1$ is always odd.

You can also solve this problem by Plugging In. After plugging in several values for x and calculating $x^2 - x - 1$, you will discover that the result is always odd. The correct answer is A.

21. D The question stem tells us that the average high temperature for the five-day period was 86°; therefore, the sum of the high temperatures for those days was $5 \times 86 = 430°$. Statement (1) tells us that the average high temperature for the first four days was 87°; therefore, the sum of the high temperatures for those days was $4 \times 87 = 348°$. $430 - 348 = 82°$, the high temperature on Friday. Statement (1) is sufficient; the answer is A or D. Statement (2) tells us that Friday's temperature reduced the average high for the five-day period by 1 degree. This means that the average high for the first four days was 87°; thus, (2) is sufficient for the same reason that (1) is sufficient. The correct answer is D.

QUESTIONS

22. What is the value of $x^2 - y^2$?

(1) $x + y = 0$

(2) $x - y = 2$

(A) Statement (1) ALONE is sufficient, but statement (2) alone is not sufficient.
(B) Statement (2) ALONE is sufficient, but statement (1) alone is not sufficient.
(C) BOTH statements TOGETHER are sufficient, but NEITHER statement ALONE is sufficient.
(D) EACH statement ALONE is sufficient.
(E) Statements (1) and (2) TOGETHER are not sufficient.

23. If P is the perimeter of an equilateral triangle, which of the following represents the height of the triangle?

(A) $\frac{P}{3}$

(B) $\frac{P\sqrt{3}}{3}$

(C) $\frac{P}{4}$

(D) $\frac{P\sqrt{3}}{6}$

(E) $\frac{P}{6}$

EXPLANATIONS

22. **A** Don't get caught making a careless assumption on this question. You may have immediately recognized that $x^2 - y^2$ factors to $(x + y)(x - y)$. Seeing that Statement (1) provides a value for $(x + y)$ and Statement (2) provides a value for $(x - y)$, you might have automatically assumed that the correct answer to this question is C. Look more closely, however; Statement (1) tells you that $(x + y) = 0$. Zero times any number equals zero. Therefore, Statement (1) is sufficient to tell you that $(x + y)(x - y) = 0$. Statement (2), however, is not sufficient. Since Statement (2) says that $x - y = 2$, plug this number back into the factored expression from the question stem. Without the value for the other factor (or the values of x and y), Statement (2) cannot be used on its own to answer the question. The correct answer is A.

23. **D** This is an excellent Plugging In problem. Plug in a value that is easily divisible by 3 for P; let's use 18. That would make the length of each side of the equilateral triangle 6.

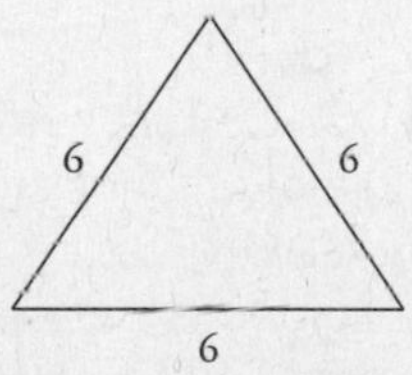

Draw a height for the triangle. Note that the height of an equilateral triangle divides the triangle into two 30–60–90 triangles, each with a base of 3.

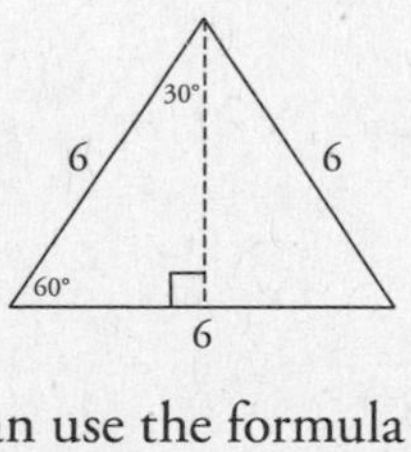

Now you can use the formula for the sides of a 30-60-90 triangle to determine that the height of the triangle is $3\sqrt{3}$ when $P = 18$. Finally, simply plug in 18 for P in every answer choice and eliminate those that do not yield a result of $3\sqrt{3}$. The correct answer is D.

QUESTIONS

24. If 75 percent of all Americans own an automobile, 15 percent of all Americans own a bicycle, and 20 percent of all Americans own neither an automobile nor a bicycle, then what percent of Americans own *both* an automobile and a bicycle?

(A) 0%
(B) 1.33%
(C) 3.75%
(D) 5%
(E) 10%

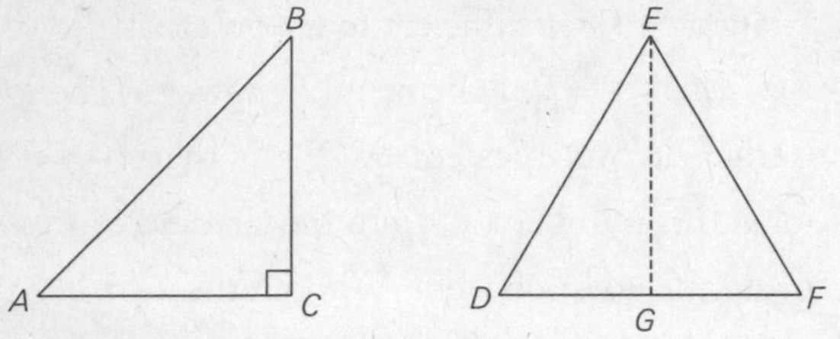

25. Triangle *ABC* is an isosceles right triangle and triangle *DEF* is an equilateral triangle with height *EG*. What is the ratio of the area of *ABC* to the area of *DEF* ?

(1) The ratio of *BC* to *EG* is 1:1.

(2) The ratio of *AC* to *DF* is $\sqrt{3}:2$.

(A) Statement (1) ALONE is sufficient, but statement (2) alone is not sufficient.
(B) Statement (2) ALONE is sufficient, but statement (1) alone is not sufficient.
(C) BOTH statements TOGETHER are sufficient, but NEITHER statement ALONE is sufficient.
(D) EACH statement ALONE is sufficient.
(E) Statements (1) and (2) TOGETHER are not sufficient.

EXPLANATIONS

24. **E** This is a group formula problem. The group formula is Total = Group 1 + Group 2 – Both + Neither. Assume the total is 100. If there are 100 total Americans, then 75 own an automobile (which is Group 1), 15 own a bicycle (Group 2) and 20 own neither. So the equation now reads 100 = 75 + 15 – Both + 20. Solve for Both and discover that it equals 10. 10 is 10% of 100. The correct answer is E.

25. **D** The formula for the area of a triangle is $A = \frac{\text{base} \times \text{height}}{2}$. Therefore, if we know the ratio of the bases and the heights of these triangles, it would be safe to assume that we know enough to calculate the ratios of their areas. This makes C a very tempting answer, because Statement (1) provides the ratio of the heights of the two triangles and Statement (2) provides the ratio of the bases of the two triangles.

The reason that the answer to this question is D lies in the special nature of isosceles right triangles and equilateral triangles. Their sides are in a fixed proportion to one another, so when you have information about one side, you have information about all the sides and, consequently, the area of the triangles. For this reason, each statement is sufficient on its own.

To prove that to yourself, you can plug in values for the sides of the triangles. For example, in Statement (1), the ratio of *BC* to *EG* is 1 to 1. So, let's say *BC* and *EG* are both one meter long. Since *ABC* is isosceles, that means *AC* = 1, too, and the area of *ABC* is $\frac{1}{2}$. Since *DEF* is equilateral, that means *DG* and *GF* are each $\sqrt{3}$ and *DF* is $2\sqrt{3}$. Therefore, we can find the area of *DEF* ($\sqrt{3}$).

QUESTIONS

26. What is the value of integer x ?

(1) $\sqrt[x]{64} = 4$

(2) $x^2 = x + 6$

(A) Statement (1) ALONE is sufficient, but statement (2) alone is not sufficient.
(B) Statement (2) ALONE is sufficient, but statement (1) alone is not sufficient.
(C) BOTH statements TOGETHER are sufficient, but NEITHER statement ALONE is sufficient.
(D) EACH statement ALONE is sufficient.
(E) Statements (1) and (2) TOGETHER are not sufficient.

EXPLANATIONS

26. A The only one solution to the equation in Statement (1) is $x = 3$. Therefore, the answer to this question is A or D.

To determine whether Statement (2) is sufficient, subtract $2x + 8$ from both sides of the equation to get

$$x^2 - x - 6 = 0$$

This equation can be factored to

$$(x - 3)(x + 2) = 0$$

Thus, the equation has two solutions: x can equal 3 or –2. Statement (2) is not sufficient. The correct answer is A.

MATH BIN 4

QUESTIONS

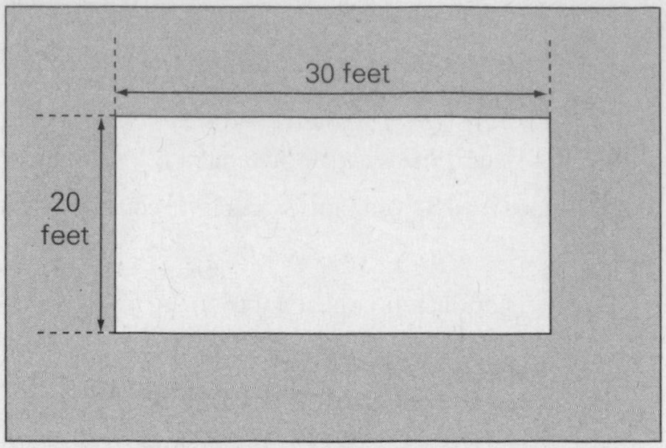

1. A rectangular garden with dimensions 20 feet by 30 feet is surrounded by a rectangular brick walkway of uniform width as shown in the figure above. If the area of the walkway equals the area of the garden, what is the width of the walkway?

(A) 1 foot
(B) 3 feet
(C) 5 feet
(D) 8 feet
(E) 10 feet

EXPLANATIONS

1. C To answer this question, first recognize that the area of the walkway can be calculated by subtracting the area of the smaller (white) rectangle from the larger rectangle in the figure. The difference between the areas of the two rectangles equals the area of the shaded region. This problem is ideal for Plugging In the Answers. Start with answer choice C; if it is incorrect, you may be able to tell whether it is too large or too small, and you will be able to eliminate not only C, but also two other answers.

If C is correct, then the walkway is 5 feet wide. With a walkway of that width, the dimensions of the large rectangle in the figure are 30 feet (the width of the garden—20 feet—plus 5 feet on each side to account for the width of the walkway) by 40 feet (the length of the garden—30 feet—plus 5 feet on each side to account for the width of the walkway). The area of the large rectangle, then, is $40 \times 30 = 1{,}200$ square feet, and the area of the shaded region is $1{,}200 - (20 \times 30) = 1{,}200 - 600 = 600$ square feet.

When the width of the walkway is 5 feet, the area of the walkway equals the area of the garden. That's the result we're looking for, so the correct answer is C.

QUESTIONS

2. If a fair two-sided coin is flipped 6 times, what is the probability that tails is the result at least twice but at most 5 times?

(A) $\frac{5}{8}$

(B) $\frac{3}{4}$

(C) $\frac{7}{8}$

(D) $\frac{57}{64}$

(E) $\frac{15}{16}$

EXPLANATIONS

2. C As is often the case with difficult probability questions, the bottom part of the fraction—the total number of possibilities—is a permutation problem in itself. In this case, we need to figure out how many different outcomes we can get if we flip a coin 6 times. Since we have 6 events with 2 possible outcomes each, our total number of different outcomes is $2 \times 2 \times 2 \times 2 \times 2 \times 2$, or 2^6, or 64. Now we just need to figure out how many of those possibilities meet the requirement.

For this problem, however, since there are so many different ways to meet the requirement, we'll be better off figuring out how many outcomes *don't* meet our requirement; we can then subtract this number from the total of 64. There are only three ways to *not* meet the requirement of 2 to 5 tails on 6 flips—we could get 0, 1, or 6 tails—and these can be quickly and easily counted out. There is only one way to get 6 tails, and, likewise, there is only one way to get 0 tails, which is another way of saying 6 heads. That's two possibilities. And there are only six different ways to get tails once: The single tails can come up in the first spot, the second spot, and so on. That's 8 out of the total of 64 possible outcomes that don't meet our requirement, so 56 do. The probability, therefore, is $\frac{56}{64}$, which reduces to $\frac{7}{8}$. The correct answer is C.

QUESTIONS

3. The new recruits of a military organization who score in the bottom 16 percent on their physical conditioning tests are required to retest. If the scores are normally distributed and have an arithmetic mean of 72, what is the score at or below which the recruits are required to retest?

(1) There are 500 new recruits.

(2) 10 new recruits scored at least 82 on the physical conditioning test.

(A) Statement (1) ALONE is sufficient, but statement (2) alone is not sufficient.
(B) Statement (2) ALONE is sufficient, but statement (1) alone is not sufficient.
(C) BOTH statements TOGETHER are sufficient, but NEITHER statement ALONE is sufficient.
(D) EACH statement ALONE is sufficient.
(E) Statements (1) and (2) TOGETHER are not sufficient.

EXPLANATIONS

3. C Statement (1) is not sufficient to answer the question by itself. It does let us determine *how many* recruits will have to retake the test, but we don't know anything about their scores. The possible answers are B, C, or E. Statement (2) is also insufficient by itself—while those 10 recruits are certainly impressive, we don't know what part of the overall recruiting class they represent. We're down to C or E.

When we combine the statements, though, we have enough information to answer the question. We can now calculate that those 10 top-scoring recruits make up the top 2% of the class as a whole—and since the scores are normally distributed, the top 2% represents the third standard deviation above the mean. If the mean is 72, and the third standard deviation above the mean begins at 82, then there are 2 standard deviations (the first and the second) between 72 and 82. The dividing line between them, then, falls at the score halfway between 72 and 82, or 77. We now know the entire upper half of the curve: The first standard deviation runs from the mean of 72 to 77; the second standard deviation runs from 77 to 82; and the third standard deviation runs from 82 to 87. More importantly, we now know that one standard deviation equals 5 points, so that bottom 16%—also known as the second and third standard deviation below the mean—are those who score at or below 67. The correct answer is C.

QUESTIONS

4. Each of the integers from 1 to 20 is written on a separate index card and placed in a box. If the cards are drawn from the box at random without replacement, how many cards must be drawn to ensure that the product of all the integers drawn is even?

(A) 19
(B) 12
(C) 11
(D) 10
(E) 3

EXPLANATIONS

4. C To determine how many cards must be drawn to ensure that the product is even, determine the worst-case scenario. Let's start by figuring out the maximum number of cards that can be drawn so that the product of the numbers on the cards is odd. The first card, obviously, is an odd-numbered card. If the second card is an odd-numbered card, then the product of the numbers on the cards is odd. If the third card is odd, then the product remains odd. As long as the numbers on the cards drawn are odd, the product of those numbers is odd. Thus, in the worst-case scenario, all ten odd numbered cards are drawn in succession. At this point, the eleventh card must be even, which would make the product of the 11 cards even. Therefore, 11 cards must be drawn to ensure an even product. The correct answer is C.

QUESTIONS

5. The average (arithmetic mean) of integers r, s, t, u, and v is 100. Are exactly two of the integers greater than 100 ?

(1) Three of the integers are less than 50.

(2) None of the integers is equal to 100.

(A) Statement (1) ALONE is sufficient, but statement (2) alone is not sufficient.
(B) Statement (2) ALONE is sufficient, but statement (1) alone is not sufficient.
(C) BOTH statements TOGETHER are sufficient, but NEITHER statement ALONE is sufficient.
(D) EACH statement ALONE is sufficient.
(E) Statements (1) and (2) TOGETHER are not sufficient.

EXPLANATIONS

5. E This is a yes-or-no question. Statement (1) tells us that three of the five integers are less than 50. This information by itself does not ensure that the other two integers *are* greater than 100. Both remaining values *could* be greater than 100; the solution set {10, 20, 30, 140, 300}, for example, satisfies this condition. However, the set {1, 2, 3, 4, 490} *also* satisfies the conditions of the problem, and it contains only one value greater than 100. Statement (1) is insufficient on its own; the correct answer must be B, C, or E. Statement (2) tells us only that none of the integers is equal to 100. By itself, this is clearly not sufficient to tell us that exactly two of the integers are greater than 100; eliminate answer B. In fact, the statement provides no more useful information than that provided in Statement (1); both of the solutions provided above satisfy this statement as well. The correct answer is E.

QUESTIONS

6. Paul jogs along the same route every day at a constant rate for 80 minutes. What distance does he jog?

(1) Yesterday, Paul began jogging at 5:00 P.M.

(2) Yesterday, Paul had jogged 5 miles by 5:40 P.M. and 8 miles by 6:04 P.M.

(A) Statement (1) ALONE is sufficient, but statement (2) alone is not sufficient.
(B) Statement (2) ALONE is sufficient, but statement (1) alone is not sufficient.
(C) BOTH statements TOGETHER are sufficient, but NEITHER statement ALONE is sufficient.
(D) EACH statement ALONE is sufficient.
(E) Statements (1) and (2) TOGETHER are not sufficient.

EXPLANATIONS

6. **B** Statement (1) clearly is not sufficient to answer the question because it tells us only Paul's starting time. The correct answer to this question must be B, C, or E. Statement (2) tells us that Paul had jogged 5 miles by 5:40 P.M. and 8 miles by 6:04 P.M. You might be tempted to answer C at this point; after all, you now know when Paul began jogging and how far he had jogged at various intervals, so you could easily figure out how far he had run by 6:20 P.M., the end of the 80-minute period beginning at 5:00 P.M. Resist the temptation! Let's look more closely at Statement (2). It tells us that Paul covered 3 miles between 5:40 P.M. and 6:04 P.M. Thus, we know that Paul ran eight-minute miles during that 24-minute period. The question stem tells us that Paul jogs at a constant rate, and that he jogs for 80 minutes. Therefore, Statement (2), in combination with the question stem, provides all the information we need; Paul jogs eight-minute miles for 80 minutes, so the route along which he jogs is 10 miles long. The correct answer is B.

QUESTIONS

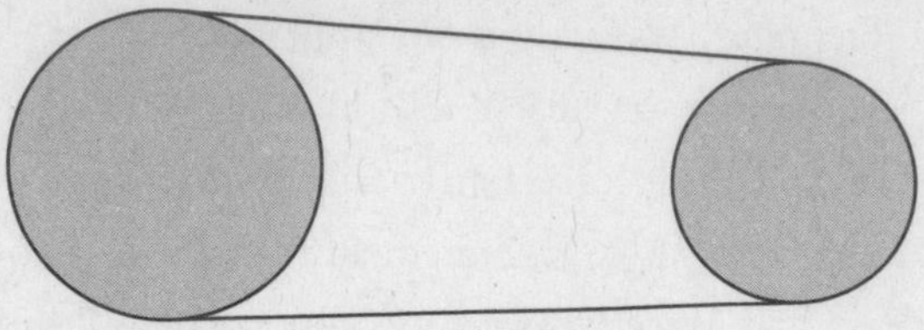

7. The diagram above shows two wheels that drive a conveyor belt. The larger wheel has a diameter of 40 centimeters, and the smaller wheel has a diameter of 32 centimeters. If each wheel must rotate the exact same number of centimeters per minute, and the larger wheel makes *r* revolutions per minute, then, in terms of *r*, how many revolutions does the smaller wheel make per hour?

(A) $\frac{1,280\pi}{3}$

(B) $75r$

(C) $48r$

(D) $24r$

(E) $\frac{64\pi}{3}$

EXPLANATIONS

7. **B** Because the problem has variables in the answer choice, Plugging In is a great way to solve. Plug in an easy number, one that will make your calculations and answer checking simple. For the purposes of this explanation, let's set *r* equal to 2. With each rotation, each wheel rotates the length of its circumference. Thus, the wheel with diameter 40 centimeters rotates 40π centimeters with each rotation; the wheel with diameter 32 centimeters rotates 32π centimeters with each rotation. The larger wheel makes *r* revolutions per minute; because we've set *r* equal to 2, it makes 2 revolutions per minute and thus rotates 80π centimeters per minute. According to the problem, the smaller wheel must rotate the same distance. Therefore, the smaller wheel also rotates 80π centimeters per minute, meaning it rotates $60 \times 80\pi = 4,800\pi$ centimeters per hour. The smaller wheel covers 32π centimeters per rotation, so it must rotate $4,800\pi \div 32\pi = 150$ times per hour. Plug 2 in for *r* in each of the answer choices. The correct answer is B, $75r$.

QUESTIONS

8. An automobile dealership sells only sedans and coupes. It sells each in only two colors: red and blue. Last year, the dealership sold 9,000 vehicles, half of which were red. How many coupes did the dealership sell last year?

(1) The dealership sold three times as many blue coupes as red sedans last year.

(2) The dealership sold half as many blue sedans as blue coupes last year.

(A) Statement (1) ALONE is sufficient, but statement (2) alone is not sufficient.
(B) Statement (2) ALONE is sufficient, but statement (1) alone is not sufficient.
(C) BOTH statements TOGETHER are sufficient, but NEITHER statement ALONE is sufficient.
(D) EACH statement ALONE is sufficient.
(E) Statements (1) and (2) TOGETHER are not sufficient.

EXPLANATIONS

8. **C** Create a table to solve this proportions question. It should look something like this:

	Red	**Blue**	**TOTAL**
Coupes			
Sedans			
TOTAL	4,500	4,500	9,000

The question stem tells us how many cars were sold last year. Because it tells us that half the cars sold were red, it also tells us the number of blue cars sold last year.

Statement (1) tells us: "The dealership sold three times as many blue coupes as red sedans last year." Enter this information into the table in algebraic terms:

	Red	**Blue**	**TOTAL**
Coupes		$3x$	
Sedans	x		
TOTAL	4,500	4,500	9,000

Because two unknowns—red coupes and blue sedans—remain, Statement (1) does not provide enough information to solve the problem. The correct answer is B, C, or E.

Use the same procedure to test Statement (2): "The dealership sold half as many blue sedans as blue coupes last year":

	Red	**Blue**	**TOTAL**
Coupes		$2x$	
Sedans		x	
TOTAL	4,500	4,500	9,000

Again, two unknowns remain. *This* time, though, we have all the information we need to write a solvable equation. We know that $2x + x = 4{,}500$. Therefore x equals 1,500. We now know the following:

	Red	**Blue**	**TOTAL**
Coupes		3,000	
Sedans		1,500	
TOTAL	4,500	4,500	9,500

QUESTIONS

EXPLANATIONS

Unfortunately, this still isn't enough information to answer the question. The answer is C or E. Combine the information from the two statements. Statement (2) tells us that the dealership sold 3,000 blue coupes; combined with Statement (1), this tells us that the dealership sold 1,000 red sedans. We can now subtract 1,000 from 4,500 to determine that the dealership sold 3,500 red coupes. Therefore, it sold 6,500 coupes last year. The correct answer is C.

9. At a college football game, $\frac{4}{5}$ of the seats in the lower deck of the stadium were sold. If $\frac{1}{4}$ of all the seats in the stadium are located in the lower deck, and if $\frac{2}{3}$ of all the seats in the stadium were sold, what fraction of the unsold seats in the stadium are in the lower deck?

(A) $\frac{3}{20}$

(B) $\frac{1}{6}$

(C) $\frac{1}{5}$

(D) $\frac{1}{3}$

(E) $\frac{7}{15}$

9. **A** Solve this one using Plugging In. First, plug in a number of seats for the entire stadium. Choose a number that divides easily by 3, 4, and 5. For the purposes of this explanation, let's say the stadium seats 60,000 people. The problem states that $\frac{2}{3}$ of all the seating in the stadium was sold, meaning that 40,000 of the 60,000 seats were sold. It also states that $\frac{1}{4}$ of the seating is located in the lower deck. Because $\frac{1}{4}$ of 60,000 is 15,000, that means the stadium has 15,000 seats in the lower deck. Of those 15,000 seats, according to the problem, $\frac{4}{5}$, or 12,000, were sold. The question asks what fraction of the unsold seats in the stadium were in the lower deck. Because 40,000 seats were sold in the entire stadium, a total of 20,000 were unsold; of the 20,000 unsold seats, 15,000 – 12,000 = 3,000 were in the lower deck. The fraction $\frac{3{,}000}{20{,}000}$ reduces to $\frac{3}{20}$, so the correct answer is A.

QUESTIONS

10. At Company R, the average (arithmetic mean) age of executive employees is 54 years old and the average age of non-executive employees is 34 years old. What is the average age of all the employees at Company R ?

(1) There are 10 executive employees at Company R.

(2) The number of non-executive employees at Company R is four times the number of executive employees at Company R.

(A) Statement (1) ALONE is sufficient, but statement (2) alone is not sufficient.
(B) Statement (2) ALONE is sufficient, but statement (1) alone is not sufficient.
(C) BOTH statements TOGETHER are sufficient, but NEITHER statement ALONE is sufficient.
(D) EACH statement ALONE is sufficient.
(E) Statements (1) and (2) TOGETHER are not sufficient.

EXPLANATIONS

10. **B** Statement (1) provides no information about the non-executive employees at Company *R*. It is not sufficient by itself and the correct answer is B, C, or E. Statement (2) provides a ratio of executive employees to non-executive employees at Company *R*. This information is sufficient on its own to determine the average age of all employees at Company *R*. Regardless of whether Company *R* has 2 executives and 8 non-executives or 200 executives and 800 non-executives, the resulting average for all employees is the same, because the proportional contribution of each group to the average remains fixed. The best way to prove this is simply to plug in some numbers and see for yourself. The average age of 1 executive and 4 non-executives is $\frac{54+4(34)}{5}=38$. The average age of 30 executives and 120 non-executives is $\frac{30(54)+120(34)}{150}=38$. Thus, the correct answer is B.

QUESTIONS

11. If a, b, c, d, and x are all nonzero integers, is the product $ax \cdot (bx)^2 \cdot (cx)^3 \cdot (dx)^4$ negative?

(1) $a < c < x < 0$

(2) $b < d < x < 0$

(A) Statement (1) ALONE is sufficient, but statement (2) alone is not sufficient.
(B) Statement (2) ALONE is sufficient, but statement (1) alone is not sufficient.
(C) BOTH statements TOGETHER are sufficient, but NEITHER statement ALONE is sufficient.
(D) EACH statement ALONE is sufficient.
(E) Statements (1) and (2) TOGETHER are not sufficient.

12. A four character password consists of one letter from the English alphabet and three different digits from 0 to 9. If the letter is the second or third character of the password, how many different passwords are possible?

(A) 5,040
(B) 18,720
(C) 26,000
(D) 37,440
(E) 52,000

EXPLANATIONS

11. A Statment (1) tells us that a, c, and x are negative. Instinctively, we might conclude that this isn't enough information, because it tells us nothing about b or d. Look at the expression in the question stem again, though; b and d appear only in the expressions $(bx)^2$ and $(dx)^4$. Both of these expressions contain even exponents; we know, therefore, that these expressions are positive regardless of the values b and d represent, because nonzero integers raised to an even power are always positive. From Statement (1) we know that ax is positive (a negative times a negative equals a positive) and, similarly, that $(cx)^3$ is positive. Statement (1) is sufficient even though the answer to the question is no. The possible answers are A or D. Statement (2) provides no valuable information. The values of b and d do not matter as they are only used in expressions that result in positive numbers. The values of a and c, however, do matter because they are raised to an odd exponent. Any number raised to an odd exponent retains the positive or negative nature of the original number. There is no way to ensure, then, that ax or cx, when raised to an odd exponent, is positive or negative. The correct answer is A.

12. D According to the problem, an acceptable password consists of either *DLDD* or *DDLD*, where *D* represents a digit and *L* represents a letter of the alphabet. Remember also that the digits must be different. First, let's consider *DLDD*. The first character can be any of the ten digits, 0 through 9. The second character can be any of the 26 letters of the English alphabet. There are only 9 possible digits for the third character, because the third character cannot repeat the digit used for the first character. By the same reasoning, there are only 8 possible digits for the fourth character. Thus, there are $10 \times 26 \times 9 \times 8 = 18{,}720$ possible

QUESTIONS

EXPLANATIONS

passwords that follow the *DLDD* pattern. Now consider *DDLD*. There are an equal number of possible passwords that follow this pattern. The first character can be any of 10 digits; the second character can be any of the 9 remaining digits; the third character can be any of the 26 letters of the alphabet; and the fourth character can be any of the remaining 8 digits.
$10 \times 9 \times 26 \times 8 = 18{,}720$. There are 18,720 + 18,720 = 37,440 different passwords possible, and the correct answer is D.

13. If x is a positive integer, is x divisible by 48 ?

(1) x is divisible by 8.

(2) x is divisible by 6.

(A) Statement (1) ALONE is sufficient, but statement (2) alone is not sufficient.
(B) Statement (2) ALONE is sufficient, but statement (1) alone is not sufficient.
(C) BOTH statements TOGETHER are sufficient, but NEITHER statement ALONE is sufficient.
(D) EACH statement ALONE is sufficient.
(E) Statements (1) and (2) TOGETHER are not sufficient.

13. E This is a yes-or-no question. If we plug in numbers for x in Statement (1), we can get both a "yes" answer (by plugging in 48) and a "no" answer (by plugging in 16), so the possible answers are B, C, or E. The same is true with Statement (2). If $x = 48$, which is divisible by 6, the answer to the question is yes. But, if $x = 6$, the answer to the question is no. The possible answers are C or E. Now, combine the state ments. If $x = 48$, which is divisible by both 6 and 8, the answer to the question is yes. However, if $x = 24$, which is also divisible by both 6 and 8, the answer to the question is no. So, the statements are not sufficient when combined. Therefore, the correct answer is E.

QUESTIONS

$$\begin{array}{r} FGF \\ \times\ G \\ \hline HGG \end{array}$$

14. In the multiplication problem above, *F*, *G*, and *H* represent distinct odd digits. What is the value of the three-digit number *FGF* ?

(A) 151
(B) 161
(C) 171
(D) 313
(E) 353

EXPLANATIONS

14. **A** At first it looks as though you'll have to substitute every odd digit for the three variables until you stumble onto the correct answer, but there's a trick to this problem that eliminates such guesswork. Look at the units column of the problem and you'll see that $F \times G$ yields a product with a units digit of *G*; therefore, it is quite possible that *F* is 1. Actually, you can go even further: *F must* equal 1, because *G* cannot equal 1 (otherwise, the product of this multiplication problem would be *FGF*, not *HGG*). Plus, if both *F* and *G* were odd digits greater than 1, the product of this multiplication problem would be a four-digit number. Because the product is the three-digit number *HGG*, *F* equals 1. You can now eliminate answer choices D and E, and you also know that *G* must equal 5 or 7 (*G* cannot equal 6 because the problem says *G* must be an odd digit). When *G* equals 7, the product is a four-digit number; therefore, *G* is 5, and the correct answer is A. But you could have just plugged the answer choices into the problem, one at a time, to see which one works.

QUESTIONS

15. A group of 20 friends formed an investment club, with each member contributing an equal amount to the general fund. The club then invested the entire fund, which amounted to *d* dollars, in Stock *X*. The value of the stock subsequently increased 40 percent, at which point the stock was sold and the proceeds divided evenly among the members. In terms of *d*, how much money did each member of the club receive from the sale? (Assume that transaction fees and other associated costs were negligible.)

(A) $800d$

(B) $\frac{7d}{5}$

(C) $\frac{d}{20} + 40$

(D) $\frac{d}{2}$

(E) $\frac{7d}{100}$

EXPLANATIONS

15. E The variables in the answer choices should tell you that this is a great problem for Plugging In. Choose a value easily divisible by 20 (the number of friends in the group) and one for which percentages are easy to calculate (because the value of the stock increases by a percentage). Let's set *d* equal to 100. The general fund of $100, then, was invested in Stock *X*, which subsequently increased in value by 40 percent; thus, its value increased to $140. At this point, the club sold the stock and divvied up the proceeds. Each member received $140 ÷ 20 = $7 in the process. Therefore, when *d* equals 100, the correct answer choice yields a result of 7. Check each answer choice, plugging in 100 for *d*. The correct answer is E.

QUESTIONS

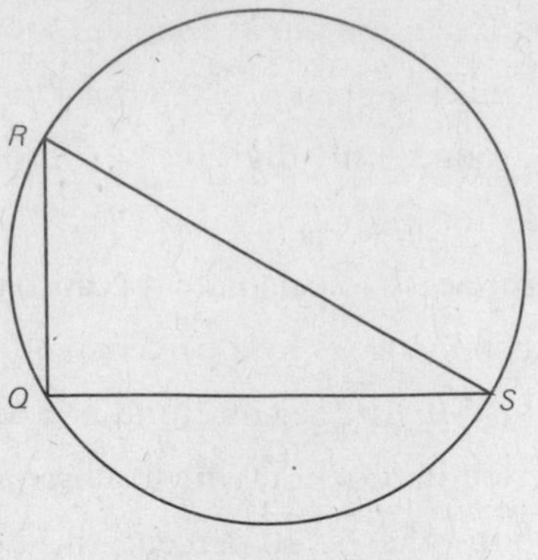

16. Triangle *QRS* is inscribed in a circle as shown above. Is *QRS* a right triangle?

(1) *RS* is a diameter of the circle.

(2) *QR* = 3 and *RS* = 5

(A) Statement (1) ALONE is sufficient, but statement (2) alone is not sufficient.
(B) Statement (2) ALONE is sufficient, but statement (1) alone is not sufficient.
(C) BOTH statements TOGETHER are sufficient, but NEITHER statement ALONE is sufficient.
(D) EACH statement ALONE is sufficient.
(E) Statements (1) and (2) TOGETHER are not sufficient.

EXPLANATIONS

16. **A** This problem requires you to clear two hurdles. First, you must remember a rule about inscribed angles in semicircles. Then, you must avoid succumbing to the power of suggestion. First, the rule about inscribed angles. Statement (1) tells us that *RS* is a diameter of the circle. That means we are dealing with two semicircles. The question stem tells us that triangle *QRS* is inscribed in a circle; thus $\angle RQS$ is inscribed. A triangle inscribed in a semicircle is always a right triangle. Therefore, $\angle RQS$ measures 90°. Statement (1) is sufficient, and the correct answer is A or D. Statement (2) can trick you if you don't forget all about Statement (1) first. It suggests that *QSR* is a right triangle, because the ratio of *QR* to *RS* recalls the familiar 3-4-5 triangle that satisfies the Pythagorean theorem. However, Statement (2) does not preclude the possibility that *RS* is *not* a diameter and that therefore side *QS* does *not* measure 4. There is no way to determine whether *QRS* is a right triangle from Statement (2). The correct answer is A.

QUESTIONS

17. Square *G* has sides of length 4 inches. Is the area of Square *H* exactly one half the area of Square *G* ?

(1) The length of the diagonal of Square *H* equals the length of one side of Square *G*.

(2) The perimeter of Square *H* is twice the length of the diagonal of Square *G*.

(A) Statement (1) ALONE is sufficient, but statement (2) alone is not sufficient.
(B) Statement (2) ALONE is sufficient, but statement (1) alone is not sufficient.
(C) BOTH statements TOGETHER are sufficient, but NEITHER statement ALONE is sufficient.
(D) EACH statement ALONE is sufficient.
(E) Statements (1) and (2) TOGETHER are not sufficient.

EXPLANATIONS

17. **D** Statement (1) tells us that the diagonal of Square *H* is 4 inches long. That is enough information to determine the length of a side of Square *H*, because the diagonal and two adjacent sides of a square form a 45-45-90 triangle, and the lengths of the sides of a 45-45-90 triangle are in the proportion $1:1:\sqrt{2}$. One side of Square *H* has a length of $\frac{4}{\sqrt{2}} = \frac{4\sqrt{2}}{2} = 2\sqrt{2}$ inches. The area of Square *H* is 8 square inches, which is indeed half the area of Square *G*. The correct answer is A or D. Statement (2) mentions the diagonal of Square *G*, which we know to be $4\sqrt{2}$ inches because question stem tells us that the length of one side of Square *G* is 4 inches. Thus, the perimeter of Square *H* is $8\sqrt{2}$ inches, and the length of one side of Square *H* is $2\sqrt{2}$ inches. As in Statement (1), this information is sufficient to answer the question. The correct answer is D.

MATH BIN 4

QUESTIONS

18. In a certain state, 70 percent of the counties received some rain on Monday, and 65 percent of the counties received some rain on Tuesday. No rain fell either day in 25 percent of the counties in the state. What percent of the counties received some rain on Monday and Tuesday?

(A) 12.5%
(B) 40%
(C) 50%
(D) 60%
(E) 67.5%

EXPLANATIONS

18. **D** Use the group formula to solve this problem. The group formula is Total = Group 1 + Group 2 – Both + Neither. The problem specifies that the answer is the percent of counties that got rain on both days, so the answer depends on finding the "Both" category of the formula. Now, fill in the values for the formula. Plug in 100 for the total number of counties. Therefore, 70 counties received rain on Monday (which is Group 1), 65 counties received rain on Tuesday (Group 2), and 25 counties received no rain. Put these into the formula, so 100 = 70 + 65 – Both + 25. Solve the equation to find that Both = 60. 60 is 60% of 100, so the correct answer is D.

QUESTIONS

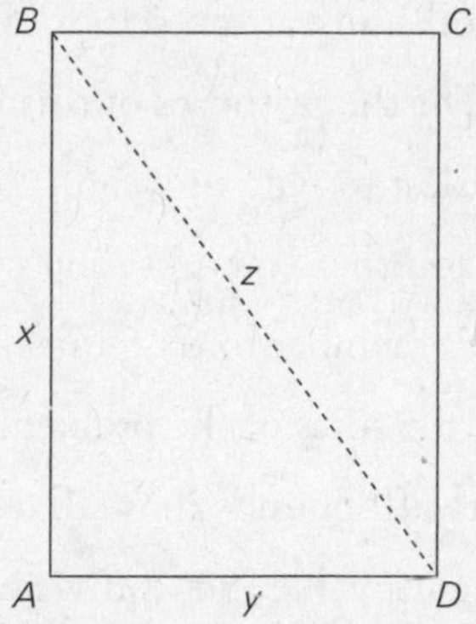

19. *ABCD* is a rectangle with sides of length x centimeters and width y centimeters, and a diagonal of length z centimeters. What is the perimeter, in centimeters, of *ABCD* ?

(1) $x - y = 7$

(2) $z = 13$

(A) Statement (1) ALONE is sufficient, but statement (2) alone is not sufficient.
(B) Statement (2) ALONE is sufficient, but statement (1) alone is not sufficient.
(C) BOTH statements TOGETHER are sufficient, but NEITHER statement ALONE is sufficient.
(D) EACH statement ALONE is sufficient.
(E) Statements (1) and (2) TOGETHER are not sufficient.

EXPLANATIONS

19. C Statement (1) tells us that $x - y = 7$. An infinite number of combinations satisfy this equation, yielding an infinite number of perimeters for *ABCD*. Statement (1) is not sufficient, and the answer is B, C, or E. Similarly, there are many different ways to draw a rectangle with diagonal 13. Not all of these rectangles have the same perimeter. Statement (2) is not sufficient by itself, and the correct answer is C or E. At first glance, the two statements together don't appear to offer much more help. However, by applying a bit of algebraic trickery and the Pythagorean theorem, we can wring more information from these two statements than is immediately apparent. Start by squaring Statement (1); this yields the equation $x^2 - 2xy + y^2 = 49$. The Pythagorean theorem tells us that $x^2 + y^2 = z^2$, so we can use Statement (2) to substitute 13^2, or 169, for $x^2 + y^2$. This yields the equation $169 - 2xy = 49$, which can be simplified to $xy = 60$. There's just one more step. We know that $x^2 + y^2 = 169$, and we know that $xy = 60$. Thus, we know that $x^2 + 2xy + y^2 = 289$. The square root of $x^2 + 2xy + y^2$ is $(x + y)$, so we also know that $x + y = 17$ (it cannot equal -17 because x and y are centimeter lengths). This equation can be used in conjunction with Statement (1) to solve simultaneously for x and y, thus allowing you a way to calculate the perimeter of the rectangle. The correct answer is C.

QUESTIONS

20. Together, Andrea and Brian weigh p pounds. Brian weighs 10 pounds more than Andrea, and Andrea's dog, Cubby, weighs $\frac{p}{4}$ pounds more than Andrea. In terms of p, what is Cubby's weight in pounds?

(A) $\frac{p}{2}-10$

(B) $\frac{3p}{4}-5$

(C) $\frac{3p}{2}-5$

(D) $\frac{5p}{4}-10$

(E) $5p-5$

EXPLANATIONS

20. **B** Variables in the answer choices mean it's time to plug in. For the purposes of this problem, it's probably easiest to plug in weights for Andrea and Brian, add them, and use the sum for the value of p. Remember to plug in values that conform to the rules of the problem; Brian must weigh exactly 10 pounds more than Andrea. Try to make p a value that is divisible by 4; that will make it easier to calculate Cubby's weight. Let's say Andrea weighs 45 pounds and Brian weighs 55 pounds. That makes p equal to 100, a nice, round number that is easily divisible by 4. Cubby weighs $\frac{p}{4}$ pounds more than Andrea, so he weighs 25 pounds more than Andrea, or 70 pounds. Plug 100 in for p in each of the answer choices and eliminate those that do not yield an answer of 70. The correct answer is B.

QUESTIONS

21. A first-grade teacher uses ten flash cards, numbered 1 through 10, to teach her students to order numbers correctly. She has students choose four flash cards at random and arrange the cards in ascending order. If she removes the cards numbered 2 and 4, how many different correctly ordered arrangements of the four selected cards are possible?

(A) 70
(B) 210
(C) 336
(D) 840
(E) 1,680

EXPLANATIONS

21. **A** This question is easier than it first appears. At first glance, the restrictive rules—the cards must be arranged in order, some cards have been removed from the deck—seem to complicate the problem. In fact, they do not; because there is only one correct solution for each set of cards chosen, you need only figure out the number of possible combinations of the cards in order to determine the number of possible correct arrangements. The one-to-one correlation between combinations and correct solutions actually simplifies the problem. Because the teacher has removed two cards from the deck, only 8 cards remain. The values on the selected cards are immaterial, and are presented merely as a distracter; the answer to this question is the same regardless of the values written on the two cards she removes. Make four spots for the cards chosen, then fill in the number of options for each spot: $8 \times 7 \times 6 \times 5$. Then, divide by the number of ways to arrange these four cards: $4 \times 3 \times 2 \times 1$. Reduce and solve to find 70. The correct answer is A.

QUESTIONS

22. If A and B are two-digit integers that share the same digits, except in reverse order, then what is the sum of A and B ?

(1) $A - B = 45$

(2) The difference between the two digits in each number is 5.

(A) Statement (1) ALONE is sufficient, but statement (2) alone is not sufficient.
(B) Statement (2) ALONE is sufficient, but statement (1) alone is not sufficient.
(C) BOTH statements TOGETHER are sufficient, but NEITHER statement ALONE is sufficient.
(D) EACH statement ALONE is sufficient.
(E) Statements (1) and (2) TOGETHER are not sufficient.

23. A university awarded grants in the amount of either \$7,000 or \$10,000 to selected incoming freshmen. If the total amount of all such awards is \$2,300,000, did the university award more \$7,000 grants than \$10,000 grants to its incoming freshmen?

(1) A total of 275 freshmen received grants in one of the two amounts.

(2) The amount of money awarded in \$10,000 grants was \$200,000 more than the amount of money awarded in \$7,000 grants.

(A) Statement (1) ALONE is sufficient, but statement (2) alone is not sufficient.
(B) Statement (2) ALONE is sufficient, but statement (1) alone is not sufficient.
(C) BOTH statements TOGETHER are sufficient, but NEITHER statement ALONE is sufficient.
(D) EACH statement ALONE is sufficient.
(E) Statements (1) and (2) TOGETHER are not sufficient.

EXPLANATIONS

22. E As you consider each statement, you might be tempted to think, "How many numbers can possibly satisfy all the constraints of the question stem *and* this statement?" Or, you may figure that both statements together, in addition to the information in the question stem, *must* be sufficient to answer the question. That, of course, is just what the test writers *expect* you to think. It turns out that several values satisfy each of the statements: 61 and 16; 72 and 27; 83 and 38; and 94 and 49 all satisfy Statements (1) and (2). Thus, neither statement is sufficient on its own, nor are they sufficient together. The correct answer is E.

23. D This is a simultaneous equation problem dressed up as a word problem. The question stem tells us that two types of grants were awarded; it also provides the sum of the grants. Let's call the group of freshmen who received \$7,000 grants x and the group of freshmen who received \$10,000 grants y. The question stem tells us that $7{,}000x + 10{,}000y = 2{,}300{,}000$. That's one equation; to solve simultaneous equations we need two equations. Statement (1) provides a second equation. That equation is $x + y = 275$. You can solve simultaneously—although, of course, you don't have to because this is Data Sufficiency, not Problem Solving—to determine that $x = 150$ and $y = 125$. Statement (1) is sufficient; the answer is A or D. Statement (2) also provides a second equation. That equation is $10{,}000y = 7{,}000x + 200{,}000$. Again, you can solve to determine that $x = 150$ and $y = 125$. D is the correct answer.

MATH BIN 4

QUESTIONS

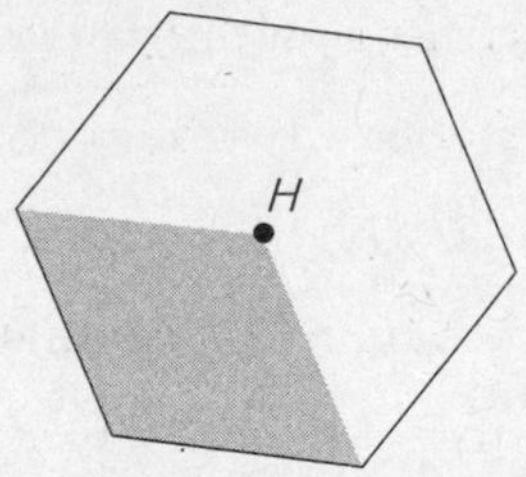

24. The figure shown above is a regular hexagon with center H. The shaded area is a parallelogram that shares three vertices with the hexagon and its fourth vertex is the center of the hexagon. If the length of one side of the hexagon is 8 centimeters, what is the area of the unshaded region?

(A) $16\sqrt{3}$ cm^3

(B) 96 cm^3

(C) $64\sqrt{3}$ cm^3

(D) $96\sqrt{3}$ cm^3

(E) 256 cm^3

EXPLANATIONS

24. C When a problem includes a regular hexagon, you know a lot more than you might think. That's because you can divide a regular hexagon into 6 congruent equilateral triangles, all meeting at the center of the hexagon. Furthermore, if you know the length of one side of an equilateral triangle, you can determine its area by dividing the equilateral triangle into two 30-60-90 triangles and applying the 30-60-90 ratios to determine the height of the equilateral triangle (the ratio of the sides of a 30-60-90 triangle is $1 : \sqrt{3} : 2$). The problem tells you that the length of one side of the hexagon is 8 centimeters. That means that the equilateral triangles that make up the hexagon have sides of 8 centimeters. Divide one into a 30-60-90 triangle and you'll get a triangle with sides $4 : 4\sqrt{3} : 8$; this tells you that the height of the equilateral triangle is $4\sqrt{3}$ and that its area is $\frac{8\left(4\sqrt{3}\right)}{2} = 16\sqrt{3}\text{ cm}^2$. The area of the unshaded region consists of four of the six equilateral triangles (the shaded region consists of the other two), so the area of the shaded region is $4 \times 16\sqrt{3} = 64\sqrt{3}\text{ cm}^2$. The correct answer is C.

QUESTIONS

25. A fish tank contains a number of fish, including 5 Fantails. If two fish are selected from the tank at random, what is the probability that both will be Fantails?

(1) The probability that the first fish chosen is a Fantail is $\frac{1}{2}$.

(2) The probability that the second fish chosen is a Fantail is $\frac{4}{9}$.

(A) Statement (1) ALONE is sufficient, but statement (2) alone is not sufficient.
(B) Statement (2) ALONE is sufficient, but statement (1) alone is not sufficient.
(C) BOTH statements TOGETHER are sufficient, but NEITHER statement ALONE is sufficient.
(D) EACH statement ALONE is sufficient.
(E) Statements (1) and (2) TOGETHER are not sufficient.

EXPLANATIONS

25. D To figure out this problem, you need to know the total number of fish. Looking at Statement (1) in combination with the question itself, you can see that if there are 5 Fantails, and the probability that the first selection is a Fantail is $\frac{1}{2}$, that means we actually know the total number of fish: $\frac{1}{2} = \frac{5}{x}$ or 10. You might think that the probability of the second fish being a Fantail is also $\frac{1}{2}$, but in fact that's not the case: There are only 9 fish left in total when the second selection is made, and there are only 4 possible Fantails from which to chose. So the probability of them both being chosen is $\frac{1}{2} \times \frac{4}{9}$, or $\frac{2}{9}$. We are down to AD. Now, looking at Statement (2), if the probability that the second fish will be a Fantail is $\frac{4}{9}$, that means that the probability of the first fish being a Fantail is $\frac{5}{10}$, which means we can answer the question based on Statement (2) alone as well. The correct answer is choice D.

VERBAL BIN 1

QUESTIONS

1. As its reputation for making acquisitions of important masterpieces has grown, the museum has increasingly turned down gifts of lesser-known paintings they would in the past have accepted gratefully.

    (A) they would in the past have accepted gratefully
    (B) they would have accepted gratefully in the past
    (C) it would in the past have accepted gratefully
    (D) it previously would have accepted gratefully in the past
    (E) that previously would have been accepted in the past

2. Over the past few decades, despite periodic attempts to reign in spending, currencies in South America are devalued by rampant inflation.

    (A) are devalued
    (B) are becoming more devalued
    (C) which have lost value
    (D) have become devalued
    (E) have since become devalued

3. A fashion designer's fall line for women utilizing new soft fabrics broke all sales records last year. To capitalize on her success, the designer plans to launch a line of clothing for men this year that makes use of the same new soft fabrics.

    The designer's plan assumes that

    (A) other designers are not planning to introduce new lines for men utilizing the same soft fabrics
    (B) men will be as interested in the new soft fabrics as women were the year before
    (C) the designer will have time to develop new lines for both men and women
    (D) the line for men will be considered innovative and daring because of its use of fabrics
    (E) women who bought the new line last year will continue to buy it this year

EXPLANATIONS

1. **C** The pronoun *they* in this stem sentence doesn't agree with the noun it refers to: the museum. In everyday speech, of course, we often say "they" when we are referring to a large institution—but on the GMAT, the test writers won't let us get away with such imprecision. Choices A and B can both be eliminated because they use the plural pronoun. Choices D and E both fix the problem in different ways, but both add a redundancy: There is no need to have "previously" and "in the past" in the same sentence. The best answer is choice C.

2. **D** This is a tense question. *Over the past few decades* implies a continued action over time—which needs the perfect tense. This eliminates choices A and B. Choice C creates a sentence fragment. E isn't bad, but the word *since* is a bit redundant because the sentence began with *over the past few decades*. D is best.

3. **B** This is an analogy argument. The men's line is being introduced in the hope that men will like the new soft fabrics as much as women did the year before. The key word in the passage that might have alerted you to the analogy was the word *same*. The assumption on which this argument depends is that men and women will like the same new fabric. Choices A, C, D, and E are all outside the scope of the argument. The best answer is B.

QUESTIONS

4. The standard lamp is becoming outmoded, and so too is the incandescent light bulb, it is Edison's miraculous invention to use so much more energy than the new low-wattage halogen bulbs.

(A) so too is the incandescent light bulb, it is Edison's miraculous invention to use
(B) so too is the incandescent light bulb, Edison's miraculous invention that uses
(C) so too the incandescent light bulb, Edison's miraculous invention using
(D) also the incandescent light bulb, it is Edison's miraculous invention that uses
(E) also the incandescent light bulb, which is Edison's miraculous invention to use

5. Over the last 20 years, the growth of information technology has been more rapid than any other business field, but has recently begun to lag behind as newly emerging fields seem more enticing to new graduates.

(A) the growth of information technology has been more rapid than any other business field
(B) the growth of information technology has been more rapid than any other fields of business
(C) information technology's growth has been more rapid than any other fields of business
(D) the growing of information technology has been more rapid than that of any other business field
(E) the growth of information technology has been more rapid than that of any other business field

EXPLANATIONS

4. **B** This is basically an idiom question, but your checklist may first uncover a pronoun issue. The pronoun *it* clearly refers back to *light bulb*, but in this case the pronoun isn't actually necessary: *Edison's miraculous invention* refers directly back to *light bulb* without the need of a pronoun. This eliminates choices A and D, both of which are actually run-on sentences. Next, you should turn your attention to the end of the underlined phrase. Do you have an invention *to use* energy (choices A and E), an invention *that uses* energy (choices B and D), or an invention *using* energy (choice C)? If you said *that uses*, then you are doing just fine. Since we've already eliminated choice D, the best answer is B.

5. **E** The clue that tells you this is a potential parallel construction problem is the word *than*. This sentence is supposed to compare the *growth* of information technology to the *growth* in other fields. However, as written, the sentence is comparing the *growth* of information technology directly to other fields. Once you spot this, you should immediately start looking for the replacement phrase, *that of*. Only two answer choices contain it, D and E. However, Choice D uses the awkward and unidiomatic phrase *the growing of information technology*. The best answer is E.

QUESTIONS

6. According to mutual fund sales experts, a successful year for a stock fund should result not only in increased investor dollars flowing into the fund, but also in increased investor dollars flowing into other mutual stock funds offered by the same company. However, while last year the Grafton Mutual Company's "Growth Stock Fund" beat average market returns by a factor of two and recorded substantial new investment, the other stock funds offered by Grafton did not report any increase whatsoever.

Which of the following conclusions can properly be drawn from the statements above?

(A) When one of the mutual funds offered by a company beats average market returns, the other mutual funds offered by that company will beat average market returns.
(B) The mutual fund sales experts neglected to consider bond funds in formulating their theory.
(C) The performance of the Grafton "Growth Stock Fund" was a result of a wave of mergers and acquisitions that year.
(D) Investors currently dislike all stock mutual funds because of market volatility.
(E) The success of one mutual fund is not the only factor affecting whether investors will invest in other mutual funds run by the same company.

7. With <u>less than thirty thousand dollars in advance ticket sales and fewer</u> acceptances by guest speakers than expected, the one-day symposium on art and religion was canceled for lack of interest.

(A) less than thirty thousand dollars in advance ticket sales and fewer
(B) fewer than thirty thousand dollars in advance ticket sales and less
(C) fewer than thirty thousand dollars in advance ticket sales and fewer
(D) lesser than thirty thousand dollars in advance ticket sales and fewer
(E) less than thirty thousand dollars in advance ticket sales and as few

EXPLANATIONS

6. **E** This is a causal argument. According to experts, the high returns of one mutual fund *cause* investors to invest in other mutual funds run by the same company. However, in the case of the Grafton "family" of mutual funds, that was not the case. What conclusion can we draw from this? The best answer is E, which asks us to consider that there might be alternate causes. Choices A, B, and C are outside the scope of the argument, while D is too extreme and illogical because the argument makes it clear that investors liked at least *one* stock mutual fund: Grafton's "Growth Stock Fund."

7. **A** This question is about quantity words, as you probably suspected just from looking at the answer choices. When it comes to money, you use *fewer* if you are referring to the number of actual bills you have, but *less* if you are referring to the total amount and don't know the actual number of bills. This would get you down to choices A and E. Acceptances, however, can be counted, so in the second half of the underlined portion of the underlined sentence, you would use *fewer*. If you were tempted by choice E, you didn't notice that it created a new idiomatic error: Would you say as few *than* or as few *as*? The best answer is choice A.

QUESTIONS

8. New technology now makes it feasible for computer call-in help desk services to route calls they receive to almost anywhere, theoretically allowing employees to work from home, without the need for a daily commute.

   The adoption of this policy would be most likely to increase productivity if employees did not ____________.

   (A) commute from a distance of fewer than 10 miles
   (B) commute by car as opposed to by rail
   (C) live in areas with dependable phone service
   (D) need to consult frequently with each other to solve callers' problems
   (E) have more than one telephone line

9. The port cities of England in the 19th century saw a renaissance of ship construction, with some innovative designs breaking new ground, stretching the limits of ship-building theory, and <u>received</u> acclaim from around the world.

   (A) received
   (B) it received
   (C) receiving
   (D) would receive
   (E) it had received

EXPLANATIONS

8. **D** The tricky part of this inference question is dealing with the "did not." Choice A is outside the scope of the argument because eliminating such a short commute would presumably not have much effect on productivity. Choice B is also outside the scope since the *method* of the commute employees would no longer have to make is probably irrelevant. If employees did not live in areas of dependable phone service, that would likely *decrease* productivity, so that eliminates C. For similar reasons, if employees did not have more than one phone line, it might decrease productivity since they would presumably get some personal calls at their place of residence. Choice D is best, because if employees needed to consult each other to answer callers' questions, they would be at a distinct disadvantage if they were all in separate locations.

9. **C** This is a parallel construction question, in which the second half of the sentence contains a list of three actions, which must all be expressed in the same way. The three actions are *breaking*, *stretching*, and...*received*. Hmm. Which of the three is wrong? Well, since only *received* is underlined, that might be a pretty good clue that we should change it to match the others. The best answer is choice C. None of the other choices is parallel to the other two verbs. Choices B and E also add the needless pronoun *it*, which has no clear referent.

VERBAL BIN 1

QUESTIONS

10. According to a consumer research group survey, the majority of kitchen appliances purchased in the United States are purchased by men. This appears to belie the myth that women spend more time in the kitchen than men.

    The argument is flawed primarily because the author __________.

    (A) fails to differentiate between buying and using
    (B) does not provide information about the types of kitchen appliances surveyed
    (C) depends on the results of one survey
    (D) does not give exact statistics to back up his case
    (E) does not provide information on other appliances such as washers and dryers

11. <u>A contribution to a favorite charity being sent instead</u> of flowers when a colleague dies is becoming more the rule than the exception when it comes to funeral etiquette.

    (A) A contribution to a favorite charity being sent instead
    (B) A contribution being sent to a favorite charity as opposed
    (C) To send a contribution for a favorite charity instead
    (D) Sending a contribution to a favorite charity instead
    (E) Sending a contribution to a favorite charity as opposed

EXPLANATIONS

10. **A** The faulty assumption of this argument is that the buyers of the kitchen appliances are also the users of the kitchen appliances. We do not know that this is true. While more men may buy kitchen appliances, they are not necessarily the ones who use them. Choice B is wrong because knowing the individual types of kitchen appliances would not enhance the argument. Although Choices C and D might seem tempting, the problem with this argument is not so much that the survey might not be representative, but rather that the author is using information about buying patterns to extrapolate how these appliances are later going to be used and by whom. Choice E is outside the scope of the argument. The best answer is A.

11. **D** The GMAT test writers have an aversion to the word *being*, which usually creates a passive voice. This eliminates choices A and B. Generally, when a sentence begins with the infinitive verb form (*To send…*), you would need a parallel infinitive verb form in the second half of the sentence, which is not the case in choice C (which also uses the incorrect idiomatic expression *contribution for*). Choice E might seem tempting except that the last two words—*as opposed*—don't go idiomatically with *of.* The best answer is D.

QUESTIONS

EXPLANATIONS

Questions 12–15 are based on the following passage:

As a business model, the world of publishing has always been a somewhat sleepy enclave, but now all that seems poised to change. Several companies have moved aggressively into a new business endeavor whose genesis comes from the question: Who owns the great works of literature?

Text-on-demand is not a completely new idea, of course. In the 1990s, the Gutenberg project sought volunteers to type literary classics that had expired copyrights into word processing files so that scholars would have searchable databases for their research. Most of the works of Shakespeare, Cervantes, Proust, and Molière were to be found free online by as early as 1995.

However, now large-scale companies have moved into the market, with scanners and business plans, and are looking for bargain basement content. These companies are striking deals with libraries, and some publishers, to be able to provide their content, for a price, to individual buyers over the Internet.

At stake are the rights to an estimated store of 30 million books, most of which are now out of print. Many of these books are now also in the public domain, giving any company the right to sell them online. Still, a good portion of the books a general audience might actually want to buy is still under copyright. The urgent question: Who owns those copyrights? In the case of all too many books put out more than 20 years ago by now-defunct publishing companies, the answer is unclear—a situation the new text-on-demand companies are eager to exploit. An association of publishers has sued, claiming massive copyright infringement. The case is several years away from trial.

12. The primary purpose of the passage is to

(A) present the results of a statistical analysis and propose further study
(B) explain a recent development and explore its consequences
(C) identify the reasons for a trend and recommend measures to address it
(D) outline several theories about a phenomenon and advocate one of them
(E) describe the potential consequences of implementing a new policy and argue in favor of that policy

12. **B** Process of elimination is useful here. Does the author present a statistical analysis? No, so eliminate choice A. While the author might be said to identify the reasons for a trend, does she recommend measures to address it? No, so eliminate choice C. Does the author advocate anything whatsoever? No, so eliminate choice D. Does the author argue in favor of any policy? No, so eliminate choice E. The best answer is B.

QUESTIONS

13. It can be inferred from the passage that the works of Shakespeare, Cervantes, and Molière

(A) are some of the most popular works of literature
(B) are no longer copyrighted
(C) are among the works for which the association of publishers is suing text-on-demand companies
(D) do not currently exist as searchable databases
(E) were owned by now-defunct publishing companies

14. Which of the following is an example of a book that a text-on-demand company would not have to acquire the rights to?

(A) a book still under copyright
(B) a book more than 20 years old
(C) a book in the public domain
(D) a book a general audience might want to buy
(E) a book not already owned by publishers the company has a deal with

EXPLANATIONS

13. **B** This specific question has several good lead words: *Shakespeare*, *Cervantes*, and *Molière*, and they all come from the end of the second paragraph. As always, read several lines above and below the lead words to make sure you understand what's going on. Remember, in Reading Comprehension, inference questions are not really about inferring. You are looking for an answer that restates something already said in the passage. While undoubtedly the works of these great authors are some of the most popular works of literature (choice A), how do we infer that from the passage? It was never stated. Choice C is outside the scope of this question: lawsuits are not discussed anywhere near the lead words. Choice D directly contradicts the passage. Choice E might be true but requires too big an inference for the GMAT. The best answer is B—a restatement right from the passage.

14. **C** A text-on-demand company would not need to acquire a book if it was already free, which leads us to choice C. Choice B might have appeared tempting, but if you read the passage, you will note that books more than 20 years old are still usually under copyright, even if in some cases it is often difficult to determine who owns the copyright.

QUESTIONS

15. It can be inferred from the passage that text-on-demand companies are

(A) using scanners to find books they want to acquire
(B) creating business plans well before they have any actual business
(C) buying content at premium prices
(D) acquiring the rights to books for as little as possible
(E) attempting to supplant the role of traditional publishers

16. Exit polls, conducted by an independent organization among voters at five polling locations during a recent election, suggested that the incumbent mayor—a Democrat—was going to lose the election by a wide margin. But, in fact, by the time the final results were tabulated, the incumbent had won the election by a narrow margin.

Which of the following, if true, would explain the apparent contradiction in the results of the exit polls?

(A) The people chosen at random to be polled by the independent organization happened to be Democrats.
(B) The exit poll locations chosen by the independent organization were in predominantly Republican districts.
(C) The exit polls were conducted during the afternoon, when most of the districts' younger voters, who did not support the incumbent mayor, were at work.
(D) The incumbent mayor ran on a platform that promised to lower taxes if elected.
(E) An earlier poll, conducted the week before the election, had predicted that the incumbent mayor would win.

EXPLANATIONS

15. **D** In this inference question, the trick is not to infer too far. Perhaps it could be argued that these new companies might come to supplant the publishing industry, but it isn't said in the passage, so eliminate choice E. The same could be said for creating business plans before they have any business; it could well be true, but it isn't said. Eliminate choice B. Choice A is not said in the passage and is illogical. Choice C is the opposite of what was stated in the passage, while choice D is a nice restatement of the passage: "looking for bargain basement content."

16. **B** The key to this statistical argument is to understand that the sampling of the voters might not be representative of ALL the voters. Choice A says the voters chosen by the pollsters happened to be Democrats. But in that case, we would expect that the incumbent mayor, a Democrat, would have been predicted the winner of the election. Choice C says the exit poll was conducted at a time of day in which many people who disliked the mayor could not vote, implying that the actual election results for the incumbent would be worse, or at least no better. Choices D and E are outside the scope of the argument. The best answer is B, which gives a statistical reason for the skewed results: The exit polls were conducted in locations where the incumbent had little support—leaving open the possibility that his results would be stronger elsewhere.

VERBAL BIN 1

QUESTIONS

17. The spread of Avian flu from animals to humans has been well-documented, but less understood is the mechanism by which it is spread from one bird species to another. **In order to avoid a world-wide epidemic of Avian flu, scientists must make that study a first priority.** To solely tackle the human dimension of this possible pandemic is to miss half of the problem: its spread from one hemisphere to another.

    The bolded phrase plays which of the following roles in the argument above?

    (A) The bolded phrase states a premise of the argument.
    (B) The bolded phrase contradicts the author's main point.
    (C) The bolded phrase makes a statement that the author is about to contradict.
    (D) The bolded phrase states the author's conclusion.
    (E) The bolded phrase states an assumption the author is making.

18. Successful business leaders not only anticipate potential problems and have contingency plans <u>ready, instead proceeding as if they are likely to occur at any time</u>.

    (A) ready, instead proceeding as if they are likely to occur at any time
    (B) ready, but also proceed as if such problems are likely to occur at any time
    (C) ready, but also proceeding as if the occurrence of them is at any time likely
    (D) ready; they instead proceed as if their occurrence is likely at any time
    (E) ready; such problems are likely to occur at any time, is how they proceed

EXPLANATIONS

17. **D** Although there is no "therefore" or "hence" in front of it, the bolded phrase is the conclusion of the argument. The other phrases are premises of the argument. If you suspect a phrase may be the conclusion, it sometimes helps to imagine a "therefore" in front of it, to see if the sentence would make sense. If it does, chances are that's your conclusion. The best answer is D.

18. **B** The phrase *not only* must be followed by the phrase *but also* in order to complete the sentence properly. The answer must therefore be either B or C. Choice C lacks parallel structure in the words *anticipate* and *proceeding*. Correctly formulated, this sentence should read *business leaders not only anticipate...but also proceed...* The best answer is B.

QUESTIONS

19. An artist who sells her paintings for a fixed price decides that she must increase her income. Because she does not believe that customers will pay more for her paintings, she decides to cut costs by using cheaper paints and canvases. She expects that, by cutting costs, she will increase her profit margin per painting and thus increase her annual net income.

Which of the following, if true, most weakens the argument above?

(A) Other area artists charge more for their paintings than the artist charges for hers.
(B) The artist has failed to consider other options, such as renting cheaper studio space.
(C) The artist's plan will result in the production of inferior paintings which, in turn, will cause a reduction in sales.
(D) If the economy were to enter a period of inflation, the artist's projected increase in income could be wiped out by increases in the price of art supplies.
(E) The artist considered trying to complete paintings more quickly and thus increase production, but concluded that it would be impossible.

20. Although tapirs reared in captivity are generally docile and have even been kept as pets by South American villagers, <u>it is nonetheless a volatile creature</u> prone to unpredictable and dangerous temper tantrums.

(A) it is nonetheless a volatile creature
(B) it is nonetheless volatile creatures
(C) being nonetheless volatile creatures
(D) they are nonetheless a volatile creature
(E) they are nonetheless volatile creatures

EXPLANATIONS

19. **C** To weaken an argument, look first at its conclusion. This argument concludes that the artist will *increase her profit margin...and thus increase her annual income* by using cheaper art supplies. Which answer choice undercuts this conclusion? Choice C does; if the artist's sales decrease, then her increased profit margin may not lead to an increase in annual income, because the decrease in sales may offset the increase in per-painting profit. The best answer is C.

20. **E** This is a pronoun agreement question. The subject of the sentence is *tapirs*; therefore, the pronoun that refers to the subject must be plural. The answer, therefore, must be D or E. Choice D contains a new pronoun agreement error, because *they* is plural and *a volatile creature* is singular. Choice C has no pronoun at all. The best answer is E.

QUESTIONS

21. According to a recent report, the original tires supplied with the Impressivo, a new sedan-class automobile, wore much more quickly than tires conventionally wear. The report suggested two possible causes: (1) defects in the tires, and (2) improper wheel alignment of the automobile.

Which of the following would best help the authors of the report determine which of the two causes identified was responsible for the extra wear?

(A) a study in which the rate of tire wear in the Impressivo is compared to the rate of tire wear in all automobiles in the same class
(B) a study in which a second set of tires, manufactured by a different company than the one that made the first set, is installed on all Impressivos and the rate of wear is measured
(C) a study in which the level of satisfaction of workers in the Impressivo manufacturing plant is measured and compared to that of workers at other automobile manufacturing plants
(D) a study that determines how often improper wheel alignment results in major problems for manufacturers of other automobiles in the Impressivo's class
(E) a study that determines the degree to which faulty driving techniques employed by Impressivo drivers contributed to tire wear

EXPLANATIONS

21. **B** Because the report identifies two possible causes of the tire wear, the best answer must identify a study that focuses on one of these possible causes. Studies focusing on car models other than the Impressivo (A and D), worker satisfaction C, or driver error E are all irrelevant to this study. The study described in B removes onc of the two possible causes. If the newly installed tires made by another manufacturer also turn out to wear abnormally, then the authors will have good reason to suspect that faulty alignment caused the initial problem. If the new tires wear normally, then they will know that the original tires were faulty.

Questions 22–25 are based on the following passage:

Line
(5)

(10)

(15)

(20)

(25)

(30)

(35)

(40)

(45)

(50)

Founded at the dawn of the modern industrial era, the nearly forgotten Women's Trade Union League (WTUL) played an instrumental role in advancing the cause of working women throughout the early part of the twentieth century. In the face of considerable adversity, the WTUL made a contribution far greater than did most historical footnotes.

The organization's successes did not come easily; conflict beset the WTUL in many forms. During those early days of American unions, organized labor was aggressively opposed by both industry and government. The WTUL, which represented a largely unskilled labor force, had little leverage against these powerful opponents. Also, because of the skill level of its workers as well as inherent societal gender bias, the WTUL had great difficulty finding allies among other unions. Even the large and powerful American Federation of Labor (AFL), which nominally took the WTUL under its wing, kept it at a distance. Because the AFL's power stemmed from its highly skilled labor force, the organization saw little economic benefit in working with the WTUL. The affiliation provided the AFL with political cover, allowing it to claim support for women workers; in return, the WTUL gained a potent but largely absent ally.

The WTUL also had to overcome internal discord. While the majority of the group's members were working women, a sizeable and powerful minority consisted of middle- and upper-class social reformers whose goals extended beyond labor reform. While workers argued that the WTUL should focus its efforts on collective bargaining and working conditions, the reformers looked beyond the workplace, seeking state and national legislation aimed at education reform and urban poverty relief as well as workplace issues.

Despite these obstacles, the WTUL accomplished a great deal. The organization was instrumental in the passage of state laws mandating an eight-hour workday, a minimum wage for women, and a ban on child labor. It provided seed money to women who organized workers in specific plants and industries, and also established strike funds and soup kitchens to support striking unionists. After the tragic Triangle Shirtwaist Company fire of 1911, the WTUL launched a four-year investigation whose conclusions formed the basis of much subsequent

(55)

(60)

(65)

workplace safety legislation. The organization also offered a political base for all reform-minded women, and thus helped develop the next generation of American leaders. Eleanor Roosevelt was one of many prominent figures to emerge from the WTUL.

The organization began a slow death in the late 1920s, when the Great Depression choked off its funding. The organization limped through the 1940s; the death knell eventually rang in 1950, at the onset of the McCarthy era. A turn-of-the-century labor organization dedicated to social reform, one that during its heyday was regarded by many as "radical," stood little chance of weathering that storm. This humble ending, however, does nothing to diminish the accomplishments of an organization that is yet to receive its historical due.

QUESTIONS

22. The primary purpose of this passage is to

(A) describe the barriers confronting women in the contemporary workplace
(B) compare and contrast the methods of two labor unions of the early industrial era
(C) critique the methods employed by an important labor union
(D) rebuke historians for failing to cover the women's labor movement adequately
(E) call readers' attention to an overlooked contributor to American history

EXPLANATIONS

22. **E** The author of the passage makes this point twice in the opening paragraph (*the nearly forgotten Women's Trade Union League...the WTUL made a contribution far greater than did most historical footnotes*) and again in the final sentence of the passage. The entire passage serves to focus readers' attention on "an overlooked contributor to American history," the WTUL.

Process of Elimination is helpful here: A is incorrect because the passage is about a defunct historical union, not contemporary working women; B is incorrect because the main focus of this passage is a single organization, the WTUL; C is incorrect because the WTUL's achievements, not its methods, are the focus of the passage; and D is incorrect because no such rebuke is ever stated. Remember also that the answer to a primary purpose question must apply to the entire passage, not just to one paragraph or section.

23. Which of the following best characterizes the American Federation of Labor's view of the Women's Trade Union League, as it is presented in the passage?

(A) The WTUL was an important component of the AFL's multifront assault on industry and its treatment of workers.
(B) Because of Eleanor Roosevelt's affiliation with the organization, the WTUL was a vehicle through which the AFL could gain access to the White House.
(C) The WTUL was to be avoided because the radical element within it attracted unwanted government scrutiny.
(D) The WTUL offered the AFL some political capital but little that would assist it in labor negotiations.
(E) The WTUL was weakened by its hesitance in pursuing widespread social reform beyond the workplace.

23. **D** This answer is a good paraphrase of this excerpt from the second paragraph: *Because the AFL's power stemmed from its highly skilled labor force, the organization saw little economic benefit in working with the WTUL. The affiliation provided the AFL with political cover, allowing it to claim support for women workers...*

QUESTIONS

24. Each of the following is cited in the passage as an accomplishment of the Women's Trade Union League EXCEPT

(A) It organized a highly skilled workforce to increase its bargaining power.
(B) It contributed to the development of a group of leaders in America.
(C) It provided essential support to striking women.
(D) It helped fund start-up unions for women.
(E) It contributed to the passage of important social and labor reform legislation.

25. The passage suggests which of the following about the "middle- and upper-class social reformers" mentioned in lines 32–33?

(A) They did not understand, nor were they sympathetic to, the plight of poor women workers.
(B) Their naive interest in Communism was ultimately detrimental to the Women's Trade Union League.
(C) It was because of their social and political power that the Women's Trade Union League was able to form an alliance with the American Federation of Labor.
(D) They represented only an insignificant fraction of the leadership of Women's Trade Union League.
(E) They sought to advance a broad political agenda of societal improvement.

EXPLANATIONS

24. **A** This answer choice describes the AFL, not the WTUL. The passage specifically states that the WTUL *represented a largely unskilled labor force [and so] had little leverage against [its] powerful opponents* (lines 14–15).

25. **E** Process of Elimination is helpful on this question. Choice A defies common sense; if these reformers had not been sympathetic to the plight of poor women workers, they never would have joined an organization called the Women's Trade Union League. B and C can only be justified—poorly—by "reading between the lines," a definite no-no on Reading Comprehension. Because neither the reformers' interest in Communism nor their influence within the AFL is mentioned in paragraph three (the paragraph pertinent to this question), neither answer can be correct. D is contradicted by the passage, which states that the reformers constituted a *sizeable* minority within the WTUL. E is a good paraphrase of this excerpt from the passage: …*the reformers looked beyond the workplace, seeking state and national legislation aimed at education reform and urban poverty relief as well as workplace issues.*

VERBAL BIN 2

QUESTIONS

1. As its performance has risen on all the stock indexes, the bio-tech start-up has branched out into new markets to look for opportunities <u>they would previously have had to ignore</u>.

   (A) they would previously have had to ignore
   (B) they would have had to ignore previously
   (C) that previously they would have had to ignore
   (D) it previously would have had to ignore in past years
   (E) it would previously have had to ignore

2. Scientists wishing to understand the kinetic movements of ancient dinosaurs are today studying the movements of modern day birds, which many scientists believe are descended from dinosaurs. A flaw in this strategy is that birds, although once genetically linked to dinosaurs, have evolved so far that any comparison is effectively meaningless.

   Which of the following, if true, would most weaken the criticism made above of the scientists' strategy?

   (A) Birds and dinosaurs have a number of important features in common that exist in no other living species.
   (B) Birds are separated from dinosaurs by 65 million years of evolution.
   (C) Our theories of dinosaur movements have recently undergone a radical reappraisal.
   (D) The study of kinetic movement is a relatively new discipline.
   (E) Many bird experts do not study dinosaurs to draw inferences about birds.

EXPLANATIONS

1. **E** If you go through your mental checklist, you will probably spot the pronoun *they*. To whom does that pronoun refer? Even though there are a lot of plural nouns in the front half of the sentence, *they* must refer to the start-up company, which is singular. Never mind that many people in spoken English refer to a large company as *they*. On the GMAT, a singular noun needs a singular pronoun. That eliminates choices A, B, and C. To choose between D and E, look for a new error. That's what you'll find in choice D which uses both the words *previously* and *in the past*, creating a redundancy error. The best answer is E.

2. **A** In this passage, the author is questioning an analogical argument. To understand the kinetic movement of dinosaurs, says the argument, we should study the kinetic movement of birds, which are a lot like dinosaurs. The author is trying to weaken this analogy by saying that dinosaurs and birds are actually not very similar. Your job is to weaken the author's attempt to demonstrate that the argument is flawed. How do you do that? By showing that dinosaurs and birds *are* in fact alike. Choice B, if anything, actually strengthens the author's criticism of the analogy. Choices C and D are outside the scope of the argument. Choice E seems to strengthen the author's criticism of the analogy. It is also out of scope since the fact that some bird experts don't study dinosaurs doesn't mean that dinosaur experts shouldn't study birds. Choice A is best because it shows how birds and dinosaurs are alike.

QUESTIONS

3. A factory in China has two options to improve efficiency: adding robotic assembly lines and subcontracting out certain small production goals that could be done more efficiently elsewhere. Adding robotic assembly lines will improve efficiency more than subcontracting some small production goals. Therefore, by adding robotic assembly lines, the factory will be doing the most that can be done to improve efficiency.

   Which of the following is an assumption on which the argument depends?

   (A) Adding robotic assembly lines will be more expensive than subcontracting some small production goals.
   (B) The factory has a choice of robotic assembly lines, some of which might be better suited to this factory than others.
   (C) The factory may or may not decide to choose either alternative.
   (D) Efficiency cannot be improved more by using both methods together than by adding robotic assembly lines alone.
   (E) This particular factory is already the third most efficient factory in China.

4. <u>Just as the early NASA space explorers attempted on each flight to push the frontiers of our knowledge, so too</u> are the new private-consortium space explorers seeking to add to man's general understanding of the cosmos.

   (A) Just as the early NASA space explorers attempted on each flight to push the frontiers of our knowledge, so too
   (B) The early NASA space explorers attempted on each flight to push the frontiers of our knowledge, and in the same way
   (C) Like the case of the early NASA space explorers who attempted on each flight to push the frontiers of our knowledge, so too
   (D) As in the early NASA space explorers' attempts on each flight to push the frontiers of our knowledge, so too
   (E) Similar to the early NASA space explorers attempted on each flight to push the frontiers of our knowledge, so too

EXPLANATIONS

3. **D** As always, if you don't immediately grasp the reasoning behind an argument, scope is key to eliminating wrong answers. For example, the expense of implementing these goals (choice A) was never mentioned and thus is outside the scope of the argument. The same goes for choice B: Choosing between different types of robotic assembly lines is not part of this argument. As for choice C, the argument does not depend on whether the two actions being considered are ever actually implemented—again it is outside the scope. And, come to think of it, so is choice E, which tells us that the factory is already quite efficient; the argument is about making it *more* efficient. By process of elimination, you have your answer. However, here's the logic: The conclusion of the argument is that choosing *one* of these two methods will result in the factory becoming the most efficient that it can be. What the argument is ignoring is the possibility that the factory could be even more efficient if it implemented *both* changes. The best answer is D.

4. **A** The idiom *just as…so too* is correct as written. Each of the other choices uses variations on an unidiomatic expression instead. The best answer is A.

QUESTIONS

5. A proposal for a new building fire safety code requires that fire-retardant insulation no longer be sprayed on steel girders in the factory, but be sprayed on once the girders have arrived at the building site. This will eliminate the dislodging of the insulation in transit and reduce fatalities in catastrophic fires by an estimated 20%.

Which of the following, if true, represents the strongest challenge to the new proposal?

(A) The fire-retardant insulation will also be required to be one inch thicker than in the past.
(B) Studies have shown that most dislodgement of insulation occurs after the girders arrive on site.
(C) Catastrophic fires represent only 4% of the fires reported nationally.
(D) The proposed safety code will add considerably to the cost of new construction.
(E) In most of Europe, spraying fire-retardant insulation onto steel girders at the building site has been required for the past ten years.

6. An effort <u>to control the crippling effects of poverty in Brazil's interior cities, begun almost thirty years ago,</u> has been partially successful, despite the setback of a major drought and the interruption of aid during an extended economic crisis.

(A) to control the crippling effects of poverty in Brazil's interior cities, begun almost thirty years ago,
(B) begun almost thirty years ago for controlling the crippling effects of poverty in Brazil's interior cities,
(C) begun for controlling the crippling effects of poverty in Brazil's interior cities almost thirty years ago,
(D) at controlling the crippling effects of poverty in Brazil's interior cities begun almost thirty years ago,
(E) that has begun almost thirty years ago to control the crippling effects of poverty in Brazil's interior cities,

EXPLANATIONS

5. **B** The words *strongest challenge* in the question mean that you are trying to weaken the argument. Choice A, if anything, appears to support the argument rather than weaken it, so you can eliminate it. Choices C and D do seem negative toward the argument, but both are outside the scope, as is choice E. Choice B is best because if the insulation comes loose *after* the girders arrive on site, then making an effort to prevent its dislodgement in transit to the building site will not have any effect and will not necessarily reduce fatalities.

6. **A** This is an idiom question. Do you attempt *to* do something, do you attempt *at* something, or do you attempt *for* something? Choice E uses the idiom correctly but creates a new tense error. The best answer is A.

QUESTIONS

7. A newly discovered disease is thought to be caused by a certain bacterium. However, recently released data note that the bacterium thrives in the presence of a certain virus, implying that it is actually the virus that causes the new disease.

 Which of the following pieces of evidence would most support the data's implication?

 (A) In the absence of the virus, the disease has been observed to follow infection by the bacterium.
 (B) The virus has been shown to aid the growth of bacteria, a process which often leads to the onset of the disease.
 (C) The virus alone has been observed in many cases of the disease.
 (D) In cases where the disease does not develop, infection by the bacterium is usually preceded by infection by the virus.
 (E) Onset of the disease usually follows infection by both the virus and the bacterium.

8. The company was not even publicly traded until 1968, when the owner and founder sold it to David P. Markham, a private investor, who took the company public and established a long and generous policy of stock options for valued employees.

 (A) who took the company public and established a long and generous policy of stock options for
 (B) who, taking the company public, established a long and generous policy of stock options to
 (C) who, when he took the company public, established a long and generous policy of stock options to
 (D) who had taken the company public, establishing a long and generous policy of stock options as
 (E) taking the company public and establishing a long and generous policy of stock options for

EXPLANATIONS

7. **C** The last line of this argument gives away its type: *...the virus that causes...* The cause of a certain disease was thought to be one thing, but now is believed to be something else. Recent evidence suggests that the cause is a virus (which also nourishes the bacterium once thought to be the cause of the disease). To support a causal argument, you take away possible alternate causes. Choice C does this by showing that while both virus and bacterium are often present at the same time, the virus has been found *without* the bacterium in many cases of the disease. Choice A directly contradicts this, suggesting that the bacterium is the sole cause. B and E suggest that the virus plays a supporting role to the bacterium. D is outside the scope of the argument. The best answer is C.

8. **A** The second half of this sentence contains a correctly constructed parallel list. The private investor *took* and *established*, both verbs in the simple past. In choices B and D, the construction is less than parallel. In addition, several choices also use the unidiomatic *established...for* as opposed to *established...to*. In choice E, the construction is parallel, but it now seems to modify *the owner and founder* rather than *Markham*. The best answer is A.

VERBAL BIN 2

QUESTIONS

9. Because of a quality control problem, a supplier of flu vaccines will not be able to ship any supplies of the vaccine for the upcoming flu season. This will create a shortage of flu vaccines and result in a loss of productivity as workers call in sick.

   Which of the following, if true, most seriously weakens the argument above?

   (A) The quality control problem of the supplier is not as severe as some experts had initially predicted.
   (B) Other suppliers of flu vaccine have not been affected by the quality control problem.
   (C) Last year there was also a shortage of flu vaccine available.
   (D) The price of flu vaccines is expected to fall in the next ten years.
   (E) The flu season is expected to last longer than usual this year.

EXPLANATIONS

9. **B** You might have been tempted by choice A, which seems to weaken the argument by saying the quality control problem of the supplier is not as severe as experts had predicted. However, the initial predictions of experts are outside the scope of the argument, because they don't change the fact that this supplier will not be supplying any vaccines, regardless of how minor the problems might be. Similarly, what happened last year (choice C) or what will happen in the next 10 years (choice D) is also outside the scope of the argument; we want to know what will happen *this* year. Choice E seems to strengthen the argument since a longer flu season will presumably result in more people getting sick. The best answer is B, because if other suppliers have not been affected by quality control problems, then the overall shortage may be less severe.

QUESTIONS

10. Never before had the navy defeated so many foes at once as it had in the battle of Trafalgar in 1805.

(A) so many foes at once as it had in
(B) at once as many foes as
(C) at once as many foes that there were in
(D) as many foes at once as it did in
(E) so many foes at once as that it defeated in

11. The changes that may be part of a general global warming trend include an increase in the frequency and severity of hurricanes, a gradual rise in sea level, depleting the ozone layer, and raising the temperature of the earth.

(A) depleting the ozone layer, and raising the temperature of the earth
(B) depleting the ozone layer, and a rise in the earth's temperature
(C) a depletion of the ozone layer, and raising the earth's temperature
(D) a depletion of the ozone layer, and a raise of the temperature of the earth
(E) a depletion of the ozone layer, and a rise in the temperature of the earth

EXPLANATIONS

10. **D** This question is a swirling mixture of idiom and parallel comparison. The correct idiom in question: *as many…as*. When you say it out loud, does *so many…as* seem right? Of course, it's much easier to notice that it doesn't when the expression has already been pulled out of the problem for you. During the GMAT, you have to do your own pulling, but remember, you always have five sensational clues: the answer choices. Even if you initially have no idea what might or might not be wrong with this sentence, you can figure it out by scanning the answers; you'll see that you have a collection of *so many as*'s and *as many as*'s to choose from.

The other thing going on in this sentence, of course, is parallel comparison. Words such as *as* or *than* often mean a comparison is being made. The correct comparison would read: "Never before had a navy defeated as many foes at once as it *defeated*…," but as you know from reading our chapter on Sentence Correction, the test writers like to see if you know that you can replace the second verb with a replacement verb: *did*. The best answer is D.

11. **E** This sentence has what should be a parallel list of nouns, beginning with *an increase* and *a rise*, but then the last two items on the list are suddenly verb-like things: *depleting* and *raising*. Since it is the last two items that are underlined, these are the items that must change. Choices A, B, and C all have verb-like things in them. Choice D, with two noun-like things, seems tempting at first, but do you say *a raise of the temperature*? Nope, it's unidiomatic. Choice E is best.

Questions 12–16 are based on the following passage:

It has long been a tenet of business theory that the best decisions are made after careful review and consideration. Only after weighing all the options and studying projections, say most professors of business, can a practical decision be made.

Now, that model is being questioned by some business thinkers in the light of the theories of Malcolm Gladwell, who states that human beings often make better decisions in the blink of an eye.

It is, at first glance, a theory so counterintuitive as to seem almost ludicrous. Behind any decision, Gladwell posits, there is a behind-the-scenes subconscious process in which the brain analyzes; ranks in order of importance; compares and contrasts vast amounts of information; and dismisses extraneous factors, seemingly almost instantaneously, often arriving at a conclusion in less than two seconds. Citing a multitude of studies and examples from life, Gladwell shows how that split-second decision is often better informed than a drawn-out examination.

Evanston and Cramer were the first to apply this theory to the business world. Evanston videotaped the job interviews of 400 applicants at different firms. He then played only 10 seconds of each videotape to independent human resources specialists. The specialists were able to pick out the applicants who were hired with an accuracy of over 90%.

Cramer took the experiment even further, using only five seconds of videotape, without sound. To his astonishment, the rate of accuracy with which the HR specialists were able to predict the successful applicants fell only to 82%.

Critics argue that these results illustrate a problem with stereotyping that impedes human resources specialists from hiring the best candidates even when they have the time to get below the surface: going for the candidate who "looks the part." Gladwell argues that, on the contrary, the human mind is able to make complicated decisions quickly, and that intuition often trumps an extended decision-making process.

Line (5) *(10) (15) (20) (25) (30) (35) (40) (45)*

QUESTIONS

12. The primary purpose of the passage is to

(A) discuss reasons an accepted business theory is being reexamined
(B) present evidence that resolves a contradiction in business theory
(C) describe a tenet of business practices and how that tenet can be tested in today's economic environment
(D) argue that a counter-intuitive new business idea is, in the final analysis, incorrect
(E) present evidence that invalidates a new business model

13. According to the passage, all of the following are examples of the subconscious processes by which the brain makes a decision EXCEPT

(A) analysis of information
(B) ranking of information
(C) comparison and contrast of information
(D) rejecting information that is not pertinent
(E) consulting a multitude of studies and examples

14. The author's attitude toward the long-held view that decisions should be made carefully over time expressed in lines 1–5 can best be described as

(A) dismissive and scornful
(B) respectful but questioning
(C) admiring and deferential
(D) uncertain but optimistic
(E) condescending and impatient

EXPLANATIONS

12. **A** In this passage, the accepted practice of making thoughtful business decisions based on careful review is being questioned in light of a new theory. Both choices D and E imply that the author has rejected this new model. Choice C uses a catchy word from the passage (*tenet*) and fails to indicate that there is a new idea that goes against that tenet. Choice B implies that the contradiction between the theory of making decisions based on careful review and the theory of making split-second decisions has in fact been resolved. The answer is A.

13. **E** Where do you find the key words *subconscious process*? In the third paragraph. Choices A, B, C, and D are all paraphrases of examples of the processes cited in that paragraph. Only choice E is not. In fact, the multitude of studies and examples are cited in support of Gladwell's hypothesis. The answer is E.

14. **B** Both choices A and E are too extreme to be the correct answer on the GMAT. But clearly, the new theory being described is an attempt to go beyond the conventional wisdom. The best answer is choice B.

QUESTIONS

15. The author most likely mentions the results of Cramer's extension of Evanston's experiment in order to

(A) show that Cramer's hypothesis was correct while Evanston's hypothesis turned out to be incorrect
(B) show that Evanston's hypothesis was correct, while Cramer's hypothesis turned out to be incorrect
(C) demonstrate that while both experiments were scientifically rigorous, neither ended up being scientifically valid
(D) illustrate that the principle of subconscious decisions continues to work even when less information is available
(E) demonstrate that Cramer's experiment was 8% more accurate than Evanston's, even though his subjects had less information to work with

16. It can be inferred that the critics referred to in line 36 believed the excellent results of the two experiments had less to do with the innate decision-making of the subjects than with

(A) the excellent decision-making of Evanston and Cramer
(B) the expertise of Malcolm Gladwell, who originated the theory
(C) not choosing candidates who "looked the part"
(D) the use of videotape as a method of choosing candidates
(E) their unconscious use of visual stereotypes in making their selections

EXPLANATIONS

15. **D** Cramer's experiment took Evanston's experiment even further, depriving the subjects of even more information as they tried to make a decision—and yet the subjects did nearly as well in choosing candidates. If you chose E, you got reversed: Cramer's experiment was 8% *less* accurate than Evanston's. The answer is D.

16. **E** This inference question asks us to go only slightly further than the passage itself—to realize that what the critics objected to was a potential tendency of the subjects to choose candidates who *looked the part* without really looking at their actual qualifications. If you chose C, you missed the word *not* in the answer choice, which turns the meaning around completely. The answer is E.

QUESTIONS

17. The women's volleyball team at a local college finished fifth in its division, prompting the college to fire the team's general manager. The manager responded by suing the college, saying that the team's performance put it among the top teams in the country.

Which of the following statements, if true, would support the claim of the team's manager, and resolve the apparent contradiction?

(A) The team won all of its "away" games during the season in question.
(B) Attendance at the volleyball team's games was up 35% from the year before.
(C) Of the starting team, three team members were unable to play for at least half the season because of injuries.
(D) There are 80 teams in this particular volleyball team's division.
(E) The team lost more games this year than it did the year before.

18. Country A recently broke off diplomatic relations with Country B when it was reported that Country B had been running a covert intelligence operation within the borders of Country A. While a spokesperson for Country B admitted the charge, the spokesperson said that it was common knowledge that all countries do this, and that Country A was no exception.

Which of the following inferences can be drawn from the argument above?

(A) Country B should apologize and dismantle its intelligence operation in Country A.
(B) The spokesperson for Country B claims that Country A engages in intelligence gathering too.
(C) Because all countries engage in this practice, Country A's outrage was disingenuous.
(D) Relations between Country A and Country B will be strained for some time.
(E) Country B would be just as outraged if it was reported that Country A was running a covert intelligence operation with Country B's borders.

EXPLANATIONS

17. **D** The manager was apparently fired because of his team's end-of-season statistics. If this made you wonder if the statistics were actually representative, your thinking was right on the money. To support the manager's claim we have to show that the team's fifth-place finish was actually better than it looked. Choices A, B, and C, while generally positive about the team (and by extension, perhaps, its manager) are outside the scope of the argument. Choice E actually puts the team's performance in a more negative light. On the other hand, Choice D puts the team's fifth-place finish in a very positive perspective: If the division was made up of 80 teams, finishing in fifth place is actually extremely good. The best answer is D.

18. **B** All of the answers to this inference question infer way too much to be the correct answer to a GMAT question—except for choice B, which simply restates a sentence from the argument itself. Choice A says an apology is needed, which is way beyond the scope of this argument. Choice C goes further than the argument to make a value judgment. Choice D looks into the future. And choice E takes a "what if" position and builds on it. The best answer is choice B.

QUESTIONS

19. Because cellular telephones emit signals that can interfere with cockpit-to-control-tower transmissions, airplane passengers' use of these instruments at all times that the airplane is in motion, even while on the ground, are prohibited.

(A) at all times that the airplane is in motion, even while on the ground, are
(B) at all times during which the airplane, even while on the ground, is in motion, are
(C) during airplane motion, even when it is on the ground, are
(D) during times of the airplane being in motion, even on the ground, is
(E) when the airplane is in motion, even while on the ground, is

20. In contrast to classical guitars, whose owners prefer the dulcet, rounded tones produced by nylon strings, folk guitar owners prefer the bright and brassy sound that only bronze or steel can create.

(A) folk guitar owners prefer the bright and brassy sound
(B) folk guitar owners prefer to get a sound that is bright and brassy
(C) with a folk guitar, the owner gets the preferably bright and brassy sound
(D) folk guitars produce a bright and brassy sound, which their owners prefer,
(E) folk guitars produce a preferred bright and brassy sound for their owners

EXPLANATIONS

19. **E** The subject of this sentence, *use*, is singular. Therefore, answers A, B, and C are incorrect; each states that *the passengers' use of these instruments...are prohibited*. Choice D is unidiomatic, and the phrase *even on the ground* is unnecessarily vague. Choice E is concise, clear, and employs the correct verb. The best answer is E.

20. **D** Choices A, B, and C include a parallel comparison error; A and B compare *classical guitars* and *folk guitar owners*, while C compares a plural (*classical guitars*) and a singular (*a folk guitar*) noun. Choice E incorrectly suggests that the *bright and brassy* sound is universally preferred rather than preferred specifically by folk guitar owners. Furthermore, the placement of *for their owners* is unnecessarily confusing, as it separates two elements of the sentence that should be closely connected (*bright and brassy sound...that only bronze and steel can create*). Choice D corrects this error by setting the interceding phrase off with commas. The best answer is D.

QUESTIONS

Questions 21–22 are based on the following passage:

A system-wide county school anti-smoking education program was instituted last year. The program was clearly a success. Last year, the incidence of students smoking on school premises decreased by over 70 percent.

21. Which of the following assumptions underlies the argument in the passage?

    (A) Cigarettes are detrimental to one's health; once people understand this, they will quit smoking.
    (B) The doubling of the price of a pack of cigarettes last year was not the only cause of the students' altered smoking habits.
    (C) The teachers chosen to lead the anti-smoking education program were the most effective teachers in the school system.
    (D) The number of cigarettes smoked each day by those students who continued to smoke last year did not greatly increase.
    (E) School policy enforcers were less vigilant in seeking out smokers last year than they were in previous years.

EXPLANATIONS

21. **B** The argument presented is a causal argument. The significant underlying assumption of the argument, therefore, relates to the causal link between the anti-smoking education program and the reduction in smoking on school premises. The argument assumes that the program, and not some other set of circumstances, caused the reduction. It thus assumes that other possible causes—such as an increase in the price of cigarettes—were not substantial contributors to this result.

Process of Elimination is effective on this question, as it is on all Critical Reasoning questions. Because the argument hinges on one crucial piece of evidence—a decrease in the incidence of smoking on school premises—you can eliminate all answers that do not speak directly to that reduction. Thus you can eliminate A, C, and D. Choice E, if true, would weaken the argument and therefore cannot be correct. The best answer is B.

QUESTIONS

22. Which of the following, if true, would most seriously weaken the argument in the passage?

(A) The author of this statement is a school system official hoping to generate good publicity for the anti-smoking program.
(B) Most students who smoke stopped smoking on school premises last year continued to smoke when away from school.
(C) Last year, another policy change made it much easier for students to leave and return to school grounds during the school day.
(D) The school system spent more on anti-smoking education programs last year than it did in all previous years.
(E) The amount of time students spent in anti-smoking education programs last year resulted in a reduction of in-class hours devoted to academic subjects.

23. Mild exercise throughout pregnancy <u>may reduce the discomfort associated with pregnancy and result in</u> a speedier, easier birth, according to a recent study.

(A) may reduce the discomfort associated with pregnancy and result in
(B) may reduce the discomfort associated with pregnancy, with the result
(C) may cause a reduction in the discomfort associated with pregnancy and as a result
(D) might lead to a reduction in the discomfort associated with pregnancy and as a result
(E) might reduce the discomfort associated with pregnancy and resulting in

EXPLANATIONS

22. **C** Once again, your focus should be on the evidence supporting the causal link between the anti-smoking education program and the reduction in smoking on school premises. What, other than the effectiveness of the program, would explain the reduced incidence of smoking on school premises? Choice C provides a possible alternate explanation: School policy made it easier for students to leave and return to campus. It is therefore possible, then, that the reduction in smoking on school premises was simply the result of students leaving school premises to smoke, then returning afterward.

Choice B, while tempting, does not provide an alternate cause for the observed result. None of the incorrect answers addresses the evidence supporting the conclusion of the passage; therefore, none of them truly weakens the argument. The best answer is C.

23. **A** The sentence, as written, maintains correct parallel construction between *reduce the discomfort*...and *result in a speedier*.... Each of the incorrect answers violates the rule of parallel construction. The best answer is A.

QUESTIONS

EXPLANATIONS

Questions 24–27 are based on the following passage:

What is it that keeps the developing world in an apparent state of perpetual poverty? Poor education, lack of basic medical care, and the absence of democratic structures all certainly contribute to these nations' plight. However, according to Peruvian economist Hernando de Soto, the overriding cause is the overwhelming prevalence of black market activity, well outside the formal economy, in these countries. The losses incurred from this condition are twofold. First, they deny the government tax revenues which could be used to improve education, medical treatment, and government efficiency. More important, however, they deny earners the chance to accumulate assets recognized by law and thus prevent them from leveraging those assets to borrow. Reforming these nations' legal systems in order to confer ownership through titling, de Soto argues, would help the poor there access the assets their work should be generating. These assets could then be used to buy homes and construct businesses, thus building a more stable and prosperous economy. De Soto estimates the value of these assets, which he terms "dead capital," at nearly $10 trillion worldwide.

De Soto is not the first to locate the developing world's problems in the domain of property rights. Others have tried property rights reform and failed. According to de Soto, this is because his predecessors attempted to model their plans on existing, successful property rights systems. In other words, they tried to transplant American and British property law to an inhospitable host. De Soto argues that, within many of the extralegal markets of the developing world, mutually agreed upon rules for distributing assets and recognizing property rights already exist. Rather than force these markets to adjust to a new, foreign system of property titling, reformers should focus on codifying the existing systems wherever it is practical to do so. This would facilitate a quicker, more natural transition to an economy that builds wealth rather than squanders it.

QUESTIONS

24. The author's primary goal in the passage is to

(A) compare several failed attempts to address a problem
(B) respond to criticism of a new theory
(C) identify the problems inherent in a new economic theory
(D) describe a novel approach to an old problem
(E) compare different property rights systems in the industrial world

25. According to the passage, de Soto believes that the quickest way to address poverty in the developing world is to

(A) increase funding for education
(B) build the infrastructure to support lending
(C) ensure medical care for all citizens
(D) aggressively root out corruption in government
(E) increase tax rates on all citizens in developing countries

EXPLANATIONS

24. **D** The passage describes an old problem—poverty in the developing world—and a new approach to it, that proposed by Peruvian economist Hernando de Soto. D is the best answer.

You can use Process of Elimination to get rid of all incorrect answers. Because the passage focuses on one approach and not several, its purpose cannot be to draw comparisons between two or more ideas; therefore, A and E are incorrect. The passage does not address criticism of de Soto's plan, so neither B nor C can be correct.

25. **B** This answer summarizes the following information from the first paragraph: *However, according to Peruvian economist Hernando de Soto, the overriding cause is the overwhelming prevalence of black market activity, well outside the formal economy, in these countries...Reforming these nations' legal systems in order to confer ownership through titling, De Soto argues, would help the poor there access the assets their work should be generating. These assets could then be used to buy homes and build businesses, thus building a more stable and prosperous economy.* The best answer is B.

QUESTIONS

26. The author's assertion that "reformers should focus on codifying the existing systems wherever it is practical to do so" (lines 39–41) suggests that

(A) in some instances, current systems are inadequate to meet the needs of a market economy
(B) these systems are already written down and need only be enacted as law
(C) where it is impractical to codify existing systems, countries should adopt American property law
(D) the existing systems are superior to those currently in use in modern industrialized countries
(E) improving education and medical care in these countries should take priority over reforming property laws

27. The term "dead capital" (line 24) refers to

(A) loans that are never repaid
(B) failed investments in new businesses
(C) cities ruined by over-industrialization
(D) the proceeds of extralegal commerce
(E) property passed from generation to generation

EXPLANATIONS

26. **A** The key phrase in the excerpted text is *wherever it is practical*, which suggests that in some cases, it may be impractical to codify the existing systems. Because the purpose of codifying the existing systems is to allow developing nations to acquire market economies, it follows that where it is impractical to codify existing systems, the reason is that the systems do not meet the needs of a market economy. The best answer is A. The incorrect answers are either unsupported by information in the passage (B, D) or directly contradicted by information in the passage (C, E).

27. **D** In lines 23–24, de Soto refers to *these assets* as *dead capital*. To answer this question, we have to find out more about *these assets*. Earlier in the paragraph, we learn that they are the result of black market activity. The answer is D.

VERBAL BIN 3

QUESTIONS

1. Unlike <u>Franklin D. Roosevelt's bootstrap program that helped</u> to restart economic growth in the 1930s through public works, Ronald Reagan proposed a program of trickle-down economics to restart the economy.

   (A) Franklin D. Roosevelt's bootstrap program that helped
   (B) Franklin D. Roosevelt and his bootstrap program which helped
   (C) Franklin D. Roosevelt, whose bootstrap program helped
   (D) the bootstrap program of Franklin D. Roosevelt that has helped
   (E) Franklin D. Roosevelt and his bootstrap program helping

2. In the 1970s, it became evident <u>that writing about someone else's research was much easier for social scientists who wanted to make a quick name for themselves</u> than it was to do their own research.

   (A) that writing about someone else's research was much easier for social scientists who wanted to make a quick name for themselves
   (B) that for social scientists who wanted to make a quick name for themselves, it was much easier to write about someone else's research
   (C) that for social scientists wanting to make a quick name for themselves, writing about someone else's research was much easier
   (D) for social scientists who wanted to make a quick name for themselves that writing about someone else's research was much easier
   (E) for social scientists who wanted to make a quick name for themselves, writing about someone else's research was much easier

EXPLANATIONS

1. **C** What can we say? You're in Bin 3. Part of what normally makes misplaced modifiers easy to spot is that the test writers generally ask you to fix the second phrase; this time, you have to fix the first phrase. The modifying phrase *Unlike F.D.R's bootstrap program* is supposed to modify the noun *Ronald Reagan*, which, of course, is not possible. You can't directly compare a program to a person. We could fix the second half of the sentence (*unlike F.D.R.'s program...Reagan's program...*), but since the second half of the sentence isn't underlined, we'll have to fix the first half. Choices B and E still directly compare F.D.R.'s program to Ronald Reagan. So does choice D. Only choice C avoids the modifier error by directly comparing F.D.R. to Reagan.

2. **B** The problem in the stem sentence is that there are two actions that ought to be parallel but are not. *Writing* (about someone else's research) was easier than *to do* the research themselves. You could fix this two ways in the real world: *Writing* was easier than *doing*, or it was easier *to write* than *to do*. Each of the other answer choices mixes and matches these two ways incorrectly, except for choice B. Putting the phrase *for social scientists* first, as choices D and E do, would not necessarily be wrong if the verbs were parallel. Choices D and E also do not have the idiom *evident that*. The best answer is B.

QUESTIONS

Questions 3–4 are based on the following passage:

To improve the town's overcrowded school system, the town council has proposed an ambitious education plan to reduce classroom size and make capital improvements—a plan they intend to pay for with an increase in property taxes for homes valued over $500,000. Although the school system desperately needs improving, the town council's plan should be defeated because the majority of the people who would end up paying for the improvements receive no benefit from them.

3. Which of the following, if true, most strengthens the argument above?

(A) The town's school system is currently ranked among the worst in the state.
(B) Other towns nearby that have made similar capital improvements did not find that the improvements translated to a better quality of education.
(C) The town will need to spend additional money on architect's plans for the capital improvements.
(D) An examination of the tax rolls shows that most homeowners in this category no longer have school-age children.
(E) Some homeowners will delay home improvement projects in order to keep the value of their homes below $500,000.

EXPLANATIONS

3. **D** The author is arguing to nix the plan to improve the schools. We want to strengthen his argument, but before we do, there is usually at least one answer choice that actually weakens the argument. It is helpful to get rid of these first, since they are usually easier to spot. In this case, choice A gives a compelling reason to *improve* the school system; eliminate it. Now, the reason the author gives for defeating the plan is that the people who pay for it will not benefit. To strengthen this argument, we need to show why this would be true. Choice B is against the school improvements, but for a different reason: in other towns, similar improvements didn't increase the quality of education. While important in the real world, this is slightly outside the scope of this argument. Choice C provides another possible negative of the plan, but again it doesn't show why the people who pay for it will not benefit. Choice E implies that taxpayers will delay their own capital improvements to avoid paying for the schools' capital improvements, but again this doesn't strengthen the author's particular argument—that the plan should be defeated because the people who must pay for it do not benefit. The best answer is D, which explains how this could be true: Most of the people slotted to pay for the school improvements don't even have school-age children.

QUESTIONS

4. Which of the following, if true, provides the town council with the strongest counter to the objection that its plan is unfair?

(A) Even with the proposed increase, property taxes in the town are well below the national average.
(B) Paying for the school system improvements using existing town funds will result in shortfalls that will force the town into arrears.
(C) The teachers in the town's school system receive some of the lowest salary packages in the immediate area, which is a major cause of attrition.
(D) Smaller class sizes and capital improvements in a school system tend to increase property values in the surrounding community.
(E) A feasibility study has shown that the cost of the improvements will likely be 20% higher than projected.

5. The rules of engagement under which a border patrol station can decide to use deadly force <u>includes responding to an invasionary incursion and the return of</u> hostile fire.

(A) includes responding to an invasionary incursion and the return of
(B) includes responding to an invasionary incursion and returning
(C) include responding to an invasionary incursion and the return of
(D) include a response to an invasionary incursion and the return of
(E) include a response to an invasionary incursion and returning

EXPLANATIONS

4. **D** The author says the plan is unfair to the people who must pay for it. How do we counter that? By showing that they actually do receive a benefit. Before we weaken the author's argument, let's eliminate any answers that strengthen it. In this case, that means only choice E. Now, choice A points out that property taxes would still be quite low even after the increase, but that doesn't mean the increase is fair. Choice B tells us why an alternate way to finance the improvements won't work, but doesn't address the fairness of the way being discussed. Choice C tells us why the funds are urgently needed, but again doesn't show that the people who have to supply the funds actually would receive a benefit. Choice D finally gives us a reason the property tax increase might actually benefit those who pay for it: Good schools translates to higher property values.

5. **D** As you know, GMAT test writers like to put as many words between the subject and the verb of a sentence as they can, in hopes that you will forget to check for agreement. The subject of this sentence was the plural *rules*. The verb: the singular *includes*. This eliminates choices A and B. Choices C and E are not parallel (neither is choice A), because they mix verb-like forms with noun-like forms. The best answer is D.

VERBAL BIN 3

QUESTIONS

6. Although the word "phonetician" is popularly associated with Henry Higgins's task of improving the diction of Eliza Dolittle in *My Fair Lady*, in linguistics, <u>it is someone who studies</u> the formation of language.

(A) it is someone who studies
(B) it is a person studying
(C) it refers to someone who studies
(D) they are people who study
(E) it is in reference to people who study

7. Experts studying patterns of shark attacks on humans have noted that attacks tend to diminish when the water temperature drops below 65 degrees Fahrenheit. Until recently, researchers believed this was because sharks prefer warmer water, and thus are present in fewer numbers in colder water. However, new research shows that sharks are present in equal numbers in cold and warm water.

Which of the following, if true, best explains the apparent paradox?

(A) In general, humans prefer warm water.
(B) Sharks' keen sense of smell is enhanced in cold water.
(C) In the Pacific, shark attacks tend to occur more frequently in the daytime.
(D) Of the more than 200 types of sharks present in the ocean, only three attack humans.
(E) The average temperature of the earth's oceans is 55 degrees.

EXPLANATIONS

6. **C** The question here is: to what does the pronoun *it* refer? You might think it refers to *phonetician*, (in which case you might have thought the sentence was fine the way it was), but in fact it refers to *the word*. Choices A, B, and D could give the impression that *the word* is a person or persons. Choice E is awkward, and, like choice D, needlessly uses the plural *people*. The best answer is C.

7. **A** We tend to try to explain shark attacks by thinking about the *shark's* behavior. But choice A points out that it takes two to tango. A shark attack requires A) one shark and B) one human to be attacked. One reason there might be fewer shark attacks on humans in cold water is that there are fewer humans swimming in cold water in the first place. If you were looking at choice B and saying, "Hmm, if a sharks' olfactory powers were enhanced by cold water, then presumably he'd be better at attacking," or if you were thinking that if his olfactory powers were enhanced he would know enough *not* to attack a human, then either way, you were having to think way too hard for this to be inside the scope. Choice C is outside the scope, too, since it is dealing with only one ocean and does not address temperature at all. Choice D provides extraneous information, and choice E does not help to explain the apparent paradox. The best answer is A.

QUESTIONS

8. As a result of surging economic indicators, most analysts upgraded the company's stock to a strong "buy," ignoring the advice of the head of a watchdog organization who warned that the company's product would prove not only dangerous but ineffective in the long run.

(A) who warned that the company's product would prove not only dangerous but
(B) warning that the company's product would prove not only dangerous and also
(C) warning that the company's product would prove itself to be both dangerous and
(D) who warned that the company's product would prove to be both dangerous and
(E) who was warning that the company's product would prove not only dangerous but

9. Scientists today accept that the increased severity of hurricanes in the last 10 years has been a result of warmer water in the Caribbean, which "feeds" the storms as they pass over it by a mechanism not yet completely understood. Thus, these severe hurricanes are yet more evidence of global warming.

Which of the following, if true, would most strengthen the argument above?

(A) Accurate statistics on the warming of the earth do not go back more than 100 years.
(B) Scientists have now discovered a new undersea current, fueled by an undersea volcano, which could have funneled warmer water into the Caribbean.
(C) The arctic ice caps have been losing three feet of circumference each year for the past five years.
(D) A new modeling computer program projects that the severity of hurricanes will increase over the next 10 years.
(E) Some scientists believe they will soon prove that the mechanism by which a storm picks up energy from warm water is based on convection.

EXPLANATIONS

8. **D** The sentence, as written, needs a *but also* to complement its *not only*. Choices A and E bite the dust. In choice B, the same idiom comes into play, but this choice has bigger problems: Without the *who warned*, it is no longer clear who is doing the warning. Choice C can be eliminated for the same reason. The best answer is D.

9. **B** To weaken a causal argument, propose an alternate cause. To strengthen a causal argument, *remove* an alternate cause. Choice A weakens the argument, so cross that off. Choices C and D both appear to strengthen the case for global warming in general, but do not make the important connection between the warming of the waters of the Caribbean and global warming in general. Choice E promises that the mechanism that creates more severe storms will soon be better understood, but that doesn't help to make the case that the warm water causing more severe hurricanes is related to global warming. The best answer is B. While choice B might seem unlikely, it strengthens this causal argument by removing a possible alternate cause. If there *were* an undersea volcano heating the Caribbean, then that might be what was causing the severe hurricanes, *not* global warming.

QUESTIONS

10. A new influx of unprecedented private investment should create a bright new future for manned space exploration, making the possibility of commercial space tourism much more viable than 10 years ago.

(A) making the possibility of commercial space tourism much more viable than 10 years ago
(B) and make the possibility of commercial space tourism much more viable than 10 years ago
(C) making the possibility of commercial space tourism much more viable than it was 10 years ago
(D) and make the possibility of commercial space tourism much more viable than it was 10 years in the past
(E) making the possibility of commercial space tourism much more viable than 10 years in the past

EXPLANATIONS

10. C The key word here is *than*—and if you spotted it, you knew to look for a parallel comparison problem. Two actions are being compared in this sentence, so we need the words "it was" after *than* to make that clear. If you spotted this error, you could eliminate Choices A, B, and E. D might seem possible (and parallel in a different kind of way) until you get to the last words: *10 years in the past*. This is just not the same as *ago*. The best answer is C.

VERBAL BIN 3

QUESTIONS

EXPLANATIONS

Questions 11–15 are based on the following passage:

As the American workforce gets grayer, age discrimination will likely become a more prominent issue in the courts. It is, of course, illegal to discriminate against an employee because of his or her age, and yet it is not illegal to dismiss a worker because he has a high salary and expensive health care.

This apparent contradiction is at the heart of a raft of cases now making their way through the courts. The outcome of these cases will have broad implications for the workplace in the coming years. By 2010, the Bureau of Labor Statistics has projected that more than half of all workers will be over 40—many of whom, by dint of seniority and promotions, will be earning higher than median salaries, eligible for more stock options, and carrying higher health care costs as a result of a larger number of dependents and the increased cost of health care for older workers.

Is it any wonder that a bottom-line oriented business might want to shed those workers, whose productivity is likely to plummet in the next few years, even as they become more expensive employees?

Still, the legal challenges of implementing this policy are daunting. Businesses have the right to rate workers on their productivity and to rank them against their peers. But they are not allowed to prejudge individuals based on their sex, race or age. Each worker must be treated on his or her own merits, rather than by how they fit into a larger profile of the group they belong to.

For companies looking to lay off these workers, the cost of making a mistake is high; while only one in three age discrimination suits are won by the plaintiff, the awards tend to be steep and the political fall-out harsh.

11. The primary purpose of the passage is to

(A) advocate on behalf of the older American worker who could soon face dismissal
(B) describe the origin of two theories of labor law and their effects on the workplace
(C) present an overview of the legal ramifications of a practice some call discriminatory
(D) describe the process by which America's workforce is getting older
(E) describe the methods by which a company could reduce its bottom line

11. **C** This passage presents an overview of the legal issues involved in age discrimination. Choices A and E are wrong because they imply that the passage takes sides on the matter. B is tempting, but the passage doesn't discuss the *origins* of the issues. Choice D implies that the passage is describing the aging process itself. The answer is C.

VERBAL BIN 3

QUESTIONS

12. Which of the following best describes the organization of the second paragraph of the passage?

(A) An assertion is made and then briefly contradicted.
(B) A contradiction is stated and then quickly resolved.
(C) A new theory is described and then qualified.
(D) An apparent inconsistency is stated and its consequences outlined.
(E) A conventional model is described and an alternative is introduced.

13. Which of the following, if true, would most effectively weaken the author's assertion that a "bottom-line oriented business" might want to fire older workers?

(A) A new study shows that, on average, younger workers earn less and have lower associated medical costs than older workers.
(B) Older workers have a higher rate of absenteeism than younger workers.
(C) A new study shows that older workers are in fact more productive and have fewer medical expenses compared to younger workers.
(D) A forecasted downturn in the economy will erode profits in may American businesses.
(E) A new bill scheduled to become law will make it easier for employers to employ illegal aliens.

EXPLANATIONS

12. **D** The contradiction highlighted at the beginning of the second paragraph is not resolved or qualified; it is stated, and then its ramifications are outlined. The answer is D.

13. **C** To weaken the assertion that it might be in the interest of employers to fire older people, it is necessary to show why employing older people would be GOOD for companies. C is the only answer that does so, suggesting that older employees are actually more productive and have fewer health care costs.

VERBAL BIN 3

QUESTIONS

14. It can be inferred from the passage that

(A) what is good for American companies is not necessarily good for older Americans
(B) American companies are prohibited by law from practices that discriminate based on gender, color of skin, or age
(C) large monetary judgments from age discrimination suits might prove more expensive than paying older employees' salaries
(D) by the year 2020, the percentage of older employees will be even higher than in the year 2010
(E) some older employees may well be more productive than some younger employees

15. The author mentions all of the following as driving up the cost to employers for employing workers over the age of 40 EXCEPT

(A) the cost of out-placement services
(B) a larger number of dependents
(C) increased cost of health care
(D) higher median salaries
(E) the cost of employee stock options

EXPLANATIONS

14. **B** The trick in any inference question is not to infer too far. Many of the possible answers here might well be inferred in a normal interchange, but on the GMAT, the best answer will generally seem almost laughably self-evident. In this case, that is B. Choices A and C are much too cynical to be correct answers on the GMAT, and choices D and E go well beyond the scope of the question.

15. **A** All of these costs were cited with one exception: the cost of out-placement services. The answer is A.

QUESTIONS

16. A pharmaceutical company claims that its new drug promotes learning in children. To back up its claims, the company points to a study of 300 children who were given the drug, along with a control group of 300 children who were given a placebo. The 300 children who were given the drug reported that they were able to retain new information much more easily.

Which of the following statements, if true, would most tend to weaken the claims of the pharmaceutical company?

(A) The 300 children in the control group also reported that they were able to retain new information much more easily.
(B) The drug has also been shown to prevent common skin rashes.
(C) The drug has been proven to have severe side-effects.
(D) The children in the study were not given any other medications during the study.
(E) The children who were given the drug did better on cognitive measurement tests after the drug therapy than before.

EXPLANATIONS

16. **A** The drug company says its drug caused enhanced learning ability. To weaken this causal argument, look for an alternate cause. Choices B, D, and E appear to strengthen the argument, so we can eliminate them. Choice C, while clearly a negative aspect of the drug, does not weaken the argument itself, which states simply that the drug enhances learning capability in children. Side effects are outside the scope of the argument. Choice A may not seem at first like an alternate cause, but if the control group (which did not receive the medicine) reported the exact same results as the children who did receive the drug, then clearly there is some other, as yet unnamed, alternate cause. The best answer is A.

VERBAL BIN 3

QUESTIONS

17. In order to understand the dangers of the current real-estate bubble in Country *Y*, one has only to look to the real-estate bubble of the last decade in Country *Z*. In that country, incautious investors used the inflated value of their real estate as collateral in risky margin loans. When the real-estate market collapsed, many investors went bankrupt, creating a major recession. Country *Y* is in real danger of a similar recession if more-stringent laws restricting margin loans are not enacted promptly.

    The answer to which of the following questions would be most useful in evaluating the significance of the author's claims?

    (A) Was the real estate in Country *Z* located principally in rural areas or was it located in more urban communities?
    (B) Could the bankruptcies in Country *Z* have been prevented by a private bailout plan by the nation's banks?
    (C) Does Country *Y* currently have any laws on its books regarding margin loans?
    (D) Are there business ties and connections between Country *Y* and Country *Z*?
    (E) Were there other factors in the case of Country *Y* that would make the comparison with Country *Z* less meaningful?

EXPLANATIONS

17. **E** To evaluate the significance of the author's claims, we need to recognize what kind of argument it is: an analogy. The author is saying that the situation in Country *Y* is analogous to that of Country *Z*. To weaken an analogy, you merely have to question whether the two situations were really analogous. Choices A and B are outside the scope of the argument. Choice C is incorrect because the author's argument stated that *more-stringent laws* were needed, making it irrelevant whether Country *Y* had any laws about this in the first place. Choice D goes off on an interesting tangent by asking if there were business ties between the two countries, but it does not weaken the argument's analogy. Only choice E questions whether the two situations are in fact analogous. E is the best answer.

QUESTIONS

18. Rules governing participation in a new extreme sports fantasy camp require that applicants should be physically fit enough to endure the demanding activities in which they will be engaging.

(A) that applicants should be physically fit enough to endure the demanding
(B) that applicants be physically fit enough to endure the demanding
(C) applicants should have enough physical fitness to allow enduring the demands of
(D) applicants are physically fit enough as to endure the demands of
(E) physical fitness in applicants, enough for endurance of demanding

19. During the summer of 2002, the Outer Banks suffered a massive toad infestation, discouraging many vacationers from visiting the area.

(A) suffered a massive toad infestation, discouraging
(B) suffered from a massive toad infestation and discouraged
(C) suffered a massive infestation of toads, which discouraged
(D) was suffering a massive infestation of toads and discouraging
(E) had suffered from a massive toad infestation and this discouraged

EXPLANATIONS

18. B This question tests two concepts. The first is idiomatic and concerns the word *require.* Because the word *require* indicates something that is compulsory (as opposed to optional), it cannot be followed by the word *should*; in other words, you can't require that something should happen, because then it's not really a requirement. This eliminates A and C.

The second concept is a little more arcane. Requirements, like hypothetical situations posited in the future, take the subjunctive mood. In the subjunctive, the proper way to phrase the idea expressed in this sentence is *the rules require that applicants be physically fit*. Tough and obscure, but that's why this question is in Bin 3. If you get this question wrong, suck it up and move on, confident in the knowledge that you can miss this one and still score a 790.

19. C This question presents two ways to discuss the unfortunate toad incident on the Outer Banks. Was there a *massive toad infestation* or a *massive infestation of toads*? The second option is better, because the first leaves it unclear whether *massive* refers to the infestation or the toads themselves. Under the first option, it is theoretically possible that the Outer Banks was infested by a single 50-foot-tall toad. Thus, A, B, and E are all incorrect. Choice D incorrectly suggests that the Outer Banks, not the infestation of toads, discouraged vacationers.

QUESTIONS

20. A prolonged period of low mortgage rates resulted in a period of the most robust home sales ever. At the same time, the average sale price of resale homes actually dropped, when adjusted for inflation.

Which of the following, if true, would explain the apparent contradiction between the robust home sales and the drop in the average sale price of resale homes?

(A) The inflation rate during this period exceeded the increase in the average salary, thus preventing many buyers from securing mortgages.
(B) Resale homes represent the best value on the real estate market.
(C) Without the adjustment for inflation, the price of resale homes actually increased by a very slight amount.
(D) The decrease in mortgage rates was accompanied by a widening of the types of mortgages from which borrowers could choose.
(E) The increase in home sales was due entirely to an increase in the sale of new homes.

EXPLANATIONS

20. **E** During a period of robust home sales, one would expect the prices of all homes to increase; that would be the natural effect of the law of supply and demand. The question tells us, however, that the real price of resale homes during this period actually decreased. Thus, it is reasonable to assume that the demand for resale homes decreased. How can we resolve this apparent contradiction? If all the increased demand for homes was in the new home market, then it would be possible that the overall increase in home sales would not result in an increase in resale home prices and may, in fact, even accompany a drop in those prices. The best answer is E.

QUESTIONS

21. Luis is taller than Rei. Kiko is taller than Marcus. Therefore, Kiko is taller than Rei.

The conclusion drawn above is not supported by the argument; however, the addition of one additional piece of information would make the conclusion logically sound. All of the following could be that additional piece of information EXCEPT:

(A) Kiko is taller than Luis.
(B) Luis is taller than Marcus.
(C) Luis and Marcus are the same height.
(D) Marcus and Rei are the same height.
(E) Marcus is taller than Rei.

EXPLANATIONS

21. **B** This question is best solved by drawing a diagram to represent the information in the question stem.

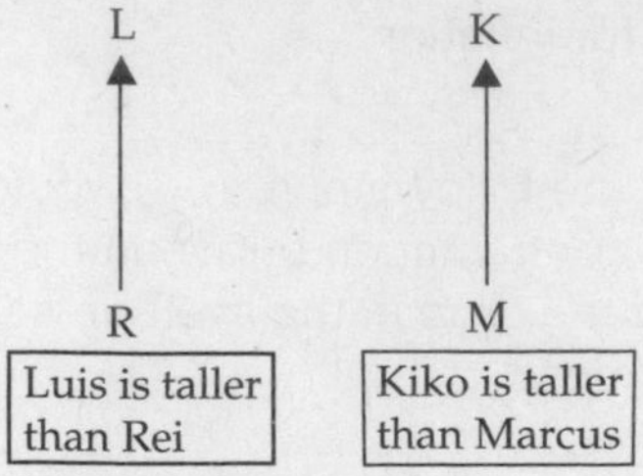

We are looking for information that will allow us to draw the diagram

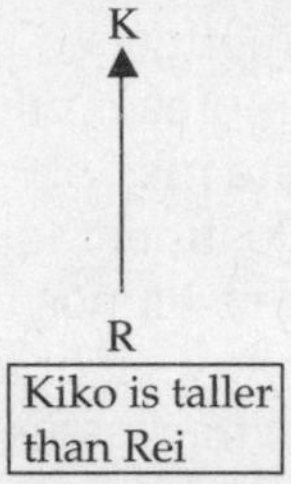

According to the question stem, four of the answer choices are sufficient to accomplish this. Your job is to find the one that is NOT sufficient.

Choice A is sufficient; if Kiko is taller than Luis and Luis is taller than Rei, Kiko must be taller than Rei.

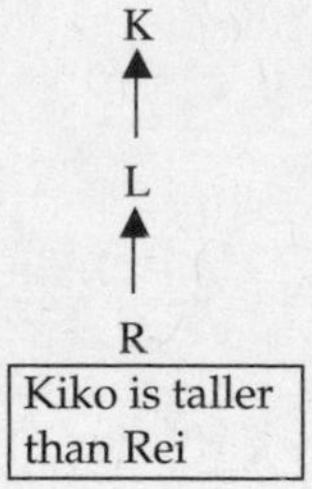

Choice B is NOT sufficient; if Luis is taller than Marcus, then it is conceivable that Luis is taller than Kiko. Consequently, it is also possible that Rei, who is shorter than Luis, is also taller than Kiko; however, Rei may also be shorter. The best answer is B.

Use the diagrams we have already created to demonstrate, on your own, that C, D, and E are sufficient to make the conclusion logically sound.

QUESTIONS

22. It has been estimated that an increase in average regional temperature of even 0.5 degrees Fahrenheit could cost the southern United States more than $10 billion in lost agricultural income annually.

(A) an increase in average regional temperature of even 0.5 degrees Fahrenheit could cost the southern United States more than $10 billion in lost agricultural income annually
(B) every year, $10 billion in agricultural income could be the cost to the southern United States as a result of an increase in the average temperature of the region of even 0.5 degrees Fahrenheit
(C) the cost to the southern United States could be more than $10 billion in income from agriculture that results from a regional increase in average temperature of even 0.5 degrees Fahrenheit annually
(D) annual income losses in agriculture of more than $10 billion could be the cost from increasing average temperatures in the southern United States of even 0.5 degrees Fahrenheit
(E) annual income losses to the southern United States from the increase in average regional temperature of even 0.5 percent costing more than $10 billion in agricultural income each year

EXPLANATIONS

22. **A** Well, you've got five choices here and none is particularly good. Only four, however, contain grammatical errors, so the best way to proceed on a question like this one is to eliminate as many answer choices as you can, take your best guess from among the remaining answers, and move on. Choice B is an endless string of prepositions; furthermore, the placement of the phrase *of the region* between *increase in the average temperature* and *of even 0.5 degrees Fahrenheit* is needlessly confusing. Choice C incorrectly suggests that it is agriculture, and not lost income, that results from the temperature increase. In D, *cost from* is unidiomatic; the correct phrasing is *cost of.* Choice E is redundant, as it refers to *annual losses* that occur *each year.* The best answer is A.

QUESTIONS

23. Within the Green Party, an internal debate is raging among those who believe in compromising with mainstream politicians in order to achieve some goals with those who believe the party must not abandon any of its principles.

(A) among those who believe in compromising with mainstream politicians in order to achieve some goals with those who believe the party must not abandon any of its principles
(B) among those who believe that achieving some goals requires compromise with mainstream politicians and those believing that none of the party's principles must be abandoned
(C) between those believing in compromising with mainstream politicians in order to achieve some goals with those who believe the party must not abandon any of its principles
(D) between those who believe in compromising with mainstream politicians in order to achieve some goals and those who believe the party must not abandon any of its principles
(E) between those believing that achieving some goals means compromising with mainstream politicians and those who believe that the principles of the party must not be abandoned

EXPLANATIONS

23. **D** This is a tricky *between/among* question. The rule is that *between* is used to compare two items, *among* to compare three or more. Here we are talking about thousands of people, so you might think that *among* is the correct choice. However, because the sentence compares two groups of people, the correct answer is *between*. The argument is between the two groups, not among the thousands of people who make up those groups. Eliminate A and B.

We can eliminate C because it is unidiomatic: It draws a comparison between one group *with* another when it should draw a comparison between one group *and* another. Choice E can be eliminated because it lacks parallel structure: It compares *those* ***believing*** *that achieving some goals*...and *those who* ***believe*** *that the principles of the party must not be abandoned*. The best answer is D.

QUESTIONS

24. In comparison to the drivers who live in Mountainview, a greater proportion of the drivers who live in Oak Valley exceed the speed limit regularly. This explains why there are more accidents each year in Oak Valley than in Mountainview.

    All of the following statements, if true, weaken the conclusion drawn above EXCEPT:

    (A) Oak Valley has a greater proportion of blind intersections and sharp turns than has Mountainview.
    (B) There is a greater number of drivers in Oak Valley than in Mountainview.
    (C) Drivers in Mountainview must travel to Oak Valley to shop and work.
    (D) Per capita, there are fewer police officers monitoring traffic in Oak Valley than there are in Mountainview.
    (E) The roads are icier for a greater proportion of the year in Oak Valley than in Mountainview.

EXPLANATIONS

24. **D** Answer D may explain why people are more likely to exceed the speed limit in Oak Valley than in Mountainview, but it has no necessary correlation to the number of accidents in the two towns; therefore, it does nothing to weaken the conclusion that the greater proportion of speeders in Oak Valley results in a greater number of accidents there.

    Answers A and E provide an alternate explanation: Driving conditions are poor, which certainly could contribute to accidents. Choice B indicates that there is much more traffic in Oak Valley, which could well explain why there are more traffic accidents there. Choice C states that many Mountainview residents travel to Oak Valley regularly; it is possible, then, that they, not the drivers who live in Oak Valley, cause the accidents.

QUESTIONS

25. A study showed that only ten percent of American dog owners enroll their dogs in formal obedience training classes. More than 20 percent of these dog owners, the study also showed, participate in dog shows. Thus, it is obvious that people who train their dogs are more likely to participate in dog shows than are people who do not train their dogs.

The conclusion above is correct provided which of the following statements is also true?

(A) It is impossible for a dog to compete in a dog show if the dog has not completed at least one formal obedience training class.
(B) The proportion of dog owners who enroll their dogs in formal obedience training classes is representative of the proportion who train their dogs outside such classes.
(C) Dog owners who participate in dog shows only train their dogs by enrolling them in formal obedience training lessons.
(D) Participation in dog shows is a reliable indicator of how much attention a dog owner pays to his dog.
(E) Only purebred dogs can participate in dog shows, so many owners who enroll their dogs in formal obedience training classes are excluded from this activity.

EXPLANATIONS

25. **B** The statement draws a conclusion about *people who train their dogs* based on statistics relating only to people who take their dogs for formal obedience training classes. In order for the statement to be correct, then, these statistics must be valid for all people who train their dogs, not only those who train them in formal classes. Choice B plugs this hole in the argument, thus making the conclusion necessarily true.

QUESTIONS

26. A bullet train travels in excess of 150 miles per hour. Therefore, if a train travels slower than 150 miles per hour, it is not a bullet train.

Which of the following most closely parallels the reasoning used in the argument above?

(A) An orange ripens only on the vine. If it ripens on the vine, then it is not an orange.
(B) Newspapers are often read by more than one person. Therefore, magazines are also likely to be read by more than one person.
(C) An earthquake of 5.0 or above on the Richter scale causes massive damage. If there is not massive damage, then the earthquake did not attain a 5.0 or above.
(D) A supersonic plane travels at speeds in excess of Mach 1. If it is not supersonic, then it will travel at speeds below Mach 1.
(E) Fluoride generally prevents cavities. If there are no cavities, then there was no fluoride used.

EXPLANATIONS

26. **C** To answer this parallel-the-reasoning question, you have to break down the original argument, and then find an answer choice that mimics it exactly. In this case, the argument says a bullet train travels in excess of 150 miles per hour (if A, then B). Therefore, if a train travels less than 150 miles per hour, then it is not a bullet train (if not B, then not A). Now all you have to do is find an answer choice that mimics that reasoning exactly. Choice A, broken down, reads, "if A, then B…so if B, then not A." This isn't it. Eliminate it. Choice B breaks down to "if A, then B…therefore C will also cause B." That's not it either. Choice C breaks down to "if A, then B…therefore if not B, then not A." This is the best answer.

Choice D might seem tempting because it also has to do with a fast means of transportation, but what counts here is the reasoning: if A, then B…if not A, then not B. This is close, but no cigar. Choice E is also appealing; you may even think it mimics the argument exactly. But there's a trick. The first half of the sentence reads, "Fluoride generally prevents cavities" (if A then B). Note that the B part is about the prevention —not the presence —of cavities. So the second half, "If there are no cavities, there was no fluoride," actually breaks down to "if B, then not A."

About the Author

Geoff Martz attended Dartmouth College and Columbia University before joining The Princeton Review in 1985 as a teacher and writer. Geoff headed the development team that designed The Princeton Review's GMAT course, now taught in more than 50 cities around the country. He is the author or coauthor of *Cracking the ACT, Paying for College Without Going Broke,* and *Cracking the GED.*